# Business Ethics and Values

## Individual, Corporate and International Perspectives

**Second edition**

Colin Fisher and Alan Lovell

Nottingham Business School, Nottingham Trent University

**FT** Prentice Hall
FINANCIAL TIMES

*An imprint of* **Pearson Education**

Harlow, England • London • New York • Boston • San Francisco • Toronto • Sydney • Singapore • Hong Kong
Tokyo • Seoul • Taipei • New Delhi • Cape Town • Madrid • Mexico City • Amsterdam • Munich • Paris • Milan

**Pearson Education Limited**
Edinburgh Gate
Harlow
Essex CM20 2JE
England

and Associated Companies throughout the world

*Visit us on the World Wide Web at:*
www.pearsoned.co.uk

_____

First published 2003
**Second edition published 2006**

© Pearson Education Limited 2003, 2006

ISBN-13: 978 0 273 69478 6
ISBN-10: 0 273 69478 2

**British Library Cataloguing-in-Publication Data**
A catalogue record for this book is available from the British Library

**Library of Congress Cataloging-in-Publication Data**
A catalog record for this book is available from the Library of Congress

10 9 8 7 6 5 4 3 2 1
10 09 08 07 06

Typeset in 10pt Palatino by 30
Printed and bound by Ashford Colour Press Ltd., Gosport

The publisher's policy is to use paper manufactured from sustainable forests.

# Business Ethics and Values

Visit the *Business Ethics and Values, second edition* Companion Website at **www.pearsoned.co.uk/fisherlovell** to find valuable **student** learning material including:

- Links to relevant sites on the web
- New case material and discussion and commentary on case studies contained within the book
- Commentaries on suggested assignment briefs contained within the book
- Answers to the quick revision tests
- Updates including group work exercises and postings concerning contemporary issues and how the ethical arguments and theories discussed in the book relate to current 'hot topics'

# Brief contents

# Contents

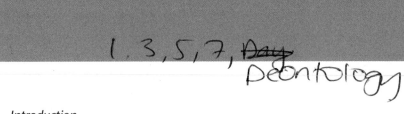

*1, 3, 5, 7, ~~Any~~ Deontology*

## Chapter 10    Ethical conformance: codes, standards, culture, leadership and citizen power          377

| Chapter 13 | Moral agency at work and a modest proposal for affecting ethics in business | 501 |
|---|---|---|

**Supporting resources**
Visit **www.pearsoned.co.uk/fisherlovell** to find valuable online resources

**Companion Website for students**
- Links to relevant sites on the web
- New case material and discussion and commentary on case studies contained within the book
- Commentaries on suggested assignment briefs contained within the book
- Answers to the quick revision tests
- Updates including group work exercises and postings concerning contemporary issues and how the ethical arguments and theories discussed in the book relate to current 'hot topics'

**For instructors**
- PowerPoint slides that can be downloaded and used as OHTs
- Thoughts on the quick revision tests
- Commentary and ideas on the in-chapter activities and the end-of-chapter group activities

For more information please contact your local Pearson Education sales representative or visit **www.pearsoned.co.uk/fisherlovell**

# Introduction

Business ethics is an important subject. Notions of ethics have been debated for millennia, relating as they do to beliefs concerning the nature of human practice and action. Business ethics as a specific area of applied ethics, and as a subject of academic enquiry, is of more recent vintage, possibly dating from around the 1920s (Lovell, forthcoming).

Corporations represent the arenas within which most people spend much of their waking lives and the sheer scale of some of their operations makes many multinational corporations more influential in world affairs (not just business affairs) than some governments. Hence the actions of corporations, whether judged 'good' or 'bad', can affect many, many people, both within the organisations and outwith. Minimising the negative effects of corporate behaviour thus becomes an issue, not just for business, but for the political and social spheres of human activity.

However, the simple labels of 'good' and 'bad' will often represent gross oversimplifications of what could be complex and dynamic issues and situations. We are often faced with dilemmas, with the options available to us containing both positive and negative aspects. This book has been written to allow you to understand the ethical underpinnings of such complex situations, but also to allow you to determine where the weight of evidence might lie in any given case or situation.

At the time we wrote the first edition of the book the bankruptcies of Enron and WorldCom were just beginning to unfold. As we apply the finishing touches to this second edition, the senior officials of Enron have yet to stand trial, but Bernie Ebbers, the chief executive of WorldCom, has been found guilty of an $11bn fraud. His sentence has yet to be announced, but the crime carries a maximum 84-year prison term. However, for the companies who were part of WorldCom's supply chain, the company's employees, its investors and other involved groups and individuals, this is scant consolation. Many will have lost their livelihoods, with the personal turmoil and distress that invariably follows. The business, or economic, sphere of human activity cannot exist for long without an ethical base. Mistrust, cheating, conniving, deceit and fraudulent behaviour are the quicksand upon which no business system can be built.

Far more than many other books on business ethics we have devoted considerable attention to business ethics at the individual level, without underplaying the need also to look at business ethics at the corporate level. The reason for this attention to the individual is that ultimately the actions taken in the name of corporations will in fact be decisions made by individuals, acting either in groups or alone. This is not to deny that corporations can develop a form of persona, what we might call ethical culture, which can be transmitted and maintained through stories, myths, legends and artefacts, which we explore in Chapter 1. The effects of these actions and cultures will be felt by (other) individuals, either collectively or singly. It is for these reasons that we give to the individual such attention.

A second major feature of our approach is to stress the centrality of argumentation within business ethics. At its heart the subject is devoid of facts. It is a collection of theories, beliefs and arguments. It is no less important because of this; indeed we believe it to be profoundly important. With its roots set in argumentation we need to help you gain confidence in understanding the various ethical perspectives or stances. Most ethically charged situations are arenas for competing arguments, even if some of the arguments are judged weak, or fraudulent. Dealing with controversial issues must inevitably involve debate and argument and we believe that a primary aim of a book on business ethics should be to develop the skills of argumentation, or what are known as rhetorical skills.

We do not advocate particular positions in the book, for that would be hypocritical as educators. However, we do advance, in the closing chapter, a tentative manifesto for affecting ethics in business as a way of crystallising the issues and arguments raised in the book. Such a proposal also plots a possible way forward.

We make the case throughout the book that, whilst there are competing arguments concerning where the ethical high ground might be on particular issues, the competing arguments are unlikely to be equally valid or meritorious. Our objective has been to provide you with the knowledge and understanding necessary to be able to form your own reasoned arguments and ethically informed positions on the many varied and complex issues that permeate business life.

The opinions we may each hold and the behaviours we may display in different situations are likely to be affected by a range of issues, including the support of others, our dependents, the risks associated with the issue, where power lies and our respective values. Indeed, we devote time to the subject of values as reflected in the title of the book, because we believe values to be important elements in understanding both ethical reasoning and moral behaviour. Values can be said to act as filters and triggers for stimulating responses to ethically charged situations and we devote a whole chapter to considering the nature of values and their roles. However, we do not claim certain values to be superior to others. This is a matter about which each of us should come to our own conclusion. Our task, as authors, has been to help you analyse, explain, interpret and interrogate ethical situations, but not to prescribe how you should view the situations.

Our emphasis upon argument explains another feature of the book. As well as providing you with the basic material you would expect to find in a textbook on business ethics, we also develop new arguments that are subject to challenge and dispute. Consequently the book is not designed as a definitive work of reference (although where the material is standard we have treated it as authoritatively as we can). Instead, the book is intended to provide thoughts, ideas and provocations to stimulate your own thinking.

The book is designed for both undergraduate and postgraduate students; each may take from it what they need. The materials on ethical theories and ethical reasoning should be of use to both undergraduate and postgraduate students.

These theoretical materials are provided to give you resources for developing arguments for and against particular positions on issues in business ethics. Undergraduate students tend to have limited business experience to draw upon when considering different ethical stances and theories. Thus, we have provided many case studies which are designed to illustrate the application of the various ethical theories. Postgraduate students may like to extend the case studies featured in the book by referring to their experiences in handling, or being aware of, ethically complex business situations. The case studies perform two roles. First they provide practical applications of ethical theories and arguments, making the arguments more accessible and understandable. Secondly they show, unequivocally, the relevance of business ethics for both individuals and societies by illustrating the pain and anguish that can ensue from corrupt, deceitful or other practices that might be judged immoral.

In addition to the case studies within each chapter, there are small tasks to undertake or challenges to respond to. At the close of each chapter we have provided 'quick test' questions. Sometimes these are objective test questions, and you have to select the correct answer from those presented; in other chapters the questions are typical 'short answer' questions such as you might find on an exam paper. These are complemented by suggested assignment briefs and activities that can be undertaken by groups, probably in seminar rooms.

The book provides more material than might be possible to cover in either an undergraduate or postgraduate programme, thereby making a helpful complement to lectures and seminars, taking the subject beyond what might feasibly be explored in the time available for lectures and seminars. Thus, you should follow your tutor's guidance on which parts of the book are critical to your course, and where you can usefully extend your studies by studying parts of the book not able to be covered in the required depth during lectures or seminars. For postgraduate students and practising managers, the book should aid reflection upon personal and organisational experience.

The benefits offered by the study of the book are:

- a comprehensive review of standard/classical ethical theories, complemented by new perspectives to equip you for the challenges of organisational environments;

- a wealth of diagrams and charts that present overviews and contexts of the subject, which also act as useful study aids;

- 'definition' boxes that highlight and explain key themes;

- connexion boxes, which make links between ethical theories that are considered in one part of the book with particular applications or arguments featured elsewhere in the book;

- real-life case studies that contextualise theory and provide springboards for debate;

- simulations and exercises that encourage you to reflect upon your own values and ethical standards;

- activities for group and seminar work that enliven study; a blend of academic theory and concrete issues that reflect the challenge and excitement of the subject;

- a tentative proposal, offered by the authors for affecting ethics in business, as a way of 'making sense' of the many issues and arguments considered in the book and as a possible schema for debate.

## The structure of the book

The book is divided into four main parts, each representing an important subset of business ethics.

## Part A – Business ethics matters: what is it and why does it matter?

This opening section groups together the chapters that lay the foundation for the book.

Chapter 1: *Perspectives on business ethics and values*. This scene-setting chapter considers a range of issues, in preparation for the more focused chapters that follow. The chapter opens with the way values can be created, maintained and communicated via the medium of stories. The chapter moves on to provide an early exposure to the 'business case for business ethics'. There follows a consideration of stakeholder theory and then four dominant theories of the firm, each with its own underpinning set of assumptions as to what constitutes ethical behaviour. The chapter closes with a review of other theoretical positions, namely descriptive, normative and reflective approaches.

Chapter 2: *Ethical issues in business*. The purpose of this chapter is to move from the big questions to the particular issues. A 'map' is used to identify the range of ethical and moral issues to be found in business, organisations and management. Detailed case studies are provided to give you a clear understanding of the issues, many of which are referred to throughout the book.

Chapter 3: *Ethical theories and how to use them*. Having presented you in Chapter 2 with the range of ethical problems, this chapter describes the formal ethical theories and principles that are available for use in analysing them. The theories are largely drawn from the history of western philosophy (other philosophies are considered in Chapter 11). Few of the theories were developed with reference to business and so the chapter draws out the implications of the theories for organisations and the people within them.

## Part B – Individuals' responses to ethical issues

A feature of our approach is our consideration of ethics in business from the perspective of the individual. This section groups together Chapters 4 to 7, with each chapter dealing with an important aspect of this broad focus.

Chapter 4: *Personal values in the workplace*. This chapter deals with the subject of values, which we show to be a multifaceted subject. The chapter provides a general underpinning to our more focused application of personal values in Chapter 5.

Five distinct perspectives on values are introduced and discussed to provide a thorough understanding of the issues involved.

Chapter 5: *Values and heuristics.* Having presented the introduction to personal values in Chapter 4, we consider here how people might think through an ethically charged situation. We argue that personal values can be seen as filters through which the elements of any ethically charged situation are sieved (along with other filters such as perceptions of power, and the support of others), as an individual wrestles with an ethically complex situation. Heuristics are a form of 'cognitive short-cut', allowing us to handle complex, ill-defined and/or incomplete information in ways that have a logical rationality, at least from the perspective of the individual.

Chapter 6: *Individual responses to ethical situations.* Here we consider how an individual might define, or 'label', an ethical situation. The two dominant processes involved in 'labelling' are categorisation and particularisation and the choice will be heavily influenced by an individual's personal values. Categorisation, for example, would describe the situation where someone decided that an issue was a matter of following the core values set by an organisation, or that an issue was a question of loyalty. However, the particulars of a situation might make that person think that the categorisation is not right. It is the details of a situation that make people debate under which value an issue should be categorised or indeed whether it should be put in a separate category of its own.

Chapter 7: *Whistleblower or witness?* The concluding chapter in Part B considers ethical behaviour and specifically the employee who rails against an organisational practice to such an extent that, following failure to achieve resolution within the formal organisational structures, s/he reveals their concerns to another individual, whether inside the organisation or outside.

## Part C – Organisational responses to ethical issues

This group of chapters moves our focus to the organisational level of analysis and considers the ethical obligations and accountabilities of corporations.

Chapter 8: *Corporate responsibility, corporate governance and corporate citizenship.* These three related themes provide the initial focus for our consideration of business ethics as seen at the organisational level. Corporate governance is the term given to the structures within and external to organisations that are intended to ensure that corporate objectives are met. In theory and at law this is the maximisation of shareholder wealth. High profile corporate scandals, such as Maxwell Communications and BCCI, and more recently Enron, WorldCom, Parmalat and Global Crossing, have raised profound questions concerning a raft of corporate governance issues. However, for many these debates are stunted, concerning themselves with only the interests of shareholders. The terms corporate responsibility and citizenship are employed to stretch the arguments concerning corporate responsibilities beyond shareholders. We explore the ethical bases of these arguments through the medium of case studies and other examples.

Chapter 9: *Sustainability and the responsible corporation.* In this chapter we consider the issue of sustainability from a variety of perspectives, including, but not limited to, environmental sustainability. We debate the current preference for a market-based 'business' solution to the problem of greenhouse gas emissions and the more general case of ethical egoism being the underpinning assumption of human behaviour in developing policy responses to the challenges of sustainable corporations and societies.

Chapter 10: *Ethical conformance: codes, standards, culture, leadership and citizen power*. In this chapter we discuss the more formal mechanisms that organisations employ to try to inculcate and maintain particular ethical practices and to identify those practices that are unacceptable. The most common of these mechanisms are codes of conduct and codes of ethics. Such codes can be developed by organisations to apply to their own internal processes and contexts, but codes are also developed by external bodies, sometimes in collaboration with large corporations to whom the codes relate, but sometimes without their cooperation.

## Part D – The international context

This section considers the international context of business ethics, but in the final chapter, Chapter 13, we bring the individual perspective back into consideration within both the international and the corporate contexts.

Chapter 11: *Global and local values – and international business*. It is a cliché to say that values and cultures vary, but recognition of the notion of 'difference' is an important issue for international organisations as they endeavour to operate in various cultural contexts without offending a wide range of sensibilities, values and laws. This chapter provides insights and comparisons between western operating contexts and those in the Asia, notably China and India.

Chapter 12: *Globalisation and international business*. Globalisation is a term that can arouse considerable passions, often negative. We consider the full gamut of issues that corporations operating at a global level face: their potential as forces for positive developments, but also their involvement in cases that illustrate the issues that trouble many concerning their power and their practices.

Chapter 13: *Moral agency at work and a modest proposal for affecting ethics in business*. This is much more than just a 'summing-up' chapter. Whilst we draw upon many of the issues, arguments and theories we have discussed in the preceding chapters, we take these forward by initially worrying about the implications of democratic ideals of what is termed 'globalisation', but more than this we also offer a tentative proposal for affecting ethics in business. The latter is a risky venture because it smacks of prescription, as if 'we know best'. That is why we have qualified our proposal with the adjective 'tentative'. However, the proposal addresses two important issues for us as authors. The first is that it pulls together into a coherent framework the key issues that we have highlighted and discussed in the book. Secondly it provides a framework around which debates and arguments can be framed and possibly moved forward.

A range of support materials is available to lecturers and students on the website for this book at www.pearsoned.co.uk/fisherlovell

# Acknowledgements

We are grateful to the following for permission to reproduce copyright material:

Figures 1.1, 1.2, 1.3 and 1.4 from *Does Business Ethics Pay?*, London, Institute of Business Ethics, with permission of the Institute of Business Ethics (IBE), www.ibe.org.uk (Webley, S. and More, E., 2003); Figure 6.1 from 'Managing messy moral matters' in J. Leopold, L. Harris and T. J. Watson (eds) *Strategic Human Resources, Principles, Perspectives and Practices*, London, Pearson Education, with permission of Pearson Education (Fisher, C. M. and Rice, C. 1999); Figure 11.1 from *Culture's Consequences*, 2nd Edn, London, Sage, p. 377, with permission of Professor Geert Hofstede, copyright © Greet Hofstede; Table 4.1 adapted with the permission of The Free Press, a Division of Simon & Schuster Adult Publishing Group, from THE NATURE OF HUMAN VALUES by Milton Rokeach, copyright © 1973 by The Free Press, all rights reserved; Table 8.1 from the *Guardian GC*, 27 April 2001, p. 2, copyright © Guardian Newspapers Limited 2001; Table 10.2 featuring a selection of extracts from Johnson & Johnson, with the permission of Johnson & Johnson, from the UK Civil Service Code, Crown copyright material reproduced with the permission of the Controller of the HMSO and the Queen's Printer for Scotland; Table 11.5 from 'Boxing with shadows: competing effectively with the overseas Chinese and the overseas Indian business networks in the Asian arena', *Journal of Organisational Change Management*, Vol. 11, No. 4, pp. 301–320, figure 111 (Haley, G. T. and Haley, U. C. V. 1998), Activity 3.10 from 'Principles of business ethics: their role in decision making', in *Management Education*, Vol. 128, No. 8, p. 21 (Carroll, C. B.), with permission of MCB University Press.

Texas Instruments for an extract 'The TI Ethics Quick Test' taken from TI.com © TI 2002; Taylor Francis for an extract adapted from 'Monksbane and feverfew' in *Resource Allocation in the Public Sector: values, priorities and markets in the management of public services* by C M Fisher published by Routledge 1998 and Anita Roddick for her letter to the *Guardian*, 13 July 2001.

We are grateful to the Financial Times Limited for permission to reprint the following material:

Case study 2.3 Inside Track: Big pharma and the golden goose, © *Financial Times*, 26 April 2001; CS 2.5 Leader: Spy trap, © *Financial Times*, 22 August 2000; CS 2.7 Rough justice in the talent market, © *Financial Times*, 4 May 2001; CS 2.9 National News: Medicines arbiter delays decision on beta-interferon: Clinical Excellence Multiple Sclerosis Society angry that drug ruling is only likely after election, © *Financial Times*, 23 December 2000; CS 2.10 Racism remains rife in the Metropolitan Police, © *Financial Times*, 14 December 2000; CS 2.11 Leader: Changing track, © *Financial Times*, 9 May 2001; CS 2.16 A hole dug over 30 years, Companies Section © *Financial Times*, 20 February; CS 2.22 Supermarkets facing more scrutiny after election, © *Financial Times*, 11 April 2001; CS 2.26 Hit squad to tackle animal rights activists, FT.com, © *Financial Times*, 27 April 2001, and Brands feel impact as activists target customers, © *Financial Times*, 18 July 2001; Chapter 13 Leading article: A tale of greed and gullibility, © *Financial Times*, 9 April 2005.

In some instances we have been unable to trace the owners of copyright material, and we would appreciate any information that would enable us to do so.

# PART A

# Business ethics matters: what is it and why does it matter?

# Perspectives on business ethics and values

## Learning outcomes

Having read this chapter and completed its associated activities, readers should be able to:

■ Identify the good, tragic, comic, satirical and farcical elements in the way in which people and organisations deal with matters of ethics and morality.

■ Explain the basic features of stakeholder theory.

■ Evaluate the business case for business ethics and the validity of its claims.

■ Give an account of the various arguments about the moral status of business, organisations and management.

## Stories and business ethics

The study of business ethics begins with stories. Families and societies have always used stories to illustrate and reinforce their sense of values, justice and fairness. And so it is in business and organisations. There are the stories often found in organisational glossy newsletters of good deeds done by staff volunteering to work among disadvantaged groups and the benefits that the organisation has brought to the communities it works within. Then there are the more gossipy stories that are told, and half told, as episodes are interrupted by work or authority figures, that tell of jealousies and spites, corruption and abuse, lying and distortion.

Czarniawska (2004: 21) pointed out that there are four types of dramatic story in the European classical tradition – romances, tragedies, comedies and satires, each of which has its characteristic figure of speech. Each of them can represent different kinds of business ethics issues.

## Figures of speech

### Metaphor

Makes comparisons by referring to one thing as a different thing. So calling all the employees in an organisation 'assets' is a metaphor. If you said of a chief executive officer 'she is a Branson among business leaders', this would be a use of metaphor and a means of making a hero of her. It could also be a kind of paralipsis in which attention is drawn to something – that the CEO is a woman and Branson a man – while pretending to pass over it. As a form of irony this paralipsis could be taken as a criticism of the CEO.

### Metonymy

Uses an attribute of something to represent the thing itself. Chairpersons sit in a chair when they hold a board meeting. The chair is their attribute, so they become known as chairs. In tragedy a single attribute can undermine a person's integrity; a good person is often brought low because of a part of their behaviour or character.

### Synecdoche

Uses a part of something to represent the whole. Business people wear suits and so that particular aspect of them comes to represent them and their role. Others refer to them as suits, as in 'are the suits arriving today to check us out?'. Suits are also a means by which business people present a good image of themselves. In comedy synecdoche points out the comic pretensions between ambition and reality. The smartness of the clothes can emphasise the vacuity of the wearer.

### Irony

Speaking or writing in such a way as to imply the opposite of what is being said. Often used to imply mockery or jest. It is therefore the basis of much satire.

Romances are based on the quest of a single individual to achieve some noble goal that is only achievable because human beings have an innate, if sometimes well disguised, goodness. The Quaker heroes of the past such as Joseph Rowntree who built model factories and villages for model workers, or more modern heroes such as Anita Roddick who sought, against the odds, to make selling beauty products a beautiful process, are good examples. Such heroes become metaphors for their particular brand of ethical management.

Tragedies tell of people who try to behave well but who, by challenging fate, come to personal grief. The stories of whistleblowers who reveal corporate wrong-doing but in so doing lose their families, their homes and their livelihoods are a good example. Tragedy is based on metonymy, as in the film *The China Syndrome* (Bridges, 1979) in which Jack Lemmon plays an engineer in a malfunctioning nuclear power station who is the only person to be troubled by a vibration felt as a test procedure was conducted. The vibration is a metonym for the potential cataclysm that is waiting to happen.

Comedies are stories about how human imperfections and weaknesses make the achievement of a happy ending difficult. The ways in which companies that are foreign to a new country they have begun to operate in often get their attempts to integrate wrong are a strong source of comedy. The western business-men, for it is mostly men who would do this, who ignorantly offend their Arab business partners by putting their feet up on their desk after concluding a deal in an attempt to show that the formal business is over and everyone can relax, and so revealing the soles of their shoes, have a degree of comic potential. The dirty soles of the shoes act as a synecdoche, a part of the businessman, which stands for the unwholesomeness of the whole man.

Satires work ironically. By contrasting people's behaviour with their words, or by defining the context in which the words are said, it is made clear that people meant the opposite of what they said. When corporations are accused of not taking care of

- customers, by not closing the doors on the *Herald of Free Enterprise* (*see* p. 328), or

- employees, as in the Bhopal incident in which 20,000 people were killed or harmed by a chemical leak from an American owned chemical works in the city (*see* p. 469) (the leak could have been prevented if procedures, management and maintenance had been rigorous), or

- the environment when the oil companies are accused of despoiling the Niger Delta (*see* p. 475),

organisations often reply by saying that the objects and subjects they have damaged are in fact their top priority. They thereby make themselves the object of satire. People then take such claims as ironies. In the film *Super Size Me*, Morgan Spurlock (2004) tested McDonald's claim that its food is not intrinsically unhealthy by living for a month on its products. Of course such a diet made him an unhealthier person (that is irony).

### Connexion point

The ethical issues raised by the film *Super Size Me* are discussed in Case study 2.23 (pp. 91–2).

There is, in business ethics as in life generally, a narrow point of balance

- between romance and satire

- and between tragedy and comedy.

These tensions are the narrative dynamic behind business ethics issues. The heroes of romances can easily become the subject of satirists' scorn. In the struggles between heroes and villains the heroes can overreach themselves and believe they really do have magical powers, in some cases literally. In 1999 in the oil producing delta region of Nigeria members of a cult known as the *Egbesu* began a violent campaign against, as they saw it, the despoliation of their homeland by the oil companies (Ibeanu, 2000: 28). It was believed that the charms they wore made them impervious to bullets. The heroes may then become ridiculous and the villains begin to look more benign. Tragedy can, uncomfortably, have comic elements. As Marx (1963: 1) pointed out, history repeats itself, 'first time as tragedy, second time as farce'. Just as commonly comedy can descend into tragedy. The difference between an organisational comedy of incompetence and a tragedy may be no more than the operation of chance. If luck remains with the organisation then we can all laugh at its bumbling, but if luck runs out the story can become tragic, for some. In December 2004 (Harding, 2004) a Delhi school-boy from one of the elite schools, doubtless anxious to show off his new mobile phone with built-in camera, used it to take a video clip of his girlfriend providing him with oral sex. Unfortunately for him within a few days the video clip was on sale on Bazee.com, the Indian version of eBay, and indeed owned by eBay. The company took the item off the website as soon as they became aware of it but nevertheless an uproar ensued in India and a mildly, if in poor taste, comic event turned serious. The boy was taken to juvenile court and expelled from school. Avnish Bajaj, the CEO of Bazee.com and a US citizen, was arrested and thrown into the notoriously overcrowded Tihar gaol. For three people at least tragedy was a tale of prosperity, for a time, that ended in wretchedness. The matter was debated in the Indian parliament and the BJP party denounced the incident as the result of American 'interference'. The American government in its turn was taking a serious interest in Mr Bajaj's imprisonment. Condoleeza Rice, the soon to be American Secretary of State, was reported to be furious at the humiliating treatment meted out to an American citizen. The Indian software industry association called for Bajaj's immediate release.

It would appear that the issues and problems that form the subject of business ethics can appear in different forms, sometimes as romances, sometimes as tragedies, sometimes as comedies and sometimes as satires. It follows that stories are a good mechanism through which business issues can be studied and understood. If we can understand how the plots of these stories can lead to either good or bad outcomes we can develop an intuitive knowledge of how to encourage more happy endings than bad ones. Or at least the stories might palliate, or help us come to terms with, the dilemmas we face (Kirk, 1974: 83).

| Case study 1.1 | **The _Hindustan Times,_ Monday 29 November 2004** |
| --- | --- |

I am writing this part of the chapter in a hotel room in New Delhi, India. A copy of the newspaper has been slid under the door to my room. A number of its stories show the range of business ethics issues. The lead story is a _romance_: a hero entrepreneur and philanthropist, in this case Sir Richard Branson, is reported to have attended a party in New Delhi at which 4.5 crore (a crore is ten million) rupees had been raised for a children's educational charity. 'The creation of wealth is fine. But businesses need to pay back to the society in a number of ways', said Branson. The next day it was also reported that the Government of India might allow Branson to buy a personal stakeholding in a domestic airline, even though the rules on foreign direct investment would not allow Virgin Atlantic, his own airline, to buy such a stake.

_Tragedy_ was represented by a story that a former High Court judge was likely to be charged with receiving bribes and manipulating judgments to favour the person who had paid the bribes. It is a tragedy because a judge appointed to uphold the law, and who no doubt originally intended to do so, allowed himself to give way to external pressures and so destroyed his reputation.

A story that *satirises* itself is that twenty years after the Bhopal incident American scientists are proposing to recreate the gas leak under controlled experimental conditions. In particular they want to discover whether deadly chemicals such as carbon monoxide and hydrogen cyanide were released as well as other chemicals in the original leak. The irony is that it seems that, when only Indian citizens had been harmed and killed by such a leak, the Americans had been content to ignore the possibility that these two gases were involved. But, by 2004, when it was possible that American citizens might be subject to such a chemical attack by terrorists, then it was suddenly important to know the truth. The *Hindustan Times* reported that Indian scientists already know the truth, from their clinical studies of the victims, that these gases had been released. The report was also *ironic* (in the technically incorrect meaning of its being an unhappy coincidence) in that on the same day *BBC World* reported that an Amnesty International report had condemned both Union Carbide and the Government of India for not ensuring that past and continuing victims of the incident were properly compensated.

*Comedy* was represented by a report on how fog was, as in the past, causing airline passengers at Delhi's airport to become unhappy because it delayed their flights. This should not have been the case, but the proposed anti-fog landing system had not been implemented as planned. The *Hindustan Times* poked gentle fun at the airport's management who had proposed to avert passengers' displeasure by providing a gallery of pictures of Delhi's ancient monuments to entertain and inform them. This apparent dedication to customer service when their solution was comically inadequate ('but what if, after viewing all the sketches, the foreign tourist still has time to kill before he could catch his flight?') indicates a bureaucratic disdain for customers. (When I arrived at the airport the sketches were found to be few in number, unexceptionable and unviewed by anyone but me.)

There is one other story in the paper that suggests a fifth dramaturgical genre is needed – *farce*. The characteristic figure of speech of farce is hyperbole or excessive exaggeration to the point of silliness. Laloo Prasad Yadav is a notorious figure in Indian politics (Dalrymple, 1999: 10–25). When he was imprisoned for corruption, while Chief Minister of the State of Bihar, he was replaced in the post by his wife. When the new national government was formed in 2004, Laloo was made Minister for Railways. The paper reported he was in a bitter spat with a ministerial colleague, Ram Vilas Paswan, who had been railway minister in the 1990s. Both wanted the railway job: allegedly it is a rich source of kickbacks. In a speech to a political rally in Patna, the capital of Bihar, Laloo said 'Lots of money was made in that time [when Paswan had the portfolio]. I will make all those files that show corruption public. He is now in deep trouble.' The farcical elements are that the pot is calling the kettle black; that a government department has had files proving alleged corruption for ten years but has not taken any action; and that a politician has claimed the moral high ground by the unethical practice of revealing confidential official papers in an attempt to gain a political advantage over a rival.

## Activity 1.1

Choose a daily newspaper or weekly magazine and identify as many stories in it as you can that deal with an aspect of business ethics. Read each story in turn and decide whether it has elements of romance, tragedy, comedy, satire or farce within it.

One of the long running business ethics stories concerns a moral decision that faces profit seeking organisations. It is a conflict between public duty and self-interest. Should they only exercise their social and environmental duty if it coincides with the financial interests of their owners? In this case they will be heroes in the stories of the owners but villains in the tales of everyone else. Or should they prevent the organisation harming society and the environment, beyond the demands of the law if necessary, even if it will hurt the owners' immediate interests? In this case their ascription to the roles of hero and villain in the stories will be reversed.

Following the Asian tsunami in 2004 many Australian companies made donations to the appeal fund. Stephen Matthews, a spokesman for the Australian Shareholders' Association, criticised the companies, saying that they had no approval for their philanthropy. He implied that companies should not make such donations without expecting something in return.

> Boards of directors don't have a mandate from their shareholders to spend money in this way. [ ] There is a role for business to make a contribution in relation to the tsunami, particularly those businesses who have activities up in South Asia. [ ] Where their businesses are dependent on those sorts of markets there could possibly be a benefit for shareholders in them making donations to relief.
>
> (ABC News Online, 2005a)

Later the Association's chief executive tried to limit the damage of the ensuing public disdain by clarifying the statement. The ASA was not opposed to companies making donations because 'it is in everyone's interests that the affected communities and economies recover as soon as possible'. Companies should however disclose to the shareholders the extent of their giving (ABC News Online, 2005b). Some commentators thought, uncharitably, that the rapid donations of cash and goods to the affected regions by some large companies was an attempt to have their brands associated with humanitarian good works (Simpson, 2005).

The story illustrates the question of whether a business case should be proven for acting in a socially and environmentally responsible way before it is necessary for an organisation to adopt the role. This is dealt with in the next section.

## The business case for business ethics

Should private, profit seeking organisations behave in a socially responsible and moral way, beyond the requirement of the law, because it is the right thing to do or because it pays them to do so? This might be seen as a moral dilemma; indeed in many ways it is the central issue in business ethics. If it is true that corporations that behave in a responsible and ethical manner do in fact make better returns for their owners than do those organisations that cut corners or behave badly, then the philosophical question of whether organisations ought to behave well is redundant. Do the well-behaved hero companies actually achieve their reward and despite their tribulations win through and enter into a successful long-term relationship with their investors and reach the top of the corporate financial performance league tables, or, in folk story terms, marry the princess and ascend the throne (Czarniawska, 2004: 78)? Several people have sought to answer this question.

There are sensible arguments that can be used to suggest that corporate bad behaviour can be bad for business. It would be logical to assume that a business that was seen to behave badly would lose the esteem and respect of its customers and so lose sales and profitability. A poor image would counteract the large sums that companies spend on developing their brands. Conversely if a company is associated with good behaviour, using renewable resources, not employing child labour in its factories in developing countries and providing good training and development opportunities for its staff, it should be good for sales. This is one of the motivations behind the fair trade movement.

## The fair trade labels

The fair trade (or alternative trade) movement began in the late 1960s as an attempt to give small and independent farmers and artisans in the third world a better return on their efforts. As such, small-scale producers did not have access to first world markets and as they were many and the purchasers were relatively few they received only a small percentage of the price that their products eventually sold for in the developed countries. This situation was made worse because much of the processing and packaging of the basic products, which adds much of the value to a product, was done in the developed countries and not in the countries of origin. At this stage large NGOs such as Oxfam started selling third world products in their shops at terms that were beneficial to the producers. They also encouraged the setting up of cooperatives and credit unions and local processing plants that all added value to the producers.

In the 1980s a Dutch priest who worked, with the support of a church-based NGO, alongside small-scale Mexican coffee producers realised that there could be a marketing advantage in selling the coffee under a 'fair trade' label. The development of such labels meant that fair trade products were not just available in charity and ethnic shops but in mainstream supermarkets and retailers (IRC, 1998). Some research conducted in Belgium (de Pelsmacker *et al.*, 2003) distinguished four groups of coffee buyers:

- Fair trade lovers – 10% of sample who are willing to, and sometimes do, pay the premium price for fair trade coffee.
- Fair trade likers – 40% of the sample who were well disposed to fair trade products and could be encouraged to buy them by effective marketing.
- The flavour lovers (24%) and the brand lovers (25%) were not influenced at all by the fair trade label.

As the range of fair trade label goods increased to include tea, honey, chocolate and clothes, the researchers concluded a large potential and profitable market would open up for such products.

In 2002, the Co-op in the UK announced that it would make all its own brand chocolate products fair trade. This was seen as a major change that would enable it to charge a premium for its products and achieve a good level of sales. Cadbury Schweppes (2004) take a different view and point out that only 0.1 per cent of worldwide cocoa sales goes through the fair trade system which pays the producers a social premium on top of the going market price. One reason why this is so is that fair trade works best through producer cooperatives and there are still very few of these in the producing countries. They also argue that if most producers were paid a social premium this would result in a cocoa glut that would eventually lead to a collapse in cocoa prices. Their approach is to work directly with producers and provide programmes that can improve the farmers' efficiency and the value they can add to their crops.

However, these benefits of good behaviour are not guaranteed. A brand untarnished by a poor reputation is most likely to affect the buying decisions of consumers, but less likely to influence business purchasers, who will rate a good deal before a sense of social responsibility. Bad corporate behaviour will only diminish reputation, and good behaviour boost it, if it becomes known. Many companies of course have public relations departments and corporate communications departments that are designed to prevent harm being done to their brands and reputation. Making bad behaviour known requires that wrongdoing is seen and made public and that there are ways of measuring good behaviour so that credit can be given to those corporations that score well on some kind of ethics scale. There are measures of social, ethical and environmental performance, but these are mostly designed to meet the needs of the ethical investment community rather than consumers and purchasers.

## Measures of corporate social, ethical and environmental performance                                    DEFINITIONS

There are a number of standard measures, or more properly indices, that are available for assessing the social and environmental performance of corporations.

**FTSE4Good:** This index is calculated from a number of factors that cover the three areas of:

- working towards environmental sustainability
- developing positive relationships with stakeholders
- upholding and supporting Universal Human Rights.

The factors are sometimes but not always measurable things. Judgements about whether a company is complying with international ethical standards are also included. A panel of experts meets to decide whether companies' performance entitles them to be included in the index.

- **Dow Jones Sustainability Indices**
  The DJSI tracks the financial performance of companies that have committed to long-term sustainability. It is a guide for those who wish to invest in companies that are ethical or that profess a philosophy of sustainability.
- **SERM rating:** This stands for Socio-Ethical Risk Management. It is designed to assess the degree to which companies are actively managing the risk they would be subject to in areas such as abuse of human rights, engagement in bribery and corruption, degradation of the physical environment, negative impacts of new technology, and many other factors.
- **Ethical Investment Research Service (EIRIS)**
  EIRIS carries out research on companies worldwide and provides information to those who wish to invest ethically. It is a charity set up in 1983 by churches and charities who did not wish to invest any of their money in ethically dubious organisations.

The indices are all professionally designed and include checks and tests to ensure that the judgements they contain are valid; this however makes starker the fact that they are judgements rather than measures of social and environmental outcomes.

Webley and More (2003) have sought an empirical answer to the question whether business ethics pays. They faced the technical problem that there is no single and definitive measure of ethical performance. They happily admit that they have had to choose proxy or surrogate measures that are indicative of whether a company is behaving in an ethical and environmentally protective way but not conclusive proof that they are. (Commentators have taken a satirical delight in the fact that Enron was often commended for its ethics policies.) Webley and More chose the following measures:

- Whether a company has a published code of ethics that has been revised within the past five years.
- Companies' SERM rating.
- Companies' ratings on *Management Today*'s 'Britain's Most Admired Companies' survey that is carried out by Michael Brown of Nottingham Business School.

Their analysis showed that companies that had a code of ethics had better ratings on both SERM and the 'Most Admired Company' league tables than those that did not. Therefore, to keep things simple all they needed to check was whether companies with a code performed better financially than those that did not.

It might have been anticipated that when Webley and More (2003) came to consider how to measure the financial performance of companies the task would be easier, but there is a wide range of possible measures. They chose:

- Market value added (MVA) – This is the difference between what investors have put into a company over a number of years and what they would get from it if they sold it at current prices.

- Economic value added (EVA) – This is the amount by which investors' current income from the company is greater or less than the return they would get if they had invested the money in something else of equal risk. In other words it is the opportunity cost of placing money in a particular company.

- Price earnings ratio (P/E ratio) – This is the market value of a share in a company divided by the shareholders' earnings.

- Return on capital employed (ROCE) – This is a measure of the return that the capital invested in a company makes for its owners.

The results of their research into the relationship between a company's ethical standing and its financial performance is shown graphically in Figures 1.1, 1.2, 1.3 and 1.4.

Two cohorts, each a little short of 50, of large companies were chosen from the FTSE 350 for the study. The results indicate, *prima facie*, that companies within the sample that have a code of ethics (and hence score better on the SERM ratings and the 'Most Admired Company' tables than those who do not) also achieved a better MVA and EVA over the four-year period 1997–2000. Between 1997 and 2000 companies without a code had a greater ROCE than those that did, but by 2001 the position had reversed and those with a code performed better. The P/E ratio was more stable over the period of the study for companies with codes than it was for companies without. There is a strong indication that having a code, managing the non-financial risks of a company (as measured by SERM), and being rated by one's peers as a reputable company are associated with higher and more stable financial returns.

1. **Is having an ethical code consistent with the generation of more added value?**

*Chart 1: Average Economic Value Added (EVA) by year for major UK quoted companies*

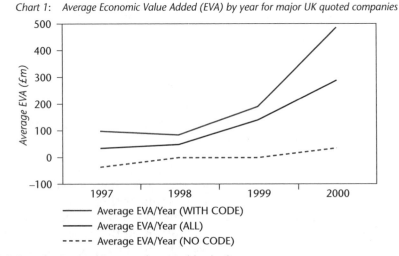

**Figure 1.1** Does business ethics pay: does it add value?

*Source*: Webley and More 2003

**2.  Is having an ethical code consistent with enhanced market value?**

*Chart 2:   Average Market Value Added (MVA) by year for major UK quoted companies*

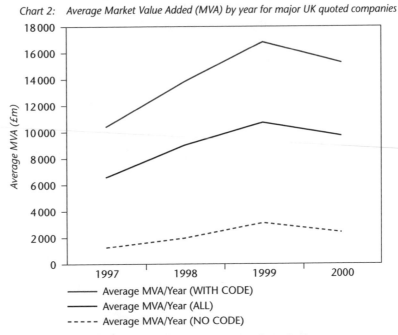

**Figure 1.2** Does business ethics pay: does it enhance market value?

*Source*: Webley and More 2003

**3.  Is having an ethical code consistent with an improved return on capital?**

*Chart 3:   Return on Capital Employed (ROCE) by year for forty-two major UK quoted companies*

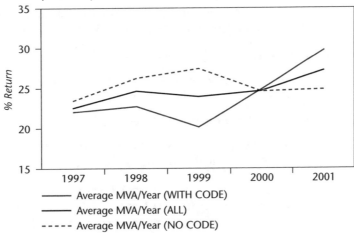

**Figure 1.3** Does business ethics pay? Does it improve return on capital?

*Source*: Webley and More 2003

**4. Is having an ethical code consistent with a more stable Price/Earnings Ratio?**

*Chart 4:  Price/Earnings Ratio (P/E) by year for forty-two major UK quoted companies*

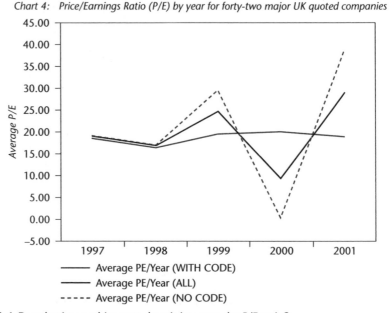

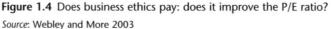

— Average PE/Year (WITH CODE)
— Average PE/Year (ALL)
- - - - Average PE/Year (NO CODE)

**Figure 1.4** Does business ethics pay: does it improve the P/E ratio?

*Source*: Webley and More 2003

However, this is not necessarily proof of the business case for business ethics. A statistical association does not mean that the adoption of ethical business practices is the cause of financial improvement. It could be the result of some different, and as yet unconsidered, factor.

Moore (2001) conducted a study of the financial and social performance of eight retail supermarket companies in the UK over a three-year period. He found a number of statistical correlations but, because of the small sample size, only one was statistically significant. The social performance of companies was measured by a sixteen-factor index prepared by EIRIS (see p. 11). The correlations were:

- That social performance got worse as financial performance improved.

- But if social performance was compared with financial performance three years earlier the association was positive.

- That older companies did better on social performance than younger ones.

- And larger companies had a better performance than smaller ones; this was the one statistically significant finding.

These findings suggested that far from good social performance leading to improved financial effects the cause and effect relationship worked the other way around. That is to say, companies that do well financially find themselves with some money that they can spend on good works and improving their social and environmental performance. It takes time to implement these policies, hence the three-year time lag. The Institute of Business Ethics research could not be expected to identify this time lag because their key indicator, the presence or absence of a code of ethics, is not one that would fluctuate year on year, but the index that Moore used would. This direction of causation, from financial to social, is known as the Available Funding Hypothesis (Preston and O'Bannon, 1997). However, giving attention to these new social projects causes companies to take their eye off their main objective, making money. This distraction of attention, plus the fact that these projects can cost a lot of money, causes the financial performance to worsen. In response the companies would return their efforts to financial performance. Commentators within the supermarket industry anticipated that as Sainsbury and Marks and Spencer were performing less well financially their social and environmental efforts would decrease.

These same commentators also speculated whether social and environmental performance might be related to the social class of its customers (Moore and Robson, 2002: 27). Tesco and Morrisons served lower socio-economic groups (on average) who were less likely to be conscious of social and environmental concerns and so there would be no advantage to the company in taking a lead on such matters. The higher status groups who shopped in Sainsbury and Marks and Spencer were more likely to be careful conservers of the natural and social world and might begin to boycott the stores if they were not seen to be sufficiently interested in sustainability.

In a later study (Moore and Robson, 2002: 28–9) a more detailed statistical analysis was carried out between the 16 social performance indicators (instead of the aggregate result as in the first study) and an extended range of financial performance indicators. Negative, and statistically significant, correlations were found between growth in turnover and the league table rank of:

- the mission statements compared with those of others;
- the proportion of women managers compared with other companies;
- the environmental policy;
- the environmental management systems;
- the social performance total.

In summary, this suggests that as companies increase their turnover their social performance worsens, or the obverse, that as their social performance improves their turnover declines. This adds support to the second part of the cycle suggested above, that social performance endangers financial performance, but does not of itself support the first part of the cycle, that companies flush with profits are inclined to spend some of the profits on social performance, even though as we saw above this is precisely what Sir Richard Branson says they should do. These results of course only apply to one industry – retailing and supermarkets.

There is an association between good social performance or ethical business practices and good financial returns. It is not clear, however, that it is the good social performance that increases profits. It may be the other way around. This conclusion is not necessarily dismissive of all concerns with business ethics from an organisational point of view. There may not be a financial case for actively and purposefully seeking to make a better social and environmental world. This does not mean that companies should not seek to minimise the potential costs of being found to have acted unethically or improperly. If a company or government department is sued for damages arising from its negligence or its bad behaviour, the costs of the case and the costs of the award can be very high. It may be wise to seek to avoid those actions and practices that could cost dearly; this management function is known as risk management. If a company can be shown though its risk management procedures to have taken every reasonable precaution to identify a potential malpractice or problem and to do what is reasonable to prevent it, then, even if the problem or malpractice happens and damages others, the company will have a legal defence.

So, unfortunately (fortunately for text book writers for if otherwise we would have to close the book at this point), it is not clear that there is a business case for business ethics, although on the defensive principle there is one for managing the financial risk of unethical or improper organisational behaviour. It is necessary to turn to other ways of deciding whether companies and organisations should act ethically and responsibly. This comes down to the question of whose interests companies and organisations should exist to serve. Should they serve the interests of society generally? Or should they serve the interest of particular groups within society? If so, which groups should they serve? It is the answer to these questions we now turn to.

## Stakeholder theory

> **Connexion point**
>
> Stakeholder theory is a key and recurring theme in this book because ethics is concerned with the harm or good done to people. As different people may be affected differently by the same action then it is important to take these various impacts, some good and some bad, into account. The simplest way of doing this is to use stakeholder theory. The theory will be used and discussed in Chapters 2, 8 and 12.

If we continue with the storytelling metaphor it is important to know who the characters in the story are. In terms of business ethics stakeholder theory provides an answer. It might be more accurate to say stakeholder theories since there are various interpretations of what the term means. They share one attribute, however, which is that for any organisation there are a number of definable groups who have an interest, or a stake, in the actions of that organisation. There is more disagreement about what constitutes a stake. It is clear that the shareholders, the owners if it has any, have a legitimate stake in an organisation. So do its employees. At the other extreme the 'phishers', who try to gain fraudulently customers' bank account details through fake, spammed emails, obviously have an interest in the banks they attack; but it is hardly a legitimate one. So the issue is three-fold:

- What responsibilities or duties, if any, does an organisation owe to its stakeholders? The fact that a stakeholder group may have a legitimate interest does not, of itself, mean that the organisation owes anything to it. At one extreme of the spectrum of possibilities an organisation may be obliged to do what its stakeholder group requires. If that group is society at large, as it expresses its will through legislation, then the organisation should submit to it. At a level below this stakeholders could have the right to participate in the organisation's decision making. This might be accepted in the case of employees who are expected to commit to the organisation's objectives and decisions. It might not be right in the case of a judicial system's obligations to those being tried in a court. A lesser obligation might be a stakeholder group's right to be consulted before major decisions are taken. If not this, then at least the group might expect the organisation to give them an account of why they did what they did. At the other extreme the organisation might owe the stakeholder group nothing.

- How should an organisation decide between its obligations to two or more stakeholders if they demand incompatible things from an organisation? What criteria should the organisation use when deciding which stakeholder group's wishes it should prioritise? Often in public service organisations the criterion used is a crude one that the group that shouts loudest is the one listened to. There is an interesting issue involved here. What if a constituency is not a person or persons but a thing or collection of things or ideas (these are known in sociological jargon as actants) such as rivers, nature reserves, spirituality? How can these things be given a voice? An easy answer might be that their voices are those of the lobby groups that support each particular cause. There is a problem here though. Some research indicates that, when lobby groups cause too much irritation to the organisation they are trying to influence, their reward is not to be listened to but to be shut out. If the cause of environmentalism is voiced by overaggressive agitation then an organisation might close its ears to the problem when the cause itself is more deserving than its supporters' actions.

- What legitimate interests justify a group of people being regarded as a stakeholder in an organisation? A criterion often proposed is that stakeholders are any group that is affected by an organisation's actions. But this would give a commercial company's competitors a voice in its activities because their performance would be affected by the organisation's performance, which would not seem fair.

The subject matter of business ethics is an attempt to answer these three questions. In the next section we consider four different answers, or perspectives, that are given in modern western, capitalist societies.

## Business and organisational ethics

In this section four broad theories of the firm, and the assumptions and implications of these perspectives for prioritising the various stakeholders' needs and for the exercise of moral agency, are considered.

> **DEFINITION**
>
> **Moral agency** within organisations is the ability of individuals to exercise moral judgement *and behaviour* in an autonomous fashion, unfettered by fear for their employment and/or promotional prospects.

Organisation, in the sense we are using the term here, refers to any configuration of people and other resources that has been created to coordinate a series of work activities, with a view to achieving stated outcomes, or objectives. At this stage we make no distinction as to whether an organisation is profit seeking, located within the public sector, or is a charitable/voluntary organisation. The issues we discuss are largely, but not exclusively, sector-blind, although the intensity with which the issues are experienced may vary significantly between organisational types.

As will become evident as we progress through the chapters, the location of an organisation within the public sector does not make it immune from economic constraints, even economic objectives. Likewise, there is a growing body of opinion that argues forcibly that profit seeking organisations should be more accountable to a body of citizens that extends considerably beyond shareholder-defined boundaries. While the distinctions between private sector and public sector, profit seeking and non-profit seeking, have become less clear-cut in recent years, we do not argue that all organisations are equivalent, and that the sector of the economy in which an organisation is located is irrelevant to understanding the ethical, political, economic and social constraints within which it operates. Penalties or sanctions for poor performance are possibly more obvious and severe in the profit seeking sectors, but it can be argued that the multiplicity and complexity of the objectives managers are required to achieve in certain parts of the public sector make managing in such a context a far more demanding and ethically fraught role. Although each perspective assumes that organisational relationships are largely, if not exclusively, mediated by market dynamics, the extent to which 'the market' is relied upon as an exclusive mediating mechanism does vary.

Table 1.1 presents the schema of four perspectives to highlight the point that different imperatives and assumptions may underpin market-based, capitalist economies.

Within the four categories in Table 1.1 different assumptions are made about the relationships between:

- organisations and the state;
- organisations and their employees;
- organisations and their various stakeholder groups (i.e. beyond the employee group).

Table 1.1 Theories of the firm and their ethical implications

| Issue | Classical liberal economic | Pluralist (A and B) | Corporatist | Critical |
|---|---|---|---|---|
| Status of the category | 1. For its advocates it is the only game in town, not merely the most efficient, but the most ethically justifiable. 2. For others the 'pure' model must be tempered by interventions to (a) minimise problems of short-termism, or (b) correct power imbalances. 3. Whilst for others the neo-classical model is a corrupting chimera that acts as a cover to camouflage the interests of the powerful. | 1. Type A. A stakeholder perspective is advocated in corporate decision making, with key interest groups physically represented on decision-making boards. 2. Type B. Individual managers weigh the full ethical and social considerations of their actions and decisions. Stakeholder groups would not necessarily be present at decisions. | Refers to the business relationships in countries such as Germany, Sweden and Japan (although the approaches adopted are not identical). The interests of employee groups, non-equity finance, and sometimes the state, are represented alongside the interests of equity shareholders, on senior decision-making boards. | Ranging from descriptive theories of the firm that portray how organisations appear to be (or are), rather than how they should be, to critical theorists who portray an organisational world beholden to the demands of capitalism or managerialism (these terms are not the same). Both approaches reflect messier and more ethically fraught worlds than tend to be suggested in the other three categories. |
| Number of objectives recognised | One – meeting the demands of equity shareholders. | Multiple, reflecting an array of stakeholder perspectives, although the actual mechanics remain problematic. | A mix of equity shareholder, employee and non-equity finance perspectives, although long-term economic interests of the firm are dominant. | Multiple, reflected by the various coalitions and power groups within an organisation, particularly economic interests. |
| Status of financial targets | Regarded as the organisation's primary or sole objective, because they will reflect the efficiency with which resources are being employed. | Important, but not to the domination of all other considerations. Ethical as well as multiple stakeholder perspectives are weighed in decision making. | Important, but greater attention paid to the medium to longer-term financial implications of decisions than appears to be the general case in Anglo-American corporations. | In highly competitive markets, or during periods of crisis, likely to be the dominant, although not the exclusive, organisational consideration. During periods of relative stability, other considerations will gain in significance and could dominate. |
| Significance of ethical behaviour (both individual and corporate) | Defined by national and international laws, which are seen as both the minimum and maximum of required ethicality. The neo-classical model is argued to be the only approach that allows the primacy of individual interests to be reflected in economic and social coordination. | At the heart of the debate for those who bemoan what is seen as the exclusive, or overly dominant, economic orientation of organisations. | No clear evidence that ethical considerations feature more strongly in corporate decision making, although the lack of an exclusive shareholder perspective might offer greater potential for a broader societal perspective. | An important, but variable, element in defining the reputation of the organisation. Will be shaped by the power of influential individuals and groups within and external to the organisation. |

Table 1.1 Continued

| Issue | Classical liberal economic | Pluralist (A and B) | Corporatist | Critical |
|-------|---------------------------|---------------------|-------------|----------|
| Role of managers | Portrayed as functionalist, technicist and value neutral. | Type A. Managers come into direct contact with specific sectional interest groups, which should affect decision making. Type B. Individual managers are required to have internalised a societal ethic into their decision making. | The structures of organisations reflect a formal involvement of employee representatives, non-equity financiers, and sometimes state representatives, alongside shareholder interests, on corporate decision-making boards. | Complex, with competing and sometimes/often mutually exclusive interests and demands being required to be satisfied, including the managers' own agendas. |
| Status of employees | Resources to be used by the organisation in its quest to satisfy shareholder interests. | Employees represent an important interest/stakeholder group within the organisation, although economic considerations are not ignored. | Employee representation is guaranteed on some of the organisation's senior decision-making boards, e.g. supervisory boards in Germany. | Operating within a capitalist mode of production, employee interests will vary between organisations, depending upon the power of individuals and groups of individuals. |
| Values | Competition seen as the bulwark against power imbalances. Efficient resource allocation facilitated by profit-maximising behaviour. | Inherently societal in orientation, but the views of those actually making decisions will be important. | Those of the shareholders, employees, non-equity financiers (possibly the state) are likely to dominate. | A complex interaction of multiple individual and corporate values. Critical theorists would single out the values that underpin capitalism. |
| The possibilities for moral agency in organisations | The individual as consumer, as chooser, is the personification of moral agency, but the individual as moral agent when selling his or her labour is troublesome. The atomisation of society, which appears to be an inevitability of this form of individualism, is seen by many as leading to feelings of alienation and anomie. | Type A. Multiple perspectives offer heightened possibilities, but medium to long-term organisational survival will dominate concerns. Type B. Very similar to Type A, but the confidence and integrity of individual managers becomes a critical issue. | With employee representatives on the supervisory boards of organisations (as in Germany), the possibilities again appear stronger than with the liberal-economic perspective. However, economic considerations will remain dominant. | Empirical evidence indicates that the suppression of moral agency might be more than minor and isolated aberrations in an otherwise satisfactory state of organisational affairs. Critical theorists would see these problems as an inevitable consequence of the demands of capitalism. |

We need to understand these perspectives because they are helpful in appreciating the potential for, and the constraints we each face in exercising, moral agency within business contexts.

With the exception of the 'classical-liberal' category, each of the categories is an amalgam of a variety of theories, ideas and practices. The corporatist approach is referred to by Crouch and Marquand (1993) as 'Rhenish'. This latter term refers to a particular (German) approach to a market-based, capitalist-oriented economy, although the writers broaden their consideration beyond Germany to take in a wider group of non-Anglo-American market-based economies. Whilst the German approach displays important differences from the Japanese and the Swedish approaches, they have, for our purposes, been grouped together as representing a more corporatist approach, where the overt involvement of the state and employees in the running of individual organisations is an accepted practice.

This is not to say that the Anglo-American approach to economic development can be simply categorised within the 'classical-liberal-economic' group. Notwithstanding the rhetoric of various UK and US governments, state involvement has been required and forthcoming on many occasions in these two countries, often to overcome what is known as market failure. However, the common belief in the UK and America leans towards the need for less, or minimal, government interference in business, and a drive towards market dynamics to facilitate organisational coordination.

The following is a closer examination of the four theories of the firm and their implications for moral behaviour within, and of, organisations.

## The classical-liberal-economic approach

A classical-liberal theory of the firm places the organisation within an economic system that is made up of a myriad of interconnecting but legally separate parts, and where relationships between these many parts are defined in terms of free exchange. Money acts as the facilitator of exchange, thus performing the role of the oil that greases the economic system's wheels. The 'invisible hand' that Adam Smith spoke of is the force that drives the mass of individual transactions. The argument is that, with no individual person or company able to affect price, the resulting transactions, and the prices that draw both suppliers and customers into the marketplace, reflect people's wishes. This is the strength of the claims for the ethicality of 'free' markets as espoused by writers such as Milton Friedman, Friedrick von Hayek and Ayn Rand. Individual choice, free of government coercion, is seen as the only ethical influence in shaping economic and social development.

Rand is probably the least well known of the three advocates of free markets mentioned above, although her advocacy appears to have been influential. She is reputed to be a favourite writer of Alan Greenspan, the Chairman of the American Federal Reserve at the time of writing. Friedman's arguments in defence of a business world free of government or social obligations beyond those defined in law are considered in more depth in Chapter 8, so a little more time will be given here to consider some of the key thoughts of Rand on the subject of markets as the basis of economic and social coordination.

Ayn Rand was born in Russia in 1905, but she emigrated to America when she was twenty-one, nine years after the 1917 Bolshevik uprising in Russia and four years after the civil war that followed the uprising. On arriving in America, Rand took a variety of low-paid, menial jobs. She is quoted as saying: 'I had a difficult struggle, earning my living at odd jobs, until I could make a financial success of my writing. No one helped me, nor did I think at any time that it was anyone's duty to help me.' Rand depicted man as 'a heroic being, with his own happiness as the moral purpose of his life, with productive achievement as his noblest activity, and reason as his only attribute'.

Such snippets of historical context are helpful in understanding some of the factors that might explain an individual's philosophical position on key issues. Randianism (the term used by followers of Rand) rejects government in anything other than its minimalist form, i.e. that which can be justified to protect individual rights, such as the police, the law courts and national defence forces. All other functions can and should be operated by 'the people', preferably via market mediation, and paid for (or not) by choice.

| Case study 1.2 | **Biography and philosophy** |
| --- | --- |

Bauman (1994) contrasts two philosophers, Knud Logstrup and Leon Shestov. Logstrup lived a tranquil and civilised life in Copenhagen. He wrote of human nature, 'It is characteristic of human life that we mutually trust each other ... Only because of some special circumstance do we ever distrust a stranger in advance ... initially we believe one another's word; initially we trust one another' (Bauman, 1994: 1). Shestov, on the other hand, experienced great persecution during his life, under both the tsarist and anti-tsarist regimes and as a consequence had a far more pessimistic view of human nature, portraying the individual as one who is vulnerable and must at all times be ready to be betrayed. 'In each of our neighbours we fear a wolf ... we are so poor, so weak, so easily ruined and destroyed! How can we help being afraid?' (Bauman, 1994: 2).

Rand is credited with developing the philosophical position that is known as objectivism. Objectivism has three key elements:

1. '*Reason* is man's [*sic*] only means of knowledge', i.e. the facts of reality are only knowable through a process of objective reason that begins with sensory perception and follows the laws of logic. Objectivism rejects the existence of a God, because it lacks (to date) empirical support. However, in America, some of the most strident advocates of free markets come from politically powerful religious groups.

2. *Rational self-interest* is the objective moral code. Objectivism rejects altruism (i.e. the greatest good is service to others) as an unhelpful and illogical human attribute. Individuals are required to pursue their own happiness, so long as it does not negatively affect anyone else's. This is compatible with negative

freedom, one of Isaiah Berlin's two forms of freedom. It relates to a 'freedom from' approach that grants people a right to be free from interference by others, including, and in particular, government.

3. *Laissez-faire capitalism* is the objective social system. It is important to recognise that laissez-faire capitalism is referred to by its advocates as a social system, and not just an economic system. This is an important issue and one towards which critics of the approach feel unified in their opposition, although such opponents have differing views on how to respond. Some would argue for an overthrow of the capitalist ethic and practice, whilst others would retain a market-based framework, but define boundaries of relevance and ethical justification for markets. The latter is exemplified by writers such as Walzer (1983) and is discussed below.

> **DEFINITION**
>
> **Laissez-faire** means unrestricted. So laissez-faire capitalism refers to a preparedness to let markets 'sort themselves out', even during periods of disequilibrium and apparent malfunctioning. The belief is that a 'market' will self-correct in time (a natural law, or Darwinist view within economics). Self-correction rather than external intervention is deemed infinitely preferable in the long run for all concerned.

The attachment of modern-day libertarian-economists to a myopic focus upon competition can be criticised for ignoring two other significant elements of economic systems, which are:

- *Command* (the extent to which power, coercion and hierarchy affect economic relationships), and

- *Change* (the way that capitalism effects change and is itself affected by change).

These three central elements of capitalism, competition, command and change have ethical and moral implications and it is argued here that they are interconnected, not subject to easy and simplistic separation. However, the classical-liberal perspective eschews these arguments and presents a schema in which the operations of the firm, both those within the firm and how it interacts with its external environment, are treated as if they are value neutral.

Within the simple competitive model of economic behaviour managers are expected to behave in ways that reflect what is known as economic rationality. This normative theory is open to challenge in terms of its descriptive rigour, hence the existence of alternative theories of the firm. Supporters of the neo-classical-economic perspective would accept that actual practice is likely to be variable around the preferred norm, but it is argued that economic rationality is the goal towards which organisations should strive. They argue that those organisations that get closest to the normative position will prosper, with competitors having to respond in a similar fashion, or wither on the economic vine.

## The corporatist approach

The corporatist approach does not deny the primacy of competitive market forces, but an exclusive equity shareholder perspective is eschewed in favour of a broader-based set of perspectives in some of the organisation's decision making. These additional perspectives are those of employee representatives, debt financiers, and in some cases state interests. This broadening of the decision-making base is claimed, and appears to offer, a longer-term view to certain aspects of corporate decision making. For Crouch and Marquand (1993: 3).

> The system as a whole trades-off losses in the short-term efficiency on which the Anglo-American tradition focuses against gains in consensual adaptation and social peace. It owes its extraordinary success to its capacity to make that trade-off ... In a high skilled – or would be high skilled – economy, consensual adaptation and social peace are public goods, for which it is worth paying a price in strict allocative efficiency.

The sphere of inclusion reflected in this approach goes beyond the exclusivity of the shareholder orientation of the classical-liberal perspective espoused by most Anglo-American corporations. Evidence suggests that the corporatist-type approach has avoided, or minimised, many of the worst effects of short-term economic 'adjustments' in world trade that have been experienced since about 1960. This is not to say that countries such as Germany, Sweden and Japan (examples of the corporatist perspective) can be immune from significant movements in world economic activity, but it is argued that significant economic lurches have been avoided in these countries, thus minimising significant rises in unemployment levels, with the attendant impacts upon social cohesion. The significant economic downturns experienced by a number of Asian economies in the late 1990s, including Japan, were associated more with structural factors within these economies than with inherent weaknesses in Japan's more corporatist approach to market coordination.

Whether the corporatist approach is preferred by some because it offers a greater likelihood of economic, and thus political, stability, with the greater apparent value placed upon the interests of individual citizens/employees merely an ancillary benefit, or whether the rationale for employing this approach is reversed (i.e. the ethics of the corporatist approach are argued to be the main reasons for its adoption), is not critical for our discussion. What is relevant is that both the 'classical-liberal-economic' and the 'corporatist' approaches can cite ethical justifications for their superiority as economic and social systems. The former can do so because of the primacy attaching to the notion of individual choice, the latter because of its attachment to social cohesion and the desire to avoid, or minimise, what might be deemed unnecessary social disruption and distress to individual lives during periods of economic correction or recession.

## The pluralist perspectives

There are two main pluralist perspectives. The first (referred to as Type A pluralism) sees broad stakeholder interests being represented (as far as this is possible) by elected or appointed members of corporate boards. This is a development of the corporatist perspective, but with the stakeholder groups being drawn more widely. The corporatist approach is evident in the countries cited above on a reasonable scale, whereas the two pluralist perspectives currently exist as arguments and debates, rather than as practice. Companies such as The Body Shop are very much the exceptions that prove the rule.

In Type A pluralism stakeholder groups are required to do more than argue their particular, vested-interest, case. They are expected to be representative of societal interests. Clearly the extent to which the latter are adequately represented will depend upon the composition of the stakeholder groups. Thus, as compared with the classical-libertarian-economic perspective, where the unconscious forces of individual decisions are deemed to give expression to society's preferences, within Type A pluralism societal preferences are given voice by the presence (or not) of stakeholder groups on company boards or committees.

The second pluralist perspective (referred to as Type B pluralism) does not dispute the possibility of stakeholder groups being physically represented within corporate decision-making processes, but this is neither a prerequisite, nor part of the basic arguments. This second variant of pluralism sees economic rationality being moderated by concerns for, and recognition of, wider social implications of corporate decisions, with these factors being weighed by individual decision makers. Type B perspectives can be presented as a continuum, with writers such as Casson (1991) at one pole, and Maclagan (1998), Maclagan and Snell (1992) and Snell (1993) at the other.

The perspective argued by writers such as Casson is that competition via market-based economies is the preferred economic system, but that reliance upon unadulterated economic rationality as the sole explanation of individual behaviour is both naïve and unhelpful. For the discipline of economics to retain relevance Casson argued that it must recognise behaviours that are explained by drives other than, or in addition to, economic rationality.

> These professional prejudices must be overcome if economics is to handle cultural factors successfully. They are the main reasons why, in spite of its technical advantages ... economics has not contributed more to the analysis of social issues.
>
> (Casson, 1991: 21–2)

Classical-libertarian economics retains a view of human behaviour that sociologists would describe as 'under-socialised' (i.e. unrepresentative of the complexity and variability of actual human behaviour). Type B pluralism argues for a recognition of the realities of everyday market conditions, but also a more socialised set of assumptions of human behaviour. Whilst a market-based economy is seen as the foundation upon which organisational coordination takes place, structural issues and problems within markets are recognised, e.g. power imbalances between competitors; information asymmetry between producers and customers; and the capricious nature of (the owners of) capital. Greater responsibility, ethicality and humanity are required of corporate decision makers.

In a similar vein, but with less of Casson's implicit instrumentalism, Etzioni (1988) employed a moral justification for an overt recognition of broader perspectives beyond short-term profit motives. In the following quotation Etzioni used the term 'deontological'. This is an important word in any consideration of business ethics and it is considered in more depth in Chapter 3. However, we offer a brief definition of the term here to allow you to understand the argument that Etzioni was making.

---

**DEFINITION**

A **deontological** approach to moral behaviour is one that believes that moral reasoning and action should be guided by universal principles that hold irrespective of the context in which an ethical dilemma might exist.

---

> Instead of assuming that the economy is basically competitive, and hence that economic actors (mainly firms) are basically subject to 'the market' possessing no power over it (monopolies are regarded as exceptions and aberrations), the deontological 'I & We' paradigm evolved here assumes that power differences among the actors are congenital, are built into the structure, and deeply affect their relationships. We shall see that power differentials are gained both by applying economic power (the power that some actors have over others, directly, within the economy) and by exercising political power (the power that some actors have over others, indirectly, by guiding the government to intervene on their behalf within the economy). These fundamentally different assumptions make up what is referred to here as the I & We paradigm (one of the larger possible set of deontological paradigms). The term [I & We] highlights the assumption that individuals act within a social context, that this context is not reducible to individual acts, and most significantly, that the social context is not necessarily wholly imposed. Instead the social context is, to a significant extent, perceived as a legitimate and integral part of one's existence, a whole of which the individuals are constituent elements ... The deontological paradigm evolved here assumes that people have at least some significant involvement in the community (neo-classicists would say 'surrender of sovereignty'), a sense of shared identity, and commitment to values, a sense that 'We are members of one another'.
>
> (Etzioni, 1988: 5)

Etzioni continued:

> The issues explored here range way beyond the technical, conceptual matters of what constitutes a workable theory of decision-making in economic and other matters. At issue is human nature: How wise are we, and what is the role of morality, emotions and social bonds in our personal and collective behaviour.
>
> (Etzioni, 1988: xii)

Progressing along the continuum, past Etzioni's position, one moves towards those who argue for Type B pluralism on the grounds that a broader ethic than that required by classical-liberal economics is desirable, even essential, on the grounds that society as a whole needs organisational decision-makers who understand and can exercise moral judgement in complex situations (Maclagan, 1996,

1998; and Snell, 1993). These writers see management practice as essentially a moral practice, set in a complex and challenging arena (business organisations), for individual moral development.

Thus, our pluralist continuum moves from writers, such as Casson, who argued for theories of decision making to recognise actual human behaviour and instincts in order to make economic theorising more relevant and realistic, to the arguments of writers such Maclagan and Snell, who justify the inclusion of the moral dimensions within business decision making on the grounds of the ethical demands of society as a whole.

## The critical perspective

The critical perspective is composed of many different theories about human and collective behaviour, including the politics of organisations (Simon, 1952, 1953 and 1955); expectation theory (Vroom, 1964); the use of ambiguity and hypocrisy as managerial tools (Brunsson, 1986 and 1989); the theory of coalitions (Cyert and March, 1992); the exploitation of people (Marcuse, 1991); the benefits that people seek at work and the importance of these benefits (Maslow, 1987); power and identity in organisations (Knights and Willmott, 1999); and the range of strategic resources that individual managers draw upon to allow them to cope with managerial life (Watson, 1994). This is far from an exhaustive list, but it gives a flavour of the range of research and theories that have been developed to explain actual behaviour within organisations. What these works share is a picture of organisational life that is far more complex and messy than classical-liberal economics would prefer to work with. The behavioural and critical theories are not normative theories (i.e. theories of how things should be, such as the classical-libertarian-economics perspective), but what are referred to as descriptive theories, i.e. theories of how things actually appear to be. However, behavioural theorists and critical theorists do vary in terms of the intentions of their respective arguments.

Behavioural theories are amoral in their stance in that, unlike the liberal-economic, corporatist and pluralist perspectives, they do not put forward a preferred ethical foundation for their theorising. They might however highlight examples of laudable, contentious or downright immoral behaviour. They do so by acting as organisational windows through which we can observe the ways in which employees at all levels in organisations appear to react, and behave, when faced with ethically complex situations. For example, you become aware that a friend and work colleague, who you know has a very difficult financial situation at home, unlawfully takes a small toy (a company product) home to one of their children. Such situations could involve divided loyalties between either colleagues or concepts, where the ethics of a situation are not clear-cut or neat; or where moral agency is compromised by power imbalances that jeopardise future employment and promotional prospects.

Critical theorists, however, have an avowed commitment to societal change, for the emancipation of employees from the shackles of capitalism. However, critical theorists make different analyses (for example, Foucaudian perspectives, e.g. McKinley and Starkey, 1998, and neo-Marxist perspectives, e.g. Alvesson and

Willmott, 1996) and there is no consensus on the preferred replacement for market-based societies. Habermas (whose ideas are discussed in Chapter 3) does, however, outline the necessary conditions for a societally acceptable economic set of relationships to develop.

## Boundaries of jurisdiction or spheres of justice

The fear of market-based relationships as the bedrock upon which all societal and interpersonal relationships are based is articulated by a number of writers. Walzer (1983), for example, wrote:

> One can conceive of the market as a sphere without boundaries, an unzoned city – for money is insidious, and market relations are expansive. A radically laissez-faire economy would be like a totalitarian state, invading every other sphere, dominating every other distributive process. It would transform every social good into a commodity. This is market imperialism.

(Walzer, 1983: 119–20)

Taking his cue from Walzer, Keats (1993) argued that:

> It is as if their [liberal economists'] theoretical energy has been so fully utilised in demonstrating the virtues of the market that little has been left to deal with the arguably prior question of what it is that defines the nature – and hence limits – of that 'economic' domain with respect to which market and state are seen as the chief rival contenders.

(Keats, 1993: 7)

As a way of handling this problem Walzer argued that societal life should be seen as a series of spheres, which contain and constrain differing elements of societal existence. One of these spheres is the economic, in which markets are recognised as the most effective mediating mechanism, and competition the most defensible form of organisational coordination. Whilst markets, contract and competition are seen as appropriate mediating elements, their relevance is largely constrained within this sphere. Within the spheres representing non-economic interpersonal relationships we find notions of trust, care, welfare, sharing, friendship, leisure and possibly even altruism (although this is not highlighted by Walzer). There is some similarity between Walzer and the earlier work of the German philosopher Hegel (1770–1831) who also used the notion of spheres to conceptualise the social world (Singer, 1983). Hegel spoke of the spheres of state, family and civil society, and to these Walzer adds the economic as worthy of consideration.

McMylor comments upon the development of market-based capitalism from feudal societies. He presented the development from non-market societies as a process whereby the economic moved from being enmeshed 'within other dominating frameworks' to a situation in market societies when:

the economy, with a capital 'E' is no longer so embedded. The market means that there is in some sense, a differentiation of economic activity into a separate institutional sphere, no longer regulated by norms that have their origin elsewhere. The individual economic agent is free then to pursue economic self-interest, without 'non-economic' hindrance.

(McMylor, 1994: 100)

From a moral perspective one of the problems with dividing the human world into separate spheres is that it might suggest the spheres are independent to the point of allowing differing forms of behaviour to prevail within each. Behaviour might be accepted, or at least tolerated, in one sphere that would not be acceptable in another. It has been argued that this is a recognition that people sometimes act (or feel they need to act), when in 'business mode', in ways that they would not employ within their private, domestic lives. Walzer recognised this and argued that the spheres should not be seen as totally autonomous and independent. Rather, he portrayed a dynamic set of relationships between the spheres in which shifts between spheres of particular facets of societal life do happen, and that a sphere's scope and importance may wax and wane. Boundary conflict thus becomes endemic:

The principles appropriate to the different spheres are not harmonious with one another, nor are the patterns of conduct and feeling they generate. Welfare systems and markets, offices and families, schools and states are run on different principles: so they should be.

(Walzer, 1983: 318)

However, Walzer went on to say that 'the principles must fit within a single culture' (1983: 318). This is highly problematic, unless the single culture is one that recognises difference, a multiplicity of cultures. Within such a complexity of perspectives, the notion of wisdom becomes an important mediating factor, but this has to be an active wisdom, i.e. it is always in a state of emerging through dialogue and debate. Within this perspective the dynamic of change is recognised, is debated and matures through processes that are demanding but which, it must be stressed, are subject to 'social capture' by active groups and voices if participation is shirked by the general polity.

---

### DEFINITION

**Social capture** is a term used to describe a mechanism, e.g. a committee, a regulatory body or a political process, which is established to oversee a particular facet of social life, but which becomes dominated by, or heavily influenced by, the very sectional interests the mechanism was intended to monitor or control. The original intentions behind the creation of the mechanism thus become at best neutralised, and at worst subverted.

To minimise the risk of social capture and other such distorting influences within political, economic and social systems requires an active citizenry, prepared to be interested in, even involved in, micro- and macro-level debates about equity and justice – the very morality of life's various spheres. Hegel spoke of the dialectic, the processes of debate and argument that are required to surface and (possibly) resolve differences of view and contradictions. The dialectical approach is to be found in the teachings of Socrates, certainly in the way that Plato presents the work of his master. Billig (1996) makes a plea for a resurgence of the practice of rhetoric, not in the pejorative sense in which the term tends to be viewed in contemporary society, but as a return to an engagement in debate and argument, for these are the mechanisms and processes by which civilised societies develop and progress.

## Defining the boundaries of the economic sphere

One of the principal virtues of competitive markets, as the mechanisms by which business and social interaction is mediated, is that the 'invisible hand' of the market is amoral, i.e. value neutral. Although some may suffer as a result of market-based outcomes, through unemployment or loss of capital, the outcomes are not intended from the start. They are simply the unintended consequences of the multitude of transactions that comprise a free market. Sir Keith Joseph, a notable politician of the 1970s and 1980s and an architect of the political period and philosophy referred to as Thatcherism, was a devotee of Hayek and Friedman. As Heelas and Morris (1992: 19) observed:

> Policies designed to effect more equal distribution of resources, Joseph claims, are not only coercive and threaten individual liberty but are counterproductive and give rise to a series of negative consequences (economic, psychological, moral and political) ... Liberty is primarily to be exercised by the self-interested consumer in the market place, including the political, educational and medical 'markets'.

Plant (1992), taking up the theme of markets being the most appropriate mediating mechanism for medical services, explored the possibilities for a free market in body parts (human organs), as well as the justification for a market-based ethos replacing a service ethic in non-voluntary, public service organisations. With regard to a market for human body parts Plant (1992: 91) observed:

> On a strictly capitalist view of market principles, it is very difficult to see why there should not be such a market. The scope for a market is clearly quite wide. There could be a market in blood and blood products; in kidneys; in sperm; in renting out a uterus for surrogate pregnancy; and so forth.

Plant argued that, from a market perspective, at least three principles would favour a market in these areas:

1. There is a clear demand.

2. The current donor system is failing to meet demand.

3. Ownership of the human organs is clear and would not be undertaken by the donor if it were not in their personal interest.

Despite strong advocacy for such markets, broad public support was (and appears to continue to be) lacking. Plant argued that this reluctance reflected a boundary being drawn by society, with human organs currently residing outside the boundary that defines the limits of market application.

Titmuss (1970), in a seminal work on the marketisation/commercialisation of blood donor services, observed, when responding to arguments that blood should be seen as a commodity and thus private blood banks should be introduced to improve the productivity of the blood giving process:

> In essence, these writers,[ ] are making an economic case against a monopoly of altruism in blood and other human tissues. They wish to set people free from the conscience of obligation. Although their arguments are couched in the language of price elasticity and profit maximisation they have far-reaching implications for human values and all 'social service' institutions ... The moral issues that are raised extend beyond theories of pricing and the operations of the marketplace.
>
> (Titmuss, 1970: 159)

Titmuss worried about the wider implications of commercialising the blood donor service in the UK. If the altruism that, it is argued, is reflected in the voluntary and unpaid giving of blood is replaced by a commercial relationship, what, asked Titmuss, fills the space that used to be occupied by the sense of community inherent within the existing system?

> There is nothing permanent about the expression of reciprocity. If the bonds of community giving are broken the result is not a state of value neutralism. The vacuum is likely to be filled by hostility and social conflict, a consequence discussed in another context ... the myth of maximising growth can supplant the growth of social relations.
>
> (Titmuss, 1970: 199)

Titmuss discussed four economic and financial criteria, excluding the much wider and unquantifiable social, ethical and philosophical aspects to concentrate upon those aspects that economists (the focus of his criticism) would recognise. These were:

1. Economic efficiency.

2. Administrative efficiency.

3. Price – the cost per unit to the patient.

4. Purity, potency and safety – or quality per unit.

On all four criteria the commercialised blood market fails. However, paradoxically ... the more commercialised a blood distribution system becomes (and hence more wasteful, inefficient and dangerous) the more will the GNP be inflated. In part, ... this is the consequence of statistically 'transferring' an unpaid service (voluntary blood donors, voluntary workers in the service, unpaid time) with much lower external costs to a monetary and measurable paid activity involving costlier externalities.

(Titmuss, 1970: 205)

The discussion so far in this chapter has laid out the arguments for claiming that the market system is:

- The only defensible economic and social system for protecting the freedom of the individual to exercise personal choice, which allows the development of economic and societal relationships that are free from government coercion and intervention. This is the liberal-economic perspective.

- Something that is preferable to alternative economic systems, but which needs to be carefully watched and, if necessary, modified from time to time to ensure that the economic system is compatible with broader societal aims. This incorporates the corporatist and pluralist perspectives.

- An intrinsically corrupting system that pits human beings against each other, with only an elite few dictating the life chances of the many. This is the critical perspective.

The argument has been about the place of ethics in business life, and the place of business in the ethics of life.

## Descriptive, normative and reflective approaches

Two ways of discussing ethical matters, normatively and descriptively, are often proposed. Normative discussion is concerned with rules and principles that ought to govern our thoughts and actions. Normative arguments are focused in particular on how such prescriptive claims can be shown to be legitimate or valid. Descriptive discussion focuses on how things *are* rather than how they should be. A descriptive approach to ethics would give an account of the values and ethics of particular groups and try to explain how they have emerged. It would analyse value systems to look for norms and the tensions between them. The word normative is troublesome in a subject, such as business ethics, that spans both philosophy and sociology. In sociology, normative refers to that which is the norm within a group or society. The term is both descriptive – the norms are those of a particular group, and also normative – they define right and wrong within that group. In philosophy normative and descriptive are seen as opposing terms. In this book normative will be used in its philosophical sense.

Many business ethics textbooks take a normative approach. They identify ethical difficulties in business, rehearse the arguments about what should be done about them and then present a resolution or a set of principles. Rather than taking a normative and prescriptive approach this textbook takes a descriptive and analytical approach. It attempts to describe how people in organisations interpret and respond to ethical issues at work. It does not propose solutions to the many ethical dilemmas and problems that face managers and organisations. However, by explaining how others think about and respond to ethical matters, and by providing you with the appropriate tools for thinking, we hope the book will enable you to analyse the issues and to come to your own conclusions.

The intention of the book brings us to a third way of talking about business ethics, the reflective and reflexive approach. Reflection implies careful consideration of ethical issues. Reflexive means to turn back on one's own mind and to consider one's own values and personality. This textbook therefore tries to help you examine your own positions and thoughts. This can be done in part by reflecting on the material in this book and other publications. But this is vicarious learning, piggy-backing on the experiences of others. Reflexive learning occurs when you use your values to challenge your actions and your experiences to challenge your values.

## Reflections

One of our concerns in this book is the possibility of the existence of moral agency and ethical practice within organisations. Integrity is one of the concepts that would form part of any definition of business ethics. The importance of integrity within organisational life in general, and executive decision making in particular, is discussed by Srivastva and Cooperrider (1988), although they stress that the way forward is not easily mapped. It can only be navigated and negotiated through dialogue, reflection, learning, tolerance and wisdom.

> Executive integrity is dialogical. Executive integrity is more than the presence of morality or the appropriation of values; integrity involves the process of seeing or creating values. Whereas ethical moralism is blindly obedient, integrity represents the 'insightful assent' to the construction of human values. In this sense, organisation is not viewed as a closed, determined structure but is seen as in a perpetual state of becoming. Dialogue is the transformation of mere interaction into participation, communication, and mutual empathy. Executive integrity is, therefore, a breaking out of a narrow individualism and is based on a fearless trust in what true dialogue and understanding might bring, both new responsibilities and new forms of responsiveness to the other.
>
> (Srivastva and Cooperrider, 1988: 7)

The big weakness of a heavy reliance upon the notion of a dialectic transformation of society is that the associated processes are subject to the risk of social capture. The best chance of minimising this possibility is for all of us to take ourselves seriously and to believe that our individual voices count in shaping the societies in which we live.

We end this opening chapter on a qualified, optimistic note. Spaemann (1989) refused to accept that conscience is either purely instinct or exclusively a function of upbringing:

> In every human being there is the predisposition to develop a conscience, a kind of faculty by means of which good and bad are known.
>
> (Spaemann, 1989: 62–3)

However, Spaemann went on to say that conscience has to be nurtured and supported – shown good practice in order for it to flourish and mature. Fail to do this and the development of a strong conscience becomes 'dwarfed'. The term 'dwarfing' is used by Seedhouse (1988) when discussing the growing attention to a 'business mentality' within UK health care, at the expense of a prioritising of the individual. Both Spaemann and Seedhouse saw the individual as central to any challenge to the primacy of business interests, although, as you will see in Chapter 7, conscience is often the victim of the need to maintain organisational and personal relationships.

Hannah Arendt (cited in Bauman, 1994) also placed the individual at the centre of any developments towards making ethics a live and legitimate subject for debate within organisations. Arendt wrote, 'there are no rules to abide by ... as there are no rules for the unprecedented'. Bauman continued

> in other words, no one else but the moral person themselves must take responsibility for their own moral responsibility.
>
> (Bauman, 1994: 14)

With this in mind, this book is intended to inform your understanding of some of the key issues that bear upon this critical element of modern society – the possibilities for business ethics.

## Summary

In this chapter the following key points have been made:

- Business ethics issues can be illustrated through stories; sometimes these are expressed as romances, as tragedies, as satire, as comedies and sometimes as farces.

- Many writers, and indeed organisations, argue that there is a business case for companies to behave ethically and responsibly. There is an association between the two, but whether good companies are profitable because they are good, or good because their profitability means they can afford to be, is not easily proven one way or the other.

- Many business ethics issues are best understood by using a stakeholder approach.

- Four different perspectives: the classical-liberal, the corporatist, the pluralist and the critical, on the question of whether organisations, and their role within market systems, are ethically proper.

- The doubts about the classical-liberal model place a premium on the role of the moral agency of individuals within organisations. Moral agency involves reflection on what is right and wrong and working for the good within organisations.

## Quick revision test

1. What is meant by the term 'moral agency'?

2. Ayn Rand is credited with being the founder of the philosophical position known as 'objectivism'. What are objectivism's three core elements?

3. What does the criticism of neo-liberal economics being 'under-socialised' mean?

4. What is the difference between 'normative' theories and 'descriptive' theories of ethical behaviour within organisations?

## Typical assignments and briefs

1. Is there an effective 'business case' for corporations acting in a socially, ethically and environmentally responsible way?

2. Compare and contrast the four approaches to the involvement of stakeholders' business decision making (classical liberal, pluralistic, corporatist and critical) outlined in this chapter.

3. How should a company decide which interest groups should be treated as stakeholders and which should not?

4. What can we learn about business ethics issues at work by studying the stories in which they are reported?

## Group activity 1

### A delphi exercise on reasons to be an ethical organisation

Delphi is a technique for creating a consensus on difficult matters of prioritising or forecasting. In this instance it will be used to answer the question:

*Why should organisations choose to behave ethically and socially responsibly?*

The exercise needs the group to divide into groups of between five and eight people. Each group should then follow the following steps.

1. Each person, working on their own, should think of as many reasons as they can why an organisation should behave ethically and socially responsibly. Write each reason down on a Post-it note and make a pile of them.

2. Everyone then posts their Post-its in random order on a convenient board.

3. The group should gather around the Post-its and sort and cluster them, putting similar points together, until the mass of Post-its has been reduced to about five or six reasons.

4. The group should then write a simple, one-page, questionnaire that lists the five or six reasons and asks respondents to score each reason according to its importance. The scoring should be done using percentages, the larger the percentage the more important the reason. Photocopy a batch of the questionnaires (or, if you are inclined, create a small spreadsheet).

5. Each member of the group then completes the questionnaire on their own.

6. The scores are then totalled and averaged and presented to the whole group.

7. Each group member then completes a new questionnaire taking into account the average scores of the whole group.

8. The process continues through cycles of individual scoring and group feedback until the group reaches a consensus, or nearly does, on the scoring and importance of the five or six reasons.

9. You will then have decided why organisations should behave ethically and socially responsibly.

10. Discuss in the group how the arguments you have identified are similar to or differ from those presented in this chapter.

## Useful websites

| Topic | Website provider | URL |
|---|---|---|
| Business Ethics A general website including articles, corporate codes of ethics, resources and so on. | Sharon Soerger | http://www.web-miner.com/busethics.htm#additional%20 |
| Business case for ethics | World Economic Forum | http://www.weforum.org/site/knowledgenavigator.nsf/Content/_S3576 |
| A news digest service that provides useful updates on stories about business ethics. | Institute of Business Ethics | http://www.ibe.org.uk/ethicsnews.html |
| A website on a research project into stakeholder theory. It includes a bibliography of articles on stakeholder theory. | | http://www.mgmt.utoronto.ca/~stake/Articles.htm http://www.mgmt.utoronto.ca/~stake/index.htm |
| Business case for ethics | World Economic Forum | http://www.weforum.org/site/knowledgenavigator.nsf/Content/_S3576 |
| FTSE4Good Home page | FTSE | http://www.ftse.com/ftse4good/index.jsp |
| Dow Jones Sustainability Index Home page | Dow Jones STOXX Ltd | http://www.sustainability-index.com/ |
| EIRIS home page | Ethical Investment Research service (EIRIS) | http://www.eiris.org/index.htm |

# CHAPTER 2

# Ethical issues in business

## Learning outcomes

Having read this chapter and completed its associated activities, readers should be able to:

- Describe the range of ethical and moral issues that arise in management, business and organisations.

- Distinguish between ethical, moral and legal wrongdoing and assess the importance of a particular misdeed.

- Analyse the complex consequences and motives that typically attend ethical and moral issues in management, business and organisations.

## Introduction

Identifying the range and variety of ethical issues in business and management is the main focus of this chapter. It includes many case studies and so is longer than the other chapters. The case studies are provided because understanding of theoretical issues, which are not dealt with until the next chapter, is made easier if the reader first has some concrete examples to refer to. They also provide resources that will be referred to in other chapters. When reading this chapter it is not necessary to read all of the case studies. Only read those that have taken your interest or where you feel you need to think some more about the general issues raised. To make the chapter more manageable it has been divided into five parts.

- Part one: The map of business ethics issues
- Part two: Encouraging goodness
- Part three: Creating a level playing field, benign-ness
- Part four: Preventing indifference to others
- Part five: Discouraging badness.

## Part one: The map of business ethics issues

If the variety of business ethics issues is going to be explained we need a map, and that in turn needs a set of coordinates to explain how the range of issues relate to each other. In practice the field of business ethics has been divided into specialist fields dominated by academics and consultants with backgrounds in different forms of knowledge.

- Corporate social responsibility (CSR) – dominated by social policy experts and environmentalists

- Corporate governance – largely dominated by lawyers and accountants

- Corporate citizenship – lawyers

- Sustainability – environmentalists

- Ethical investment – market analysts

- Employment rights and human rights – human resource management specialists and lawyers

- Fair trade and the regulation of international trade – economists

- Risk management – accountants

- Reputation management – marketing and public relations specialists.

We will not divide the issues between these sub-fields because it prevents the holistic approach that business ethics issues commonly demand. Our map will use two coordinates.

- Degree of morality, or from bad to good.

- Legality, illegality and justice.

## Good and bad

### The semiotic square

The semiotic square, under the name of the square of opposition (Parsons, 1999), has been used by philosophers since classical times as a tool for logical analysis. It was reinvented in the twentieth century by Greimas (1987) as a method of analysing the structures in stories and narratives. We will use it to identify the structures within stories about business ethics matters. It has been popularised in the UK by Chandler (2001). All semiotic square analyses begin with a key theme and continue by plotting three types of relationships that necessarily stem from it (*see* Figure 2.1). As we are dealing with ethics we will begin the semiotic square with the notion of good.

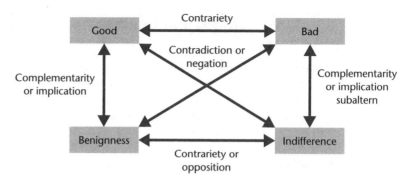

**Figure 2.1** A semiotic square analysis of the concept of 'good'

The first type of relationship is opposition or contrariety. If we begin with good its opposite is bad. Both of these two terms then has its contradiction – the second form of relationship. In the semiotic square opposites and contradictions are not the same thing. Contradictions occur through particulars and practicalities that negate formal, universal terms. An example is the poet Edna St Vincent Millay's remark 'I love humanity but I hate people'. In other words, in formal, general terms Millay approved of humanity, but her dislike of individuals, in all their, sometimes unpleasant, diversity, contradicted that belief. If the good is negated we are left with an absence of good, which is not the same as the bad; it may be mere indifference. Indifference however, in its connection with 'bad', represents the third kind of relationship – complementarity – because, as in the quotation famously (but probably incorrectly) attributed to Edmund Burke, 'the only thing necessary for the triumph of evil is for good men to do nothing'. Indifference may permit badness but is not the whole of it. It is, to use the term of the original square of opposition, subaltern to it. The most complex relationship is now left, which is the contradiction of 'bad', the negation of the negation. If we absent the bad we are left with benignness (as incorporated in the famous precept 'first of all do no harm'). This is the opposite of indifference. Benignness allows the good to occur and avoids the bad, but on its own does not constitute the good. Benignness may only consist in avoiding the doing of harm and not concern itself with doing good.

The semiotic square identifies four degrees of rightness and wrongness in behaviour, which in order of goodness are:

- the good,
- benignness,
- indifference,
- and the bad.

These four categories, which form a scale from good to bad, are the first dimension in Table 2.1, which will be used to illustrate and explain the range of ethical issues facing businesses, organisations, managers and those affected by them. The scale from good to bad may also be seen from a different perspective. In terms of moral action what is required at the 'good' end of the spectrum is encouragement, or prescription, while at the 'bad' end distraint, or proscription, is necessary. Some writers (Vardy and Grosch, 1999 and Taylor, 2001) distinguish between the terms ethics and morality to point up this contrast. Ethics is focused on doing good. It deals with defining the good life for humankind. Morality in contrast is a concern for justice, which is about preventing wrongs and making restitution if wrongs are done. Ethics, in these terms, can be thought of as developmental whereas morality is judgemental. In Christian terms the Ten Commandments represent morality but ethics is represented by the Beatitudes. The Ten Commandments specify what it is wrong to do, for example commit murder or adultery (Deuteronomy, 6). The Beatitudes are the virtues that Jesus commended in a sermon to his followers. They include meekness, mercy, pureness of heart and peacemaking (Matthew, 5.).

## Legal, illegal and just

The second dimension in Table 2.1 is based on the following categories:

- things that it is legal to do but which the law does not require to be done;
- things that must be done or not done according to law;
- and finally things that are illegal but that may well be justified (i.e. a requirement of justice)

that can be used to judge the rightness of actions. Legality and illegality are defined by the criminal or civil law. A criminal offence is one so grievous that the state takes action to protect society. Civil law is concerned with the compensation that people who are damaged by others (by tort or breach of contract) may seek. Four combinations of legality and justice are identified.

### 1 Actions that are good and legal but not a legal obligation

Some actions may raise ethical issues because, although they are good and legal, people do not take them because the law does not require them to do so. The question is whether people, and corporations, should do them even though they are not obliged to do so.

### 2 Actions that are wrong and illegal

In the next category ethical or moral questions arise because an action is both wrong and illegal. Such actions ought to be straightforward to condemn. However, on issues that many would place in this category, others might argue that the action is neither wrong nor illegal.

### 3 Actions that are legal but not necessarily just

Another category includes actions that may be legal but are also, arguably, bad. Many of the moral and ethical issues that affect business and management fall into this category. They are a reflection of the big question, raised in Chapter 1, of whether business has moral obligations beyond the proprietary claims of the

Table 2.1  Illustrative cases of the major issues in business ethics

Ethics ← → Morality

Prescribing the good life ————————————————————— Proscribing bad actions

| | Good — Positive action for good or to prevent harm being done | | Benign — Avoiding doing harm, supports the doing of good but takes no positive action to do good | | Indifferent — Ignoring harm done by or to others and disregarding the rights of others | | Bad — Taking action to do harm / Taking no action to prevent harm being done | |
| | Social development and Caring | Social responsibility and Supporting | Reciprocity | Fairness | Lying and dishonesty | Cheating and Selfishness | Bullying and Social irresponsibility | Harming and Social & environmental disengagement |
|---|---|---|---|---|---|---|---|---|
| **Legal, but not a legal obligation** | The Nationwide Foundation Case study 2.1, p. 48. | AIDS drugs and patent rights in South Africa. Case study 2.3, p. 51. | Paying for staff's professional training. Case study 2.6, p. 58. | Providing new drugs for MS sufferers. Case study 2.9, p. 64. | BAT, Nottingham University and the honorary professor. Case study 2.13, p. 75. | | | |
| **Legal** | British Sugar and Sunday trucking. Case study 2.2, p. 49. | Child labour in developing countries. Case study 2.4, p. 53. | Executive fat cats. Case study 2.7, p. 60. The oil companies and the 2000 fuel crisis. Case study 2.8, p. 62. | The British railway system: priorities, profits and governance Case study 2.11, p. 67. | Economy with the truth when dealing with the tax authorities. Case study 2.15, p. 77. | The retention of dead babies' organs in hospitals. Case study 2.19, p. 85. | The hospital consultants. Case study 2.21, p. 88. Supermarkets' treatment of their supply chains. Case study 2.22, p. 89. | The Firestone Tire recall issue. Case study 2.25, p. 93. The 'Super size Me' sales promotion. Case study 2.23, p. 91. |
| **Illegal** | | | | Discriminating against employees. Case study 2.10, p. 65. | The case of Shell's missing oil barrels. Case study 2.12, p. 72. The Jonathan Aitken story. Case study 2.14, p. 76. | The rise and fall of Parmalat Case study 2.16, p. 79. Lord Black and Hollinger International. Case study 2.17, p. 81. BAT and allegations of cigarette smuggling. Case study 2.18, p.83. | British Airways and Virgin Atlantic. Case study 2.20, p. 86. | Sexual harassment. Case study 2.24, p. 92. |
| **Illegal but just?** | David Shayler and whistleblowing on MI5. Case study 2.5, p.55. | | | | | | | Huntingdon Life Sciences Case study 2.26, p.94. |

shareholders. The claim that there are no ethical obligations on a private company other than to obey the law and meet the demands of their shareholders was most famously articulated by Milton Friedman (1970).

**Connexion point**

Milton Friedman is an economist who is one of the major participants in debates about business ethics. His views are discussed in Chapter 8.

Friedman's position can be criticised from several perspectives. Solomon's (1993) critique is based on the Aristotelian idea of virtue (*see* p. 101). He argued that the belief that business is simply about the financial 'bottom line' is untrue. However, he claimed this misconception has generated many false metaphors for business that hide the truth from people. The idea of cowboy entrepreneurs who are driven by greed and profit and who see themselves as loners in competition with all others is one such metaphor. Rather, he argued, the purpose of business is to provide for the prosperity and happiness of the community. This cannot be achieved if people make a distinction between their business and their personal lives. People are social animals but their social needs are ignored if their business lives are focused on the individualistic pursuit of profit. The problem is intensified if working lives are associated with necessary drudgery in contrast to the pleasure that can be had from personal and social lives. Virtues, according to Aristotle, are formed from the ability to find a sensible mean between such extremes as dreary work and pleasurable personal lives.

> The bottom line of the Aristotelian approach to business ethics is that we have to get away from the 'bottom line' thinking and conceive of business as an essential part of the good life, living well, getting along with others, having a sense of self respect, and being part of something that one can be proud of.
>
> (Solomon, 1993: 104)

There is a religious objection to the Friedmanite view of business that can be exemplified from the Roman Catholic position as expressed in the encyclical *Centesimus Annus* (John Paul II, 1991). Humans, it argued, have a capacity for transcendence – the ability to give themselves away to others, and to God. The role of capitalism and profit seeking has to be seen within this context.

> The church acknowledges the legitimate role of profit as an indication that a business is functioning well. When a firm makes a profit, this means that productivity factors have been properly employed and the corresponding human needs have been duly satisfied. But profitability is not the only indicator of a firm's condition. It is possible for the financial accounts to be in order and yet for the people, who make up the firm's most valuable asset, to be humiliated and their dignity offended ... In fact the purpose of a business firm is not simply to make a profit, but it is to be found in its very existence as a community of persons who in various ways seek to satisfy their basic needs and who form a particular group at the service of the whole society.
>
> (John Paul II, 1991: §35)

Large companies, such as Shell, are adopting forms of accounting that attempt to balance traditional financial accounting with a concern for environmental sustainability and social justice. This is known as triple bottom line accounting, which provides output and performance measures in the, potentially contradictory, fields of financial, social and environmental performance. The idea, similar to that of the balanced scorecard, is to make it obvious if financial success is only being achieved at a social and environmental cost. The technical problem of identifying measures that can illuminate a company's performance on environmental quality and social justice is difficult. Comparing the many possible measures against each other and against financial performance is a matter of judgement rather than of accountancy calculation (Elkington, 1999).

> **Connexion point**
>
> The triple bottom line reporting concept is discussed in more detail in Chapter 9, pp. 371–2.

The issues that arise from legal, but unethical, managerial and business actions all reflect one or more of these criticisms of the Friedmanite perspective.

## 4 Actions that are just but illegal

The final category of the dimension is one that will always generate controversy. It concerns actions that may be illegal but are morally or ethically good. It concerns the perennial question of when a law can be said to be immoral and when it is justifiable to break or defy it. Campaigning against a law one disapproves of is acceptable within a democratic system; the ethical problem only emerges when a person moves from campaigning to disobedience. The dilemma is two-fold.

The first problem is defining the conditions or circumstances in which it would be proper to defy the law. In a democratic system does a general acceptance of governmental authority imply that it is never acceptable to disobey a particular law? Political obligation does not exhaust moral obligation. This is the case with conscientious objectors, for example, who refuse to take a combatant role in a war. But before refusing to obey a law the person needs to consider carefully the balance between their political and moral obligations (Raphael, 1970: 115–16). If in general the state seeks to achieve justice and the common good, and if the law has been passed with the assent of the majority and according to the rule of law, then there is a presumption in favour of complying with the law. Conversely where laws are arbitrary and the state is not just, the contrary presumption may hold. Lyons (1984: 214) argued that the presumption should be that a legal system does not automatically deserve respect. Respect has to be earned. Greenawalt (1987: 222), however, pointed out that there are no plain rules available to guide people on when it is proper to disobey a law.

The second problem is the nature of the defiance, which can extend from passive civil disobedience through to violent direct action. Gandhi, in his campaigns against British rule in India, practised passive resistance. His belief was that people should disobey immoral laws but should not resist when the forces of the law took action in response. His concept of *Satyagraha* was based on the Hindu Vaishnavite principle of *ahimsa* (or non-violence) and the importance of suffering (Brown, 1972: 6). He believed that passive resistance would eventually cause the authorities, through shame, to right the injustices. This increasingly appears to be the position of the Catholic Church. The Pope wrote, concerning the fall of the Soviet bloc:

> It seemed that the European order resulting from the Second World War and sanctioned by the Yalta Agreement could only be overturned by another war ... Instead it has been overcome by non-violent commitment of people who, while refusing to yield to the force of power, succeeded time after time in finding effective ways of bearing witness to the truth.
>
> (John Paul II, 1991: §23)

At the other extreme some anarchist and other radical groups argue that harming property, and in some cases people, can be justified by the importance of their cause. As will be seen in Case study 2.26 some animal rights activists argue that the evil of vivisection, practised by some pharmaceutical companies, justifies violent action against those companies, their employees and backers.

Deciding when, if ever, violence against an organisation is justified is similar to arguing about which circumstances can make war just. The concept of the just war has concerned theologians since the time of St Augustine. St Thomas Aquinas set down the main tests of a just war in the thirteenth century. They were:

- The war must be declared by a lawful authority (*auctor principis*).

- The cause must be just (*justa causa*).

- Those going to war must intend to advance the good and avoid evil (*recta intentio*) (D'Entreves, 1965: 159).

- The test of 'proper means' (*debito modo*), which requires that minimum force be used in accordance with the rules of war and that peace should be established at the end of the conflict, was added to the list later.

An additional requirement, that all other means of resolving the issue should have been exhausted before resort is made to violence, seems to be a twentieth-century addition.

In considering the question of the justness of violent action against organisations, rather than war between states, the first criterion does not apply. If the actions that people condemn as immoral also happen to be legal then the state could not be expected to take action against the company. However, the criterion does alert us to the dangers of validating violent action that is not carried out in the name of some legitimate body. Allowing self-legitimating groups the right to define who is evil, and to use force to attack it, could lead to the intolerance displayed by fascism. Sometimes civil associations or non-governmental organisations (NGOs), such as Greenpeace, take this legitimating role upon themselves.

The cause of militant animal rights activism can illustrate the impact of the other criteria. Even if the cause, for sake of argument, were just, its narrow focus on destroying an alleged evil, rather than the creation of a peaceful solution, violates the requirement that the violence should serve the establishment of long-term peace. Nor do the movement's tactics meet the requirement for minimum use of force and adherence to the 'rules of war'. Its actions have included intimidating 'civilians' such as investors and bankers who had only an indirect connection with vivisection. These also violate one of Greenawalt's (1987: 235) considerations for disobeying a law: that the law objected to and the laws being broken are closely connected. The final criterion has not been met in the case of violent actions in support of animal rights because, in a democratic society, there are always non-violent means of protest that can be adopted. Pacifists of course object to the notion of a just war and would claim that, as violence begets violence, its use to stop evil is never justified.

The business world of Russia since the collapse of the Soviet Union provides an example of the issues that surround behaviour that may be illegal but just. Tax evasion (not just the legal tax avoidance) is rife among companies in Russia. Corporations evade their tax liabilities by constructing the accounts so as never to show a profit, by transferring the company's income to a third-party organisation a few days before the tax is due, providing loans and insurance cover for employees to reduce the taxable revenue and so on. These practices are clearly illegal, but in a study into Russian executives' views on these practices Meirovich and Reichel (2000) reported that 36 out of 40 interviewees regarded such practices as ethical while the remaining four took the neutral position that the practices were neither ethical nor unethical. Their arguments in support of this view were that:

- the legal and environmental conditions for businesses in Russia are draconian and businesses would not survive if they paid tax at 90 per cent on all their profit;

- the government itself is corrupt and inefficient and they merely waste or embezzle the taxes received, therefore it is good to deny the government the money and instead direct it to the society at large by enabling economic growth.

There are of course suitable counter arguments such that the illegal behaviour of private organisations further encourages the growth of corrupt institutions. Also the loss of revenue to the government prevents it from meeting the many pressing social needs of the Russian population.

**Connexion point**

The battle between the Russian government and the oil company Yukos is instructive on this matter. It is described in Chapter 12, p. 471. Some see it as a proper attempt by the Russian government to make large corporations pay their taxes, which can then be used for the good of society at large. Others see it as an attempt by the Russian government to renationalise a major industry and curtail the growing political power of the oligarchs – business men who have become very rich after they bought many state enterprises during the time of privatisation.

## The cases

Table 2.1 plots some recent issues in business against the two dimensions just discussed. The cases (presented later in this chapter) are located in positions on the grid according to whether, on the face of it, they are examples of goodness, benignness, indifference or badness and whether they represent actions above and beyond legality, conformance to the law, illegality or unjust legality. These grid positions are not indictments of the people and organisations discussed in the cases. The cases are located at certain coordinates in the grid because it forces us to ask questions about legality, morality and ethicality, not because they are definitive illustrations of good or bad behaviour.

## Part two: Encouraging goodness

## Social development

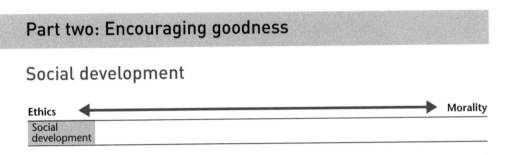

Social development is defined as actions taken by an organisation or company that are undertaken to improve the social, economic, cultural or environmental conditions of a society. In an earlier period such actions would have been termed philanthropy. Andrew Carnegie, who was a poor Scottish immigrant to the USA in the nineteenth century, provides a classic example. He built an industrial empire and when he sold his business he was thought to be the richest man in the world. He disposed of his wealth philanthropically. A particular interest was the public libraries, of which he founded 2,509 throughout the English-speaking world. He thought libraries important because of the role they could play in helping the poor to participate in what he saw as a meritocratic society in which people could become successful through learning. He also saw libraries as a means by which immigrants such as he could learn about the countries in which they had chosen to live.

Between 1985 and 2000 the generosity ratio of UK companies (the percentage of their philanthropic donations to their pre-tax profits) rose from 0.10 per cent at the start of the period to 0.40 per cent at the end (all statistics are from Moore, 2003). This rate of growth in the ratio was much faster than it had been in the previous decade. There is a Percent Club in the UK, an association of corporations committed to giving 0.5 per cent of their pre-tax profits to good causes, though none of the members has yet achieved this. In the USA where there is a form of social contract which requires low corporate tax rates to be offset to some degree by higher levels of philanthropy the average level of donations is five times higher than in the UK, although the generosity ratio is in decline there.

A company's social development activities need not be directly connected with its business activities. However, even if they are not it may be argued that organisations are hoping to improve the standing of their business indirectly as a result of their good works. Motives, corporate and philanthropic, are nearly always mixed and this should not detract from the value of development activities. Other organisations, such as non-governmental organisations (NGOs), have social development as their prime purpose.

Corporate citizenship is sometimes used as an alternative term for social development. British Airways, for example, define their citizenship objective as 'To succeed in partnership with the communities in which we work, not at their expense' (British Airways 2000: 26). Among its activities, which focus on education, it provides training for school governors and provides a Community Learning Centre at Heathrow. It sponsors the British Olympic and Paralympic teams. It has provided high-profile sponsorship, in the tourism field, for the Millennium Dome (which probably did little for BA's reputation) and the British Airways London Eye (which probably did much for the company's reputation). The company's report also commends the initiative of its staff who have carried out charitable work for children in Africa and the Indian subcontinent.

The first case study reports on an organisation that is seeking to respond to social problems and raises the question of whether philanthropy necessarily must arise from altruism or whether the point is to bring social good from strategic necessity.

| Case study 2.1 | **The Nationwide Foundation** |

Building societies are mutual organisations. Their customers own them. This reflects their origins as self-help organisations designed to help people buy their own homes. In the 1990s, and into the twenty-first century, there was a move to demutualise building societies. This process involved converting a society into a public limited company (plc). The new plc would give the previous owners (the customers) shares in the new company to compensate them for their loss of ownership. The new owners could either keep or sell these new shares. If they sold them they would make a windfall profit. They would receive a cash sum for a property that had cost them nothing except the constraint of saving with, or accepting a mortgage from, that particular building society. Some building societies wish to remain as such. The pressure to demutualise is more keenly expressed by their customers.

The Nationwide Building Society wishes to remain mutual. In 1997 it created the Nationwide Foundation to become the channel for its charitable giving. Everyone who became a member of the society from November 1997 onward also became a member of the foundation and agreed to assign to the foundation their rights to any future conversion payments. This meant that should the society demutualise or be taken over in the future then any connected payment of any sort which would otherwise be received by the society members would be passed to the foundation to create a fund for charitable giving. Bluntly, there would be no windfall payments. A number of the society's members who had been members since before 1997 also agreed to become members of the foundation.

The foundation supports schemes throughout the United Kingdom using money donated by the society, its staff and its members. These include a Time Bank scheme in London. In this scheme people give of their time and skills and receive credits that they can use when they need help. It also supports schemes in the areas of adventure training, support for people with hearing difficulties, sport in disadvantaged areas and providing community information services. Its priority in 2001 was a project called the New Generation Initiative that was designed to help parents face the problems of bringing up children.

(*Source for further information*: www.nationwidefoundation.org.uk)

### Discussion activity 2.1

Does the use of the fund as a means of meeting the society's own purpose of remaining a mutual institution detract from the worth of its activities?

Case study 2.2 is about a company that was accused of disengaging from the largely rural community within which it operated. Although its plans were legal it drew back from implementing them because people objected to the disruption they would cause to the pattern of weekend life in East Anglian villages.

### Case study 2.2

### British Sugar and Sunday trucking

East Anglia is sugar beet territory. There is an annual sugar beet harvest that lasts for five months when the crop has to be taken to British Sugar's factories for processing. For many years there had been an agreement between British Sugar and the National Farmers Union (NFU) that deliveries would take place for five and a half days each week with no lorries on Saturday afternoons or Sundays. Most residents in the villages through which the large and heavy beet lorries rumble accept the beet harvest as part of country life. In 2000 British Sugar, in an attempt to diminish the queues of lorries that formed during the mornings at the factories, decided to switch to seven-day-a-week deliveries and they came to an agreement with the NFU to do so. There was immediate outcry. As a resident in one of the affected villages said, 'We do appreciate that they have a job to do. The noise of these lorries is quite considerable. All we want is for them to leave us in peace for one day of the week.' The hauliers who delivered the beet met at Peterborough and came out against seven-day deliveries. As one of them said, 'Imagine big sugar beet lorries driving past country churches on a Sunday morning while people are trying to worship. It simply won't work – we won't do it.' The campaign against the additional deliveries carried on and within a few weeks British Sugar announced that it was suspending its agreement with the NFU to deliver beet for seven days each week.

(*Sources*: Moore, 2000; Bradley, 2000; Pollitt and Ashworth, 2000)

**Discussion activity 2.2**

Was British Sugar right to forego the efficiency and cost benefits that could have been gained from a seven-day working week?

## Social responsibility

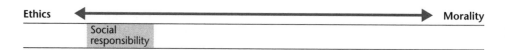

Social responsibility, in the way the term is used in this chapter, covers a narrower canvas than social development. It can be defined as conducting the business of an organisation in a manner that meets high social and environmental standards. It differs from social development in not requiring organisations to do good works beyond the commercial purposes of the organisation. Also social responsibility affects fewer arenas than social development. Social responsibility excludes the social and cultural good works that are appropriate to social development. Social responsibility is important to organisations 'not least because of the devastating impact that even isolated acts of wrong doing can have on an organisation's reputation among its stakeholders' (Arthur Andersen and London Business School, 1999). Many large companies report their performance as socially responsible organisations; for an example see British Petroleum's social and environmental report (BP, 2001).

The nature of a socially responsible approach to redundancy illustrates some of the factors that distinguish social responsibility from social development. It is possible to argue that redundancies, especially on a large scale, are morally wrong because they harm individuals, families and communities. The counter argument is that the welfare of families and communities is not the concern of a company or organisation. Another possible defence is that the loss of some jobs protects the jobs and livelihoods of many more. Social responsibility would suggest a middle position. It would argue that redundancy may be justified but that a responsible organisation will take trouble to help those affected. This might involve using outsourcing consultants to provide counselling and career advice to those losing their jobs. It could involve setting up agencies or funds to encourage the introduction of new businesses in affected localities, or helping those made redundant to start their own companies. Social responsibility is an obligation to minimise the collateral harm caused by the organisation's actions and decisions.

The next case study provides an example of assertive public and governmental opinion which judged companies' protection of their patent rights as socially irresponsible. The pressure of global media scrutiny became such that the threat to the companies' reputations became greater than the economic loss caused by the challenge to their patents.

Case study
2.3

## AIDS drugs and patent rights in South Africa

There is an epidemic of AIDS in southern Africa. There is therefore a great need for drugs (anti-retro-viral – AVR) with which to treat the disease. One of the drugs, Ciprofloxican, cost South Africa's public health sector 52p for each pill when bought from the company that had developed it and that held the patent. A generic version of the drug could be imported from India for 4p a pill. The cost of these drugs was a heavy burden on the health services and the South African government proposed a new law that would allow the cheaper generic drug to be imported. The world's largest pharmaceutical companies opened a lawsuit against the South African government to claim that their property and patent rights were thereby put at risk. However, in May 2001, as the case was about to commence in the South African High Court, the pharmaceutical companies withdrew the claim.

The following article from the *Financial Times*, which includes an interview with the chief executive of one of the major pharmaceutical companies, rehearses the arguments.

**FT**    Very sick people need drugs. The world's largest pharmaceutical companies charge plenty for them but they channel that money into research to find new medicines. The companies, now suffering an unprecedented onslaught over the prices they charge and lack of access to their medicines, want to refocus public attention on what they see as the main issue. 'You can kill the golden goose,' says Hank McKinnell, chief executive of Pfizer, of demands for lower prices. 'You'll eat well today but the cupboard will be bare in future.'

Mr McKinnell is a staunch defender of the prices that his company, the world's largest drugs group, charges. He is also very aware that a humanitarian and economic disaster is unfolding in Africa, where 27m Africans are now HIV-positive and only a fraction of them have access to or can afford even deeply discounted western Aids medicines. But in an interview he points out that Aids was first identified by medical researchers in the early 1980s. By 1987, he says, there was one treatment. Now, 64 Aids drugs are available and more than 100 are in development. 'What was the right thing to do in 1981?' asks Mr McKinnell. 'Say the prices are too high and take away the incentives for the research? That doesn't help patients or their families.'

But many believe this is an argument the drugs industry will never win. Companies are supplying Aids drugs in Africa at up to 90 per cent discounts but they face demands for larger cuts. This is on the grounds that the products are still unaffordable for almost all HIV-positive patients or their governments. Meanwhile, companies in countries such as India and Thailand are making cheap, often illegal, copies of western drugs and promising to save thousands of lives at a fraction of the cost. And in the US there is speculation that it will not be long before patients lose patience and refuse to pay up to 10 times the price for treatments. Whichever way they turn, Mr McKinnell and his peers will be accused of placing a different value on the lives of people on different continents.

▶

Pfizer's chief executive concedes the industry appears to have lost its way trying to formulate a response to the unprecedented wave of bad publicity. Changing that is one of his new responsibilities. This month he became chairman of the Pharmaceutical Research and Manufacturers of America, the industry's most powerful lobby group. Drugs companies have been caught off-guard by the sheer size of the attack. As well as being criticised for their drugs pricing policy in sub-Saharan Africa, they have endured closer scrutiny of pricing and patent regimes worldwide.

Federal and state regulators in the US have been investigating abuses of marketing to physicians and consumers. Influential Washington politicians have proposed revisions to US patent law that make it easier for cheap copies of drugs to come on the market. Meanwhile, Mr McKinnell says, Indian companies have been lobbying the World Trade Organisation to preserve their ability to break patent laws being ushered in as part of the WTO's Agreement on Trade Related Intellectual Property. He has little sympathy: 'The Indian companies have been making billions of dollars stealing our technology and selling it, not only in India but any place around the world they can get away with it.'

He believes the pharmaceutical industry has convinced people it genuinely wants to help, particularly in Africa. Last week, in a high-profile dispute, 39 pharmaceutical companies abandoned their case against the South African government in which they had said their patent rights were in danger. Bad publicity was an important factor behind the decision to drop the case and the companies have escaped a disastrous legal situation. Mr McKinnell says the companies have also been increasing their efforts to work with aid agencies, non-governmental organisations and local governments to improve distribution.

'Unfortunately, we haven't expanded them rapidly enough,' he says. 'But there is now a realisation that if we don't provide access, we're going to stay as part of the problem ... I think we've been pretty successful in becoming part of the solution.'

But prices are still too high in countries where any price is unaffordable. The answer, says Mr McKinnell, is to forge partnerships with agencies and governments to bring in more resources. 'If the sole problem is the high price of drugs, you give up. But the industry has been smart enough to take that off the table. When the drug is free or at cost, now what's the problem? It's national will, it's distribution, and it's medical treatment.' In other words, drugs companies have knocked 90 per cent off the price but it is up to someone else to find the rest and to help deliver the drugs.

(*Sources*: A. Michaels, *Financial Times*, 26 April 2001. Copyright © The Financial Times Limited. Reproduced with permission; McGreal, 2001; Clark and Borger, 2001)

The main pharmaceutical companies began to cut their prices for ARV drugs in developing countries. Glaxo SmithKline reduced the price of its main drug three times in 2003. The large companies also began to come to understandings with the generic drug producers in India and began to license generic producers in South Africa (Dyer, 2003a). In some cases regulatory bodies such as the South African Competition Commission argued that the international companies were breaking competition rules by over-charging and threatened to force the companies to grant generic licenses to local producers (Dyer, 2003b). Much of the movement on the issue was attributed to pressure from institutional investors who were worried that the damage being done to the reputation of the pharmaceutical industry might reduce its ability to charge premium prices in the industrialised countries. The focus of the debate shifted more to the ability and commitment of governments in some African countries to take action against AIDS. It took the South African Government, for example, a long time to agree to a programme to provide free ARVs and in 2004 there were criticisms that the roll-out of the programme was being delayed (Degli Innocenti and Reed, 2004).

## Discussion activity 2.3

What are the arguments for saying that knowledge that is medically beneficial to humanity should not be private property?

The next case study raises similar issues to those in Case study 2.3 as it reviews why a company acted more responsibly than was required by law.

## Case study 2.4

## Child labour in developing countries

The use of child labour by multinational companies, in their factories in the third world, to produce cheaply the products they sell in western markets became an international issue in the 1990s and the first decade of the new millennium. The United Nations' Convention on the Rights of the Child, and the International Labour Organisation's Declaration on Fundamental Principles and Rights at Work (United Nations 1989) condemn the use of child labour. NIKE in particular has been the subject of public campaigns against its labour practices in South East Asia.

The Adidas-Salomon group is a sportswear retailer and manufacturer. Many of its shoes are made in six factories in Vietnam. The factories are not directly owned. They are owned by Taiwanese businesses. The factories are all modern, light, spacious and equipped with the basic facilities that people need at work.

Adidas became aware of child labour issues during the 1998 football World Cup when it was alleged that its footballs were stitched by child labourers in Sialkot, Pakistan. In response it set up a department of social and environmental affairs and developed a code of conduct known as SOE (Standards of Engagement). On child labour the SOE states:

> Business partners shall not employ children who are less than 15 years (or 14 years old where the law of the country of manufacture allows), or who are younger than the age for completing compulsory education in the country of manufacture where such age is higher than 15.

▶

In Vietnam the local managers made a decision that they would introduce a minimum age for employment of 18 years. This was not only a more stringent policy than the company required globally; it was also tougher than Vietnamese law that specified that children should not be in full-time employment until they finished their compulsory education at 15 or 16.

The reasons for adopting a more demanding ethical stance were not necessarily entirely altruistic. The local managers were anxious to avoid bad publicity and the two-year margin of safety made it less likely they would unintentionally employ child labourers because of difficulty in establishing their ages. The local managers also argued that the rigours of the footwear production line were inappropriate to people less then 18 years old.

An audit of labour practices was carried out in the Vietnamese factories. In one particular factory it was found that, out of 3,500 employees, there were 12 girls aged 14 and 15 years. Most of these had already worked in the factory for between one and three years. They had obtained the jobs by presenting false documents that belonged to aunts or sisters. In addition there were 130 staff of 16 and 17 years. The employment of this latter group was of course legal.

The local management decided that the children in the younger age group would be provided with a full-time, two-year education programme but would continue to be paid a basic wage. The older group of child workers would be provided with some part-time educational input. The company was keen to adhere to the SOE requirements because it valued the contract with Adidas for which 80 per cent of their output was made. The educational programme was being delivered by the USA-based NGO that had carried out the initial labour practice audit although the cost was borne by the local factory management. The visibility caused by the NGO's presence may have encouraged the company to pay the cost of educating the 12 employees. They would have been entitled to dismiss the children and free them to attend school in the normal way.

A Vietnamese teacher in a well-equipped classroom next to the factory floor taught the 12 children. There was formal tuition in the morning. The children were expected to return to the classroom in the afternoon for private study. This expectation did not become practice and the children disappeared after lunch. The factory had decided to teach the children in the factory because it was feared that, if they were sent to normal school, they would truant and find employment in another factory. The children believed they were in 'paradise'. The notion of being paid to be educated was almost impossible to believe. What the other workers thought was not recorded.

(*Source*: Based on Winstanley, Clark and Leeson, 2001)

## Discussion activity 2.4

What action do you think companies should take when they find their suppliers use child labour contrary to their company policy?

The next case introduces a new aspect of social responsibility that considers when it is proper for a person to break their duty of confidentiality to their employer if they know that their employer is acting irresponsibly.

**Connexion point**

This issue, also known as whistleblowing, is discussed in detail in Chapter 7.

**Case study 2.5**

## David Shayler and whistleblowing on MI5

David Shayler is an ex-employee of MI5. He alleged that the service had plotted to kill the President of Libya. Having made the allegation he fled to France where attempts by the British government to extradite him were unsuccessful. However, he decided to return to Britain where he was arrested and charged. As a member of MI5 he had signed the Official Secrets Act of 1920 that banned him from revealing official secrets for life. The Public Interest Disclosure Act (*see* p. 285), which gives some limited protection to whistleblowers, does not apply to the security services. Shayler's intention was to use the Human Rights Act 1998, which incorporated the European Convention on Human Rights into English law, in his defence. The Act provides a right to freedom of expression and if a court makes a declaration of incompatibility between the Human Rights Act and a particular piece of legislation, such as the Official Secrets Act, the government would have to consider amending the law. Some of the issues are raised in the following leading article from the *Financial Times*.

FT Here's a paradox for Britain's spymasters. Three years ago, David Shayler, the former secret agent, fled to Paris after claiming that the security service had tried to kill President Muammar Gadaffi of Libya. Robin Cook, the foreign secretary, said the allegation was 'pure fantasy'. Yesterday on his return to Britain, Mr Shayler was arrested. But he would only be guilty in relation to the Gadaffi affair under the Official Secrets Act if what he said about his former employment was fact, not fiction.

The authorities seem to have avoided this difficulty by charging him with unauthorised disclosure related to his other allegations of mess-ups and impropriety in the service. Even so, the case shows up a huge problem for spymasters in dealing with former agents who talk too much. In James Bond's world, the solution was easy – perhaps something nasty with an exploding cigar, or a shark.

Outside spy fiction, the authorities face harder options. They may dismiss mud-slinging agents as mercenary fantasists. But then some of the mud may stick. If the authorities prosecute the agent for a serious disclosure, they risk giving credence to his allegations. If they bring charges for a technical breach, they look heavy handed. If they mount a full investigation into the agent's allegations, they risk further embarrassing revelations – even if the allegations prove false. If true, the agent faces huge difficulties in proving them in court.

▶

Clearly the secret services must be allowed to keep their secrets. But such secrecy is only tenable in peaceful democracies if the agencies are seen to act within the law and the principles of civil liberty. This requires a good deal more openness than they have shown in recent decades – and more vigorous scrutiny by the parliamentary committee set up to watch over them 11 years ago.

In the present case, the authorities must show that they have not done a shabby deal by promising to soft-pedal charges in exchange for silence. If Mr Shayler has revealed important secrets – as the authorities appear to believe – he must be prosecuted vigorously, however embarrassing his defence might prove.

Equally, the police, who are now investigating his charges against the service, must find ways to demonstrate that they are doing the job properly. Mr Shayler's accusations may be found eventually to be insubstantial or wildly exaggerated. But if the authorities take Mr Shayler seriously enough to prosecute him, there must be a presumption that his allegations against the service deserve, at the least, serious investigation.

(*Source*: Leader article, *Financial Times*, 22 August 2000. Copyright © The Financial Times Limited. Reproduced with permission)

Shayler appeared in Court in August 2002 and was charged with passing on information without the consent of his employers. He pleaded not guilty but was found guilty and sentenced to six months in prison. He appealed on the grounds that he was acting in the public interest but he was denied this defence by the Court of Appeal and by the House of Lords.

### Discussion activity 2.5

Was David Shayler's whistleblowing justified?

Were the British authorities acting in a socially responsible way in choosing the offence David Shayler was charged with?

## Part three: Creating a level playing field, benign-ness

### Reciprocity

Ethics ←————————————————————————→ Morality

Reciprocity

If the avoidance of doing good and behaving well is irresponsibility, then selfishness is doing harm through a pursuit of self-interest. This section discusses human beings' inclinations to act either selfishly or altruistically. The assumption that selfishness is the norm in the behaviour of human beings may be unsafe. Research into the evolution of insects and animals suggests that altruism, sacrificing oneself to benefit others, may be the result of evolutionary selection. Reciprocity is perhaps a more appropriate term than altruism because such behaviour anticipates a future benefit for the individual's near relatives, if not for the individual. One form of reciprocity is called kin selection. It accounts for the altruistic behaviours found among ants, bees and wasps. Individuals in these species, it is suggested, forego their own opportunity to breed in order to support the queen, their sister, in rearing large numbers of offspring. By doing this they will increase the total number of offspring that are born bearing genes similar to their own. This characteristic is particularly noticeable among bees, ants and wasps because their odd genetic system means that they are more closely related to their sisters than they are to their offspring. Reciprocity can also be a successful evolutionary allele (genetic trait) in animal evolution. Some writers, such as Dugatkin (2000), argued, controversially, that studies of altruism in animals and insects can provide clues for improving human cooperation. Of course this behaviour will only develop if in the long run 'cheats' (individuals who accept but do not return the favour) are 'punished'. This issue is most often studied through the medium of a games theory scenario known as the Prisoners' Dilemma.

---

**DEFINITIONS**

The **Prisoners' Dilemma** involves two imaginary prisoners who have jointly committed a murder. They have been arrested by the police and put in separate cells. They have not been able to talk to each other since the murder and the police make sure that they cannot communicate in the police station. The police have inadequate information to charge them with murder but they could charge both of them with possessing illegal weapons. The two prisoners are interrogated separately. They have a choice of two options, to confess or to keep silence. The consequences of each option, in terms of number of years in gaol, are shown in the pay-off figure (Figure 2.2).

If both prisoners confess they will each receive the

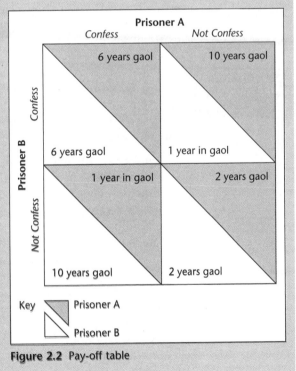

**Figure 2.2** Pay-off table

normal sentence for murder of six years' imprisonment. If they both keep silent the police have insufficient evidence and they will be charged for the weapons offence for which the sentence is two years in prison each. This is the best option for both of them. However, if one confesses after doing a deal with the police, he will only get one year in prison but the one who kept silent will have the book thrown at him and will receive the maximum penalty of ten years. Neither prisoner knows what the other will do because they cannot communicate. If each prisoner feels they can trust the other then neither will confess and both will receive a relatively light tariff of two years' prison each. However, if one keeps silent, but the other 'cheats' and confesses, the silent one will receive a harsh ten years. If a prisoner feels he cannot trust the other then the best bet is to confess. The worst that can happen is six years in prison but the worst that can happen if he does not confess is ten years. This is the Prisoners' Dilemma, whether they can trust each other enough to achieve the best outcome for both of them by both not confessing.

The Prisoners' Dilemma can only be avoided if the players exist in a continuing community in which cheats are punished. In these circumstances the players have to continue to meet, which enables trust to develop. Selfishness will occur, on this analysis, where there is a lack of trust or where people do not see themselves as being in the same community as those whom they harm by their selfishness.

These issues can be seen in the following case studies. In Case study 2.6 altruism was present because all the players saw themselves as part of the same community and there were opportunities for the altruism to be reciprocated. But even in this situation the person explaining the situation found it hard to decide whether the recipients were trustworthy and who were likely to reciprocate his altruism.

| Case study 2.6 | **Paying for staff's professional training** |

The case study is an extract from an interview with a partner in an accounting firm who was responsible for the professional training of new staff.

Well, treating people properly and fairly is always an interesting one; it is a very subjective area. In my role as training partner there are undoubtedly incidents every time anybody doesn't pass an exam; we have to decide what to do about it. Whether to terminate their contract, or whether to pay for absolutely everything. There is a whole spectrum of solutions. Yes, and there is never, I don't think, a right or wrong answer. Well, we had a situation a few weeks ago where we had two students, sat the same exams, got very similar results, both marginally failed.

One of them had cruised through the year, not really done enough, but was a bright lad. The other, a girl, had sweated blood throughout the year and still wasn't quite good enough. Then you get a situation where, some people would think, well, Claire deserves another chance because she worked so hard, some people think you should treat Chris better, he is the brighter one, he will be the more marketable one, he will be more use to us. Some people think you should treat them the same. Some people think that people should be allowed to keep sitting exams at our expense for as long as it takes. Some people think we should just terminate people's contracts for failure.

So, I suppose, I take a business decision basically, rather than a moral judgement when anyone fails. I would say that in practically no instance would more than a small minority agree with my decision, some people think they should be treated harsher, some people think they should be treated more leniently. I gave them both a week's study leave and I paid for their exams, so it gave them both another week and a half to find out of their holiday and about £200 to find for the course. It was a close call, it was a difficult call.

But what you have to do as well is consider the impact on the other students, what message it sends to them. I will have a dilemma within the next year, because I have only been training partner for just over a year. The exam results here; I don't believe they are good enough. I don't think they have been good enough basically because there has been tolerance of failure in the past and I have said repeatedly that in certain circumstances I will terminate people's contracts for failing. That has not happened here for about five years. Sooner or later I am going to have to do it, otherwise people won't believe me. I will only have to do it once. The difficulty is, one person has got to pay the price.

Everyone knows the rules but no one will believe the rules. Now the brighter one of those two, the one who had cruised, the Monday when I spoke to them about it, I was in a foul mood. I didn't terminate his contract – the only reason I didn't – I was sorely tempted to, because (a) I think he deserved it and (b) it would have made an example of him – the reason I didn't was because I was in a bad mood and I thought, there is a risk that I could let my mood take my decision. Had I been in a good mood, I think I would have terminated his contract.

(*Source*: Research interview conducted by the authors)

### Discussion activity 2.6

Why do you think the training partner acted altruistically when, by not supporting the trainees, he might have better met the (selfish) needs of the firm?

In the next case study it is clear that the highly paid executives do not feel they need to act altruistically towards the generality of employees because they see themselves as belonging to a small elite group of world-class CEOs. This is the market argument, which holds that executives are entitled to whatever salary they can command on the international market. This argument only holds good of course if the market is an open and fair one. The second argument in support of high executive rewards is that it can be justified if they secure good performance and results for the organisation. Researchers from two Business Schools

(Erturk *et al.*, 2004 cited in Caulkin, 2004) studied chief executive pay in a sample of FTSE 100 companies. They reported that between 1978/9 and 2002/3 CEO pay in those companies rose by 536.9 per cent but net profits only increased by 118.9 per cent. At the same time the differential in remuneration between the CEOs and average employees rose. CEOs now earn on average 50 times as much as the ordinary employees but 20 years ago the figure was only nine times average pay. The article in Case study 2.7 was written at a time when the question of executive pay was first becoming a matter of public concern and debate.

| Case study 2.7 | **Executive fat cats** |
|---|---|

An article from the *Financial Times*:

**FT**    **Rough justice in the talent market**

Luc Vandevelde, the Marks and Spencer executive chairman who last week turned down an £816,000 ($1.2m) bonus, is unlikely to inspire many imitators. While his gesture was not unprecedented, it is extremely unusual. With thousands of staff being made redundant in the US and Europe in response to the recent market downturn, chief executives have shown little inclination to share their pain. It is not just greed that prevents them from doing so. Those who turn down money risk giving the lie to one of the central tenets of chief executive lore: that their pay is set by forces beyond their control and that they are merely the grateful recipients.

Most chief executives react angrily to news reports that a particular corporate leader has 'paid himself' an impressive-sounding sum. Senior executives do not set their own pay, they point out. The job is done by a remuneration or compensation committee, which carefully examines the market for chief executives' services, researches the going rate and approves a bonus only if the chief executive meets exacting targets. For a chief executive to refuse to accept any of this money would be to sweep aside the committee's careful deliberations.

Gerald Corbett, former chief executive of Railtrack, the UK railway organisation, and one of the few other company heads to have waived a bonus, did so in extreme circumstances. Mr Corbett gave up a bonus of £100,000 after the 1999 Paddington rail crash in which 31 people died. Even Mr Vandevelde's sacrifice was not all it seemed. M&S announced he was giving up his bonus after critical press comment and anger from shareholders and staff that the bonus came at a time when the retailer was doing so badly. But Mr Vandevelde will not go hungry. When he was recruited last year from Promodes, the French retailer, M&S awarded him nearly £2m in shares. And this year's bonus is not so much cancelled as postponed. M&S said it would grant him £352,000 in shares next year, and an equivalent cash sum if he meets specific targets.

Charles Morgan, head of Acxiom, a data management company based in Little Rock, Arkansas, recently made a more substantial gesture. Mr Morgan decided he did not want to lose employees that he would find hard to rehire when the economy recovered. Instead, he imposed a 5 per cent mandatory pay cut on all staff earning more than $25,000 a year and gave them share options in return. He then offered staff the option of taking a further 15 per cent voluntary pay cut in exchange for options. Mr Morgan led the way by cutting his own pay by 20 per cent. 'Acxiom has a shared-fate culture,' the company said. 'Just as the successes of the company have been shared broadly, so are the sacrifices.' Mr Morgan's US colleagues, however, show little appetite for shared sacrifice. Chief executive remuneration climbed 16 per cent last year, giving the average company head total pay of $10.9m, a new record, according to Pearl Meyer & Partners, the consulting firm. The highest-paid US chief executive last year was John Reed, who stepped down as chairman and co-chief executive of Citigroup. Mr Reed gained $293m, followed by Sandy Weill, now Citigroup's sole chief executive, on $224.9m, according to Standard & Poor's and Business Week. Third place was held by Gerald Levin of AOL Time Warner on $163.8m, followed by John Chambers of Cisco with $157.3m. In the UK, the highest-paid company head last year was Martin Read, chief executive of Logica, the information technology group, who gained £27.4m, according to data collected by the Monks Partnership.

Do these pay packages really reflect the demand for executive talent or do they result from remuneration committees looking after their own? The committees are, after all, usually made up of serving or retired senior executives from other companies. By approving large salaries, are they not simply looking after friends and improving the chances that their own pay committees will offer similar sums? Chief executives, particularly in the UK, argue, usually privately, that such questions reflect a culture of envy and a bias against business. They point out that far fewer questions are asked about the huge sums paid to footballers and pop stars.

There is one difference, however. In the case of David Beckham, the Manchester United star, for example, the best clubs in Europe would pay high sums to attract him. Manchester United has to pay him enough to persuade him to stay. The workings of an international market for talent are clear to see. Mr Beckham's salary is not determined by a committee made up of Gary Lineker, Michael Owen and Zinedine Zidane.

Pay specialists argue that competition for chief executives' services, particularly in the US, is just as efficient. 'We still have a tight labour market for senior executives that can manage business of the scope of today's global companies,' says Yale Tauber, senior compensation consultant at William Mercer. Mr Tauber argues that trends in executive pay do partly track company performance. His firm examined 350 companies which had a median increase in net income of 8.9 per cent. The increase in chief executive total compensation in those companies was 10 per cent. The bottom 25 per cent of companies saw net income fall 22 per cent; their chief executives' compensation fell 3.2 per cent. Pay does not track performance precisely, Mr Tauber concedes. 'But there's a rough justice in all of this,' he argues. Employees losing their jobs might not feel that way but, Mr Vandevelde aside, there is little chance they will embarrass their bosses into giving up much more.

## Discussion activity 2.7

Are chief executives inclined to selfishness?

Case study 2.8 raises questions about whether there is an obligation on companies to avoid selfishness in times of national crisis.

**Case study 2.8**

### The oil companies and the 2000 fuel crisis

The UK experienced an oil crisis in July 2000. A combination of self-employed lorry drivers, owners of small haulage companies and farmers took objection to the high price of petrol (the bulk of the price of which in the UK is determined by the excise duty). In a Poujadist protest they used their mobile phones to create a network of supporters who blockaded the country's oil storage depots and led slow-moving convoys up and down motorways causing traffic queues. Any modern country depends on the internal combustion engine and the shortage of fuel caused by the action soon threatened chaos. The National Health Service was put on Red alert and businesses could not carry out their normal business. There were fears that food would not be delivered to the supermarkets.

The government was caught unawares. The prime minister declared that the situation would be back to normal within 24 hours; but it was not. It looked for scapegoats and blamed the international oil companies for selfishness. The government argued that the oil companies should take strong action to break the blockades and ensure that oil was delivered to the nation's petrol station forecourts. The oil companies argued that it was not their responsibility to take risks with the safety of their employees. They would not order their drivers to drive through the pickets if there was a danger that they might be hurt. They were suspected by some politicians of secretly agreeing with the protestors. It was reported that there was a 'chummy camaraderie' between the protestors blockading a refinery and the management within in it; even to the extent that the protestors were served tea and bacon sandwiches from the canteen within the refinery (Weaver, 2000). The oil companies claimed to make only small profits of a penny a litre on retailing petrol, and if the protest led to a reduction in excise duties it could only be of benefit to the industry. Oil transport was outsourced to small independent companies and self-employed drivers (some of whom had been sacked by the companies only to be re-employed as independents for less pay) who did have real complaints about the cost of the diesel that fuelled their lorries. The oil companies had little leverage to force these drivers to break the blockade. The view of the *Observer* (2000) leader writer was that the oil companies were too concerned with maximising their shareholders' returns by carrying low contingency stocks of oil and using a just-in-time logistics system that meant there was no buffer in the case of a crisis. There was a view that the companies owed an obligation to the wider community when they traded in a material that was so vital to the functioning of society.

The blockade melted away as quickly as it had formed as people began panic buying at the supermarkets. The Prime Minister said he would not be forced into cutting the duty on fuel.

**DEFINITION**

**Poujadism** is a set of political beliefs named after Pierre Poujade, a small-town shopkeeper in France in the 1950s. It objects to state interference such as taxation, the investigation of tax evasion and any regulation of small businesses. It also opposes big corporations and large-scale labour organisation.

**Discussion activity 2.8**

Do the oil companies have a moral obligation to maintain fuel supplies in a country?

## Fairness

Ethics ⟵————————————————⟶ Morality

Fairness

Fairness concerns the proportions in which resources are distributed between people or causes. The resources can be money, respect or any possession that a community can allocate among its members. Aristotle expressed the central concern, about the appropriateness of the proportions, in a system of distributive justice. He saw it as a matter of algebra in which there are at least four terms: two persons and two shares. A just distribution is one in which the ratio between the first person and the first share is equal to the ratio between the second person and the second share. If Fred is twice as worthy as Jane then Jane's portion should be half of Fred's. In this case the two ratios will be the same. The arithmetic is fine but the question is how the two people involved are to be assessed. Aristotle said it should be done by assessing their merit. But he admitted that people define merit in different ways.

> People of democratic sympathies measure degrees of merit by degrees of freedom, oligarchs by degrees of wealth, others judge by good birth, those who believe in the rule of the 'best' go by moral and intellectual qualifications.
>
> (Aristotle, 1976: 146)

This does not exhaust the possibilities. Marx measured it according to need, 'From each according to his ability, to each according to his needs' (in Marx and Engels, 1962: 24). Others might measure merit by personhood and insist that, since all are equal in this particular aspect, then everyone should receive equal shares.

The debates under the ethical heading of fairness concern the appropriate measure of a person's merit and the fairness of the ratios between one person's merit and share and those of others. The case studies in this section give examples of these debates. Case study 2.9 focuses on need, 2.10 on personhood and 2.11 contrasts the property rights of shareholders with the needs of customers.

| Case study 2.9 | **Providing new drugs on the NHS to people with multiple sclerosis** |

Multiple sclerosis is a debilitating and incurable disease. A new drug, with the generic name of beta interferon, has been shown to alleviate the effects of the disease but it costs £10,000 per patient per year. The National Institute for Clinical Excellence (NICE) in the UK investigated the drug to see whether, on clinical and economic grounds, it should be made freely available on the NHS. The belief of those who suffer from the disease, and of those who support them through membership of lobby groups, is that it would be unfair to deny this drug to sufferers. The following article from the *Financial Times* identifies some of the politics and anger that surround the issue.

**FT**   The National Institute for Clinical Excellence has put off a decision on the use of beta-interferon, the drug for multiple sclerosis sufferers, until at least July next year. The decision to delay has been taken to allow a publicly available economic model of the costs and benefits of the drug to be built. The delay brought a furious reaction from the Multiple Sclerosis Society that accused the institute of putting back the decision to ensure that it came after the likely date of the general election. Peter Cardy, the society's chief executive, described the decision to delay as 'astonishing' and 'breathtaking bungling' given that beta-interferon and glatiramer, another MS drug, have been reviewed by the institute for almost a year.

Mike Wallace, a former managing director of Schering, which manufacturers beta-interferon, said: 'I find it appalling. You have to wonder what these guys are playing at. I feel desperately sorry for the people with MS who have had their hopes raised and dashed and raised and dashed again by the NICE process.'

The institute initially judged that MS drugs were not cost effective and should be supplied only to patients already receiving them. Appeals led to that decision being reconsidered, but the institute is unhappy with the economic models that Schering and Biogen have supplied. The appeals committee described as 'flawed' a model built by Biogen that claimed the drug might save money when the cost of working days lost by patients and carers was taken into account. Schering has submitted a new model, but has told the institute that it is commercially sensitive – a stance which appraisal committee members say makes it difficult for the institute to explain its objections to the model's conclusions.

The committee has, therefore, decided to build its own model – an approach that may force manufacturers to reveal more of the assumptions behind their results. Mr Cardy said it was 'impossible to understand why NICE has only now decided to look at the cost effectiveness of these drugs in a different way'. He demanded that Alan Milburn, the health secretary, 'sort NICE's ineptitude out'. Andrew Dillon, the institute's chief executive, said: 'The evidence relating to the cost effectiveness of these medicines is critically important in this appraisal.' It was 'of the utmost importance that the institute's guidance is both evidence-based and seen to be fair', and the delay to achieve that was in the best interest of those with MS. The appraisal committee originally said that a big price reduction would be needed before the drugs became cost effective. The process of deciding what would go into the institute's model, and the commissioning and evaluation of its results would be transparent, said Mr Dillon. The results would be published in full, with interested parties free to comment on it.

(*Source*: D. Pilling and N. Timmins, *Financial Times*, 23 December 2000. Copyright © The Financial Times Limited. Reproduced with permission. Additional material from Barlow, 2001; NICE, 2001 and 2002)

In 2002 NICE decided it would not recommend beta interferon or glatimirer for the treatment of MS.

### Discussion activity 2.9

Should the decision whether or not to provide these drugs to MS sufferers be based solely on clinical grounds or should cost-effectiveness criteria also be considered? What influence should powerful lobby groups have on such decisions?

The next case study raises the issue of unfair discrimination at work. In the last three decades of the twentieth century this was one of the major areas of ethical concern in business and organisational life. In the UK discrimination on grounds of race has been illegal since the Race Relations Act 1975 was passed. The Sex Discrimination Act came into force in 1975; it was amended and broadened in 1986. The Equal Pay Act took effect in 1975 and was amended in 1984. In 1995 an Act of Parliament made discrimination on the grounds of disability illegal. There is currently much debate about discrimination on the grounds of age but at the time of writing this was not illegal.

**Case study 2.10**

### Discriminating against employees – the Metropolitan Police Service

One of the most high-profile cases of race discrimination at work involves the Metropolitan Police. It was accused of institutional racism by the McPherson report into the police's investigation of the murder of Stephen Lawrence. The following extract from an article from the *Financial Times* in 2000 reports on discrimination against staff from ethnic groups within the Metropolitan Police.

**FT**  Racism remains rife in the Metropolitan Police, according to an internal report by Sir Herman Ouseley, former chairman of the Commission for Racial Equality who is now a senior lay adviser to the force.

[ ] Sir Herman's report, the result of a four-month investigation, says that white officers claim government oversensitivity on the race issue is undermining their ability to fight crime. But it also says that black, Asian and other ethnic minority officers complained of discrimination at all levels of the organisation.

'A vast majority of staff appear to regard the racism issue as overplayed and overemphasised unnecessarily,' it says. But evidence taken from non-white police officers 'strongly confirmed the existence and reality of institutionalised racism'.

As a result, potential black recruits were discouraged from applying, contributing to a recruitment crisis, and government targets of recruiting 6,500 black and other minority ethnic officers by 2009 were unrealistic. 'This is very unlikely to be achieved for another 50 years at the present rate of [ethnic] recruitment,' Sir Herman says.

Non-white police officers regarded the Met as 'an organisation in denial, still wanting, too often, to pretend that there is not a problem of racism and other forms of exclusion. They (ethnic minority officers) see the closed networks, personal relationships and social interactions in self-selected groupings as perpetuating the exclusive inclusion of like-minded people to appointments panels and assessment and review boards which work against equality and fair treatment.'

(*Source*: J. Burns and R. Shrimsley, *Financial Times*, 14 December 2000. Copyright © The Financial Times Limited. Reproduced with permission)

The issues of discrimination later became focused on the case of Superintendent Ali Dizaei who was Iranian born and one of the most senior officers in the Metropolitan Police from an ethnic minority background. In 1999 he became officer in charge of operations at Kensington Police Station. The Metropolitan Police made him the subject of an undercover operation called 'Helios' that investigated suspicions that he was involved in drugs and prostitution. This enquiry became the most expensive ever undertaken against a single officer. He was suspended from office in 2001. He was eventually charged with attempting to pervert the course of justice, misconduct in public office and submitting false expenses claims. In April 2003 he was found not guilty of perverting the course of justice and in September of the same year the prosecution withdrew the expenses charges. His lawyers claimed that the prosecution had been a 'witch hunt' and a campaign of 'Orwellian proportions' (Tait, 2003).

The criminal proceedings being concluded, the Metropolitan Police service then began a disciplinary process against Dizaei. In 2003 nine allegations were identified and an investigation began. Subsequently the National Black Police Association (NBPA) called for a boycott of the Metropolitan Police Service by anyone from the ethnic minorities who might have considered joining the service. This was something of a blow when the service was intent on increasing the proportion of its officers from the ethnic minorities. Before the investigation was completed the Home Secretary urged Dizaei and the Metropolitan Police to come to a settlement. A deal was brokered by the

Arbitration and Conciliation Advisory Service. Under this deal Dizaei admitted that his conduct had fallen 'far below the standards expected of a police officer' and he agreed not to take his employer to an employment tribunal. In return he received £80,000 compensation, a statement that his integrity was intact and a return to work (BBC News, 2004a). The NBPA dropped its boycott. However, the Police Complaints Authority (PCA) was unhappy that the disciplinary process had not taken its proper course and had been pre-empted by a private agreement between the parties. The chairman of the PCA stated,

> Every police officer should face a consistency of treatment as far as the disciplinary process is concerned – we can't have one officer getting special treatment because he is a senior black officer and because there are concerns about race in the police service.

*(Source*: BBC News, 2004b)

The Metropolitan Police resisted the demand to continue disciplinary action against Dizaei and in March 2004 the PCA directed the Metropolitan Police to take disciplinary action. However, the PCA was then replaced by a new body called the Independent Police Complaints Commission (IPCC). They reconsidered the issue. They also were unhappy about the private deal but they thought it not in the public interest to pursue the disciplinary action. They thought the charges against Dizaei were capable of proof but that if he were found guilty any penalty would likely be modest. They pointed out that he had admitted errors and was to receive 'Words of Advice from his Chief Officer'. They therefore revoked the instruction to continue the disciplinary proceedings (IPCC, 2004). A separate enquiry by another Police Force into Operation Helios continued.

## Discussion activity 2.10

Should efforts to eliminate discrimination be given priority even if they were leading to a reduction in the morale and effectiveness of the police service?

Can the formal and fair processes of a disciplinary policy become a means of discrimination?

Case study 2.11 considers whether Railtrack , the company that oversaw the operations of the British railway system, was fair in its treatment of its stakeholders, in particular the travelling public, in relation to its solicitude towards shareholders.

## Case study 2.11

### The British railway system: priorities, profits and governance

In May 2001 Railtrack, the company responsible for running the infrastructure of Britain's rail system, published its financial results. It made a worse than expected loss of £534m. This was largely due to the cost of renewing the ▶

permanent way after the Hatfield crash in 2000. Despite a disastrous year the company maintained the dividend payment to its shareholders. It was argued that it had to keep the confidence of the financial markets because it would need to borrow millions of pounds in the future to invest in the rail system.

The following leading article was published in the *Financial Times*.

 That profits conflict with safety on the railways can no longer be in doubt. The draft report of the official inquiry into the Hatfield derailment reveals a catalogue of management and engineering failures.

After privatisation in 1996, the top executives of Railtrack, the infrastructure company, focused too much on immediate value for shareholders and too little on maintenance of the track. This might have been predicted; for although the rail regulator set targets for infrastructure improvement, every pound saved on maintenance helped to increase dividends.

Railtrack would have been entitled to keep such savings if they had resulted from extra efficiency. But the inquiry shows that it lacked managerial and technical skills, was slack in its maintenance discipline and communicated poorly with subcontractors. New management brought in after the fatal crash has admitted past failings and has made some progress towards putting them right. But broader remedies are needed. The company must be subject to a new set of incentives that more explicitly recognises its status as a public service utility in receipt of large government subsidies.

At the time of privatisation, it was decided to adopt the regulatory model used in the gas, electricity and telecommunications industries. This sets a price that the utility may charge, leaving an incentive to make extra profits from greater efficiency.

It is now obvious that this was a bad model for the railways – partly because of the importance and unpredictable costs of safety and partly because the fragmented structure of the industry creates perverse incentives. If Railtrack closes a line for unexpected safety work, for example, it must pay penalty charges to train operating companies.

Regulation should move closer to the US model. That would involve tighter supervision and replace the profit motive with the guarantee of a 'fair' rate of return – provided the company does its job properly. There are disadvantages: the spur to efficiency is blunted and, when the return is assured, managers may try to over-invest.

But since Railtrack has failed to convince its shareholders, the markets and the general public that it can find the right balance between profit and maintenance expenditures, stronger regulation must be the way ahead.

(*Source*: Leader article, *Financial Times*, 9 May 2001. Copyright © The Financial Times Limited. Reproduced with permission)

The case raises the question of whether public utilities, which are necessaries of a civilised life, are ethically different from other products and services. The chairmen of UK regulated utilities, according to a survey (Brigley and Vass, 1997: 164), thought they were not, and that the ethical obligations on a private utility company should be no different from those placed on any private company.

In 2001 Railtrack plc was declared insolvent and put into administration. The shareholders demanded that they should be compensated by being paid the value of the Railtrack shares when the company was floated on the stock exchange. The government retorted that taxpayers' money would not be used to spare shareholders the consequences of their poor investment.

The successor body is called Network Rail. It is a not-for-profit public interest company. It has no shareholders but it does have 116 members. The members have no financial interest in the company and receive neither dividends nor capital. Nevertheless they are expected according to Network Rail to ensure that 'Network Rail is managed in line with high standards of corporate governance' (House of Commons, 2004). Two-thirds of the members are members of the public who were appointed from those chosen from 1,200 applicants by a membership selection panel that was appointed by Network Rail. The public members therefore are the appointees of Network Rail. Some public members represent special interest groups such as The Royal Society for Disability and Rehabilitation (Gosling, 2004). In addition the key industry stakeholders, franchise holders who actually run the train services, railway undertakings and operators of railway assets who look after the rolling stock and property such as stations are represented. The Parliamentary Select Committee on Transport (House of Commons, 2004: §59) argued that this structure would create no strong accountability to the public interest.

> We were also concerned that the industry members were virtually self-appointing. These members include contractors [to Network Rail] and while members may have a duty to the company, there was always some possibility of the appearance of a conflict of interest. Finally the public members are appointed by the Board of the company and represent no one but themselves.

There was much scepticism regarding whether members without a financial interest would have sufficient influence on the Board. The rail regulator thought the members would not have the motivation to drive down costs. It is arguable that such a consequence reflects a better balance of influence between stakeholders and between the demand for profit and other demands such as safety. If this argument is correct then the governance of Network Rail might be a powerful new model of governance.

## Discussion activity 2.11

What is a fair balance between interests of the owners of a company that provides a public utility and the interests of the customers? Was Railtrack right in its approach? Will the structure of Network Rail, which has no shareholders, redress the balance?

## Part four: Preventing indifference to others

Ethics ←————————————————————————→ Morality

|  | Lying |  |

## Lying

Lying is wrong; except that in everyday usage it is not always so. The acceptability of a lie depends partly on the context in which it is made. Perjury, lying under oath in a court of law, is not acceptable; indeed it is a crime that carries heavy punishment. In the context of business negotiations lying, in the form of bluffing, may be acceptable as Carr argued (1968) in a classic article. Lies, in such a context, may be no more than putting a spin on an unpalatable truth.

**DEFINITION**

Winston Churchill used the phrase **terminological inexactitude** in a speech on Chinese labour in South Africa. The phrase was not actually used as a euphemism for a lie. He argued that although the labourers' contracts might not be proper or healthy they could not be classified as slavery without 'some risk of terminological inexactitude'. However Alexander Haig, the American politician, is credited with saying, 'It is not a lie, it's a terminological inexactitude'.

The reprehensibility of a lie may also depend upon its nature. Telling an absolute untruth is often worse than failing to tell the whole truth. A cabinet secretary to a British government famously objected to a suggestion that he had lied. He had, he claimed, merely been 'economical with the truth'. Managers often find difficulty when they have to keep silent about privileged or confidential information, as when they know there are proposals to make people redundant but have been required to say nothing until the plans are finalised and can be announced. Their loyalty to their staff conflicts with their commitment to their company's needs. Conflicts of interest are a particular problem for professionals and public officials whose judgement should be seen to be free of private or opposing interests. They should be open about any such conflicts. Recruitment consultants finding new jobs for staff being made redundant would be regarded with suspicion if they received fees from both the organisation buying the out-placement service and the company in which they placed the redundant staff. The Nolan Committee's (1995) seven principles for public life are all focused on ensuring that private or sectional interests do not prejudice people's decisions on matters of public interest.

**The Nolan principles** are:                                    `DEFINITIONS`

*Selflessness*
Holders of public office should act solely in terms of the public interest. They should not do so in order to gain financial or other benefits for themselves, their family or their friends.

*Integrity*
Holders of public office should not place themselves under any financial or other obligation to outside individuals or organisations that might seek to influence them in the performance of their official duties.

*Objectivity*
In carrying out public business, including making public appointments, awarding contracts, or recommending individuals for rewards and benefits, holders of public office should make choices on merit.

*Accountability*
Holders of public office are accountable for their decisions and actions to the public and must submit themselves to whatever scrutiny is appropriate to their office.

*Openness*
Holders of public office should be as open as possible about all the decisions and actions that they take. They should give reasons for their decisions and restrict information only when the wider public interest clearly demands.

*Honesty*
Holders of public office have a duty to declare any private interests relating to their public duties and to take steps to resolve any conflicts arising in a way that protects the public interest.

*Leadership*
Holders of public office should promote and support these principles by leadership and example.

Another test of the dishonesty of a lie is its purpose. There is a range of names for acceptable lies, including fibs and white lies, that are intended to avoid giving offence or causing distress to individuals. Not all managers see such lying as acceptable, as one told us in a research interview.

> I think for me the most important thing is honesty and what I find difficult is when managers maybe are doing something for one reason but are telling staff it's for another reason. Something like that I would find, and do find, quite difficult. Rather than actually saying to staff, you didn't get the job because your performance isn't as accurate or whatever else; what they give is fairly obscure reasons rather than actually facing the real reason.

A lie involves intent to deceive; if there is no such intent there is no lie. We fill our conversations with figures of speech such as hyperbole ('I'm so hungry I could eat a horse') and metaphor ('That man is a pig') that do not lead people to accept the literal truth of what we are saying. Advertising is a common area in which companies may seek to deceive their customers. The Advertising Standards Authority, in a typical example, criticised Virgin Trains for claiming in their advertisements that all fares were half-price when conditions meant that many were not (Milmo, 2001).

| Case study 2.12 | **The case of Shell's missing oil barrels** |
| --- | --- |

The Royal Dutch/Shell company, or rather group of companies, has been accused of being over-large, out of control, secretive and hidden behind a bland façade. Theses claims have centred on the story of Shell's missing oil reserves.

The problem began in the late 1990s. One of the figures used by observers of the oil industry is the reserve replacement ratio (RRR). Shell's RRR was one of the poorest in the industry. It was not finding new sources of oil fast enough. Managers assumed that the policy for 'booking' new reserves was too restrictive. There was management fashion at the time for using problem solving teams to come up with radical and creative solutions and Shell established four such teams to improve the exploration and production function that was led by Sir Phillip Watts. New guidelines for booking reserves were implemented. In Shell's 1998 annual report there was a brief note reporting that 'Estimation methods have been refined during 1998'. The RRR consequently increased by 40 per cent and the director was rewarded for improving the efficiency of his directorate. Shell had adopted the system of determining senior managers' rewards and bonuses according to their performance against critical performance indicators. Rewards were triggered by numbers and targets and not by the rounded judgements of appraisers.

In 2001 the American Securities and Exchange Commission (SEC) published new guidelines for assessing the commerciality of new oil discoveries. These were to be used to determine whether finds were certain enough to be accounted as a reserve. Shell's booked reserves in Australia, Norway and Nigeria did not comply with the new SEC guidelines. However, there was great pressure within Shell to keep the RRR as high as possible. Nor was there much internal auditing pressure to review the reserve figures, the auditing of which was done part-time by one engineer who had no staff to back him up.

It is clear that several top executives within Shell knew of this problem by 2002. However nothing was made public. This was largely a result of feuds between senior managers, particularly between Sir Philip Watts (who had been promoted to Chairman) and Walter van de Vijver, head of exploration. After what van de Vijver considered an unfair performance appraisal from Sir Philip Watts the former sent the latter an email stating 'I am becoming sick and tired about lying about the extent of our oil reserves issues and the downward revision that needs to be done because of far too aggressive/optimistic bookings'.

On 9 January 2004 the Shell group announced through its investor relations staff that they had downgraded their reserves by 20 per cent, or 3.9 billion barrels of oil. The markets were not happy and the stock market valuation of Shell dropped £2.9bn. That the announcement had not been made by Sir Philip Watts personally increased investors' anger. The pressure led to Watts and van de Vijver resigning. At first it was reported that Watts left by mutual consent although later it was admitted that he had been pushed. Nevertheless he received a £1m compensation package for the breaking of his contract. Jeroen van der Veer from Royal Dutch became the new chairman. There was some negative comment in the business press that the new chairman was an insider, although given the reported friction between the British and Dutch wings of the group Shell insiders would be more likely to see the appointment as a Dutch coup d'état. The Finance Director resigned in July. There was no question of financial impropriety on her part but there were questions about her effectiveness in ensuring compliance with good accounting practice.

Shell argued that the differences between its criteria for booking reserves, and those of the SEC, are largely a technical matter. The de-booking of reserves, they pointed out, does not mean that the oil is not there and they anticipate that 85 per cent of the missing barrels will prove to have been there all along. Shell's approach to internal control is on a risk assessment basis that is designed to manage rather than to eliminate the risks to achieving the company's objectives. In September 2004 Sir Philip Watts announced that he planned to challenge the FSA in the Financial Services and Markets Tribunal (the appeal court for FSA decisions). He was claiming that he was treated unfairly by the FSA who criticised him implicitly in their report, although not by name, and did not give him an opportunity to rebut the criticisms (Hosking, 2004).

Shell's audit committee instigated an internal review that was carried out by external accountants. There was pressure for an independent inquiry both in the UK and the USA. In the UK the charge was that the company had breached Stock Market regulations by not reporting in good time matters and information that could have an impact on the share price. The UK Financial Services Authority (FSA) started an investigation as did the SEC in America.

Shell cooperated fully with the investigations. In August 2004 the FSA fined the company £17m and the SEC fined it £66.29m. The FSA accused Shell of 'unprecedented misconduct' and a failure to put internal controls in place to prevent misleading information being given to the market. In its agreement with the SEC Shell did not admit any illegality but it did agree to spend nearly £3m on developing better internal compliance systems. These official punishments may be only the start of the problem for Shell as lawyers in the USA are clamouring to start class actions against the company on behalf of various pension funds who believe that the misinformation caused them financial losses. Shell may be one of the first cases to feel the weight of the Sarbanes-Oxley Act that was passed in the USA following the Enron and WorldCom cases. Under this Act's provisions the senior managers of the company signed a declaration concerning the 2002 annual report that 'based on my knowledge, this annual report does not contain any untrue statement of a material fact'.

Royal Dutch Shell has an unusual, but not unique structure. It is a dual listed company. This means that the Shell group operates as a single organisation but

▶

legally it is two organisations, the Royal Dutch Petroleum Company, which is based in Holland and listed on the Dutch Stock exchange, and the Shell Transport and Trading Company, which is based in London and whose shares are listed on the London Stock Exchange. These two companies are the parent companies. The shareholders of Royal Dutch are mostly Dutch and those of Shell Trading mostly UK based, although there is a substantial block of American depository receipts (ADR) held in the USA. A series of legal agreements governs the relationship between the two parent companies. This arrangement dates from 1907 when Shell (which was founded in 1833 as a shop selling seashells to naturalists) merged with the Royal Dutch Company for the Exploration of Petroleum Wells in the Netherlands East Indies. Under this deal Royal Dutch controls 60 per cent of the group's assets and Shell Trading controls the remaining 40 per cent.

Royal Dutch and Shell Trading do not undertake any operations. Instead they own the shares of two holding companies, Shell Petroleum N.V. and the Shell Petroleum Company Ltd. These in turn own the large number of companies that carry out the group's operations around the world. The two parent companies each have a board of directors (Royal Dutch has a supervisory board as well) that have different memberships. The combined group is overseen by an executive board known as the committee of managing directors (CMD). The members of the CMD are appointed by the boards of the parent companies. In such a structure there is clearly tension as to who has the greatest influence and who carries oversight and responsibility for the organisation's compliance with laws and conventions. It appears that Royal Dutch is the dominant partner. The supervisory board of Royal Dutch controls a number of foundations that own 'priority shares' that confer voting rights but no economic benefit. These enable the supervisory board to control nominations to both parent company boards and thus to the CMD. The CMD is not formally covered by the joint venture agreement that defines the merged company and so it has no formal authority over the parent companies' assets.

Investors have complained that the legal structure of Royal Dutch/Shell makes it difficult for shareholders to gain information from the group and to influence its policy. This, taken together with the divisionalised structure of the group that leads to a high level of decentralisation, raises questions about the effectiveness of internal control. This said, the group has the full panoply of policies, codes of ethics and operating principles, which all large companies have, to ensure good governance. Economists have studied the tensions between insider ownership and insider control (through such devices as priority shares) in dual class companies. Some have suggested that when the insiders, in this case the Dutch boards, have great voting muscle they use it to support their own position as against the interests of outsiders such as share holders. This tendency itself would make it difficult for shareholders to hold the company to account. Although it can equally be argued that the system in Royal Dutch/Shell, which gave the managers low ownership but high voting rights, contributed to the development of a strong and flexible corporate culture.

The reserves revaluation has led to calls for changes in corporate governance of Royal Dutch/Shell to prevent the reoccurrence of similar problems.

Shell has now adopted a single board structure. In 2005 Shell announced the largest profit ever made by a British based company, largely attributable to the increase in world oil prices in 2004.

*Sources*: Doran and Mansell (2004), Gompers *et al.* (2004), Harrington (2003), Harris and Michaels (2004), Morgan (2004), Plender (2004), Shell Group (2004), The *Guardian* (2004a and 2004b), Watchman (2004).

## Discussion activity 2.12

- In your opinion did Shell lie?

- If you believe it did what were the factors and influences that may have caused them to lie?

- Is this a good news story because the regulatory agencies punished Shell?

- Why did Shell's shareholders get so vexed about the corporate governance issues?

- What changes in corporate governance if any might be necessary?

Refusing to be true to one's own beliefs can be a form of self-deception. This can happen when a person justifies continuing their connection to an organisation even though they object on ethical grounds to the organisation's behaviour.

## Case study 2.13

### BAT, Nottingham University and the honorary professor

Nottingham University accepted £3.8m from British American Tobacco (BAT), the world's second biggest tobacco company, towards setting up an international Centre for Corporate Responsibility. There was of course nothing illegal about the gift but many individuals and groups thought it was wrong. The problem was that Nottingham University carried out medical research into cancer and its treatment, some of it funded by medical charities. This was thought to fit ill with accepting money from a company that sells products known to cause cancer.

Richard Smith was editor of the *British Medical Journal* (BMJ) and an unpaid honorary professor of medical journalism at Nottingham University. He believed the university's acceptance of BAT's money was a 'serious mistake'. He polled readers of the BMJ to discover their views on whether he should resign from his post at Nottingham University. Of the 1,075 votes cast 84 per cent said the university should return the money and 54 per cent said that Professor Smith should resign if the university did not do so. The latter vote was closer than had been anticipated and this was because some argued that the professor should stay within the university and argue his case internally. The professor did resign, both because he said he would abide by the result of the poll and because he firmly believed the university was wrong in its actions.

(*Source*: Meikle, 2001)

## Discussion activity 2.13

Is it better to retreat and live to fight another day or to take a stand on a matter one sees as an injustice?

The next case study in this section has the character of an ancient Greek tragedy. Jonathan Aitken, who had publicly defended the freedom of the press in his early career, committed hubris over a weekend spent in the Paris Ritz, received his nemesis and was reported to be looking for catharsis.

## Hubris, nemesis and catharsis                    DEFINITIONS

The first two terms represent the themes of Greek tragedy and the third is the experience of the audience watching the play. **Hubris** is a great pride and belief in one's own importance. **Nemesis** is a deserved punishment that cannot be avoided; and **catharsis** is the release of strong emotion caused by the experience of fear, albeit only expressed on the stage.

### Connexion point

This story is technically a tragedy, but at the time the press and its readers took delight in treating it as a comedy. On the types and roles of the stories in ethics, see Chapter 1, pp. 3–5.

### Case study 2.14

### The Jonathan Aitken story

Jonathan Aitken is a great-nephew of Lord Beaverbrook, the 1950s newspaper magnate. He was at one time a journalist and in 1992 he became a member of John Major's cabinet. In 1995 he was being talked about as a potential prime minister and successor to John Major. He had become a Member of Parliament in 1974 and in 1992 he was appointed a Minister of State for defence and two years later Chief Secretary to the Treasury. He resigned from the Cabinet, to much surprise, in 1995. Here is the story.

In 1993 he stayed at the Paris Ritz. The *Guardian* newspaper took an interest in this visit and enquired why a cabinet minister was staying at a very expensive hotel at someone else's expense. Aitken said he had paid for the stay himself. He lied. But at the time there was no proof he had. The *Guardian* kept running the story and Aitken, saying that he was going to fight 'the cancer of bent and twisted journalism ... with the simple sword of truth', sued the newspaper for libel. He persuaded his wife and his daughter to lie in support of the claim that he had paid for the stay himself. When documents were presented that showed that he had lied on oath in the court the libel case collapsed. He was charged with perverting the course of justice and perjury in 1998 and sent to prison in 1999.

Why had he lied over such an apparently trivial issue? Aitken had long had contacts with the Saudi royal family and had been involved in the arms trade with Saudi Arabia. The *Guardian* reported that:

> We know that Mr. Aitken's business in Paris that weekend was closely tied up with multi-million pound arms deals involving his close friend, Said Ayas, and the Saudi royal family. For that to have become public would have been devastating for Mr. Aitken, for the Saudis and the government.

Lying to protect business confidentiality led to perjury. Rumours that Aitken was planning to become a priest after finishing his 18-month sentence were denied by him. He did enrol to study theology at Oxford. He is currently available as an inspirational and motivational after-dinner speaker who offers topics including 'From power to porridge – a journey through prison' (SpeakersUK, 2005).

(*Sources*: Harding, 1999; *Guardian*, 1999; Wilson, 1999)

## Discussion activity 2.14

What would you have done in Aitken's position?

Many of the issues related to lying, as in the following case study, concern the failure to tell the whole truth rather than the telling of falsehoods.

## Case study 2.15

### Economy with the truth when dealing with the tax authorities

This is an extract from an interview with the finance director of a private company.

> Most of the ethical issues revolve around disclosure to the revenue and tax authority. The issues are whether we should disclose all the material facts and secondly, when arguing a case with the revenue, whether we should make a case even when we know it is weak. The rule is 'we will make a case as long as we have one argument – however obtuse'. As long as we have an arguable position we won't be embarrassed.
>
> I have just had a conversation with someone on an issue ... actually tax again, on whether we give the Inland Revenue a letter or not at this particular point in time. It could be slightly prejudicial, only slightly, to our case, and as we are going to have a meeting and it may settle it, do I need to give it to him [the tax inspector] now? This is a question of timing. If I can settle it without giving it to him I might do.
>
> It's just to do with tax planning and why we actually had done a transaction. It may make the revenue renege on something they have just agreed. Unlikely, but you don't want to raise doubts in somebody's mind

▶

who has actually spent some time looking at it. Tax is always slow anyway, so why shouldn't I delay sending the letter? We are likely to have a meeting in July. I would see how that went and if they decide they still want the correspondence – we'll give it to them. It is actually the fact that we know we have got a meeting due that enables us to prevaricate.

(*Source*: Research interview conducted by the authors)

## Discussion activity 2.15

In what circumstances might it be right not to tell the whole truth?

## Cheating

This category of ethical issues concerns keeping the rules. However, for many in organisations the important question is whether the benefits of bending the rules are high enough, and the chances of being caught low enough, to justify taking a risk. This ethical calculation can be made both at a corporate level and as a matter of individual discretion.

Rules are not always bent to benefit the person doing the bending. In bureaucratic systems rules are often bent to protect people who would otherwise be harshly treated by the system. One example we came across during our research concerned a production line worker in a factory that made prepared foods for supermarkets. The employee was diabetic and, on the day of the incident, had been careless of his diet. Consequently at work he felt the start of a hypoglaecemic attack and took, and ate, one of the products from the production line. This prevented him from collapsing. But he was threatened with dismissal because company rules made theft of company property punishable by instant dismissal. The personnel officer thought the man had been foolish but thought it unjust to sack him. The rules were ignored.

In many cases, however, rules are broken and lies are told by people who simply seek their own benefit at others' expense. The case of the rise and fall of Parmalat provides the most recent and biggest example. The Tanzi family who were the major shareholders benefited themselves to the cost of bond holders and other investors.

| Case study 2.16 | **The rise and fall of Parmalat** |

In 1961 Calisto Tanzi started a milk pasteurisation plant to supply milk to the Italian city of Parma. From that starting point it grew to become a multi-national, publicly owned corporation in the food and milk business. Until December 2003 Tanzi led the company, which employed 36,200 people in 146 plants in 30 countries on five continents. In December 2003 Parmalat defaulted on payment of a €150m bond despite having €4.2b of liquidity. Tanzi handed over control to a company doctor. Then the Bank of America announced that the claim that Bonlat, a Parmalat subsidiary, had an account in the Cayman Islands with €2.95m was untrue and that Parmalat had a €4.9m hole in its accounts. It sought bankruptcy protection and the Italian Prime Minister Silvio Berlusconi said he found the revelations 'almost unbelievable' but he pledged to save the company which was Italy's eighth largest corporation (CNN International, 2003).

As time went on the financial hole in the company was discovered to be larger – €14.8bn. Kapner (2004a) provides an overview of the scandal.

**FT**     Investigators seeking to reconstruct the events leading to one of Europe's most spectacular frauds are starting to create a clearer picture. But it remains unclear precisely how the hole grew and how much was siphoned off by the controlling Tanzi family and top managers.

Although investigators and creditors still hope to find a 'Tanzi treasure chest' among bank accounts held in the Cayman Islands, Switzerland, Monaco, Liechtenstein, Malta and the US, virtually all of the missing money was burned up by the company's global operations.

To hide the losses, Parmalat invented false billings, false inter-company credits and bank accounts, including the infamous Euros 4.4bn that it claimed was held in what turned out to be a fictitious Bank of America account in New York. Investigators and people familiar with the group believe the fraud began in the 1970s, when Parmalat grew rapidly by acquiring numerous unprofitable milk processing plants from state entities.

Parmalat often overpaid, and did so as a favour to local politicians eager to preserve jobs and votes and to bolster municipal coffers. Said one former executive: 'The margins on milk are not high. If you buy a dozen loss-making plants and don't close any because that's the deal with the political class, there's little you can do other than cook the books.'

The losses continued through 1988, when Calisto Tanzi, chairman, briefly flirted with selling out to US-based Kraft and denied rumours of debt problems. In 1990, Parmalat undertook a massive capital increase. After that, the company embarked on an aggressive acquisition spree in Latin America, notably Brazil, that was financed through numerous bond issues underwritten by US banks. Again, Parmalat often overpaid by a factor of two, according to one former executive familiar with that region. Parmalat was losing €350m–€450m a year from the mid-1990s through to 2001,

▶

according to testimony from Fausto Tonna, the former chief financial officer now being held in an Italian prison. During that period, Parmalat's accounts claimed profits of €926m.

The losses from South American units were at least 500bn lire (€258m) a year. Parmalat SpA (the Italian unit) also had large losses that were between 200bn and 300bn lire, Mr Tonna told interrogators, according to an arrest order. The order was issued this week against teight former executives of Parmalat and Parmatour, the unprofitable travel and leisure group owned entirely by the Tanzi family.

(*Source*: A hole dug over 30 years, *Financial Times*, 20 February 2004. Copyright © The Financial Times Limited. Reproduced with permission)

The company's operating principle seems to have been that, in ensuring the long-term survival of the firm, acquiring influence among local politicians was more important than making a profit. In this of course they were proved wrong. However, they applied this system in countries other than Italy. A *Financial Times* investigation identified that Parmalat considered, but never completed, a deal to buy a near-bankrupt Nicaraguan Bank in 2001 in a effort to 'build influence in Central and South America' (Barber and Parker, 2004).

A letter writer to the *Financial Times* generously saw Parmalat's policy of subsidising European farmers (by making a loss of from €350m–€450m per year in the late 1990s) as more efficient than the European Union's Common Agricultural Policy. He pointed out that the farmers received a subsidy at no cost to European tax payers because the financial strain was being borne by largely American Parmalat bond holders. So the farmers were better off, as were the taxpayers, and the consumers were no worse off (Carter, 2004).

When this policy proved expensive and the company was making losses the Tanzi family, several of whom apart from Calisto were arrested, tried a number of devices for covering up the losses and protecting their own interests. One technique was to transfer money from the publicly owned Parmalat to family controlled companies such as the travel firm Paratours (Kapner and Minder, 2004). They also used sophisticated and legal financial devices. In one deal with a bank called Buconero (black hole in Italian) the bank made an 'investment' in Parmalat of €117m in return for a share of the company's net profit. By setting up the loan as an investment Parmalat's borrowing costs were made to look smaller than they were (ExecutiveCaliber 2004). On occasions the company resorted to plain lying and forgery. When the auditors enquired about the money in the Cayman Islands branch of the Bank of America they received a reply from the bank, confirming the existence of the account, which had in fact been forged at Parmalat's headquarters.

The Italian Courts decided in 2004 that the 29 people arrested as a result of the scandal and the Italian subsidiaries of the Bank of America and auditors Grant Thornton Deloitte could not be tried under a fast-track procedure and it was therefore likely that the trial would last for several years (Kapner, 2004b). The pre-trial hearing that will decide who will be charged and with what over the Parmalat case began in Milan in October 2004.

## Discussion activity 2.16

Neo-institutionalism is a theory which argues that societies have templates of formal and informal rules, values and acceptable ways of behaving; and that organisations in those societies fit in with, and organise themselves to fit in with, those institutional templates. The technical name for this process is isomorphism. Can the story of Parmalat be interpreted using this theory? Can it be argued that Parmalat's way of operating by keeping local politicians and others happy reflected the institutional world of a small company in Italy in the 1960s, but that it was too risky to sustain when Parmalat had become a huge multi-national corporation?

The next case study tells a similar story but the history and motivations were probably very different from those seen in the Parmalat Case study.

**Case study 2.17**

## Lord Black and Hollinger International

At the beginning of 2004 Conrad Black, Lord Black of Crossharbour , was chairman and chief executive of Hollinger International, an organisation based in the USA that owned many newspapers including the *Daily Telegraph* in Britain and the *Chicago Sun-Times* in the USA.

The group has a complex structure. Hollinger International Inc. is the holding company that oversees the group's assets and operations. Hollinger Inc. (a Canadian registered company) holds 18.2 per cent of the equity in Hollinger International; and 80 per cent of Hollinger Inc. is held by Ravelstone which is a private company belonging to Lord Black. One particular feature of the structure is that although Hollinger Inc. only owns a small part of Hollinger International it owns 68 per cent of the voting rights. This was possible because Hollinger International has a dual class of shares. Those held by Hollinger Inc. were super-voting shares carrying more votes per share than ordinary shares. This discrepancy between ownership and control gave Black control of the main company and control over appointments to the board.

This situation led to a conflict between Lord Black and the rest of the board of Hollinger International. In 2003 Lord Black lost his position as CEO of Hollinger International but remained chairman. However, Lord Black's announcement in January 2004 that he had made a deal, to sell the Daily Telegraph to the Barclay brothers, which prevented the ordinary shareholders of Hollinger International benefiting from the sale, brought the crisis to a head. The 'non-interested' board members challenged the deal by setting up a corporate review committee to scrutinise the deal. Lord Black responded by using his controlling interest to change the company's by-laws by written consent, a technique that by-passed the other shareholders. The new by-laws abolished the review committee and put practical constraints on the board's freedom to act. The matter went to court in Delaware and Lord Black lost the case.

▶

After these battles the board of Hollinger International commissioned a detailed investigation into Lord Black's business affairs in relation to Hollinger International. The investigation was conducted by Richard Breeden, a former chairman of the American Securities and Exchange Commission (SEC). The Breeden report that arose from the investigation was published in September 2004 and accused Lord Black of 'fiduciary abuses' and fraudulent acts. According to Breeden, Black had taken £223m from the company in a six-year period up to 2003. This represented 95.2 per cent of its entire adjusted net income. Most of this money, it was claimed, came in the form of excessive management fees paid to Black and his associates and in expense claims. Lord Black challenges these claims and has hired forensic accountants to work on his case. He argues that there was no misconduct and that his actions were approved by the board.

One of the main accusations was that Lord Black and Mr Radler, a former deputy Chairman, broke their fiduciary duties to the company's shareholders by causing Hollinger International to pay them unjustifiable management fees through Lord Black's private company Ravelstone. This matter was the cause of Lord Black losing his position of CEO in 2003 when he was found to have overcharged for his services by $32m, a sum that he subsequently repaid to Hollinger International. Some of the fees were paid to shell companies registered in Barbados which does not tax dividends and charges only 2.5 per cent income tax. One particular device that was used by Black was non-compete payments that were made between 1999 and 2001. When Hollinger International wished to sell one of its publications Black and his associates would demand a fee to sign a non-competition agreement with prospective purchasers which ensured that they would not enter the competition to buy the titles. The Breeden report considered this a conflict of interests because, as a board member of Hollinger International, Black had responsibilities to maximise the sale price of the company's assets. If these non-competition deals had not been made then the fee paid to Black (as compensation for not acquiring the assets) would most likely have gone to pay a higher purchase price to Hollinger International.

The second main charge against Black made by the Breeden report was that Black and Radler and their families had used Hollinger International as a 'piggy bank'. The company paid for much of their living expenses, their housing expenses and their personal travel. Radler was given a private aircraft by the company, worth $11.6m, and Black had a Gulfstream IV leased for him at a cost of $3m–$4m a year. The running costs of these aircraft between 2000 and 2003 were $23m. Two of the more high profile items mentioned in the report were $43,000 spent by the company on Lady Black's birthday party and the $2,436 handbag she was given as a gift.

KPMG, who were auditors for Hollinger International, Hollinger Inc. and Ravelstone, did not initially question or raise with the company's audit committee the matter of whether the management fees and non-compete contracts contradicted Lord Black's fiduciary duties to Hollinger International. However, it did so in late 2003 and resigned as auditors in December.

Some of the journalists who worked and socialised with Conrad Black saw him as an intelligent and scholarly man who acted with propriety in editorial matters concerning the papers he controlled. Some saw him as leading a revival of newspapers in Canada. The journalist who uses the pseudonym Taki (2004) wrote:

> Conrad Black took the *Telegraph* company, which was moribund, and turned it into a powerful weapon for the values we conservatives believe in. He was a great proprietor, but more important, a great visionary. He and his wife should get their good name back and the sooner the better.

Black was rewarded in 1999 when he was made a British peer, though the Canadian Prime Minister forced him to renounce his Canadian citizenship in order to accept the honour. Black was also a generous host.

*Sources*: Burt (2004), Hollinger international Inc. (n.d.), Investor Responsibility Research Centre (IRRC) (2004), Paris *et al.* (2004), Parker (2004), Rees-Mogg (2004), Rubin (2004), *Observer* (2004).

## Discussion activity 2.17

- Can a greedy person be a good visionary and corporate leader?
- What ethical problems might flow from dual-voting structures and 'super shares'?
- Conrad Black was the effective owner of Hollinger International; could he not do as he wished with his property?
- What rights, if any, did or should the minority shareholders have in such companies?
- Have you ever manipulated your expenses or used organisational resources for personal benefits?

## Case study 2.18

### BAT and allegations of cigarette smuggling

An oddity in the world market for cigarettes was discovered in 1997. When global exports were compared with global imports one-third of the total inventory was unaccounted for. The reason was not hard to find. Up to one-third of cigarettes sold are smuggled. The charge made by investigators and journalists against British American Tobacco (BAT) was that it colluded with tobacco smuggling and factored the sales of smuggled cigarettes into its strategic planning. The charge was not that BAT employees actually took cigarettes across borders without paying the excise duties. It was that they sold cigarettes to distributors whom they knew would avoid paying tax. This conclusion was drawn from a study of BAT's internal documents that were made public as a result of legal cases in the USA and in the UK.

BAT used a series of euphemisms for smuggling in its documentation. They included DNP (duty not paid), GT (general trade) and transit goods. Legal ▶

goods were known as DP – duty paid. One extract from the documentation illustrates the process. It concerns a 1995 dispute in Colombia between BAT and Philip Morris over the ownership of a cigarette brand called Belmont. One memorandum proposed a contingency plan to be used in the event that BAT lost the case. The plan was 'to launch a new brand in DP and maintain Belmont in a GT channel'. One problem with selling Belmont through GT was that the 'company could not support Belmont in GT through advertising'. Advertising a product that was not officially imported might have caused the revenue authorities to ask questions.

Kenneth Clarke, the deputy chairman of BAT, and a one-time Chancellor of the Exchequer who had been responsible for UK duties on tobacco, responded to these criticisms when they were published in the *Guardian*. He pointed out that smuggling was a major problem in the tobacco business. Cigarettes are easily transportable and of high value. These factors, combined with the high rates of duty and the high differentials between the taxes of neighbouring countries, provide incentives for smuggling. He pointed out that BAT was always willing to cooperate with governments who wished to crack down on smuggling. He added:

> However, where governments are not prepared to address the underlying causes of the problem, businesses such as ours who are engaged in international trade are faced with a dilemma. If the demand for our brands is not met, consumers will either switch to our competitors' brands or there will be the kind of dramatic growth in counterfeit products that we have recently seen in our Asian markets. Where any government is unwilling to act or their efforts are unsuccessful, we act, completely within the law, on the basis that our brands will be available alongside those of our competitors in the smuggled as well as the legitimate market.

Audrey Wise, a Member of Parliament and a member of the House of Commons Health Committee, said of BAT's policy:

> If there was ever a case of being within the letter of the law but clearly outside the spirit of the law then this is a gem. Smuggled goods are illegal goods, so if you're deliberately making your goods available for smuggling knowingly and deliberately you are an accessory to the fact.

(*Sources*: Center for Public Enquiry, 2000; Clarke, 2000; Maguire, 2000)

## Discussion activity 2.18

Should companies accept being placed at a competitive disadvantage by following the spirit as well as the letter of the law?

The next case study raises a large number of ethical issues. One is whether doctors used people's ignorance of the law and the regulations to 'cheat' parents grieving for their dead children.

Case study
2.19

## The retention of dead babies' organs in hospitals

In the UK, when a child died, the coroner could order a post-mortem examination to discover the cause of death. A hospital could also order a
post-mortem with the parents' consent to study the disease that had killed the
child. After post-mortems organs from the child were often retained for
research or educational purposes. Doctors assumed, wrongly, that a coroner's
request for a post-mortem allowed them to retain organs. In other cases the
law merely required that the parents should not object. Over a period of years
a collection of 50,000 organs from dead children was established in a number
of English hospitals. The general public were unaware of these collections;
more importantly the parents of the children were not aware the organs had
been retained. Even where parents had given consent to post-mortems they
were not necessarily aware that the hospital could remove and retain the
organs. The parents had not been given the opportunity to give full and
informed consent. This is a form of cheating that arose, as Professor Kennedy
argued, 'from a type of professional arrogance that ignored – indeed did not
acknowledge, the views and voices of parents'.

The issue exploded into the public's consciousness because of the Alder
Hey hospital case. Professor van Velzen at that hospital had developed an
obsession with organ retention. The Redfern report into Alder Hey found that
van Velzen had ordered illegal retention of children's organs, had falsified
records and had failed to catalogue the specimens. The identification of this
particular example of illegal activity triggered the investigations that revealed
a culture of mendacity over organ retention in many hospitals. The issue
released raw emotions as parents who believed they had buried their dead
child requested that they be allowed to bury their child's retained remains.

The impact of these new stories was a tightening-up of rules for organ
retention and an unwillingness of the public to allow organs to be retained.
Researchers began to complain that research into cancers was being prevented
because of the difficulty of obtaining human material for use in trials and
experiments. The pharmaceutical companies were removing clinical development from UK to Europe because of the difficulties in obtaining materials for
work on breast and prostate cancers.

(*Sources*: Anon., 2001; Boseley, 2001a; Boseley, 2001b; Redfern Report, 2001)

## Discussion activity 2.19

Was the general practice (rather than the particular practice of Dr van Velzen)
of retaining organs without proper consent a case of actions being ethical
but illegal?

## Part five: Discouraging badness

### Bullying

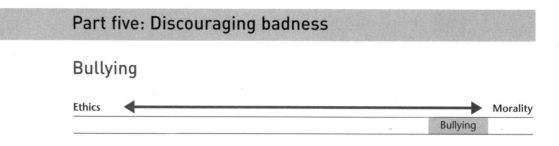

In organisations bullying is the misuse of power to abuse, humiliate or cajole others. Unlike bullying in the school playground, which may also involve physical harm, organisational bullying is more likely to be social. Some bullying may be too insignificant or transient to be turned into an issue. But where should the line between the insignificant and the significant be drawn? At what point does proper assertion, within a negotiation for example, become an improper use of aggression? The problem is made worse by people's differing perceptions of acceptable, and unacceptable, behaviour. What may be harassment from a supervisor, from a subordinate's point of view, may be an effective example of leadership from the team leader's perspective.

One answer to the problem of bullying is to allow the victim to define it. This empowers the weak against the strong by accepting that if someone says they are being bullied then they are. If a legal perspective were to be taken this would put the burden of proof on the accused and not on the victim. The accused would have to prove they were innocent. This of course is the opposite of the legal custom that the accused is innocent until proved guilty.

The following case may not look like bullying but it is an example of a company using its dominant position to control the actions of its agents. It raises the question of when assertive marketing and selling practices cross the line and become illegal.

| Case study 2.20 | **British Airways and Virgin Atlantic** |

British Airways and Virgin Atlantic have for many years been in intense competition. In 1993 Virgin had accused British Airways (BA) of 'dirty tricks' that discouraged customers from buying tickets from Virgin. In the subsequent libel proceedings BA paid Richard Branson, the chairman of Virgin, £610,000 to settle the case. Virgin started proceedings in the United States courts seeking damages for BA's unfair and illegal marketing practices.

The core of Virgin's complaints was that BA, by far the larger of the two airlines, was using its dominant position in the market to coerce travel agents to sell its flights. This was done by only paying agents certain commissions when they had sold a quota of BA flights, and by packaging discounts on flights. People who travelled to destinations where BA had little competition were offered additional discounts if they bought BA connecting flights in areas where there were many alternative carriers. In November 1997 Virgin formally complained to the European Commission that these 'illegal' practices were in breach of Article 86 of the Treaty of Rome, which covers abuse of dominant market position.

In 1998 BA accused Virgin Atlantic, in its in-house magazine *BA News*, of using similar marketing techniques to those that BA was accused of using. In November of that year Sir Colin Marshall, chairman of BA, apologised to Richard Branson for the accusations and destroyed all copies of the magazine.

In 1999 the European Commission fined BA £4.5m for operating an anti-competitive loyalty scheme with travel agents. The Competition Commissioner said, 'It is well established in community law that a dominant supplier cannot give incentives to its customers and distributors to be loyal to it, so foreclosing the market from the dominant firm's competitors'. BA announced they would appeal. In October of the same year a New York judge threw out Virgin Atlantic's claim against BA. One lawyer pointed out that the notion of a 'dominant company' did not exist in American law.

At the end of 1999 it appeared that BA's ticketing practices were illegal in the European Union but legal in the United States.

(*Sources*: Anon., 1997; Skapinker, 1998; Anon., 1999a; Anon., 1999b)

The story entered the mythology of business and Richard Branson did his best to keep it fresh; especially as in one version first published in 1994 (Gregory and Rufford, 1994) he was presented as a hero – a combination of a 'corporate Peter Pan' and a 'misty eyed Corinthian' (Tilney, 2000). (Unfortunately Corinthian has a range of meanings from 'a wealthy sports enthusiast', through 'a fashionable man' to 'someone given to elegant dissipation'.) Virgin republished the book in 2000. In 2003 Richard Branson sought to take over the operation of Concorde from BA when the latter announced it would be taken out of service. BA announced this intervention as a 'stunt' and Branson retorted that BA was acting in ways reminiscent of its dirty tricks campaign in the 'bad old days' (Done, 2003).

The ill-feeling between the two companies has also had significant commercial effects. The case of airline routes to India is an example. The commercial flights between India and the UK have long been constrained and controlled by a bilateral treaty. Consequently the supply of direct services was much less than the demand. In 2004 the two countries agreed a new deal that would increase the number of flights between them from 19 to 40 a week. BA had held the rights to all of the flights under the old treaty and Virgin only provided a limited service to Delhi through a deal with Air India. The Civil Aviation Authority held a competition for the new services because BA had applied for all 21 and Virgin for 18 (Done, 2004). BA were awarded seven, Virgin ten and British Midland four.

## Discussion activity 2.20

Is corporate bullying as common as personal bullying? Is it more or less of an ethical wrong than personal bullying?

This next case involves powerful individuals within an organisation exploiting their strength.

| Case study 2.21 | **The hospital consultants** |
|---|---|

The following is an extract from an interview with an accountant in a hospital.

You will be aware I am sure, through the media, that the government this year has made available an extra £500 million or £600 million for trying to reduce the waiting lists [of patients awaiting treatment]. What that means with a hospital like this is that suddenly you have got to do an extra lot of work, very quickly over a short period of time and it doesn't really give you time to get additional staff employed. You are really talking about expecting either existing staff to do overtime or to get some agency staff in to help. Also we haven't had confirmation that this money will be recurrent, although it is likely to be. But because we haven't had that specific guarantee hospitals are reluctant to employ people on open-ended contracts.

One of the problems we then face is with consultant surgeons, a lot, if not all, of whom have private work as well, and there are some of them who say, 'Right, I will do this extra work, provided I am paid such and such a rate'. The rates that they are inclined to quote will be what they would charge privately. I think they forced the hospital's arm into agreeing to it. They got what they wanted then ... They will see their job probably in a wider context than just their work in the NHS, because it is regular, their private work. What their stance of course is, if you are wanting me to do this extra NHS session, in theory I am foregoing doing a private session somewhere else, so I want to be compensated at least somewhere near the level of income that I would have earned.

It causes me some unease. I suppose in terms of unfairness. If we haven't got additional nurses in the hospital prepared to do extra hours, then we won't get the operations done because it needs a team in the operating theatres, both the consultants and the nurses. But of course the nurses haven't got the option of doing private work and being able to earn more money so they haven't got the clout. Yeah, I think, I am sure whoever you speak to, they will see it is the consultants who have got the most clout in the hospital. It is them who can bang the table. Why is it that they can do this? Is it right that they should do this? Don't get me wrong, I am not saying that every surgeon in the hospital has taken a slider, some think the stance taken by most people is totally wrong and unjustified. I know that when there was a meeting of surgeons to discuss it, one particular [consultant] said 'well, he didn't think that any of the surgeons should get additional money for this extra work because they all earned quite enough anyway'. In some ways it can be helpful, because in theory you can maybe marginalise those that have taken a more extreme stance, but that depends really if they are very forceful personalities within the hospital; it depends then whether the hospital management wants to stand up to them.

(*Source*: Research interview conducted by the authors)

**Discussion activity 2.21**

Were the consultants exercising their market power legitimately or were they bullying the hospital management?

The bullies in the next case study were organisations rather than an individual or a group.

**Case study 2.22**

## Supermarkets' treatment of their supply chains

In recent years there have been many criticisms of the power that the major supermarket chains exercise in the UK. Among these criticisms were the charges that they were using oligarchic power to keep prices to the consumer high and that, by building large out-of-town stores and requiring people to drive to them, they were damaging the environment. The Competition Commission investigated several of these arguments. They found that the market was competitive and that profits were not excessive. However, they did uphold the claim that the big supermarkets did bully (to use our word, not theirs) the farmers and smaller companies locked into their supply chains. The following extract from a *Financial Times* article rehearses some of the arguments.

**FT**   The relationship between food suppliers and retailers will again come under the microscope. In the meantime, ministers want to use a new code of practice between supermarkets and suppliers, one of the recommendations of the Competition Commission report, to clamp down on some of the extreme practices, such as retailers imposing retrospective price cuts to contracts.

A draft code has been drawn up by the Office of Fair Trading with the supermarkets. Food suppliers are being consulted on the results and have signalled their dissatisfaction with what they have seen so far. Instead of calling a halt to some of the practices criticised by the Competition Commission, such as asking suppliers to meet the cost of shop refurbishment or staff hospitality, the code suggests retailers should not 'unreasonably' ask suppliers to foot the bill. But Whitehall officials expect the code to be toughened up during the consultation process. 'The code has to be robust. It has to end the practices the Competition Commission criticised, not just say it would rather they didn't happen. If there is no confidence in the new code, a future government may have to consider further legislation,' said one. Colin Breed, Liberal Democrat agriculture spokesman, believes the code will not help suppliers stand up to supermarkets. 'The only sensible way to proceed is to appoint an independent retail regulator who would not be in the pockets of the supermarkets,' he said.

The industry may also come under the scrutiny of the [House of] Commons' trade and industry committee. Members have praised the sector for helping to deliver lower food prices through fierce competition, but say they are aware suppliers further down the chain often pay the price. Martin

▶

O'Neill, committee chairman, said there could be room for an inquiry around the time of the planned sweeping review of the farming industry. 'I would hope that review will spark off a broad debate about the future of retail and the protection of consumer choice just as much as consumers' rights,' he said.

Retailers are, of course, keen to avoid any inquiry that focuses directly on their role, although all say they are happy to take part in any wider-ranging review of the supply chain. Inquiries are costly and time consuming. They can also depress share prices across a sector. For many retail analysts, constant carping about supermarket profits risks damaging the industry, leaving it susceptible to overseas predators. 'One day people are weeping and wailing about the fact that Marks and Spencer does not make £1bn profits any more,' said one analyst. 'The next thing, they are complaining that Tesco does just that. Do they want a successful retail industry in this country or not?'

(*Source*: R. Bennett and S. Voyle, *Financial Times*, 11 April 2001. Copyright © The Financial Times Limited. Reproduced with permission)

## Discussion activity 2.22

How easy is it for supply chain partnerships, that are proposed as a new and better way to manage procurement, to become abusive relationships? How might this tendency, if true, be prevented?

## Harming

This category involves questions of harm to individuals, animals, institutions, organisations or the environment. One area of controversy is whether a degree of harm is acceptable if the overall results of the harmful action are good. Another concerns the accuracy of the forecasts of the amount of harm and good a particular action will do. An interesting case, which involved such judgements, was that of the Brent Spar oil platform. The issue was whether it was safe to dump the disused platform at sea or whether it would be better to take it ashore and dismantle it. Some time after the issue had been resolved the environmental group Greenpeace admitted that it had exaggerated the amount of environmental harm the sinking of the platform would have done.

Many of the examples of harm being done within or by organisations concern harm to individual employees, as in the following case study.

**Case study 2.23**

## The *Super Size Me* sales promotion

The film *Super Size Me* was directed by Morgan Spurlock (2004) and gives a cinematic account of the results of living for 30 days by eating only the food he bought from McDonald's. The question of whether a sensible person would eat such a monotone diet is at the centre of the ethical issue raised by the film. It was a question that had been considered by the American courts in 2002. Ashley Perelman, aged 14, and Jazlyn Bradley, aged 19, were both obese and had many of the health problems associated with the condition. They also ate hugely at McDonald's restaurants. They blamed the McDonald's Corporation and sued it. The judge pointed out that this was a conflict between personal responsibility and public health and thought the girls were sufficiently knowledgeable and rational to realise that eating too much of what they fancied would not do them good. But the judge's rejection of the girls' claim was not an unalloyed victory for McDonald's (United States District Court, Southern District of New York, 2003). He pointed out that in certain circumstances it could be possible to show that McDonald's might be responsible for its customers' obesity related ill health. If restaurants do nothing to encourage people to overeat, and provide all the proper nutritional information, then if the customers still decide to eat more than they should that was the customers' problem. If, however, it was shown that any restaurant intended and encouraged customers to eat its food at dangerous rates then 'proximate cause' could be established. Many American restaurants do encourage gluttony by offering a free dessert if a customer can eat, for example, an impossibly sized steak. If it could be shown that McDonald's staff were encouraging people to eat a meal far larger than anyone should eat at a single sitting then the legal situation might be very different. The judge commented,

> The plaintiffs fail to cite any advertisement where McDonald's asserts that its products may be eaten for every meal of every day without any ill consequences [and] if plaintiffs were able to flesh out this argument in an amended complaint, it may establish that the dangers of McDonald's products were not commonly well known and thus that McDonald's had a duty towards its customers.

(United States District Court, Southern District of New York, 2003: 12, 17)

This comment must have acted as the trigger that led Spurlock to make his film, in which there were three rules he chose to follow.

1. He had to eat everything on the McDonald's menu at least once.

2. He could only consume what was on offer at McDonald's, including the water.

3. Whenever McDonald's offered him the option to super size his meal by the addition of extra French fries and sodas he had to take it.

At the start of the month he was fit, healthy and slim; he was checked by doctors who confirmed his healthy condition. Thirty days later he was 35 pounds heavier, with a liver in poor condition and all the symptoms of

▶

addiction – twitches, chest pains, headaches. He was also impotent. Some of the latter symptoms, it may be supposed, could have been reinforced by his need for a good film narrative. As one reviewer pointed out,

> Obviously the more rapidly his health deteriorates; the better it is for his career. [ ] When one of his doctors tells him that his liver is malfunctioning and he must stop the diet at once, he keeps a straight face; but we can tell that inwardly he is cheering.

> (Wilson, 2004: 17)

The film was a critical success and McDonald's felt it necessary to take out advertisements in the daily newspapers in the UK arguing that it was irresponsible for anyone to eat such an imbalanced diet; and that no sensible person would eat their products alone. They pointed out that eating at McDonald's, if part of a balanced diet, would not cause people problems. They also pointed out that they had introduced healthy options into their menus. Though others pointed out that if the dressings provided with the salads were eaten then the meals had as many calories as the burgers. The messages were reinforced by a special website set up to counter the film's claims (www.supersizeme-thedebate.co.uk). They did, however, cease the *Super Size Me* promotion. As Wilson concluded her review of the film,

> The best the food giant can do is to accuse Morgan Spurlock of having acted 'irresponsibly' – by eating too much of its own food.

> (Wilson, 2004: 17)

### Discussion activity 2.23

1. To what extent should people be protected against their own ignorance and frailties? (This by the way is a standard revealing question because it gives away the feelings of the writer – so you might wish to re-frame it.)

2. Is there a litigation culture developing in other regions of the world following US precedents? Is it a bad thing?

### Case study 2.24

### Sexual harassment

This case study is an extract from a research interview.

> I mean I haven't had it personally but a very close friend of mine was a secretary in a very large organisation in London and worked for the Assistant Chairman and she felt she was being harassed. Well she was being harassed and when she actually spoke to her personnel department they said, 'Well yes, you're probably right, we've had complaints before but nobody in this organisation will remove the Assistant Chairman. We will help you find another job.' So their compassion went to the individual in getting her

another job because their knowledge was, what could they do? The organisation would not support [her], whatever claim she put in, at the end of the day it would not result in his dismissal. It may have resulted in a rap over the knuckles but she could not work for him and ... sometimes you know that that is the approach you are going to have to take. Fortunately I've never been in that sort of situation of something quite as clearly wrong.

(*Source*: Research interview conducted by the authors)

### Discussion activity 2.24

What are the longer-term consequences of not confronting behaviour such as that discussed in the case study?

The next case describes the harm that can be caused by corporate inaction, although in this example there is a dispute as to which of two corporations was culpable. It also raises the question, to be discussed in Chapter 8, of when harm done by corporate indifference can, or should, invite criminal charges as well as civil liabilities.

### Case study 2.25

### The Firestone Tire recall issue

In August 2000 Ford and Firestone announced the product recall of 6.5 million tyres used on Ford's sports utility vehicle (SUV), the Explorer. The recall was limited to tyres made at Firestone's plant at Decatur in Illinois. Tyres made at other plants were not recalled. The problem was that the treads on the tyres were prone to separate in hot weather; this could cause a loss of control of the vehicle that could result in a rollover accident. Over 180 people had died in such accidents in the USA and 700 people had been injured.

It was alleged by commentators that Firestone knew the problem was not simply a quality systems fault at Decatur but a general problem that affected all of Firestone's SUV tyres. It was therefore alleged that Firestone, far from putting things right, was replacing the faulty tyres with equally dangerous ones.

The situation was made more complex by the desires of both Ford and Firestone to blame each other for the rollover accidents and the deaths. While Ford blamed Firestone, Firestone partly blamed design faults in the Explorer. In a report on the accidents Firestone identified some problems for which it was responsible, but also claimed that Ford's recommendation that the tyres should be inflated to a pressure significantly below the tyres' maximum capacity (to overcome a design fault in the Explorer) increased the temperature of the tyres and increased the possibility of tread separation. Ford, in its 'root cause' report, claimed that design problems played no role in the crashes and that underinflation was not a contributory factor. The argument continued during 2000 and was the subject of Congressional hearings.

▶

On 22 May Firestone announced that it would no longer be a supply partner of Ford, ending a relationship that had lasted nearly a century. On the same day Ford announced that it was recalling 13 million tyres at a cost of $2.1 billion. On the previous day it had recalled 47,000 of its SUVs because of fears, unconnected with the Firestone issue, that tyres had been damaged on the production line.

The case paralleled that of the Pinto model which exercised Ford in the 1970s (De George, 1999: 240–1). The Pinto was a car produced in a hurry. When it was tested for rear-end impact it was found to be below the standard of comparable cars. There was a danger, because of the positioning of the fuel tank, that the tank could be punctured in a crash and the car would explode. Ford undertook a cost–benefit analysis. They estimated that the cost of inserting a protective baffle was greater than the cost of legal claims that might arise from deaths attributable to the design fault. The design of the car was not changed between 1971 and 1978 and the customers were not informed of the potential problem. Between 1976 and 1977 thirteen Pintos exploded after rear-end crashes. The cost of the legal compensation proved to be much greater than the cost of the alteration and in 1978 the cars were recalled and protective baffles were fitted.

(*Sources*: Turner, 2001; Firestone Tire Resource Center, n.d.; Bowe, 2001)

## Discussion activity 2.25

Had Ford's strategic attitude to safety fears concerning its vehicles changed in over 20 years?

This last case study concerns when it might be right to break the law to prevent an organisation doing harm. It also, as it centres on the issue of the moral status of animals, questions the definition of harm.

## Case study 2.26    Huntingdon Life Sciences

This case raises questions about whether there are situations in which it is appropriate to take illegal action because either the law is immoral or the law has to be broken to prevent some greater harm being done. This case study concerns Huntingdon Life Sciences (HLS), a company that carries out pharmaceutical testing on laboratory animals. The company's activities are highly regulated by government agencies and the testing it does is legal.

Animal rights activists argue that testing drugs on animals is cruel and immoral. The case raises difficult questions about whether animals have rights. The traditional view was that animals are not accorded moral status or rights because they lack the power to reason. The obvious response is that this does not prevent them from suffering. This argument may justify minimising the pain caused during experiments, but it does not necessarily mean that the experiments are bad in themselves, especially if they contribute to a greater benefit for humanity through the development of better drugs and medical treatments. The arguments around this issue, which are not primarily the concern of this text, can be explored in Tester (1991) and Scruton (2000). When people claim the existence of rights they may be exhibiting emotivism. This simply means claiming something is right because it feels right. Moral judgement becomes a subjective emotional reaction to a situation.

Animal rights activists believe they are justified in using violence, or the threat of violence, to stop vivisection. The shareholders of HLS, as well as its managers and employees, have been intimidated. The activists threatened to identify and protest to the shareholders. Various institutional shareholders decided in consequence to cease investing in HLS and a number of brokers advised shareholders to sell after threats from activists. Two of HLS's marketmakers had also withdrawn and this made it difficult for investors to trade their shares. The company responded by proposing to set up a rarely used shareholding structure to keep investors' identities anonymous and to protect them from intimidation. The proposed corporate nominee scheme is within the rules set out by the Financial Services Authority.

The government felt it had to take action, as described in the following article from the *Financial Times*, to protect a legitimate business.

**FT** The authorities on Thursday stepped up their fight against animal rights activists with the launch of a police hit squad and a top-level government committee. The two measures are aimed at preventing violent attacks against companies that carry out medical research, their customers and financial backers. The police announced the creation of a squad 'to target the ringleaders of animal [rights] extremist activity who are organising and taking part in serious criminal offences'.

The group will draw officers from different police forces and will work under the National Crime Squad. It aims to prevent attacks such as those suffered by directors, staff and customers of Huntingdon Life Sciences, the drug-testing group. Over the past year, activists have set fire to Huntingdon workers' cars, sent hate mail to staff and assaulted Brian Cass, its managing director. No one has been arrested in connection with these attacks.

The Association of Chief Police Officers denied that the police had acted slowly in dealing with animal rights extremists. It would 'not say [the squad] was late. We felt this was the right time to act.' The squad will liaise with the new government committee, which includes five ministers and is chaired by Jack Straw [at the time, Home Secretary]. The committee will coordinate government action against the activists. The home secretary, who on Thursday visited Huntingdon's laboratories in Cambridgeshire, said: 'We will not tolerate a small number of criminals trying to threaten research organisations and companies.' Some 15 protesters stood outside the gates but were denied a meeting with the home secretary. Greg Avery of Stop Huntingdon Animal Cruelty said the campaign group had no involvement in the violent attacks.

(*Sources*: F. Guerrera, www.FT.com, 27 April 2001, *Financial Times*, 18 July 2001. Copyright © Financial Times Limited. Reproduced with permission)

### Discussion activity 2.26

In what situations do you think it might be justified to break, or defy, the law, to end an injustice?

## Reflections

This chapter has presented a panorama of the ethical and moral issues that affect managerial and organisational life. Some patterns can be seen to emerge from plotting the case studies on the matrix in Table 2.1. Many of the issues that cause difficulty and controversy in the business and organisational world concern actions that are, arguably, wrong but legal. These cover the range of matters from the ethical to the moral. Issues that centre on actions that are wrong and illegal mainly concern questions of morality rather than ethics. They are about stopping organisations doing harm. Conversely, issues arising from actions that are good and legal, but are not legal obligations, rest mostly at the ethical end of the spectrum in Table 2.1. The most contentious issues, and perhaps the least common, are those concerning illegal actions that are ethically and morally justifiable.

All the case studies are matters of controversy; every claim that an act is illegal or wrong can be challenged. As Watson (2002: 455) argued, ethical ambiguity and ethical dilemmas are inevitable in organisational and managerial life.

## Summary

In this chapter the following key points have been made:

- The major virtues of corporate and organisational behaviour are:
  - **Doing good**
    - social development
    - social responsibility

  - **Acting benignly**
    - reciprocity
    - fairness

- The major vices are:
  - **Ignoring harm done to others**
    - Lying and dishonesty
    - Cheating and selfishness

  - **Doing harm**
    - bullying and social irresponsibility
    - doing social and environmental damage

- Under each of these headings issues at work may raise questions about what is right and what is wrong. What is right may in many cases also be legal but not necessarily a legal obligation. In other cases what is right may not be legal. Conversely, things that the law allows might not be right.

- Ethical issues are not easy to categorise. They appear as dilemmas in which arguments can be made for all sides. The protagonists in the cases, however, may see and present only a single point of view.

## Quick revision test

1. The prisoners' dilemma is ...
   (a) how to stop being bored in the cell
   (b) an account of the dilemma people face when they know they should collaborate with others for their own advantage but may not trust the others
   (c) a theory that explains how altruism is a natural result of evolutionary pressures

2. How does the rate of corporate philanthropy in the UK compare with the rate in the USA?
   (a) Higher
   (b) Lower
   (c) About the same

3. Which of the following forms of discrimination at work are illegal in the UK?
   (a) Sex discrimination
   (b) Discrimination because of disability
   (c) Age discrimination

4. The Nolan principles are ...
   (a) guidelines to help UK civil servants avoid conflicts of interest;
   (b) guidelines concerning executive remuneration in the USA;
   (c) guidelines on the retention of human organs in hospitals.

## Typical assignments and briefs

1. In what circumstances might it be right to break the law in an effort to prevent a company behaving in a way that is legal, but, in the eyes of some, immoral?

2. Discuss the proposition that companies should behave in a socially responsible manner but are not obliged to contribute to social development.

3. Are there degrees of lying? Can some forms of lying be acceptable in business and management practice?

4. Should dual class share systems (in which some shares carry more voting weight per share than others) be made illegal? Illustrate your reasons from recent cases.

## Group activity 2

Locating issues in the grid shown in Table 2.1 is not straightforward. An issue may involve several of the moral and ethical problems identified. It might, for example, exhibit an unfair distribution of resources as well as lying and bullying. It might also be possible to argue about which categories of rightness and legality the issue best fits. Different readings of the facts of the case might lead to different opinions about whether an action was, *prima facie*, illegal or not.

In class identify current business ethics issues that are being discussed in the media. Identify as best you can the facts of the issue and discuss where, on the grid in Table 2.1, the issue might best be placed. It might be necessary to plot different aspects of the issue in different places on the grid.

## Recommended further reading

A good review of current issues in business ethics is P.W.F. Davies (ed.) (1997) *Current Issues in Business Ethics*, London: Routledge. D. Winstanley and J. Woodall (2000) *Ethical Issues in Contemporary Human Resource Management*, London: Macmillan is a very useful guide to ethical issues related to human resource management.

## Useful websites

| Topic | Website provider | URL |
|---|---|---|
| Business ethics resources: topics and issues | Chris MacDonald: ethicsWeb.ca | http://www.ethicsweb.ca/resources/business/topics.html |
| Materials and updates on current issues in business ethics | Business and Human rights resource centre: a charitable not-for-profit organisation set up to promote discussion of human rights issues in business | http://www.business-humanrights.org/Home |
| Most of its services are subscription based but it does provide press releases which identify emerging business ethics issues | EIRIS (Ethical Investment Research Service) | http://www.eiris.org/Pages/TopMenu/News.htm |
| Good exposé style stories on business ethics matters | Jon Entine Online, a website focused on business ethics issues by a campaigning journalist | http://www.jonentine.com/business_ethics.htm |

# Ethical theories and how to use them

Having read this chapter and completed its associated activities, readers should be able to:

- Compare and contrast four approaches to ethical theory.

- Describe the implications of different ethical theories for businesses, organisations and management.

- Apply the theories to ethical issues in business, organisation and management.

## Introduction

In Chapter 2 the range of ethical issues that can affect businesses, organisations and managers was plotted and examples were given that you were invited to think about. This chapter will give you tools for ethical thinking that you can use in analysing such issues. We have called them ethical theories because they are speculations or mental conceptions about how one should think about ethical matters. They should help you to move from an intuitive response to ethical matters to a systematic and analytical approach. However, the theories do not provide an easy resolution. One reason for this is that there are many theories and it may not be obvious which should be applied to any particular set of circumstances. A second reason is that the theories are general. It is not always clear how they should be applied or interpreted in specific cases. The fact that some of these theories have been the subject of philosophical debate for many centuries implies that there is no consensus, or final resolution, to be had on these questions. It may be best to consider that the theories provide means of legitimating the stances you take on an issue rather than as sources of definitive or authoritative solutions.

## A map of ethical theories

As there are many ethical theories, they will be plotted on a map (Figure 3.1) based on that developed by Petrick and Quinn (1997: 48). A note of warning is needed. Figure 3.1, as are all two-by-two matrices, is a work of simplification. It is only intended to give you a broad overview. It does not capture the subtleties of the writers included in it because to do so would make it impossible to constrain them within any one quadrant of the figure.

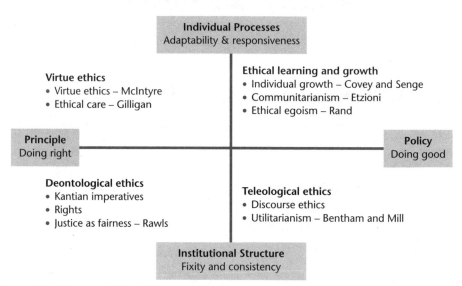

**Figure 3.1** A framework for ethical theories

The two elements of the horizontal axis of Figure 3.1 are policy and principle. The terms are taken from Dworkin's (1977: 22) work on rights.

- **Policy** is defined as an approach that *sets out a goal to be reached, generally an improvement in some economic, political or social feature.*
- **Principle**, in contrast, *is a standard that is to be observed, not because it will advance an economic, political or social situation, but because it is a requirement of fairness or justice or some other dimension of morality.*

Those ethical theories on the left of this dimension determine what is right and wrong from predetermined principles and standards. They take no regard of the consequences of an action – 'let justice be done though the heavens fall', a maxim of Roman law that was famously used in 1772 by Lord Mansfield during a legal case concerning slavery. Those theories to the right of the dimension measure the rightness of a thing according to whether it brings us to, or closer to, a desired state. The vertical dimension in Figure 3.1 contrasts a focus on ethical individuals with a focus on ethical institutions. The theories in the top half of the framework emphasise individuals' responsibility to develop themselves and the groups they belong to, by acquiring judgement and self-knowledge. The theories in the lower half of the framework are concerned to develop fixed structures, institutions, that are independent of us but which determine our principles and govern our ethical deliberations.

## Virtue ethics

We will begin our consideration of Figure 3.1 by focusing upon those theories and ethical perspectives shown on the left-hand side, the principle-based perspectives. This does not mean that those ethical positions on the right-hand side of Figure 3.1 are unprincipled, not at all. Principle, in the sense being used here, refers to beliefs that are not affected by, or shaped by, the people involved, or what might result if a particular course of action is followed. This disregard for the consequences that could result from an undiluted adoption of these approaches is why they are sometimes grouped under the broad heading of 'non-consequentialist' positions. This, as you will see, can sometimes lead to awkward and fraught situations.

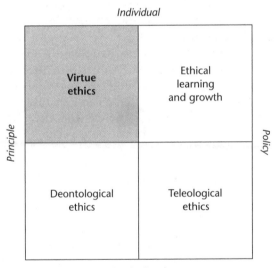

Virtues are not 'ends'; rather they are 'means'. They are personal qualities that provide the basis for the individual to lead a good, noble, or 'happy' life. Whilst the notion of what is virtuous behaviour has changed over time, the person most associated with virtue ethics is Aristotle, a philosopher of great eminence who lived in Greece between 384 and 322 BC. Not only have the characteristics of a virtuous life undergone significant changes, but the meanings attached to the terms used to describe particular characteristics are also a source of difference.

The Greek word, εὐδαιμονία (eudaemonia) is loosely translated as 'happiness'. However, as MacIntyre (1967) pointed out, in Greek the term actually embraces the notion of both behaving well and faring well. Its use in ancient Greece was not concerned with hedonistic notions of happiness. It concerned itself with the individual's behaviour, and thus the way others perceived the individual. The latter was an essential ingredient to personal happiness. The 'good life' had, and retains, strong connotations of a 'whole' life, and places the individual within a social context. Even though social structures were deeply class-ridden during Aristotle's life, within the social and political elite there was a strong sense of being part of a whole.

Aristotle, reflecting the ideas of his age, placed the 'great-soul-man' on a pedestal. As you will see, the great-soul-man displays those virtues that were regarded as of the highest order. In ancient Greece the views of one's peers were critical to feelings of self-worth. Whilst the individual is the focus of Aristotle's attention, it is an individual within a society. Some social commentators, like MacIntyre (1967, 1987), have argued that since the eighteenth century liberalism has placed the individual outside of society. In this latter context, society is at best the sum of its parts. At worst, in Margaret Thatcher's famous words, 'there is no such thing as society'.

Virtue ethics is not a system of rules, but rather a set of personal characteristics that, if practised, will ensure that the individual is likely to make the 'right' choice in any ethically complex situation. Thus, the question for the individual, caught in the maelstrom of an ethically complex situation and appealing to virtue ethics as a guide for action, would ask, 'What would a virtuous person do in this situation?'

Plato, Aristotle's teacher, had identified four virtues, those of wisdom, courage, self-control and justice. For Aristotle, justice was the dominant virtue, but he expanded upon the number of personal qualities that could be regarded as virtues. Thus, into the frame came qualities such as liberality (the virtuous attitude towards money); patience (the virtuous response to minor provocation); amiability (the virtue of personal persona); magnanimity, truthfulness, indifference (in relation to the seeking of public recognition of achievement), and wittiness. It must be stressed that these virtues were not seen as of equal merit. The original Platonic virtues were seen as central to the attainment of a 'good' life, whereas the other virtues were seen as important for a civilised life. To understand the nature of a virtue we must understand how they are derived, and to do so we introduce the concept of the 'mean'.

For Aristotle, those personal qualities that were regarded as virtues were reflected in behaviours that represented a balance, or mean, in terms of the particular personal quality being considered. Thus, if the response of an individual to the threat of 'danger or significant personal challenge' was being considered, we can envisage a continuum with cowardice at one extreme and recklessness at the other (as in Table 3.1). Neither of these personal qualities (what Aristotle termed 'dispositions') is appealing as they are both likely to lead to detrimental outcomes in the long run. In the face of danger the 'noble' or 'great-soul-man' (and it was always the male that was considered in ancient Greece) would have to overcome his fears (i.e. suppress feelings of cowardice), but avoid acts of rashness, which would be likely to reduce the chances of success. Thus, an intermediate-point is required. This mean, or disposition, in this context is termed 'courage'.

Aristotle also considered modesty (used by Aristotle to mean 'respect', or 'sense of shame') as a possible virtue, but he dismissed it, other than as a virtue in the

**Table 3.1** Aristotle's moral virtues

| Context | The vice of deficiency | Virtue (mean) | The vice of excess |
|---|---|---|---|
| *Danger or a significant personal challenge* | Cowardice | Courage | Rashness |
| *Physical pleasures* | Indifference (being unable to recognise the joy that physical pleasures can offer) | Self-control (knowing when and where to enjoy oneself) | Greed |
| *Wealth* | Meanness | Liberality (discriminating generosity) | Profligacy |
| *Money* | Miserliness | Magnificence (knowing when to spend, how much and on what) | Spendthrift |
| *View of self* | Meekness | Magnanimity (being able to feel and display personal pride when it is deserved, but without vanity) | Vanity |
| *Personal recognition* | False modesty | Indifference (good deeds are done for their own sake and not for personal recognition) | Careerist |
| *Minor irritants* | Defeatism | Patience | Irascibility |
| *Personal demeanour* | Obsequious (fawning and grovelling) | Amiable | Quarrelsome |
| *Sincerity in expression* | Self-deprecating | Truthfulness | Boastfulness |
| *Sociability* | Boorishness | Wittiness | Buffoonery |

younger man. In the latter case, Aristotle saw it as a curb on youthful indiscretion, but he considered that the virtuous mature man should not require modesty for he should not commit acts of which he could be ashamed.

For Aristotle, the 'great-soul-man' was magnanimous, which was defined as 'possessing proper pride, or self-control' (Aristotle, 1976: 153). It is not surprising that, in the class-ridden society of ancient Greece, the virtues described by Aristotle were only available to the elite of society. McMylor (1994), citing MacIntyre, observed:

> Certain virtues are only available to those of great riches and high social status, there are virtues which are unavailable to the poor man, even if he is a free man. And those virtues are in Aristotle's view ones central to human life.
>
> (McMylor, 1994: 103)

Wealth, however, was not a necessary prerequisite of a magnanimous man.

> It is chiefly with honours ... that the magnanimous man is concerned; but he will also be moderately disposed towards wealth, power, and every kind of good or bad fortune, however it befalls him.
>
> (Aristotle, 1976: 155)

Indeed when discussing the virtuous approach towards wealth Aristotle identified liberality as the virtue (the mean). Illiberality or meanness was one extreme vice, while prodigality or profligacy was the other. However, Aristotle did not regard the two extremes as vices of equal unacceptability, judging profligacy as less objectionable than meanness. This ranking of profligacy over meanness underscores the slightly lower importance attached to money and wealth, although this is not to say that wealth was unimportant.

Magnanimity was not equated with self-deprecation or undue humility. These were seen as approximating to vices, but so too were vanity and boastfulness. Being *rightly* proud of who you were, or what you had achieved, was not a vice; only unjustified high self-esteem was unacceptable.

> A person is considered to be magnanimous if he thinks that he is worthy of great things, provided that he is worthy of them; because anyone who esteems his own worth unduly is foolish, and nobody who acts virtuously is foolish or stupid.
>
> (Aristotle, 1976: 153)

The point about this statement is that it is the perception of others that determines whether behaviour is vain or deserving. In one sense a person can be both vain and deserving, but for Aristotle vanity implied a degree of exhibitionism above that which could be justified by one's achievements or social standing. Thus, vanity becomes a relative term in this context, relative to the state of deservingness attached to the achievement of the individual or his position in society.

Aristotle gave justice prominent consideration, but the notion of justice in ancient Greece was quite different from that which we articulate today. As is further explored below, the accepted standards of ethical behaviour are a product of their times, notwithstanding that notions of justice feature in most philosophies of ethics. Aristotle, while he spent some time differentiating between differing forms of justice, nonetheless offers a less than precise definition of justice, with the notion of the 'mean' again featuring strongly.

> To do injustice is to have more than one ought, and to suffer it is to have less than one ought and justice is the mean between doing injustice and suffering it.
>
> (Aristotle, 1976: 78)

This concentration upon the notion of justice as the bedrock of ethical behaviour is not universally shared, with the invisibility and muteness of women within such debates a cause for concern.

## A challenge to the primacy of justice

The role of women in ancient Athenian society did not register on political and social seismographs. Thus, the virtues as articulated by Aristotle can be said to be virtues from a masculine perspective. This is a relevant observation when we consider, as we do later, the work of psychologists, such as Lawrence Kohlberg, who developed a hierarchy of moral reasoning, based upon the assumption that justice is the ultimate test of the superiority of one form of moral reasoning over another. Within this framework, hard choices can be made between competing claims using justice as the decision criterion. The hypothetical scenarios employed by Kohlberg during his studies presented research subjects with choices to be made, but compromises were not available. Under this approach, one claim could be successful, while all others would fail.

Gilligan (1982), a former student of Kohlberg, has taken issue with the use of justice as the pre-eminent determinant of moral reasoning. Within Kohlberg's studies fewer females than males have displayed the form of moral reasoning that has allowed them to be classified as reasoning at the highest levels of Kohlberg's hierarchy. Gilligan has argued that this should not be interpreted as a lower level of reasoning than is possible, rather that the form of reasoning often displayed by women is *different* from that held by men. It is argued that women's early socialisation processes (particularly observing their mothers) encourage them to seek out compromises, not to allocate blame exclusively to one side or another, nor to distribute prizes or plaudits exclusively to only one member of a group. Rather the resolution of competitions, games or arguments is achieved with a sense of 'everyone gets something'. This approach is adopted with one eye on the medium to long term, that is, if a family is to develop cohesively there must be give and take from all sides at one time or another. From Gilligan's perspective the wisdom of Solomon involves more than the simple application of all-or-nothing justice to resolve a family dispute. Gilligan's argument contains a strong sense of the wisdom of the female perspective that she referred to as 'care'.

The need for wisdom to temper justice is possibly best exemplified in recent times by the approach adopted by President Mandela's government in South Africa when, on coming to power, it established the Commission for Truth and Reconciliation. The Commission was charged with investigating the myriad of stories and accusations of atrocities, murder and brutality inflicted upon the black and coloured communities by individuals, the police and the army during the apartheid years. Under the chairmanship of Archbishop Desmond Tutu, the Commission for Truth and Reconciliation continues to investigate a wide range of cases, with the accused giving evidence in the knowledge that they will not be prosecuted for their crimes. It is hoped that the truth relating to each case will thereby emerge (a critical issue for the bereaved), and gradually the nation's shame will be exorcised. In the process a potential bloodbath of retribution will have been avoided. Whether the Commission's work has satisfied everyone is a moot point, but it represents an understanding that justice, if exercised exclusively in the form of retribution ('an eye for an eye'), would be unlikely to serve the longer-term interests of the people of South Africa.

Gilligan argued that the concept of 'care' should be regarded as highly as justice when interpreting responses of research subjects to moral reasoning scenarios. This is not care (which is too often interpreted as compromise) born out of an 'anything-for-a-quiet-life' approach. Rather, care is reflected by an approach that seeks to find a way forward that not only provides some form of equitable resolution to a conflict (although not necessarily reflecting 'full' justice in an Aristotelian or Kohlbergian form), but also holds out the possibilities for maintaining a working relationship between the protagonists, so that future cooperation might be possible. This is not to deny that there are times when guilt or success should be identified with individuals, to the exclusion of all others. Gilligan's argument is that such an approach is undoubtedly appropriate on occasions, but not as a universal maxim.

If we think about this issue from an Aristotelian perspective, we can employ the notion of a mean as in Figure 3.2. You may wish to consider this perspective when you tackle Activity 3.1.

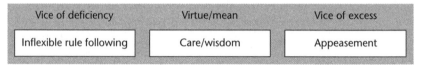

| Vice of deficiency | Virtue/mean | Vice of excess |
| --- | --- | --- |
| Inflexible rule following | Care/wisdom | Appeasement |

**Figure 3.2** Care and wisdom as a virtue

## Changing perceptions of virtue

The notion of virtue is heavily dependent upon the period in which the concept is being considered. As MacIntyre (1967: 174) observed,

> it [virtue] always requires for its application the acceptance of some prior account of certain features of social and moral life, in terms of which it has to be defined and explained.

As centuries have passed, so shifts can be detected in what becomes regarded as virtuous behaviour.

- In the time of Homer (who lived some 400 years before Aristotle and during a period of constant hostilities), the warrior was the model of human excellence and achievement.

- During the Greece of Aristotle's time, with its relatively stable Athenian city-state, the virtues embodied in the privileged, Athenian gentleman were paramount.

- From a western perspective, the rise of Christianity, as reflected in the New Testament, brought with it a fundamental shift in the perception of virtuous behaviour. Contra Aristotle, the New Testament presents an image of goodness that is unattainable by the wealthy and the privileged. Only the poorest are deemed worthy, with slaves (the lowest class within Aristotle's Athenian society) more likely to be seen as virtuous than the rich.

- The coming of the Industrial Revolution, in the eighteenth century, found new personal qualities becoming valued. Benjamin Franklin, for example, espoused the virtues of cleanliness, silence and industry, as well as punctuality, industry, frugality, plus many others, but always with utilitarian motives (McMylor, 1994).

- Solomon (1993: 207–16) identified honesty, fairness, trust and toughness (having a vision and persevering in its implementation) as the important virtues for managers in modern corporations.

The Aristotelian and Christian perspectives recognise different virtues but both link means and ends. Unethical means cannot be justified by good outcomes. A good deed is not a good deed if it is done with bad motives, e.g. to avoid pain, or to ingratiate oneself with the recipient. In Aristotelian terms, a virtuous life is one that allows individuals to achieve their *telos*, or end, to its full potential. Practice of the virtues makes this potential realisable. The emphasis is thus upon both means (virtues) and ends (*telos*). From this perspective the relationship between means and ends is an internal one, not external. Both are within the control of the individual.

For Franklin, however, virtue was dependent upon some specified notion of utility. Achievement of socially acceptable ends (which have increasingly become articulated in material terms) can justify less than virtuous means. Understanding the values, social structures and key discourses of an era is crucial to understanding what will be regarded as virtues.

Within the Franklinian conception of virtues we have some of the seeds of what troubles many people about juxtaposing ethics and business. Some of the virtues articulated by Franklin can be achieved most effectively by the suppression of individual rights, e.g. silence and industry, whilst others, e.g. punctuality and cleanliness, are regarded as virtues, not primarily because they benefit the individual concerned, but because they contribute to the economy and efficiency of business. Thus, whilst the ends (punctuality and cleanliness) can be regarded as beneficial in themselves, they would not be regarded as virtues from an Aristotelian perspective, because they are driven by a concern with ends and not means.

## Activity 3.1

Briefly analyse Case study 2.14 (*The Jonathan Aitken story*) employing a virtue ethics perspective.

1. Which virtues would you prioritise?

2. Are there any personal characteristics that so far have not been mentioned that you would regard as virtues and that might contribute to addressing the issues raised in the case?

One of the problems with this instrumentality is that it turns people into means rather than ends. This was of considerable concern to another major figure in the development of the philosophy of ethics – Immanuel Kant.

## Deontological ethics

### Kantian ethics

Kant's ethical philosophy was that actions must be guided by universalisable principles that apply irrespective of the consequences of the actions. In addition an action can only be morally right if it is carried out as a duty, not in expectation of a reward. From a Kantian perspective, principles exist *a priori*. By this is meant that, knowing what to do in a situation will be determined by a set of principles that have been established by deductive reasoning, independent of, or before, the specifics of the decision in hand have been considered. Indeed, for Kantian ethics the context and consequences of a decision are irrelevant. Lying, for example, is invariably employed to illustrate the inflexibility of Kantian ethics. Lying, irrespective of the context, is wrong. So, for Kant, truth telling, even if the telling of a lie would save a human life, has to be strictly adhered to – no deviations, no exceptions.

For Kant actions have moral worth only when they spring from recognition of duty, and a choice to discharge it. The 'duties' to which Kant refers were a response to the question, 'What makes a moral act right?' They were formulated around the concept of the 'categorical imperative'.

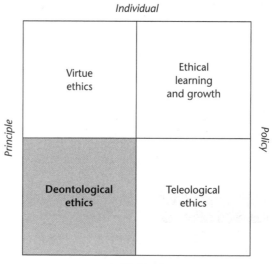

| | Individual | |
|---|---|---|
| | Virtue ethics | Ethical learning and growth |
| Principle | Deontological ethics | Teleological ethics |
| | Institutional | Policy |

| Categorical imperative | DEFINITION |
|---|---|

**Categorical** means unconditional (no exceptions), while **imperative** means a command or, in Kantian terms, a principle. Thus a categorical imperative refers to a command/principle that must be obeyed, with no exceptions. If the categorical imperative is conceptually sound we should be able to will all rational people around the world to follow this particular law. This is the concept of universalisability.

The Ten Commandments of the Old Testament are written in the form of categorical imperatives, i.e. 'Thou shalt not ...', although the extent to which they are universalisable is problematic. (The commandment 'thou shalt not kill' is debated below.)

For Kant an act is morally right if it can be judged by all reasoning people to be appropriate as a universal principle of conduct, irrespective of whether they are to be the doers, receivers or mere observers of an act. The issue of putting oneself in a state of ignorance as to one's own position within a situation is an interesting one, and one to which we will return when we discuss the ideas of John Rawls.

The 'Golden Rule', which is normally expressed as 'do unto others as you would have done unto yourself', is an example of a categorical imperative. It is a rule that can be willed as universalisable. Indeed, Shaw and Barry (1998) cited the scriptures of six world religions, that go back over millennia, identifying quotations from each that are examples of the 'Golden Rule'.

Bowie (1999), in his proposal for business organisations built upon Kantian principles, provided three formulations of the categorical imperative.

**1** The first is that universalisability provides a theory of moral permissibility for market interactions. Interactions that violate the universalisability formulation of the categorical imperative are morally impermissible. This might appear reasonable, but it must be remembered that under this rule someone who is prepared to allow others to exploit, harm and cheat him could, within the universalisability principle, proceed to exploit, harm and cheat others. Bowie tackled this issue when he cited Carr (1968), who argued for a different set of rules and morality for business. Carr observed:

> The golden rule for all its value as an ideal for society is simply not feasible as a guide for business. A good part of the time the businessman is trying to do to others as he hopes others will not do unto him ... The game [poker] calls for distrust of the other fellow. It ignores the claim for friendship. Cunning, deception and concealment of one's strength and intentions, not kindness and open-heartedness, are vital in poker. And no-one should think any worse of the game of business because its standards of right and wrong differ from the prevailing traditions of morality in our society.
>
> (Carr, 1968: 145–6)

A further example of this attitude is provided by Pava (1999) who, drawing upon the work of Badaracco (1997), referred to the case of the pharmaceutical company, Roussel-Uclaf, and its chairman, Edouard Sakiz. The case concerned the abortion drug, RU 486. Sakiz wished to market the drug, but a range of powerful interest groups opposed the drug's sale, including Roussel-Uclaf's majority shareholder, the multinational Hoechst organisation. One of Hoechst's drugs (Zyklon B) had been used by the Nazis in their pogrom against the Jews in the Second World War. Since then the company had committed itself to 'placing our energy, our ideas and our dedication to the service of Life' (Pava, 1999: 82). Sakiz is claimed to have employed a devious and high-risk strategy, in which he forced a vote of the executive committee on the drug's launch, voting against the decision himself. However, in so doing he compromised the French government, which was keen to see the drug launched. The French government threatened to move production of the drug to another company, which forced Roussel-Uclaf to reconsider its decision. This it did, but now 'under the seeming protection of the government' (Pava, 1999: 83). Pava observed:

> Sakiz obtained his ultimate goal and avoided the pitfall of publicly proclaiming his real intentions. Badaracco justifies such seeming hypocrisy by stating that public leaders must follow a 'special ethical code', one that differs from their private morality and from Judeo-Christian ethics. Badaracco elaborates that 'only a naive manager would think otherwise'.
>
> (Pava, 1999: 83)

A Kantian refutation of this argument would avoid a consequentialist assessment, that businesses could not work effectively if lying and deviousness was the universal norm, on the basis that Kant refused to allow considerations of consequences to enter into issues of ethics. Instead a Kantian refutation would take the form of a rebuttal of the logic of the attempted categorical imperative, 'always lie, always be devious'. If everyone always lied or was devious, there would be no point in listening to what anyone had to say. Conversation, language even, would be meaningless and would therefore become redundant. Thus, 'always lie, always be devious' cannot be universalised. Because categorical imperatives are derived deductively, they can be successfully challenged, if flawed.

**2** Bowie's second formulation of the categorical imperative is 'respect for humanity in persons'. This is normally taken to mean treating fellow human beings as ends not means. However, Bowie's formulation is looser than this, and might fail to achieve this objective. Bowie's argument is that this formulation provides the basis for a moral obligation in the employment of people. Employees would cease to be commodities. Everyone involved in market transactions – employees, suppliers, customers and indeed all stakeholders – should be treated with respect. However, this presupposes that it is not possible to treat a commodity with respect. If it is possible to do so, then this formulation fails to achieve its stated aim – to treat people as ends not means. The ultimate test of this formulation would be the reaction of the Kantian organisation to a dramatic fall in demand for its goods or services. If the economics of the situation demanded cost-cutting measures for the firm to survive, with redundancies high on the agenda, the people-as-ends-not-means philosophy is severely tested. It is possible to show respect to those who are being made redundant, for example by providing as generous a financial severance package as is feasible, providing counselling sessions and assistance in interviewing techniques, but, in the end, the redundant employees are redundant because they are judged to be a resource that can no longer be justified (economically) by the firm. They are ultimately a means, not an end.

This particular circle can only be squared if it is acknowledged at the outset that a market-based economy is the backdrop against which the Kantian firm is located. Thus, it is within the actions permitted by market dynamics and economic logic that the Kantian perspective is being argued. In which case, short-term pressures from financial markets to protect the company's share price are likely to take precedence over desires to accept lower profit figures in order to protect employment levels. Any significant deviation from this set of relationships would require a different set of institutional arrangements between a business and its significant investors from that which currently exists. These issues are taken up further when we discuss the stakeholder perspective later in the chapter.

**3** The third formulation is an attempt to further minimise or remove the 'people-as-means' accusation. It is an argument for greater democracy in the workplace – the moral community formulation. For example, by involving all employees (or at least their representatives) in corporate decision making, as with the 'Type A' pluralist model discussed in Chapter 1, the Kantian firm will seek out the most equitable solution when faced with a severe downturn in its markets, arriving at a 'way forward' that reflects the views of the employees. Whether this will be the majority view, or some other formulation, would presumably be left to the firm to decide.

The criticisms levelled at Kantian ethics, over the rigidity of the categorical imperative, are challenged by both Beck (1959) and Bowie (1999). Kant is partly to blame for the criticism, argued Beck, because of the examples he used to illustrate his principles (Kant actually argued for truth telling in a situation in which a lie would save an innocent life). One possible way out of this cul-de-sac is to create a hierarchy of categorical imperatives. In this way the categorical imperative of 'always tell the truth' would be inferior to the categorical imperative of 'lie if it will save an innocent life'. Whether this form of hierarchical formulation is permissible, within a strictly Kantian categorical imperative perspective, is debatable. The notion of categorical imperatives being ranked contains a logical inconsistency. If categorical imperative 'A' can be overridden on occasions by categorical imperative 'B', then it cannot be a categorical imperative because it is not universalisable. We will return to this issue when we discuss *prima facie* obligations, but for the moment we will concentrate upon those writers and arguments that have sought to stay true to an undiluted version of the categorical imperative, but have offered ways of overcoming its rigidity.

De George (1999) offers one such resolution. The scenario depicted by De George addresses the truth-telling categorical imperative. It involves the shielding of an escaped slave who is being pursued by his slaveholder. For De George an untruth that might be told to the slaveholder to throw him off the scent would *not* be construed as a lie, on the basis that slavery is immoral, irrespective of what the law of the land might say. The slaveholder is not judged to have a legitimate interest in the information being sought. Under this interpretation the telling of an untruth is not lying if the person seeking information has no legitimate (ethically acceptable) interest in the information.

This approach is arguing that the telling of an untruth to someone who does not possess a morally legitimate interest in the information being sought is not merely acceptable, but accordingly not actually a lie. The enquirer's lack of moral legitimacy does not warrant the same level of truthfulness from the respondent, as would be required if the enquirer had possessed a legitimate interest.

Kant's use of truth telling has created many problems for the principle of categorical imperatives. The above, rather tortuous, attempts to try to overcome them are not altogether convincing. Purposely misconstruing known facts is a lie, to whomever the lie is to be told, and whatever the justification for the lie. By adopting a pure Kantian perspective, the concealer of the slave is left with no option but to reveal the whereabouts of the slave. However, if the protection of an innocent person is judged more important than telling an untruth, at a *universalisable* level, then there is something wrong with making truth telling a categorical imperative.

The critical question with regard to the truth-telling example used by Kant thus becomes: is the flaw within the principle of a categorical imperative, or is the problem the use of truth telling as an example of a categorical imperative? Whilst Kant did indeed cite truth telling as an example of a categorical imperative, this is not to say that the example is an appropriate or helpful one. If the way out of this difficult situation is simply to reject truth telling as an example of a categorical imperative, then further questions arise, namely:

(a) Is it possible to identify a categorical imperative? and/or
(b) Is it not possible to think of at least one exception to every categorical imperative that might be suggested, thereby nullifying its claim to being universalisable?

You might, for example, suggest 'one should not kill another human being' as a categorical imperative. But would a mother be morally wrong to respond to the pleas of her child who was being attacked by someone intent on taking the child's life? The killing of the assailant might be unpremeditated, unintentional even, but in an unequal struggle between mother and crazed assailant, how does the mother defend her child and herself? This is not to say that the killing of the assailant is the only outcome possible from such a scenario, but what is the status of a categorical imperative of 'no-taking-of-life', if the mother does ultimately stab or shoot the assailant? This is an extreme example, but a categorical imperative is intended to be universalisable and must therefore be able to withstand such tests.

Writers such as Ross (1930) have felt the need to develop a more flexible form of principled reasoning, but remaining emphatically within a non-consequentialist perspective. Ross employed an approach known as *prima facie* obligations.

**DEFINITION**

A literal translation of the Latin term *prima facie* is 'at first sight' or colloquially 'as it seems'. '*Prima facie* evidence' is a legal term that refers to evidence that is deemed sufficient to establish a presumption of truth about an incident, unless or until counter-evidence is discovered. Thus, we can define a *prima facie* obligation as one that should be respected in one's practice, unless and until a different *prima facie* obligation, with a superior claim for adherence, is presented.

Thus, whilst supporters of *prima facie* obligations would see truth telling as a *prima facie* obligation, in a situation where truth telling would lead to the probable death of an innocent human being (e.g. by revealing the whereabouts of an innocent fugitive), the *prima facie* obligation of 'lying to protect a wrongly or unjustly accused person' would override the obligation to tell the truth.

---

### Activity 3.2

Employing a Kantian perspective, briefly analyse Case study 2.19 (*The retention of dead babies' organs in hospitals*).

1. Can you develop a categorical imperative that would be appropriate for this case?

2. Would *prima facie* obligations be more helpful? If so, what would they be?

---

Notwithstanding the above problems, Kant and others who argued for principle-based ethics did so out of a belief that there are certain principles upon which societies need to be based if they are to develop in positive ways. With the emphasis on the atomised individual in modern society, non-consequentionalists feel that principle-based ethics are particularly relevant in the present day. At the root of consequentionalist concerns are the issues of justice and human rights. It is to these issues that we now turn.

## Justice and rights

The notion of justice has featured throughout our discussion of non-consequentialist ethics, and Aristotle spent much time discussing different aspects of justice. While Aristotle's understanding was a particular one, with the 'great-soul-man' able to benefit from all the splendours that his station in life might afford, the issue of human rights has progressed since the time of Aristotle. The United Nations' Declaration of Human Rights made human rights universal, not limited to the male of the species, let alone a small subset of the male population. While inequality of opportunity could be justified by Aristotle (and was the accepted norm throughout ancient Greece), others have worried more intensely about the issue of inequalities in society. Barry (1989: 3) observed, 'In Plato's time, as in ours, the central issue in any theory of justice is the defensibility of unequal relations between people'.

In the political ferment that existed during much of the eighteenth century, some significant works were published that had an influential bearing on political matters in France and America. Thomas Paine (1737–1809) and Jean-Jacques Rousseau (1712–78) were two writers whose publications are said to have provided a philosophical justification to those who sought to wrest control from the then ruling authorities in France and America. In England, Mary Wollstonecraft (1759–97), inspired by Rousseau and the revolution in France, wrote what Held (1987: 79) described as 'one of the most remarkable tracts of social and political theory', the *Vindication of the Rights of Women*. Along with Paine and Rousseau,

Wollstonecraft argued that liberty and equality were intertwined. She argued that the then debates on 'rights of man' needed to embrace the rights of women, but this was a distinctly minority view. Rousseau was himself dismissive of women's rights. Pateman cites Rousseau's comments in *Emile*:

> Woman is made to please and to be in subjection to man, ... they must be trained to bear [a] yoke from the first ... and to submit themselves to the will of others.
>
> (Pateman, 1985: 157)

Wollstonecraft's work was published in 1792, but it was not until 1948 that the principle of one person one vote was finally established in the UK, and Swiss women were not fully enfranchised until 1971 (Pateman, 1985: 5). While major developments in human rights legislation have taken place in relatively recent times, justice remains a problematic concept and practice. The debates concerning human rights are ongoing ones, and many of them concern or involve business organisations.

This brief sojourn in a particular field of political philosophy is offered to provide at least a feel for the troubled and protracted history of the notion of rights in human practice and relations. Notions of liberty and equality are central elements of social justice and the philosopher upon whom we will focus (although not exclusively) to explore contemporary thinking is John Rawls. However, we begin with Robert Nozick (1974), a leading advocate of the libertarian position on justice and rights.

The libertarian perspective adopts the notion of negative freedoms. That is, it holds as its primary tenet the individual's right of 'freedoms from'. The most significant of these is freedom from government interference in all but the most critical of property rights protection systems, e.g. police forces for private property and military forces regarding property of the realm. From a libertarian perspective, there is little outside the maintenance of property rights that represents legitimate government activity. Differences in personal wealth, talent, physical attributes and intelligence are seen as being obtained in the 'natural' sense, in that their ownership owes nothing to social or political institutions. If they are obtained in this way, nothing can deny the owner possession of them, or the value that derives from that ownership. Differences caused to the life-chances of individuals by the possession, or not, of these qualities/characteristics are not seen as justifying the meddling of governments in attempts to redistribute some of the associated benefits.

Within the libertarian frame of reference, and as long as what an individual wishes to do is within the law, then nothing should prevent the individual from fulfilling those desires. It is for this reason that taxation (and particularly the taxes levied on inherited assets) is such a vexed subject. From a libertarian perspective, taxation is the forcible, involuntary withdrawal of economic resources from individuals to be spent by governments in ways that might fail to satisfy or be compatible with the desires and values of the taxed individuals.

Nozick coined the term 'entitlement theory' to express the view that what has been acquired legally and fairly (although fairly is an ill-defined concept) cannot be taken away within a libertarian concept of justice. This is despite the fact that practices that are regarded as immoral and illegal today, e.g. slavery, have not always been so, yet they represent an important factor in explaining the present distribution of wealth that shapes so many people's life-chances. Interestingly, in his later works, Nozick recognised the problems associated with resources obtained or lost by dubious methods and modified his views a little with respect to inherited wealth, an example being the plight of the American Indians. However, inherited resources and life-chances remain central issues within this debate.

Entitlement theory attempts to draw a veil over the means by which wealth may have been acquired. The ramifications of being denied an equal opportunity to education, health care, legal justice are seen as irrelevant within a libertarian conception of justice, or at least a greater injustice would be to transfer 'legally' acquired assets from those that have to those that have not. With no limits attached to what individuals can achieve in a liberal society, it is for every individual to improve their own life-chances.

## Rawls, justice as fairness

Rawls takes a different view of distributive justice from Nozick. In 1971 Rawls published a book (revised in 1999) that has had a significant impact upon debates about theories of justice. While Rawls does not argue that his theory is a practical one for everyday decision making, it presents a normative approach to deciding what a just society would look like in what he describes as 'the original position'. It offers a reference point against which contemporary social, political and economic systems can be contrasted. We then have to decide, as individuals and as societies, what we want to try to do about the differences between these two states – the should-be and the actual.

The original position is an artifice of Rawls that allows each of us to contemplate a 'just' society without the burden of our life experiences and prejudices tainting our views. We are required to envisage a situation in which we have no knowledge of who we are. The distinctive personal characteristics that we will ultimately possess (assuming we will actually have some bestowed upon us) are unknown within the original position. We have no knowledge of any natural or social advantages, or disadvantages, we might ultimately possess. We do not even know where in the world we would live, and therefore under which type of political system we might be governed. We do not know our ethnic origins; whether we will have a privileged or deprived upbringing; whether we would be intelligent or slow-witted; male or female; be sexually abused or lead an idyllic childhood; be short or tall; born with profound physical disabilities or be an Olympic-grade athlete; or experience a very poor or excellent educational system. We are placed behind what Rawls refers to as a 'veil of ignorance'.

From this position of total ignorance we are then asked a series of questions about the type of society we would like to live in. We are expected to employ actual knowledge of the chances of being placed within a privileged or elite position when answering a series of questions relating to issues such as social, political and economic governance; health care; education; social norms; wealth distribution and hereditary wealth; race, gender and religious equality; and employment opportunities. It must be emphasised again that the world we construct from the original position is a world in which we do not know where we will ultimately fit.

Faced with this challenge, Rawls argued that the rational person would adopt a maximin strategy. This is a risk-averse strategy that works on the basis of studying all the worst-case scenarios that exist within each option before us. Having identified all the worst-case possibilities, we then select the one that is the least worse. Thus, we opt for the option that gives us the greatest possible benefit, assuming we were unfortunate enough to be dealt a position at the bottom of the economic and social ladders in any of the choices with which we are confronted. The following illustrates the approach.

---

## The veil of ignorance

You are in the 'original position' and the choice of political systems in which you will live are feudal, dictatorship, democracy and anarchy. You can imagine a range of outcomes for yourself in each system. In a feudal state, a dictatorship or a centrally controlled state, history has shown that the lives of those in power can be privileged ones, and that such an outcome is a possibility for you. However, maybe only a few can be expected to enjoy such lives. For the rest of the population, life is likely to be miserable. In a democracy the distribution of power will be far greater, going beyond political democracy and taking in workplace democracy. The opportunities to exercise moral agency should be higher than in the other options, although the opportunities to enjoy the sumptuous lifestyle of the elite of the feudal or dictatorship systems would be slight. Anarchy might possess certain attractions, but the uncertainty surrounding the notion of anarchy is likely to prove unappealing to you. Remember, Rawls anticipates that you are a calculating, risk-averse individual. Thus, considering the options before you, Rawls assumes you will judge that if you were to be one of the general members of the public (and there is a 90–99 per cent chance that this will be the case), it would be better for you to live in a full democracy.

---

A way of rationalising Rawls' original position is to see it as a mechanism to free each of us from our personal prejudices and life experiences. By removing us from the shackles of the inequities of how things are, it can enable us to focus upon what we believe distributive justice would/should look like, without the distortions born of history or fate.

Flowing from the assumption that the individual in the original position will desire not to be dealt a station in life that is unpalatable, Rawls argued that there are two guiding principles that will explain the reason for each choice made. These are:

1. Each member of society would be entitled to the same civil and political rights, and

2. Open competition for occupational positions exists, with attainment being based upon merit, but with economic inequalities being arranged so that 'there is no way in which the least advantaged stratum in the society could as a whole do any better' (Barry, 1989: 184).

The second principle is referred to as Rawls' difference principle. This is because Rawls was not arguing that everyone could be or should be the same. He recognised that differences relating to qualities such as intelligence, acumen, technical skills, physical abilities and so on will exist. However, he viewed the arbitrary and random distribution of social and natural attributes as no justification for the individuals blessed with these attributes prospering to the detriment of others less fortunate. Rawls thus rejected Nozick's entitlement theory. As Shaw and Barry observed,

> Rawls' principles permit economic inequalities only if they do in fact benefit the least advantaged.
>
> (Shaw and Barry, 1998: 114)

In dealing with differences in personal attributes and qualities, Rawls argued that contingencies must be set in place to handle the issues raised by such differences. These contingencies would be mechanisms, established at the original position, built upon cooperation and mutual respect.

> We are led to the difference principle if we wish to set up the social system so that no-one gains or loses from his arbitrary place in the distribution of natural assets or his initial position in society without giving or receiving compensating advantages in return.
>
> (Rawls, 1971: 101–2)

Thus, before you would be asked questions about your preferred political system, education, corporate governance, etc. (and still in a state of ignorance about your personal position), you would have to identify the mechanisms that would need to be in place to minimise the worst effects of the differences that would exist between individual members of society, and between societies, when the final allocation of roles was made.

You may have detected a form of schizophrenia within Rawls' theory, inasmuch as the first principle has a strong socialist egalitarian moral perspective, while the second principle clearly assumes market-based, self-interest-driven behaviour. Rawls has been challenged on this 'inconsistency' from a variety of sources. Meade (1973) observed:

> In my view the ideal society would be one in which each citizen developed a real split personality, acting selfishly in the market place and altruistically at the ballot box ... [It] is ... only by such altruistic political action that there can be any alleviation of 'poverty' in a society in which the poor are in the minority.
>
> (Meade, 1973: 52)

Rawls also acknowledged that there have to be limits to what people can reasonably be expected to do on behalf of others less fortunate than themselves. He termed this limit the 'strains of commitment'. In doing so Rawls accepted that there would be boundaries to the demands that the least privileged could make of those more fortunate than themselves. However, Rawls' theory does demand far more of individual citizens than that advocated by free market theorists. The 'hidden hand' of Adam Smith delivers an impoverished form of justice from a Rawlsian perspective. Incentives are acknowledged, albeit in a reluctant way. As Barry observed:

> Inequalities are not ideally just, but ... once we concede the need for incentives, inequalities permitted by the difference principle are the only defensible ones.

(Barry, 1989: 398)

## Activity 3.3

Briefly analyse Case study 2.3 (*AIDS drugs and patent rights in South Africa*) from a Rawlsian perspective.

We will conclude our discussion of non-consequentialist ethical theories by focusing upon the use of child labour in the present day. The use of poorly paid children, often tied, as labourers has a long and troubled history in all parts of the world. Where the children are 'tied' they are the property of adults (slaveholders), with their parents sometimes having received a payment from the slaveholder. Some of the worst examples involve the use of children in prostitution. The practice of child (sometimes slave) labour is still prevalent in certain parts of the world, and a number of western multi-national corporations have been heavily criticised for sourcing their supplies (e.g. designer clothes and sportswear) from companies that operate sweatshops involving more than, but including, child labour. How would the respective ethical positions we have considered, i.e. virtue ethics, Kantian and Rawlsian perspectives, perceive this situation?

- A *virtue ethics* approach would reflect the behaviours regarded as virtuous at any given time. In this context, we must remember that child labour has not always been regarded as a social ill. In the UK child labour was a regular feature of Victorian life. For a virtue ethics perspective to be able to reject the use of child labour, there would need to be a high-status virtue that expressly spoke of equality, the preciousness of children and the need to protect them from exploitation and abuse. With virtue ethics being about the personal qualities of individuals, where the perception of one's peers (thereby emphasising the importance of social norms) is of critical importance in judging the 'virtuous person', virtue ethics does not offer an automatic disqualification of child labour as unethical and immoral. A virtue would need to exist that explicitly addressed the relationship between adults and children, and particularly the rights of children.

- A *Kantian* perspective would not be equivocal. Respect for fellow human beings, and the need to treat other people as one would want to be treated oneself, would make exploitation in general, not just against children, immoral. The vulnerability of children would merely emphasise the importance of these categorical imperatives.

- *Rawlsian* notions of justice in the context of child labour will depend upon the parameters established in the original position. Assuming that no adult would volunteer themselves to be subject to exploitation, deprivation and possibly prostitution in childhood, then such acts would be unjust and immoral.

The above analysis has shown a range of non-consequentialist positions with regard to ethical theories. The degree of variation is significant within the non-consequentialist group, but they in turn offer an orientation towards ethical reasoning that is quite distinct from that of consequentialist theories. It is to the consequentialist theories that we now turn.

## Ethical learning and growth

The ethical theories in the top right quadrant hold that policy ends should be the yardsticks against which the morality of actions should be judged, and that they can only be achieved indirectly. An ethical organisation cannot be achieved by decree. A CEO publishing an ethical code will not of itself bring about its implementation. The end has to be approached obliquely by encouraging processes of learning that enable people to decide for themselves to act ethically.

### Individual growth and organisational learning

There is a large literature, and indeed an industry, that explains how people can develop and make themselves more effective. Stephen Covey's (1992) *The Seven Habits of Highly Effective People* can stand as an example. He raised two themes that place him firmly in the upper right quadrant of Figure 3.1. He taught that people should 'begin with an end in mind' (Covey, 1992: 97). This is clearly a policy orientation. He also argued that people develop their character ethic through a process of deep self-reflection. He distinguished character ethic from personality ethic (Covey, 1992: 18–21). The character ethic proposes basic principles of effective living, things like integrity, fidelity, humility, courage and so on. These are hard precepts to live by. In contrast the personality ethic proposes 'quick-fix solutions' drawn from a public relations approach that aims to present a good image of oneself and easy behavioural tricks used to manipulate others. It is the character ethic that people should concentrate on.

Covey (1992: 36) adopted the 'principle of process' of personal growth in the spheres of emotion, human relationships and character formation. These processes cannot, he argued, be short-circuited; people have to go through the necessary stages to achieve greater effectiveness. He applied these lessons not only to people's personal lives but also to working lives. His book has become a very popular guide for managers. Senge, in his book *The Fifth Discipline* (1990), also stressed the importance of individuals' learning, which he saw as necessary for the development of learning organisations. These, he argued, were the only kind of organisation that will be successful. For Senge learning is not simply an acquisition of useful information; it is a personal moral development. He used the classical Greek term *metanoia* (Senge 1990: 13–14) to describe the sort of learning that learning organisations should aspire to. It means a shift of mind. The word was used by the Gnostics who, in the early years of Christianity, saw gnosis, or knowledge, as an awareness of a person's relationship with God. Gnosis involves relating to the divine power of creativity by truly learning to know oneself (Pagels, 1982: 133–4). Senge's view of organisational development parallels this view of learning as ethical and spiritual growth.

> Real learning gets to the heart of what it means to be human. Through learning we recreate ourselves. Through learning we reperceive the world and our relationship to it. Through learning we extend our capacity to create, to be part of the generative process of life.
>
> (Senge, 1990: 14)

Individual growth and learning is not simply learning how to use new leadership or financial appraisal techniques. It is a process of becoming aware of one's ethical potential. Learning becomes an ethical end in itself.

### Activity 3.4

Briefly analyse Case study 2.25 (*The Firestone Tire recall issue*) from a learning organisation perspective.

## Communitarianism

The communitarian approach to ethics is a reaction to the liberal view that sees the individual as more important than social groups. The communitarian approach argues that people are inherently social and that they can only achieve their moral potential by being part of growing and developing communities. By contributing to the ethical growth of a group people also become ethical individuals. These communities may be based on place, such as a neighbourhood, on shared group memories, such as in immigrant communities, or on a host of voluntary associations such as golf clubs, parent teacher associations, churches and so on. A tenet of the communitarian perspective is that different communities might be expected to develop their own values and moral principles. The universalism of liberalism's claim, that democratic, free market systems are the correct solution for all societies, as argued by Fukuyama (1993) in his book *The End of History*, is false. This acceptance of particularism or relativism will become important when we discuss international business in Chapter 11. Amitai Etzioni (1993) is the most high-profile advocate of a communitarian approach.

It follows from a communitarian point of view that anything that limits the potential for communities to grow and be responsible for themselves is reprehensible. Such threats may come either from the political left, with its concern for creating centralised, bureaucratic welfare structures for dealing with social problems, or from the right, whose protagonists do not see why granting rights such as flexible working hours, parental leave and child care facilities to support families should be tolerated in a free market system.

Communitarian ethics raises a number of questions for businesses and organisations:

- Should business try to create a homogenous world in which everyone consumes the same products and shares the same values? This would maximise industry's efficiency. Or should business respond to the particularities of different societies and groups by diversifying their products and business models?

- To what extent should businesses and organisations contribute to the growth and development of local communities? Should they provide resources and managerial expertise to encourage the development of self-help groups in the communities in which they work? Should such support be philanthropic or be part of commercial sponsorship deals? The development of 'family friendly' employment practices (Elshtain *et al.*, n.d.) is important from a communitarian perspective. These matters of corporate citizenship are considered in Chapter 8.

- Should organisations attempt to create themselves as communities? The Foster architectural partnership has long sought to design office buildings that encourage the development of community bonds, as well as employment relationships, between the staff. Their buildings include 'streets', cafés, restaurants, swimming pools and games areas so that in one building the staff described working in the building as 'homing from work' (Foster, 2001: 206). The commercial pressures on organisations mean that such facilities are often converted to a more directly productive use.

## Activity 3.5

Briefly analyse Case study 2.1 (*The Nationwide Foundation*) from a communitarian perspective.

## Ethical egoism

J.S. Mill praised those who would sacrifice their personal happiness to gain a greater happiness for others. Ethical egoists would not understand such an act. They argue that an individual should pursue their own interests by applying their reason to the task of identifying and achieving their own best interests.

Ethical egoism gained popularity in America during the twentieth century through the novels of Ayn Rand (1905–82), who has already been discussed in Chapter 1. Her ethical stance is known as objectivism. It gives primacy to people's capacity for rational thought. This facility, when applied to a knowledge of the world gained through the senses, leads to an objective understanding of the world that leaves no room for the sceptical belief that all knowledge is mere opinion. The theory's ethical position is that each individual should seek their own happiness through a productive independent life in which their own rational judgement is their only guide. The main virtues of objectivist thought are independence, integrity, honesty, productiveness, trade and pride. It encourages a robust belief in self-help and accepts that people who cannot or will not take responsibility for themselves would have to bear the consequences. They should not expect the state or society to bail them out. An individual should not sacrifice themselves to others or expect others to sacrifice themselves for him.

We will illustrate the main themes of objectivism through Kirkpatrick's (1994) defence of advertising. He used objectivism to counter the social criticisms made of advertising, which are that advertising can be manipulative and offensive. His broad argument is that laissez-faire capitalism is good because, according to Rand, the principle of trade is the 'only system consonant with man's rational nature' (Kirkpatrick, 1994: 28). If capitalism is good then advertising, which is a necessary part of it, must also be good. Kirkpatrick blames Kant for the common mistake of seeing advertising as unethical. He attributed to Kant the ideal that human reason cannot objectively comprehend reality because reason is always affected by the innate structures of a person's mind. If this were so then human reason would not be adequate to cope with the blandishments of advertising. But he argued that Kant is wrong and Rand is right. Objective knowledge is possible and human reason is capable of properly evaluating the advertisers' messages. As to the charge of offensiveness, he argued that values are not intrinsic to objects. So a cigarette for example is not in itself a bad thing; only the way people use it can make it good or bad. If cigarettes are not intrinsically immoral and individuals have free will then 'tobacco advertisers defraud no one' (Kirkpatrick, 1994: 80).

The only necessary constraint on advertising is the common law one against fraud. 'Anything less than that turns both marketers and consumers into victims of subjective law, that is, of "rule by men" [i.e. *by bureaucrats*] rather than the "rule of law"' (Kirkpatrick, 1994: 51). The American-ness of the argument was emphasised when he quoted Daniel Boorstin arguing that advertising is the American epistemology – the way in which Americans learn about things. Kirkpatrick's argument for advertising only stands, of course, if objectivism is held to be objectively true.

The difficult question for ethical egoism is how far self-interest would cause individuals to give away some of their independence in order to accommodate others. Kirkpatrick argued that obeying the common law should be the limit of the surrender. Hobbes, who wrote in the seventeenth century, identified the key problem. People are very similar in wit and strength and therefore,

If two men desire the same thing, which nevertheless they cannot both enjoy, they become enemies; and in the way to their end, which is principally their own conservation, and sometimes their delectation only, endeavour to destroy, or subdue one another.

(Hobbes, n.d.: 81)

Self-interest, therefore, would cause people to

be willing, when others are so too, as far-forth, as for peace, and defence of himself he shall think it necessary to lay down this right to all things; and be contented with so much liberty against other men, as he would allow other men against himself.

(Hobbes, n.d.: 85)

Of course, in modern business terms, it is a matter of dispute as to the degree of liberty a person, or a company, would rationally agree to forego.

## Activity 3.6

Briefly analyse Case study 2.21 (*The hospital consultants*) from an ethical egoism perspective.

## Teleological ethics

The theories in the final quadrant of Figure 3.1 combine an intention to work towards an end with a particular view of what institutions are necessary to achieve it. These institutions govern the way in which the appropriateness of an

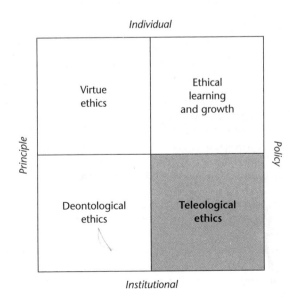

act to an end should be evaluated. These theories are called teleological. This term means that the rightness or goodness of an action is not intrinsic to that action but can only be judged by its consequences. These theories are sometimes therefore called consequentialist.

## Discourse ethics

Discourse ethics is a normative approach that deals with the proper processes of rational debate that are necessary to arrive at a resolution of ethical questions. It does not lay down what is right and wrong but it does distinguish right and wrong ways of arguing about right and wrong. It is an ancient idea that the process of argument, or rhetoric, is key to discovering the truth. Some, such as Protagoras, argued that there are always two sides to any argument (Billig, 1996: 72). This implies that dialogue cannot lead to a definitive truth because there are always arguments to be made for or against any proposition. However, Protagoras was prepared to argue, as reported by Socrates, that although opposing arguments could be presented some were more useful than others. Whether or not argument and debate can lead to true or useful statements about what is right and wrong, these classical concerns established an importance for forensic debate, and the classification of rhetorical techniques, that has remained in western culture.

The approach in modern times is most closely associated with Jürgen Habermas, of the Frankfurt school of critical theorists (Pusey, 1987). Habermas built upon the philosophical heritage of Kant; and so perhaps should not be included in the lower right quadrant of Figure 3.1. However, he breaks with Kant in his belief that knowledge develops through social interaction and discourse. Knowledge is not, as Kant argued, a matter unaffected by social and cultural processes. Habermas holds that disagreement can be resolved rationally through debate which is free of compulsion, in which no disputant applies pressure to another, and in which only the strength of the arguments matters. This calls for linguistic skill but it also requires a critical self-reflection in which those involved in a debate challenge their own arguments at:

- The objective level – at which a statement is tested against an observed state, checking for example whether the statement that 'the balance sheet does not add up' is true.

- The inter-subjective level – when a statement is made and heard it creates a social relationship between the hearer and the speaker. At the inter-subjective level it has to be questioned whether this relationship is legitimate. If the statement that the balance sheet doesn't add up implies, without evidence, that the listener is accused of cooking the books the relationship may be unfair, especially if the speaker is the listener's boss.

- The intra-subjective level – at which a speaker has to consider whether their speech sincerely or authentically mirrors their internal thoughts and values.

It is these processes of validation that Habermas refers to as discourse. The application of these in organisations would be very difficult. However, writers have attempted to put these ideas into operation. Some have focused on the skills of debate. Schreier and Groeben (1996) looked at the advice, given in popular books on how to persuade and influence people, about which tricks of presentation were unfair. They asked a panel of experts to categorise 84 of the rhetorical tricks against four ethical categories that are used to assess whether an argument in a debate was proper. Using the results they were able to identify some possible rules or tests for assessing the ethical integrity of any debate. A few examples follow.

- **Formal validity** – Are the arguments logically rigorous? *e.g. do not select only those cases to use in your argument that support your point of view.*

- **Sincerity/Truth** – Are the arguments intentionally misleading, inconsistent or economical with the truth? *e.g. misrepresenting an opponent's position or exaggerating a point.*

- **Content justice** – Treating your opponents unfairly or imposing impossible requirements on them. *e.g.* ad hominem *attacks on an opponent in which the opponent is vilified rather than his or her arguments criticised. Making mutually exclusive demands on an opponent.*

- **Procedural justice** – Preventing an opponent from fully and freely participating in the debate. *e.g. unnecessary use of technical jargon in a way intended to confuse the opponent.*

Steinmann and Lohr (quoted in Preuss, 1999: 414) also propose the use of discourse to achieve a consensus on ethical business issues. They simplified the characteristics of ideal discourse, against which actual discussions may be assessed, as:

- impartiality

- non-coercion

- non-persuasiveness and

- expertise.

They had an opportunity to put these guidelines into practice when they organised and chaired a series of corporate dialogues within Procter & Gamble on the question of self-medication by selling over-the-counter cold medicines. Others have proposed rules and procedures for debate. This has been particularly common in the field of public policy making. Fischer (1983) made a case for forensic skills to be applied to the process of evaluating public policy options through ethical discourse. He drew upon a method he called normative logic. This was based on studies of how people discuss and decide normative issues in everyday speech and life. He concluded that despite the lack of final ethical truths, people resolved value matters by combining questioning based on empirical knowledge with a lawyer-like process of marshalling a supportable case, by drawing upon their knowledge of:

- the consequences of the different positions or actions they may take;

- the alternative positions and actions open to them;

- established norms, values and laws;
- the facts of the situation;
- the network of circumstances that preceded the situation;
- the 'fundamental needs of humankind'.

People can construct defensible cases for taking particular actions or positions. According to some philosophers this process is untenable because it requires decisions, about what ought to be, to be derived from descriptions of how things actually are, and this they claim is illogical.

Fischer's response was to say that the purpose of drawing up guidelines for debate is not to establish ultimate values but to arrive at pragmatic resolutions through a rigorous, if ungrounded, process that is not anchored in immutable values.

**Connexion point**

In philosophy this argument is known as the naturalistic fallacy, as is discussed further on p. 437. Fischer's response is argued from the point of view of pragmatism which is explained on p. 161.

So far the discussion has focused on fair and open debate of ethical matters. But the question of who should have a voice in the debate is also an important ethical matter. This question can best be considered by looking at the application of stakeholder theory to ethical matters. This theory proposes that, for every organisation, stakeholder groups can be identified:

- who are affected by,
- who can affect, or
- whose welfare is tied into

the actions of a corporation. It may be necessary to add a criterion of legitimacy to the identification of stakeholders. As Whysall (2000) pointed out, a shoplifter's welfare may be affected by a retailer's actions but that does not make them a legitimate stakeholder.

Donaldson and Preston (1995) presented four perspectives on the roles of stakeholder management.

- *Descriptive* – that the stakeholder theory describes what corporations are, i.e. constellations of interconnected interest groups.

- *Instrumental* – that if corporations adopt stakeholder management they will, all other things being equal, be more successful than those organisations that do not.

- *Managerial* – that the theory enables managers to identify options and solutions to problems.

But underpinning each of these roles was the fourth *normative* one: stake-holder theory can be used to develop moral or philosophical guidelines for the operations of corporations. In particular it forces corporations to make a broad ethical appreciation of its actions that considers its impact on communities as well as on the profit and loss account. Whysall used the case of companies that retail goods, at premium prices to affluent consumers, which were manufactured in sweatshop conditions in third world countries. A traditional management approach would only consider the benefits of the business model to the corporation and its customers. A stakeholder approach would also involve consideration of the impact upon the workforces, the communities and governments of the countries involved as well as activists and lobbyists.

### Activity 3.7

Briefly analyse Case study 2.11 (*The British railway system: priorities, profits and governance*) from a stakeholder perspective.

## Utilitarianism

Utilitarianism theory accepts utility, or the greatest happiness principle, as the foundation of morals. It holds that actions are right in proportion, as they tend to promote happiness, wrong, as they tend to promote the opposite of happiness. Or as Jeremy Bentham, the eighteenth-century philosopher who proposed the principle, put it:

> The greatest happiness of the greatest number is the foundation of morals and legislation.
>
> (Bentham, 1994: 142)

The term utilitarianism, however, was coined by John Stuart Mill, a nineteenth-century writer, and not by Bentham. One interesting question that arises from utilitarianism is, 'What is happiness?' Most philosophers were at pains to suggest that it is not simply sensual pleasure. As J.S. Mill argued, 'It is better to be a human being dissatisfied than a pig satisfied' (Mill, 1998: 140). The importance of the higher pleasures over the lower has long been a theme in western ethics. St Augustine recognised that worldly pleasures were not of themselves bad but that they were insufficient to achieve an admirable life. He saw the sensual, material world as but part of human experience that has to be understood within the wider context of the intelligible world, which is one of clear and enduring ideas. Utilitarianism, according to Mill, who took a similar view, is not concerned only with material and sensual pleasures.

Utilitarianism is a calculating approach to ethics. It assumes the quantity and quality of happiness can be weighed. Bentham (1982) identified the following features of happiness that ought to be considered when measuring it:

- Intensity.
- Duration.

- Certainty – the probability that happiness or pain will result.
- Extent – the number of people affected.
- Closeness (propinquity) – pleasure or pain now or deferred in time.
- Richness (fecundity) – will the act lead to further pleasure?
- Purity – is the pleasure unalloyed or is it mixed with pain?

It is often assumed, in a business context, that maximising happiness is the same as maximising profit or return on capital invested. Plainly, improved profitability will generate happiness for some. But to apply the utilitarian principle properly one must consider the possibility that the pleasure derived from increased profitability has been achieved at the cost of a greater pain to other people. Mill (1998: 151) pointed out that most of the time someone applying the utilitarian principle need only concern themselves with their private interest. This is not necessarily so when the 'person' in question is a corporation.

Cost–benefit analysis is a natural tool of a utilitarian approach because it measures not only the direct costs and benefits to an organisation but also externalities. Externalities are defined in economics as social costs and benefits that are not reflected in the price of a product because they do not accrue directly to the organisation concerned. When people smoke the cigarettes produced by a tobacco company they are more likely to fall ill and so create costs for health care systems. But the costs of that health care are not reflected in the costs of the cigarettes because the medical bills are not the tobacco company's responsibility. In the USA, however, the claim that tobacco companies misled their customers as to the harmful effects of smoking led the courts to require the companies to reimburse states with the cost of the medical treatment of smoking-related diseases. In this case an externality was converted into a private cost of the companies.

**DEFINITION**

**Cost–benefit analysis** is a form of project appraisal. The costs and outputs of the project are identified and priced. If the outputs will arise over an extended period of time, and inputs are needed over a similar time span, the benefits and costs are discounted. If the benefits are greater than the costs then investment in the project would be sensible. If the project were, for example, a malaria control programme in a poor country, it is clear that the benefits would be widespread. Many lives would be saved; the health of the population would be improved. But these benefits are intangible and difficult to measure in financial terms. It might be thought that the costs of such a project would be easier to identify. Some, such as the cost of the labour and the insecticide, would be. But there may be wider, and less easy to measure, costs such as increased costs of education because more children survive and are fit enough to attend school.

Cost–benefit analysis is based on the premise that both elements in the equation can be measured in monetary terms. To do this some limitations have to be accepted. An example of a study undertaken by Lambur *et al.* (2003) illustrates the point. The question was whether a programme of nutrition and health education in schools created more benefits than costs by altering children's eating habits in ways that made them healthier and less prone to illness. The costs of the programme were tangible and could be measured. Three main types of benefits were anticipated:

1. Direct tangible benefits – the savings on medical treatment of people who would have become ill had they not changed their eating patterns. These benefits could be measured financially because the costs of treating medical conditions are known.

2. Indirect tangible benefits – the additional economic productivity that is achieved by preventing or delaying the onset of illness.

3. Intangible benefits – these are such things as the improved quality of life and improved self-esteem associated with healthier eating. The analysts in this case, as do all cost–benefit analysts, listed the intangible benefits but did not measure them or include them in the quantitative analysis.

Analysts have to make further, technical, choices, about how to conduct the analysis. There are three main issues:

1. Cost : benefit ratio. This is the monetary value of the benefits per pound or dollar or euro spent. If the ratio is greater than 1 then benefits exceed costs.

2. Discount rate. The value of money to be spent or received at some future time is less than money spent or received in the present. In cost–benefit analysis it is necessary therefore to choose a rate at which future income will be discounted.

3. Net present value. This is a way of showing the result of a cost–benefit analysis in present-day values. The streams of benefits and costs in future years are discounted, using the chosen discount rate, so that all costs and benefits are presented in terms of their present value.

In the study we are looking at it was decided that the cost : benefit ratio was the appropriate method and it was found to be $10.64 worth of benefits for every $1 spent. There are two problems that emerge from this form of analysis.

1. So many assumptions have to be made, and so many things have to be left out of the calculation that the validity of the results is brought into question.

2. A cost–benefit analysis may show, as indeed the example given does, that the expenditure would be worthwhile. But it does not show whether that expenditure is affordable or what its priority is in relation to other projects that could be undertaken, unless the simple criterion is used that priority should be established according to the cost : benefit ratio, with projects with higher ratios having the greater priority. Fisher (1998) has argued that establishing priorities is a more complex matter.

One danger of utilitarianism, which cost–benefit analysis is designed to address, is that organisations seek to maximise *a good* rather than *the good*. In the

British National Health Service, for example, the government set a target for reducing the size of the waiting lists for treatment, maximising a good – the number of patients treated. However, many hospitals achieved this by treating patients with minor problems that could be quickly and cheaply resolved and leaving those who needed lengthy and difficult treatment at the back of the queue, and so they failed to maximise the overall good.

In the case of public policy, public, and not simply private, good has clearly to be taken into account. Kemm (1985) used a utilitarian approach in a discussion of the ethics of food policy. He was interested in the ethical issues involved in modifying the eating habits of the population through regulation, facilitating measures (such as differentially taxing foods) and education. He argued that a policy is ethical if it produces more beneficial outcomes than harmful ones. But his suggestions about how policy makers might analyse issues sheds light on the limitations of technical means such as cost–benefit analysis.

Kemm stressed the interconnections between subjective and objective thinking in assessing the outcomes of policies. The three stages in this process are:

1. Determining the inherent goodness or badness of an outcome. This is a subjective value decision such as that involved in stating that dental mottling is less bad than carcinoma of the colon.
2. Measuring the probability that the desired outcome will be achieved. This is a scientific and objective activity.
3. Assessing the degree of certainty with which the probability of the outcomes has been estimated. This is a matter of judgement rather than measurement.

The subjective element can be illustrated by an example from the first item in the above list. Utility's concern for populations makes these subjective judgements difficult. How, for example, should moderate good for the majority be weighed against great harm to the minority? Fortifying chapatti flour would provide some health benefit for most chapatti eaters, but for the rare individual with vitamin D sensitivity it might cause serious vitamin D toxicity. The ethical problem can be exacerbated by the fact that the majority may not be aware that they have received benefits from the fortified flour. To give another example, if food policies increase the amount of fibre in the diet this will benefit people by protecting them from diverticulitis. However, they will not be aware of this. But those who suffer from flatulence as a result will be in no doubt that they have suffered, albeit the pain is not critical.

> Most would take the view that a very small harm to a very few individuals could be outweighed by a sufficiently large benefit to a sufficiently large number of individuals.
>
> (Kemm, 1985: 291)

One of the criticisms of utilitarianism is that it is unconcerned with equity. As Sen said:

> The trouble with [utilitarianism] is that maximising the sum of individual utilities is supremely unconcerned with the interpersonal distribution of that sum.
>
> (Sen quoted in Barr, 1985: 177)

The problem of forecasting future consequences, as identified in the last two items of Kemm's list, is a general difficulty with utilitarianism. If people cannot make accurate predictions about the consequences of particular actions then it is hardly worth the bother of weighing the anticipated pleasures and pains. Common experience, as expressed in Murphy's Law (if it can go wrong it will), suggests that people's forecasting skills are not to be overestimated. There is psychological evidence that people are overconfident when they make predictions. Fischoff, Slovic and Lichtenstein (1977) asked people a series of general knowledge questions (e.g. is absinthe (a) a liqueur or (b) a precious stone?) and found that when people said they were 100 per cent certain they had given the right answer they had in fact only done so on 80 per cent of occasions.

The form of utilitarianism that has been discussed so far is known as act utilitarianism, which calculates the net pleasure or pain to be obtained from a particular act. One of the practical problems with it is that the calculations it would require are too many and too complex. Let us consider a decision over whether 25 per cent of a company's employees should be made redundant to reduce costs and prevent the company going into insolvency. Table 3.2 lays out the calculations that might be required. The example is fictitious and the numbers are invented; the purpose of the table is to explain the nature of the calculations required.

The first step in the calculation is to identify the groups, stakeholders, who would be affected by a decision to make people redundant and the ways in which they might be affected. The following have been chosen although doubtless other groups could be identified.

- The shareholders who own the company. If the company becomes bankrupt they face losing their investment. If making people redundant saves the company then their capital is secured and they might even make slightly higher returns on it in future. Even if the company is saved from insolvency the situation would have increased their worries about the long-term future of the company.

- The managers will have to decide who to make redundant and also tell people that they have lost their jobs. The psychological effect of this on some managers will be to cause them much anxiety and worry because they dislike inflicting distress on others. Some managers, however, will gain a psychological boost from the event because it will confirm their self-impression that they are strong managers capable of making tough decisions.

- Those employees who will keep their jobs will have a weight of worry lifted from their shoulder but this may be balanced by feelings of guilt that they kept their jobs while their friends and colleagues lost theirs. They may also feel less confident about the long-term prospects of keeping their jobs. There would also of course be pleasure that they are still receiving a salary and in response to both these feelings they may work harder.

- The people made redundant would suffer a degree of psychological trauma and suffer a loss of self-esteem. Some may find a new and better job quite quickly, or discover that a different lifestyle not based on employment is more to their liking. These people would gain some pleasure from having been made redundant. Those who only find a worse and less well-paid job or remain unhappily unemployed will only experience pain.

Table 3.2 A utilitarian calculation concerning making employees in a company redundant to prevent bankruptcy

| Stakeholder | Impact Positive (+) Or Negative (-) | The probability that the impact will happen | Amount of pleasure or pain (JOLLIES) per person | No. of people who might be affected | Intensity & duration Scale 1-5 | Propinquity Scale 1-5 | Purity Scale 1-5 | Fecundity Scale 1-5 | Net totals (millions of JOLLIES) |
|---|---|---|---|---|---|---|---|---|---|
| Shareholders | Insolvency is avoided (+) | 0.6 | 5 | 2000000 | 2 | 5 | 3 | 1 | 66 |
| | Financial returns are increased (+) | 0.4 | 3 | 2000000 | 2 | 3 | 4 | 2 | 26.4 |
| | Worry about long-term future of the company (-) | 0.7 | -2 | 2000000 | 3 | 1 | 2 | 3 | -25.2 |
| Managers | Psychological pain at dismissing staff (-) | 0.7 | -20 | 150 | 3 | 5 | 2 | 2 | -0.0252 |
| | Psychological benefit from seeing oneself as able to make the tough decisions (+) | 0.3 | 20 | 150 | 2 | 5 | 4 | 4 | 0.0135 |
| Employees who keep their jobs | Removal of worry and anxiety (+) | 0.5 | 30 | 60000 | 2 | 5 | 1 | 4 | 10.8 |
| | Continued receipt of salary (+) | 1.0 | 50 | 60000 | 2 | 5 | 1 | 3 | 33 |
| | Work harder in gratitude (+) | 0.6 | 5 | 60000 | 3 | 5 | 1 | 3 | 2.16 |
| | Sense of guilt at having kept their job (-) | 0.7 | -20 | 60000 | 2 | 4 | 3 | 2 | -9.24 |
| | Fear that may lose job in future (-) | 0.3 | -10 | 60000 | 4 | 1 | 3 | 4 | -2.16 |
| Employees made redundant | Psychological trauma (-) | 0.9 | -50 | 20000 | 5 | 5 | 4 | 4 | -16.2 |
| | Quickly find a better job or lifestyle (+) | 0.15 | 100 | 20000 | 3 | 3 | 5 | 4 | 4.5 |
| | Find a job that is worse than the one you lost | 0.50 | 5 | 20000 | 4 | 2 | 1 | 4 | 0.55 |
| | Find no job and suffer a loss of income (-) | 0.35 | -100 | 20000 | 5 | 5 | 5 | 5 | -14 |
| Families of those made redundant | Psychological & economic impact on families of those who lost jobs | 0.8 | -40 | 50000 | 3 | 5 | 2 | 4 | -22.4 |
| Taxpayers | Additional social security benefits paid and loss of revenue | 1.0 | -0.001 | 29400000 | 2 | 2 | 3 | 1 | -0.2352 |
| | | | | | | | | TOTAL | 53.9631 |

The JOLLIES calculator

- The families of those who lost their jobs will also share some of the psychological and economic impact. They may all become more stressed yet not be able to afford a holiday to help them relax.

- Finally, in this list, the taxpayers may have to pay for additional social security benefits for those who have lost their jobs.

The next two tasks involve identifying the number of people in the stakeholder groups who may experience the impact of the downsizing; and the probability that they will. Some of these groups are large. In the UK for example there are 29.4m income tax payers and it is certain (a probability of 1.0) they would all have to bear a portion of the increased public expenditure on social security caused by the redundancies. Other groups are quite small. In this fictitious example there are only 150 managers who have to make the redundancy decisions. The fictitious company has 80,000 employees and the proposal to make 25% redundant would result in 20,000 job losses. In the table it is estimated that 90 per cent of them would suffer symptoms of psychological trauma. It is also estimated that 15 per cent would find a better job, 50 per cent would accept a new job that was less good than their previous one and 35 per cent would fail to find a new job (accounting for 100 per cent of those made redundant).

A further element needed in the calculation is a unit of measurement for pleasure and pain. We will have to invent one. In cost–benefit analysis in health care health economists created a measure called QALYs (Gudex, 1986) to measure the consequences of medical and surgical interventions. In a similar spirit we have invented the JOLLIES (Judged, Outcome Leveraged, Life Improvement Expected Sum – OK, we admit – it is a joke). Pleasure is measured by positive JOLLIES, the greater the pleasure the more JOLLIES. Pain is measured in negative JOLLIES. In Table 3.2 the number of JOLLIES per person caused by each consequence of the redundancies is assessed. Some consequences are obviously high but some are very low. For example, because there are so many taxpayers, the extra amount of tax an individual would have to pay to cover the cost of extra social security payments would be so low that it might not even be noticed. Consequently the pain caused to an individual is very small.

## Utility    DEFINITION

In economics the measure of happiness or satisfaction received from an act – mostly goods and services – is known as utility. It is the formal term for what we have jokingly called JOLLIES, which would cover a wider range of acts than simply the provision of goods and services. Utility is of course difficult to measure and so economics is largely based on preferences which can be measured. In plainer language there is no objective way to measure the happiness I get from a shot of vodka. It is however possible to measure whether I prefer vodka to tequila. So it is not possible to measure the amount of happiness gained from the drinks, which is what utilitarianism requires, but preferences can be put into rank order even though we cannot know the happiness gaps that separate them.

The other economic approach to the problem of measuring utility is to use money as a proxy measure. In other words we can assume that the more ▶

money we have the more it enables us to put ourselves into positions that make us happy. This assumption is the basis of much cost–benefit analysis because it allows things that cannot be measured directly to be incorporated into formal economic analysis. The problem is that there are disputes about what the exact relationship between the intensity of happiness and money is. It is generally thought not to be a straight line; increase of wealth suffers from diminishing marginal returns in the amount of pleasure it delivers but the shape of the relationship is not proven (Lane, 1995: 276–8).

The first calculation to be done is to multiply the number of people who might be affected by the probability that they will be affected. This number can then be multiplied by the number of JOLLIES to identify the amount of pleasure or pain caused by the redundancy decision. This is not the end of the calculation however. As we have seen, pleasure and pain have different qualities (*see* pp. 127–8 intensity, duration, certainty, extent, propinquity, fecundity and purity). The total, raw quantity of pleasure and pain has to be weighted by these factors. In Table 3.2 each of these factors is assessed on a five-point scale on which 1 equals very low and 5 equals very high. We will give a few examples.

- The intensity and duration of shareholders' relief at the avoidance of insolvency is marked but it will not last long as their minds move on to other issues and concerns. The psychological impact of redundancy on those made redundant however is likely to be intense and last a long time and so this has been scored high at 5.

- Propinquity is concerned with whether the pleasure or pain is felt immediately or only occurs at some future time. The managers' delight at confirming their self-estimation as tough managers will be close in time to the decision. Contrarily the psychological impact of redundancy may only emerge some time after the family member has been made redundant. The guiding principle involved is similar to that of discounted cash flow – pleasure and pain deferred to the future carry less weight than that experienced immediately. Future pleasure and pain carry lower weighting therefore in the calculation.

- Purity is concerned with the degree to which pleasure and pain are alloyed with each other. The pleasure those who keep their jobs feel will be mixed with anxiety about how much longer their jobs will be secure, and so this scores low on purity. Those who find themselves in a better position since being made redundant will experience a relatively pure pleasure and so this is scored high at 5.

- Fecundity concerns the extent to which an act will create future pleasure or pain. The psychological stress caused to the job losers is likely to create more problems for them in the future and so this is scored high, whereas the typical short-sightedness of investors will mean that their pleasure at receiving increased dividends will not produce much future pleasure because they will be hungry for the next reward.

In the next stage of the calculation the raw total of JOLLIES is multiplied by all the weighting factors added together (and then divided by a million to keep the numbers manageable). As the purpose of a utilitarian analysis is to balance the total amount of pain caused against the total amount of pleasure, the final calculation is to add up the total JOLLIES, remembering that the pain JOLLIES are negative to get the net impact. If the result is positive then the pleasure outweighs the pain and the act is ethical; if the total is negative the act would result in more pain than pleasure and so would be unethical. In Table 3.2 the total is positive and so the redundancies would be an ethical act.

We have written a simple Excel spreadsheet to do the calculations in Table 3.2 and it would not be too difficult to devise a small program that prompted users to make the various judgements needed and then perform the calculations. The example also identifies some of the limitations of this approach to ethics.

- If all the stakeholders and all the impacts that an act may have upon them were included then the matrix of data and calculations would become very large. One obvious one that has been ignored in the example is the impact on local businesses and economy of making 20,000 people redundant.

- People are not good at judging the consequences of actions and so it is quite likely that the probability figures in the third column are wrong.

- There are many problems in creating a measure of pleasure and pain because these are essentially subjective. The system of QALYs mentioned earlier used a matrix of pain and mobility to make the assessment and a large sample survey. A real measure such as a QALY or a fictitious one such as JOLLIES can only give an average value for the pain or pleasure caused by a particular event and cannot capture the individual experience.

- The weighting scales for the features of pleasure and pain are also subjective and so will suffer the problem of inter-rater comparability; in other words different raters may make different assessments on these scales. The overall problem is that it is difficult to identify precise and agreed numbers to put into the calculations. This means that each number has a large margin of error and if calculations were done using one extreme of the range the act might be calculated as ethical, yet if numbers at the other extreme were used the act might be shown to be unethical.

**Connexion point**

It seems unlikely that managers go through such a complex calculation whenever they have to make a decision. Indeed, psychological research suggests they use an intuitive, heuristic approach that reduces the complexity of decisions and restricts the amount of information that is brought to bear upon it. Heuristics in decision making are the subject of Chapter 5.

Some writers have tried to overcome this difficulty by proposing rule utilitarianism. This approach looks at the general consequences, in terms of pleasure and pain, of particular rules of conduct. The rule, the following of which produces the best results, is the best rule to follow. This approach does not, however, necessarily make matters simpler. A rule such as 'you should always keep your promises' would probably have to be followed by so many exceptions that it would be no simpler than act utilitarianism.

A further criticism of utilitarianism is that it is implicitly authoritarian. This tendency can be illustrated by the public debate, in the early part of the nineteenth century, over the sources and mechanisms of revenue collection in the Indian provinces ruled by the East India Company. James Mill, the father of John Stuart Mill, was at the centre of this debate and through him the utilitarian philosophy of Bentham became a dominant theme in the argument. The utilitarians argued that the company had a duty to decide how best to spend the tax revenue of the country. As Holt Mackenzie argued in 1820:

> Holding 9/10ths of the clear rent [revenue] of the country as a fund to be administered for the public good, the government may, I think, justly be regarded as under a very solemn obligation to consider more fully than has hitherto been usual, how it can dispose of that fund so as to produce *the greatest sum of happiness*.
>
> (Stokes, 1959: 113, emphasis added)

There was a clear authoritarian and paternalistic strand in the thinking of these utilitarians. They believed they had a mission to transform India, but this mission could only be achieved by strong government. They would decide how the revenue should be spent. Utilitarianism requires the presence of a powerful figure who can calculate where the happiness of the country lies and then take the necessary action to bring it about. This strain of thought can be found in Bentham's own writings in which he argued that the will of the executive should not be checked by constitutional or popular devices (Stokes, 1959: 72, 79). It can also easily take root in companies and organisations where management become the judges of utility.

Despite the criticisms that can be made of utilitarianism its core ideas are commonly expressed by managers when they talk of 'business cases'. These are arguments that a thing should be done because it would be good for the business; the good of the wider society is not always considered.

## Activity 3.8

Briefly analyse Case study 2.9 (*Providing new drugs on the NHS to people with multiple sclerosis*) from a utilitarian perspective.

## Applying ethical theories

There are many ethical theories. Even if you find it easy to discount some of them, because you think them trivial or ill-founded, several will remain. This raises a question for someone who wishes to think ethically. Should all or several theories be applied when thinking about an issue or should one approach be adopted that seems best suited to the matter in hand? Petrick and Quinn (1997:

55–6, 63) argued that those managers who are temperamentally attached to one of the theoretical perspectives on ethics 'fanatically rush to judgement'. They claimed that there can be no 'quick fixes' when dealing with matters of managerial integrity and that managers ought to use the ethical insights from all four quadrants of Figure 3.1 to make balanced ethical decisions.

The matrix in Activity 3.9 is a way of evaluating options, for responding to an ethical issue, that considers a wide range of ethical perspectives. The criteria in the matrix are based on the ethical perspectives that have been discussed in this chapter. There are many ways of constructing such mechanisms. This is a simple one because it is based on a series of yes/no questions about the importance to be given to the various ethical principles and about the principles' implications. The matrix allows four levels of weighting or importance to be given to each of the criteria.

1. *The 'trigger' level.* A criterion is of such importance that a position or action can be chosen because it meets this criterion alone, irrespective of how it fares on the other criteria.

2. *The 'veto' level.* A veto criterion can veto a particular position or decision that negatively affects the criterion, no matter how well the action or decision does on all the other criteria. However, it is not important enough to be the single trigger for an action. For example, someone might reject an option because it does not meet his or her self-interest criterion but would not be prepared to choose an option simply because it met his or her self-interest needs.

3. *The ordinary level.* A criterion that deserves to be considered but carries no more weight than the other criteria.

4. *Reject level.* A criterion that you feel should not be considered.

The scoring part of the framework encourages you to assess whether each criterion would positively suggest acceptance of the option or negatively suggest rejection.

| Activity 3.9 | **An ethical evaluation framework** |
| --- | --- |

**The issue**

*For example – Bribery and corruption in international business deals.*

**Your proposed decision/position on the issue and the action you will take**

*For example – to pay a large commission to an intermediary to obtain his influence to secure a large overseas deal.*

**Instructions**

1. Identify any criterion you see as a veto item. Circle Y. Otherwise N.
2. Identify any item you see as a trigger item. Circle Y. Otherwise N.
3. Identify any criterion you see as a reject item. Circle Y. Otherwise N.
4. Answer each question. Circle + for a positive answer or – for a negative answer.
5. Ignore any criterion you have rejected.
6. Total the number of circles in the positive and negative columns.

▶

A veto item is any criterion that is so important to you that if your decision and plan score negatively on it you will reject the proposal even if, overall, it scores more positives than negatives.

A trigger item is any criterion that is so important to you that if your decision scores positively on it you will accept the proposal even if, overall, it scores more negatives than positives.

| *Ask the following questions of your proposed decision and plan of action* | Reject | Veto | Trigger | Positive | Negative |
|---|---|---|---|---|---|
| **Virtue ethics** | | | | | |
| 1 **Light-of-day test.** Would I feel good or bad if others (friends, family, colleagues) were to know of my decision and action? | Y/N | Y/N | Y/N | + | − |
| 2 **Virtuous mean test.** Does my decision add to, or detract from, the creation of a good life by finding a balance between justice, care and other virtues? | Y/N | Y/N | Y/N | + | − |
| **Deontological ethics** | | | | | |
| 3 **Veil of ignorance/Golden Rule.** If I were to take the place of one of those affected by my decision and plan would I regard the act positively or negatively? | Y/N | Y/N | Y/N | + | − |
| 4 **Universality test.** Would it be a good thing or a bad thing if my decision and plan were to become a universal principle applicable to all in similar situations, even to myself? | Y/N | Y/N | Y/N | + | − |
| **Ethical learning & growth** | | | | | |
| 5 **The communitarian test.** Would my action and plan help or hinder individuals and communities to develop ethically? | Y/N | Y/N | Y/N | + | − |
| 6 **Self-interest test.** Do the decision and plan meet or defeat my own best interests and values? | Y/N | Y/N | Y/N | + | − |

| Ask the following questions of your proposed decision and plan of action | Reject | Veto | Trigger | Positive | Negative |
|---|---|---|---|---|---|
| **Consequentialist ethics** | | | | | |
| **7 Consequential test.** Are the anticipated consequences of my decision and plan positive or negative? | Y/N | Y/N | Y/N | + | – |
| **8 The discourse test.** Have the debates about my decision and plan been well or badly conducted? Have the appropriate people been involved? | Y/N | Y/N | Y/N | + | – |

If any trigger item scores positive – **accept the decision and action.**

If any veto item scores negatively – **reject the decision and action.**

Otherwise **accept the decision and plan** if there are more positives than negatives or **reject the decision and plan** if there are more negatives than positives.

We will now give a possible analysis of the problem using the ethical evaluation framework. It does not claim to provide the 'correct' or even a satisfactory solution. The benefit of all such analytical frameworks is the discipline and system they impose on the decision maker. Their value lies in the process they insist on, rather than on the decisions they generate. In other words the following example represents one person's analysis of the problem, others would make a different analysis. However, the framework could be used as a vehicle to help a group of people trying to come to a consensus view on the issue.

Sometimes using such a framework leads to a conclusion that the decision maker finds intuitively repugnant. This at least reveals to the decision maker what their strongest values actually are. As with Edgar Schein's (1985) concept of 'career anchors' people are often unaware of what values they really take seriously until a practical issue challenges them.

### A possible analysis of the issue

**The issue**

*Whether to accept the bribery and corruption in international business deals.*

**Your proposed decision/position on the issue and the action you will take**

To pay a large commission to an intermediary to obtain his influence to secure a large overseas deal. It is generally recognised that paying such bribes is a long established part of doing business with this country.

▶

**Instructions**

1. Identify any criteria you see as a veto item. Circle Y. Otherwise N.
2. Identify any item you see as a trigger item. Circle Y. Otherwise N.
3. Identify any criteria you see as a reject item. Circle Y. Otherwise N.
4. Answer each question. Circle + for a positive answer or – for a negative answer.
5. Ignore any criterion you have rejected.
6. Total the number of circles in the positive and negative columns

A veto item is any criterion that is so important to you that if your decision and plan scores negatively on it you will reject the proposal even if, overall, it scores more positives than negatives.

A trigger item is any criterion that is so important to you that if your decision scores positively on it you will accept the proposal even if, overall, it scores more negatives than positives.

| Ask the following questions of your proposed decision and plan of action | Reject | Veto | Trigger | Positive | Negative |
|---|---|---|---|---|---|
| **Virtue ethics** | | | | | |
| 1 **Light-of-day test.** Would I feel good or bad if others (friends, family, colleagues) were to know of my decision and action? | | | | | – |
| 2 **Virtuous mean test.** Does my decision add to, or detract from, the creation of a good life by finding a balance between justice, care and other virtues? | Y | | | | |
| **Deontological ethics** | | | | | |
| 3 **Veil of ignorance/Golden Rule.** If I were to take the place of one of those affected by my decision and plan would I regard the act positively or negatively? | | | | | – |
| 4 **Universality test.** Would it be a good thing or a bad thing if my decision and plan were to become a universal principle applicable to all in similar situations, even to myself? | | | | | – |

| Ask the following questions of your proposed decision and plan of action | Reject | Veto | Trigger | Positive | Negative |
|---|---|---|---|---|---|
| **Ethical learning & growth** | | | | | |
| **5 The communitarian test.** Would my action and plan help or hinder individuals and communities to develop ethically? | | | | | − |
| **6 Self-interest test.** Do the decision and plan meet or defeat my own best interests and values? | | | | + | |
| **Consequentialist ethics** | | | | | |
| **7 Consequential test.** Are the anticipated consequences of my decision and plan positive or negative? | | Y | | + | |
| **8 The discourse test.** Have the debates about my decision and plan been well or badly conducted? Have the appropriate people been involved? | | | | | − |

Let's start with the reject column. We think that all the criteria are relevant apart from the 'virtuous mean' test that we have excluded on the grounds that it is not the purpose of businesses to define or implement the good life. We have checked the 'Y' response for this test and so we ignore it for the rest of the analysis. In the veto column we have checked the 'consequential test'. This is because, we think, if the decision to pay bribes would lead to more harm than good then we would not pay the bribes no matter how good the option might score on all the other criteria. In the 'trigger' column we could have checked the 'self-interest test' because if the option to pay the bribe would meet that criterion we would accept the option even if it failed on all the other criteria, but we decided not to.

We can now move on to assess the option against each of the criteria/tests in turn.

- *Light-of-day test* – If we paid the bribe we would try to keep it secret from friends and colleagues (who were not complicit in the act) because we would feel a bit bad about it . Our actions would not appear virtuous to others. The option scores negatively on this criterion.

- *Virtuous means test* – Unsurprisingly, for we are decent people at heart, we do not think supporting corruption represents an aspect of the good life. Nor do we think it represents a proper mean between the two extremes of a puritan refusal to give small tokens and hospitality and the other extreme of blatant bribe giving. However, we also do not think that it is the job of businesses to provide role models for virtue or to promote conceptions of the good life. This test has been rejected and so is not scored.

- *Veil of ignorance/Golden Rule* – Certainly our competitors would think it unfair if we got the contract through bribery. If we were to decide this issue under the conditions of the veil of ignorance, not knowing whether we would be the bribe receiver, the bribe giver or a member of the general community whose welfare is damaged by corruption, we might sensibly choose against bribery. We would score the option to pay bribes negatively on this test.

- *Universality test* – We think that it would be a bad thing if bribe paying were to become the norm in international business. The bribe paying option therefore scores negatively on this criterion.

- *Consequential test* – If we pay the bribe the consequences will be good for our company and lots of employees, who might otherwise have been made redundant, will keep their jobs with all the economic and social benefits that will accrue from that. The products we are selling will benefit the country that buys them. There may be some disadvantages in that we will be reinforcing the corrupt practices of that country but this downside is insignificant compared with the benefits. We therefore score the option positive on this test. As the option has not scored negatively the veto is not brought into action. If it had been activated the option would have been rejected without any further consideration.

- *Self-interest test* – Yes. If we pay the bribe and get the contract we will be in for a big performance bonus and our promotion prospects will be much increased. So the bribe paying option scores positively on this option.

- *The communitarian test* – The payment of bribes would reinforce a culture that accepted bribery and this would not be good for the ethical development of either individuals or of the society at large.

- *The discourse test* – Because of the sensitivity of the issue all our discussions about it with the directors have been conducted huggermugger and 'off-the-record'. The discussions have not been open nor have they included as wide a range of interested parties as possible. The option scores negatively on this criterion.

If we now add up the positive and negative scores we have two positives and five negatives. Clearly, we should reject the option to pay the bribe. If having done this we are left with a nagging, intuitive feeling that we should pay the bribe then this implies that really we think that either or both the consequential test and the self-interest test should have been classified as trigger items. In other words as the bribe option scored positively on both these tests we should proceed with the option and ignore the negative ratings on most of the other criteria.

If you use this framework and you end up with an equal balance of positive and negative scores you should reconsider the decisions you made in the veto and trigger columns. If you do not make any changes here that help you clarify the action you should take, then toss a coin.

Although we claimed that this evaluation framework was a way of integrating many ethical perspectives it will have occurred to you that, through the use of the 'reject', 'trigger' and 'veto' options as trump cards that can rule out some ethical tests, the framework allows the rejection or prioritisation of ethical positions.

This thought leads us to an alternative approach – to choose one ethical approach and to ignore others, or at least to put the approaches into rank order of preference. Carroll (1990) proposed a simple exercise (Activity 3.10) for people who wish to reflect on the relative importance they give to a range of ethical perspectives. The list of principles he proposed included both normative approaches, methods for thinking about the right response, and norm approaches, which invite a person to accept the values and standards of a particular group. The categorical imperative, the Golden Rule and the utilitarian principle are all methods for normative thinking whereas the disclosure rule, the organisation ethic and the professional ethic concern decisions about which social group one wishes to belong to. These norm-based questions could be seen as an application of a stakeholder analysis.

| Activity 3.10 | Prioritising your ethical principles |
| --- | --- |

Here are a number of 'principles'. Identify your top three and rank them 1, 2, 3 in order of importance/relevance to you and your decision making. Then mark your least relevant 9, 10 and 11.

| Principle | Description | Rank |
| --- | --- | --- |
| Categorical imperative | You should not adopt principles of action unless they can, without inconsistency, be adopted by everyone else | |
| Conventionist ethic | Individuals should act to further their self-interest so long as they do not violate the law | |
| Golden Rule | Do unto others as you would have them do unto you | |
| Hedonistic ethic | If it feels good, do it | |
| Disclosure rule | If you are comfortable with an action or decision after asking yourself whether you would mind if all your associates, friends and family were aware of it, then you should act or decide | |
| Intuition ethic | You do what your 'gut feeling' tells you to do | |
| Means–ends ethic | If the end justifies the means, then you should act | |
| Might equals right ethic | You should take whatever advantage you are strong enough and powerful enough to take without respect for ordinary social conventions and laws | |
| Organisation ethic | This is an age of large-scale organisations – be loyal to the organisation | |
| Professional ethic | You should only do that which can be explained before a committee of your professional peers | |
| Utilitarian ethic | You should follow the principle of 'the greatest good for the greatest number' | |

*Source*: Carroll (1990)

Carroll used the list in Activity 3.10 as the basis of a research project and found that the Golden Rule was given the highest ranking by his respondents. The disclosure rule came second in the study.

Some ethical checklists, such as the Texas Instruments Ethics Quick Test, emphasise the social acceptability of an ethical decision rather than the philosophical correctness of the mode of thought used to achieve it. Use the questions of the Quick Test to decide whether an action you are planning to take is right.

---

### Activity 3.11    The TI Ethics Quick Test

- Is the action legal?
- Does it comply with our values?
- If you do it, will you feel bad?
- How will it look in the newspaper?
- If you know it's wrong, don't do it!
- If you're not sure, ask.
- Keep asking until you get an answer.

(*Source*: Texas Instruments, 2001)

---

## Reflections

This chapter has provided the formal, philosophical tools that can be used when you have to think about an ethical problem. These tools are not, however, easy to handle. There is first the problem of which theories you are going to use. If all the theories were to give the same answer to a problem then admittedly there would be no problem. But this is not always the case and then you have the difficulty of choosing which theories to ignore or deciding how much weight to give to the various theories. Once you have chosen a theory there remains the difficulty of applying it to the particular circumstances of the issue confronting you. It may be these problems that make the TI Ethics Quick Test (Activity 3.11) look so attractive. The 'quick and dirty' approach it uses leads us into the matter of how people actually decide about ethical issues – which is the subject of the next chapter.

## Summary

In this chapter the following key points have been made:

- Ethical issues at work might be best approached by concentrating on developing people who are virtuous and have the judgement to be able to make moral decisions and act upon them when faced with ethical problems.

- Ethical issues at work might best be approached by seeing organisations as networks of individuals who learn personally and collectively through experience, reflection and the sharing of that learning. Learning about learning, learning how to deal with ethical issues, is more important than learning pre-packaged solutions.

- Ethical issues at work might best be tackled by applying sound moral principles that should guide our actions.

- Ethical issues at work might best be tackled by forecasting which actions will bring about the greatest amount of good.

## Quick revision test

1. Eudæmonia is a classical Greek term for...
   (a) the good life, an ethically complete life
   (b) pleasure
   (c) failing to find the golden mean between extremes

2. What is the 'veil of ignorance'?
   (a) a technique of debate proposed by discourse ethicists
   (b) a means of disguising unethical corporate behaviour
   (c) a thought experiment used to identify fair principles of justice

3. What is the difference between act and rule utilitarianism?
   (a) one calculates the pleasure and pain caused by distinct actions whereas the other simply compares the pleasure and pain consequent upon the adoption of different sets of rules governing actions
   (b) act utilitarianism allows individuals to decide what creates the greatest pleasure but rule utilitarianism gives that responsibility to governments
   (c) none, they are both fictitious terms

4. Which writer has brought virtue ethics back into modern debates about morality?
   (a) Alasdair MacIntyre
   (b) Ayn Rand
   (c) John Rawls

## Typical assignments and briefs

1. How relevant to business and management is a Kantian approach to ethics?

2. Discuss the use of child labour in factories in developing countries from two different ethical perspectives (you might choose between virtue ethics, Kantian ethics, Rawls' theory of justice or utilitarianism).

3. It is sometimes argued that a major flaw of utilitarianism is that it is only concerned with maximising the total amount of good and is not concerned with the distribution of that good between people and groups. Is this true?

4. How might an organisation implement the practices implied by discourse ethics?

## Group activity 3

Form into groups. As a group, choose one of the case studies from Chapter 2. Each member of the group should then choose a different ethical perspective – utilitarian, fairness, ethics of care and so on, and individually produce an analysis of the case from that perspective. Come back together as a group and debate the issue.

## Recommended further reading

P. Vardy and P. Grosch (1999) *The Puzzle of Ethics*, London: Fount, is a good introduction to the main ethical theories. Simon Blackburn's (2001) *Being Good. A Short Introduction to Ethics*, Oxford: Oxford University Press, is an elegant reflection on the main issues in ethics. Anne Thomson's (1999) *Critical Reasoning in Ethics*, London: Routledge, is a good guide to the application of theories to issues.

## Useful websites

| Topic | Website provider | URL |
|---|---|---|
| Ethics Updates This site provides some helpful materials on all the major ethical theories and perspectives. It is a general ethics site rather than a business ethics site. | Edited by L. M. Hinman, The Values Institute, University of San Diego | http://ethics.acusd.edu/values/index.html |
| Business ethics resources Brief materials on a wide range of theoretical and applied issues in business ethics. A useful crib and ready reference. | Business Open Learning Archive (The BOLA project), Brunel University | http://sol.brunel.ac.uk/~jarvis/bola/ethics/index.html |

| Topic | Website provider | URL |
|---|---|---|
| Some useful learning material on this site. If you click on 'toolbox' a cartoon Socrates guides you through some basic ethical concepts. When you click on 'cases and surveys' a cartoon Simone de Beauvoir acts as your mentor on a number of brief cases. | Centre for Ethics and Business | http://www.ethicsandbusiness.org/whoweare.htm |
| Ayn Rand's official website | Leonard Peikoff | http://www.peikoff.com/ |
| The Bentham project, University College London Jeremy Bentham's auto icon (his embalmed and preserved body, although the head is waxen, the original having decayed and been ill-treated by students), bequeathed in his will for the inspiration of future generations, can be seen in the south cloisters of the main building of University College. An image of the auto icon can be seen on the website | University College London | http://www.ucl.ac.uk/Bentham-Project/index.htm  http://www.ucl.ac.uk/Bentham-Project/Faqs/auto_where.htm |
| A virtue ethics scale and an article to explain its use | Michael Cawley III, James Martin and John Johnson, Penn State University | http://www.personal.psu.edu/faculty/j/5/j5j/virtues/VS.html  http://www.personal.psu.edu/faculty/j/5/j5j/virtues/Virtue.pdf |
| A framework for ethical decision making | Markula Center for Applied Ethics | http://www.scu.edu/ethics/practicing/decision/framework.html |
| A package on ethical decision making by a non-profit organisation based in Washington DC | Ethics Resource Centre (ERC) | http://www.ethics.org/plus_model.html |

# PART B

# Individuals' responses to ethical issues

## CHAPTER 4

# Personal values in the workplace

## Learning outcomes

Having read this chapter and completed its associated activities, readers should be able to:

- Define values and distinguish them from attitudes and beliefs.

- Explain the idea that a set of values may be fragmented or integrated.

- Explain how traditionalists, modernists, neo-traditionalists, postmodernists and pragmatists may have different perspectives on their values; and consider which position might explain their own stance.

- Argue that to divide managers into the moral and the bad is too simple and explain how different managerial roles carry their own characteristic ethical dangers, and consider which they think they might be prone to.

- Argue a case (even if they do not actually agree with it) that those who propose ethical leadership as a way of creating a value consensus within an organisation are taking a naïve view of the nature of human values.

## Introduction

It is difficult to discuss ethics in a business and organisational context without talking about values. As both are central themes in the book it is necessary to distinguish one from the other.

The broad distinction we wish to make is that ethics is a branch of philosophy and is therefore concerned with formal academic reasoning about right and wrong, but values are the commonsense, often taken-for-granted, beliefs about right and wrong that guide us in our daily lives. Imagine a situation at work where you have to decide whether to take action against a manager who you know to be fiddling their expenses. Ethics provides principles and arguments, drawn from ethical theory, for thinking about the issue. The emotional force of your values in contrast would lead you to an intuitive feel for the right thing to do. Of course, how much weight you give to your analysis and your emotions is another matter.

Ethics and values have different sources. Ethics are drawn from the books and debates in which philosophical theories about right and wrong are proposed and tested. Ethics have to be studied. Values are acquired informally through processes of socialisation. We acquire values from our interactions with our friends, family and colleagues and, most importantly for our purpose, from the organisations we work for or belong to. Values are learned, not studied. It is true that our employing organisations may make formal attempts, through induction courses and corporate videos, to inculcate their formal values. We are not required to study them, which would involve a critical engagement with them; we are simply required to 'buy into them', to 'mark, learn and inwardly digest' them. If values are learned rather than studied they must be few and simply expressed so that all in a society can understand them. Ethics in contrast need to be studied, not simply learned, because they are more complicated.

There are overlaps between ethics and values. The processes through which values are formed, adopted and modified within groups and societies may be influenced by debates between philosophers. Equally the rational discourses of ethics may be swayed by the emotional undertow beneath the participants' arguments. Within a group of philosophers social learning, conforming to the group's norms, may be more emotionally comfortable than challenging it. Conversely, critical study and the reading of books may challenge the values people acquired through life. Nevertheless the distinction between learned values and studied ethics is still a useful one.

It follows from the above argument that values are social. They exist and are communicated through social connections. Rokeach defined values as:

> a small number of core ideas or cognitions present in every society about desirable end-states.
>
> (Rokeach, 1973: 49)

---

### DEFINITIONS

**Values** are core ideas about how people should live and the ends they should seek. They are shared by a majority of people within a community or society. They are simply expressed generalities, often no more than single words such as peace and honesty. As they are very broad they do not give guidance on how particular things should be evaluated.

**Attitudes**, like values, are evaluations of whether something is good or bad. But unlike values they are evaluations of particular things, issues, people, places or whatever. Attitudes, because they relate to specific circumstances, are more changeable than values.

A **belief** is an acceptance that something is true or not. This acceptance does not imply any judgement about whether that thing is good or bad.

---

Rokeach's work is helpful because it distinguishes between different types of values that might affect thinking about ethical issues.

- *Moral values* – concern interpersonal behaviour, e.g. being honest is desirable.
- *Competence values* – concern one's own valuation of one's behaviour, e.g. behaving imaginatively is desirable.
- *Personal values* – concern the ends, or terminal states, that are desirable for the self, e.g. peace of mind.
- *Social values* – concern the ends that one would desire for society, e.g. world peace is desirable.

The first two items in this list concern instrumental values that are about how a person should live and behave. The second two items are terminal values that concern the ends or purposes that we should be striving for. Table 4.1 lists the instrumental and terminal values identified by Rokeach's survey of a sample of Americans.

**Table 4.1** The instrumental and terminal values of Americans

| Terminal values | Rank order (females) | Rank order (males) | Instrumental values | Rank order (females) | Rank order (males) |
|---|---|---|---|---|---|
| A comfortable life | 13 | 4 | Ambitious | 4 | 2 |
| An exciting life | 18 | 18 | Broadminded | 5 | 4 |
| A sense of accomplishment | 10 | 7 | Capable | 12 | 8 |
| A world at peace | 1 | 1 | Cheerful | 10 | 12 |
| A world of beauty | 15 | 15 | Clean | 8 | 9 |
| Equality | 8 | 9 | Courageous | 6 | 5 |
| Family security | 2 | 2 | Forgiving | 2 | 6 |
| Freedom | 3 | 3 | Helpful | 7 | 7 |
| Happiness | 5 | 5 | Honest | 1 | 1 |
| Inner harmony | 12 | 13 | Imaginative | 18 | 18 |
| Mature love | 14 | 14 | Independent | 14 | 11 |
| National security | 11 | 10 | Intellectual | 16 | 15 |
| Pleasure | 16 | 17 | Logical | 17 | 16 |
| Salvation | 4 | 12 | Loving | 9 | 14 |
| Self-respect | 6 | 6 | Obedient | 15 | 17 |
| Social recognition | 17 | 16 | Polite | 13 | 13 |
| True friendship | 9 | 11 | Responsible | 3 | 3 |
| Wisdom | 7 | 8 | Self-controlled | 11 | 10 |

*Note*: 1 represents the highest value and 15 the lowest.

(*Source*: Reprinted with the permission of The Free Press, a division of Simon and Schuster Adult Publishing Group, from *The Nature of Human Values* by Milton Rokeach, p. 58, Copyright © 1973 by The Free Press.)

The rank orders in Table 4.1 are averages, and individuals will, to a greater or lesser extent, have different views on the proper order of the values. Billig has also pointed out (1996: 240) that Rokeach's view of values is positive and aspirational. He argued that values may be negative. We may, for example, all agree that cruelty is bad.

## Activity 4.1

Put the two lists in Table 4.1 (terminal values and instrumental values) into rank order according to your personal preferences. Compare these with the American average scores (male or female as appropriate) by subtracting the American ranking from your ranking (and ignoring whether the result is positive or negative). For example, equality is ranked 9 by American men. If my ranking was 12 the difference is 3. Then total up all the differences. The smaller the number, the greater the similarity between my ranking and that of Americans. If the difference is zero then the two sets of rankings are almost certainly (but not entirely, because there may be differences that cancel each other out) identical. Ask some friends or colleagues to do the ranking. Compare their average score with yours.

Consider: Is the difference between your ranking and the American's ranking greater or lesser than that between you and your friends?

Different organisations, different groups, different cultures and different countries may have different values. Ethical theory, however, is disdainful of societies. It does not matter to the validity of a theory if it is not accepted by the generality of people. The truth of an ethical theory cannot be judged by an opinion poll. It will be a constant theme of this book that in business and organisation there can be great tensions between how an ethical theory says people should behave and how their social values incline them to behave.

### Connexion point

The diversity of values relating to business and management in different countries and societies is explored in Chapter 11.

## Perceptions of values

Just as in the first chapter we discussed different views on whether there is a normative ethical order that applies to business so we can ask similar questions about the nature and role of values. It is convenient to do this by using the notion of fragmentation to explain the nature of values. Fragmentation is the idea that things in the social world are disordered and disconnected. A fragmented view of values would see them as diverse, various and expressed through conflict between different views and opinions. There are no wholes in a fragmented social and ethical world, only discordant parts that clash against each other. The philosopher Thomas Hobbes expressed this view in the seventeenth century. He argued that even a single person's view could be fragmented.

> Nay, the same man, in divers times, differs from himself; and one time praiseth, that is, calleth good, what another time he dispraiseth, and calleth evil: from whence arise disputes, controversies, and at last war.
>
> (Hobbes, n.d.: 104)

The contrary view is the one we have already noted that Rokeach expressed. He claimed that values, far from being fragmented, are simple and whole. Billig (1996: 240) agreed that the values of a group or society are simple and whole. But he pointed out that this makes them difficult to apply to particular situations. A society may have clear views on the importance of telling the truth and on loyalty. However, there may be situations in which such simple nostrums do not help much. There are two reasons for this.

1. The demands of truth telling and loyalty may conflict in a particular case. Should a government spokesman tell the truth about a military operation if it would cause danger to the soldiers who might expect him to show them loyalty? In such cases the simplicity and wholeness of values is broken by not knowing which value should be applied.

2. Simple and whole values can only provide general guidance. When it comes to dealing with specific situations values need interpretation. Can there be situations, as the behaviour of politicians often implies, when truthfulness can be interpreted as not telling lies but equally as not telling the whole truth? Once interpretation is necessary, values that were simple and whole become fragmented.

Ambiguity can arise in organisations when simple values are inadequate because they cannot deal with new circumstances or are in conflict with other values. When ambiguity occurs those who seem to offer a resolution gain power and they bring with them their new values and ideologies (Weick, 2001: 47). Weick sees this as a process of sense-making in which, through communication and interaction, people interpret and construct a view of their organisation and their roles within it. From this perspective values do not exist prior to and separate from organisational life (as Rokeach would suggest); instead they emerge and become pervasive in organisations as a consequence of a dynamic process within organisations. In his earlier book Weick (1995) identified seven properties of sense-making. These can be illustrated by considering how values about telling the truth (or not; manipulating performance measurement information for example) might emerge from a sense-making process.

- **Identity Construction.** When someone considers deceiving others at work by manipulating performance statistics they will consider how they see themselves: whether they believe themselves to be macho managers, who will change the management information to give a better impression of their efforts, or whether they value themselves as truthful individuals who can bear the truth even if it hurts them.

- **Retrospective sense-making**. According to Weick sense-making will occur after people have acted – in other words values follow actions and do not precede them. The case of the Russian business people (*see* p. 46) who justified their avoidance of taxes by arguing that they only did this because the state was too corrupt to be the rightful guardians of tax revenues is a good example.

- **Sense-making is done through enactment**. People make sense of things by taking action. If people decide to manipulate performance management information they do so by choosing an action that fits with their environment (they might decide that to actually change the performance numbers might be unacceptable), but by their choice of method of deception (say, hiding the poor figures in a great many other numbers) they also change the environment by creating a climate where that particular form of deception becomes acceptable.

- **Sense-making is social**. If people talk with their colleagues about what they have done then the practice may become accepted through use. It has been discovered that different occupational groups have different perceptions of right and wrong. Different occupational groups as a consequence may have different views about what is and is not acceptable behaviour. Some groups of programmers for example think it more acceptable than other groups to violate intellectual property rights (Stylianou *et al.*, 2004), probably because they are great users of the Web, which diminishes the idea of property rights in knowledge by making it so accessible.

- **Sense-making is ongoing**. As situations change, for example, if a member of staff is dismissed for violating intellectual property rights, then people will reformulate their position on the matter in discussion with each other.

- **Sense-making is focused on 'extracted cues'**. This means that people in an organisation will concern themselves with some things in the daily stream of events and ignore others. Those cues become the raw material from which a view and actions are taken. The vicarious experience of others (for example, whether others who are known to have deceived the performance management system flourish or are caught and punished) will become part of the sense-making process.

- **Sense-making is driven by plausibility**. The process of sense-making is based on personal assessments of risk and benefit. It is not a process of fine judgement based on incontrovertible facts. In other words people take a calculated gamble. When deciding to manipulate performance management systems they are chancing that the benefits of doing so will be great enough to outweigh the probability of being caught and the severity of the punishment.

This brief review would suggest that values can be seen as something that emerge from dynamic processes of sense-making as well as being one of the process inputs. Agreed sets of values in organisations can be changed through this process. Values express a potential tension between wholeness (wanting a consensual set of values) and fragmentation (the value sets are broken up and reformed). People's responses to this tension and their method of making sense of it can be classified under five headings:

- Traditionalist
- Modernist
- Neo-traditionalist
- Postmodernist
- Pragmatist.

## The traditional view of values

From the traditional viewpoint a group – whether a work group, an organisation, a profession or a country – is defined by its possession of shared values. The idea of value fragmentation therefore is considered anathema and a contradiction in terms. A group's values either derive from the ancient traditions of the group or are presented as if they did. In organisations these traditional values are often presented as those of the firm's founder. In companies that were not blessed with a charismatic founder a mythical one is sometimes created for public relations and advertising purposes and to act as a fount for the values the company wishes to present (Mr Kipling of Kipling's Cakes is an example). A group based on traditional values sees them as a whole. By turning their gaze inwards and not outwards to other groups and societies, they fail to recognise the fragmentation and diversity of values that surrounds them.

This inward-looking-ness identifies a disapproval of questioning as a feature of traditionalism. Education and training are seen as the processes of attaining knowledge burnished by age. To challenge that knowledge by asking why it should be so is unacceptable. In broad historical terms it can be argued that the Enlightenment, which occurred in Europe in the eighteenth century, was a time when thinkers began to challenge with empirical observation and study things that had long been accepted as unchallengeably true because they were stated in ancient religious and classical texts (Sloan and Burnett, 2004). A consequence of the lack of questioning is that traditionalism is often experienced as a moral traditionalism that defines which behaviours are acceptable in and beyond organisations. This may be seen in the movement in the Bible Belt of the USA to run businesses according to fundamental Christian precepts. Riverview Bank in Minnesota was set up as America's first evangelical bank. Its founder believed it to be a good commercial proposition because born again Christians do not smoke or gamble or drink and are dedicated to their families, all of which make them a good credit risk (Doran, 2004).

| The Enlightenment | DEFINITION |
| --- | --- |

This was a historical period during the eighteenth century when academics and writers began to question truths and beliefs that had been long held because they were sanctified by the Church or by the ancient writings of Greek philosophers. Traditionally it was thought to have been dominated by European philosophers such as Immanuel Kant (*see* p. 108) who defined the Enlightenment (*die Aufklärung* in German) as emancipation from humankind's self-incurred immaturity. But it was also seen in the work, for example, of anti-quaries and amateur geologists who began to discover and collect fossils, rocks, minerals and finds from what we would now call archaeological sites. The study of these objects began to raise doubts about the previously accepted fact that the world was created in 4004 BC, a date that Ussher had calculated from the Bible. From such practical activities rational analysis based on observation began to undermine traditionalism's criteria of antiquity and the Bible as the tests of truth. It was also a period when morals drawn from these sources were challenged by rational analysis in such works as Mary Wollstonecraft's *Vindication of the Rights of Women* (*see* p. 113).

## The modernist view of values

The modernist position is that the twentieth and, so far, the twenty-first century have been characterised by value fragmentation. However, this is seen as a transitory phase and it is thought that, through the application of reason, the pieces can be put back together and true values defined. Those who take this position believe that values are tangible, and can be unambiguously stated and defined through formal and rational debate. They accept deductive reasoning that allows truths to be logically developed from first principles. The modernist believes that values can be determined by ethical study. Jürgen Habermas, for example (Pusey, 1987: 78ff.), constructed a complex theory of communicative action that defines how the validity of spoken understandings between people can be tested. Modernism sees this as an individual task. Progress, both moral and technical, is thought possible through individual effort and rationality.

> [modernist identity] is epitomized by the notion of the self-developing individual, rootless yet constantly evolving to new heights.
>
> (Friedman, 1994: 39)

At the least other modernists believe that values can be defined and clarified (Kirchenbaum, 1977; Smith, 1977) as a preliminary to rational discussion about an organisation's mission and core values.

**Connexion point**

Habermas' idea of communicative action is discussed within the general framework of what is known as discourse ethics in Chapter 3, pp. 124–6.

The rationality that Habermas talks about is not the same as that spoken of by many managers. The former can be labelled as critical and emancipatory whereas the latter is instrumental rationality. Instrumental rationality is focused on achieving a set of given aims. Much managerial effort, for example, goes into maximising return on capital or increasing the number of hospital beds without giving much thought to whether these ends are in themselves the right ones. Questions about whether growth at all costs is a good thing, or whether, for example, a focus on preventive health measures might not be better than simply building bigger hospitals, are forgotten. Emancipatory or critical rationality (Legge, 1995: 288) asks these deeper questions. It challenges the conventional wisdoms of modern life so that people become aware of the constraints that deform their lives. Both forms of rationality have a place in the modernist perspective. They develop the 'cognitive adequacy' (Giddens, 1985: 100–1) that organisations and societies might use to improve and unify their values.

## The neo-traditional view of values

The neo-traditional approach emphasises the function of culture as a device for mediating the tensions between fragmented values and the need of societies and organisations for a common purpose and mutual understanding. Neo-traditionalists see values in the context of organisational and social cultures; indeed, cultures are defined by the values that characterise them. They argue that the fragmentation of values can be overcome and that organisations and societies can have unified values. But such an end cannot be achieved by rational analysis, which sees values as objects for analysis and not as shared myths, which is how neo-traditionalists view them. Myths can act as the glue that holds an organisation or society in unity because of their simplicity (which needs no sophisticated explanation) and because of their ability to finesse dilemmas. Sometimes the glue is weak and sometimes strong. There is agreement, however, among neo-traditionalists that values, presented as vision and myth and not as cold rationality, are the keys to overcoming fragmentation. This perspective is a form of 'back to basics' and traditional values. Historically, this may be dated to the publication of Peters and Waterman's (1982) *In Search of Excellence*. This book advocated replacing the 'paralysis by analysis' of modernism with an emphasis on values and organisational culture. Those who take this approach stress that organisations are culture-creating mechanisms and that cultures can change. This thought leads to the notion that culture may be a critical lever or variable with which managers can lead or direct their organisations. As Smircich put it,

> Overall the research agenda arising from the view that culture is an organisational variable is how to shape and mould the internal culture in particular ways and how to change culture, consistent with managerial purpose.
>
> (Smircich, 1983: 346)

Values, from this view, can be deliberately used as a means of overcoming fragmentation and improving organisational effectiveness. As Smircich also pointed out there is an alternative view that cultures are too complex for managers to be able to mould them into a desired form.

A second form of neo-traditionalism can be seen in the wave of interest in 'New Age' therapies and philosophies that encourage the spiritual growth of individuals through the rejection of materialism. It might be thought that this would fit ill with the self-interest of organisations but Covey's work (1992) has led to many agreeing that concerns with individual and organisational growth can be combined.

**Connexion point**

These neo-traditional views are also discussed in Chapter 3 under the heading 'Ethical learning and growth,' pp. 119–21.

## The postmodern view of values

The postmodern stance sees nothing in the social and intellectual world as tangible or fixed. At this vantage point fragmentation is accepted as part of the human condition. In Lyotard's (1988: 46) famous phrase, there is 'incredulity towards metanarratives'. This means that the large ideological schemes, such as capitalism and communism, that used to dominate people's thinking no longer have credibility. In the postmodern view there are no eternal truths or values. What we think of as objectively true emerges through discourses that are embedded in power and knowledge relationships where some have more influence on the outcomes of the discourses than others. But what emerges is in any case uncertain because the language we use is opaque and carries no single, clear messages (Legge, 1995: 306).

The words we use to express our values have no fixed meaning. Statements of value have to be treated as texts and deconstructed. *Différance* is Derrida's device for exploring the limitless instability of language. One aspect of *différance* is that no word has a positive meaning attributed to it; it only has meaning to the extent that it is different from other words. Another aspect is deferral because the meaning of one word is always explained by reference to another and the search for meaning can involve a complex chain of cross-references as one chases a word through a vast thesaurus. Let us take an innocuous statement about public management:

> The first steps to achieving accountability for performance must be to clarify objectives and develop a recognised approach to measuring and reporting performance.
>
> (Dallas, 1996: 13)

This is enough to cause a deconstructionist to salivate. Most of the words in the sentence do not have an unambiguous or uncontested meaning. Accountability, for example, can only be defined by relating it to other words such as hierarchy, responsiveness, transparency and so on. Accountability may be viewed from different discourses such as political accountability, audit and accounting, consumer rights and investigative journalism. If we had the time to explore this sentence in detail and to plot its webs of signification we would find that the sentence could mean almost anything.

The search for meaning may not be endless; but the end will be terminal confusion rather than clear understanding. The function of deconstruction is to reach a final impasse.

Deconstruction is not intended to overcome fragmentation but simply to map the instabilities, paradoxes and aporetic states that define it. From this position there is no hope that the fragmented values can be put back together again. As Harvey (1989: 45) expressed it, disapprovingly, postmodernism

> swims and even wallows in the fragmentary and chaotic current of change as if that was all there was.

The political passivity of postmodernism annoyed him:

> The rhetoric of postmodernism is dangerous for it avoids confronting the realities of political economy and the circumstances of global power ... meta-theory cannot be dispensed with.
>
> (Harvey, 1989: 116)

This form of postmodernism could be called hard postmodernism because it seems to lead to the impossibility of business ethics, or any other kind of ethics, in a world that desperately needs it. However, as Derrida (Derrida with Bennington, 1989: 221) said, to deconstruct the enlightenment project (which seeks to raise humanity's moral status through the application of reason) is not necessarily to criticise it. Just because someone points out that the language used, when people attempt to analyse the realities of global power, is inadequate does not mean the task is unworthy. As Gustafson (2000: 648) points out, Derrida does not say that all ways and options are of equal value, though it is not possible to say that there is one best way. This softening of the stereotypical view of postmodernism does allow postmodernists to have an ethical agenda, but this will be described in the next section under the more suitable heading of pragmatism.

## The pragmatic view of values

The pragmatism of this stance is that of the American philosopher Richard Rorty (1989, 1990). He shares the postmodernists' scepticism about the possibility of an objective truth and of a fixed hierarchy of values. In this circumstance the issue for Rorty is not how to represent, or mirror, the world in our thinking but how to cope with its ambiguity:

> All descriptions (including one's self description as a pragmatist) are evaluated according to their efficacy as instruments for purposes, rather than their fidelity to the object described.
>
> (Rorty, 1992: 92)

The notion of usefulness is a hermeneutic one. If a belief helps us to interpret our other beliefs and vice versa then it is useful. The justification of belief is therefore conversational. A dialogue between developing beliefs is necessary, not because it will bring us to an ultimate truth, but because it keeps the conversation going (Mounce, 1997: 185–9). The line taken by pragmatists is that the inability to ground our values in some grand overarching theory such as Christianity, Marxism, Islam or capitalism does not prevent people making sensible and practical arrangements for living a civil and well-mannered life. As Rorty expressed this view,

No such metanarrative is needed. What is needed is a sort of intellectual analogue of civic virtue – tolerance, irony and a willingness to let spheres of culture flourish without worrying too much about their 'common ground', their unification, the 'intrinsic ideas' they suggest or what picture of man they presuppose.

(Rorty, 1985: 168)

He argued that the lack of a metanarrative could be overcome by dealing with the concrete and practical concerns of a community and by finding ways of harmonising, but not abolishing, the conflicts of values within the community.

Zygmunt Bauman (1993) developed a pragmatic notion of ethics that he called, adding to the confusion surrounding the term, postmodern ethics. (The title of one of his other books – *Life in Fragments* (Bauman, 1995) – reinforces the importance of the idea of fragmentation in a postmodern sensibility.) He saw the techniques of rational analysis and technological development, as proposed by modernism, as part of the problem of business ethics. Organisations take a bureaucratic approach to the matter by defining rules and regulations that deny and quash employees' natural tendency to act morally towards each other. Such rules enable them to settle for the lower standard of obeying the regulations rather than aspiring to the higher level of behaving well. The failure of rationality to solve ethical problems does not mean that we should not continue to try to solve them. The contribution of postmodern ethics, however, may lie more in asking important questions than in finding the answers.

Gustafson (2000: 652–4) identifies a number of characteristics of postmodern (though we would prefer to call it pragmatic) ethics.

- Not separating personal values and principles from those applied at work. Dividing one's life into a series of disconnected boxes is a typical modernist way of reducing complexity and ambiguity to a seeming sense of order. A postmodernist would much rather face up to the conflicts between their personal values and those they are called upon to apply at work.

- As postmodernists do not accept any grand metanarrative ethical theories they have to look instead at particulars and circumstances. These can only be expressed in stories and myths that express humanity's fears, confusions and expectations. Concrete illustrations of moral issues are a more assured route to ethical awareness than mental abstractions divorced from substance. Some people have gone as far as to recommend that we should return to meditation upon the lives of saints to help us deal with the ethical dilemmas and tensions that we experience (Wyschograd, 1990: xiii). As the medieval historian Gervase of Canterbury wrote in the twelfth century,

There are many people whose minds are induced to avoid evil and to do good more easily by example than by prohibition and precepts.

(Bartlett, 2000: 629)

- A disbelief in Utopian ideas. As Bauman expressed it, a postmodern thinker uses history (particularly that of the twentieth century and even more specifically of the Holocaust) as evidence of modernists' belief in instrumental thinking and technological development is wrong. Even on a more mundane level the belief held in the 1960s that technological development would lead to a world in which everyone would have huge amounts of leisure has proved false.

- Finally, Gustafson sees postmodern ethics as a 'tempered quest'. By this he means that the search for ethical answers to the problems of business ethics is conducted with the one item of knowledge that is certain – that no definitive answer can be found.

Living in an ungrounded ethical system may call upon people's resources of humour and tolerance. These are needed because value conflict will be endemic in such a situation. Irony is helpful because people's purposes may require them to act in ways that seem naïve in the absence of a metanarrative that justifies simple behaviours. Let us explain this point by quoting Umberto Eco (1985: 67). In his reflections on his best-selling novel, *The Name of the Rose*, he used the example of the pragmatist lover. The lover wishes to say to his partner, 'I love you', but he cannot do so because everyone is aware that the proliferation of romantic novels has devalued that particular metanarrative. He would feel too naïve and unsophisticated if he said that simple sentence even though it is the emotion he wishes to express. Being a pragmatist he does not give up, and stalk away undeclared. Instead, he says, 'As Barbara Cartland would say "I love you"'. He has thereby expressed his purpose but in a way that reveals his knowledge that such sentiment can no longer be justified by reference to transcendental values. Irony, by which an apparently straightforward statement is undermined by its context, is essential to the pragmatist's stance.

From a pragmatic view, in summary, it is recognised that there is confusion and conflict over the ends of a good organisation or society and that the meanings people ascribe to values change and develop as they debate and discuss issues with others. Nevertheless the pragmatist believes that by maintaining the conversation with good humour and irony it is possible to make organisations and societies more bearable.

The five stances can be characterised in relation to their position on ethical fragmentation. A traditionalist sees a unified world united by time-hallowed values. From the other four positions the ethical world is seen as fragmented but with different responses to this perception. The modernist believes that unity can be restored through rational development of individuals. The neo-traditionalist believes unity can be restored only by a return to concern for neglected values. The postmodernist accepts the inevitability of fragmentation and enjoys it. Pragmatists learn to live with fragmentation. The following exercise is designed to test your understanding of the five stances. Read Case study 4.1. Although it is an invented case study many of the incidents have been taken from interviews with managers. Then answer the questions in Discussion activity 4.1.

Case study
4.1

## Chris's managerial development: A fable

Chris is a newly qualified social worker. She didn't start training until she was in her late twenties but she had much previous experience of acting as an unpaid worker with a voluntary agency. In her first role as a field social worker she brought much of the enthusiasm and motivation that she developed during her early experience and training. She liked to see her clients as whole persons and she tried to spend as much time with them as possible so that she could come to a proper understanding of their situation from their point of view. It is important, she believed, not to take action without the full and active consent of the client.

After some years the pressure of Chris's caseload made it difficult to find the time she needed to spend with clients. She often felt frustrated that she had to foreshorten important discussions with them. On occasions this frustration caused her to be short and less than helpful with those clients who seemed to enjoy creating their own misfortune and yet were ungrateful for any help she provided. Although some of her clients were often short-changed on the service they received because of this reaction it did not undermine her essential belief in the need to work with her clients in a way that maintained and developed their dignity.

After a few years Chris was promoted to team leader and she became responsible for the management and professional supervision of a team of workers. In a small way her attitude towards the clients changed. She no longer spent the bulk of her time working face to face with them. She also had the managerial responsibility of dividing her staff resources between all the clamouring demands for service. Her attitude towards clients was more objective. She made sure that careful, measured and objective assessments were made of all clients so that those with the greatest needs received priority.

A few years later Chris was appointed as a Services Manager for a particular category of clients in the northern area of the county. Two important themes within her new job were service quality (as expressed by performance indicators) and budgets. Cost-effectiveness became a worrying issue. She had to convince her managers that she was providing value for money and this caused her to question whether the range of services wasn't too wide and whether some of them could be ended or reduced. There was talk within the department about only providing the high 'value added' services. She came to the view that better IT, better information and more rational decision-making processes would improve the service's effectiveness. She was studying for an MBA and its heavy emphasis on IT and management science convinced her that the department needed to put more effort into producing a computer-based needs profiling and resource allocation system. She started, in a small way, to produce such a system for use within her own locality.

A few years later Chris was still a services manager, but she had moved sideways and was now working with a different client group. The move made her realise the differences in professional values between people who worked with different client groups. It was the failure to address these differences, she thought, that was at the root of organisational conflict within the department. She came to believe that it was very important that everyone in her area subscribed to a central vision and mission that would motivate and inspire all staff. To this end she organised a couple of away-day sessions at which she and her fellow managers tried to hammer out some key goals and core values for the service as a whole. The software she had developed in her previous job had proved very valuable but it had failed to deliver easy solutions to the resource allocation problems. As a result of this experience Chris thought that focusing the department on some basic core values was a better way of managing than relying too much on IT systems.

After a few years in this job Chris was more aware of its political dimension. Managers seemed to spend their time fighting their corner and the person who shouted loudest got the most. For example, whilst the IT system optimised the allocation of staff to clients it caused as many problems as it solved. It gave some groups of clients a very low priority ranking. Some managers felt that this was correct ('it would be more effective to pay for them all to go to Lourdes', as one senior manager put it) but there was a powerful and critical lobby from the relatives of the clients.

When she was trying to develop core values she began to see it as a game. People were trying to control the language that was to be used in framing the values. It was also clear that when they wrote a core value everybody bought into it while retaining the right to define it in their own way. Everyone was smart enough to play the language games of anti-oppressive practice but there was no consensus about its meaning. Indeed at meetings Chris thought they were playing a circular word game in which *client focus* was identified with quality of service, which in turn was defined as providing equal opportunities, which in its turn was seen as responding to the diversity of clients. The debates' ends were their beginnings. The inconclusive debates over policy documents often led to a point where everything seemed ineluctably confused.

Some years later Chris was a senior manager. Her enthusiasm for the importance of social services was undimmed but her expectations were less ambitious. She was aware that things in organisations do not always work as planned. She no longer believed that the answer to organisational management was more and better computers; nor did she think that the publication of a nicely printed and laminated card proclaiming the Mission Statement actually meant that everyone shared the same values. She saw the organisation as having many stakeholder groups, internal and external, and the task of managers was to keep them sweet. But this ironic awareness did not mean that Chris became cynical, although this is precisely what has happened to some of her colleagues. Chris continued to work for improvement (whatever that is) but perhaps in a different way. She came to believe in proceeding on a Ready – Fire – Aim basis. This meant trying things out in a small way, without too much prior planning, and building on them if they worked, and modifying or abandoning them if they didn't. No more rational masterplans. She no longer believed in acronyms (such as CFI – Clients First Initiative) any more. Truth lay in aphorisms not acronyms. Aphorisms are a statement of a general principle memorably expressed in a condensed form. For example, 'He who is too busy doing good finds no time for being good' (Tagore quoted in Gross, 1987: 197). Aphorisms make you think about fundamental issues, acronyms just require blind acceptance. Chris accepted both the fragmented nature of the managerial role and the plurality of values within the organisation, and she could become a little manic-depressive as a result. Nevertheless, Chris tried to maintain manners and tolerance when managing the service. Her attitude was 'pessimistic wishful thinking'.

### Discussion activity 4.1

The fable implies that managers' responses to value issues at work may change as their careers progress. In this fable can you detect the periods when Chris's approach was:

(a) traditional,

(b) modernist,

(c) neo-traditional,

(d) postmodern, and

(e) pragmatic?

We will give one possible interpretation of the fable in Case study 4.1. You may have made a different reading of it. Chris starts her career as a field social worker as a traditionalist. She had acquired a set of values about how social work clients should be treated. To some extent this would have been values acquired as she grew up and through her voluntary work. These would have been reinforced by her social work training. She had picked up the traditional values that are associated with her chosen profession. As her workload pressures increased she found it increasingly difficult to apply these values. Her next two jobs gave her responsibility for setting priorities, managing budgets and achieving performance targets. In response she began to adopt a more modernist stance. She had to assume that clients' needs can be objectively measured and ranked in order of importance so that she can make sure the neediest will receive services. She extended this view into a belief, fostered by doing a master's degree in management science, that the difficult decisions about the rationing of services, when need exceeds the resources available to meet it, could be made easier by more data and more rational decision making. Up to this stage in her career Chris had been working in the same specialist field. Her next job takes her into a different one and she realised that different groups have different values and norms. This, together with the failure of more data and better software systems to solve the management problems, leads her to take a neo-traditionalist stance and to try to make the service more effective by developing an organisational set of values that everyone could 'buy into'. However, this proved to be more difficult than she had expected as attempts to create a unified organisational culture floundered on organisational politics. Chris began to view things from a postmodern perspective and observed wryly the games playing with language that went on in the organisation. However, by the time she had become a senior manager she had become a pragmatist, who saw no quick fixes to organisational problems, but nevertheless continued to work to improve things, even though progress, even if everyone could agree it was progress, was slow and piecemeal. Success, she felt, lay in maintaining the importance of concern for others and for good manners even though this seemed an endless task.

# The ethical limitations and dangers of managerial roles

If, as argued in the previous section, there are various stances people may take in relation to their values then different people may have different potential strengths and weaknesses in their approach to ethical issues in organisations. In this section it will be argued that managers can take one of five positions in their approach to ethical issues, and that each has characteristic ethical strengths but also its own ethical dangers or limitations. The analysis may also apply to others than managers in organisations, but for simplicity the analysis will be presented in relation to managers only. The analysis is shown in Figure 4.1 and it illustrates how twelve managerial roles show varying degrees of closeness to the five positions of:

- Prophets
- Subjectivists
- Rhetoricians
- Quietists, and
- Balancers.

The degree to which the twelve roles reflect the four stances will be in proportion to their distance in the matrix of Figure 4.1 from each stance.

| **Prophets** A monocular ethical vision & an unwillingness to debate | | | | **Subjectivists** Their subjectivism can lead to ethical fragmentation & distorted dialogue |
|---|---|---|---|---|
| | Radical critiquer | Systems developer | Cynic | |
| | Guru | Culture designer | Counsellor | |
| | Mentor | Transactional manager | Ritualist | |
| | Intellectual | Pragmatist | Games player | |
| **Quietists** Disengagement from ethical problems in the world | | | | **Rhetoricians** The accommodations necessary to stay in the game may lead to a loss of moral agency |

Figure 4.1 The managerial ethical roles as a semiotic square

The roles are defined by two dimensions. The first dimension concerns a person's beliefs about the whole or fragmentary nature of the wider cultural field in which they live and work.

The four stages in this scale, modernist, neo-traditionalist, traditionalist and postmodernist, have been taken from the discussion earlier in the chapter. Pragmatism has been incorporated into the postmodern category for the purposes of this analysis.

The second dimension concerns the extent to which a person believes their own ethical values to be a whole or, to a greater or lesser degree, a changeable set. Of the three points on this scale, two, principle and policy, have been taken from Chapter 3 (*see* p. 100). The third element is new.

- Principle: this represents a low fragmentation of values – principles are fixed.

- Policy: this represents a medium fragmentation of values – policies change and adapt.

- Aporia.

The third possible position on the dimension is aporia, the state which exhibits a high degree of fragmentation of personal values. It means being uncertain because of the variety of competing values or demands. In rhetoric aporia is a figure of speech in which, according to an illustrative quote from a work of 1657 provided by the Oxford English Dictionary,

> the speaker sheweth that he doubteth either where to begin for the Multitude of Matters, or what to do or say in some strange or ambiguous thing.

Aporia therefore means a position of moral uncertainty or confusion, either genuine or feigned.

The two dimensions can be used to identify twelve ethical roles for managers (see Figure 4.2). The definition of ethical used here is 'pertaining to the science of ethics or morality'; it is not being used as a synonym of good. The roles are not descriptions of fixed positions that people occupy. They are accounts of positions that people may adopt and abandon according to preference and circumstances.

|  | principle | policy | aporia |
|---|---|---|---|
| **Modernist** | *Radical critiquer* | *Systems developer* | *Cynic* |
| **Neo-traditionalist** | *Guru* | *Culture designer* | *Counsellor* |
| **Traditionalist** | *Mentor* | *Transactional manager* | *Ritualist* |
| **Postmodernist** | *Intellectual* | *Pragmatist* | *Games player* |

**Figure 4.2** Defining the managerial roles

The use of labels to characterise the roles can be dangerous. Terms such as counsellor and mentor have multiple, and not necessarily consistent, meanings. On some definitions the terms we have used may not fit the description of the role. The benefit of a catchy label is at the price of a loss of subtlety.

The ethical characteristics of the five stances will now be discussed to identify the characteristic dangers they may be prone to.

## The ethical limitations of prophets

Prophets want to act on the world, or at least their organisation, without the constraint of comment or caution from others. Their monocular ethical vision means they may do great harm if their vision happens to be wrong or bad. The top leadership of Enron for example developed a creative approach to accountancy that brooked no challenge but which led to its bankruptcy. Its leaders were thought charismatic and this, together with the lavish lifestyle given to those employees who survived their appraisals, protected them from challenge (Moon, 2003). The metaphor of prophets is very apt for Enron because, as Wheen (2003: 276–8) has pointed out it was a company run much as an Evangelical church and its leaders behaved like American TV preachers. Ken Lay, the Chief Executive, was a Methodist lay preacher. Not paying attention to questioning voices was seen as a small price to pay for share price growth. Such managers can be labelled systems designers; the purposes of the system are ignored but the organisation must be brought into compliance with the system.

Gurus are positive prophets who have a prescription for how things should be changed and people developed. They require disciples who will 'buy into' the particular values and principles they offer. Gurus offer a package, a commodified route to development. The stance seems particularly attracted to fads and fashion. Feng Shui has provided the latest source from which gurus can extract managerial wisdom. The 'Beyond Strategy' organisation, for example, that works in the Internet business has based its logo and its organisational philosophy on Feng Shui principles (Beyond Strategy, 2001).

Radical critiquers are an example of prophets who wish to change the world, or at least organisations, but may not have a clear idea of how. They are driven by disapproval of what is, rather than a vision of what might be. Parker (1998b: 35), for example, produced a critique of business ethics that argued that the concept could lead to a worsening of, and not an improvement in, organisational behaviour. It was sufficient for a critiquer to have identified the paradoxes within the concept.

> The problem I find it difficult to address in the rest of the paper will be what options are left for a project like 'Business Ethics' if all the above [paradoxes] are accepted. It would simply be inappropriate for me to tie up a paper like this at the end as if I really did have a magical solution to these problems.
>
> (Parker, 1998b: 35)

Radical critiquers' disapproval may have many sources including anti-globalisation, feminism and sustainability. It is arguable that such challenging of organisational values is good for organisations. The ethical danger is that such devil's advocacy can become unchallenged zealotry. Examples of this phenomenon are highly contested. Showalter (1997: Ch. 12) argued that some psychiatrists and social workers used the concept of satanic ritual abuse (SRA), the existence of which she disputed, as a means of radically critiquing society. Through seminars and discussions on the 'SRA conference circuit' professionals and patients 'learn to tell their stories' of SRA (Showalter, 1997: 180). In the UK some workers in the early 1990s acted on this new understanding and children were taken from their parents into care because of allegations of SRA. In two high profile cases subsequent investigation found no evidence to support the claims of ritual abuse and the social workers involved were criticised (Showalter, 1997: 172). Although such instances are rare they do show the ethical pitfalls the radical critique role may fall into.

The ethical danger posed by prophets is that they are closed to the challenges and dialogue that can test whether their criticisms, nostrums or systems are good.

## The ethical limitations of subjectivists

Subjectivists are doubters. They are the opposite of the prophets who doubt little. Questioning the way things are done shows engagement with the world, but it is beset with anxieties as the grounds of their questioning constantly shift. This is the Sartrean position that recognises that individuals make themselves through their own choices but also that people 'cannot transcend human subjectivity'. By this, Sartre (1957: 14) means that when we make a choice for ourselves we also, because we would never make an evil choice, make an implicit choice about how we believe all others should be. The ethical limitation of the subjectivists is that they do not believe in the existence of objective ethical standards and think everyone has to make their own choices while recognising that individuals' own choices implicitly impose expectations on others. They suffer an instability caused by the collective implications of their individualism.

The ethical dangers of the stance can be illustrated by western companies' uncertainty about how to respond to other countries and cultures in which they trade. A subjectivist may believe that the payment of 'grease' is wrong but may also think it inappropriate to insist on this principle when doing business in countries where corruption is the norm. Their reluctance of course may be purely practical but there are more principled examples of accommodations to local cultures against the individual's own preferences. An example might be western trainers' uncertainty about imposing their philosophy of learning in programmes delivered in post-soviet countries and designed to prepare managers, accustomed to the communist system, to operate within a free market economy. Hollinshead and Michailova (2001) for example report how western trainers' commitment to experiential learning waned when working with managers in Bulgaria and how they adapted their learning techniques to local expectations. Because they are unwilling to impose their views on others, subjectivists often end up with having others' views imposed on them.

Counsellors do not have the gurus' preferred solutions or the culture designers' concern with the corporate. They are subjectivists who seek to understand the individuals' own values and concerns and help them identify their own solutions.

The cynic is the epitome of the subjectivists who fail to cope with this existential angst.

As Chaudhuri (1987: 128) pointed out,

> cynicism tries to compensate for the loss of moral courage by airing malice.

Team or cascade briefings sometimes illustrate this effect. Marchington (*et al.*, 1989: 26, 28) discovered that managers who delivered such briefings could be sceptical, apathetic and casual towards the process.

> The briefers ... often made comments on the core [messages from the top management] which succeeded in diminishing its impact on the audience, either by using a poor example to convey a general message or by querying the basis on which the message was built.

Gamble and Kelliher (1999: 275) reported that briefings were often unsuccessful; briefers saw the sessions as 'ends in themselves as opposed to a means to an end' and such cynicism may have contributed to their reported poor, or even negative, impact on the listeners. This may have been less to do with cynicism than with the briefers' modernist concern with producing rational and instrumental communications systems that were safely within the culture of the organisation. They were not challenging that culture, as radical critiquers might, or despising it as cynics would. In this the briefers were taking the systems developer stance, which placed them between the radical critiquers and the cynics.

The ethical risk the subjectivists take is uncertainty. This can be an arbitrary subjectivism in which everyone acts for themselves. At a more sophisticated level it is an instability caused by only wishing to be responsible for oneself but accepting that this is impossible. Schwartz (1998) argues that this is the explanation of Peter Drucker's rejection of the concept of business ethics. Drucker takes the view that ethical responsibility lies with individuals. It cannot rest with collectives such as organisations and therefore codes of business ethics are pointless because they detract from individuals' accountability. However, individual responsibility can only be discharged and tested through dialogue within a community. The constant tug of individual expression against collective or communal action leads to ethical fragmentation or a distortion of ethical dialogue.

## The ethical limitations of rhetoricians

Rhetoricians enjoy debates in which some win and others lose. In appropriating the term rhetoric we are aware that it ought not to be seen pejoratively (Watson, 1994: 183) but as a common, unavoidable human skill. Games players however have allowed their skill at argument to become separated from their own convictions. The point for them is not to be right but to win. They create façades much as postmodern architects disguise industrial sheds behind jokey elevations when building factories or supermarkets. The façades that managers build are the performance metrics and annual reports that are required to keep top management content. Such material will be provided by managers despite their doubts about their worth. Games players will try to hype their role in the organisation in order to maintain their position and status (Legge, 1995: 317–24). The façades that (Human Resource Development HRD) practitioners for example build are the evaluation studies and annual reports that provide the 'bums on seats' and 'happy sheet' statistics that top management wish to see. In their professional magazines HRD practitioners are sometimes exhorted to

> toot your own horn. All the bottom line data in the world are worthless unless you can use them to market and promote HRD's services to the organisation.
>
> (Lookatch, 1991)

It follows that the characteristic ethical dangers of the rhetoricians' stance are persiflage, economy with the truth and lying. The case of Shell (*see* p. 72), not disclosing that its estimates of its oil reserves were inflated until it was forced to, is a good, recent example. An example of the dangers of the stance can be taken from a research interview we conducted as part of an earlier project (Fisher, 2000: 66). It concerned a manager who had just been appointed as Human Resource Director of a retail fashion chain. The company was taken to industrial tribunal over alleged discriminatory recruitment practices. The new director believed the allegations were true but nevertheless successfully defended the company at the tribunal because 'you have to put it right from the inside'. She had relished her skill at defending an unjust cause and felt the compromise was a necessary one to enable her to establish herself within the company and improve things in the long term.

The game player, the ritualist and the pragmatist make compromises and accommodations in their day-to-day work. Ritualists are like priests who no longer believe in God but who still find the liturgy comforting. They value the activity of management while having doubts about its point. Pragmatists are torn between a desire to disengage with the world because they know there are no easy fixes and a wish to make things better. Consequently they, like the ritualists and the games players, might risk allowing bad things to happen. They may lose their own sense of moral agency because compromise shifts responsibility, in part, to others.

## The ethical limitations of quietists

Quietism is the resignation of self to achieve contentment. It is a disengagement from the ethical problems of the world. Its ethical limitation is that a quietist manager would not see it as their role to react to wrongdoing within their organisation. The intellectual role exemplifies this ethical danger. It combines a willingness to stand on principle with a belief in the indeterminacy of languages and values. The instability of this combination leads them to value the internal intellectual process for itself. That is their principle and it leads to disengagement.

> More generally one should see the intellectual as having a special, idiosyncratic need, a need for the ineffable, the sublime, a need to go beyond the limits, a need to use words that are not a part of anyone's language game, any social institution. But one should not see the intellectual as serving any social purpose when he fulfils this need.
>
> (Rorty, 1985: 174)

The mentor role has quietist features but it allows an engagement with the world but only through the passing on of traditional values. The mentor sees themselves as a role model whom others should follow. But they are not evangelists and those who learn from them do so by observation and emulation.

Quietists are inclined not to act against unethical organisational behaviour. The most action a quietist might take is to resign from an organisation of whose behaviour they disapproved.

## The balancers

There are two managerial roles, the culture designer and the transactional manager, that are intermediate between the four stances. They are located in the middle of the matrix in Figure 4.1. Culture designers and transactional managers are at the point of balance between the four stances. Their ethical problem is maintaining the equilibrium. If culture designers lose their balance they will become either more like prophets or more like subjectivists. If the transactional manager becomes unbalanced they are more likely to move towards either the quietists' or the rhetoricians' stances.

Culture designers for example try to obtain employees' commitment to organisational values and missions while not undermining the employees' own values. Such attempts can easily become distorted and lead to the organisational values becoming more important. This can be illustrated by some HRD practitioners who, as was reported in the literature, used the metaphor of a car's service logbook to explain the purpose of personal development plans.

> As with any product, if they [the staff] become out of date, no longer meet their customers' requirements or ceased to offer a competitive product they would lose their share of the market and their ability to attract customer interest. Learning logs were also encouraged in this way – 'who would buy a second hand car without the service history and the log book?'
>
> (Floodgate and Nixon, 1994)

There is a contradiction within this approach. It requires an employee to confront and take responsibility for the limitations in their portfolio of competencies, but those limitations are defined by a comparison with a competency framework and set of core values that were designed to meet the needs of the organisation and not necessarily those of the individual. In developing themselves to conform to these expectations the employee might be distorting or denying their own values and ethical positions. In these situations the culture designer takes on the prophet's mantle.

The transactional manager is often stereotypically presented as the opposite of a 'can-do', transformational leader. Those in this role are unlikely to become prophet like. The ethical danger results from a lack of ambition. This can take one of two forms. If the transactional manager lacks commitment they will become games players with little more expectation than to keep their jobs. If they lack belief in their power to make things better they will become quietists.

These twelve roles have not simply been divided into good and bad roles. All the roles have been argued to possess potential ethical dangers though they are not necessarily all equally damaging. The logic of Figure 4.1 suggests that the culture designer and transactional manager roles are potentially less harmful than the other roles. It is not argued the ethical dangers will necessarily be realised. Most prophets do good, not harm; the angst of the subjectivists does not automatically hurt others. It is simply being argued that the different roles may fail ethically in distinctive ways, and the purpose of this discussion has been to identify the natures of those potential ethical failures.

## Activity 4.2

Think of a situation at work, or perhaps in some other context such as within a club or association you belong to, when you faced an ethical worry or issue. Which of the five stances – prophet, subjectivist, rhetorician, quietist or balancer – do you think was the one closest to your own in that situation? Did you avoid the ethical traps that the stance presented?

## Reflections

Our values are our ethical anchors. However, we each may find our values difficult to pin down. Schein (1993) has argued that we each have a 'career anchor', a value that is so important to us that we would rather lose our jobs, or in some other way be disadvantaged, rather than offend against it. The problem is that we may be uncertain about what that anchor, among our many professed values, may be until we are actually tested by some crisis or hurtful dilemma. At the same time we have argued in this chapter that when we fail morally at work we tend to fail in a way that is characteristic of our temperament and our stance. In other words it is not just what our values *are* that matters, but also how important those values are to us. Cathexis is a term from psychoanalysis; it refers to the strong sense of attachment that people may have towards their values and it is this commitment that drives people to act in the world (Young, 1977). The nature of a person's emotional attachment to a particular value may have many forms. A particular value may be

- something we keep to ourselves and use only to manage our personal lives (quietists) or

- things that we are aspire to for others (prophets and modernists) or

- straightforward truths that we do not question (traditionalists and neo-traditionalists) or

- things over which we agonise and debate (rhetoricians and pragmatists) or

- things that we can conveniently and playfully use to persuade people in arguments at work (rhetoricians and postmodernists).

All of these possibilities indicate that our connections with our values are not straightforward. This suggests that the belief, often put forward by management writers, that the role of senior management is to promulgate a mission and a set of values that everyone can accept looks naïve. People's response to their organisation's published values will be complex. They may accept them, for example, as ones they can work with even though they are not the same as their personal values. Or they may accept them ironically or mockingly such that their listeners are not sure whether they actually agree with them or not. More commonly they may agree with the values but doubt whether the top managers who published them have committed to, and are willing to act in accordance with, them. Such qualified acceptance of an organisation's values by managers and staff might not be a bad thing. As has been argued in the case of Enron the over-enthusiastic acceptance of an organisation's values may give it the characteristics of a cult, and that carries its own dangers. The Enron case also reminds us that there is no particular reason to believe that people who reach the top of organisational career ladders will be particularly ethical and therefore capable of being ethical leaders.

The complexities of people's connections with their values and with those of their organisations also raise doubts about the value of ethical leadership.

**Connexion point**
Ethical leadership is discussed in more detail in Chapter 10.

Employees may consider their leader a good ethical role model who exhibits, what Blanchard and Peale (1988) argued were, the cardinal virtues for organisational leaders: the five 'Ps' – pride, patience, prudence, persistence and perspective. The employees may not follow their leader's example to the extent of becoming role models themselves, or indeed even follow their leader's good example. The very act of putting a leader on an ethical pedestal may indicate that such good behaviour is only for those special enough to be leaders, and who can aspire to such ethical behaviour, and that other more ordinary people cannot possibly emulate them.

People do not simply 'have' values. Their values are constantly being redefined and prioritised as they find themselves in different situations and talking to different people. It is rare for people to be driven to such extremes that they discover what their value anchors, to misquote Schein, actually are. This analysis means those who believe an organisation should and can be managed so that everyone accepts the organisation's values are misguided. The term often used for such acceptance – buy-in – suggests a limited form of engagement. You only buy into something because you think it will be advantageous, not because you think it is right.

## Summary

In this chapter the following key points have been made:

- Ethics represents an intellectual approach to matters of morality at work whereas values represent a response based on beliefs that people hold with emotional attachment. Both perspectives need to be considered when dealing with business ethics matters.

- People may take one of five viewpoints on the role of values in business ethics: the traditional, the modernist, the neo-traditional, the postmodernist and the pragmatist. The position they take will reflect their responses to ethical issues at work.

- Which of these they adopt will depend, among other things, on their career history and experiences in organisation and on their education and training.

- It is not helpful to divide people in organisations into the ethical and the unethical. All managers have the potential to act badly, but the manner of the temptation, and the nature of their unethical activities will depend upon whether they see themselves as
  - Prophets
  - Subjectivists
  - Rhetoricians or
  - Quietists.

## Quick revision test

1. Which changes least quickly?
   (a) opinions
   (b) basic assumptions
   (c) attitudes

2. Pragmatism is ...
   (a) always taking the quick and easy option
   (b) a philosophy about how to live with the impossibility of an objective truth
   (c) a philosphical view that argues that corporations have no ethical responsibilities other than obeying the law

3. What are metanarratives?
   (a) Grand overarching ethical beliefs such as Marxism or Roman Catholicism
   (b) Folktales that carry moral messages
   (c) A technical term for the corporate identities and histories that companies present to their customers

4. What is quietism?
   (a) A stress busting technique
   (b) The belief a quiet approach can be an effective style of leadership
   (c) A commitment to passive contemplation and a withdrawal from the world (as far as possible!)

## Typical assignments and briefs

1. Compare the traditional view of values, as exemplified for example by the work of Rokeach, with the view that values emerge from a process of sense making. Which view might be more helpful in understanding the role of values in management?

2. How might people with different sensibilities (traditional, modern, neo-traditional, postmodern and pragmatist) understand the nature and role of values in organisations?

3. What criticisms can be made of a postmodern view of organisations and management? Are they justified?

4. 'The commonly accepted idea that management should define and publish a set of organisational core values may create as many problems as it resolves.' Discuss vigorously.

## Group activity 4

### The Rice Orientation Test (ROT)

This test was devised by our colleague Chris Rice. It is designed to alert you to your approach to ethical issues. It uses a distinction between hedonism, moralism and pragmatism. It is not a statistically validated test and so its results must be used as a trigger for reflection and no more.

Think about each of the headings in the boxes in turn. Decide whether that term causes you to think in terms of:

A – right and wrong
B – pleasure or pain
C – success or failure

Then decide whether the concept (A, B or C) that you have chosen is of High (Hi), medium (Me) or low (Lo) importance in your thinking about the headword in the box.

Then place a tick in the appropriate cell of the grid within the box. If you think about the lottery in terms of pleasure or pain but that this is only of medium importance in your thinking then place a tick in the central cell in the grid.

Carry on to complete all the boxes.

▶

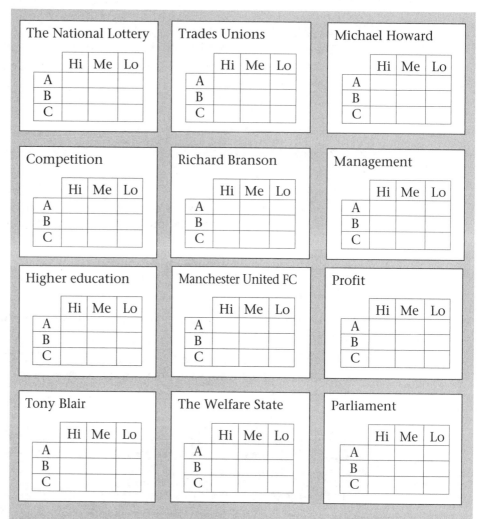

The twelve matrices, each with rows A, B, C and columns Hi, Me, Lo:

**The National Lottery** — Hi, Me, Lo / A, B, C

**Trades Unions** — Hi, Me, Lo / A, B, C

**Michael Howard** — Hi, Me, Lo / A, B, C

**Competition** — Hi, Me, Lo / A, B, C

**Richard Branson** — Hi, Me, Lo / A, B, C

**Management** — Hi, Me, Lo / A, B, C

**Higher education** — Hi, Me, Lo / A, B, C

**Manchester United FC** — Hi, Me, Lo / A, B, C

**Profit** — Hi, Me, Lo / A, B, C

**Tony Blair** — Hi, Me, Lo / A, B, C

**The Welfare State** — Hi, Me, Lo / A, B, C

**Parliament** — Hi, Me, Lo / A, B, C

Add up the number of ticks placed in each of the cells in the above matrices and transfer the totals into the table below. Calculate the weighted totals; and their percentage of the grand total, for each of the three rows in the table. The percentages show the relative importance to the respondent of moralism, hedonism and pragmatism.

| Scoring ROT | | | | | |
|---|---|---|---|---|---|
| | Hi (Nx3) | Med (Nx2) | Low (Nx1) | Total | % |
| A = Moralism | | | | | |
| B = Hedonism | | | | | |
| C = Pragmatism | | | | | |

Discuss your results with your colleagues in the group.

## Recommended further reading

Milton Rokeach's (1973) *The Nature of Human Values* is the classic work on the subject but pages 239–47 of Michael Billig's (1996) *Arguing and Thinking* provides a contrary view on the subject. The whole book is worth reading because it offers a new perspective based on the idea that thinking is entirely an argumentative process in which there are no fixed points, only constant debates, both within our heads and with other people. An implication of this is that the arguments never come to a definitive end, although people might have the last word on a particular occasion. This view has interesting implications for the role of values in business ethics that are followed up in Chapters 5 and 6. Terry Eagleton (1996) is not a management writer but he provides an intriguing introduction to postmodernism, *The Illusions of Postmodernism*. It is particularly relevant to the themes of this chapter because he treats postmodernism as a sensibility, a particular way of looking at the world, rather than as a set of philosophical ideas, although he also discusses many of these with a degree of humour. If you want to read a critique of the more (mostly French) extreme writings in a postmodernist mode then Sokal and Bricmont's (2003) *Intellectual Impostures* is good fun. An interesting book that explores management issues from a postmodern perspective is Gibson Burrell's *Pandemonium: Towards a Retro-organizational Theory* (1997, London: Sage). It has the distinction of being capable of being read back to front as well as in the normal direction.

For a wider account of how values can be fragmented or integrated in societies see Jonathan Friedman (1994) *Cultural Identity and Global Process*. On the topic of the role of values in management see Paul Griseri's (1998) *Managing Values*. There is an excessive number of 'how to manage with values' books. Two worth looking at are Rabindra Nath Kanungo and Manuel Mendonca (1996), *The Ethical Dimensions of Leadership* and Stephen Covey's (1991) *Principle Centred Leadership*.

## Useful websites

| Topic | Website provider | URL |
|---|---|---|
| Postmodernism resources and links | Roehampton University | http://www.roehampton.ac.uk/hacs/Links/PoMo.asp |
| Contemporary Philosophy, Critical Theory and Postmodern Thought | University of Colorado at Denver | http://carbon.cudenver.edu/~mryder/itc_data/postmodern.html |
| A useful overview on values and the issues of moral education and development | Huitt, W. (2004). Values. *Educational Psychology Interactive*. Valdosta, GA: Valdosta State University | http://chiron.valdosta.edu/whuitt/col/affsys/values.html |
| A very simple personal values questionnaire | Florida International University | http://www.fiu.edu/~pie/pvquestionnaire.htm |

## CHAPTER 5

# Values and heuristics

## Learning outcomes

Having read this chapter and completed its associated activities, readers should be able to:

- Explain the role of heuristics in decision making.
- Explain the concept of values and their role in thinking about ethical issues.
- Reflect upon how individuals' values may impact on their thinking about ethical issues.

## Introduction

This chapter considers how people think about and make ethical decisions in practice. It is in contrast to Chapter 2, which considered how philosophers and writers on ethics argued that people should think about ethical matters. The central theme of the chapter is the role of heuristics in human thinking. The argument is that people do not use a comprehensively rational process when they come to a view on moral matters. Rather, it will be argued, people use heuristics to ease the process of arriving at a view or taking a decision, and to simplify the mass of competing views and information that surround any issue.

### Connexion point

This chapter builds on the previous one because it gives an important role in ethical decision making to personal values.

The account of ethical thinking provided in this chapter is to some extent speculative. It presents an argument about how people might make up their minds on ethical matters. The argument is based on well-established ideas as well as on newly emerging theories, but their application to thinking on ethical matters is incomplete. Unusually for a textbook therefore it remains for you to make up your mind on the arguments presented.

> **DEFINITION**
>
> **Heuristics** are a means of discovering or finding out something. They are mental tricks of the trade or rules of thumb that are used, almost unconsciously, to simplify the process of decision making. They are cognitive devices that limit the need to search for, and evaluate, further options. The term also carries with it the idea of discovering things by trial and error rather than by systematic analysis of all appropriate information.

## Heuristic thinking

The idea of heuristic thinking can be illustrated by contrasting it with a rational approach to making a non-ethical decision such as choosing a car to buy. If this decision were to be approached from an analytical and rational position you would have to go through the following stages.

- Identify all the cars available on the market.

- Identify all the factors that are important to you in a car, such as cost, reliability, acceleration, colour and so on.

- Decide on the relative importance to you of the above criteria by either putting them into rank order or assigning weights to them.

- Research each car on the market and decide how they score against each of the criteria.

- Calculate the degree to which each car would satisfy your wishes by combining the cars' performances against each criterion with the criterion's importance, so that cars that do well against the more important criteria will have the higher scores.

- Choose the car that scores highest in these calculations.

The process just described is called subjective expected utility. This is because the decision-maker makes a personal (subjective) assessment of both what is important to them about a car (utility) and the chances (expected) that any particular car would actually provide that value.

This is obviously a time-consuming process. A heuristic approach would simplify it. A large number of heuristics could be involved in deciding which car to buy. Here are just a few. To begin with you would probably not evaluate every car available on the market but simply focus on those you have been made aware of by advertising. This is the availability heuristic. The recency heuristic might mean that a pleasurable trip last weekend in a friend's new car weighs heavily in your preference for that model. Your dislike of the colour purple might mean that the purple car you have been considering seems to have a lot of factors that turn you against it. This is an example of the halo and horns heuristic that is explained on p. 184. The application of one or more of these heuristics will leave you with a narrow range of cars to choose from and an intuitive inclination to buy one particular car.

Let us move on to consider decision making about ethical matters. Benjamin Franklin proposed, in the eighteenth century, the use of a moral algebra to resolve such issues (Gigerenzer *et al.*, 1999: 76). This was similar to the rational and analytical model, described above, for choosing a car. He would divide a sheet of paper into two columns and head one 'Pros' and the other 'Cons'. He would then identify the factors for or against a particular course of action. On further consideration he would strike out some pros and cons because they cancelled each other out. If two cons were, in his view, equal to one pro he would strike out all three. As a result of this process he would come to a balanced view about the right thing to do.

If we applied moral algebra to an ethical question we might find, but not necessarily, deontological pros ranged against consequentialist cons. Rights would have to be weighed against justice and equity and the virtuous mean might be hard to find. Giving equal consideration to potentially mutually exclusive ways of thinking about ethical questions may lead to confusion. Some writers (Kaler, 1999) suggest that the way business schools teach business ethics ('well, you could look at it from a deontological viewpoint or alternatively from a consequentialist position') encourages such confusion. It will be argued, contrarily, that people tend not to combine all the ethical perspectives on an issue but choose one and use it in a heuristic manner.

It is further argued in this chapter that values and emotions can perform the role of decision-making heuristics. Two examples of the role of values as heuristics in ethical decision making are provided to illustrate the process.

- The first example focuses on priority setting and uses the case of resource allocation in health care management.

- The second example concerns ideas of integrity and loyalty as decision-making heuristics. Each of these is explained, and illustrated by an Activity.

## Decision-making heuristics

The idea has long been recognised that people do not possess the capacity to obtain and process the amounts of information necessary in order to take a rational approach to decision making. Herbert Simon's (1983) concept of bounded rationality is the classic formulation of this viewpoint. Search behaviour is the process of looking for the information and options necessary to make a decision. Bounded rationality sets limits on the extent of such searches. He introduced the concept of satisficing, which is the process of searching for and evaluating options until one finds one that is good enough. He recognised that this solution may not be the best or optimal one. If the decision-maker had continued to identify and assess options better ones might have been found. But, he argued, once a solution has been found that will do, the psychological and practical costs to the decision-maker of looking for the best solution outweigh the additional benefits of a best solution that may not, in any case, be found. Simon's work emphasised that fully rational decision making was at best an aspiration and that the way people actually made up their minds about things was less analytical and was based more on trial and error – which is one definition of a heuristic.

## Base-rate neglect

In the 1970s psychologists, among them Kahneman, Slovic and Tversky (1982) studied the exercise of judgement. In particular they investigated how people made estimates about the probability or likelihood of situations and events. The research was carried out using questionnaires. The box below presents an example of the questions they asked.

---

### Blue taxi or green taxi?

A taxi was involved in a hit and run accident at night. Two taxi companies, the green and the blue, operate in the city. You are given the following data:

(a) 85 per cent of the taxis in the city are green and 15 per cent blue.
(b) A witness identified the cab as blue. The court tested the reliability of the witness under the same circumstances that existed on the night of the accident and concluded that the witness correctly identified each of the two colours 80 per cent of the time and failed 20 per cent of the time.

What is the probability that the cab involved in the accident was blue rather than green?

(*Source*: Kahneman *et al.*, 1982: 156–7)

---

This example identifies a heuristic (known as base-rate neglect) that leads people to pay more attention to immediate sources of information (the witness's statement) and to ignore background information (such as the relative frequency of the two types of cabs). The correct answer, derived from Bayes' theorem (which takes both items of data into account), is 0.41.

---

### DEFINITION

**Bayes theorem** includes both prior and current information when calculating a probability. It is not necessary for you to know the mathematics but for those who are curious there is a useful Bayes' theorem calculator on the Web at http://faculty.vassar.edu/lowry/bayes.html.

If you put into this calculator

- the probability that the taxi will be blue – 0.15 (P(A)),
- the probability that the witness will correctly identify the taxi as green if it is green, which is 0.68 (P $(B|{\sim}A) = 0.8 \times 0.85$) and
- the probability of the witness identifying the taxi as green if it is green, which is 0.12 (P $(B|A) = 0.15 \times 0.8$ .

it gives the probability of the taxi being blue as 0.41.

Most people, when asked to answer this question, however, ignored the data in point (a) because they were considered too general and distant from the event, and produced an answer around 80 per cent, which was based on the information given in point (b) alone.

The research questions were constructed so that if a heuristic were present respondents would misuse or neglect important information and give incorrect answers. The inference was then drawn that heuristics were a source of bias and prejudice in judgement. In hindsight it can be objected that the questions were so deviously constructed that they did not represent the kinds of judgement people have to make in real life. If so, the possibility remains that in everyday situations the heuristics might not be a cause of error.

## Other heuristics

A large number of heuristics are identified in Hogarth (1980). Just a few will be mentioned here. The recency effect was mentioned in the example of the car-buying decision mentioned above. This heuristic causes people to put more weight on information they have collected recently and to undervalue things they may have learned in the past. The halo and horns heuristic has long been known to selection and recruitment specialists. This heuristic leads people to latch on to one aspect of an interviewee to which they have a strong like or dislike. It may be the fact that the interviewee has a moustache or is wearing blue suede shoes. This one feature then dominates the recruiter's whole assessment of the individual. They might think that a man with a moustache cannot really be trusted, or that anyone who wears blue suede shoes must be just the sort of creative person the company needs. The heuristics-and-biases programme of research established the existence of heuristics in judgement but suggested that they were a problem.

A current programme of research led by the ABC research group, based in Berlin, has revisited heuristics and come to the conclusion that far from being a distortion of decision making they are both necessary and effective. The programme is intended to 'capture how real minds make decisions under constraints of limited time and knowledge' (Gigerenzer *et al.*, 1999: 5). They reject the rational, subjective, expected utility model as a description of decision making and instead propose the idea of fast and frugal heuristics. These are rules for limiting the search for information and options, and for making choices, that employ a minimum of time, knowledge and computation. They argue that fast and frugal heuristics are bounded rationality in its purest form.

The working of fast and frugal heuristics can best be explained by an example. One of the heuristics is the recognition heuristic that applies to situations where a person has to decide which of two objects has a higher value on a particular criterion. The heuristic is defined as follows: 'If one of the two objects is recognised and the other is not, then infer that the recognised object has the higher value' (Gigerenzer *et al.*, 1999: 41). In an experiment they asked students at the University of Chicago and the University of Munich the question, 'Which city has more inhabitants: San Diego or San Antonio?' Sixty-four per cent of the Chicago students got the answer right, but 100 per cent of the Munich students gave the correct answer. Why did the German students do better? They had heard of San Diego but not of San Antonio. They applied the recognition heuristic and got it right. The American students recognised both cities and could not apply the recognition heuristic. They had to search their memories for further clues as to the right answer. The additional information merely confused them. There is of course logic to the recognition heuristic; cities of which you have heard are more likely to be bigger than those that are unknown to you. The heuristic uses this logic as the basis of a very simple decision rule. But because of the logic the heuristic is not only simple; it is effective.

Of course there are many situations in which the recognition heuristic cannot be used because both of the options are recognised. Gigerenzer *et al.* (1999: Chapter 4) used a computer simulation to evaluate some simple heuristics for searching through data for solutions in such circumstances. As in their work reported above the simulation was based on the task of deciding which, of pairs of cities, was the larger. They built into the simulation a series of ten cues or clues about each of the cities. Whether a city was a capital or not was one clue. In the database of information, which was to be searched in the simulation, the cue was recorded as positive (if it was a capital city) because a capital city was likely to be larger than a city that was not, as negative (if it was not) or as a 'don't know'. Some additional information was included about the reliability of each cue (how often its use could give the right answer) and how often it would prove useful (as only one city can be a capital city you will not often have an opportunity to use it to discriminate between pairs of cities). In the simulation six search strategies were tested. The first three were based on heuristic principles.

1. *Minimalist.* Choose one of the ten cues at random. If one of the pair of cities you have to decide between scores a positive on this cue and the other a negative then choose the positive city as the larger one. If not go on trying cues randomly in turn until one provides an answer.

2. *Take the last.* Choose whichever cue worked well last time this kind of decision had to be made.

3. *Take the best.* In this strategy some of the information about the reliability and usefulness of the cues is used to decide which cue is likely to provide the most accurate answer.

The other three search strategies were all based on the rational model. They were:

- Franklin's rule

- Dawe's rule

- Multiple regression.

We will not explain each of these in detail. It is sufficient to point out that they all shared one common feature, that, when choosing between two cities, they aggregated all ten cues about each city in order to decide which was likely to be bigger. The heuristic strategies, in contrast, only used cues one at a time and when a decision had been reached ignored all the other cues.

The results from the simulation are shown in Table 5.1. The results suggest that not only are heuristics efficient because they give answers by using less

**Table 5.1** The results of the simulation comparing heuristic and rational research strategies

| Type of strategy | Strategy | Frugality (no. of cues looked up) | Accuracy (% of correct answers) |
|---|---|---|---|
| **Heuristic** | Take the last | 2.6 | 64.5 |
| | Minimalist | 2.8 | 64.7 |
| | Take the best | 3.0 | 65.8 |
| **Rational** | Franklin's rule | 10.0 | 62.1 |
| | Dawe's rule | 10.0 | 62.3 |
| | Multiple regression | 10.0 | 65.7 |

Source: Gigerenzer et al., 1999: 87

information than the rational strategies, but they are also as accurate as the rational techniques. The fast and frugal researchers see heuristics as (generally) effective strategies for making decisions. This leaves open the possibility that ethical thinking, as well as judgement, might be a heuristic process.

## Values as heuristics in ethical reasoning

In this section we want to move away from what is established in the literature and to speculate about how the fast and frugal heuristics may apply to ethical decision making. The argument is that heuristics operate in ethical decision making and that values are the basis of these heuristics.

Gigerenzer et al. (1999: 30) pointed out that, while most of the fast and frugal research concerns cognitive heuristics, emotions and social norms can also act as heuristics. For example a social norm such as 'copy the choices made by your social peers' acts as an efficient heuristic for stopping further searching for other options. This heuristic might be particularly powerful in academic recruitment procedures in which academics apparently appoint those whom they think their colleagues would approve of. Emotions, such as love for one's child, prevent wasteful ethical dithering. If a child screams in the night the emotional response forces the parent to get out of bed and comfort the child. Such parents do not calculate whether the greatest utility is achieved by this action or whether staying in bed so that they might be fresher for work the next day might do greater good. Four categories of moral emotions have been identified (Haidt, 2003) that, once elicited by some event, act as a trigger or create a tendency to act in a particular way. They are:

- Other condemning – contempt, anger and disgust.
- Self-conscious – shame, embarrassment and guilt.
- Other suffering – compassion.
- Other praising – gratitude and elevation.

If emotions and social norms can act as heuristics then it is possible that values can also do so. This is because values are closely related to emotions and social norms. Values are like emotions because people find it hard to give a rational account of why their values are important to them; they just are (Eden *et al.*, 1979). The link with social norms derives from the fact that values are acquired as part of the process of growing up and becoming socialised in a society. It is this early acquisition of values, according to Rokeach (1973: 17–18) that makes values simpler and more robust than attitudes.

## Illustration of values acting as heuristics

The ways in which values may act as heuristics can be illustrated by considering a well-known management development exercise called *Cave Rescue* (Woodcock, 1979, 1989: 81). In this exercise groups have to decide how to allocate scarce resources between people who are described in thumbnail sketches which are deliberately brief and partisan. *Cave Rescue* concerns six volunteers in a psychological experiment that requires them to be in a pothole. The cave is flooding and the research committee in charge of the experiment have called for a rescue team. When the team arrive they will only be able to rescue one person at a time because of the narrowness of the cave's entrance. The committee have to decide the order in which the volunteers will be saved from the cave when the rescue party arrive. The exercise provides a good opportunity to study the values that are articulated in such debates.

Observations of people doing the exercise suggest that they used their preferred values to select the information from the thumbnail sketches that they consider useful. Each of the characters in the *Cave Rescue* exercise has positive and negative aspects included in their thumbnail sketches. Some material about each of the characters has to be edited out for other information to become useful in making the necessary ranking decisions. A number of different values are used that include:

- Maximising the number of people who are saved by rescuing first those likely to panic and hamper the rescuers.

- Maximising the happiness of society by rescuing first those who can make the greatest contribution to society (utilitarianism).

- Rescuing first those who have the most family or other dependants.

- Rescuing the youngest first because the oldest have already had their opportunity for life.

- Rescuing the morally worthy before the morally unworthy.

The heuristic use of values can be explained by reference to volunteer Paul who, according to the information given to the participants, has been convicted of indecent assault. But he also has, in his working notes, details of a cheap cure for rabies. People who used the morality criterion to choose whom to rescue assumed that the cure could be understood from the working notes (and that in any case he was bound to have a research assistant who understood and could continue the work) and that there was, consequently, no barrier to using his behaviour to decide his order of rescue. Other people, using a utilitarian value, assumed that it was impossible to make sense of the working notes. This allowed them, when making their decision, to ignore Paul's criminal activities and concentrate on his potential contribution to society. People edited out, or rationalised into insignificance, that information which inhibited the application of their preferred values.

## How values are used as heuristics

So far, the argument seems straightforward. Values are simple but strongly held beliefs such as the importance of honesty. People, it is suggested, use values as filters to reduce the amount of information they take into account when making a decision. Values may act as a fast and frugal heuristic for limiting the amount of search behaviour. To the three heuristic search strategies proposed by Gigerenzer *et al.*, 1999 – *see* p. 185 – might be added another one: choose a cue that you like because it fits with your values.

If people do not change their values ethical decisions ought to be easy. But it is not. Ethical issues are often seen as dilemmas that are not easily resolved. According to Billig (1996: 238–47) values may be simple in themselves but in at least two ways they are complex matters of controversy.

- The first concerns the interpretations of the values. Their very simplicity makes them banal. This in turn means that they have to be interpreted before they can be of use in making decisions. An example can be taken from health care management. Everyone in the field would agree that patients come first. But different health care professionals may make sense of this value in different ways. For some it would mean improving the patients' clinical condition. Others might say it is empowering the patients to take control of their treatment and their condition. Yet others might claim it means making the patient physically comfortable and at psychological ease.

- The second source of argument and conflict over values is the multiplicity of conflicting values in any given society. This can be illustrated by referring to Table 4.1. Ambition, for example, may clash with honesty. Ethical issues are often difficult because it may not be certain which value, from a variety of contradictory values, should be applied in any given situation.

The problem for someone faced with an ethical matter is to choose which of many values to apply to the situation. This brings us back to a feature of fast and frugal heuristics as described by Gigerenzer *et al.* (1999: 30). They proposed that people are equipped with a psychological adaptive toolbox that is filled with a jumbled collection of one-function tools. Just as a mechanic manages to choose the right tool to repair a car so people choose the best heuristic to hand to help them make their mind up or take a decision.

In the next two sections we explore the ways in which particular values might be used.

# Value heuristics and priority setting

Resource allocation is a particular form of priority setting. It involves deciding which things are more important and which less. In this section it is argued that right answers to problems of priority setting cannot be found by technical means. Priority setting is a matter of values. The person setting the priorities has to decide which values they will use to determine relative importance. Whether a particular set of priorities is right or wrong depends upon the values used to judge it. This makes that priority setting an ethical matter.

This section explores the use of values as heuristics for making decisions in ethical matters, using a simulation exercise called *Monksbane and feverfew*. The exercise is based on a problem in health care management. A limited budget has to be divided between two health care programmes, one aimed at the diagnosis and treatment of monksbane and the other at the diagnosis and treatment of feverfew, both dangerous diseases. The problem is to decide which programme should be given priority. Fisher (1998) identified six values concerning priority setting in the allocation of resources. They are listed here but will be defined later in the chapter:

1. utility

2. individual need

3. deservingness

4. ecology

5. fairness

6. personal competence and gain.

In *Monksbane and feverfew* there are opportunities to apply each of these values in setting your priorities between the two programmes. Whichever you choose will lead to a different allocation of resources. It may be that you will change your mind as you work through the simulation. Do Activity 5.1 now and then the different values will be explained.

| Activity 5.1 | Monksbane and feverfew: A diagnostic instrument about values in public sector resource allocation |
|---|---|

### Introduction

In this questionnaire you imagine yourself to be a manager responsible for screening programmes for two diseases, feverfew and monksbane.

You have a total budget of £70,000 (£70k) to spend on these two programmes. In this questionnaire you will be presented with some initial information and asked to say how you would divide up the budget between the two diseases. In the subsequent sections you will be given additional information, and for each additional piece of information you will be asked to review the use of the budget available to you.

▶

- All the information you will be given is mutually consistent, i.e. information at the end of the questionnaire will not invalidate earlier information.

- Answer the questions in order. Do not look ahead.

- Once you have answered a section please do not return to it later and change it.

- There are no 'right' answers to the questions in this questionnaire. It's all a matter of your own values.

- Please make your allocations of the budget between monksbane and feverfew in units of £5,000 (£5k), i.e. £0, £5k, £10k and so on.

(*Source*: Fisher, 1998)

**Section 1**

The graph below tells you the number of lives that will be saved as a consequence of different levels of expenditure on the two diseases. The graph is based upon sound research conducted by the Paracelsus Epidemiological Institute. You need have no doubt about its accuracy.

The result of splitting the £70k equally between the two diseases would be:

| | |
|---|---|
| No. of lives saved as a result of spending £35k on monksbane | 7 |
| No. of lives saved as a result of spending £35k on feverfew | <u>59</u> |
| Total no. of lives saved | <u>66</u> |

Feverfew and monksbane affect men and women equally and also affect the same age group and social classes.

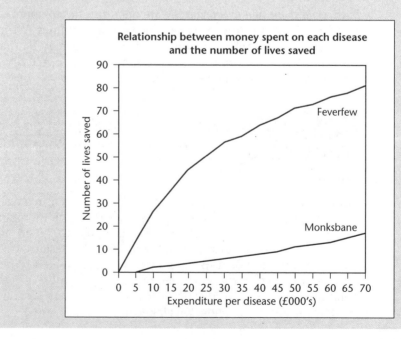

How much of the £70k do you think ought to be spent on monksbane?

£

When you have written your decision in the box please go to Section 2.

### Section 2

Monksbane is a much more dangerous disease than feverfew. If people with early signs of the disease are not identified through screening and treated there is a certain (100 per cent) chance they will die of the disease. Feverfew on the other hand can be fatal but the chances are smaller. If sufferers with feverfew are not identified and treated there is only a 57 per cent chance that they will die of the disease.

There have been great advances in the medical understanding of monksbane and only 5 per cent of people treated die from the disease. The death rate among patients treated for feverfew is 38 per cent.

Assume that currently no money at all is being spent on monksbane. How much of the £70k do you think ought to be spent on monksbane and how much on feverfew, as a result of the information given on this page?

| Monksbane | £ |
|-----------|---|
| Feverfew  | £ |

If the figure you have put in the monksbane box is £10k or less please go to Section 3b. If it is more than £10k please go to Section 3a.

### Section 3a

Feverfew is a disease that can be caught by anybody. Monksbane, however, is much more likely to be contracted by people with certain habits and lifestyles which they have chosen to adopt.

Another characteristic of monksbane is the tendency for sufferers to be of a particular personality type. They are of a choleric disposition: aggressive, demanding and ungrateful. This relationship has been well researched by the eminent group of scientists from St Barty's who have recently published their work on personality and disease. This relationship has always been well known in popular folklore. It is the origin of the disease's name since sufferers were the bane in the life of monk almoners and hospitalers in medieval monasteries.*

Bearing in mind this information how much do you now think ought to be spent on monksbane?

£

Please go to Section 4 when you have put your decisions in the box.

*Adam of Barnsley (1372) *De Natura et Nomine Opus Malleficarum.*

### Section 3b

Monksbane is a disease that can be caught by anybody. Feverfew, however, is much more likely to be contracted by people with certain habits and lifestyles which they have chosen to adopt. Another characteristic of feverfew is the tendency for sufferers to be of a particular personality type. They are of a choleric disposition: aggressive, demanding and ungrateful. This relationship has been well researched by an eminent group of scientists from St Barty's who have recently published their work on personality and disease. However this relationship has always been known in popular folklore. As Victorian doggerel had it,

'e's a gringer and as poisonous as yew is the man whats got feverfew.'*

Bearing in mind this information how much do you now think ought to be spent on feverfew?

£

Please go to Section 4 when you have put your decision in the box above.

*F. Smith Jnr (1978) *Semiotics and Ethnomethodology of Disease in Victorian England*, California: Albertus Publishers.

### Section 4

A recent television programme in the 'Medicine and Society' series has highlighted the problems of monksbane sufferers and it has caused a tremendous increase in the donations received by the MRC (Monksbane Research Society). This money is only available for research and cannot be used for screening or treatment. There is a very powerful national pressure group representing the needs of monksbane victims and they have the ear of several key members of your health consumer watchdog body. In addition your organisation employs a number of consultant medical staff who have made their reputations developing treatments for monksbane.

There is pressure from these groups to spend *more* on monksbane than you are currently spending, i.e. more than you have agreed to spend on monksbane in any of the previous sections.

Bearing in mind this new information how much of the £70k do you now think ought to be spent on monksbane?

£

When you have entered your decision in the box please go to Section 5.

### Section 5

Your research indicates that the percentage of the population that can be screened for each disease, and therefore the proportion of sufferers from each disease that can be identified and treated, is as shown in the following table.

*Identifying and treating sufferers*

| Amount spent on screening £K | Percentage of feverfew sufferers identified | Percentage of monksbane sufferers identified |
|---|---|---|
| 10 | 30 | 5 |
| 20 | 51 | 10 |
| 30 | 63 | 15 |
| 40 | 72 | 20 |
| 50 | 79 | 25 |
| 60 | 86 | 30 |
| 70 | 92 | 40 |

This means that an expenditure of £10k on feverfew and £60k on monksbane will enable you to treat 30 per cent of the sufferers from both diseases. To put it in other words, people with the two diseases will have an equal chance of being identified and treated.

Assume that at present the £70k available is split between the two diseases as follows:

feverfew        £40k
monksbane       £30k

Bearing in mind this new information how much of the £70k do you now think ought to be spent on monksbane?

£

Please go to Section 6 when you have written your decision in the box.

**Section 6**

It would be possible to treat the £70k budget for feverfew and monksbane as a combined budget and not allocate it between the two diseases. That means you would treat feverfew and monksbane sufferers as they presented themselves through their GPs until the budget ran out (if it did).

Would you take up this option to run a combined budget and work on a first come/first served basis?

Please tick the appropriate box and then go to Section 7.

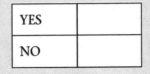

| YES | |
|---|---|
| NO | |

## Section 7

What is your current allocation of the £70k between the two diseases?

Monksbane  £ [        ]    Feverfew  £ [        ]

If you are planning to spend most of the £70k on feverfew complete this section.

You have just been told that someone very close to you is suffering from monksbane. How would you now allocate the budget between the two diseases?

Monksbane  £ [        ]    Feverfew  £ [        ]

If you are planning to spend most of the £70k on monksbane complete this section.

You have just been told that someone very close to you is suffering from feverfew. How would you now allocate the budget between the two diseases?

Monksbane  £ [        ]    Feverfew  £ [        ]

Now proceed to the scoring and interpretation information.

### Scoring and interpretation of monksbane and feverfew

Evaluate your answers by working through the boxes below.

### Section 1

How much did you decide to spend on monksbane?  £ [        ]

- If it is zero (£0) then you score HIGH on UTILITY.
- If it is £20k or less then you score MEDIUM on UTILITY.
- If it is more than £20k you score LOW on UTILITY.

### Section 2

How much did you decide to spend on monksbane?  £ [        ]

- If it is £15k or less you score LOW on INDIVIDUAL NEED.
- If it is more than £15k but less than £35k you score MEDIUM on INDIVIDUAL NEED.
- If it is £35k or more you score HIGH on INDIVIDUAL NEED.

If you answered Section 3b ignore this box.

## Section 3a

How much did you decide to spend on monksbane?    £ [            ]

- If this is the same amount as you decided in Section 2 you score LOW on DESERVINGNESS.
- If you have reduced the amount spent on monksbane by a third or less compared with the amount in Section 2 you score MEDIUM on DESERVINGNESS.
- If you have reduced the amount spent on monksbane by more than a third compared with the amount you spent in Section 2 then you score HIGH on DESERVINGNESS.

If you answered Section 3a ignore this box.

## Section 3b

How much did you decide to spend on feverfew in Section 2?    £ [            ]

How much did you decide to spend on feverfew in Section 3b?    £ [            ]

- If the two amounts are the same you score LOW on DESERVINGNESS.
- If you have reduced the amount spent on feverfew by a third or less compared with the amount in Section 2 you score MEDIUM on DESERVINGNESS.
- If you have reduced the amount spent on feverfew by more than a third compared with the amount in Section 2 then you score HIGH on DESERVINGNESS.

## Section 4

How much did you decide to spend on monksbane?    £ [            ]

- If this is the same as you spent on monksbane in Sections 3a or 3b you score LOW on ECOLOGY.
- If the amount is £5k more than you spent in Sections 3a or 3b you score MEDIUM on ECOLOGY.
- If the amount is £10k or more than you spent in Sections 3a or 3b you score HIGH on ECOLOGY.

## Sections 5 and 6

How much did you decide to spend on monksbane in Section 5?    £ [            ]

▶

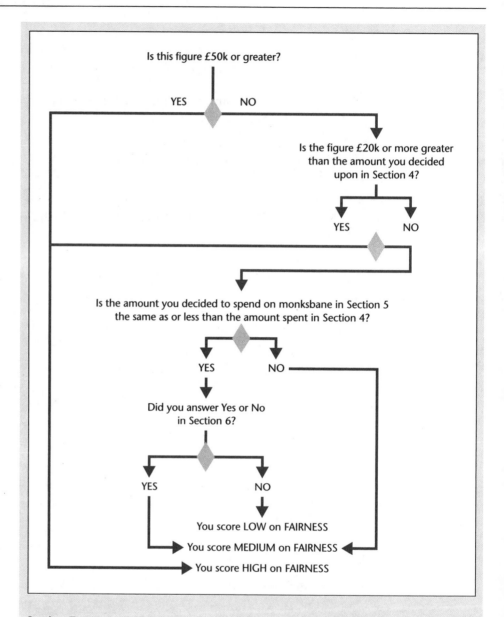

Is this figure £50k or greater?

YES    NO

Is the figure £20k or more greater than the amount you decided upon in Section 4?

YES    NO

Is the amount you decided to spend on monksbane in Section 5 the same as or less than the amount spent in Section 4?

YES    NO

Did you answer Yes or No in Section 6?

YES    NO

You score LOW on FAIRNESS

You score MEDIUM on FAIRNESS

You score HIGH on FAIRNESS

**Section 7**

- If you increased the sum spent on the disease which affects you personally, then you score HIGH on PERSONAL COMPETENCE AND GAIN.

- If you kept the allocation the same you are LOW on PERSONAL COMPETENCE AND GAIN.

- If you decreased the allocation you are VERY LOW on PERSONAL COMPETENCE AND GAIN.

Transfer your score to the grid in the table below by placing ticks in the appropriate cells.

| Heuristic | Low | Medium | High |
|---|---|---|---|
| Utility | | | |
| Individual need | | | |
| Deservingness | | | |
| Ecology | | | |
| Fairness | | | |
| Personal competence and gain | | | |

*Source*: Fisher (1998)

# The value heuristics of resource allocation

Each of the six value heuristics for resource allocation will be explained by reference to the information provided to the decision-maker in *Monksbane and feverfew*.

## Utility

Utility is a value concerned with allocating resources in a way that maximises the common good (or the beneficial impact of services). Utility values the maximisation of the quantity of good done. It is a form of utilitarianism.

In Section 1 of *Monksbane and feverfew* you are given enough information to apply utility as a value. If the graph is studied carefully it is clear that at any point money spent on feverfew will always save more lives than will be saved by spending it on monksbane. The way to save the most lives is to spend all the money on feverfew and none on monksbane. Those who make this decision are using the utility value. Not everyone can bear to do this. Those who know that rationally any money spent on monksbane costs the lives of feverfew sufferers, who might otherwise have been saved, may find themselves unable to spend nothing on monksbane at all. They therefore decide to spend a small amount on its treatment. This suggests that they are not entirely at ease with the utility value.

Utility is the heuristic that underwrites much management theory, and management science in particular. The development of QALYs, in health policy studies, provides an illustration of this approach. QALY stands for quality-adjusted life years (Gudex, 1986) and is a measure of the benefit, to the average patient, of a medical treatment in terms of additional years of life and of the quality of life. Once the benefit of a medical intervention is measured its cost can be calculated to produce a ranking of treatments in cost-effectiveness terms. Haemodialysis produced a cost per QALY of £9,075 while for scoliosis surgery the cost was £194. The latter treatment will therefore produce more benefit for any given sum of money than the former. There have been many criticisms of the utilitarian QALY approach, as reported in Pereira (1989) and Baldwin *et al.* (1990), but it is still persuasive to many.

**Connexion point**

The heuristic of utility relates to the general ethical tradition of utilitarianism that is discussed in Chapter 3, pp. 127–36.

## Individual need

Individual need is the value that can be triggered by the cues and information given in Section 2 of *Monksbane and feverfew*. This value holds that resources should be allocated in proportion to people's needs. Needs can of course be attributed to groups of people but those who adopt this value prefer to consider people as individuals. Needs are not the same as wants or demands, however. A need can only be defined by an expert in the field, in the cases of monksbane and feverfew by a doctor. Needs have two further characteristics: they can be objectively described, which means that it is possible for someone to have a need they do not know about, and, secondly, they can be ranked so that some are seen as more pressing than others.

The information provided in Section 2 of *Monksbane and feverfew* suggests that people who suffer from monksbane have greater need than those ill with feverfew. Monksbane patients are much more likely to die if not treated than feverfew patients. The information in Section 2 also highlights another aspect of individual need. It is the belief that if there are the means and the technology to improve people's lot then we are obliged to use them. In a medical setting it is the belief that everything that can be done, that has some chance of providing some benefit to the patient, should be done. It is to be noted that more can be done to treat people with monksbane than can be done for those with feverfew. If someone adopts the individual need value therefore, they will decide to spend significant sums of money on the treatment of monksbane.

The problem with individual need as a value is that it wills the expenditure of money without any regard for the availability of that money.

## Deservingness

The deservingness heuristic, which is made available in Sections 3a and 3b of Activity 5.1, divides people into two moral classes, the deserving and the undeserving. When resources are being distributed according to the deservingness heuristic the favourable allocation is given to the former and the unfavourable portion to the latter. Deservingness is an Edwardian concept. This traditional view saw the provenance of all poverty and need in individual moral failure and indolence. The growing depersonalisation and alienation of social life, caused by nineteenth-century industrialisation, made this view untenable, and a distinction was drawn between the deserving poor, brought low by social and economic factors beyond their control, and the undeserving poor, whose failure was of their own doing. New possibilities for morally classifying people have emerged since Edwardian times. People can be allocated to moral categories according to whether they are, on the one hand, greedy, truculent and ungrateful or, on the other, meek, humble and full of gratitude. The final moral criterion is group membership. The deserving person is one of us; the undeserving person is an outsider.

In more recent times the debate about the funding of treatment for sufferers from AIDS suggests that the distinction between the morally deserving and the undeserving is still current. Academic writing on the subject has been concerned with whether the treatment of AIDS sufferers is cost effective (Eastwood and Maynard, 1990). But there were arguments put forward, particularly in the press, which suggested that AIDS patients should be seen as 'less eligible' for treatment because they had visited the illness upon themselves through homosexual behaviour or drug abuse. It is, perhaps, the effect of deservingness that accounts for the different public perceptions of the plights of haemophiliacs, who acquired the disease through the necessary treatment of their primary illness, and that of homosexuals who, more likely, acquired it as a result of chosen behaviours. Whilst the UK government was initially curmudgeonly in the question of compensation for haemophiliacs, who had become HIV positive from being treated with infected blood products, public opinion clearly thought they should be compensated quickly (Mihil, 1990). There was a popular temptation to see haemophiliacs as deserving, and homosexuals as undeserving, and to fund their programmes accordingly.

In *Monksbane and feverfew* you are informed that people with the disease to which you have given the biggest share of the budget are ungrateful and truculent and that their behaviour has contributed towards their condition. If you are attracted to the value of deservingness you will have little patience with these people and decide to spend less on their treatment. However, if you do not hold this value you will probably regard all the information given in this section as irrelevant to the problem and decide to leave the budget allocation unaltered.

> **Connexion point**
>
> The heuristic of deservingness has some connections with the largely American philosophy of objectivism that is associated with Ayn Rand whose ideas are discussed in Chapter 3, pp. 122–3. This philosophy emphasises the moral independence of individuals. Those who do not rise to this challenge are undeserving.

## Ecology

The apologists for the ecology heuristic take a very different approach. They see clients as morally autonomous agents who are not passive recipients of services but actors within the resource-allocation process. Put simply the ecology value states that the voices of all the parties interested in a decision should be heard. Those who value this perspective are pluralists who assume there will be many different points of view that have to be accommodated.

The ecology heuristic is concerned with identifying the different perceptions of the many groups involved with a service and trying to create a consistent policy from that variety. Ultimately this concatenation is achieved by giving more weight to the views of those who are most closely involved with the service. Some groups, particularly the most powerful in respect to the decision-makers, will be listened to more intently than others. In other words an ecological resource allocation is one that meets the expectations and aspirations of the most significant interest groups. But such allocations also have to meet the minimum requirements of all the interest groups. If they do not, then those disregarded groups will seek to make themselves more significant to the organisation and so reach a condition in which the decision-makers have to listen to them.

Section 4 of *Monksbane and feverfew* provides enough clues for people who adopt this value to act upon it. Some very powerful interest groups are pressing for more money to be spent on the monksbane programme. People who accept ecology respond by putting another five or ten thousand pounds into the programme. Most of those who reject ecology as a value simply ignore the demands of the pressure groups. Some respondents however are so incensed by what they see as bullying by the pressure groups, that they reduce the expenditure on monksbane to punish those who would seek to bring pressure to bear.

## Fairness

Fairness is concerned with impartiality between individuals. Fairness emphasises the importance of giving everyone equal access to services or at least an equal chance of access. This makes the use of arbitrary mechanisms for allocating scarce resources possible. Some managers, for example, when faced with too many job candidates, all of whom fit the employee specification, believe the only fair way of choosing the successful candidate is to draw lots. People who apply the fairness heuristic are interested in the standardisation and consistency of services to customers and clients. One of the clearest definitions of fairness, as it is defined here, can be found in a medieval Islamic story.

> A child and an adult both of the True Faith are in Heaven, but the adult occupies a higher place. God explains that the man has done many good works whereupon the child asks why God allowed him to die before he could do good. God answers that he knew the child would grow up to be a sinner and so it was better that he die young. A cry rises up from the depths of Hell: 'Why O Lord did you not let us die before we became sinners?'
>
> (Russell, 1985: 85)

The Lord was obviously working on an ad hoc basis, dealing with individuals as they appeared before him for judgement. For some reason this child was noticed and saved while many others were not, a lapse on God's part that those in Hell naturally thought unfair. Fairness therefore must operate according to universally applied rules. Either all potential sinners die young or none.

Fairness is only concerned with equality of access and opportunity, not with equality of outcomes. In Section 5 of *Monksbane and feverfew* the table shows that if £10,000 is spent on feverfew and £60,000 on monksbane then 30 per cent of sufferers from feverfew and 30 per cent of sufferers from monksbane would be identified and treated. This would be fair because, irrespective of which disease a person had, their chances of treatment would be the same. This does not of course mean that they would all have the same chances of being made well. Some people favour the value of fairness but would not wish to impose it by dividing up the budget 10 : 60. Section 6 of *Monksbane and feverfew* therefore provides another option for applying the fairness heuristic. In this section you are given the opportunity to leave the allocation of resources between the two treatment programmes to chance. This is done by treating patients as they present themselves, irrespective of their diagnosis, and by stopping all treatments when the budget is spent. This alternative puts everyone in a queue and so everyone is dealt with in the same way – fairly.

## Personal competence and gain

Personal gain and competence is a heuristic which, when applied to the allocation of resources, causes decisions to be made to the decision-maker's benefit. The benefit can be of two different kinds. The first is the sense of worth and self-esteem that can come from having done a job properly. This implies that the decision has been made using appropriate methods and that no short cuts, which offend against the decision-maker's beliefs, have been used. The second sense relates to personal advantage. In this sense the decision-makers allocate resources in a way that brings some material or personal benefit to them – this may be an increase in organisational influence, professional satisfaction, something which eases the burden of daily life, cash or a bottle of whisky. Personal gain does not necessarily imply gain for the decision-maker because they may value being able to help their friends or family, but it does imply that decisions are made according to private rather than public considerations.

In *Monksbane and feverfew* respondents are invited to respond to this value in Section 7. It suggests that someone very dear to the respondent is suffering from the disease that is being given the smaller amount of money. Clearly that person's chances of recovery would be better if more money were spent on the screening and treatment for that disease. If the respondent increases the money allocated to the disease of the person close to them they are using the personal gain value. A range of other factors could of course trigger this value. The person making the decision might, for example, have a research or clinical interest in the treatment of one of the two diseases. We do not necessarily think people will answer this part of the simulation honestly. We suspect people do not know how they would behave in such a situation until they are in it. However, Section 7 does illustrate how this value could be used as a heuristic for making the decision.

## Values as heuristics in *Monksbane and feverfew*

We are suggesting that *Monksbane and feverfew* illustrates how values can operate heuristically in the way that people search for solutions to a priority-setting problem. Although it does not prove that people use values heuristically when making real-life decisions it does provide some interesting issues for you to think about.

When completing *Monksbane and feverfew* some people apply a range of values and change their minds as they work through the exercise. Some use only one. These people might, for example, adopt the utility value and decide in Section 1 to spend nothing on monksbane. They do not veer from this decision as they work through the simulation. In either case the use of a particular value causes them to look for some kinds of information and to ignore others. A person who has the deservingness value will look for and respond to information about people's moral failings. A person who favours the utility value will be much taken by the graph in Section 1 (Activity 5.1), which offers the prospect of the information necessary to calculate cost–benefit figures for the two diseases. Someone who favours individual need will tend to reject the information in Section 1 because it is 'just statistics' and provides no information about the needs of the people behind the statistics. Values act heuristically by allowing people to select the information they believe is important to making the decision. Once this has been done the process of making a decision is relatively straightforward. If someone accepts the ecology heuristic, and they know what the demands of the most powerful interest groups are, then they know immediately what has to be done to please those groups.

The complexity of *Monksbane and feverfew* arises from the fact that the application of different values leads to very different conclusions. Utility would lead to nothing being spent on monksbane. Individual need would lead to a large amount being spent on it. These kinds of dilemmas are of course very common in health management (*see* Case study 2.9). However, it is suggested that the six value heuristics identified in this chapter can be seen in any priority-setting or resource-allocation decision. They can be seen, for example, in decisions about the allocation of budget cuts or increases between departments, in deciding whom to make redundant in a round of downsizing and in decisions about responding to different market segments.

## Integrity and loyalty as value heuristics

There are two other values that, it will be argued, play an important role as heuristics for deciding what to think, say or do in an ethical matter. They are integrity and loyalty. A commitment to either loyalty or integrity can act as a heuristic for deciding what should be done in a situation. The process may be complicated, however, by the extent of a person's ethical horizon, the breadth of the arena in which they wish to exercise their loyalty or integrity. This will also influence their decisions. All of these issues need to be explained in more detail.

## Defining integrity and loyalty

Integrity is defined as basing action on sound judgement and seeking a unity or wholeness of thought and action. The medieval scholar Aquinas, after Aristotle, argued that the practice of virtue requires people to act knowingly, voluntarily and according to a fixed principle or habit (D'Entreves, 1965: 147–8). Winstanley and Woodall reflected these ideas when they argued that

> The development of integrity [is] based upon ethical judgement and a sense of responsibility, the development of appropriate virtues.

> (Winstanley and Woodall, 2000: 285)

Integrity therefore is defined by its possessor's self-reflection and awareness. As C.P. Snow, quoted by Adair (1980: 171), epigrammatically expressed it:

Give me a man who knows something of himself and is appalled.

A sense of self-doubt, as well as the tension between integrity and loyalty, can be illustrated by an account of an incident given during a research interview we conducted. The interviewee was a senior manager. His company required all managers to attend a series of development workshops that were designed to apply the precepts of an eastern mystical tradition to modern management practice. The respondent was a man of strong Christian belief who believed the philosophy of the seminars was contrary to his Christian principles. He felt that he should not in conscience attend the seminars. He was aware that taking this stance to maintain his integrity was at odds with his sense of loyalty. His loyalty was not particularly directed at the company but was focused on the rest of the management team who would be going to the seminars. The other team members told him that they thought him an important team member and they wished him to attend the seminars. The respondent reported that the issue caused him to think deeply about his beliefs and his responsibilities to others. His final position on the issue spoke of a self-conscious attempt to meet the demands of both integrity and loyalty. He attended the seminars but made a personal statement at the commencement in which he stated his personal objections to the values that informed them.

In contrast to integrity, loyalty is an unthinking faithfulness to a person, group or purpose. If a loyal person were to reflect on their actions they would have to question whether they were being loyal to the right thing. As Snell (1993: 82) characterised it, loyalty can range between a high commitment, analogous to a marriage, and a low level, which requires only the performance of actions contractually agreed. In a situation where high loyalty is demanded, but there is no opportunity for developmental openness (which would allow an individual to develop their own values and ethical reasoning),

> Unquestioning conformity is expected of members: one must suppress individuality, ignore one's own arguments and perspectives and accept what one has to do.
>
> (Snell, 1993: 82)

The unreflective nature of loyalty can be illustrated by another account of an ethical issue given by a manager in a finance department. When he moved to a new job he asked a colleague with whom he had previously worked to move with him and to support him in his new role. The manager was aware that the colleague was a discharged bankrupt who had invested unwisely when he had worked in the City. The financial accountant, who also reported to the manager, warned him of suspicions about the colleague's use of the credit card that the company had given him for business expenses.

> I had to take a view whether to expose him or to bring him to account, make him pay it back, and to carry on ... Either to keep it to myself and the financial accountant, or to let other people know. I think there was enough going on that could have cost him his job: and I chose the latter. I had known him for a number of years, he was an extremely hard working individual, played hard as well, and played hard sometimes in my time. But if

someone is working for me I take a balanced view. I don't expect them to work like an automaton ... He was always getting phone calls at home in the early hours of the morning from the department, 'can't do this and can't do that', and he solved it ... he was also being hounded by the CSA [Child Support Agency] so he wasn't having an easy time. All this encouraged me to take a lenient view. I also knew of his background and he was probably finding life a bit tough.

The colleague had spent £600 improperly using the credit card. The manager challenged him privately and, instead of starting disciplinary proceedings, made him pay the sum back within two weeks. The manager's loyalty towards the employee was at a cost to his honesty and integrity. He thought the colleague reciprocated the feeling of loyalty:

I felt that as he was working for me he would behave himself and he would not wish to implicate me. I thought I was entitled to more consideration than somebody he didn't know.

However, within a short space of time the colleague had found himself a new, better-paid, job with a different company and in his last few weeks of his old employment he again misused his credit card.

And so I felt as if I had paid my dues ... I had no loyalty to him then once he had done it twice ... On many occasions I have gone back and questioned my initial judgement. I find it quite difficult to think of abstract examples and decide what I would do, *because most things are instinct.* I am nearly forty-six years of age and so I have had a fair amount of experience; I am not sure I would do the same thing again.

(Research interview: our emphasis)

Loyalty, in this account, is seen as a matter of instinct and experience and not as a matter of self-reflection. The instinctive wish to act loyally can easily be destroyed, as here, by an act of betrayal by the person to whom loyalty is given.

## Ethical horizons

People in organisations may experience conflicts of loyalties. There may be situations, concerning whistleblowing for example (De George, 1999: 248, 412–16), in which they have to choose between being loyal to the organisation, to a professional body, to society at large or to themselves and their families. Less obviously conflicts may also emerge within the sphere of integrity. The issue is well illustrated by a conversation imagined by Watson (1998: 266).

*David*:   Alright for the sake of argument, imagine we set up a business to murder people.

*Colin*:   Murder Incorporated.

*David*:   OK; it's been done. But say we did this and we followed all the culture and empowerment stuff. We could have democratic management, lots of trust and all that. There's good pay for everybody, welfare arrangements, good pensions, and Christmas parties for the kiddies. There's a moral code – just like the Mafia – that holds everything together. Everything we have said so far makes this a moral business. But it is not. Murder isn't moral is it?

Legge expressed the dilemma, raised by this thought experiment, in a more formal way when discussing human resource management (HRM):

> If capitalism is, or has the potential to be viewed as ethical, then HRM similarly has a good chance. If not, it is difficult to imagine how an ethical system for managing people at work can emerge from an essentially unethical economic order.
>
> (Legge, 1998: 166)

The dilemmas in the quotations hinge on the question of ethical horizons. A person's assessment of whether the situations in the two quotations given above represent integrity and morality depends on their choice of ethical horizon. The broader the horizon the less likely is a person to see the situations as showing integrity. If their horizon is local, focused within the organisation, then the more likely they are to represent these situations as ones showing morality and integrity. It is argued therefore that perceptions of loyalty and integrity, and the actions that each demands, are affected by the extent of the subject's ethical horizon. A simplified analysis of the range of ethical horizons is shown in Table 5.3.

**Table 5.3** The ethical horizons of loyalty and integrity

**The limits of loyalty**

The limits of loyalty concerns the breadth of the unit to which a person gives their loyalty. Four levels are identified.

1  Loyalty to self, family. This horizon may be represented by the alleged judgement on many East End gangsters that they were essentially good because they 'were good to their mothers'.
2  Loyalty to the groups and associations a person has chosen to belong to (civil society). This is perhaps exemplified by E.M. Forster's (1975) remark, 'If I had to choose between betraying my country and betraying my friend, I hope I should have the guts to betray my country'.
3  Loyalty to the employing organisation. As the Civil Service code of ethics states, 'Civil servants owe their loyalty to the duly constituted government' (Cabinet Office, n.d.).
4  Loyalty to society at large.

**The limits of integrity**

The limits of integrity concerns the breadth of the arena in which a person seeks to achieve a unity of their thoughts and actions. Four levels are identified.

1  The personal and private arena.
2  The personal and public arena of associations and networks (civil society).
3  The corporate and organisational arena within which a person is employed.
4  The arena of the wider society, polity and economy.

A preference for either loyalty or integrity, together with a preference for an ethical horizon, can be used to identify someone's likely actions when they find themselves embroiled in an ethical question such as what to do when one's organisation is discovered to be behaving badly. The options are shown in Table 5.4.

**Table 5.4** An analysis of the actions open to an employee, when they discover wrongdoing by their organisation, according to the levels of ethical horizons

| Ethical horizon | Loyalty | Integrity |
| --- | --- | --- |
| Society | *Sacrifice of self for other's benefit* <br> • Anonymous whistleblowing | • Public whistleblowing |
| Civil associations | *Sacrifice to show membership and commitment* <br> • Lying to protect the group <br> • The group members agree to maintain silence to protect the the group | • The group collectively offers to help management find a way to make things right <br> • The group collectively blows the whistle on the organisation – a form of collective civil disobedience |
| Organisations | *Acting as a scapegoat* <br> • Offering to keep silent <br> • Cover up the wrongdoing | • Trying to persuade the organisation to reveal its wrongdoing and to put things right |
| Self | *Sacrifice to maintain or increase personal benefit or status* <br> • Seek personal advantage from the situation <br> • Protect self by lying <br> • Protect self by telling lies about others <br> • Refusing to be bought off by the organisation | • Keeping silent – inaction is believed not to damage integrity <br> • Resigning when the organisation will not take the right action |

The first level in the hierarchy of ethical horizons in Table 5.4 is the broadest one and encompasses a concern for the well-being of society as a whole. At this level people see themselves as parts of the whole, as flakes of rock chipped from the mountain. It is more difficult to say how society might view its members because society has no single view or form of expression. The diversity of society makes it difficult for its members to believe that society could see them as anything more than a small part of the whole. Such a sense of personal inconsequence, yet commitment to society, creates a willingness to sacrifice the self for the greater good. The difference between loyalty and integrity is the amount of personal loss the whistleblower is prepared to risk for the good of society at large. Loyalty to society requires the subject to blow the whistle on the organisation's wrongdoing, but anonymously and secretly. Integrity requires the whistleblower to take a public stand. The loyalist sacrifices openness to minimise loss and retribution; the person exercising integrity does not. The degree of risk also depends on people's circumstances. Some public whistleblowers are at less risk by taking a public stand because they have no dependants and may not be reliant on their salary from their employer.

At the ethical horizon of civil association there is an imbalance in the relationship between a member of a civil group and the group itself. Members of such groups see themselves as a mere part of the associations they belong to, but the associations see them as a metaphor for the whole. Each member stands for the whole group. This can be illustrated by popular attitudes about teamwork. Team members can only see themselves as a part of the whole team. As in Belbin's (1981) analysis of teams the individual team member is less than the whole because they cannot fulfil all roles necessary for effective team functioning. In contrast a team, it is often argued, is only effective because the team subsumes the members in a team unity and sees them as metaphors for itself. These perceptions lead people to wish to protect the group, which values them so highly, while minimising the threat to themselves by acting as part of a larger, supportive whole. Loyalty to a civil association, in the scenario, is represented by the subject encouraging the group to protect itself by keeping silent about the organisation's wrongdoing. This has the advantage, to the member who sees their link with the association as only partial, of saving them from an obligation to sacrifice themselves for the group's integrity. The group jointly blowing the whistle on the wrongdoing, on the other hand, represents integrity. This collective responsibility protects the individuals within the group.

The next level in the hierarchy of ethical horizons is the organisation. If employees set their focus on this horizon they believe themselves to be at one with the wider organisation, but the organisation does not reciprocate; it sees them as mere cogs in something bigger. When, out of integrity, an employee seeks to persuade the organisation to do the right thing they are assuming a unity, a metaphorical relationship between themselves and the organisation. But the organisation in this case may see the employee as an irritating and replaceable component. There is a danger that the employee in this situation, by raising their head above the parapet of organisational bad behaviour, will be made into a scapegoat by the organisation and dismissed or by other means punished. Loyalty, at this level of ethical focus, is expressed by the employee offering, because they assume an affinity with the organisation, to protect the organisation by covering up its wrongdoing. The organisation, however, may still feel threatened by such help; the employee may, after all, decide the organisation has done wrong and blow the whistle on both the original wrongdoing and the subsequent cover-up. This fear may cause the organisation to punish the employee even though the employee has shown loyalty (Fisher, 2000). Within the ethical horizon of the organisation the employee becomes a scapegoat for the wrongs of the organisation. In the biblical origin of the term the scapegoat is not killed but is allowed to escape into the wilderness. This is an appropriate image for the ways in which modern organisations 'let go' those who carry the taint of organisations' bad behaviour.

When the ethical horizon does not extend beyond the self the focus of actions will be on the protection and improvement of the self's position. Protecting the self's integrity can be achieved in two ways. The first involves drawing the ethical horizon so tightly around the self that any wrong action is kept beyond it. In plainer terms the subject claims or feigns ignorance of the wrongdoing. This approach to integrity has similarities with the concepts of ethical closure and ethical bracketing (Jackall, 1988; Kärreman and Alvesson, 1999). If the situation makes this stance untenable then people can maintain their integrity, not by attempting to put things right, but by removing themselves, by resigning from the organisation. When a person acts with integrity, by resigning from an organisation that they cannot prevent from behaving unethically, they sacrifice their material well-being, their job and their salary, to protect their ethical well-being.

Loyalty to the self involves sacrificing integrity for material benefits. In the scenario described in Activity 5.2 it is represented by using knowledge of the organisation's wrongdoing to gain advantages for the self. The subject believes their integrity justifies self-seeking behaviour, and that the self-seeking legitimates their integrity.

In summary, what has been argued is that a preference for integrity or loyalty and a preference for a particular ethical horizon can act in a heuristic manner. The combination of the two values leaves a person with a restricted range of actions to choose from. The values act as a heuristic for closing down and restricting search behaviour and so make coming to a conclusion easier. As has been pointed out earlier the problem for the person facing the situation is to decide what values to apply. Integrity and loyalty are commonplaces in western society; both are regarded as good things. Each of the ethical horizons is valued in society. How then does a person choose between them? You can see which values you favour, at least under simulated conditions, by completing Activity 5.2.

| Activity 5.2 | Dilemma: A diagnostic inventory of managers' ethical horizons |
| --- | --- |

### Instructions

This inventory is in the form of an action maze. You take the part of a manager and you have to make decisions about how to react to a problem at work. You start the inventory with Section 1. In each section the situation you are facing is explained and a range of possible actions that you can take is presented. *Tick the option that is closest to the one you would take in the circumstances.* Then go to the next section as indicated. When you have finished the inventory please complete the scoring sheet.

### Section 1

You are a middle-ranking manager in an organisation. You report to a board level manager and your responsibilities include managing the budgets of several operational areas. As part of your personal development you attended a seminar on tax and VAT liability. You realise from what you learned at the seminar that a practice that had been going on for years in the organisation was liable for VAT but had never been declared for VAT purposes. You have quietly and anonymously checked out your suspicions and confirmed their truth. You do not know whether the undeclared liability is the result of ignorance or an oversight, or whether it is a deliberate attempt to reduce the tax bill. However the amount of unpaid tax is large.

Which of the following actions would you take? Tick the option you choose.

| Option | Action | Go to |
|---|---|---|
| 1 ☐ | Keep quiet and say nothing to anybody. | Section 2 |
| 2 ☐ | Inform senior management about the situation and try to convince them that the situation should be disclosed to the tax authorities. | Section 3 |
| 3 ☐ | You send a signed letter to the tax authorities informing them of the undeclared liability; and you send a copy with an explanatory covering letter to senior management. | Section 4 |
| 4 ☐ | You have an informal discussion with the senior managers in which you let them know that you know about the tax liability. You keep them wondering about whether you will report the matter to the tax authorities while assuring them of your commitment to achieving success in the organisation. | Section 5 |
| 5 ☐ | You report the tax liability anonymously and secretly to the tax authorities. | Section 6 |
| 6 ☐ | You tell senior management about the tax liability and offer your help in keeping the matter quiet. | Section 3 |

## Section 2

You are a member of a professional development group. This is a private association of people with an interest in their own professional development, and with improving the public's perception of the profession's integrity. The group was formed when the original members were on a postgraduate management course together. It so happens that many of the group members also work for the same organisation as you do. All members of the group have agreed that its discussions should be kept confidential unless they agree otherwise.

You are attending one of the group's regular six-weekly meetings. As the meeting is coming to an end, under 'any other business', a couple of members say that they have discovered that the organisation has not been declaring its VAT liability for one of its activities. The group is concerned about the organisation's apparent lack of integrity, although they realise that the financial consequences for the organisation of declaring the liability would be heavy. You have good relationships with the group and you are very committed to it. The group ask you for your advice about what to do because of your important role in the organisation.

▶

Which of the following actions would you take? Tick the option you choose.

| Option | Action | Go to |
|---|---|---|
| 1 ☐ | Tell them to keep quiet about the matter because the organisation can be hard with people, insiders or outsiders, who stir up trouble. | Section 14 |
| 2 ☐ | Inform senior management, on behalf of the group and yourself, of the tax liability issue and try to convince them that the situation should be disclosed to the tax authorities. | Section 3 |
| 3 ☐ | Tell the group to keep quiet about the matter and that you will tell senior management and try to convince them that the situation should be disclosed to the tax authorities. When you have the opportunity you do what you told the group you would do. | Section 3 |
| 4 ☐ | Tell the group to keep quiet. Without telling the group what you are going to do you tell the senior managers about the situation and offer your help in keeping the matter quiet. | Section 3 |

### Section 3

You are called to a meeting with the senior management team. The subject of the meeting is the undeclared tax liability. The senior managers tell you that they have decided to stop the activity that caused the tax liability and not to reveal the past liability to the tax authorities. They call upon your loyalty to the organisation, and your obedience as an employee, to support this decision. They ask you to sign a memorandum that disguises the existence of the tax liability.

Which of the following actions would you take? Tick the option you choose. N.B. You may visit this section more than once.

| Option | Action | Go to |
|---|---|---|
| 1 ☐ ☐ ☐ | Disagree with the senior managers and continue to argue that the organisation should be honest with the tax authorities. | Section 8 (If you tick this box a third time then go to the Scoring Grid on p. 141) |
| 2 | You disagree with what the senior managers have decided and after further fruitless discussions with them you offer your resignation. | Section 9 |

| Option | Action | Go to |
|---|---|---|
| 3 ☐ | You agree with the senior managers and sign the memorandum. | Section 13 |
| 4 ☐ | You hedge a little and point out that you might consider it your duty to inform the tax authorities. You also hint that it might be easier to sign the memorandum if you were certain that your long-term prospects in the organisation were good. | Section 5 |
| 5 ☐ | You tell the senior managers that you cannot agree with their decision. You send a signed letter to the tax authorities informing them of the undeclared liability, and you send a copy with an explanatory covering letter to senior management. | Section 4 |
| 6 ☐ | You play for time in the meeting. As soon as it ends you report the tax liability anonymously and secretly to the tax authorities. | Section 6 |

### Section 4

The senior managers meet with you and point out that because they no longer have faith in your commitment to the organisation they wish to end your employment contract with the organisation. They are willing to compensate you for breaking the contract. If you agree to accept the compensation it will avoid the necessity for the disciplinary action they would otherwise have to take against you for breaking your duty of confidentiality to the organisation. However, the compensation would be dependent upon your signing a gagging clause, which would prevent you from discussing the organisation's business with any third party.

Which of the following actions would you take? Tick the option you choose.

| Option | Action | Go to |
|---|---|---|
| 1 ☐ | Refuse to accept the deal on offer. | Section 10 |
| 2 ☐ | Accept the deal on offer. | Section 11 |

### Section 5

The senior managers decide to call your bluff on the implied threats you have been making. They demand that you commit to maintaining silence about the tax liability. They insist you sign a memorandum that disguises the existence of the tax liability.

▶

Which of the following actions would you take? Tick the option you choose.

| Option | Action | Go to |
|---|---|---|
| 1 ☐ | You agree to keep silence and you sign the memorandum. | Section 13 |
| 2 ☐ | You cannot agree to the cover-up and you give your resignation. | Section 9 |
| 3 ☐ | You play for time in the meeting. As soon as it ends you report the tax liability anonymously and secretly to the tax authorities. | Section 6 |
| 4 ☐ | You tell the senior managers that you cannot agree with their decision. You send a signed letter to the tax authorities informing them of the undeclared liability, and you send a copy with an explanatory covering letter to senior management. | Section 4 |

## Section 6

The tax authorities have been asking senior management some difficult questions about the undeclared tax liability. It is clear to senior management that someone must have tipped off the authorities. Senior management confront you and accuse you of being the source of the leak.

Which of the following actions would you take? Tick the option you choose.

| Option | Action | Go to |
|---|---|---|
| 1 ☐ | Admit that you informed the tax authorities and offer your resignation. | Section 12 |
| 2 ☐ | Admit that you informed the tax authorities. You do not offer to resign because, as you argue to the senior managers, you were only doing the right thing when faced with the organisation's unethical and illegal position. | Section 10 |
| 3 ☐ | Deny that you were the source of the leak. | Section 4 |
| 4 ☐ | Admit you were the source of the leak. Admit that you were wrong to inform the tax authorities and offer to write a letter to them withdrawing the accusation and claiming it was the result of a misunderstanding. | Section 10 |

## Section 7

You have the prospect of a successful career in the organisation. You anticipate rapid promotion.

*End of exercise. Go to the scoring sheet on p. 216.*

## Section 8

You have had a meeting with senior managers and you have made your best effort to convince them that the organisation should do the honest thing and disclose the past tax liability to the authorities. However, your argument, that the tax liability on the particular activity that is causing the difficulty is an obvious anomaly and that the regulations will be changed as soon as the tax authorities are aware of it, does not suit the cynical mood of the senior managers.

*Go to Section 3.*

## Section 9

As you know, you are a member of a professional development group. This is a private association of people with an interest in their own professional development, and with improving the public's perception of the profession's integrity. The group was formed when the original members were on a post-graduate management course together. All members of the group have agreed that its discussions should be kept confidential unless they agree otherwise.

The group know about the undeclared tax liability. This is not surprising as many of the group, as well as you, work in the organisation. They also know that you have resigned over the issue rather than take action to put the situation right. They argue with you that the situation is wrong. They believe that the ethical thing to do is to declare the tax liability to the tax authorities. They believe that, in the period of notice before you leave the organisation, you may be able to help them put the situation right.

Which of the following actions would you take? Tick the option you choose.

| Option | Action | Go to |
|---|---|---|
| 1 ☐ | Tell them to keep quiet about the matter because the organisation can be hard with people (insiders or outsiders) who stir up trouble. | Section 12 |
| 2 ☐ | Support the group in their decision to inform the tax authorities of the tax liability. You agree to sign the letter to the tax authorities along with the rest of the group. | Section 12 |
| 3 ☐ | Tell the group to keep quiet, and protect their own careers, and that you will send a signed letter to the tax authorities informing them of the undeclared liability, and you will also send a copy, with an explanatory covering letter, to senior management. | Section 12 |
| 4 ☐ | Tell the group to keep quiet but agree to inform the tax authorities anonymously of the tax issue. | Section 12 |

▶

### Section 10

A few months later you receive notification that you are being made redundant from the organisation. This appears to be part of a general de-layering process designed to reduce the organisation's costs.

*Go to Section 12.*

### Section 11

You have been looking for a new job. It is difficult to get interviews for new jobs that are at the same level as your old one. You do wonder whether your old employer has put the word around on the grapevine that you are not a loyal employee. At least you have the substantial pay-off from your old job to keep you going and you are not yet in major financial difficulties.

*End of exercise. Go to the scoring sheet on p. 216.*

### Section 12

You have been looking for a new job. It is difficult to get interviews for new jobs that are at the same level as your old one. You do wonder whether your old employer has put the word around on the grapevine that you are not a loyal employee. Your financial situation is beginning to look desperate.

*End of exercise. Go to the scoring sheet on p. 216.*

### Section 13

As you know, you are a member of a professional development group. This is a private association of people with an interest in their own professional development, and with improving the public's perception of the profession's integrity. The group was formed when the original members were on a postgraduate management course together. All members of the group have agreed that its discussions should be kept confidential unless they agree otherwise.

The group, as you may be aware, know about the undeclared tax liability. You are not the only group member to work for the organisation. The group also know that you have worked with senior management to keep the matter quiet. They argue with you that the situation is wrong. They cannot believe that you are going along with the cover-up. 'We thought you were better than that', they say. They believe that the ethical thing to do is to declare the tax liability to the tax authorities. They believe that you may be able to help them work towards a more honest outcome.

Which of the following actions would you take? Tick the option you choose.

| Option | Action | Go to |
|--------|--------|-------|
| 1 ☐ | Tell them to keep quiet about the matter because the organisation can be hard with people (insiders or outsiders) who stir up trouble. | Section 7 |

| Option | Action | Go to |
|---|---|---|
| 2 ☐ | Support the group in their decision to inform the tax authorities of the tax liability. You agree to sign the letter to the tax authorities along with the rest of the group. | Section 10 |
| 3 ☐ | Tell the group to keep quiet, and protect their own careers. You, however, undertake to send a signed letter to the tax authorities informing them of the undeclared liability, and also to send a copy, with an explanatory covering letter, to senior management. | Section 10 |
| 4 ☐ | Tell the team to keep quiet but agree to inform the tax authorities anonymously of the tax issue. | Section 6 |

**Section 14**

The tax authorities have been asking senior management some difficult questions about the undeclared tax liability. It is clear to senior management that someone must have tipped off the authorities. The senior managers have come to the conclusion that the professional development group, of which you are a member, must be the source of the leak. Senior managers know that several of their key staff are members of the group and they are suspicious that membership may conflict with their obligations to the organisation.

The senior managers invite you to a meeting. They tell you about the tax liability problem and that the tax authorities are suspicious. They know you are a member of the group and they ask you to confirm their suspicion that the group is the source of the leak.

Which of the following actions would you take? Tick the option you choose.

| Option | Action | Go to |
|---|---|---|
| 1 ☐ | Deny that the group is the source of the leak and claim that, to the best of your knowledge, the group is not aware of the situation. | Section 3 |
| 2 ☐ | You agree that the group must be the source of the leak. | Section 3 |
| 3 ☐ | You agree that the group must be the source of the leak. You also offer to help senior management to cover up the problem and you sign a memorandum that disguises the existence of the liability. | Section 7 |

▶

| Option | Action | Go to |
|---|---|---|
| 4 ☐ | You say that you do not know how the tax authorities became aware of the possible tax problem, but you are pleased that it is in the open and you recommend that senior managers are open with the tax authorities and negotiate with them to overcome the problem. You point out that the tax liability on the particular activity that is causing the difficulty is an obvious anomaly and that the regulations will be changed as soon as the tax authorities are aware of it. | Section 6 |
| 5 ☐ | You point out that the discussions of the development group are confidential. The group could not function if it were otherwise. Therefore you are not able to make any comment on the group and its actions. | Section 3 |
| 6 ☐ | You point out that you cannot discuss the business of the group because of its rule of confidentiality. However, you offer to discuss the issue with the group and encourage them to enter into dialogue with the organisation. | Section 3 |

**Scoring grid**

*Instructions*

Tick, in the second column of the grid below, those sections of the inventory that you completed. Transfer your decisions from each of the sections you completed by circling the option number of the action you took. If, for example, you took option 2 in Section 3 then circle the number 2 in the sixth column in the second row of the scoring grid. When you have finished this task for all the sections you completed (remembering that you may have visited some sections more than once) add up the number of circles in each column and write them in the 'Total' row.

| Section | √if done | L1 | In1 | L2 | In2 | L3 | In3 | L4 | In4 |
|---|---|---|---|---|---|---|---|---|---|
| 1 | | 5 | 3 | | | 6 | 2 | 4 | 1 |
| 2 | | | | 1 | 2 | 4 | 3 | | |
| 3 | | 6 | 5 | | | 3 | 1 | 4 | 2 |
| 4 | | | | | | | | 2 | 1 |
| 5 | | 3 | 4 | | | 1 | | | 2 |
| 6 | | | | | | 4 | 2 | 3 | 1 |
| 9 | | 4 | 3 | 1 | 2 | | | | |
| 13 | | 4 | 3 | 1 | 2 | | | | |
| 14 | | | | 1 | 6 | 3 | 4 | 2 | 5 |
| Totals (row A) | | | | | | | | | |
| % of total responses (row B) | | | | | | | | | |

Transfer the figures from row B on to the chart that follows.

**Interpreting the results**

Transfer your scores from the scoring grid into the chart below.

|  | *Limits of loyalty* | *Limits of integrity* |
|---|---|---|
|  | L1 | In1 |
| *Focus on society* |  |  |
|  | L2 | In2 |
| *Focus on civil society* |  |  |
|  | L3 | In3 |
| *Focus on the organisation* |  |  |
|  | L4 | In4 |
| *Focus on self* |  |  |

## Discussion of the dilemma simulation in Activity 5.2

The exercise you have just completed has been tested on a sample of undergraduate business students. Studying the sequence of choices they made as they worked their way through the action maze can identify their ethical horizons. In the first section of the maze just over half of the respondents chose integrity in the organisational arena and tried to convince the management to admit the tax liability and to regularise the situation. Nearly 30 per cent continued with this position when the management at first refused to concede. A small percentage of respondents (5.8 per cent) found themselves in a closed loop, by continuing to suggest, despite the management's intransigence, that the tax liability should be admitted. But most of the respondents, when rebuffed by the management, chose integrity at the level of self and resigned from the organisation. Twenty-five of the 30 respondents who chose resignation subsequently took a position of integrity at the civil association horizon, by whistleblowing on the organisation, when urged by their professional peers to do so. The most common route through the maze took, at every opportunity, a path of integrity rather than loyalty, but the ethical horizon changed as circumstances changed. Practising managers may not share undergraduates' commitment to integrity.

A minority of respondents took the route of loyalty but changed the focus of their loyalty. Nineteen per cent of the respondents initially opted for loyalty to self, by using their knowledge of the tax liability to gain advantage for themselves. But in Section 5 of the maze most of those who had chosen loyalty to self changed their focus to loyalty to the organisation as they helped in the cover-up.

People's commitments to the sometimes competing demands of loyalty and integrity illustrate the importance of values as heuristics in decision making on ethical questions.

> **Connexion point**
>
> The issue of whistleblowing, raised in Activity 5.2, is explored more fully in Chapter 7.

## Reflections

Many textbooks on business ethics have relatively little to say about values. When they are discussed it is in the context of corporate codes of ethics or statements of organisational core values. The materials and arguments put forward in this chapter suggest that values may be central to people's thought processes when they are deciding what to say or do in response to an ethical issue. There is a paradox however. Values can be used heuristically to *simplify* the process of making up one's mind, but the problem of which particular value to apply to an issue, when there are many values within organisations and society, all of which are valued but which conflict with one another, is *complex*.

The account of values as heuristics in this chapter may provide a good description of how people make decisions on ethical issues. This does not imply that this is how such decisions should be made. Indeed, if heuristics are more a matter of habit than conscious thought they may merely be ways of avoiding complex value and ethical choices. Choices involve thinking about what we ought to do, not recalling what we normally do. In the next chapter we will explore these tensions between taking habitual stances on ethical issues, bred from our upbringing and experiences, and having to knowingly challenge our habits because the ethical matters we face contain novel circumstances or inconvenient facts.

## Summary

In this chapter the following key points have been made:

- Rational and analytic theories explain how decision making ought to be done.

- Heuristic theories probably explain how people make decisions in practice.

- Research into heuristics used to see them as sources of bias and distortion; the fast and frugal research programme sees them as efficient and effective procedures for decision making.

- Values probably act in a heuristic manner in decision making about ethical matters.

- Values can be used to limit and stop decision-makers' searches for further information and options.

- In decisions such as setting priorities and deciding how to respond to wrong-doing in an organisation the problem is to choose which of many mutually exclusive values should be applied.

## Quick revision test

1. What is a heuristic?
   (a) a cognitive device that the mind uses to make decisions
   (b) a form of decision making by trial and error
   (c) a five-stage procedure for decision making

2. Do Gigerenzer and Todd think heuristics are:
   (a) effective
   (b) a source of error
   (c) nonsense

3. Ethical bracketing means:
   (a) basing your decisions on certain ethical principles
   (b) putting your personal values to one side, and not applying them, while at work
   (c) making sure that your personal values do not contradict each other

4. Integrity is defined as:
   (a) basing your conduct on fixed and sound principles
   (b) ensuring that your actions and your values do not contradict each other
   (c) respecting others.

## Typical assignments and briefs

1. Compare rational and heuristic models of decision making. How might the heuristic model be applicable to decision making on ethical matters?

2. Loyalty or integrity: which should be the most important to organisational employees?

3. Analyse a resource allocation decision that has been taken in an organisation by reference to the six resource allocation heuristics.

4. What role do emotions and value play in an individual's decision making on ethical matters?

### Group activity 5

Obtain a copy of the *Cave Rescue Exercise*, which can be found in Woodcock (1979, 1989: 81) and in the appendix to Fisher (1998). Another version of this exercise can be found in Francis and Young (1979). Both are variations on a classic management game theme, of which *The Kidney Machine* is another popular version (Jones and Pfeiffer (1974)).

Divide into groups of between six and ten people and do the exercise.

## Recommended further reading

If you are interested in the role of heuristics in decision making, *see* G. Gigerenzer, P.M. Todd, and the ABC Research Group (1999) *Simple Heuristics That Make us Smart*, Oxford: Oxford University Press. On the topic of the role of values in management see P. Griseri (1998) *Managing Values*, London: Palgrave.

## Useful websites

| Topic | Website provider | URL |
| --- | --- | --- |
| Thinking about risk. Information on some of the heuristics of judgement. | Centre for Informed Decision Making | http://www.cygnus-group.com/CIDM/risk.html |
| Home page of the ABC Centre | Centre for Adaptive Behaviour and Cognition | http://www.mpib-berlin.mpg.de/en/forschung/abc/index.htm |

## CHAPTER 6

# Individual responses to ethical situations

Having completed this chapter and completed its associated activities, readers should be able to:

- Explain the different ways in which people may respond to ethical issues at work.

- Use this understanding to think about their own reactions to ethical issues.

- Explain the processes of categorisation and particularisation in ethical thinking.

- Explain the range of factors that influence how people respond to ethical issues at work.

## Introduction

This chapter concerns people's responses to ethical issues at work. The previous chapter dealt only with ethical thinking. Responses to ethical situations obviously involve thinking about the issue but also go beyond it. Responses include what people say, how they say it and how they behave. There are two main cognitive processes involved in choosing responses, categorisation and particularisation (Billig, 1996). The first of these involves putting an issue into a box or category and saying, 'That is the way in which I will deal with this matter'. These categories are often based on values. Someone might decide, for example, that an issue is a matter of following the core values set by an organisation, or that an issue is a question of loyalty. However, the particulars of a situation might make someone think that the categorisation is not right. It is the details of a situation that make people debate under which value an issue should be categorised or indeed whether it should be put in a separate category of its own.

The first part of the chapter describes and explains different categories of ethical response. Later the chapter explores the possibility that people do not adopt a single categorisation but debate with themselves and with others about a range of competing possible categorisations. The exercise in Activity 6.1 later in the chapter also raises the possibility that people's categorisations may change over time as they become aware of new information and different perspectives on the issue. The third section of the chapter discusses the range of factors that may influence how someone chooses to categorise an issue. The final section summarises the arguments of the chapter and gives the reader opportunities to reflect upon them.

## Categories of response to ethical issues

In this section we will use a matrix to describe the categories, let us call them stances, that people at work may use to classify ethical issues. The model is shown in Figure 6.1. Before the eight categories it contains can be described we will explain the two dimensions that form the matrix.

### Ethical integrity, the horizontal axis in Figure 6.1

The dimension of ethical integrity will be described first. The position at the extreme left of the horizontal axis in Figure 6.1 represents clarity and certainty about values. A person at this point on the scale sees moral issues in a straightforward way, which helps them to know what should be done in a situation or how an issue should be analysed and resolved. A person at the extreme right of the dimension, however, is more likely to be confused or even aporetic (this term is defined in Chapter 4, p. 168). A person in this condition will find the plurality of views on an issue difficult to reconcile and they will often change their minds. If integrity is defined as the congruence, or fit, between a person's thoughts on an issue then the left-hand column in Figure 6.1 represents a high degree of integrity and the right-hand column a low degree of integrity.

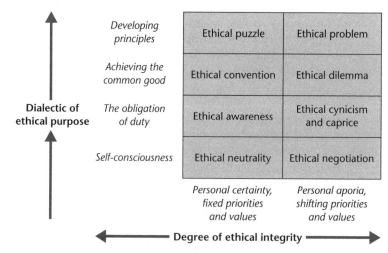

**Figure 6.1** Managers' perceptions of ethical issues – a framework
*Source*: Fisher and Rice (1999)

# The dialectic of ethical purpose, the vertical axis in Figure 6.1

The vertical dimension represents stages in the dialectical development of a personal and conscious view of right and wrong. It models a developing personal responsibility for recognising the presence of ethical issues at work and addressing them. In the initial stage, at the origin of the framework – self-consciousness – a person sees their moral universe as a personal one. They accept responsibility for themselves but wish to remain apart from ethical issues in the wider world. They show this unwillingness to accept a moral responsibility by turning a blind eye. But an individual's moral isolation is an ideal: it cannot be sustained; it is contradicted by the clamorous demands from others, bosses, colleagues, customers and so on, that they become involved.

---

**DEFINITION**

The **dialectic** is a method of analysis (associated with the German philosopher Hegel (1770–1831)) in which an initial, formal concept (thesis) is challenged by practical contradictions contained within it (antithesis) until a synthesis comes about that overcomes, or transcends, the tensions between thesis and antithesis. The thesis is a blank ideal because it has not been expressed in reality. It is when it confronts social reality that the messy detail of life negates the formal ideal. The synthesis negates this negation and the dialectic moves to a new, positive stage. The synthesis does not abolish the tensions but moves beyond them. The synthesis becomes a thesis and the cycle begins again.

---

**Connexion point**

A detailed example that shows how the dialectic works is given in pages 445–51.

---

The contradiction at the self-consciousness stage is between a person's sense of their own moral worth and their defensive refusal to take a moral stand on ethical issues. Ethical duty is the synthesis of this contradiction. People at this stage take a stand and, without much critical reflection, do what their backgrounds and their consciences tell them is their duty. However, doing one's duty can lead to an awareness that others have contrary conceptions of what their duty is.

> Unreflective duty can take its imperatives from the dooms of Zeus, from priest or parent, from the custom of a tribe or city, and act in peace and faith. But the first conflict unveils an Antigone and the question 'Whose standard?' soon brings down all standards.
>
> (Mabbott, 1967: 44)

Antigone, in Greek myth, followed her conscience by giving a ritual burial, against custom and the decree of King Creon, to her brother Polynices who had tried to usurp the throne. The formal idea of doing one's duty is undermined by uncertainty about what that duty is in any particular circumstance. This tension causes this stage to be expressed either as sincerely, but uncritically, held principle or its opposite – cynicism.

The lack of grounding, or legitimisation, of the idea of duty leads to the next stage in the dialectic, which is the search for the common good as a basis for moral certainty. In this phase people try to reconcile competing ethical demands by using such notions as organisational values and mission statements, economic utility or the public interest. This stage involves difficult debates about values and priorities. Consequently attempts to create a consensus or a common ethical convention constantly threaten to dissolve into ethical plurality and dilemmas.

When, and if, attempts at consensus building stumble or fail a person may move into the final phase of the vertical dimension. In this phase, through self-analysis and debate, people create their own set of moral precepts and values. At this level on the dimension people are aware of the plurality and fragmentation of the moral world and make choices about how to respond to it. They may either take a postmodern route, and learn to live with an ungrounded moral plurality, by playing with problems, or they may seek to re-integrate the fragments by reason and categorisation, as if they were doing a jigsaw puzzle.

Now that the dimensions in Figure 6.1 have been described the eight categories of ethical issue can be defined in relation to them. The categories are important because they define the range of possible reactions to a moral issue.

## The ethical categories

### Ethical neutrality

People put ethical issues into the category of ethical neutrality when they argue that nothing should be done about an issue that troubles them. There may be many reasons for this response. People may have applied ethical bracketing (Jackall, 1988) or ethical closure (Kärreman and Alvesson, 1999: 10–11). This causes them to suspend their normal ethical standards when they would obstruct them in getting the job done. This may lead people to argue that an issue, such as redundancy for example, has no moral dimension and should be seen as a practical question. De George (1999: 112) identified the range of excusing conditions people may use to justify their neutrality. These included the arguments of inability (you cannot be expected to save a drowning person if you cannot swim) and ignorance (you cannot be culpable if you were unaware of the consequences of not taking action).

### Ethical awareness

Ethical awareness is a category of ethical responses that causes a person to feel uncomfortable because an issue offends against their instinctively held values. At this stage the individual has an intuitive knowledge of what their duty is. As Mabbott (1967: 45) argued,

> everyone knows what in any particular set of circumstances his duty is ... I know my duty in each particular case and that I can give no reasons, nor are

there any, why I should assert this act or that to be my duty, except the self-evidence of every particular instance.

In the stage of duty a person knows what is right but cannot say why. Their reaction to an issue may only involve making their feelings known but it may extend to active opposition to the proposal under consideration. Ethical awareness is the same as emotivism, which is discussed in Chapter 2. A feature of emotivism, which is important in the context of ethical awareness, is the apparent irresolubility of moral disagreements as one person's statements of their values, in relation to an action, person or situation, contradict others' value statements.

## Ethical convention

An issue is allocated to the category of ethical convention when it is thought that it can best be resolved by applying accepted norms to it. They may be social norms, the expectations and standards of professional behaviour or the constraints of organisational cultures and sub-cultures. A feature of conventional ethical norms is that they are informal and unwritten or, if they are written, they are expressed in general terms and not as detailed prescriptions. In one incident that was described to us the respondent, a personnel manager, believed there was a norm in her organisation that one should not turn against people who had come looking for professional advice and assistance. She consequently felt a little guilt when she suspended a manager who had initially come to seek her help in disciplining a member of his staff, but who was later ensnared in the investigations he had initiated.

## Ethical puzzle

A puzzle is a conundrum, such as a mathematical teaser or a crossword puzzle, to which there is a technically correct or best answer. Arriving at the correct solution may be no easy matter, involving much hard thought and work, but the effort is justifiable because a best answer can be obtained. A puzzle can only exist in a clear moral context in which there is little argument about the values appropriate to its resolution. The wish to transform ethical difficulties into puzzles can be illustrated by those who argue that if only we had, in the National Health Service in the UK for example, better information (on clinical effectiveness, public views on medical priorities, costs and hospital activity rates) and better decision-making software to process the data, then questions of medical priorities could be settled technically, optimally, without recourse to messy political arguments about competing values in which, quite commonly, the one who argues the loudest gets the most resources (*see* Case study 2.9).

A decision to see an issue as a puzzle requires the puzzle solver to place the issue within a coherent moral framework and to ignore the demands of contrary values and perspectives. This often enables a puzzle solver to construct detailed mechanisms and steps (rules, procedures and techniques) for resolving an issue.

## Ethical problems

A problem is a conundrum to which there is no optimum solution. It may be necessary to take action on a problem, but the action will not remove the difficulty. A problem may be ameliorated or modified but it is unlikely to be resolved. Problems are complicated entities that form, develop and disappear according to their own dynamics. An issue is likely to be categorised as a problem because it involves many different values, and principles which, when taken in isolation, make perfect sense, but which, when taken together, fall into conflict. In these situations there has to be a debate between the differing conceptions of value, and part of the difficulty, for people who see issues as ethical problems, is to ensure that the arguments in the debate are conducted rigorously and fairly. The discussion of discourse ethics in Chapter 3 is relevant to this stance.

## Ethical dilemma

A dilemma is a perplexing state involving difficult or unpleasant choices. The options presented by a dilemma are often unpleasant because they demand a choice between conventions. If the person decides to act according to one set of conventional norms or rules then they will break another set of expectations. As conventions are social constructs it follows that dilemmas are essentially social and political issues. Breaking out of a dilemma necessitates choosing to support one group, by accepting their rules and values, but annoying another group by offending against theirs. It is not unsurprising therefore that categorising an issue as a dilemma can lead to indecision and inaction.

## Ethical cynicism and caprice

Cynicism emerges when ethical duty turns bitter. In the category of ethical awareness a person tries to do what their conscience tells them is right. The cynical person, however, has given up on this aim and become, as in the original definition of the word, like a surly dog. The cynic believes that all ethical issues will be resolved in ways which primarily meet the personal and private interests of those involved. Sometimes, the cynic thinks, it would be better to leave matters to capricious chance than to try to improve things. The cynics' aim, apart from maintaining their safely detached position, is to cast blame on those who are trying to deal with an issue.

## Ethical negotiation

Ethical negotiation is the process followed when someone is seeking to protect their self-interest (keeping their heads down and getting on with their work), by remaining ethically neutral, but find themselves caught between powerful groups with different views and values. Ethical negotiation therefore is a search for consensus or compromise between differing positions. This category is not concerned with the rightness of a decision but with the correctness of the process used to arrive at it. Put another way, the morality of an action is ignored; only a broad acceptability of an action, as determined by voting, opinion polling, consensus seeking, deal cutting and negotiation, is required. Responding to opinion becomes more important than doing the right thing. This was a barb frequently thrown at the Labour Party during the 2001 election campaign as they responded to feedback from focus groups. This category involves defending oneself by responding to the demands of competing interest groups.

## The stances in practice

The model presented in Figure 6.1 represents a range of stances or reactions to an ethical issue at work. However, the descriptions of them are very general and summary. They would be difficult to identify in everyday life. Table 6.1 identifies the sorts of arguments and values, arising from each of the stances, that people would use in their discussions.

**Table 6.1** A summary of the eight categories of ethical response

| Stances | Grids | Way of thinking about the issue | Likely actions |
|---|---|---|---|
| **Ethical neutrality** | Keeping out of trouble/jobsworth | People decide to ignore what they see as an injustice because to raise the issue would cause them trouble. | Inaction and keeping quiet. |
| | Getting the job done | For example a team leader might choose not to respond to concerns raised about the unethical behaviour of some staff working on a contract, because it would have disrupted the staff scheduling that had been planned with much difficulty. | |
| **Ethical awareness** | Dignity of persons | A sort of pop Kantianism which is triggered when it is thought that people are used as means and that their proper dignity is not respected. | Assertion of, and acting upon, one's values. Expressing surprise that others may see things differently. |
| | The importance of truth | The moral imperative of always telling the truth. | |
| | Just desserts | Rewarding people according to their merits. A form of deservingness. One respondent, working in government, regarded the catering management as feckless and shed no tears when they were threatened by competitive tendering; but he thought it unjust when the laundry, which the respondent believed provided an excellent service, lost out to an external bidder. | |
| **Ethical convention** | Professional norms | The argument that people should adhere to professional and organisational norms and standards. | Seeking advice and help from others on what the normal and acceptable response would be. Applying norms and conventions. |

**Table 6.1** Continued

| Stances | Grids | Way of thinking about the issue | Likely actions |
|---|---|---|---|
| | Fairness | Keeping a level playing field and being fair, treating all the same. | |
| **Ethical puzzle** | Policies, rules and procedures | The belief that things are best kept ethical and proper by sticking to the rules and regulations and not bending them to allow for special cases. | Applying the rules of an organisation or institution. |
| | Utility | Belief in the maximisation of an objective or of utility. This is the philosophy of utilitarianism. | Calculating the consequences of an action. Acting to resolve the issue on the basis that they have the correct or best solution. The assumption is that, the correct action having been taken, this will be an end to the matter. |
| **Ethical problem** | Moral judgement | The application of moral judgement rather than the moral calculation of utility. Moral judgement, the ability to define the ethical mean proportionately is acquired through the development of virtues. One respondent argued that ethical codes were unnecessary because the organisation's staff were virtuous and honest. | Clarifying how the conflicts between different values would lead to different actions or decisions. Acting upon one's best judgement. |
| | Learning from moral exemplars | The argument that ethical lapses can be temporarily tolerated if people have the opportunity to learn new and better ways. | |
| **Ethical dilemma** | Personal relationships | In a wicked world one should concentrate on the development of personal relationships. See Case study 6.1 for an example. | The emphasis of action is on maintaining discussion about the issue rather than seeking closure on it. When conflicts about issues are serious it is important to maintain good manners and interpersonal relationships. |
| | Ironic liberalism and pragmatism | This notion is taken from Rorty (1989). It is a view on how sanity can be maintained in a world where values are ungrounded. The key techniques are the separation of private and public domains and giving priority to 'keeping the conversation going' (Mounce, 1997: 197, 207). | |
| | Relativism | The argument that different cultures have different moral precepts and that what may be unethical in one culture, or organisation, may not be so in another. | |

**Table 6.1** Continued

| Stances | Grids | Way of thinking about the issue | Likely actions |
|---|---|---|---|
| | Holism | Trying to take the whole position into account. At its most extreme it is like the Buddhist belief that great effort is needed to see beyond the illusion of fragmentation to the unity beyond (Kjonstad and Willmott, 1995: 457). | |
| **Ethical cynicism** | Façadism | One person thought others wanted to be seen to follow the proper recruitment procedures even though the person they wanted to have the job had been decided beforehand. This grid includes being economical with the truth and the belief that business involves games playing and bluffing (Carr, 1968). | The cynic will withdraw from any action or decision but will snipe from the sidelines at any action or decision that others may have taken. |
| | Personal gain and selfishness | The argument that people are distorting situations and procedures to their own private advantage. | |
| **Ethical negotiation** | Complex politics | 'There are high-level politics concerning this issue to which I am not privy – so I keep my own views to myself.' A person working with this perspective tries to steer a compromise route through the competing demands of different groups. The problems of allocating scarce car parking spaces at work are often a good example. | Seeking out others' views and supporting or acquiescing in the wishes of the most powerful. |
| | 'Dodgy deals' | Bending rules, or acquiescing in rule bending, to accommodate the interest of powerful groups. | |

# Competing stances: the possibility of cognitive dissonance

It would be convenient to claim that people opted for one of the eight categories just described, when dealing with an ethical issue, and kept to it. In practice people may change their categorisation of an ethical issue; indeed they may hold conflicting views in their minds at the same time. This latter possibility will be explained first.

Let us consider how someone might hold conflicting views. When someone is thinking about an ethical issue it can be speculated that there are at least four perspectives from which the issue can be addressed:

- What is it that is ethically or morally wrong about a situation? What has triggered the recognition of the issue as an ethical one? What in other words has triggered their *conscience*?

- What ideally should be done about the situation? When they apply their *ethical reasoning* to the situation what will they think is the proper course of action?

- What do they think all the other interested persons and parties think about the situation? What are the *demands and expectations* that other stakeholders in the situation wish to impose?

- What, in practical terms, should be done about it given all the constraints and complexities of the 'real' world? What are their *options for action*?

The theory of cognitive dissonance claims that people try to make all their perspectives fit neatly together in their own minds. Instead it will be argued that people may hold contradictory views. Each of these perspectives can be discussed in more detail.

## Conscience

Aspects of an issue might cause some pain or difficulty because they are thought to be wrong. This feeling may be termed conscience, defined as an anxiety caused by the belief that a thought or act is wrong. Conscience is the starting point for the analysis of people's response to ethical incidents. It is conscience that causes, as one of our interviewees phrased it, 'the ethical twinges' that lead us to identify an issue as an ethical one. Conscience, or the superego to use a psychoanalytic term, is the function that keeps bad impulses in check. It does this by drenching the mind with anxiety whenever temptation is on hand and by creating feelings of remorse and humiliation when bad impulses are succumbed to. Conscience does not, however, tell us what is right; that is more the province of social norms and ethical reasoning.

## Ethical reasoning

Ethical reasoning is a person's rational, or rationalised, analysis of what they think should be done in relation to an incident or issue (Snell, 1993). If conscience defines the problem then ethical reasoning identifies the solution. It is the actions (or inactions) that the person thinks, on the basis of their values and analysis, they should take.

## The demands and expectations of others

From the perspective of the demands and expectations of others a person undertakes a mini 'stakeholder analysis'. They identify the motives they attribute to the speech and actions of others. It is important to note that this perspective cannot pretend to know what the other's motives actually are. It is focused on what the person thinks the others involved in the story are thinking and why.

## Options for action

If conscience is the expression of the superego then the perspective of options for action represents the ego. In psychoanalysis the ego is the instinct for self-preservation. It is the aspect of the self that is aware of the external world and rationalises how one should act within it. From this perspective therefore the concern is not what should, in moral terms, be done, but what it is sensible and practical to do.

These four perspectives and the eight categories of ethical response can be used to analyse someone's (or one's own) position on any particular ethical issue. An illustration of how this might be done is shown in the following example.

---

### An ethical issue

This illustration presents an example of an ethical incident, described by a research interviewee (R), analysed using these four perspectives.

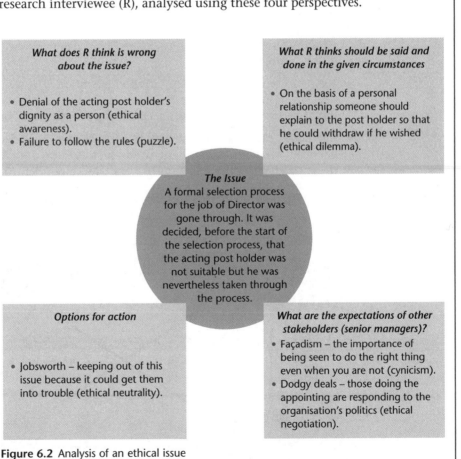

**What does R think is wrong about the issue?**

- Denial of the acting post holder's dignity as a person (ethical awareness).
- Failure to follow the rules (puzzle).

**What R thinks should be said and done in the given circumstances**

- On the basis of a personal relationship someone should explain to the post holder so that he could withdraw if he wished (ethical dilemma).

**The Issue**
A formal selection process for the job of Director was gone through. It was decided, before the start of the selection process, that the acting post holder was not suitable but he was nevertheless taken through the process.

**Options for action**

- Jobsworth – keeping out of this issue because it could get them into trouble (ethical neutrality).

**What are the expectations of other stakeholders (senior managers)?**

- Façadism – the importance of being seen to do the right thing even when you are not (cynicism).
- Dodgy deals – those doing the appointing are responding to the organisation's politics (ethical negotiation).

**Figure 6.2** Analysis of an ethical issue

## Conflicts between perspectives

The above example illustrates how a person can hold different views on an issue at the same time. People may think that something is wrong, and suffer pangs of conscience about it, but simultaneously believe that it may not be ethically proper to do anything about it. It is also clear, as Snell (1993) pointed out, that just because someone is capable of thinking at an advanced ethical level it does not mean that this will be reflected in his or her actions. There is no necessary connection between reasoning and action.

When people experience conflict because they adopt contradictory stances at some or all of the four perspective points they may experience a number of states, as shown in Figure 6.3. We argue that if people adopt different stances in the four perspectives, which clash with each other, then certain consequences can be predicted. Six types of conflict have been identified.

- Type 1 conflict occurs when conscience and ethical reasoning are at odds and this produces feelings of anxiety. There was no type 1 conflict in the illustration because, although there are differences between the respondent's conscience and ethical reasoning (denial of personal dignity and personal relationships), a personal approach would have restored the personal dignity of the acting director.

- A type 2 conflict could be seen in the illustration. The respondent took a position of neutrality on an issue her conscience told her was wrong and this might be expected to produce feelings of guilt, shame or remorse.

- The illustration also suggests a type 3 conflict because there was disagreement between what the respondent thought should be done and the position of those conducting the selection process. The respondent thought the selection procedure should have been properly applied with no prior decision being taken about the suitability of any candidate. The senior managers however

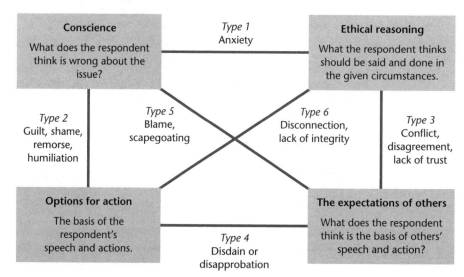

**Figure 6.3** The consequences of conflicting perspectives: six types of conflict

were happy to maintain a façade of keeping the rules and spirit of the recruitment policy while ensuring that the acting director did not get the job. This conflict might be expected to reduce the respondent's trust of the senior managers. If they were capable of 'shafting' one individual then they might just as easily do it to others.

- The respondent's position, in the illustration, of neutrality in the 'action' box prevented a type 4 clash with the views of others.

- There was a type 5 conflict in the illustation because the respondent blamed the others for behaving wrongly.

- Type 6 conflict, in which a person acts contrary to their ethical reasoning, will damage people's sense of integrity because they cannot consider their thoughts and actions to be of a piece. This was the situation in the illustration because the respondent did not do what her ethical reasoning told her to do.

Festinger's theory of cognitive dissonance (1957) held that the consequences of holding conflicting ideas in our heads were so unpleasant that we jerk our attitudes and actions into line so that they all fit comfortably together. Billig (1996: 202) pointed out that dissonant thoughts are not in themselves a cognitive problem. They only become an issue if an external opponent makes a public criticism of them. Even in this case, if it can be argued that the dissonances are trivial and not to be taken seriously, then the contradictory thoughts need not be a problem to the possessor of the ambiguity. Many may find little difficulty in taking different stances from each perspective.

---

**Case study 6.1**

## Disabled access

### Extract from an interview with a personnel manager

The fact [is] that both sites are not access friendly in a way that they would need to be for a lot of disabled people. So we've had a small audit of access and mobility type issues. You think it's small when you start out and then you get into it and there are major changes that would be required and therefore the money comes into it and how much we should be spending. So there's fairly wide ranging discussions going on at the moment about whether any of those changes should be made up front of employing anybody, or whether we wait to be pushed along that line by the employment of somebody. The law says you can obviously wait for the latter. There's two distinct camps. Those in slightly more senior positions, those with the clout, are favouring small changes now and delaying big spend on bigger changes until there's a need because we already employ a couple of individuals who fall into the definition of disabled, and both are perfectly well able to carry out their jobs with the arrangements that we have currently. But then we do have some people who strongly believe that we should make ourselves more overtly accessible and as a result we would attract a greater range of people.

Well, we have a working party set up and there are some people on it who are motivated by different things. Some are not often invited on to a working party and have taken the issue to heart so strongly that they feel that you

▶

should do something with it. Others have members of their family, or people that they know, who have disabilities and are therefore fighting from a particular corner for it. You do get into a moral argument with some people about, you know, it's the proper thing to do, we should do it. But there's quite a lot of proper things to do and at some point in time they have to be slotted into some sort of order, to deal with them. I would argue that there are a number of lower cost areas that could be addressed that would make us [more accessible], for instance we do not have ramp access to our reception. Now that wouldn't be a big deal but would be very visible and would then allow those with access problems to get into us. We could then move from there. We tend to have a lot of people that make assumptions about the nature of disabilities of people and assume that anybody with [a] disabled nametag is in a wheelchair and therefore everything should be wheelchair related. When we know it's not like that at all. So I would much rather get into some of the more obvious things like somewhere to park that's not too far away from the front. A ramp so that people can actually get in. Some of the problems we have are huge, like upstairs [you have to go] round goodness knows how many corridors, downstairs and back up again to get to the canteen. And that's the only place where people can buy food. But on the basis that we employ a couple [of] males already who have fairly strong disabilities we can get round it. No I don't think it's easy. It's particularly difficult. I recently popped back from work to attend a conference at which one of the lads, who is disabled, was arguing very, very strongly for spending all this money – big sums of money; and it's a very sensible argument. He delivers it with force. I mean at the end of the day [he was] saying that you have your independence and you should therefore do everything to ensure other people have independence because all a disabled person wants is independence. You should therefore facilitate that however you can. Yes it is hard to argue against but at some point things have to take their place. It's hard to argue against the fact that the best person for the job could cost ten grand a year more than you've actually got available. You know you could get the value for that person but somewhere it's got to stop. It is hard and I don't sit on the working party personally but obviously I've got quite a lot to do with what they're up to. I do know that they go round in circles on that one quite a lot and they will do. We have a policy decided and we don't have a disability budget. Budgets are set for the next twelve months and have been for quite some time so it is a question of saying well if you spend the money on X it doesn't get spent on Y. Or finding it from somewhere else, well we're always looking for money from somewhere else for something

## Discussion activity 6.1

Describe, using the categories in Table 6.1, the respondent's view of the problem described, in the interview above, under the headings of conscience, ethical reasoning, the positions of others involved and practical action. The issue concerned making a building appropriate for disabled people to use.

A suggested analysis is shown in Figure 6.4. In this figure the informant's perspectives on the central issue of access improvements have been shown by quoting her words and then by categorising them using the eight ethical stances and the list of values shown in Table 6.1. The analysis could have been done more simply without recourse to the eight stances, but their use clarifies any conflicts between the four perspectives.

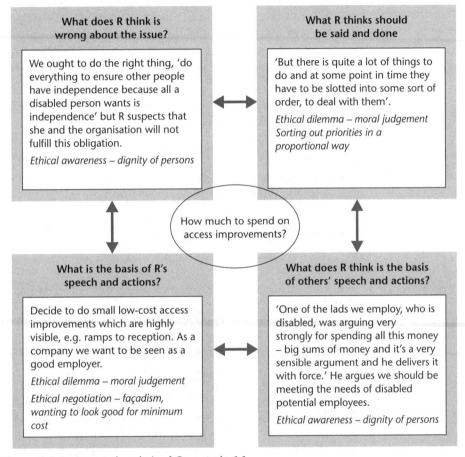

**Figure 6.4** A suggested analysis of Case study 6.1

The contradictions between the respondent's perspectives are indicated by the arrows in Figure 6.4, which shows type 1, 2, 3 and 4 tensions. Her conscience informed her that there was a major wrong that ought to be righted, but her ethical reasoning suggested that it would be wrong to do everything that needed to be done. Her conscience had sympathy for the views expressed by the member of staff but her ethical reasoning did not. So her actions (in sympathy with her reasoning rather than with her conscience) contradicted what she thought the staff were telling her. This pattern of conflicts and congruencies might be described as melancholic acceptance. With regret she thought it wrong to do what her conscience, and the consciences of others, demanded (Fisher, 1999).

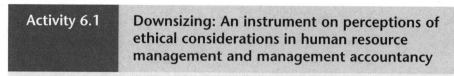

**Downsizing: An instrument on perceptions of ethical considerations in human resource management and management accountancy**

## Instructions

In this questionnaire you are put in the place of a team manager who is facing pressure to make someone in the team redundant. Please work through the various sections of the questionnaire in sequence and please do not flip through the document to see how the storyline develops and ends!

There are a few points you need to bear in mind as you work through the questionnaire.

- All the information you are given is consistent, i.e. you will not be given information in the latter part of the questionnaire that contradicts information given earlier.

- There are no right answers to the questions posed in the questionnaire. The purpose of the questionnaire is to research the variety of responses to it and not to find out how many people get it 'right'.

- Do not backtrack to earlier sections of the questionnaire when you get near the end and change your decisions.

## Section 1

You are a human resource management specialist managing a team of four professional staff. A benchmarking exercise, which you have no reason to doubt, has shown that the organisation's unit costs, in the function in which the team works, are much higher than those of similar and competing organisations. The market environment of the organisation is becoming more competitive and market share is showing a marginal decline.

Senior management have announced staff redundancies and the team's share of the overall reduction, which actually is proportionately smaller than that demanded of other teams and departments, is one member of staff. You have been lucky in previous rounds of redundancy and your team has escaped cuts. Whilst you have heard rumours on the grapevine, the actual announcement of the latest round, when it came, was unexpected.

The team members are:

**Chris** who is a willing worker and makes a good contribution to meeting the team's objectives.

**Phil** who has joined the organisation in the last few years, and

**Leslie** who has long service with the organisation. You have begun to be dissatisfied with the quantity and quality of Leslie's work.

**Nicky** who is a good worker but can be uncooperative and curmudgeonly (a curmudgeon is a surly and niggardly person).

You have had previous experience of making people redundant, in an organisation you worked for earlier in your career, and you found it very difficult. You have no doubt that this round of redundancy will be equally emotionally wearing and it is not an experience you are keen to repeat.

On balance would you:

Adopt a position of grumbling acceptance and argue that, as you were not consulted about the decision, your senior manager should decide who should be made redundant. ☐ (01)

Accept the redundancies as an unfortunate necessity and start thinking about the decision you have to make. ☐ (02)

Lobby and fight to get the redundancy decision reversed and/ or argue that redundancy is unethical. ☐ (03)

*Please go to the next section.*

## Section 2

Through your managerial position you have gained inside knowledge about the organisation and there are several things you know which some people might consider as ethical failings. The organisation has been making large profits in recent years but it is clear that it has given more priority to shareholders than to customers and staff in the way its added value has been allocated. The chairman of the organisation might also be branded a 'fat cat' because, through pay increase, bonus payments and share option schemes, his income has increased at a rate many times greater than inflation. The organisation is based in Skegmouth which has one of the highest unemployment rates in the country and there is little chance that those made redundant could obtain new jobs locally.

On balance would you:

Adopt a position of grumbling acceptance and argue that, as you were not consulted about the decision, your senior manager should decide who should be made redundant. ☐ (01)

Accept the redundancies as an unfortunate necessity and start thinking about the decision you have to make. ☐ (05)

Lobby and fight to get the redundancy decision reversed. ☐ (06)

*Please go to the next section.*

## Section 3

You have had discussions with the team, following the announcement of redundancies, and they all agree, and so do you, that in these situations the opportunities for voluntary redundancies and early retirements should be taken up before there is any consideration of compulsory redundancy. This is a strong matter of principle with you. You find it hard to explain why it is so important to you; it just seems the fair and just solution.

Chris is in his early sixties and is willing, almost desperate, to take early retirement. He has been talking to you about going early for several years. He is the only man in the team, in an organisation that has appointed more women in recent years. There is some grumbling in the organisation that a policy of accepting voluntary redundancies will discriminate against women. The older staff (who are more likely to want and to get early retirement) are disproportionately male. Therefore more men are likely to benefit from an early retirement policy than women. Whether this issue causes you any concern or not, it is clear that Chris's experience and competence in the job will be hard to replace.

Would you continue to fight against the cuts, probably by using delaying tactics? ☐ (07)

If not, would you

**Refuse** to give Chris early retirement? ☐ (08)

Agree to Chris retiring early because it seems the right thing to do, and/or ☐ (09a)

Agree to Chris retiring early because it gets you out of a tricky decision. ☐ (09b)

*Please go to the next section.*

## Section 4

Chris has recently come to see you to say that he and his partner have been discussing their retirement plans, and although he has always been keen to go, he now realises that it will not be financially possible to buy his dream retirement home in the Caribbean if he retires now. So, with some regret, he has withdrawn his offer to take early retirement or voluntary redundancy. If you had agreed to accept Chris's offer in the previous section you are no longer able to. As there are no other team members willing to take voluntary redundancy you have accepted that it is up to you to decide which member of the team should be made redundant. All the team are on approximately the same salary so there is no greater cost saving to be had by making a particular team member redundant. You also recognise that you will have to establish some clear guidelines for choosing whom to make redundant so that the process can be made open, transparent and fair.

The organisation has no policy, or joint agreements, or preference for 'last in first out' or any other criterion for choosing which jobs to make redundant. The following seem to be the decision criteria available to you.

- **Contribution** to team and organisational objectives – you make redundant the person who makes least contribution.

- **Last in first out** (LIFO).

- **Deservingness** – the least deserving person, i.e. the one who makes least effort to be a good team player, should be made redundant.

- **Career potential** – the young, who have a career ahead of them and perhaps a greater contribution to make in terms of their ability with new technology, should not be made redundant. It is the older members of staff who should bear the brunt of redundancy.

You have thoroughly studied appraisal records, 360° multi-rater returns, attendance records and work records of your team members and constructed Table 6.2 which gives your considered evaluation of each of them against the possible criteria for redundancy.

**Table 6.2** Suitability of each team member for redundancy against each criterion

|        | Career potential | Contribution | LIFO | Deservingness |
|--------|------------------|--------------|------|---------------|
| Chris  | 1                | 4            | 2    | 3             |
| Leslie | 2                | 1            | 3    | 4             |
| Phil   | 4                | 2            | 1    | 2             |
| Nicky  | 3                | 3            | 4    | 1             |

1 = most suitable for redundancy.
4 = least suitable for redundancy.

Who would you make redundant?

Chris                                                    ☐ (10)

Leslie                                                   ☐ (11)

Phil                                                     ☐ (12)

Nicky                                                    ☐ (13)

Or would you decide you cannot choose someone for redundancy because you:

Don't know/won't do it                                   ☐ (14)

*If you chose a team member to make redundant go to the next section. If you ticked the 'don't know' box, go to Section 6.*

## Section 5

You found the decision in Section 4 difficult. If you accepted the 'contribution' criterion then Leslie would have to be made redundant but you do know that her poor performance at work is because her partner is suffering from terminal cancer and she is finding it hard to keep her concentration on her work. If you accept the LIFO criterion then Phil would be the one to go. But Phil has been critical in purchasing and installing the new IT systems that are going to be the bedrock of the organisation's success in the future. The 'deservingness' criterion would lead you to choose Nicky for redundancy but she also makes a valuable contribution and often adds a useful note of scepticism in a group that can otherwise be a little too cohesive, inward-looking and blinkered in its

▶

approach. On the basis of the 'career potential' criterion then it is Chris who would be the obvious candidate for redundancy but his experience cannot be easily replaced.

The team member you chose to make redundant in Section 4 describes themselves as of an Afro-Caribbean ethnic origin. They had been recruited when the introduction of an equal opportunities policy, and the provision of formal training in selection and recruitment, were beginning to increase the number of people from minorities who were appointed. There was no affirmative action policy, however, and there is no doubt that they were appointed on merit and were the best candidate available. The organisation still does not have a good record on the employment and promotion of people from minority groups, despite the signs of improvement. Because staff from minorities were often recruited after the recent development of equal opportunities polices they generally have short lengths of service with the organisation and the use of LIFO to decide who should be made redundant would discriminate against them. The result for the organisation would be that staff from the minorities would be more likely to be made redundant than other categories of staff and the proportion of staff from minority backgrounds would diminish.

Many people feel that several of the criteria for choosing who to make redundant, and not just LIFO, discriminate against people from the minority groups. Often their contribution, or career potential, is not as great as it could be because they have had less opportunity for staff development. When, as occasionally happens, they are seen by others as not fitting in with their team and being difficult and uncooperative often the failure is as much the result of unconscious racism on the part of their colleagues as their fault.

Taking the above information into consideration whom would you now decide to make redundant?

Name of person ☐ (15)

Don't know ☐ (16)

*Please go to the next section.*

## Section 6

As you agonise about the decision you talk to more and more people about the situation, and people seek you out and lobby you to make the decision one way or another. The trade union representatives believe that LIFO is the only fair way to make the decision. The equal opportunities office is determined that the redundancy policy should not discriminate against minority groups. The senior management are firmly convinced that in a competitive market it would be folly to choose whom to make redundant on any grounds other than merit – or contribution to the organisation's goals. You find you have sympathy with each of these views when you are talking face to face with their proponents but you find it difficult to square all the conflicting viewpoints.

The senior managers are pushing you for a decision. The deadline to inform the HRM director is tomorrow morning. Do you:

Decide to make redundant. ☐ (17)

Decide to report that none of the team should be made
redundant and let senior management decide. ☐ (18)

Decide to choose the person to be made redundant by drawing lots. ☐ (19)

Decide to have a very large drink. ☐ (20)

*Please go to the next section.*

## Section 7

The decision you have to make is so complex that you decide to discuss it, and
negotiate, with others and arrive at a compromise. Which of the following
groups, if any, would you negotiate, and seek consensus, with?

*Tick as many boxes as appropriate, or none.*

The team ☐ (22)

The senior managers ☐ (23)

The equal opportunities office ☐ (24)

The trade unions ☐ (25)

You have had the discussions, and the large drink, you sit down and you feel,
in your heart of hearts, that

should be the person to go. ☐ (21)

Or you feel that you just cannot make this decision. ☐ (26)

*This is the end of the instrument.*

### Instructions for scoring Downsizing

- At first sight the scoring matrix for *Downsizing* (Figure 6.5) looks complex.
  But if you follow these instructions it should not be too difficult.

- First of all note that all the boxes you ticked in the exercise had a field
  number attached to them in brackets. You will use these to score yourself.

- Start at the left of the scoring form and work your way across it. In Sections
  1 to 4 put a cross in the cell that corresponds to the answer you have in
  that section, as follows.

- In Sections 5 to 7 it is a little more difficult because you have to apply the
  decision rules described in the cells to decide which cell is the correct one
  to describe your decision.

- Join up all the 'X's in the columns to draw a profile line across the grid that
  represents the categories of ethical response you chose in the exercise.  ▶

Use the decision rules in each box to allocate responses to an ethical category

Espoused stances and values

Forced hard choices: stances and values in practices

| | Section 1 | Section 2 | Section 3 | Section 4 | Section 5 | Section 6 | Section 7 |
|---|---|---|---|---|---|---|---|
| Ethical Cynicism | | | | If 10 ticked | If 15 is Chris | If 19 ticked | If none of 22/23/24 or 25 is ticked & if 26 ticked |
| Ethical Negotiation | | | | | | | If 22, 23, 24 or 25 ticked & if 26 ticked |
| Ethical Dilemma | | | | | | If 18 ticked or if 17 is different from 15 or if 20 ticked | If 26 ticked, or if 21 is the same as 17, or different from 15 |
| Ethical Problem | | | | If 14 ticked | If 16 ticked, or 15 different from person chosen in section 4, or if 14 ticked | If 17 is the same as 15, or if a choice is made after choosing 14 | If 21 same as 15 |
| Ethical Puzzle | | | If 08 ticked | If 10 or 11 or 12 or 13 ticked | If 15 the is same as person chosen in section 4 | If 17 is the same as person chosen in section 4 | If 21 same as person chosen in section 4 |
| Ethical Convention | | | If 09a ticked | Name of person chosen | Name of person chosen | Name of person chosen | Name of person chosen |
| Ethical Awareness | If 03 ticked | If 06 ticked | If 07 ticked | | | | |
| Ethical Neutrality | If 02 ticked | If 05 ticked | | | | | |
| Ethical Cynicism | If 01 ticked | If 04 ticked | If 09b ticked | | | | |

Figure 6.5 Scoring matrix for *Downsizing*

## Shifting stances

The discussion in the previous section has illustrated how a person might take potentially conflicting perspectives on an ethical issue and hold them simultaneously. In the changing circumstances of a working life it might be that people give emphasis to different perspectives as the situation develops and more particulars become known. Others of course might adopt an initial stance and then keep to it without distraction. This is the issue that is explored in Activity 6.1.

## Some research findings from the use of Downsizing

*Downsizing* has been completed by a large sample of financial professionals and accountants and by a smaller sample of human resource managers (Fisher and Lovell, 2000). The results are shown in Figure 6.6. You might wish to compare your results with those of these two samples.

The great majority of both accountants and human resource specialists began by taking a neutral position in Section 1. The inference would seem to be that redundancy is a common part of organisational life and there is no reason to suspect there are any particular moral issues arising from the situation. In Section 2 doubts are sown about the ethical status of the organisation in the case study. A narrow majority of the HR specialists changed their view of the case, took a position of ethical awareness, and began to protest against the redundancies. The majority of accountants continued to take a neutral stance although a minority shifted to the ethical awareness position. In Section 3 respondents were given the opportunity to adopt a conventional response to the situation (reducing numbers through voluntary redundancy) and the majority of both accountants and HR specialists took this option.

The opportunity for a conventional response is removed in Section 4 when Chris withdraws his or her offer to take voluntary redundancy. The respondents are given sufficient information to treat the problem as a puzzle. A number of criteria that can be used to select candidates for redundancy are provided and all the team members are ranked against each of the criteria. These can be used to make a rational choice of who should be made redundant. Over 80 per cent of the accountants, and over three-quarters of the HR specialists, took this opportunity and used the information provided to choose the most suitable candidate for redundancy. A small percentage of respondents (although fewer accountants than HR specialists) recognised that it was not possible to identify an optimum candidate for redundancy when all of the proposed criteria were applied. Put simply, there was no candidate who was the best choice on all the criteria. These respondents took an ethical problem stance that recognised the conflicts between the values represented by the different criteria.

Further information is provided in Section 5 of the exercise. This reports a clash between incompatible values. Those respondents who chose a candidate for redundancy on apparently rational grounds are told that the choice raises other problems and ethical difficulties. Some accountants, as a consequence, did move their stance to that of ethical problem but most ignored the new complexities and continued to see the issue as an ethical puzzle. The majority of HR specialists

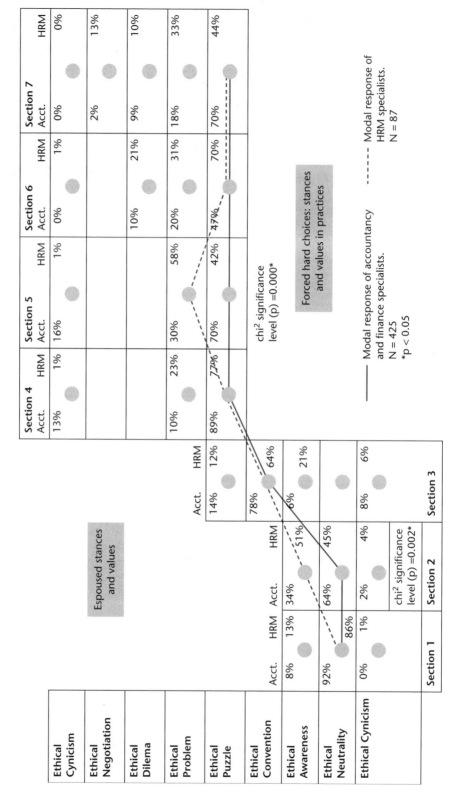

**Figure 6.6** Results from the *Downsizing* instrument: the percentage frequency with which Accounting and Finance specialists and HRM specialists chose ethical positions in the seven sections of the instruments

(*Source:* Fisher and Lovell, 2000)

however did take a new, ethical problem, stance. Further complexities are introduced in Section 6. Most of the accountants still saw the issue as a puzzle. A fifth of the HR specialists now saw the issue as a dilemma; a third saw it as a problem but the single biggest group of the HR specialists returned to a puzzle stance. The pattern was the same in the last section of the exercise in which some information was provided that was intended to encourage some to take a position of ethical negotiation. Only a small proportion of respondents did so.

In the latter half of the exercise most accountants stuck with their ethical puzzle stance, no matter what ethical difficulties they were presented with. Most of the HR specialists did initially respond to these difficulties but they subsequently returned to a pragmatic ethical puzzle stance. You can see from the scoring matrix (Figure 6.5) that the results for the second part of the exercise are labelled 'forced hard choices' whereas those in the first part are termed 'espoused stances'. Espoused values are those that people would wish others to think that they hold. These are often contrasted with those values that people use in practice, especially when under pressure.

## Categorisation and particularisation and the eight stances

The results from *Downsizing* suggest that some people pigeon-hole an issue under one category, and do not change their minds; other people change their views as the issue unfolds. This phenomenon can be explained by using the concepts of categorisation and particularisation that were mentioned at the start of the chapter. The emphasis in this chapter so far has been on categorisation but the idea of particularisation will be useful in explaining the processes that cause people to take different stances on ethical issues.

Categorisation is the process of placing an object within a general category or schema. Psychologists have claimed it is the fundamental process of thinking. As Cantor *et al.* (1982: 34) claimed:

> Categorisation schemes allow us to structure and give coherence to our general knowledge about people and the social world, providing expectations about typical patterns of behaviour and the range of likely variation between types of people and their characteristic actions and attributes.

The terms category and schema are similar in meaning. However, it is generally claimed that schemata are more general and complex than categories. It is possible for example to see schemata as formed from collections of categories.

On its own, however, Billig (1996: 154) argued, categorisation can lead to bureaucratic and prejudiced forms of thinking. The story (which may be an urban myth) of the doctor who would not give emergency treatment to a person who had a heart attack on the pavement in front of the hospital, because his employer's liability insurance did not extend beyond the hospital premises, illustrates the typical ethical costs of bureaucracy. The research finding (Galton and Delafield, 1981) that primary school teachers' ways of talking to and questioning pupils they had judged to be low performing led such pupils to do less well than they ought identified the prejudicial impact of categorisation.

Illustrations of the bureaucracy and prejudice that can emerge from categorisation were found when we interviewed people about ethical incidents they had experienced at work. In some cases the rigidity of bureaucracy was at the organisation's (rather than the employee's or customer's) cost. In one incident a young marketing manager had been partly disabled by a stroke that prevented him from driving. His job required him to work on two widely separated sites and the company paid his taxi fares and overnight costs. In other circumstances a manager of his seniority would have had a company car with free petrol. The week before his summer holiday he asked personnel to hire a car for him so that his wife could drive him about on their continental holiday. He argued that other managers were able to use company cars and petrol on their holidays and that he should be treated the same as them. Most of the personnel department, for they all became involved in discussing the case, tended to the view that the manager was trying it on, manipulating the bureaucratic rules to gain a personal advantage. They thought that the bureaucratic rules were being used to achieve an unfair and undeserved benefit for the marketing manager.

Other interviewees gave accounts of many instances in which an injustice may have resulted from the way in which people were categorised. In one case an employee was appointed to a post but was denied membership of the company pension scheme because he was too fat. In other cases managers refused, illegally, to appoint young women to jobs in case they later caused disruption by becoming pregnant and taking maternity leave.

Billig proposed that categorisation, because it can lead to distorted responses, should be understood in the context of the tension with its opposite – particularisation. Particularisation is the process of recognising the specific and unique features of a situation, which mean that it cannot be categorised. At the least particularisation causes controversy about how an issue should be categorised. It provides a counterweight to categorisation. Those whose powers of particularisation are diminished may become bureaucratic and prejudiced in ways that deny justice, or at the least provide a dulled and mechanical response to ethical issues.

Comparison of the *Downsizing* results of the accountancy and HR specialists (Figure 6.6) suggests that categorisation, evidenced by an unwillingness to change one's categorisation of an issue, need not be the dominant way of thinking about ethical issues in organisations. The HR managers were more likely than the financial specialists to change their categorisation as they worked through the instrument. They were readier to change their categorisation in response to new particulars. The greater proportion of women in the HRM profession could account for the relative strength of particularisation in the HR sample. Some research (Helson and Wink, 1992) has suggested that women have a greater tolerance of ambiguity as they get older. This tendency, if related to a greater ease with particularisation, contrasts with men's inclination to see things in the puzzle mode more often as they get older (Fisher and Lovell, 2000).

The point is not which mode, categorisation or particularisation employees ought to be encouraged to adopt, rather that they should be helped to use both. As Winter puts it (1989: 53) dialectical critique means looking for 'unity concealed behind apparent differentiation and contradiction concealed within apparent unity'. People should be helped to challenge, and argue about, how ethical issues at work should be categorised. Particularisation and categorisation need to be operated in combination because particularisation is the trigger for challenges to habitual categorisation. Billig (1996: 171) discussed

> the rhetorical strategies which turn around our schemata and unpick our categories. It will be seen that these strategies are not based upon a simple process of particularisation. Rather they are located within a continual argumentative momentum, oscillating between particularisation and categorisation.

There are two aspects to this momentum: arguing about which category it is appropriate to use in a particular case; and arguing about what the categories are, or what they mean. An issue from our research interviews can illustrate this. A company that trades with developing countries had relieved its managers of wrestling with the ethical problems associated with accepting gifts from overseas agents. It required that any employees who were offered gifts by an overseas agent should accept them (thereby avoiding giving offence to the agent), but hand them over to the company. During the year such gifts were auctioned and the proceeds donated to charities. Thus, the need to think or worry about how to handle such situations is removed from the individual manager involved by the adoption of an ethical code.

Whilst managers' lives were made easier by the code it also took away from them their personal moral responsibility. For this reason the categorisation of the issue as a matter of rule following should have been challenged. It could, for example, have been recategorised as a matter of ethical awareness, and the view taken that nothing that could be seen as corruption should be tolerated. In this case no gifts should be accepted. Or, by way of redefining the categorisations, it might have been argued that it was a question of following ethical conventions, but not those of the company's home base. Instead the norms of the country in which the business was being conducted (where giving bribes was accepted) should be followed. There is another possibility. Texas Instruments' (1999) code argued that a gift is improper if it is expected to provide the giver with an advantage. The impropriety of a gift is not judged by its scale, which customarily differs between countries, but by the intention of the gift giver. This approach categorises the issue as one of moral judgement within a problem perspective. These possibilities lead to the conclusion that ethical behaviour in organisations requires employees to balance their tendency to categorise or 'label' ethical issues by using the particularity of a situation to challenge their categorisations.

Case study 6.2 shows how particulars can suddenly challenge categorisations as one particular feature of a case acts as an epiphany that causes a major realignment in a person's view of an issue.

---

**DEFINITION**

**Epiphany** was originally a Christian term for the manifestation of God's presence in the world. James Joyce (1996, but actually published in 1914–15) took the term over, in his novel *The Portrait of an Artist as a Young Man*, to mean a commonplace object or gesture that provides a sudden insight.

## Case study 6.2

### Particularisation and categorisation

The following incident was recounted by one of our research interviewees, a senior personnel manager in a food processing company. The company had a van sales force that sold and delivered the product to small shops and catering businesses. She became indirectly involved in discussions about the fate of a van salesman who had been accused of theft. She was told that on his rounds the salesman had seen a bike on waste ground outside a shop he was delivering to, and had put it in the van to take it home to give to his son. The police had stopped him and accused him of theft and the question was whether the salesman should be summarily dismissed in line with the company's disciplinary policy. The man's manager, realistically in the personnel manager's view, said that he was loath to dismiss the salesman because he was good at his job and, in any case, 'wouldn't we all take the bike in similar circumstances; pick up an abandoned bike?' The manager also reported that the police had said it would be unfair to dismiss the salesman. Despite this the police had decided to prosecute, which seemed a little odd to the personnel manager.

The personnel manager thought it important to maintain the reputation of the van sales force for trustworthiness.

> They are out on the road on their own and we trust the van sales people. Your sales reps have to be honest because the shopkeepers have a degree of mistrust and it's important that we build up a reputation as an honest company.

This thought inclined her to dismiss the van salesman. However, there had been a number of recent cases where staff had been involved in minor theft and had been let off with a caution because they had been good employees. It seemed sensible to show leniency to the salesman especially as there was some doubt about whether it was a case of theft or simply a matter of 'finder's keepers'. On this basis the personnel manager was inclined to accept the manager's wish to retain the salesman.

Out of curiosity she asked:

> 'What sort of shop was it where the bike was taken from?' The manager replied, sheepishly, 'It was a newsagent's early in the morning'. Suspicions aroused she asked, 'Was it a newspaper boy's or girl's bike?' 'Yes it was', came the resigned response. 'It was leaning against the side wall of the newsagents – but it was on waste ground. It was just alongside the newsagents.'

This fact was enough for the personnel manager who insisted that the employee be dismissed. The manager was annoyed because he had lost a good salesman and recruiting new ones was not easy. The sudden revelation of a few particulars about the nature and position of the bike were enough to settle the personnel manager's mind on how the issue should be categorised. It was a clear puzzle, which could be easily resolved by applying company rules, not an ethical problem that called for fine moral judgements.

**Discussion activity 6.2**    **Can you think of other examples?**

This small example provides an illustration of how particulars may serve to challenge categorisations.

**Connexion point**

The implications of particularisation for making decisions on ethical questions are explored in Chapter 13, p. 520.

## Influences on choice of stance

So far this chapter has concentrated upon identifying the categories people use to label ethical issues. It has also highlighted the importance of allowing categorisations of an issue to be challenged and changed by particulars. It is now necessary to look a little more closely at these particulars. The emphasis in this section will be on the factors and influences that bear upon people's choices of the stance to be taken on an ethical issue. Some of the influences upon these choices have been pre-empted in the description of the two dimensions in Figure 6.1. The vertical axis suggests that the adoption of a stance will depend upon the sophistication of a person's ethical reasoning. The horizontal axis indicates that a person's certainty about their values will also affect their choice of stances.

There are many other factors that have a claim to influence ethical categorisation and decision making. Models of the antecedents influencing ethical decision making often include four broad areas. They are:

### 1 Cultural factors

The importance of an organisation's ethical culture or ethos is discussed in Chapter 10. Trevino and Youngblood (1990) identified a link between an organisation's culture and the ethical position adopted by organisational members that they called vicarious reward and punishment. They hypothesised that people's actions would be influenced by whether they saw the wrongdoing of others being punished and whether others' ethical actions were praised. The conclusion was that vicarious reward and punishment influenced ethical decisions if they were greater than expected. It was argued that people expected wrongdoing to be punished and ignored this effect unless the punishment was stronger than they had anticipated. Conversely they did not expect good to be praised, and when they saw it was, it did have a positive effect on their assessments of the probability that their own good actions might attract praise and reward.

### 2 Situational factors

The specifics of a situation can also affect someone's response to an ethical issue.

Some people's jobs and organisational positions make it easier for them to take a moral stand than do those of others. The degree of closeness to an ethical problem, or their formal responsibility for resolving it, is an important factor. The closer one is the greater the obligation to act. Stewart (1984) defined this as the Kew Gardens Principle. (The geographical reference is to the public gardens in New York where passive bystanders witnessed a murder and did nothing, and not to the British botanical gardens.) This principle proposed an obligation to take action against an ethical wrong where:

- there was a clear case of need;
- the agent was close to the situation in terms of 'notice' if not space;
- the agent had the capability to help the one in need; and
- no one else was likely to help.

**Connexion point**

The Kew Gardens case is discussed more extensively in Chapter 13 pp. 525–6. As well as defining the conditions under which people have a moral obligation the case also raises the problem of why people do not act on the obligation. This is a particular problem for the American ethical objectivism based on the work of Ayn Rand (see Chapter 1, pp. 21–3.) The objectivists argue that ethical good comes from reducing government interference in people's lives and giving them the maximum autonomy. If, as the Kew Gardens case would seem to show, people cannot be trusted to act well then the moral case for objectivism is undermined.

In our research interviews people often claimed their 'distance' from an issue, in terms of their managerial responsibility, justified taking a position of neutrality on some example of organisational wrongdoing. Equally a person's general situation, in terms of their responsibility for others, for family, or their degree of economic independence, will also affect their willingness to move beyond neutrality. The specific circumstance of the ethical issue will also affect a person's response to it. Most people's response to the theft of a box of paper clips from work will be different from their response to serious misuse of a company credit card.

## 3 Psychological factors

Trevino (1986) suggested a number of individual variables that could affect a person's response to an ethical issue. They included ego strength, which is the tendency to stick to one's convictions. People with high ego strength are less likely to be swayed by circumstances or impulses into changing their mind. Field dependence was another possible variable. This refers to the degree to which someone depends on information given by others when faced with an ambiguous situation. A person with high field dependence, if asked by their superior to take a possibly unethical action, would be influenced by the superior's assurances that they will not be blamed and that the action is not really improper. A person with low field dependency would wish to make up their own mind independently of the advice from others. Other writers (Verbeke *et al.*, 1996) have suggested that Machiavellianism, as a personality trait, may affect someone's response to an ethical issue.

**Machiavellianism** is named after Niccolò Machiavelli (1469–1527), whose name (rightly or wrongly) has become synonymous with cunning, amoral, devious and manipulative behaviour. The reputation is based on his book *The Prince*, in which he gave practical advice on statesmanship. He saw democracy as the best form of government but recognised that it was not always possible to behave in the most virtuous way. The dictum that 'the end justifies the means' is attributed to Machiavelli. By this he meant that there is no moral distinction between ends and means so that any badness in a proposed means can be balanced by the goodness of the outcome. It does not mean that good ends can justify any means no matter how wicked (Mackie, 1990: 159), but, as Machiavelli (1950, Ch. XVIII) put it, 'the prince must have a mind disposed to adapt itself, according to the wind, and as the variations of fortune dictate... not deviate from what is good, if possible but be able to do evil if constrained'.

Rotter's (1966) internal–external locus of control scale is another psychological construct that may affect ethical choices. It measures an individual's perception of how much control he or she exerts over events in their lives. Some people believe that most things in life are within their control. They do not believe in luck; they believe people make their own luck. Others do not believe they control their own lives. They believe in luck, fate and happenstance. Trevino's analysis found there was a relationship between this factor and people's ethical choices. It showed that people who felt in control of their actions were more likely to make ethical rather than unethical decisions than those who believed themselves influenced by external factors. To some extent this relationship was reinforced by the tendency of people with an internal locus of control to believe that they can bring about the beneficial consequences of their actions that they hoped for.

| Activity 6.2 | Scoring the locus of control scale |
| --- | --- |

Versions of the locus of control scale for you to fill in, and obtain your own score from, are to be found in plenty on the World Wide Web. Go to one of the following sites and see how you score.

**Locus of control questionnaires on the World Wide Web**

http://uhddx01.dt.uh.edu/~avenf/locus.html
http://home.hkstar.com/~ttyu/psytests/loc.htm
www.ballarat.edu.au/bssh/psych/rot.htm

## 4 Cognitive factors

The seminal work on levels of cognitive development was conducted and published by Lawrence Kohlberg (1969, 1984). His theory was originally developed in the field of developmental psychology. He researched the development of children's capacity for ethical reasoning and it was only later that the model was applied to adults and people in organisations in particular. Whether the focus is on adults or children the key idea is that people pass through an invariant and hierarchical sequence of three stages – the pre-conventional, the conventional and the post-conventional – in the development of their ethical cognitive ability. However, it is not quite as simple as this. Kohlberg originally proposed that each of the three stages be subdivided into two, giving a total of six stages. Subsequent developments have led to this being expanded to eight or possibly nine stages. We will take you through these one at a time.

# Pre-conventional stages

## Stage zero

At this stage a person has no capacity for moral reasoning. They simply act impulsively and respond to any urge no matter what the consequences.

## Stage one

People at this stage, and certainly all young children, have no innate sense of morality but they have learned that certain actions bring praise and others bring punishment. They can respond to the carrots and sticks without knowing the rationale for their subsequent behaviour. This stage of development consists of unwitting compliance with the demands of those with the ability to praise and punish. Parents clearly have this power but so do managers and supervisors in organisations.

## Stage two

Personal gain, and the wish not to miss out on good things, characterises moral thinking at this stage. People evaluate options according to the benefits that they might gain. This is a selfish stage at which a person cannot, when considering a situation, think beyond what might be in it for them. In an organisational context only the prospect of higher pay, promotion or some other benefit would be of weight.

# Conventional stages

## Stage three

It is at this level of development that a person responds to their social role by thinking about morality in terms of being, to use the phrase always used of this stage, a 'Nice Boy/Good Girl'. At this stage people accept as legitimate the social norms and expectations of the groups they belong to. This stage does not involve ethical thought about the issues. People abide by the social norms not because they have analysed them and concluded they are correct but because they wish to be socially accepted.

One of these social norms is the obligation to be caring towards others; and this lowly positioning of care (level three when eight or nine represents the highest level of morality) has been the source of a major criticism of Kohlberg's model. Gilligan (1982) showed that girls' moral development differs from that of boys (*see* p. 105). Girls place more emphasis on relationships, responsibility and caring for others than boys. Gilligan argued that care is more than a response to social norms, that philosophically it is the equivalent of the cold abstraction of justice, which, as we shall see, Kohlberg placed at the apex of his model. Kohlberg responded to this criticism by placing welfare higher in his model, but many argue (Snell, 2000: 274) that this response is inadequate.

## Stage four

At this stage the conventions that frame a person's morality are not social but organisational and institutional. Sometimes this stage is further divided into two. At the inferior of these two stages morality is framed within the rules and regulations of a specific organisation such as a company or a professional association that has defined rules of conduct and ethics. At the superior level the adherence is to the wider institutional rules of society. Some people argue that rule utilitarianism (*see* p. 135) is the guiding morality of this stage. The critical factor in both stages, however, is that the commitment to 'law and order' is a knowing one. People have chosen to apply the rules by choice because they believe them to be good for themselves individually as well as for the wider institutions of society.

## The post-conventional stages

### Stage five

At the post-conventional stages people are capable of questioning and reflecting upon the systems and principles of morality that they follow. At this stage, which is referred to as the social contract stage, people challenge the prevailing morality and seek to change it in accordance with their own reflections. They might, for example, campaign to change the law on cigarette advertising because they think it would advance social justice to do so.

### Stage six

At stage six, which in some versions is the final stage of the model, there is an acceptance of the existence of universal principles of justice (and in later versions, *pace* Gilligan) welfare. This knowledge of universal principle is not easily come by but gained through intellectual struggle and practical confrontation with injustice in the world. A person at this level takes risks to bring justice wherever they find injustice. Kohlberg's definition of level six is Kantian (*see* p. 111). It is austere and concerned with abstract principle. Not all of Kohlberg's critics were at ease with this.

The postmodernists in particular had trouble with the notion of justice as a metanarrative. Snell (1993: 20) reported, and to some extent accepted, the arguments of those who see stage six as a capacity for principled relativism rather than irrefragable justice. This mirrors Rorty's views (Mounce, 1997: 185–9) in stressing the need for continuing conversations, a celebration of doubt and paradox and a playful sense of irony when dealing with complex moral matters.

### Stage seven

This stage we find hard to define because of its transcendental nature, which means you have to achieve it to know it. It does in general draw themes from many of the world's major religions including Christianity, Buddhism and Judaism. One such is the idea of the unity of all creation, the belief that in some way all things are part of a single whole. The idea of morality at this highest level is linked with the idea of becoming at one with the whole of creation. This is the final stage in the nine-fold developmental sequence (remembering that the first phase is called stage zero and that stage four can be subdivided).

There have been many criticisms of Kohlberg's model but it has proved robust and remains a core theory. It has been pointed out that the stages may not be hierarchical. One particularly relevant form of this argument is that even though people may have acquired a capacity to think morally at one of the higher levels there is no guarantee that they will choose to do so. Nor is such a capacity a guarantee that people will act according to the highest level thinking that they are capable of. Nevertheless it is clear that a person's capacity for moral reasoning will have an impact on which of the ethical stances is chosen.

## Reflections

This chapter has presented a classification of eight stances that may be taken in response to an ethical issue at work. The question has to be asked whether some stances are more ethical than others. It might be considered in two parts. The first is to consider whether, in Figure 6.1, the stances higher in the matrix are more ethical than those lower on the vertical scale. The second part is whether those stances on the right-hand side of the matrix are more ethical than those on the left-hand side.

Kohlberg has made the case that ethical cognitive development is hierarchical. On this basis it could be argued that the ethical puzzle and problem stances are better than neutrality or negotiation. However, such a claim would suggest that people should always aspire to the higher stances. This might lead to some odd consequences. Would it be sensible to apply the relatively complex stances of ethical puzzle or ethical problem to a relatively simple matter such as the casual theft of office stationery? This question implies that a contingency approach might be sensible in which the 'higher' and more complex stances would be more appropriate for major and difficult ethical dilemmas. Snell made a suggestion of this type in relation to Kohlberg's stages of moral development. He argued that an ethical difficulty arises when a level of ethical development creates rather than solves a problem. If someone is thinking at level three (nice boy/good girl) then they will be in a dilemma if the people they want to like them are tugging them in contradictory directions. It is the level of thinking that is causing the difficulty. Snell (1993: 62) recommends overcoming the difficulty by shifting the level of ethical thinking up at least one stage. If the demands of social peers are incompatible then the difficulty can only be overcome by thinking in terms of the rules and regulations of the organisation (stage four). The general principle is that one should use the minimum cognitive level, or stance if we move from cognition to action, that is required to overcome an ethical difficulty.

The second part of the question is whether the left-hand stances are ethically better than the right-hand stances. The two sides of the matrix in Figure 6.1 can be described in terms of categorisation and particularisation. The left-hand stances give priority to categorisation. They all operate by pigeon-holing issues so that their commonalities may be stressed and standard responses applied. The right-hand stances give more emphasis to particularisation. They all emphasise the complexity and ambiguity of issues, which are things that make it difficult to categorise an issue. These stances do not dictate particular solutions to issues though they do suggest ways of dealing with or coping with the uncertainty (debating judgements, keeping the conversation going, cynical withdrawal or negotiation with stakeholders). The trade-offs between the left-hand and right-hand stances are clear. If the left-hand stances are taken, actions can be decisively chosen and implemented, but they may be inappropriate or unfair. The right-hand stances might be more responsive to the nuances and complexities of an issue but they may also lead to prevarication and inaction. The results from the *Downsizing* exercise (Activity 6.1) suggest that many managers and professionals were uncomfortable with the right-hand stances (the accountants being more uncomfortable than the HR specialists). This may be dangerous because it is the neglected right-hand stances that provide the critical element necessary to limit the left-hand stances' propensity for inflexibility and unfair discrimination. As has been suggested earlier in the chapter people at work may need to develop a momentum that swings them between the left-hand stances and the right-hand stances – between categorisation and particularisation.

## Summary

In this chapter the following key points have been made:

- There are eight stances that people may take in response to an ethical issue at work.

- People may take different stances on an issue, depending on their consciences, ethical reasoning, perceptions of others' views, and in their actions.

- Tensions between a person's conscience, ethical reasoning, perceptions of others' views and their actions can cause psychological discomfort and interpersonal conflicts.

- The particulars of a specific ethical issue will also have an influence on the stance a person chooses and their inclination to change stances.

- Their choice of stances will be affected by a number of factors such as their level of cognitive development and the values they share with a group or society.

## Quick revision test

1. What is cognitive dissonance?
   (a) when people do not understand a thing
   (b) disrespecting other people's views
   (c) when an individual's opinions and values contradict each other

2. What does ethical duty mean?
   (a) a person's moral principles developed through hard thought and reflection
   (b) the obligations placed on a person by their backgrounds and conscience without any critical reflection
   (c) obeying the rules

3. How many stages are there in Kohlberg's theory of moral development?
   (a) 9
   (b) 8
   (c) 6

4. The superego, in Freudian analysis, is...
   (a) our conscience that fills us with anxiety if tempted to act badly
   (b) the instinct for self-preservation by acting in the world
   (c) that part of the self that rationally analyses the ethical choices that confront us.

## Typical assignments and briefs

1. Analyse an ethical issue that you have experienced at work using the categories, conscience: ethical reasoning: expectations of others: options for action framework presented in Figure 6.3.

2. Discuss the ethics of downsizing using the framework of stances presented in Figure 6.1. Illustrate your arguments by reference to particular cases of downsizing.

3. How effective is Kohlberg's model of moral development, which was based on studies of children, to understanding the behaviour of managers when faced with ethical issues?

4. What range of factors might influence how a manager responds to an ethical situation at work? How important are the cultural factors in relation to other influences?

## Group activity 6

The following is an extract from an interview with a personnel manager. It gives two examples of situations where an organisation's senior managers wanted to dispense with employees whom they thought no longer fitted with the official culture and values of the organisation. The personnel manager, who was an intermediary in both of these situations, took a different stance in each case. In the first case she was in favour of parting with the employee but in the second case she thought it would be wrong to part with the member of staff.

Read the interview and discuss how the respondent might explain why she took different stances on issues that seem to involve the same matter of principle.

1.  Should employees be let go if they do not fit with an organisation's official culture?

2.  What particulars might have triggered different categorisations in each of the incidents?

The most recent example is a retail business manager who has got a consistently high appraisal rating, high performance rating over the last few years. But what is required over the next three years? Has this person the ability to move forward? Therefore there is a big question mark over where that person goes. Because we're talking about somebody who's perceived by the organisation as a high performer. Yet in terms of everything they do everyday we can see that they have the inability to change, to move forward with the change in an emerging brand.

Well, the whole style of the operation is changing. We have a new Director and General Manager and senior management team for a start. They have a different way of working. The emphasis is on empowerment. The emphasis is moving away from control culture, control type management to a more loose management culture and more sales oriented and building on development in sales. This person is not interested in development and growing sales. He's more about the old control culture. Hit them with a big stick and sack them if they don't do what you tell them mentality. But he has an excellent performance record, and if you look in terms of actual year on year profit performance he's the best achiever in the company.

Also the difficulty is because he has a reputation throughout the company for that tough management style nobody else wants to face him. So the fact is that we'll end up losing somebody [said ironically, meaning the manager] from the organisation. Which will also cause or create a huge employee relations issue. Because he will take us to tribunal. Rightly so in terms of performance.

Well we've decided he's got to go. Well it will be a severance. He'll have to go. We've looked at the other alternatives and there aren't any.

I think in terms of the organisation's culture it's absolutely right but actually this guy has worked for the company for some time and in his own way has been committed. So I think there probably is a view that maybe over the years this person hasn't been managed properly in the past and maybe if he'd been managed better in the past then maybe we wouldn't be at this point now. Yes ▶

we've worked on him, we've been working on it for the last six months. It's not even a runner. We're basically saying, up yours, you know, as good as. Well I've dealt with so many [severance cases] that I always think that if I go home at night and sleep, my conscience is relatively clear. I have a job to do and I believe when it comes round and it's right for the business, then it's part of the job. I think so, yes.

I quite often won't do something if I don't agree with it being morally right, or I'll look for a compromise. Yes, somebody who works for me who, one of the Directors felt, wasn't committed enough to the organisation because they didn't work seven days a week. He told me that I needed to do something about that person and I refused point blank. I said that they actually worked more effectively than anybody else here and no I don't intend to get rid of him. I refuse to do that. At the end of the day, just because you [the director] believe that we should work seven days a week it doesn't prove that they're not committed. So I actually did dig my heels in and said no I'm not going to do it. I refused and we've worked around that. I did then talk to that person and let that person know how he [the director] felt about it and said you know you just need to think about raising your profile and meeting part way. Well I think I responded as I did because that person is an extremely effective member of the team and actually the output is far higher than the average. And really it was more about profile. In terms of the organisation it's the nature of the business and because our business does operate seven days a week, then it becomes the accepted norm. If you've got pressure from a senior manager then it makes life difficult for you and then ultimately it forces somebody out. The director was being unreasonable, totally unreasonable, absolutely.

It's settled down again now but it was very difficult at the time. It put me in a difficult position. I'm a great believer in sticking to your guns and I'm a spade or shovel person.

## Recommended further reading

Many of the key themes and ideas of this chapter are taken from M. Billig (1996) *Arguing and Thinking. A rhetorical approach to social psychology*, 2nd edn, Cambridge: Cambridge University Press. It is not an easy read but it is very rewarding. R. Snell's book provides a good introduction to Kohlberg and has convincing case studies that relate the theory to resolving ethical problems at work: R. Snell (1993) *Developing Skills for Ethical Management*, London: Chapman and Hall.

## Useful websites

| Topic | Website provider | URL |
|---|---|---|
| A resources Web page concerned with theories of moral development | The PSI cafe | http://www.psy.pdx.edu/PsiCafe/Areas/Developmental/MoralDev/ |
| An interactive version of the defining issues test for assessing stage of moral development | D. Whetton and K. Cameron *Developing management skills surveys* | http://www.prenhall.com/whetten_dms/chap1_2.html |

# CHAPTER 7

# Whistleblower or witness?

## Learning outcomes

Having read this chapter and completed its associated activities, you should be able to:

- Examine the various issues that relate to the act of whistleblowing.
- Debate the role that whistleblowing potentially has to play within corporate governance processes.
- Discuss possible explanations of the whistleblower's plight.
- Evaluate the legislation which seeks to protect whistleblowers in the UK.

## Introduction

Chapter 6 considered possible stances or ethical positions that people facing ethical challenges may move through. The stances are ways of labelling the different forms of responses people might display in ethically complex situations. In this chapter we discuss the issue of those employees, who, for a variety of reasons, come to a position where they are so uncomfortable with a particular practice or activity within their employing organisation that they feel no alternative but to raise the matter with another person. This other person might be a work colleague, a senior member of the organisation, a family member, or a non-related third party who is external to the employing organisation. The person to whom the revelation is made can be important because in the UK, for example, it can affect the degree of legal protection that is available to the concerned employee. However, to whomever the concerned employee confides, the act is the same. It is often referred to as whistleblowing and the people who whistleblow are usually referred to as whistleblowers. However, this can be a pejorative term and some writers prefer other descriptions, e.g. Beardshaw (1981) described such employees as 'conscientious objectors at work', while Winfield (1990) preferred 'principled dissenters'. Borrie and Dehn (2002: 5) offered some thoughts on how whistleblowers might be viewed in the future and in order to help change people's perceptions they suggested the alternative nomenclature of 'witness', not 'complainant'. This is an interesting suggestion because changing people's perception of those who whistleblow is an important stepping stone in altering the likely outcomes experienced by those who reveal organisational malpractices.

### Connexion point

The issues and arguments discussed in this chapter build upon Chapters 5 and 6 by focusing attention upon those individuals who encounter an issue within their organisation that challenges their personal values and ethics in a profound way, but for which they can find no satisfactory resolution.

The words we use to describe people or things are important because they create an initial context and orientate our emotions towards the discussion that might follow. Thus, if the term whistleblower brings to mind the notion of a snitch, or a grass, then you are more likely to be inclined, initially at least, towards a negative view of a whistleblower with regard to any discussion of a particular whistleblowing case. If, however, you prefer the descriptions proffered by writers such as Winfield, Beardshaw or Borrie and Dehn, because that is how you see most whistleblowers, then your interpretation of the 'rights' and 'wrongs' of a particular case is likely to lean towards the position of the whistleblower. Our quest in this chapter is to consider the issue of whistleblowing and whistleblowers, using the terms neither pejoratively nor exaltingly, but merely descriptively.

In this chapter we will present you with the arguments surrounding whistleblowing, but also with evidence of the pressures within organisations that can constrain potential whistleblowers and the implications of such 'muteness'. We will use actual cases to illustrate the arguments, reflecting the messiness that is often to be found in organisational life, and the organisational impotency that many employees feel, irrespective of their position within the organisation. This is not to justify or to recommend an uncritical acceptance of the messiness and personal impotency that can be experienced in ethical dilemmas. The tools of analysis and the implications of the differing philosophical positions discussed in Chapters 3 and 4 will allow you to form reasoned judgements on the questions, issues and cases relating to whistleblowing that you will now consider.

However, before we progress, we would like you to work through Activity 7.1.

### Activity 7.1

On the scales shown, identify your feelings towards the person raising the alarm.

**Case A**

You are playing in a team and a player on your side fouls a player on the opposing side, but the referee misses the incident. However, one of your team mates suddenly stops the game and brings the foul to the attention of the referee.

Extremely supportive                                                 Extremely angry

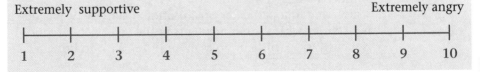

```
1      2      3      4      5      6      7      8      9      10
```

**Case B**

You read in the newspaper that an employee of a building company has provided evidence to a national newspaper of practices on building sites that contravene health and safety legislation and which have resulted in fatalities and serious injuries during the past two years.

Extremely supportive                                               Extremely angry

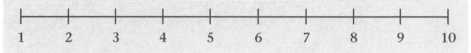

**Case C**

You work for a car manufacturer and a fellow employee, whom you do not know personally, releases information to the press of a design fault in one of the company's best-selling models that is potentially life threatening. Sales of the car plummet and significant layoffs are announced.

Extremely supportive                                               Extremely angry

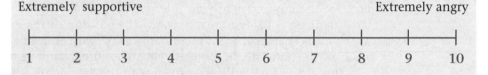

## When is a whistleblowing act performed?

A commonly held understanding of a whistleblowing act is the release of confidential organisational information to an external third party, often, but not exclusively, the media. However, as suggested above, a whistleblowing act can be a conversation, a remark even, to a work colleague or a family member in which organisational information, unknown to others participating in the conversation, is revealed. If these concerns are relayed back to 'management' before the employee concerned has raised the issue through the company's formal procedures (assuming they exist), and they are dismissed as a result of the revelation, then, in the UK, they are likely to lose the protection of the law that was introduced to protect whistleblowers. This is the Public Interest Disclosure Act 1998 (PIDA), which is discussed in more detail later in the chapter.

The PIDA was designed to provide protection to those who raise awareness of an act or practice that poses problems for public safety, or threatens other, specific areas of public interest. From the above it is clear that, whilst whistleblowing is normally a purposeful and intentional act, it might also be unintended and innocent. The law makes little, if any, distinction between intended and unintended whistleblowing.

Reacting to a particular organisational activity or practice in a way that does not comply with the requirements of the PIDA does not mean that legal recourse is denied to a whistleblower, should they wish to bring a case for wrongful dismissal. A civil action will still be possible. It is simply that the protection afforded by the PIDA will not be available.

## Why whistleblow?

The personal outcomes experienced by many whistleblowers have been damaging, whether the outcomes are considered at a psychological, financial or social level (*see*, for example, Soeken and Soeken, 1987; Winfield, 1990; Miceli and Near, 1992; Hunt, 1995, 1998). Loss of employment is common for the whistleblower, with opportunities to gain alternative employment often limited. Some whistleblowers have become unemployable as their names have been circulated among employing organisations as 'troublemakers'. Borrie and Dehn (2002) refer to such an example.

| Case study 7.1 | **Paying a heavy price** |
| --- | --- |

Robert Maxwell, who was chief executive of Maxwell Communications, stole $1M from the pension funds of the company, which included the pension funds of the *Daily Mirror* group of newspapers. He sacked a union official who had challenged what he was doing with the pension money at a Scottish Newspaper. Maxwell, a powerful businessman, was able to ensure that the man could not get another job in the industry. Subsequently the claims of the union official were found to have been accurate, but that was little consolation for the union official whose career in the print industry had been ruined.

The whistleblower and his or her family often experience great financial and emotional hardship, with break-ups in marriages or partnerships frequently reported. Suicides of whistleblowers have also been attributed to the financial and psychological fallout from their whistleblowing experiences (Soeken and Soeken, 1987). However, not all whistleblowing cases end in such unhappiness, although it is difficult to overplay the trauma that is likely to be experienced while the scenario is unfolding, even if the final outcome shows the whistleblower both vindicated and adequately compensated.\Sherron Watkins was an accountant and a former vice-president at Enron before she 'blew the whistle' on the corrupt practices at Enron. Watkins has enjoyed something of a celebrity status since her whistleblowing act, but this might have something to do with the scale of the fraud at Enron and the ease with which it was possible to identify key individuals at the top who were directly implicated in the fraud. A less clear-cut scenario, with slightly less media scrutiny, can find the potential whistleblower in a more vulnerable and exposed position. As it was, Watkins was faced with some hostility from her work colleagues. It must be recognised that the revelation of an organisational malpractice, however corrupt and indefensible it might be, risks damaging the employing organisation's share price and standing in its various product or service markets. This could place jobs at risk, the jobs of one's work colleagues and perhaps their pension funds.

The situation at Enron was complicated by the fact that many of the employees had invested heavily in the stocks and shares of Enron, believing that the phenomenal growth in the share price that had been experienced over the previous seven or so years would continue, allowing their portfolio to be converted upon retirement into a sizeable pension fund. Thus, anyone blowing the whistle at Enron would be putting at risk both jobs and personal retirement/pension funds. Without minimising the courage displayed by Sherron Watkins, her position was possibly eased slightly because she first formally raised her concerns in an internal letter to Kenneth Lay (CEO and Chairman) on 15 August 2001. This was only two months before Enron made a public announcement that it was making significant write-offs and only three and half months before Enron filed for bankruptcy. The scale of the fraud and the perpetrators became evident quite quickly, a state of affairs not often experienced by whistleblowers.

The PIDA does appear to have made a difference in some cases, and with compensation claims now having no ceiling (which was not the case when the Act was first introduced), the compensation awards to some wronged whistleblowers have been significant. The organisation Public Concern at Work has undertaken a review of the first three years' working of the Act. During this period employees lodged over 1,200 claims alleging victimisation for whistleblowing. Of these two-thirds were either settled out of court or withdrawn without a public hearing. Of the remaining one-third, 54 per cent of claimants lost, 23 per cent won their case, but under a different employment or discrimination law, and the final 23 per cent won their case under the PIDA. The highest award made was for £805,000 and the lowest £1,000. The average value of award made during this first three-year period was £107,117.

Although the protection afforded by the PIDA may encourage some potential whistleblowers to become actual whistleblowers, whistleblowers have followed their respective consciences for millennia without the protection of the PIDA, so what might explain such acts? The answer may be found in a number of tragedies, but we will focus upon only those of recent times. In these instances we often find evidence of employees who have raised concerns prior to the final incident occurring. Had these concerns been acted upon the tragedy in question might not have happened. Whether we look at examples such as the Piper-Alpha disaster or the Zeebrugge (*Herald of Free Enterprise*) tragedy, BCCI, Maxwell Communications, Barlow Clowes, the Lyme Bay canoeing tragedy, the Southall rail crash, the Clapham rail crash, or the incidence of high fatality rates among operations on young children at Bristol Royal Infirmary, we find evidence of the ignored concerns of employees.

These were tragedies in the Greek sense. They could have been predicted from their specific circumstances yet the final dénouement appeared inexorable. The circumstances in question often related to lax controls and practices and/or a failure to listen to the concerns of employees. The concerns had either been reported to management, but not acted upon, or unreported due to oppressive and authoritarian management practices or misguided feelings of loyalty. An example of the former is the case of the *Herald of Free Enterprise*, which capsized as it left Zeebrugge harbour because its bow doors had been left open, resulting in the deaths of 192 passengers and crew. A more detailed account of the case is provided in Chapter 8 in Case study 8.6 (*see* p. 328), but some relevant details are provided here. The inquiry report into the disaster, concluded,

If this sensible suggestion … had received the serious consideration it deserved this disaster might well have been prevented.

(Lewis, 2000:3)

The suggestion in question was the fitting of lights to the bridge that would have indicated whether or not the bow doors were closed. On five occasions prior to the *Herald of Free Enterprise* capsizing, P&O staff had experienced ferries leaving port without the bow doors being fully closed and had expressed their concerns, but these were not acted upon. The concerns, although communicated to the ferries' management, had not been conveyed to the top management of the company. The concerns appear to have become lost in the middle management tiers of the organisation. Tragedies, such as those mentioned above, created a sufficiently supportive socio-political climate that allowed the PIDA to be passed as an Act of Parliament in 1998 and to become operative in 1999.

| Case study 7.2 | **The Lyme Bay canoeing tragedy** |
|---|---|

Once again the term 'tragedy' is appropriate, because this appears to have been an accident waiting to happen. The company OLL Ltd offered outdoor adventure holidays, breaks and vacations for younger people. However, two of the instructors were concerned at the lack of attention to safety issues within the company. They became exasperated at the refusal of the owner of the company to take their concerns seriously, so that they felt compelled to resign, although not before they wrote to the owner, detailing their concerns. Not long after their resignations a group of school children were taken canoeing in Lyme Bay, England, by the company, but the weather and sea conditions changed and four of the school children lost their lives. Because there was evidence that the safety failings in the company had been brought to the attention of the owner, 'the guiding mind' (which is discussed in more detail in Chapter 8), a case of corporate manslaughter could be brought. The company was fined £60,000 and the owner was jailed for three years.

The penalties imposed upon the corporations and individuals found complicit in the injuries or deaths of others are not necessarily adequate to influence adherence to health and safety regulations. Slapper and Tombs (1999) cite a couple of cases that illustrate this point. The first relates to Mr Roy Edwin Hill, who was a director of a demolition company. In 1994, the company won the contract to demolish the former Lucas Building in Brislington, which is near Bristol. The factory was demolished with an excavator, but, in violation of Health and Safety legislation, no precautions were taken to prevent the spreading of asbestos and asbestos dust contained in the roofing and pipework lagging. In 1995 Mr Hill received a jail sentence of thee months and a fine of £4000. While these penalties might be surprising, what is possibly more surprising is that Mr Hill's sentence was the first custodial sentence under Health and Safety legislation in 193 years! The next case has some gruesome details, but it reveals the types of practices that are still prevalent.

| Case study 7.3 | **Dickensian practices, but in modern times** |
|---|---|

A 19-year old man, Michael Pollard, was employed as a heavy goods vehicle mechanic by a company that manufactured fibres that were used in carpet felt. Mr Pollard was not employed to maintain the equipment in the factory, but on the day in question he was instructed to correct a problem on one of the factory machines. A safety gate was not working and this allowed Mr Pollard to enter the machine while it was still operative. His arm became trapped between spiked rollers and was torn off at the shoulder and shredded in the machine. The Health and Safety Executive immediately maintained that a Prohibition Notice that was served on the company to prevent the use of the dangerous equipment was ignored by the directors. Two of the company's directors were sent to jail for ignoring the Prohibition Notice, but the maximum sentence under the legislation is six months.

The next case provides further evidence of the calculative approach companies can adopt in weighing up whether it is cost-effective to comply with legislation.

| Case study 7.4 | **What is a life worth?** |
|---|---|

James Hodgson was 21 years old. In 1996, while cleaning the chemical residues from a road tanker, Hodgson was sprayed in the face with a toxic chemical and died. The company was found guilty of gross negligence in the supervision, training and the equipment it supplied to handle dangerous chemicals. The company was found guilty of corporate manslaughter and fined £22,000 (£15,000 of which related to the corporate manslaughter) and the owner of the company was sent to prison for 12 months (subject to early release for good behaviour).

So, in response to the question 'why whistleblow?', examples, such as those above, can be cited of situations in which (many) lives might have been saved, had the concerns of employees been listened to and acted upon. Alternatively the concerned, but ignored employees might have taken their worries on to a broader public platform and made the general public aware of their concerns. So does this type of evidence make the general argument in favour of whistleblowing correct, justifiable, and to be encouraged? If so, why is the act of whistleblowing and of a whistleblower so often portrayed and perceived as a negative force within society?

A contributory factor in explaining why one person might choose to whistleblow in a given situation, while another, when faced with the same circumstances, would opt for a different strategy, is associated with the issues we discussed in Chapter 3.

**Connexion point**

Although no substantial evidence exists concerning the ethical orientation of whistleblowers (and more significantly suppressed whistleblowers), we can employ our understanding of ethical theories to hypothesise about their likely ethical orientation. In terms of the ethical theories represented in the quadrants of Figure 3.1, people who display a predominantly deontological orientation towards ethical issues, whose ethical thinking, and possibly action, reflects principle-based responses, are more likely to feel compelled to whistleblow if resolution of an ethical dilemma proves impossible.

With concepts such as justice, honesty and integrity normally included in any set of virtues, a virtue ethics orientation (the top left-hand section of Figure 3.1) would also suggest that someone possessing such an orientation would be more likely to resist pressure to compromise themselves should an ethical issue prove insoluble. Likewise, for a Kantian oriented person, whistleblowing would be a likely outcome to an intractable ethical issue.

This contrasts with someone whose ethical orientation reflects consequentialist thinking, i.e. whose decision making will be determined by a thinking through of the consequences of the available options before choosing a course of action. With this orientation, the course of action chosen will depend upon the circumstances of each situation. Given the history of whistleblowing cases (and not just the negative outcomes for the whistleblowers, but also for other employees and the organisation concerned), whistleblowing becomes a far less likely outcome if the concerned employee displays a consequentialist orientation.

The above discussion assumes, of course, that the individual is free to adopt the ethical reasoning which reflects their personal orientation. This, however, is often not possible, due to powerful pressures upon individuals to suppress personal values and to compromise their principles. We discuss the implications of these pressures in the case examples that follow.

| Activity 7.2 | What would you do? |
| --- | --- |

If your knowledge of an organisational malpractice could, if revealed, cause job losses among your colleagues and possibly harm their pension funds, do you believe that you could undertake a whistleblowing act?

What, if any, organisational issue would be likely to force you ultimately to whistleblow?

**Connexion point**

In terms of the theoretical framework presented in Chapter 3, the organisation that develops and employs a bona fide whistleblowing process can be located in the top right-hand section of Figure 3.1, the 'ethical learning and growth' section. Such an approach would suggest a reflective, thoughtful orientation towards organisational development, with employees seen as important stakeholders and contributors to that development. Such processes would reflect the best of practices.

# When might whistleblowing be justified?

Some writers have set out what, for them, are the essential conditions that make whistleblowing acts justifiable. De George (1999) argued that there are six such conditions. De George's position on whistleblowing is a consequentialist one. Because any whistleblowing act is likely to do harm to the employing organisation, the act can only be justified if the overall effects of the act are likely to be positive. There is no reference to principles or virtues. For De George, it is the overall consequences of a whistleblowing act that determine its justification. The first three conditions (shown below) are argued to make whistleblowing permissible, but not obligatory. If conditions 4 and 5 can be satisfied then whistleblowing becomes a far more persuasive option, in De George's terms, morally obligatory. Another way of interpreting these conditions is to say that, without them, an act of whistleblowing cannot be morally justified as the likely outcome will be painful and probably fruitless for the whistleblower, and detrimental to the organisation. The conditions are as follows:

1. A product or policy of an organisation needs to possess the potential to do harm to some members of society.

2. The concerned employee should first of all report the facts, as far as they are known, to their immediate superior.

3. If the immediate superior fails to act effectively, the concerned employee should take the matter to more senior managers, exhausting all available internal channels in the process.

4. The prospective whistleblower should hold documentary evidence that can be presented to external audiences. In this condition De George argues that the evidence should show that the product or policy 'poses a serious and likely danger to the public or to the user of the product' (De George, 1999: 255).

5. The prospective whistleblower must believe that the necessary changes will be implemented as a result of their whistleblowing act.

6. The sixth condition is a general one and it is that the whistleblower must be acting in good faith, without malice or vindictiveness.

These conditions will now be considered to assess their defensibility, but first we would like you to ponder their appropriateness and helpfulness.

| Activity 7.3 | Challenging the conditions for justifiable whistleblowing |
|---|---|

The six 'conditions of whistleblowing' mentioned above suggest that, if they cannot be fulfilled, then a whistleblowing act cannot be justified. Develop arguments against as many of the six conditions as possible to justify acts of whistleblowing.

## A consideration of the conditions

*1. A product or policy of an organisation needs to possess the potential to do harm to some members of society.*

At first sight it might seem difficult to find fault with this requirement, because if no public safety or public concern issue exists, where is the public interest in 'the problem'? What can be the justification for any revelation? An important caveat would be that harm must be interpreted widely and not confined to physical harm. Economic harm, as in the cases of Enron and WorldCom, or psychological harm in the form of race or gender discrimination can be just as damaging as physical harm.

*2. The concerned employee should first of all report the facts, as far as they are known, to their immediate superior, and*

*3. If the immediate superior fails to act effectively, the concerned employee should take the matter to more senior managers, exhausting all available internal channels in the process.*

These two conditions are considered together because of their obvious linkage. Some would argue that organisations should view internal whistleblowing procedures as important mechanisms within their corporate governance processes. It might seem common sense that organisations would wish to be informed about practices that threaten the well-being of their customers, or the public at large. After all, reputations and brands can take years and considerable expenditures to build, but be destroyed in a very short time by adverse publicity. Thus, enlightened self-interest would seem to dictate an interest in encouraging internal whistleblowing. So why are many organisations not more receptive to the concerns and criticisms of their employees?

The roots of the explanation are complex, but they have to include personal reputations and relationships. By suggesting that 'organisations' would wish to be informed about unsafe practices or products gives a physical status to the term 'organisation' which is, in this context, inappropriate and unhelpful. Criticisms made of products and practices will invariably be criticisms of people, usually more senior than oneself. Condition 2 implies that one's immediate superior within the organisation should be consulted, even if they are part of the problem, hence condition 3. The PIDA also recognises this potential problem and allows the whistleblower to bypass their immediate supervisor if this can be shown to be warranted.

Condition 3 assumes that some form of internal whistleblowing process exists and is operated with integrity. A good example is Nottinghamshire County Council's website, from which you can access a report prepared for the Council on its whistleblowing procedures. The County Council employs an external organisation to operate its anonymous whistleblowing procedure. This is a laudable approach and the County Council operates a refreshingly open policy to its procedures.

However, it is quite possible that the cause of one's concerns lies with the policies or practices of the senior management. For example, budgetary pressures to achieve improved output targets within existing or reduced resources might compromise quality, including safety checks. Alternatively, managers at differing levels within their organisation might each, unknown to the others, impose planned efficiency savings on budgetary forecasts in order to impress senior management (De George, 1999: 244, cites such a scenario). In the process a final budget is created that might involve production outputs and cost levels that are wholly unrealistic. As a consequence corners are subsequently cut to try to approach the agreed output or cost budgets. Any expression of concern by an employee may become 'lost' within the management hierarchy. Finding out where the blockage exists might be a far from simple task. Expecting employees who are employed 'at the coal face' to have the awareness or confidence to express their concerns higher up the management tree (assuming one can identify how far one needs to go to escape the vicious circle of partially implicated managers) could be an unrealistic assumption. In real life, raising one's concerns internally can simply mean that management can identify which employees are likely to reveal problems that are of the managers' making.

A number of cases reported on the *Public Concern at Work* website (www.pcaw.co.uk) illustrate how the PIDA has been used and several cases relate to whistleblowers being victimised following internal disclosure of concerns.

| Case study 7.5 | **Victimisation and its consequences** |
|---|---|

In the case Fernandes v. Netcom (2000), Fernandes (F) was the finance officer of a subsidiary of a large US telecoms company. F became concerned at the level of expenses claimed by the CEO of the subsidiary company. F was initially told by his contact in America to 'turn a blind eye', which initially F appears to have done. However, when the CEO's expenses went above £300,000, F took his concerns to the US Board. F was immediately put under pressure to resign (not the CEO), but F refused. F was disciplined and then sacked for authorising the CEO's expenses. F brought a claim using the PIDA. Contrary to the claims of the American parent company, the UK Employment Tribunal found that F had been dismissed for his whistleblowing, not for authorising the expenses, and because he was 58 and unable to secure similar work, he was awarded £293,000.

Returning to De George's conditions, it might be argued that conditions 2 and 3, while initially suggesting a way for concerned employees and enlightened organisations to operate open channels of communication, might in fact be more reflective of a desire to keep the problem within the organisation, as experienced by Fernandes. This implies an emphasis upon loyalty to the organisation, loyalty which history would question in terms of reciprocated loyalty and commitment.

So far we have shown that a number of circumstances can exist that make conditions 1, 2 and 3 problematic. Yet these are only considered to be conditions that would make a whistleblowing act permissible. They are argued to be insufficient on their own to constitute the necessary conditions for an act of whistleblowing to be morally obligatory. To achieve this, De George argued that conditions 4 and 5 need to be satisfied.

*4. Documentary evidence should be in the possession of the prospective whistleblower that can be presented to external audiences.*

Here it is being argued that, without hard evidence of your concerns, you are not obliged to reveal them to an external (or internal) audience. The rationale is that without strong evidence you may risk the negative outcomes experienced by many whistleblowers, without being able to expose the bad practices that concern you. This has to be a sensible, cautionary note for any potential whistleblower to weigh in their deliberations about expressing their concerns, but it does not address the moral dilemma that the concerned employee faces.

Obtaining the evidence one requires to substantiate one's concerns can be extremely difficult. First there is the problem that ownership of the information is likely to rest with the organisation. The law of property rights would make the photocopying of such evidence a criminal offence. However, to blow the whistle without such evidence would be naïve in the extreme. Most whistleblowers obtain as much evidence as they can and let the courts decide whether accusations of stealing company property are an adequate defence by the employing organisation.

The other major problem is that sometimes incriminating evidence is either too difficult to obtain or simply not available. In the example of the misappropriation of pension fund monies by Robert Maxwell, the case was so complex, due to the interlocking nature of so many of the subsidiary companies within the *Maxwell Communications* empire, that the task for one, or a few, employees of obtaining sufficient corroborating evidence to support their concerns was simply impossible. It took a team of accountants nearly two calendar years, and many more person years, to unravel the web that Maxwell had woven.

So if one has deep concerns about a particular issue (say the use of pension funds as in the Maxwell case), but a lack of hard evidence, is one absolved from one's civic responsibilities? The financial loss suffered by the pensioners of the Maxwell companies, as was experienced by the employees of Enron and WorldCom, were significant. These were not minor financial scams. A lot of people were financially hurt; in a significant number of cases their lives were damaged irrevocably.

While it is wise to counsel caution to prospective whistleblowers if their corroborating information is not strong, society as a whole might be the lesser if this condition was used as an ethical loophole, through which individuals could escape their personal dilemma, i.e. to divulge or not to divulge. It is unlikely that sufficient corroborating evidence will be gathered in many cases to prove irrevocably that a particular revelation is watertight. This is why the PIDA uses phrases such as the whistleblower should 'reasonably believe' and should believe the accusation to be 'substantially true'. UK law does not require that the accusation be 'true', only that it was reasonable to believe that it was true.

*5. The prospective whistleblower must believe that the necessary changes will be implemented as a result of their whistleblowing act.*

The emphasis here is again on the protection of the whistleblower. Given the negative personal outcomes that the majority of whistleblowers have experienced, this condition is merely saying, 'If the probabilities are that nothing will change as a result of your action, you are not duty bound to make your revelation'. Although the condition is expressed in a positive sense, i.e. 'if conditions 1–5 exist and you are of the view that your revelation will cause the offending or dangerous practice to cease, then you are morally obliged to make your revelation', the condition can be reinterpreted as possessing a negative slant. In its negative form the condition is effectively offering an escape route to the uncertain whistleblower.

*6. The whistleblower must be acting in good faith, without malice or vindictiveness.*

This is a contentious condition. It begs the question, 'Why are the motives of the whistleblower important or relevant?' If, say, the whistleblower can be shown to have grounds for harbouring resentment at being passed over for promotion at some time in the past, or for being disciplined for an organisational infraction, why should this invalidate or undermine any revelation that they might make about an organisational malpractice? If, as some managers claimed in our research interviews, the disgruntled employee was lying, out of spite, about an alleged wrongdoing, then clearly the claimed whistleblowing act would not in fact be one, because no wrongdoing took place. Such acts are simply lies, not whistleblowing.

We might prefer that those revealing organisational malpractices do so for honourable reasons, and the purity of the whistleblower's position is an oft-cited requirement for acceptable whistleblowing, but it is a doubtful argument. As you will see when we discuss the PIDA, one of the requirements of the Act is that, for a whistleblower to gain the protection of the Act, they must not profit from the whistleblowing, e.g. being paid as a result of publishing their revelations in a newspaper or book. While it might not be wholly desirable for whistleblowing to be stimulated by thoughts of personal gain, it has to be asked whether the public interest is served by denying such whistleblowers legal protection. Practices for encouraging whistleblowing are followed when rewards are offered for information leading to the successful prosecution of criminals in cases of robbery, murder, hijacking and so on, and nothing is judged to be untoward in these circumstances. One must ask what the distinctions are that make whistleblowers of organisational malpractices less valued by society than whistleblowers of other crimes?

The 'crime' of revealing corporate malpractices is sometimes seen as greater than the corporate malpractices themselves. Whilst offering rewards for the capture of, say, criminals who have robbed a bank is acceptable, the offering of rewards for evidence against companies who have 'robbed' shareholders and employees is somehow seen in a different light.

## Whistleblowing: a positive or negative force within society?

The tragedies referred to earlier in the chapter might suggest that organisations would be wise to institute internal whistleblowing procedures to allow employees to raise their concerns and thus create early warning systems upon which the employing organisations could act. Indeed, internal whistleblowing structures can be seen as essential to good corporate governance. So is whistleblowing a characteristic of a healthy, self-aware and self-critical society, with those who reveal organisational malpractices regarded as performing positive civic acts? The evidence would suggest that as a society we are some way away from such a position, although Borrie (1996) observed that the development of organisations such as *Childline* might be heralding a changing view in relation to those who reveal evidence of abuse, recklessness, and disregard for the integrity and sanctity of fellow human beings.

Sternberg (1996) argued that companies should look upon whistleblowing processes as critical elements within good corporate governance practice, and Borrie and Dehn (2002: 5) have also discussed the development of a whistleblowing culture in which, the whistleblower would be seen 'as a witness, not as a complainant'. They argued that, thirty years ago, it was rare to find a company seeking the views of its customers about the quality of the company's products or services. Now it is regarded as central to staying competitive. Borrie and Dehn suggested that perhaps by, say, 2030 whistleblowing processes will not merely be the norm, but seen as essential elements of a corporation's information gathering processes.

### Connexion point

Whilst a Kantian perspective (discussed in Chapter 3) would see the instrumental rationale implicit in such a development as reducing its ethical integrity, prospective whistleblowers might just be grateful for the development.

A more serious concern for the development of supportive whistleblowing cultures is that, if their justification is based upon economic rather than ethical grounds, then if the economic justification ceases to exist (i.e. the costs of operating a whistleblowing process are judged to outweigh the benefits being derived), then whistleblowers will once again be seen as impediments to organisational competitiveness.

As mentioned earlier, incidents such as the Lyme Bay canoeing disaster and the *Herald of Free Enterprise* disaster created the social and political conditions that allowed the Public Interest Disclosure Act to become law, but history is replete with examples of individuals who have revealed organisational malpractices, invariably to their own personal cost. Peter Drucker (cited in Borrie, 1996) referred to whistleblowers as informers and likened societies that encouraged whistleblowing as bearing some of the characteristics of tyrannies such as those of Tiberius and Nero in Rome, the Spanish Inquisition, and the French Terror, a view that not all would share. Others see the acts of whistleblowers as equivalent to referees who maintain 'the rules of the game'. However, the analogy of the whistleblower as a referee in a sporting contest is flawed and a closer examination of the acts of whistleblowing within the context of a sporting event goes some way to explaining the antipathy that some feel towards whistleblowing and whistleblowers.

A whistleblower in a sporting event would not be the referee, but a member of one of the opposing sides who, upon seeing an infringement by one of his own side, stops the game and calls the referee's and the crowd's attention to the incident. This would be referred to as displaying a Corinthian spirit, i.e. placing the

ideals and integrity of the sport above the mere winning of the immediate contest. Whether the supporters and fellow team members would see the incident in
exactly the same light is debatable.

The sporting analogy should not be taken too far, because whistleblowing
cases involve far greater consequences than the result of a game. The point of the
analogy is that whistleblowers are not the appointed referees of organisational
affairs. Neither do they claim to be so. They are usually unfortunate individuals
who become ensnared in the maelstrom of a situation, which for a variety of reasons becomes irresolvable, at least to their satisfaction. They are then faced with
the predicament of either allowing their concerns to subside and to 'keep their
heads below the parapet', or to seek to get the issue resolved by revealing their
concerns to either an internal or external audience. Some have described whistleblowing acts as heroic acts, because the outcomes for many whistleblowers tend
to be so negative. But why are whistleblowers so often maligned and cast as the
wrongdoers, in situations where others have created great potential harm?

Besides the unpleasantness of being seen as a 'snitch' or an informer, the
prospective whistleblower has to weigh the implications for an organisation of
news reaching its critical markets about the practices in question. These markets
include both product markets and securities' markets. In competitive markets,
ground lost to rival organisations can be difficult to make up, and confidence
lost by investors in the organisation difficult to restore. The threat of lost jobs
can mean that even long-term colleagues may not support the whistleblower.
Whilst the architect of such a situation is the person/s who have committed the
malpractice, the innocent employee who becomes knowledgeable of the malpractice is placed in a complex, vexed situation. In some respects they could be
damned if they do (i.e. whistleblow) by their colleagues, but damned if they
don't (i.e. stay silent) by members of the public who might subsequently be
harmed as a result of the malpractice.

The following example, which is taken from a study conducted by the authors
(Fisher and Lovell, 2000), indicates that such bad practices are not confined to small,
back-street operators who exploit the vulnerability of a low-skilled workforce. The
company concerned was a large, internationally known engineering organisation.

| Case study 7.6 | **The Engineering Company and its overseas markets** |
| --- | --- |

This company operated in a range of domestic (UK) and overseas markets. In
at least one of the overseas markets 'arrangements' were sometimes negotiated
with overseas agents that involved exported goods being artificially reclassified to reduce the level of import duties in the overseas country. For example,
a £1M order for engineered products would be reclassified for invoice purposes
as £700K engineered products and £300K consultancy services. In this particular overseas country consultancy services were not subject to import duty.

The engineering company did not suffer as a result of the reclassification,
and the importing agents acquired the goods at a lower cost (taking import
taxes into account) than they would otherwise have had to pay. The only
losers were the governments of the countries concerned. When these situations arose, the unofficial, but well understood, procedure within the

engineering company was for the requested 'arrangement' to be passed directly to the sales director and managing director of the engineering company. This ultimate decision-making unit would weigh the risks, the returns and the implications of the decision and then decree whether the proposed deal with the agent would be sanctioned. Clearly this act was illegal, yet it was argued that such behaviour was necessary in order to stay in the markets concerned and to protect jobs in the UK. Other operators in these markets were claimed to offer similar 'arrangements'. Here the consequentialist argument that all the implications of a decision should be weighed in order to identify the decision that offers the greatest good to the greatest number might be tabled. The waters become further muddied when the management of the engineering company argued that the government of the overseas country operated a repressive regime, employing punitive import taxes in order to shore up excessive government expenditure on military equipment and government largesse.

None of the claims about the foreign government could be validated, but, assuming they were accurate, what did the actions of the senior management of the company say to the employees of the engineering company? Whatever the rights and wrongs of the situation, the engineering company was employing criteria and a decision process that sanctioned law-breaking activity.

Interestingly, Tony Blair, the British Prime Minister, made the problems of Africa one of the major challenges of his 2005 G8 presidency. Having previously established the Commission for Africa, one of the principal areas of focus of the Commission was the issue of fraud within African governments and between those governments and multinational corporations. If progress ensues from the work of the Commission then the type of incident portrayed in Case study 7.6 might become a thing of the past, but history would suggest that progress may be slow and uneven. This is particularly so if the account provided by Evans (2004) is indicative of the UK Government's commitment to the principles of the Commission for Africa. Evans reported that secret documents, which were revealed in the high court on 22 December 2004, showed that the Trade Secretary, Patricia Hewitt

> overruled her civil servants to water down rules to curb corruption by companies after lobbying by the Confederation of British Industry (CBI) and Rolls Royce, BAE Systems and the Airbus aircraft maker,. ... previously confidential documents showed that the CBI had appreciated the 'full engagement and (continuing friendliness) on this very important issue' shown by Mrs Hewitt and 'our friends at the Department of Trade and Industry'... the government and business were 'really playing together now on this'!

If the argument is raised that business is not a precise and neat ethical practice and that one has to accept that in certain cases the ends justify the means, one is accepting a situation where different rules are known to apply in different contexts. No part of a code of behaviour can be seen to be inviolate and every organisational value has its price. This is not to suggest that all laws have to be respected, however repressive and immoral, but the behaviour of the engineering executives was not lawbreaking born from high ideals, but rather lawbreaking born of organisational or personal gain and/or prejudice.

| Case study 7.7 | **A postscript to Case study 7.6** |
| --- | --- |
| | An interesting development to the previous case was that the practice involving the reclassification of exported products had come to the attention of an overseas government and the major operators in this market (including the UK engineering company) were making provisions for substantial repayments of undeclared import taxes. There was also the possibility that a number of the operators could be barred from selling in the overseas market in the future. This development does not suddenly make the decision-making procedures employed invalid, when previously they could be justified on an ends–means basis. An action does not acquire the status of being ethical or unethical merely on the grounds that its existence is either publicly known or unknown. |

An obvious question regarding the engineering company is why the employees we interviewed tolerated their organisational environment. The answer to this question is not explained by one single factor, but it did appear that the most senior managers of the organisation were implicated in the practices. Fear that any form of dissent would be quickly suppressed and impair future promotional prospects was the overriding reason offered by the interviewees for their muteness. There were no whistleblowers within this organisation. Was this a state of affairs to be applauded or encouraged, and how and why can middle and senior managers possess such feelings of organisational impotence?

Within the engineering company many understood the practices, but no one possessed the courage, the will or the independence (as a result of the need to retain their employment) to raise their concerns, either within the organisations or to external agencies. The extent of the malpractices acted like a cancer, corrupting others who might otherwise have exercised moral judgement. There appeared to be a view among certain middle and junior management levels of 'what is sauce for the goose (senior management) is sauce for the gander (themselves)'.

The engineering company might seem an extreme example of modern organisational life. However, the continuing evidence of unacceptable organisational practices and whistleblowing cases (*see* for example Hartley, 1993; Hunt, 1995, 1998), and the work of organisations such as Public Concern at Work and Freedom to Care, do not provide much support for benign assumptions about respect for the moral agency of individual employees.

## Suppressed whistleblowing

For the concerned employee, there are not only potential costs associated with revealing organisational malpractices; there are also costs associated with suppressing whistleblowing. The latter costs tend to be emotional and psychological and are associated with a loss of self-esteem. This is illustrated in Figure 7.1. A fuller account of the issues relating to this framework is given in Lovell (2002).

The framework possesses two layers. The first of these is concerned with two non-organisational factors that are significant in shaping the third element, that of the individual's personal autonomy. The three elements of layer 1 are:

- The individual's personal value system, born of past experiences, including family values and perspectives (both nature and nurture are included).

- Broader societal values, which are unlikely to be homogenous or consistent.

- The feeling of personal autonomy held by the individual.

Layer 2 also possesses three elements, which are context specific. These are:

- Values derived from within the organisation.

- The ethical intensity of a situation or problem felt by the concerned employee.

- The support from others, normally organisational colleagues, both peers and hierarchical superiors, and family, but also support groups, professional associations, etc.

In Figure 7.1 the six cells are shown as the same size. However, the figure can be used to describe the relative importance of the six elements in different potential whistleblowing situations. The relative size of the cells is contingent on the specifics of each case.

The emboldened part of Figure 7.1 represents an inflexible organisational boundary. If an ethically charged situation develops in which the position of the troubled employee is at loggerheads with the senior management, it is likely that the organisational mores/strength of practices will flex and grow in scale. With the boundaries of Figure 7.1 fixed, either one or more of the other elements has to shrink, or a fracture in the boundary will occur. If this happens, then confinement of the problem within the organisation will have ceased and an external whistleblowing situation could follow.

If the troubled employee wishes to retain employment within the organisation, but retains a belief that the organisational practice is wrong, their personal autonomy will need to shrink to accommodate organisational/managerial interests. As a consequence of this diminution of personal autonomy, the ability to exercise moral agency is driven out.

| | | | |
|---|---|---|---|
| **LAYER 2** | Intensity of problem | Organisational values/ strength of practices | Support of others |
| **LAYER 1** | Personal values | Personal autonomy | Societal values |

**Figure 7.1** Elements of ethical complexity

Effectively an individual's personal autonomy acts as a type of shock absorber, allowing confinement of the issue within the organisational boundary. As a consequence, however, the confidence of the suppressed whistleblower can be severely affected. This was particularly so with respect to the individual featured in Case study 7.6. The shrinking of personal autonomy is also significant in Case study 7.8.

| Case study 7.8 | **The charity** |
|---|---|

G possessed a strong religious faith, which reflected his family upbringing. He worked for an internationally known charitable organisation, whose *raison d'être* was love, understanding, tolerance and forgiveness. During the initial interview G revealed that he had an interesting example of principle that was live at the time of the interview. Having recently attended a seminar on value-added-tax (VAT), G had realised that a practice operated by the charity was liable to VAT, but the practice had never been declared for VAT purposes. On returning from the seminar G brought the matter to the attention of the directors, believing that the correct approach would be to notify Customs and Excise and to discuss the issue with them. G was very aware that the charity could not afford to repay the sums that were now clearly owing to Customs and Excise, but G believed that Customs and Excise would agree that the VAT rules were never intended to apply to charities like his own, and at worst the charity would need to lobby Parliament and the Treasury to get the rules changed retrospectively. Being an internationally known charity that attracted widespread public support, G believed this would be possible.

At a subsequent meeting with G, he was clearly less buoyant than at the first meeting. He described how the charity's solicitors had been contacted to obtain a legal ruling on the practice in question and they had confirmed G's assessment. However, the attitude of the senior management towards G was not one of gratitude, but rather coolness, even a degree of wariness. At the third meeting with G, he revealed that the affair had been a sickening experience for him. The legal advice had been that the practice should be terminated immediately, but that no mention should be made to Customs and Excise. The belief was that Customs and Excise would demand a refund of the unpaid taxes and that the probability of the Treasury seeking a change to taxation legislation to exclude the charity from future liability was low, with no chance of retrospective legislation. G's wishes to be honest and 'come clean' with Customs and Excise' were dismissed as naïve. What particularly vexed and troubled him was that he was now, in his own words, 'perceived as a potential whistleblower'. His relationship with members of the charity's Board of Directors had changed from a close and friendly one to one characterised by considerable wariness and mistrust. He had no intention of whistleblowing (out of loyalty to the organisation, not to the senior management), but it hurt greatly to come face to face with his organisational impotency, when he had thought that he and his work were highly valued.

At the start of his ethical dilemma, G carried with him a set of values that he argued reflected a strong commitment to notions of fairness, equity and justice. These underpinned his initial reasoning of the problem. These were values that he believed corresponded with those of the broader society and the charity in question.

---

**Connexion point**

*The Golden Rule*
G enjoyed a quite senior position within the charity. A quiet and softly spoken man, G initially considered his individual autonomy to be high. He was confident of his (moral) position and his arguments. During the interviews, he even cited the 'Golden Rule', in his words, 'treat others as you would want to be treated yourself'.

---

For G, the intensity of the problem was initially high, but he quickly realised that the support of others did not exist, particularly at a very senior level. This mix of level 2 elements (high problem intensity; total resistance from senior management; and low support from others) transformed the issue from one, in G's eyes, capable of resolution within notions of justice and equity, to an ethical dilemma. G's preference to discuss the issue with Customs and Excise put him at variance with the charity's board of directors. G became isolated and was seen as a deviant. He had a loyalty to both the organisation, whose values and mission he wholeheartedly believed in, and to his fellow employees, whose livelihoods would certainly be affected if the tax authorities did demand a repayment of back taxes.

G expressed the view that, if he really believed that Customs and Excise would be successful in demanding repayment of back taxes, he too would support concealment, as the work of the charity would be affected to the point of ruin. However, he simply could not accept that this would be the ultimate outcome. He believed that the Board of Directors did not wish to be seen as having made a serious error in the decisions they had taken over the configuration of the organisation that had led to the practice in question attracting VAT liability, a ramification they had overlooked.

---

**Connexion point**

*Kohlberg's hierarchy of moral reasoning*
G's apparent willingness to 'break the law' is not necessarily a reprehensible position to hold. In G's view the particular VAT law in question represented a failing in the legislation's drafting. It was 'bad law', and could be corrected once its failings were brought to the attention of the relevant authorities. This form of reasoning would normally be considered to reflect high levels of moral reasoning, that is, 5, possibly even 6, within Kohlberg's hierarchy (see p.252-4), depending upon how hard G was prepared to fight for his convictions.

---

G considered the concealment decided upon by the directors reflected an avoidance of pain motive on their part, the very lowest stage of reasoning within Kohlberg's hierarchy. The values imposed upon the situation by the Board of

Directors effectively challenged G. He either stayed and kept quiet or he left. Due to family commitments and a strong belief in the work of the charity G stayed, but his personal autonomy was severely diminished and he viewed the future with sadness and apprehension. Figure 7.2 reflects an application of the elements of ethical complexity to the case.

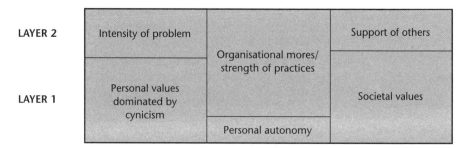

**Figure 7.2** Elements of ethical complexity (Case study 7.8)

If a whistleblower reveals an organisational practice that they consider to be against the public interest, such a whistleblowing act could be considered a civic act. In the sense used here, civic describes an act that an individual citizen carries out as a member of a community or state. The term citizen is an inclusive term. It locates the individual within a community of others. It stresses relatedness, without the integrity and specialness of the individual being lost in the blandness of a crowd. The citizen is both part of a community, but identifiable and separable within it.

There is no suggestion that in such a society every individual is perpetually and desperately seeking to achieve a utopian form of communitarian existence, a form of societal nirvana. What the term civic describes is a context in which justice and understanding are at the bedrock of social relationships. Thus, when a (potentially) significant injustice is observed, the civic-minded individual does not walk away from their civic responsibilities by ignoring the injustice or public hazard. They seek to change the practice, and if this is unsuccessful they seek to bring the problem to public attention. They act in an autonomous way, i.e. they act as free people. They act with moral agency. This is what many whistleblowers would claim for their acts. This is not an argument for a form of societal or organisational chaos that would encourage everyone to challenge everything. As with all aspects of human relations, rights should normally carry with them responsibilities. As a consequence the right to exercise moral agency requires that individuals also respect the beliefs of others insofar as they represent commonly held views.

The whistleblower can be portrayed as a somewhat heroic figure, and some writers do argue this position. While no attempt will be made to suggest that whistleblowing is a saintly act, there is no doubt that particular whistleblowing cases portray individuals who have displayed personal courage and determination to overcome legal, financial, psychological and physical obstacles in their attempts to stop a particular organisational practice, or to bring it to public attention (see Hoffman and Moore, 1990; Hunt 1995, 1998; Lovell and Robertson, 1994; Matthews, Goodpaster and Nash, 1991; Miceli and Near, 1992 for examples). But, for some, there can be an exhilaration associated with whistleblowing. Paul van Buitenen (2000) was the EU employee whose revelations about the misuse of EU funds contributed to the resignation of the entire European Union Commission in 1999. His autobiography reveals that, although his whistleblowing damaged him, he also relished the excitement of the clandestine meetings and the media attention that arose from it.

Returning to our consideration of the societal role and defensibility of whistleblowing, we consider Case study 7.9. This case provides further evidence of the psychological damage that can be inflicted upon an employee who rails against an organisational practice. The person in question occupied a senior position within the organisation concerned, but was judged to pose a threat to certain key individuals within the organisation.

---

**Case study 7.9**

### The costs of whistleblowing

W had worked for the organisation concerned for seven years and had risen to a senior position, effectively being the joint deputy head of finance. However, his unease about certain accounting 'adjustments' he was being asked to make and the obstacle that he represented to the advancement of a junior colleague whom the chief executive appeared to favour, meant that W suddenly appeared to be a 'persona non grata'. This was surprising to all those who were interviewed to corroborate this case, because, without exception, they all held W in very high esteem. A decision appeared to have been made by the chief executive that W had to go, and considerable psychological pressure was exerted on W to encourage him to resign. W's last annual appraisal spoke about his failing performance, despite glowing previous appraisals. W finally resigned, although he appeared to have been 'constructively dismissed', and an out-of-court settlement was made to remove the threat of an industrial tribunal hearing for wrongful dismissal. The words of W are illuminating:

> ... they drag you down to such an extent that your confidence is absolutely rock bottom. You have no confidence in your own ability and it takes you a long time to realise that you didn't deserve this. You hadn't done anything wrong... in the back of your mind you're thinking, did I do something wrong to deserve this? Until now, I have not said anything about my case ... You want a career and you're not quite sure what influence they have in the rest of the public sector – I still haven't got a permanent position.

---

The governance structures of W's organisation were clearly deficient.

Whistleblowing was not on the agenda of any of the central characters within the cases considered in this chapter because of their fear for their respective employment prospects. Many of those who, in a study of accountants and HR managers (Fisher and Lovell, 2000), expressed disgust over certain organisational practices felt impotent and unable to do anything to put things right.

The words of a hospital's deputy director of finance reveal behaviour that might surprise some.

| Case study 7.10 | **The hospital case** |
|---|---|

This case was recounted to the researchers by a range of middle ranking HR managers and accountants within a hospital, as well as by H, the Deputy Director of Finance. It was a situation that troubled many in the hospital (see Case study 2.21 for another interviewee's perspective).

The case relates to the waiting lists initiative instigated by the Department of Health in 1998. The intention of the initiative was to provide additional funds to hospitals to allow them to reduce hospital waiting lists in key areas. The following are the words of the Deputy Director of Finance.

> The government has just put all this money into the waiting list initiative, to treat patients and get them off the waiting list. It's taxpayers' money – the spirit of that money was not to line consultants' pockets. In theory, it's NHS money, health sector money. A number of the specialties reacted as one would hope. However, the ophthalmologists said, 'Yes, we will do this, if you pay me something like £750 per case. We will pay the nurses time and a half. ... And if you don't pay us that rate we won't do the list'. So ophthalmologists got their way – a very dirty deal – nurses get a bit and porters and cleaners get nothing. The ophthalmologists are getting about £15,000 extra per list.

> In addition to the ophthalmologists, ENT specialists and anaesthetists at this hospital also negotiated their own special deals with regard to the waiting lists' initiatives. When asked how particular specialties could drive through such arrangements, the response was, 'They confronted the organisation. The chief executive is frightened of the power of these groups, so he is prepared to do deals, rather than risk not getting patients done.'

> When asked to describe his own feelings towards this situation, H replied, 'Perhaps I am naïve, but I wouldn't have let it happen. I think all staff should be treated equally and I would have waged war with the consultants and said, I am sorry – we are not playing.'

> Had H ever been tempted to blow the whistle at any time? The answer was yes and the above situation was such a time. He had not because, 'I have to respect the chief executive's decision. My loyalty to him, my accountability – I haven't done anything wrong.'

'I haven't done anything wrong.' These are words to ponder.

---

**Connexion point**

Using De George's six criteria for justifiable whistleblowing (see p. 268) it is possible to argue that H could have responded positively to conditions 1, 2, 4 and 6.

- H would have been acting honourably, assuming he did not sell his story to the press, if he had chosen to go public with his knowledge (condition 6).

- It was disgust with the way senior consultants were using their organisational power to 'line their pockets' with public money that was at the heart of H's angst (condition 1).

- H had also discussed the issue with the finance director (condition 2), although the latter seemed resigned to the realities of organisational power within the hospital.

- H also had the documentary evidence to substantiate his case, had he chosen to use it (condition 4).

- However, H had not taken the matter to the chief executive because the chief executive was a central figure in the affair (condition 3), and

- He doubted whether a whistleblowing act would change much, after the initial furore had died down (condition 5).

Thus, against the six criteria H would have found a degree of support for an act of whistleblowing, although the belief that little if anything would change as a result of a whistleblowing act (condition 5) does provide a justification (within De George's framework) for 'keeping quiet'.

A further consideration was that H feared that the adverse publicity that such a revelation would attract would do the hospital great harm, at a time when hospitals across the UK were under considerable media scrutiny due to revelations about the concealment of negligent practices by clinicians (*see* Case study 2.19). It is not just organisations operating in the profit seeking sectors that can suffer from adverse publicity and falling 'client' confidence. H's concerns over the ramifications for 'his' hospital of any disclosure about the greed of a significant number of consultants were real.

Within this account of H's case, there are a number of issues that need to be explored further. The first is the harm that can be caused by an act of whistleblowing. Notwithstanding the existence of unacceptable organisational practices, or shortcomings in quality and/or safety, the whistleblowing act itself may inflict harm upon individuals and organisations including individuals known personally to the whistleblower. To present whistleblowing situations as always clear-cut, with 'good guys' and 'bad guys' clearly demarcated, and issues neatly packaged with 'right' and 'wrong' labels attached, would be misleading. Life is messy, and organisational life is particularly messy on occasions. However, this is not an excuse to do nothing. Judgement has to be a major factor in shaping personal decision making, but when that judgement is constrained by employment fears, moral agency is undermined and impoverished. This takes us to the second point, that of floating responsibility (Bauman, 1994).

## Floating responsibility                    DEFINITION

Floating responsibility refers to the situation where all the individuals that were potentially involved or implicated in a particular incident or problem are all able to explain that responsibility for the problem was not theirs. Responsibility becomes impossible to pinpoint. It appears to fall between the cracks of job descriptions and roles.

H's closing words 'I haven't done anything wrong' could be seen as an example of floating responsibility. It becomes an organisational defence against individual conscience. In this way the following of rules and adherence to the commands of superiors make identification of responsibility difficult to isolate. 'I was only following orders' is a plea heard from junior clerks to senior military officers.

The third point to consider is H's expressed loyalty to the chief executive. 'I have to respect the chief executive's decision. My loyalty to him, my accountability.' Besides loyalty to the chief executive, H was also thinking of his other work colleagues. As the case indicates, H was not alone in his knowledge of the affair, yet H indicated that no one else would 'rock the boat'. These others preferred to 'keep their heads down' for fear of the personal consequences. Colleagues (and their families) who choose to ignore the implications of a malpractice could be significantly affected by any revelations. These are heavy considerations to weigh in the decision of whether or not to whistleblow. The vulnerability and aloneness of the potential whistleblower, but also those who adopt a 'not my business' stance, need reflecting upon. Jos (1988: 323) argued that,

> Modern organisations require workers to do things they might not otherwise do.... [they] undermine the capacity of workers to make their own judgement about what they should do. By uncritically deferring to others, workers may become party to immoral or illegal activities and policies. In short, it is the worker's autonomy, his status as a chooser that is at stake.

Jos's lament over the demise of moral autonomy needs to be juxtaposed with the celebration of 'the individual' as evidenced in much political and corporate rhetoric. The wishes of the individual consumer are claimed to be sovereign. Citizen charters abound, and organisations, both public and private sector, claim to dance to the tune of consumer preferences. Nisbet (1953), while addressing issues of political economy, offered some thoughts that are relevant to this debate.

> The political **enslavement** of man requires the **emancipation** of man from all the authorities and memberships ... that serve, one degree or another, to insulate the individual from the external political power ... totalitarian domination of the individual will is not a mysterious process, not a form of sorcery based upon some vast and unknowable irrationalism. It arises and proceeds rationally and relentlessly through the creation of new functions, statuses and allegiances which, by conferring community, makes the manipulation of the human will scarcely more than an exercise in scientific social psychology ... there may be left the appearance of individual freedom, provided it is only individual freedom. All of this is unimportant, always subject to guidance and control, if the primary social contexts of belief and opinion are properly organised and managed. What is central is the creation of a network of functions and loyalties reaching down into the most intimate recesses of human life where ideas and beliefs will germinate and develop.
>
> (Nisbet, 1953: 202, 208, emphasis in the original)

Thus, Nisbet argued that the freedom inherent within current conceptions of individualism is a particular and partial form of individualism, located precisely in the economic sphere. This ideology has, however, facilitated the neutering of people as political actors. Yet in the economic sphere individualism is again pre-scribed, with certain forms of action almost proscribed. Sarason (1986) commented on a society in which individuals affected by social dilemmas per-ceive their dilemmas as their, and only their, responsibility. Paraphrasing Sarason,

> If **your** ethical dilemma is **your** responsibility according to **my** morality, this is quite consistent with the increasingly dominant ideology of individual rights, responsibility, choice and freedom. If I experience the issue as **yours**, it is because there is nothing in my existence to make it **ours**. And by **ours** I mean a socio-cultural network and traditions which engender an obligation to be part of the problem and possible solution.
>
> (Sarason, 1986, emphasis in the original)

What we hope is becoming evident is that whistleblowing is a complex, many-sided debate that cannot be removed from the social, cultural and economic contexts to which it relates.

Whilst individual attitudes might be difficult to change, certainly in the short term, maybe the least that might be expected of a civilised society is that those of its members who do act in ways that reflect a civic orientation in their whistle-blowing should enjoy the protection of the law. Thus, it is appropriate that we now progress to a consideration of the law relating to whistleblowing in the UK, The Public Interest Disclosure Act, 1998.

## The Public Interest Disclosure Act (1998) (PIDA)

There are two central elements to the PIDA to recognise from the outset. The first is that it does not give a right to an employee to whistleblow. The Act has been constructed upon the premise that confidentiality of corporate information is the primary principle, from which there a few exceptions. It is to these excep-tions that the Act speaks. It offers protection to those who speak out (in the parlance of the Act, make a 'disclosure') against specific types of organisational malpractices, as long as certain conditions are met. The construction of the Act encourages disclosure to be kept within the employing organisation's boundaries by increasing the conditions that have to be satisfied if one makes a disclosure outside the confines of the employing organisation.

The second element that lessens the Act's potential from the perspective of the concerned employee is that the burden of proof is upon the employee to show that a malpractice has occurred, although the burden of proof does vary depend-ing upon to whom a disclosure is made. In circumstances where the work environment is intimidatory and oppressive, obtaining supporting evidence, such as corroboration from current employees, could prove extremely difficult.

The term 'protected disclosure' relates to the type of whistleblowing act that falls within the protection of the Act. The malpractice must normally relate to the employing organisation. However, in certain, restricted situations a protected disclosure can be made against third-party organisations. Interestingly, auditors, with the exception of matters relating to terrorism and money laundering, do not have a duty to report wrongdoing, and neither are they protected by the PIDA if they do make such a revelation. It could be argued that this exclusion from protection by the Act and the omission of a duty to report wrongdoing, other than in the two areas mentioned, suits the practising members of the accountancy profession, as it avoids their coming into conflict with their clients. Audit income is but a part of the income that most practising accountancy firms earn from their audit clients. It is not in the interest of practising accountancy firms to be required to play the role of society's watchdog on the activities of their clients.

For a disclosure to fall within the protection of the Act, the disclosure itself must relate to a specified set of malpractices. These are:

- A criminal offence.

- A failure to comply with any legal obligation.

- A miscarriage of justice.

- Danger to the health and safety of any individual.

- Damage to the environment.

- Deliberate concealment of any of the above.

To comply with the PIDA (and thus to stay within its protection), an ethically concerned employee must use to the full the organisation's internal procedures for handling such concerns. Such procedures can be avoided only if:

- at the time the disclosure was made the employee reasonably believed that they would be 'subject to a detriment' by the employer if a disclosure was made to the employer;

- the employee is concerned that evidence relating to the malpractice would be concealed or destroyed by the employer;

- the employee has previously made a disclosure to the employer of substantially the same information.

> **DEFINITION**
>
> **Detriment** is defined in the Act as being penalised by the employer, e.g. being fined, demoted, sacked or denied promotion.

Internal procedures can be sidestepped if they are shown to be seriously flawed, because of legitimate fears of information being confiscated or destroyed. Other fears, such as the existence of an oppressive and threatening employment environment, can be more difficult to substantiate. This is because obtaining corroborating evidence from fellow employees (who might be fearful for their own jobs) can be extremely difficult to obtain.

One concern about the Act is that it addresses the circumstances of the employee once that employee has made a disclosure. It is possible that, if only the *threat* of disclosure is made by the concerned employee, the Act would not protect the employee in the event of the employee being sacked before a full disclosure was made. In addition, whilst expressions of concern by one employee to another employee about a particular organisational (mal)practice might constitute a breach of confidentiality (and thus create the possibility of dismissal), the PIDA would not be available to the sacked employee if he had not raised the issue with the organisation's management.

While the establishment of an internal whistleblowing procedure may, at first sight, be a laudable development by any organisation, in the hands of unscrupulous employers it might be a mere device for complying with the letter of the law but not the spirit. Warren (1993) questioned the rationale for American firms introducing corporate codes of conduct. The same might be said of internal whistleblowing procedures.

There is also the issue of gaining sufficient evidence to feel able to lodge a concern. Raising a concern within the employing organisation requires that the concerned employee must satisfy two tests. The first is that he must 'reasonably believe' that one of the above mentioned malpractices has occurred. Secondly, the disclosure must be made in 'good faith'. However, the process of gaining evidence, as mentioned in relation to the Maxwell affair, can be a big problem. In such situations, being able to prove that sufficient evidence existed to allow individuals to 'reasonably believe' there were malpractices afoot could be extremely difficult. In addition, the use of internal procedures could prove unattractive to an employee (as in the Maxwell case). This would leave the concerned employee with only external whistleblowing to contemplate. However, the burden of proof required to stay within PIDA protection increases as soon as one raises one's concerns with external third parties. If information is revealed within the firm then the 'reasonably believe' test applies. However, if concerns are expressed to an external third party then the test becomes, 'the employee ... reasonably believes that the information and any allegation contained in it are *substantially true*' [emphasis added]. Thus the concerned employee must be able to show that there were reasonable grounds for them to believe that the allegation being made was 'substantially true' – a far more rigorous criterion than 'reasonably believe'.

Even if this condition is met, the concerned employee loses protection of the PIDA if the employee is rewarded for disclosing the wrongdoing, e.g. receiving payment from a newspaper. Thus, motive for the disclosure affects the protection provided by the PIDA. As mentioned earlier, rewards for information (including that provided anonymously) that leads to the successful prosecution of a criminal are quite acceptable. So why the different treatment of those who report the criminal activity of organisations?

If the internal whistleblowing procedures of an employing organisation are judged to be unsafe by a concerned employee, they will normally be expected to use the offices of a 'prescribed body'. Such a prescribed body is likely to be a regulatory body of an industry (e.g. OFWAT for water companies, or the Financial Services Authority for financial service companies). Within the public sector, such prescribed bodies are less likely to exist. It will be important for the concerned employee to establish whether a 'prescribed body' exists to handle their concerns.

Failure to follow the required procedures might take the complaint outside the protection of the PIDA. Notwithstanding this, there exists no requirement on the part of a regulator to act in response to the information supplied by a concerned employee, other than the rules under which the regulator normally acts.

The above uncertainty over the 'actual' protection afforded by the PIDA is at the heart of concerns expressed about the Act. The evidence provided by *Freedom To Care* on those cases it has investigated is that the PIDA would not have provided the protection the whistleblowers needed to withstand losing their jobs.

Employees working in areas covered by the Official Secrets' Act are also not protected by the PIDA. There are many examples of classified information within central government and (to a lesser extent) local government that are of dubious sensitivity, yet the information is covered by the Official Secrets' Act. There is a need for a concerned employee to check whether any information that relates to the cause of their concern is of a classified nature.

If all the requirements of the PIDA are satisfied (including the requirement that the alleged malpractice be deemed to be a sufficiently serious offence, plus all the other requirements mentioned above), the Act does provide protection that previously did not exist. Additional features of the PIDA are:

**1 Gagging clauses.** Gagging clauses are restrictive clauses in employment contracts that prevent the mentioning of anything of an organisational nature to anyone outside the employing organisation. These were a very real problem for many employees prior to the PIDA, but they appear to be void under the Act – other than those covered by the Official Secrets Act.

Whilst gagging clauses appear to be outlawed by PIDA, it must still be remembered that an implied term of employment contracts is the duty of confidentiality to the employing organisation on the part of the employee. It is this 'duty of confidentiality' that explains the considerable restrictions that have been placed upon the definition of a 'protected disclosure'. Only when the conditions of the PIDA have been judged to have been complied with, can the 'duty of confidentiality' be usurped by the PIDA in the specified situations identified above.

**2. Interim Relief** (keeping one's salary if dismissed for whistleblowing). Under section 9, the PIDA extends one of the provisions of the Employment Rights Act (ERA). If an employee suffers dismissal as a result of making a 'protected disclosure', they should make representation to an Employment Tribunal within seven days of dismissal. This aspect is known as interim relief. If the Employment Tribunal considers that the disclosure is likely to fall within the definition of a protected disclosure, the Employment Tribunal *may* order the employer to reinstate the employee. If the employer fails to comply with such an order, 'the employee is deemed to remain in employment until the hearing and entitled to continue to be paid as such'. However, before these conditions are activated on behalf of the employee, three further conditions must be met.

1. The claim for an interim relief must be lodged within seven days of dismissal.

2. The Employment Tribunal must first decide that the employee is likely to be found to have made a protected disclosure (not an obvious decision without studying all the relevant information); **and**

3. An order is likely to be made to the employing organisation to reinstate the employee (and this ruling happens relatively infrequently).

Thus, an interim order, while appearing to be a positive aspect of the PIDA, is likely in practice to be much less frequently activated than it might first appear. For example, in the case, *Bladon v. ALM Medical Services ET*, reported by Myers and Dehn (2000), an application for interim relief was rejected by the Chairman of the Employment Tribunal without hearing evidence. The basis for this judgement was that the Tribunal Chairman considered the claimant's (the whistleblower) case to be 'implausible'. Yet, when the case was finally heard, the whistleblower's actions were upheld and he was awarded damages. However, in the many months between the application for an interim relief and the actual Tribunal hearing, the whistleblower was denied any salary from his former employer.

If an employee's case falls within the protection of the PIDA then:

- The employee will be entitled to a compensation payment if victimisation is experienced as a result of the whistleblowing act (e.g. the employee stays within the employing organisation but suffers demotion). The level of compensation will depend upon the specifics of each case.

- If dismissed, the employee will be entitled to a compensation payment in line with the awards available through Employment Tribunals. These rates change over time, but, as mentioned earlier, the ceiling has now been removed.

## Reflections

This chapter has considered various aspects of whistleblowing. Although examples can be cited of revelations of organisational malpractices that have been shown to be both accurate and serious, as well as examples of where the concerns of employees have been ignored or 'lost' in managerial structures and disasters involving loss of life have followed, the prospects for those contemplating whistleblowing remain uncertain. Employment law and the PIDA are written with the primary intention of protecting the commercial confidentiality of organisations that operate in legally compliant ways. There is thus a fundamental tension between, on the one hand, the need for employees to feel able to exercise moral agency and raise awareness of issues that have a genuine public interest and, on the other hand, the need for organisations to retain commercially sensitive information, and be protected from malicious and ill-founded accusations by disgruntled employees. The extent to which the balance between these competing requirements is acceptable and appropriate needs to be revisited regularly.

In modern times strong economies and vibrant business sectors are essential if political and social goals are to be achieved. It is difficult to refute the centrality of a strong economy to many societal aspirations, whether the economy is located in the so-called developing or developed worlds. As a result, businesses, and pressure groups representing business interests, act as powerful influences in the creation and maintenance of the legal frameworks that govern business activities. In this context it is perhaps not surprising that the PIDA was framed in the way that it was, if it was to receive sufficient support in the UK Parliament and thereby become law. Yet the very necessity to support and protect business interests creates loopholes for unscrupulous organisations to use. In addition there are those situations in which organisations flout the laws that society has passed, and the question then arises as to how and when society should be made aware of these infractions.

There are also questions about the relationships between business, environmental and societal interests, with the latter relating as much to future societies as to present ones. It is important that assumptions regarding the roles and power of organisations are challenged – not taken for granted. Related to, but separate from, these assumptions are the issues relating to notions of individualism and civic perspectives that have been alluded to in this chapter. These need revisiting on a regular basis to ensure that the issues and debates are themselves comprehended, and not overpowered by the pre-eminence of business interests.

## Summary

In this chapter the following key points have been made:

- Whistleblowing includes, but is not limited to, the revelation of an organisational issue to an external party.

- Whistleblowing help-lines can be both important organisational mechanisms for the raising of ethical concerns, and early warning systems of unacceptable practices.

- Protection offered to whistleblowers by the PIDA is constrained and cannot limit the trauma that tends to accompany whistleblowing acts.

- The pejorative connotation of whistleblowing needs to be reflected upon and understood. Whilst perpetual whistleblowing is an unattractive proposition, the organisational impotence reflected in the case studies cited is equally unpalatable.

- Viewing whistleblowers as witnesses rather than snitches would be a positive development.

- If it is right to reveal the identity of those who break the law outside organisational life, why is it less right to reveal those who break the law or who endanger human life in their capacities as organisational employees?

## Quick revision test

1. Is an act of whistleblowing confined to the release of organisational information to an external third party?

2. Is it appropriate or helpful to view whistleblowers as equivalent to referees?

3. What is the name of the Act that can offer protection to those who reveal an organisational malpractice in the public interest?

4. Rewards are often offered by the police to those who reveal the identity of those who commit a crime, such as robbery or theft. Does the PIDA take a similar view to those who make a financial gain as a result of their whistleblowing?

## Typical assignments and briefs

1. Debate the strength of the arguments that seek to change the terminology for describing those who reveal organisational malpractices as whistleblowers.

2. To gain the protection of the Public Interest Disclosure Act, those who reveal organisational malpractices have to satisfy a number of conditions that witnesses in other criminal investigations do not have to satisfy, e.g. deriving no financial gain from the case and not having been involved in the crime at any stage. Critically evaluate the merits of these conditions.

3. Evaluate the argument that internal whistleblowing procedures are an essential part of any learning organisation.

4. Assume that a person has responded to Activity 7.1 in the following way. He has indicated:
   - an extreme level of anger (point 10 on the scale) in response to Case A;
   - a high level of support (point 2 on the scale) in Case B; and
   - a fair degree of anger (point 6 on the scale) in Case C.

   Discuss the factors that could explain these variations in the responses to the questions posed and what this might say about ethical principles.

### Group activity 7

Consider the PIDA and make recommendations to reduce or add to the scope of the Act. Your proposals should be able to withstand critical appraisal at both a practical and theoretical level. Divide a sheet of paper into four columns. In the first column list your proposals. In the second column state against each proposal why you believe the amendment is justified. In the third column you should identify the principal objections or problems associated with your proposal. The final column should reflect your thoughts on the strengths of the objections/ problems identified in column three, and whether you believe they are surmountable.

## Recommended further reading

The two main authors writing on the topic of this chapter are Borrie and Hunt. We recommend that you read Borrie (1996), 'Business Ethics and Accountability', in Brindle, M. and Dehn, G. (1996), *Four Windows on Whistleblowing*, pp. 1–23, Public Concern at Work. Also Borrie, G. and Dehn, G. (2002), *Whistleblowing: The New Perspective*, Public Concern website, http://www.pcaw.co.uk/policy_pub/ newperspective.html. Hunt's books (1995), *Whistleblowing in the Health Service: Accountability, Law & Professional Practice*, Edward Arnold and (1998), *Whistleblowing in the Social Services: Public Accountability and Professional Practice*, Edward Arnold are also useful. A more recent work is by Lewis, D.B. (2000), *Whistleblowing at Work*, Athlone Press.

## Useful websites

| Topic | Website provider | URL |
|---|---|---|
| The website of the leading charitable organisation providing advice to both individuals and organisations on whistleblowing issues/ organisational hotlines | Public Concern at Work | http://www.pcaw.co.uk |
| An impressive organisation that acts as an advocate for those who stand up for freedom of speech in the workplace. Publishes an extremely thought provoking and important newsletter | Freedom to Care | http://www.freedomtocare.org |

# PART C

# Organisational responses to ethical issues

## CHAPTER 8

# Corporate responsibility, corporate governance and corporate citizenship

## Learning outcomes

Having read this chapter and completed its associated activities, you should be able to:

■ Discuss the development of corporate social responsibility (CSR), and the more recent attachment to the notion of corporate responsibility.

■ Critically evaluate the counter-arguments to CSR.

■ Debate the scope and appropriateness of developments in Anglo-American corporate governance since the early 1990s.

■ Discuss the challenges posed to Anglo-American development in corporate governance by the King Report.

■ Review the UN Global Compact and the development in orientation reflected in the 2004 *Gearing Up* report.

■ Understand the notion of the social contract as reflected in *Integrated Social Contract Theory*.

■ Discuss the position of corporate manslaughter as an indictable offence in the UK and America.

## Introduction

Corporate responsibility is a term that is supplanting the term corporate social responsibility. The 'social' is increasingly being omitted in order to emphasise the (claimed) broader responsibilities of business corporations, particularly their responsibilities with regard to the environment, as discussed in the next chapter.

Corporate governance is a phrase with some longevity, but which has gained greater prominence since the early 1990s. The issues of whether corporations can assume the status of citizens and, if so, whether such a development is desirable, will also be discussed. The three terms have been purposely linked in this chapter because, whilst they possess different associations, within corporate governance reforms in the UK and America, there have been strenuous and largely successful attempts to deny their relationship, or at least to contest the notion of corporate responsibility, let alone debate the notion of corporate citizenship.

## The early calls for corporate social responsibility (CSR)

The desire to encourage, nay require, corporations to assume greater responsibility for their actions can be traced back over many decades, and reflects growing concerns regarding the power and influence of corporations over people's lives and even the independence and integrity of governments. For example, Oberman (2000) refers to academic debates over corporate social responsibilities taking place in the 1920s.

As the power and influence of business corporations have assumed ever greater proportions, so too have the calls increased for mechanisms to be put in place that would make corporations more accountable as well as responsible to a wider constituency than merely their shareholders. Within this latter aspect of the debate the use of the term *stakeholder* has gained currency in recent years and is a subject to which we will return later in this chapter.

The development of the argument from one of requiring corporations to act in socially responsible ways, to more recent calls for corporations to be seen as corporate citizens, reflects a desire to lock corporations, both formally and possibly legally, into the responsibilities that this status would confer. As indicated in the definition below, the citizenry is, in theory, sovereign to the state, yet the citizenry has little or no access, and certainly few, if any, rights with respect to corporations. With corporations playing an increasingly influential role over very many aspects of social and political life, the demand for more accountability and responsibility on the part of corporations is unlikely to diminish.

---

**DEFINITION**

The term **citizen** normally relates to the relationship between an individual and the political state in which the individual lives. It carries with it notions of rights and responsibilities on the part of the individual and the state. However, this reciprocity (i.e. two-way relationship) is unlikely to be an equal one. Within democratic theories of the state, citizens have ultimate sovereignty over the state, or at least sovereignty over those who represent the citizenry within government. Practice, however, usually reflects a quite different balance of power.

---

Being described as a citizen does not of itself imply much about morality. It is a noun in need of an adjective such as 'good' or 'moral' before it can confer a positive societal influence. Wood and Logsdon (2001) referred to this issue when they observed, in the context of the corporate citizen debate,

> One important debate distinguishes the concept of citizenship-as-legal-status from the concept of citizen-as-desirable-activity. The minimum requirements to be called a citizen are very different from the requirement to be called a 'good citizen.'
>
> (Wood and Logsdon, 2001: 88)

The role of the citizen can vary from the active notion of citizenship evident in ancient Greece (for those conferred as free men) to a passive acceptance of governance from a sovereign body (à la Hobbes) or from the bureaucratic state (à la Weber). Within the corporate citizen debate, the demands made of corporations vary from a minimalist societally neutral influence, to a proactive role. The societally neutral arguments do not, however, reflect a status-quo situation, or even a single understanding of what might be meant by societally neutral. For example, would being societally neutral mean that:

- Negative and positive effects of corporate activities could be balanced out (possibly involving an international perspective), or would a corporation's impacts need to harm no one or nothing at any time?

- Acting within legal constraints would be acceptable, even if the law was judged by many to be inadequate (as a result of the political lobbying by corporations)?

- There is a general acceptance that corporations do have social responsibilities?

These debates are still developing and represent just some of the issues that make the general area of business and values both dynamic and vital.

Hobbes (*see* Pojman, 1998) held a pessimistic view of human nature, seeing people as essentially selfish and untrustworthy. Thus, Hobbes deemed that a sovereign power was necessary to which the people would owe allegiance. The relationship between the sovereign power and the citizen is, in a Hobbesian world, a subjugated one. In this context, being a citizen within a Hobbesian state is a quite different one from that which would be acceptable in the twenty-first century. However, if the idea of conferring citizenship status upon corporations is one that concerns people, due to their distrust in corporations to act in socially beneficial ways, then a Hobbesian notion of citizenship has some appeal. But much depends upon the constitution and constituent parts of the sovereign power.

As societies have developed and the scope of governments has increased, the lack of possibilities for active participation of citizens has come to be viewed as a weakness of modern conceptions of democratic states. In contemporary societies political citizenship is increasingly limited to periodic elections of political representatives, and even the relevance of these is being questioned. For example, in the 2001 general election in the UK, only 58 per cent of those eligible to vote did so, the lowest turnout for many years. In the UK, local elections and those for the European Union achieve even lower levels of elector participation. In these elections approximately two out of three people do not vote. Thus, when we, or others, use the term citizen, we need to be clear about the form of citizenship we are discussing.

The next time you are in a group – in a seminar room, pub or other social gathering, try to establish how many people voted at the last general election, and if you think the conversation will stand the enquiry, how many people voted at the last local election when it was held independently of a general election. Do you think the percentages you establish sit comfortably in a democratic state?

One of the most widely expressed concerns about modern corporations is that they have relatively unfettered authority, with only limited responsibilities (basically to keep within the laws of the land), but there is a need to be more specific about the form and level of participation in the operations of the state that are being suggested when the phrase corporate citizenship is employed. Given the significance of business organisations within democratic (as well as undemocratic) states, the presumption must be that the notion of corporate citizenship assumed by its advocates would reflect the acceptance of certain societal responsibilities, although whether there is envisaged to be an equal bestowing of citizens' rights on corporations is far from clear.

Before progressing any further, it is worth reflecting upon the observations of Charles Lindblom, a former Professor of Economics and Political Science at Yale University. In his book *Politics and Markets* (1977), Lindblom concluded his analysis of the relationships between large corporations and political systems (and the book itself) with the following paragraph.

> It has been a curious feature of democratic thought that it has not faced up to the private corporation in an ostensible democracy. Enormously large, rich in resources ... they can insist that government meet their demands, even if these demands run counter to ... citizens .... Moreover they do not disqualify themselves from playing the role of citizen ..... they exercise unusual veto powers .... The large private corporation fits oddly into democratic theory and vision. Indeed it does not fit.
>
> (Lindblom, 1977: 356)

The final five-word sentence is the last in the book and is particularly piercing. Lindblom was bringing into sharp focus the lack of compatibility between democratic aspirations for political systems and the autocratic, sometimes feudal, systems that operate in many, if not the majority of, corporations, and it is the latter in which most people spend most of their waking lives. Large corporations have influence in and upon even the most significant of political powers. Table 8.1 illustrates the sort of evidence that gives rise to such concerns. The table reflects some of the donations made to the Republican Party during the 2000 American presidential campaign and the actions taken immediately following the inauguration of George W. Bush as President of the United States of America in 2001. All the actions were taken by the President during the first three months of his presidency.

**Table 8.1** Actions taken by President G.W. Bush within three months of his inauguration in 2001

| Industry | $M donated | Actions taken |
|---|---|---|
| Tobacco | 7.0 | Removal of federal lawsuits against cigarette manufacturers |
| Timber | 3.2 | Restrictions on logging roads scrapped |
| Oil and Gas | 25.4 | Restrictions on CO2 emissions abandoned; Kyoto agreement scrapped; moves to open Arctic refuge to drilling |
| Mining | 2.6 | Scrapping of environmental clean-up rules, e.g. arsenic limits in water supply |
| Banks and credit card companies | 25.6 | Bankruptcy bill making it easier for credit card companies to collect debts from bankrupt customers |
| Pharmaceuticals | 17.8 | Medicare (government-supported health insurance) reform removing price controls |
| Airlines | 4.2 | Federal barriers to strikes introduced; back-pedalling on antitrust (mergers and monopolies) legislation |

Source: *Guardian* G2, 27 April 2001, p. 2

It would be wrong to imply that concerns are only ever expressed with regard to American corporate–political relationships. The following are just two examples taken from the UK that have raised similar concerns.

1. In 1997, the incoming Labour government had a manifesto commitment to a total ban on tobacco advertising, yet no such proposed legislation was ever formally debated in Parliament during the 1997–2001 administration. By the time the Labour Party's 2001 manifesto was published, the commitment to a complete ban on tobacco advertising was noticeable by its absence, although in March 2002 the Minister for Health announced legislative plans for an almost complete ban on tobacco advertising and sponsorship, the one exception being motor racing sponsorship. It might be just a coincidence that Bernie Ecclestone, who effectively controls world-wide Grand Prix motor racing, donated £1M to the Labour Party, which was subsequently repaid when the donation became public knowledge.

2. The Labour Party's 1997 manifesto also included a commitment to a reform of company law by recognising a stakeholder perspective (as opposed to an exclusively shareholder responsibility). Upon election the Labour government established a committee to consider how the stakeholder commitment could be operationalised. The committee deliberated for nearly two years. An interim report was published after the first year, which retained an attachment to the notion of pluralism in corporate decision making, although the wording can be seen to be becoming a little ambiguous.

The principle arguments are that the present scheme of law fails adequately to recognise that businesses best generate wealth where participants operate harmoniously as teams and that managers should recognise the wider interests of the community.

One year later the committee published its final report, but by now the term pluralism had been lost and in its place appeared the term 'enlightened shareholder value'. The removal of the commitment to pluralism led to the resignation from the committee of the finance director of *The Body Shop*. He described himself as an advocate of social and environmental responsibility and was not prepared to remain a member of the committee once the commitment to enlightened shareholder value had replaced pluralism. Newspaper reports on the outcome of the committee's work talked of frantic lobbying by business interests that ultimately led to not only the retention of the shareholders' interests being the only one formally recognised in UK law, but also the conversion of the committee's proposals for compulsory statements on corporate issues into proposals that would only be voluntary, i.e. at the discretion of directors.

The above examples are not cited to claim that all businesses are corrupt or corrupting. However, just as a few examples of negative or unethical business practices should not tar all businesses with these behaviours, neither should a few examples of positive business behaviour suggest that all is right in the corporate and political worlds. For our purposes the point the cases illustrate is the way the business lobby groups successfully influenced legislative matters. The cases illustrate the significant ramifications for social and democratic processes of the lobbying phenomenon which, by its very nature, is opaque. An image thus emerges of business interests playing an active, although not always transparent, role in political and social, as well as economic, matters.

The question is thus raised, 'To what extent is ethical egoism, with its appeal to emotive and fundamental concepts such as freedom and individuality, merely a convenient façade behind which privileged and powerful self-interests hide?'

> **Connexion point**
>
> Ethical egoism was discussed in Chapter 3 and relates to the ethical stance that sees the protection of individual freedom as the touchstone of ethics. It draws upon notions of choice, meritocracy and a form of justice, but it can conceal extreme selfishness, protectionism and callousness.

With many large corporations now (and for some time) more powerful than the majority of governments, the feudal nature of corporate realpolitik is masked by the veil of democratic political paraphernalia for the majority of people living on the planet. Thus, if large corporations are to exist within democratic states there have to be certain developments that democratise the corporations and other developments that make them less of a threat to political and social democracy.

When put in this context the subject of corporate governance ceases to be (if it ever was) an arcane and dry technical subject. As we will see, different notions of corporate governance exist in different parts of the world, with some of the most enlightened thinking emanating from South Africa.

## The recurring issue of corporate governance

As with notions of CSR, issues relating to corporate governance have featured regularly through time. For example, the 'Bubble Act' of 1719 came into being as the result of a corporate scandal which, in relative terms, involved sums of money greater than the combined value of Enron and WorldCom.

Lee (1984) and Edey (1984) referred to the manipulation of company accounting information by managers at the expense of the owners' interests during the early nineteenth century, while Carey (1984) referred to the contribution of William Z. Ripley, a Harvard professor, who, in the early 1920s wrote about the 'docility of corporate shareholders permitting themselves to be honeyfuggled'. In relation to the public utilities industries, Ridley referred to 'the hoodwinking of the shareholders', and of accountants Ripley observed, 'accountants are enabled to play ball with figures to an astounding degree' (Carey, 1984: 243).

The concerns over corporate governance continued through the latter part of the nineteenth century and into the early part of the twentieth century, culminating in Berle and Means' seminal publication in 1932. In this publication Berle and Means charted the history and implications of the decoupling of ownership (shareholders) from control (senior management) within the modern corporation. Niebuhr (1932) also wrote powerful critiques of corporate power and the exploitative and alienating tendencies of the capitalist system. Since the early 1990s there has been increasing attention to corporate governance as a result of major corporate scandals such as Maxwell Communications, BCCI and Polly Peck in the late 1980s and in the early 2000s Enron, WorldCom, Global Crossing and Parmalat. We will return to the issues raised by these corporate collapses and scandals shortly, but first we address the issue of whether we should just accept such corporate débacles as a fact of economic life and not be too concerned about them.

## Are not corporate failures just a fact of economic life?

It is clear from the very brief overview above that concerns over corporate governance are not new, but reactions to corporate scandals of the 1990s and early twenty-first century by organisations such as the major stock exchanges, professional accountancy bodies and governments appear to have been more obvious and public than before. Could this reflect a degree of vulnerability and sensitivity that was not felt in the past? It is difficult to say, although débacles such as Enron and WorldCom, Global Crossing and Parmalat pose fundamental problems for securities' markets. Investing in companies is a risky business and any investor must recognise and accept this fact. Thus, it is not the losing of money that is the problem. The problem is the failure of market mechanisms to provide the information and warning signals that the investing public has a right to expect. In all the corporate failures referred to in this chapter the most recent accounts of the corporations concerned gave little if any hint of the financial turmoil the corporations were experiencing.

In the cases of Enron and WorldCom the auditors appear to have been complicit in the deceit, whilst in the cases of Maxwell Communications and BCCI (financial scandals of the late 1980s and early 1990s) the causes of the auditors' performance are more opaque. Whatever the reasons, the important market mechanism that the role of audit is supposed to play (verifying the reliability of the financial information supplied to shareholders) failed. The accounting profession was seen to be, at best, an unreliable scrutineer of financial information. More significantly the independence and integrity of accountants and accounting firms were increasingly being called into question.

In addition to the failings of the audit function, market analysts were still recommending Enron and WorldCom stocks as 'buys' to the investing world until days before the companies crashed, although again the integrity of the market analysts concerned has subsequently been shown to have been heavily compromised. As a result of these failings of the securities' markets, confidence in their fairness, transparency and integrity was undermined, with the risk that investors might turn to other investment options, such as property, currencies, works of art, etc. Thus, while it might only be out of enlightened self-interest, the securities' markets cannot afford to tolerate unethical corporate behaviour. However, at the same time, the intensity of the demands of the securities' markets is unrelenting in terms of the enormous pressures placed upon company executives to deliver improved 'financials' (profits) year upon year, half-year upon half-year, quarter upon quarter.

## Developments in corporate governance

There has been a lot of activity with regard to corporate governance in the UK since the early 1990s and Figure 8.1 presents a schema of the various reports, with the addition of one notable reform in the USA, that of the Sarbanes–Oxley Act in 2002. A brief overview of these reports is provided so that the contestability of corporate responsibility and corporate governance can be discussed.

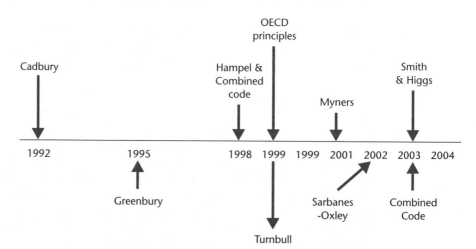

**Figure 8.1** Significant recent reports and developments in corporate governance

The **Cadbury Committee** was established as a response to some significant corporate collapses/scandals in the late 1980s and early 1990s, including BCCI, Polly Peck and Maxwell Communications. Given the comments made above regarding the questioning of the audit function performed by the large accounting firms and the resulting undermining of confidence in the London Stock Exchange, it will come as no surprise to learn that these were the two major sponsoring organisations of the Cadbury Committee. The major recommendations of the committee included the increased use of non-executive directors to counter what is referred to as the agency effect, and the splitting of the roles of chief executive and chairperson.

> **DEFINITION**
>
> The **agency effect** is derived from agency theory, which assumes that people are, at heart, untrustworthy. As a result of the privileged position that executive directors enjoy over shareholders with regard to the control of information, executive directors are deemed likely to exploit this power situation to their own advantage. This might manifest itself in 'managing' information (hence the importance of the audit function) and large remuneration packages.

The **Greenbury Committee** was set up to look into the issue of executive pay (Sir Richard Greenbury was at the time Chief Executive of Marks & Spencer and one of the highest paid directors in the UK). Even at this time the issue of executive pay, sometimes referred to as 'fat-cats pay', was a vexed issue but the work of the Greenbury Committee seems to have had little constraining effect, as indicated by Table 8.2. This table contrasts the movement in the FTSE 100 index with the average increase in the remuneration of the executive directors of the same top 100 UK corporations. If the movement in a company's market worth is a fair reflection of the performance of the company's senior management, then is it not reasonable to expect that there would be a close correlation between the change in corporate executives' remuneration and the change in market worth of the companies they manage, certainly over a reasonable period of time like three years?

Table 8.2 Average increases in the remuneration of the directors of the FTSE 100 companies for 2000–2002 compared with movements in the FTSE 100 share index over the same period

| Year | Movement in directors' remuneration | Movements in FTSE 100 index |
| --- | --- | --- |
| 2000 | + 28% | – 8% |
| 2001 | + 17% | – 15% |
| 2002 | + 23% | – 23% |
| Overall movements from Jan. 2000 to 31 Dec. 2002 | + 84% | – 40% |

A similar picture is evident in the USA. With the boundaries of self-control removed during the 1990s, but with the retention of the rhetoric of free markets, rapacious has been a frequently used adjective in discussions of corporate and executive behaviour. In both America and the UK stock options became a central part of executive remuneration packages during the 1990s, as attempts were made to tie the pay of senior executives to the performance of their companies, thereby trying to minimise the agency effect. The result was startling, although not necessarily in the way intended. Robert Monks (2003) commented upon the transfer of wealth reflected in the value of stock options held by a very small minority of senior executives in America.

> The most important component of compensation was the grant of options that, according to the accounting rules after 1994, did not have to be accounted for as an expense by the issuing company. Typically, the top five executives in a company held 75% of the total options granted; the ratio of options to the total outstanding rose in the 1990s from 2% to 12%. This must be the greatest 'peaceful' transfer of wealth in recorded history.
>
> (Monks, 2003: 165)

Two per cent or one-fiftieth, of the value of the equity capital of corporate America is a huge figure. Twelve per cent, or nearly one-eighth, is a gargantuan number and this proportion of American equity capital is held by a relatively small number of senior of executives.

Returning to reports on UK corporate governance, the **Hampel Committee** (1998) was formed to take stock of both the Cadbury and Greenbury reports and to suggest how best to implement their recommendations. Interestingly, the Hampel report, while recognising that boards of directors have a responsibility for *relations* with stakeholders, felt the need to emphasise that the *responsibility* of directors is to shareholders. Stakeholders are of concern to directors, but only in as far as they can contribute to the maximisation of shareholder wealth.

The Hampel Report led to the first '**Combined Code**', which was issued by the London Stock Exchange in 1998. The Code specifies the corporate governance practices that quoted companies should follow if they wish to have a listing on the London Stock Exchange. The Code is not backed by law and if a quoted company chooses not to follow the Code the company must explain the rationale for its different practice. For example, the supermarket chain, Morrisons, had, until it bought the Safeway group in 2004, combined the roles of chief executive and chairman, which was contrary to the 1998 Combined Code. Morrisons claimed that combining the two roles made sense for them and this was accepted by the London Stock Exchange.

The 'comply or explain' approach towards corporate governance developments in the UK is different from the approach of the United States, where changes are passed through the legislative processes and are thus legally binding. Such an example is the Sarbanes–Oxley Act of 2002. The latter was the result of two Congressmen formulating their response to a number of financial scandals, notably those of Enron, WorldCom and Global Crossing. The Act places specific responsibilities upon chief executives and the chief financial officers (in UK terms, the finance directors) to personally sign off the accounts. In addition certain accounting services that audit firms might wish to provide to their audit clients have been proscribed by the Act. This reflects the concerns that have been expressed for many years that the level of non-audit fee income earned by accounting firms from their audit clients might compromise their independence and objectivity. The fact that Andersen's (Enron's auditors) generated around $25M of non-audit fee income from Enron, on top of the $25M audit income, was felt by many to have been an unhealthy situation, and it was not unique. Interestingly, Andersen's were also WorldCom's auditors.

The **Turnbull Report** of 1999 concerned itself with internal controls and internal audit, while the **Myners' Committee** was sponsored by the UK Treasury to look into the role of institutional investors in company affairs. With institutional investors (banks, pension funds, unit and investment trusts) such influential players on securities' markets, any hope of improved shareholder activism to challenge the power of directors would need to come from the institutional investors. In a nutshell, Myners recommended that institutional investors *should* be more active, but not a lot more.

The statements of corporate governance principles by the **OECD** (Organisation for Economic Cooperation and Development) in 1999 and 2005 represent a very Anglo-American view of the subject and bear a close resemblance to the 1998 and 2003 UK Combined Codes.

The reports of the **Higgs** and **Smith** Committees were published in 2003, the former being concerned with the roles of non-executive directors (NEDs) and the latter concerned with the work and roles of Audit Committees. Higgs recommended a scaling up of the importance of NEDs, such that the majority of main board directors should be NEDs, presumably to further minimise the agency effect. The Report makes further recommendations with respect to how many NED appointments executive directors can hold etc., but these need not concern us. However, three questions remain unanswered by the Higgs Report and corporate governance developments in general.

1. The majority of directors on Enron's main board were NEDs, but this did not prevent the corruption that appears to have taken place at Enron. So why was the main recommendation of the Higgs Report that the majority of main board directors should be NEDs?

2. NEDs only attend the companies of which they are NEDs on one, possibly two, days each month. Does this not place even more power in the hands of the few remaining executive directors, who agency theory claims should not be trusted?

3. If minimising the agency effect is a key role of NEDs, why is it that the vast majority of NEDs are also executive directors in their primary employment? Why should person 'A', who is an executive director of company 'X' be subject to the agency effect and be untrustworthy in this role, but upon taking on the mantle of NED of company 'B' become a trustworthy individual whose role it is to ensure the integrity of company B's practices? What is the transformation process that turns A from untrustworthy to trustworthy?

As for the Smith Report on Audit Committees, it makes various recommendations, but it stops short of requiring accounting firms to stop providing any of their non-audit services to their audit clients. This is a far less prescriptive or punitive approach than that reflected in the Sarbanes–Oxley Act.

## What have the developments in corporate governance achieved?

What do all these reports and recommendations say about corporate governance and ethics in business? For many they say very little and what they say is inadequate, given the scale of corporate governance issues. A more inclusive view of corporate governance sees the disregard for shareholder interests displayed by executives as but one of the corporate governance issues to be addressed. All the developments in corporate governance since 1992 amount to very little. An increase in NEDs here, some concerns expressed about accounting firms there, but really it is a 'steady-as-she-goes' approach, with only minor adjustments to the tiller.

Frustration with the myopia and impotence displayed by governments to correct what are seen as the inadequate responses to profound corporate governance issues such as child labour, forced labour, inhuman working conditions, despoliation of the environment, and the connivance and corrupt practices of governments (*see* the *Transparency International* website for an examination of the latter) with corporations has led to a series of other initiatives, which are highlighted in Figure 8.2.

## The King Report on corporate governance

Before progressing to the issues reflected in the UN Global Compact, reference will be made to the second King Report, which was published in 2002 (the first having been published in 1994) and which relates to corporate governance in South Africa. The opening of the report is interesting in that it refers to a state-

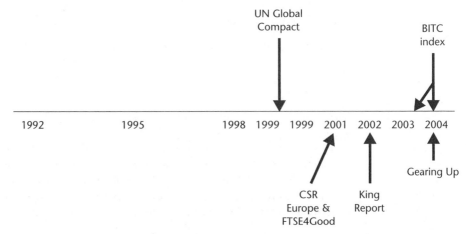

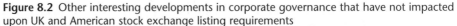

**Figure 8.2** Other interesting developments in corporate governance that have not impacted upon UK and American stock exchange listing requirements

ment made by Sir Adrian Cadbury (the same Cadbury who gave his name to the 1992 UK Cadbury report on corporate governance), but this time the statement was made by Cadbury in the World Bank's 1999 report on corporate governance.

> Corporate governance is concerned with holding the balance between economic and social goals and between individual and community goals. ... The aim is to align as nearly as possible the interests of individuals, corporations and society.
>
> (King, 2002: 6)

This is a much more expansive and inclusive view of corporate governance than that articulated in the 1992 UK Cadbury Report, or in any UK or US financial corporate governance reports since. There are further important features of the King Report that are highly relevant to the considerations of this chapter. The first is the continuation in the second (2002) King Report of the inclusive orientation of the first (1994) King Report. This orientation is reflected in the following extract.

> Unlike its counterparts in other countries at the time, the King Report 1994 went beyond the financial and regulatory aspects of corporate governance in advocating an integrated approach to good governance in the interests of a wide range of stakeholders having regard to the fundamental principles of good financial, social, ethical and environmental practice. In adopting a participative corporate governance system of enterprise with integrity, the King Committee in 1994 successfully formalised the need for companies to recognise that they no longer act independently from the societies and the environment in which they operate.
>
> (King, 2002: 6)

In contrast, Anglo-American reforms to corporate governance have been allowed to concentrate exclusively upon corporations' responsibilities to shareholders. The King Committee took an explicitly inclusive view of a corporation's stakeholders, although it was not a naïve report that ignored or undervalued the economic imperatives faced by companies. It is a thoughtful, scholarly report that distinguishes between accountability and responsibility, which UK reports on corporate governance have failed to articulate. The King Report was not a maverick study located at the margins of South Africa's economic interests. It was a study sponsored by the South Africa Institute of Directors, and whilst operating in the context of a market-based capitalist economy the King Report reflects a very different conception of the business–society debate. This is most intriguingly reflected in paragraph 38 and its subsections where the report focuses upon the values that underpin South African society. This is a dimension to corporate governance that has not only been missed by UK and US corporate governance reports; it would currently not be countenanced as it reflects a profoundly different world view of the business–society relationship.

The very first of the values considered in the King Report is 'spiritual collectiveness'. Paragraph 38.1 reads as follows:

> Spiritual Collectiveness is prized over individualism. This determines the communal nature of life, where households live as an interdependent neighbourhood.

Other values considered include:

Humility and helpfulness to others is more important than criticism of them. (paragraph 38.3)

There is an inherent trust and belief in fairness of all human beings. This manifests itself in the predisposition towards universal brotherhood, even shared by African-Americans. (paragraph 38.6)

High standards of morality are based on historical precedent. These are bolstered by the close kinship observed through totem or clan names and the extended family systems. (paragraph 38.7)

The above claims to community values and beliefs do not deny the historic tribalism that has seen African peoples at war with one another over centuries. However, it draws out the common values that unite rather than separate the tribes (which are effectively mini-nation states in western terms) and seeks to build notions of corporate governance that reflect cultural mores and values, rather than allow more recognisable business values and beliefs to migrate from the economic sphere, driving out the more inclusive, community-oriented values in the process.

Interestingly, paragraph 39 opens with the statement, 'Corporate governance is essentially about leadership', followed by the essential values that a leader should possess and display. The African 'great-soul-man' appears to being alluded to here, who is noticeable by his absence from Anglo-American debates.

The twentieth century was traumatic for South African society. The release of Nelson Mandela in 1990 heralded the ending of the brutal apartheid policies, and the King Report must be seen in this social and cultural context, but it should not be side-stepped or minimised as a result. It is a report that should demand our attention. It offers a very different perspective on corporate governance, arguing that business is a part of society rather than apart from society. This challenge to the assumptions implicit within Anglo-American corporate governance reforms leads us to a consideration of the UN Global Compact.

## The UN Global Compact

In 1999, frustrated by the lack of progress of governments to respond adequately to addressing issues such as child labour and inhuman working conditions in companies located in the developing economies, but which are part of the supply chains of large international organisations, the United Nations set up the UN Global Compact. In the words of Global Compact's Chief Executive, the Global Compact was established to fill a void, to 'respond to demands and needs that governments were either unwilling or unable to meet' (Kell, 2004).

The Compact was, and remains, a voluntary code that is intended to influence corporate practices by:

(i) gaining the support and membership of leading organisations, and then

(ii) increasing the acceptance and take-up of corporate responsibility by disseminating examples of good practice that hopefully other organisations will adopt.

The Compact focuses upon nine key principles of corporate activity, which are grouped into three categories.

*Human rights*
Principle 1 –  Businesses are asked to support the protection of international human rights within their sphere of influence; and
Principle 2 –  To ensure their own corporations are not complicit in human rights abuses.

*Labour*
Principle 3 – Businesses are asked to uphold the freedom of association and the effective recognition of the rights to collective bargaining;
Principle 4 – To eliminate all forms of forced and compulsory labour;
Principle 5 – To abolish child labour; and
Principle 6 – To help eliminate discrimination in respect of employment and occupation.

*Environment*
Principle 7 – Businesses are asked to support a precautionary approach to environmental challenges;
Principle 8 – To undertake initiatives to promote greater environmental responsibility;
Principle 9 – To encourage the development and diffusion of environmentally friendly technologies

In 1999 those responsible for the Compact saw the future for social change to be through international corporations, hence the focus on working with significant organisations to both gain their support (patronage) and stimulate corporate responsibility (CR) by highlighting examples of good practice that 'work' and that could be seen to be compatible with being a successful company.

The Foreword to the 2004 report *Gearing Up*, which was commissioned by the executive of Global Compact, reflected a development in this thinking and strategy. There now appears to be a recognition that it was unrealistic to expect corporations to respond to initiatives such as the Global Compact independent of governments. While the original Global Compact may have been a response to political failings, a voluntary initiative that appears to ask businesses to make good the failings of governments, ironically, needs the commitment and positive engagement of governments to help it develop. For this reason *Gearing Up* argues for a greater level of dialogue, collaboration and partnership between businesses and governments for the future development of corporate responsibility.

A more critical voice is that of Christian Aid. In its 2004 report, *Behind the Mask*, Christian Aid dismissed the UN Global Compact as having had 'almost no impact' (p. 16). The lack of transparency associated with the Global Compact and its lack of monitoring and verification are other failings in the initiative's credibility. For Christian Aid it would seem that the Global Compact is an example of the worst sort of CSR initiative, that is one that enjoys a lot of publicity and hype, but is in fact a toothless tiger, with few if any monitoring and/or verification powers or resources. For some it is a sham and governments are complicit, instrumental even, in this charade.

The Global Compact contains the sorts of commitments and aspirations that many supporters and advocates of CSR or CR (corporate responsibility) would welcome, as well as displaying many of the limitations of a number of CR initiatives. Thus, with the important caveat from Christian Aid expressed in the above paragraph, we return to a key aim of the *Gearing Up* report, which is stated as making 'the link between corporate responsibility … initiatives and wider sustainable development challenges', with the report linked to the Millennium Development Goals (MDGs) (*see* Table 8.3).

The *Gearing Up* report moves on, via a discussion of its findings and case studies, to identify six possible ways (or, probably more accurately, rates of change) that CR could reflect. The six possibilities reflect different levels of engagement by 'business' in economic and non-economic development, including one option (termed 'reverse') which reflects the possibility that businesses might publicly articulate a commitment to being catalysts for change, while, behind the scenes, doing all they can to frustrate and hinder developments.

**Table 8.3** The Millennium Development Goals

1  Eradicate extreme poverty and hunger

2  Achieve universal primary education

3  Promote gender equality and empower women

4  Reduce child mortality

5  Improve maternal health

6  Combat HIV/AIDS, malaria and other diseases

7  Ensure environmental sustainability, and

8  Develop a global partnership for development (this relates to trade issues, but also debt relief and access to affordable, essential drugs in developing countries).

**Connexion point**

One can construct both consequentialist and deontological arguments to support the development of CSR. Produce two brief justifications for adopting CSR based upon (i) consequentialist arguments, and (ii) deontological arguments. Refer back to Chapter 3 if you need to refresh your memory on these respective ethical stances.

**Activity 8.2    An important question**

Notwithstanding the ethical arguments you have raised in response to the above connexion point, is it fair, sensible and/or ethical to ask, let alone expect, business organisations to take on the role of correcting the world's ills? How can organisations, established to fulfil a very specific economic role, take on the responsibility for enacting or at least contributing to roles that might be expected to be the responsibility of governments?

Activity 8.2 raises a fundamental question. To explore both the implications of the question and how one might respond to the question we turn to the arguments of Milton Friedman (1970).

## Milton Friedman's arguments against corporations being charged with social responsibilities

Milton Friedman was a Nobel prize-winning economist, whose ideas were very influential in America and the UK during the 1980s and 1990s. It is worth reading Friedman's oft-cited 1970 article on why the only social responsibility of business is to increase its profits, and not to indulge in social interventions such as sponsorship of community activities, the funding of charities, community activities, or other 'good deeds'.

Friedman's article was a response to what were becoming increasingly frequent calls for corporations to act in socially responsible ways in the late 1960s and early 1970s. Precisely what was meant by 'socially responsible ways' was often left vague and poorly explained, save for concerns being expressed that corporate power was authority without responsibility. Friedman's criticisms were rehearsed by Wolf (2000) thirty years later when the latter accused those (still) calling for greater corporate social responsibility as not only distorting business activity, but confusing and misunderstanding the rationale of business. 'The role of well run companies is to make profits, not save the planet', Wolf argued.

Friedman criticised the arguments for corporate social responsibility on three fronts. The first criticism was an economic one, with ethical undertones. If corporations are required to engage in corporate philanthropy, e.g. making a donation to a charity, school or hospital, these acts will distort allocative efficiency, i.e. the profitability with which capital is employed. Friedman argued that corporations are responsible for using shareholders' funds in profitable ways, in legally acceptable ways – nothing more. Worrying about which charity to support, or which good deed/s to perform, merely 'takes management's eye off the ball', the ball being how to increase profits. Thus, the only form of corporate philanthropy that Friedman's argument would accept is where it could be shown that a donation, or good deed, would improve a company's profitability in ways superior to alternative investment opportunities. We can view this as 'prudential altruism'. In such a case the charitable donation would in fact be described more accurately as a commercial investment. Porter and Kramer (2002) makes a similar point but refers to such acts as 'strategic philanthropy', which, given the points he makes in the article, stretches the notion of philanthropy a little. Windsor (2001) reinforced the philanthropy argument with the demand that all business activities, including 'good deeds', should 'add-value', or more precisely 'add-shareholder-value'. This is most emphatically a Friedmanite position.

The second of Friedman's criticisms draws upon both ethics and political philosophy. It is that it is undemocratic for corporations to use shareholders' funds to support charities or other 'good causes'. Any such donation can only come at the expense of lower dividends, higher prices or lower wages (or a combination of all three). Friedman asked, 'How can it be ethical that a corporation should act first as unpaid tax collector (i.e. levying a tax on the shareholders, customers and/or employees) and then as unaccountable benefactor?' It is either for publicly elected representatives of the people (i.e. national or local politicians) to provide financial support to public services or charities, etc. from public funds, or for individuals to decide to which charities they wish to make private donations.

The third criticism was a philosophical one. It was that corporations cannot possess responsibilities. Corporations are social constructs, i.e. they have been brought into existence by societies passing laws that give legal protection to certain forms of business associations and structures. Without these legal and social devices, corporations could not and would not exist. In Friedman's terms only individuals can have responsibilities, not corporations.

| Activity 8.3 | Challenging Friedman |

Taking the three criticisms that are raised by Friedman, try to develop arguments that challenge Friedman's claims. It is important that you think through the arguments that Friedman is making, so take your time.

## Responding to Friedman's arguments

From the perspective of advocates of unfettered (or as unfettered as possible) market-based economies, which we referred to in Chapter 1 as the *neo-liberal economic position*, or simply neo-liberalism, the best hope for the protection of individual freedoms is the maintenance of open markets (i.e. no barriers to trade) and minimum interference in the workings of business by governments.

**Connexion point**

Adopting the stance that governments should play as small a part as humanly possible in economic and social affairs is the concept known as 'negative freedom', i.e. freedom 'from', as discussed in Chapter 3.

Not only is interference by government seen as economically counter-productive in the medium to long run, but such interventions are themselves argued to be unethical, i.e. they impose a big-brother-knows-best mentality over individual preferences and thus undermine the sovereignty of individual choice. From the perspective of the neo-liberalist position the first and second objections raised by Friedman are both strong objections. Non-accountable tax-raising, whether by government or corporate leaders, is a distortion to allocative efficiency, injurious to the sovereignty of the individual and undemocratic, and thus to be opposed.

Friedman did not argue that corporations should be above the law, but he did argue that corporations should not be expected to exceed what the law defines as minimum levels of behaviour. Laws are assumed to represent what societies deem to be acceptable behaviour (of both individuals and corporations) and only if a society increases the burden upon business in terms of legally defined levels of performance (e.g. increased levels of pollution control) should corporations have to raise their performance. This obviously ignores the pressures for increased performance resulting from normal competitive forces, although such pressures will often present countervailing forces to those emanating from environmental concerns.

Neo-liberal supporters would accept that there are sometimes considerable negative human consequences resulting from economic fluctuations. For example, large-scale redundancies and/or high levels of unemployment can result from significant economic downturns, with resulting impacts upon local infrastructure in the form of, say, lower than desired levels of expenditure on education, health care, transport, etc. The latter would be the economic consequences of lower levels of taxes being collected, coupled with increased social security benefits. These are seen as unfortunate, but unavoidable, consequences that societies must accept in order to protect the overall integrity of the market system. Yet the increasing impact of what is known as globalisation and the powerful moves towards full deregulation of markets across the world by the World Trade Organisation (WTO) have raised the political and social stakes in this debate.

Within the arguments presented by Friedman, either the role and impact of business in general must be benign, or, the more traditional argument, the acknowledged inequities and imperfections in market-based systems are more than counterbalanced by the claimed advancements and advantages that everyone ultimately enjoys, as a result of the market dynamics levering change and economic progress. That everyone does not benefit to the same extent as a result of these claimed economic advances is not disputed, but everyone is argued to be better off, to some extent, in the long run. You may recognise something of the Rawlsian position (which was discussed in Chapter 3) in this argument, that whilst the poorest of society are indeed relatively poor they are better off than they would be, or could be, under any other economic system. This claim can be considered at two levels.

(i) The first is the empirical question. Does the evidence we have of the globalising and deregulating effects on world markets display an overall elevation of people's well-being and is this elevation superior to all other options?

(ii) The second is the ethical question. Does this approach stand up to scrutiny when judged against notions of justice, fairness, wisdom and care?

The evidence that is available with regard to question (i) is incomplete, but at best it is mixed. At worst we are experiencing even greater concentrations of power over resources that lie outside the political arena, with fundamental questions regarding authority, responsibility and accountability remaining unanswered.

### Connexion point

The observations of Anita Roddick, founder of The Body Shop organisation, are interesting in this context. She was responding to an article by Philippe Legrain that had appeared in the *Guardian* newspaper (on the day before the publication of her letter). Legrain had made the case that the deregulation of world markets, in line with the actions of the WTO, should be welcomed by all, as ultimately all would benefit (the argument outlined above). The words of Ms Roddick are shown on p. 464.

It is always possible to highlight acts by individual people or specific corporations that present a poor image of the groups they are said to represent. Proverbially speaking, bad apples do not necessarily tell us much about the rest of the apples in a barrel. However, if one can point to trends, allegiances, purposeful manipulation of power by large corporations, or groups of corporations, then we might have something more than the odd bad apple. The following are just a selection of possible examples that could be used.

| **Case study 8.1** | **The tobacco industry** |

For many years, medical research had indicated a clear link between the use of tobacco products and various forms of cancer, although these findings had always been contested vigorously by the tobacco industry. Yet, in 2000, the tobacco company Reynolds broke ranks and announced in court that it was accepting liability for certain smokers' ill-health. There is evidence to suggest that the tobacco companies had confirmed the link between their products and cancer-based illnesses many years previously but concealed the evidence. Since sales of tobacco products in most western countries have been either stagnant or in decline since the early 1990s, the tobacco companies had targeted developing countries (and particularly young people) as growth markets for their products.

Notwithstanding the many previous denials of the tobacco companies of the link between cigarettes and cancer, it is now clear that such a link is accepted. This is exemplified by the use made of a study commissioned by the multinational tobacco company, Philip Morris. In 2001 the tobacco firm, one of the world's leading producers of tobacco products, and responsible for 80 per cent of the cigarettes sold in the Czech Republic, felt the need to respond to claims that cigarette smoking was costing the Czech economy significant sums by virtue of high levels of hospitalisation, absenteeism from work and thus lower tax collection levels caused by smoking-related illnesses. The study commissioned by the tobacco company concluded that, rather than impose costs on the Czech economy, cigarettes saved the Czech government over £100M each year. The basis for this assessment was that, because cigarette smokers would be dying earlier than non-smokers, due to smoking-related illnesses, this would save the government hospitalisation costs associated with old age, as well as lower pension costs and lower housing costs.

| **Case study 8.2** | **When can genetically modified crops be grown?** |

In many western countries, including the UK, the planting of genetically modified (GM) crops is limited and tightly controlled by governments. Following a series of trials the UK government announced that only one genetically modified crop had passed its tests. The principal companies concerned had accepted the need to monitor the trials and to develop a thorough body of evidence before large-scale commercial planting could be considered. Yet, at the very time the UK government was proclaiming a moratorium in the UK, in the

Indian state of Andhra Pradesh, a 384 square mile area known as Genome Valley, was being developed for GM crop production, funded by overseas aid from the UK government. In excess of £50M was allocated to this project by the UK government in 2001. Monsanto, the principal company involved in the controlled trials in the UK, was among the companies invited to participate in the development in Andhra Pradesh. Farmers in Andhra Pradesh expressed concerns that development of prairie-style fields would result in the mass migration of millions of small farmers and labourers to the cities in search of work. The Andhra Pradesh project (known as *Vision 2020*) was the result of a study undertaken by a large American consulting firm, which, critics argue, gave little, if any, consideration to alternative forms of raising agricultural efficiency that utilised local resources more effectively and sensitively. Local farmers in Andhra Pradesh wished to control their own destinies, but the fear was that this scheme, with such influential corporate involvement, involvement that will have secured governmental support before it was officially announced, would lead to a social disaster in the region.

The case of the carving up of Indonesia, following the overthrow of President Sukarno in 1966 (reported in Chapter 12), is a further example of what appear to be structural, rather than aberrational, problems in the workings of business-society-political relationships.

| Case study 8.3 | **Markets, prices and need** |
| --- | --- |

The pharmaceutical industry tends to be the target of a lot of angst when it comes to illustrating the problems/issues raised by global markets and global corporations. Among other things, the pharmaceutical corporations are often criticised for concentrating the overwhelming proportion of their research and development budgets on diseases of the rich. For example, there are new products continually coming to the market which claim to address issues of impotence, hair loss, wrinkles, obesity, etc., whereas diseases such as malaria, Ebola and HIV AIDS either remain under-investigated or the drugs available are too expensive for millions of people experiencing the diseases. However, the drugs companies point out that they are commercial corporations, subject to the disciplines of financial markets. If governments wish them to channel/divert research and development budgets into specific areas of medical treatment, then the pharmaceutical companies need to be compensated for the opportunity cost of this activity. One of the responses to these claims is that generic producers can manufacture HIV-AIDS drugs, for example, for a fraction of the price charged by the global pharmaceutical companies (around one-eighth of the price). The pharmaceutical companies respond by arguing that they need to recover the research and developments costs of those drugs that never reach their intended markets, costs that the generic producers do not incur.

Whilst the ethical weight of the above arguments are not suggested to be equal, we will sidestep offering a view on where the balance lies, but consider one of the ways the pharmaceutical companies (Big Pharma) responded to criticisms of their policies with regard to HIV-AIDS. ▶

In 2001 the South African Government took Big Pharma to court in South Africa over the pricing of retro-viral drugs (the drugs used to treat HIV AIDS). The day before the judicial decision was to be given, the pharmaceutical companies, realising that they were going to 'lose' the decision, effectively began to discuss an 'out-of-court settlement'. This took the form of initially a fifty-word statement, which, after many months of 'debate', became a massive obfuscating document. Many felt the pharmaceutical companies had pulled victory from the jaws of defeat. This feeling was reinforced when in October 2003 the US Senate announced the name of the person who was to head the American AIDS Initiative. It was Randall Tobias, a former head of Eli Lilly, one of the world's big pharmaceutical companies. He was not required to sell his share holding in pharmaceutical companies, meaning that, if Mr Tobias took any decisions that harmed the interests of Big Pharma, he would also be negatively affecting his own wealth position. The question of a conflict of interest was raised by many but never adequately responded to.

The relationship between government and business is complex and in continuous need of scrutiny. It is far more complex than the simplistic call for minimal government that is heard from free-market fundamentalists would suggest. In a market system businesses require the autonomy to respond to market signals and claim the right of freedom from government interference in business decisions. Yet, that claim is disingenuous. It ignores the role of governments in setting fiscal policies; the management of government borrowing and macro-economic affairs; the support given to businesses during times of local or national recessions; the funding provided by governments to support both pure and generic research; and the funding of major projects that might be too large for private capital formation.

In addition, business in general has a vested interest in the maintenance of particular economic and legal conditions. As part of the pluralist political system, business organisations lobby governments and parliaments to achieve the conditions and laws that suit them. In the modern era it is argued that pressure groups, particularly business pressure groups, have a far more significant influence upon the construction of legislation than the polity in general.

The ethical question is immensely complex and not just in terms of disentangling competing notions of justice, fairness and care from one another. However, it is not clear whether this question is being asked at all. The power and influence of large corporations appear to dominate political agendas, stunting debate and maybe thinking.

So, to summarise the argument so far, corporations, via their economic power, have the potential to do significant good and significant harm. The UN Global Compact was initially a reaction to multi-government failure in adequately addressing critical global issues. It was an attempt to by-pass governments and to seek social intervention by large corporations. More recently, in 2004, the *Gearing Up* report has recognised this approach as unrealistic and set itself the task of trying to facilitate greater corporate and government bi-partisanship in tackling the world's great challenges. Are we entering a period when corporate executives become engaged with addressing the world's great social and environmental challenges without jeopardising their economic well-being? It is much too early to say, but what is clear is that the issue of ethics in business has never been more relevant and high profile.

## Profit as the lever and the lure

The types of examples highlighted above regarding globalisation and deregulation issues challenge the claim that the overall effects of liberalism will necessarily be a benefit for all. An application of the Rawlsian original position test might cast doubt upon the efficacy, let alone the ethicality, of the poor being better-off as a result of MNC-influenced globalisation and WTO strictures, rather than the employment of other, more culturally and socially sensitive, approaches to economic development. For example, Chang (2002) makes the case that the principal countries that now fund and direct WTO free-trade policies did not follow WTO-type strictures when they were developing economies. The UK and the USA both employed protectionist policies to allow their economies to grow.

In a similar attack on free-trade ideology, but this time aimed at the IMF and World Bank, Burgo and Stewart (2002) used Malawi as an illustration of enforced privatisation policies that had created a food crisis. The case is explained in more detail in Chapter 13 (*see* Case study 13.3 on p. 513). In summary, in the mid-1990s the IMF insisted on the deregulation of the grain and foodstuffs agency before any further loans and aid finance were to be granted. The result, which Burgo and Stewart attribute principally to the deregulation policy, was a collapse in grain supplies and widespread famine in 2002. Interestingly, the Commerce and Industry Minister of Malawi, Mr Mpasu, was asked by the UK Government to speak to a meeting of G7 ministers in Cancun of the benefits of liberalising the Malawi economy. He stood up and said, 'We have opened our economy. That's why we are flat on our backs' (Elliott, 2003).

An issue emerging from this discussion is the complex question of how can the demands of economic imperatives be tempered within socially acceptable parameters? Nearly 200 years ago, David Ricardo (a significant figure in British economic thinking) described profit as 'the lever and the lure'. The lure because it is the indicator of how successfully capital has been invested, thereby acting as a lure to new capital investment. The notion of the lever, however, speaks to the social, as well as the economic, impact that capital migration can have on whole communities. The migration of capital from one region to another, from one country to another, as it seeks out the most advantageous investment opportunities, can have destabilising impacts upon those areas affected by the capital flows. While Friedman points to the undemocratic nature of corporate social responsibility, the argument to leave business alone ignores the profound influence of corporate decisions and their impact upon, potentially, millions of lives. Corporate decisions are made by unseen and largely unaccountable decision-makers. Critics of Friedman's 'undemocratic' argument see these issues as far more significant and serious threats to democratic processes than those raised by Friedman.

## Friedman's third argument

Moving to the third of Friedman's criticisms, we find that it is open to challenge at the levels of principle, of legal argument and empirical evidence. To remind you, the third of Friedman's arguments was that businesses cannot have responsibilities because they are not real people; they are social constructs, i.e. they are artificial entities. While accepting Friedman's argument that a corporation is a social construct, this does not deny the possibility that the passage of time may confer upon business organisations new constraints, attributes, rights and/or responsibilities. In essence, social constructs can be reconstructed. Therefore, the simple fact that corporations are social constructs does not deny the possibility that the significance of such entities can develop to such an extent that society deems it necessary to place constraints, or responsibilities, upon corporations. There would be nothing philosophically objectionable, or flawed, in such developments. Whether such moves would achieve their desired ends is, however, a quite different question and set of issues.

In addition to challenging the validity of Friedman's third criticism at the level of principle, corporations have themselves undermined the strength of the criticism by their own actions. Corporations in America have claimed the same rights as individuals under the American Constitution. For example, in 1996 the US Supreme Court unanimously overturned a Rhode Island law which had stood for forty years. This law had prohibited businesses advertising the price of beers and spirits. Referring to the First Amendment the Supreme Court ruled that corporations could claim the same rights of protection as individuals. In 1998 in *First National Bank of Boston v. Bellotti* the American Supreme Court ruled again that corporations are protected by the First Amendment in the same way that individuals are in terms of freedom of speech. Thus, notwithstanding that they are social constructs, the corporations involved in these cases were granted the same rights under the American Constitution as those available to individual American citizens.

In the King Report, a further and critical legal point is highlighted. The conventional rhetoric is that corporate executives are required to run corporations in the interests of shareholders. However, the King Report challenges this claim by referring to some jurisdictions in which, upon incorporation,

> the company becomes a separate persona in law and no person whether natural or juristic can be owned. Courts have also held that shareowners have no direct interests in the property, business or assets owned by the company, their only rights being a right to vote and a right to dividends. Shareowners also change from time to time while, as the owner, the company remains constant. Consequently, directors, in exercising their fiduciary duties, must act in the interest of the company as a separate person.
>
> (King Report, 2002: 10)

Following the logic of this separation, the corporate executives are committed to act in the interests of the company, which would suggest that, if they deem it appropriate, this could include acting in ways that could be labelled corporately socially responsible. This approach places the company's long-term economic survival above all others. The interests of shareholders and those of the company would coincide via the process known as 'the correspondence principle', in which investors select companies to invest in on the basis of each company's known objectives and performance. Thus corporate executives do not have to worry about acting in the ways shareholders would prefer. If the actions of corporate executives are consistent with past decisions and rationale, then this will correspond with the interests of the shareowners, because the shareowners would have decided to invest in the company on this very basis.

As a recognisable legal entity, it might also be argued that, if corporations can be assigned the rights of citizenship, why should they not be assigned equivalent levels of responsibilities? If this argument is accepted then it raises questions about how one operationalises a broader view of a corporation's responsibilities and this in turn heralds the notion of stakeholders.

## Stakeholding and stakeholders

The term stakeholding refers to an idea, a principle or argument, whereas the term stakeholder refers to a specifiable person or groups of people (sometimes in an organised form), with clear implications for how the interests of such groups might be incorporated or represented within organisational decisions. This distinction is important because, for some writers who support and argue for the concept of stakeholding, the operationalising of the concept presents enormous problems that possibly cast doubt upon the usefulness of the concept. Writers such as Bucholz (1998) and Rosenthal (1990) are examples of commentators who have expressed support for the stakeholding concept, but also expressed concerns about its real-world potential.

Notwithstanding these concerns, there is growing empirical evidence to suggest that an increasing number of organisations can be said to be adopting more inclusive perspectives into their ways of working that deny an exclusive shareholder focus to their decisions. This does not imply that shareholders are no longer an important consideration of managerial thought and action. Indeed, economic imperatives will often/invariably have to take precedence when stakeholder interests clash, but maybe, just maybe, the interests of shareholders are becoming more of a minimum constraint than a maximising objective.

In many ways a constraint is more demanding than an objective in that a constraint is invariably expressed as a specific number, e.g. the minimum dividend return next year must be 6 per cent, or the minimum earnings yield must be 11 per cent, whereas to state that 'we aim to maximise shareholder wealth' is a very loose statement, with no identifiable performance target. The minimum returns specified in the 'constraints' would need to take account of competing investment opportunities, so what is being suggested here is not 'pie-in-the-sky' wishful thinking, but rather a possible explanation of what might already be happening in some corporate board rooms in an osmotic sort of way. Thus the change process, if it reflects a genuine long-term change rather than something of faddish duration, is not an abrupt sea-change in perspective, which is heralded by a fanfare of trumpets, but rather a more incremental, less obvious change. Clearly more empirical evidence is required to allow more confident statements to be made on this point.

By turning shareholder considerations into a constraint, maybe seeing ordinary shareholders as becoming akin to first-order preference shareholders, managerial attention can then turn to considering how an organisation can become more a part of the societies with which it interacts, rather than apart from them. How might this work in practice?

There are various ways of approaching this issue, but one way that would *not* work is for an organisation to wait until it is confident that it will definitely achieve its shareholder 'constraint' target (i.e. the minimum dividend or earnings return) before debating how it should position itself as a social-economic entity. It might not be until, say, month eleven or later that attainment of the minimum shareholder return can be confirmed, leaving no time to begin thinking about other stakeholder issues.

If stakeholder engagement is to be a realistic and meaningful idea, then a longer-term stakeholder strategy becomes essential, just as a market strategy is essential for product or service development. Organisational development then becomes the sum of the two. To counter the concerns articulated by Friedman (and acolytes such as Elaine Sternberg, 2000), a number of organisations are firmly of the view that employee participation in social projects, which are outside the organisation's normal line of business, has a positive effect upon staff morale and aid organisational performance. The application of staff time in 'social projects' can be shown to be an effective 'value-adding' activity. Case study 8.4 is a specific example.

| Case study 8.4 | **An economically successful corporation with a view of its social position** |
| --- | --- |

Capital *One* is a credit card company that chooses not to publicise its social projects because it is uneasy that it might be accused of only undertaking its social activities in order to gain publicity. Most of its social engagements go unreported and thus unrecognised, but the following example did attract media attention and the company acknowledged its role in the programme.

The projects in question related to the development of sophisticated software to facilitate the interrogation of differing national databases by a local police force in the pursuit of suspected paedophiles. The company supported a number of its programmers in working with the local police force over many months in developing the software, which has subsequently proved to be an important advance in police work and adopted by other police forces. The programmers also committed a lot of their own free time to the project. When talking with people at the company, one of the authors was left in no doubt that everyone was extremely supportive of the project and that its effect upon staff morale had been both positive and significant, manifesting itself in enhanced levels of efficiency and innovation in all areas of the programming division's work.

The Friedmanite response might be that such an example is fine, as long as it is undertaken in the belief that it will positively affect shareholder interests. If this is thought unlikely then such activities should not be undertaken. Interestingly the senior management argued strenuously that the decision to support the project was not taken for Friedmanite reasons. The senior executives argued that decisions relating to their 'social projects' were taken on non-consequentialist grounds. The senior management review projects that have been identified by the 'Social Resonsibility Team' (which comprises four full-time staff). There also appeared to be some consultation with all the employees to help shape the 'social projects' agenda' for the coming year.

The senior management argued that they saw their company as part of the local community and wanted to be regarded as a part of that community. They wanted to be regarded as a good employer, thereby attracting not just 'good' employees, but employees coming with the right approach and commitment. Such a policy did enhance organisational efficiency, but the senior management regarded the policy decision as reflecting more of a principled than an instrumental stance. At its root, the senior management philosophy was an inclusive approach to organisational 'Being'.

The 'everybody wins' feel of the closing sentence of Case study 8.4 does not have to be seen in a cynical light. The basic argument harks back to the original conceptualisation of the word 'company'. The etymology of the word 'company' relates to a community of interest, a mutually beneficial partnership of employers, employees and investors. Such an approach does not deny the significance of competition in an organisation's financial market as well as its product and service markets, but the 'shareholder-as-constraint-perspective' offers a possible way of negotiating the conundrum that the notion of stakeholding appears to present when set in the context of market-based, capitalist systems.

## Corporate governance and trust

We discuss codes of ethics and conduct in Chapter 10, where we make the point that codes of ethics tend to be concerned with values and virtuous qualities. Certainly the most efficient and economic form of corporate governance is a relationship built upon trust, buttressed by the requisite levels of accountability and transparency. As soon as one begins to doubt a person's integrity and trustworthiness then monitoring and control processes come into play, but these are expensive and can themselves exacerbate a situation and breed an air of mistrust.

If an organisation wishes to develop a culture based upon virtues such as integrity, honesty, objectivity, justice and fairness, partly to reduce the costs of monitoring and control processes, then consistency in practices and the avoidance of double standards are essential. Unfortunately this is too often not the case, as indicated by Table 8.4.

**Table 8.4** Organisational principles and human behaviour

| Issue | General employees | Senior executives |
|---|---|---|
| Working for other organisations | Taking time off to do 'other' work would be described as moonlighting and subject to instant dismissal. Working for other organisations considered to be a vice. | Taking consulting or NED-type role with another organisation invariably seen as broadening for all concerned and a virtue. |
| Pay–motivation relationship | Paying people low wages incentivises employees to work hard. High wages merely breed sloth and inefficiency. | Senior executives need increasing levels of pay to incentivise them. The higher the pay, the higher the motivation. |
| Pensions | It is unreasonable to expect the state or organisations to provide for income after employment. | Generous pension packages are essential to entice the appropriate level of executive talent. |
| Working conditions | General working conditions should reflect basic functional requirements. To do more would reflect an unnecessary diversion of shareholder funds. | Require high-quality accommodation and to provide less will act as a disincentive to prospective appointees. |
| Perks | Very few and where they exist will need to reflect a close relationship between performance and perk. No such thing as a 'free lunch'. | Come in many forms from first-class travel to company cars (when little corporate travel is undertaken by road), to executive boxes at arts or sporting arenas, to company accommodation and company loans. Lunches may still not be free but are paid for by 'others'. |

## Moving the debate forward

So where have we arrived in terms of our consideration of Anglo-American developments in corporate governance and corporate responsibility? It brings us to the point where it is fair to ask, if the Friedmanite position on corporate responsibility can be successfully challenged, how can one operationalise notions of ethics in business which recognise the dynamics of market conditions, but which also recognise the differences in ethical perceptions and stances? Any such framework needs to have at its core some universally held principles relating to human dignity and rights, but also a flexibility to allow certain, 'acceptable' local variations to apply. This might be regarded as the Holy Grail, yet an attempt has been made to develop such a framework. What we are about to discuss is not a prescriptive approach to developing specific ethical principles in complex, multicultural contexts, but rather an over-arching framework that at least provides a general structure upon which organisations can begin to shape their respective approaches to managing in ethically complex contexts.

## The social contract and the business case

The social contract is an interesting concept that can be traced back to Plato (Bosanquet, 1906) and Aristotle (Aristotle, 1976), but more recently to Hobbes (1968), Locke (1952) and Rousseau (1913). Lessnoff (1986) provides a good introduction to the history of social contract as an idea and as an argument.

A more recent articulation of the social contract is found in the argument that corporations have to earn and maintain a 'license to operate'. The license to operate reflects a commitment to more than economic imperatives, although the approach does not ignore economic issues. Two interesting writers working in this area are Thomas Donaldson and Thomas Dunfee. They have published in various forms over the past twenty years, for example, Donaldson (1982, 1989, 1990, 1996); Donaldson and Dunfee (1994, 1995 and 1999); Dunfee (1991, 1996); and Dunfee and Donaldson (1995). Donaldson and Dunfee have taken the social contract idea and developed a distinctive approach that they call *Integrative Social Contract Theory* (ISCT). At the core of the theory are four norms, or categories of values. One way to visualise ISCT is in the form of concentric circles, with the core foundational values at the centre (Figure 8.3).

The norms are described as follows.

*Hypernorms* These are argued to be fundamental human rights or basic prescriptions common to most religions. The values they represent are by definition acceptable to all cultures and all organisations. These have the characteristics of universal norms and in order to be workable will be few in number. What is and what is not a hypernorm would be agreed by rational debate and any contender for 'hypernorm' status would fail if it could be shown not to be universalisable. The issue of universal norms raises all the problems that Kantian ethics encounter, but rather than turning to something akin to Ross's (1930) *prima facie obligations*, Donaldson and Dunfee introduce two 'lower level' norms that allow for 'local' variations to be possible. The first of these is *consistent norms*.

*Consistent norms* These values are more culturally specific than hypernorms, but they will be consistent with hypernorms and other legitimate norms, the latter being defined as a norm that does not contradict the hypernorm test (Donaldson and Dunfee, 1999: 46). Donaldson and Dunfee cite corporate mission statements as examples of 'consistent norms'.

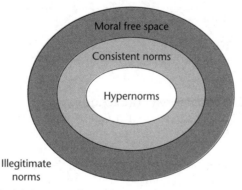

**Figure 8.3** Integrated Social Contract Theory (ISCT)

*Moral free space* This is an interesting concept and allows Donaldson and Dunfee to contain norms that might be in tension (or limited contradiction) with any of the hypernorms within ISCT. An example of such a tension could be the use of child labour. Donaldson and Dunfee cite two examples involving the company Levi-Strauss.

---

**Case study 8.5**

### Levi-Strauss

In the first example Levi-Strauss severed its links with the Tan family (and their businesses) because they (the Tan family) reportedly 'held twelve hundred Chinese and Philippine women in guarded compounds working them seventy four hours a week' (*The Clean Clothes Campaign*, 1992). These practices contravened Levi-Strauss's Business Partners Terms of Engagement'. The actions of the Tan family could be said to have contravened the hypernorms of respect for human dignity and justice.

The second example relates to the reaction of Levi-Strauss when it became aware that two of its suppliers in Bangladesh were employing children under the age of fourteen (a generally internationally accepted minimum age of employment). The company did not sever its relationship with the suppliers but chose an alternative course of action. The company required that the children be sent to school, with Levi-Strauss paying the children's tuition and associated fees, but also paying the children's wages to their families, so the latter did not suffer, but only while the children were at school. The company also agreed to re-employ the children when they reached fourteen. Whilst the exploitation of children has to addressed by the hypernorms, ISCT can cope with the actions of Levi-Strauss in this case because, whilst the use of the child labour must have been in contravention of at least one hypernorm, the practice was also recognition of a locally 'accepted' practice, something that might, for the time being, be seen to reside within the 'moral free space'. This is not to say that for all companies the 'right' action would be to react as Levi-Strauss had. For some the use of children under the age of fourteen may have meant a severing of links with the suppliers concerned, irrespective of the ripple effects of this action. In this case the moral free space would not allow the inclusion of the use of children less than fourteen years of age, notwithstanding that it is an 'accepted' local norm. ISCT allows both of these (re)actions because of the relationship of 'moral free space' to 'hypernorms' and 'consistent norms'. The example does illustrate that it is for individual groups and organisations to define what constitutes their 'moral free space'.

---

*Illegitimate norms* These norms are irreconcilable with *hypernorms*. For some this might be the case with regard to the treatment of women and children in some societies, but for others some of these 'problems' might fit within a 'moral free space' that would allow some development of understanding on all sides to see if a longer-term relationship might be possible with some modification to the 'problems' in question.

**Connexion point**

In this form of application, *moral free space* becomes something of a utilitarian concept (which, you will recall from Chapter 3, weighs ethical decisions in the context of a decision's consequences), but only on the understanding that the intention is to achieve longer-term correction of the offending practice and, to do this most effectively, it is better to work at the offending practice and to achieve change.

It would seem possible for principle-based *hypernorms* to be 'suspended', for some short passage of time, to allow utilitarian considerations to be located within the *moral free space*. This is contentious, and this interpretation might not meet with universal agreement, but it does show the flexibility that would be essential for such a framework to be useful for a multi-national corporation endeavouring to make sense of developing an ethical framework where certain practices, for example nepotism, might be unacceptable in most western cultures, but acceptable and important in others, e.g. Indian society. For an international corporation with operations in many parts of Asia and Europe, how should they handle this tension? They will require a short-term strategy guided by a longer-term principle.

As a result of the above type of example, ISCT has been criticised for being relativist. Donaldson and Dunfee refute this, arguing that ISCT is pluralist, combining the notion of universal norms of behaviour (hypernorms) with the recognition of important cultural differences (consistent norms and moral free space). The authors also recognise that, within the theory, individuals, corporations and communities have to work out for themselves what are their respective 'norms', at all levels.

> Business ethics should be viewed more as a story in the process of being written than as a moral code like the Ten Commandments. It can, and should ... adjust over time – to evolving technology, and to the cultural or religious attitudes of particular economic conditions.
>
> (Donaldson and Dunfee, 1999: viii)

Donaldson and Dunfee go on to say,

> At the heart of social contract effort is a simple assumption, namely that we can understand better the obligations of key social institutions, such as business or government, by attempting to understand what is entailed in a fair agreement or 'contract' between those institutions and society and also in the implicit contracts that exist among the different communities and institutions within society. The normative authority of any social contract derives from the assumption that humans, acting rationally, consent – or at least would consent hypothetically – to the terms of a particular agreement affecting the society or community of which they are a member. In this manner contractarian theories utilise the device of consent, albeit it is often *hypothetical* consent, to justify principles, policies and structures.
>
> (Donaldson and Dunfee, 1999: 16–7)

In order to provide a mechanism that might help operationalise ISCT, Donaldson and Dunfee employ a modified form of Rawls' veil of ignorance. Unlike Rawls' conception of the veil of ignorance, in which those (metaphorically) placed behind the veil have no knowledge of any aspect of their status, ethnic origin, physical abilities, gender, geographic location, political and economic system, etc., in Donaldson and Dunfee's conception only those aspects of a person's identity that are economic in nature, e.g. level of personal skill, nature of economic system, type of employing organisation, employment position held, etc., are concealed. This modified Rawlsian artifice is hoped to facilitate reflection and debate about an 'objective' fairness that should be inherent within an economic system and the ethical and moral base of that system.

ISCT attempts to hold on to both the integrity of universalisable norms (minimum accepted standards of behaviour irrespective of where in the world the norms are being considered), but avoiding the inflexibility of non-consequentialist stances. This is addressed by the introduction of the consistent norms and the moral free space. It is an interesting development, providing as it does a schema or framework that business people can employ to interrogate the ethical and moral issues that might be at stake in a particular situation. Donaldson and Dunfee are emphatic that ISCT is not a framework, let alone an approach, that can be employed unthinkingly. By its very nature it is a framework for facilitating discussion, debate and argument. It is not a decision-making tool, for the type of ethically charged situations that corporations are often faced with are invariably too complex and multi-faceted to lend themselves to easy formulation and calculation. However, the ideas and categories within ISCT do provide a language and a set of concepts that may help parties to a decision think constructively about the different issues and dimensions inherent within a complex business scenario.

## Corporate manslaughter

The concluding major topic in this chapter continues the theme of attempts to hold corporations to account for their roles in, or impacts upon, society. To do this, there is a need to consider both the legal position and the philosophical position of corporations with regard to this issue.

Within the UK the prosecution of corporations, as distinct from individual employees, for claimed acts of wilful neglect of a duty of care has been difficult, at least via criminal law. Actions through the civil courts against corporations have been possible for many years, but the expense and the many years involved in prosecuting such cases make the civil law option one that is rarely taken up by members of the public.

### Recent developments

Recent developments, reflected in proposals to change UK criminal law with respect to corporate manslaughter, by possibly bringing it in line with US criminal law, suggest that corporations might, in future, face the prospect of being held to account for criminal neglect of their duty of care. However, the UK administrations of Prime Minister Tony Blair have been reticent to bring the proposed law to Parliament for debate, despite a manifesto pledge since 1997. The inclusion of a corporate manslaughter bill in the 2004 Queen's Speech (the mechanism that announces the proposed bills to be discussed in the forthcoming parliamentary session) was seen by many as a deceit, because it was generally believed that the Prime Minister would call a general election in May 2005, which proved to be correct, thereby relegating all the proposed bills to the 'bills lost' bin.

Why this reticence to instigate a corporate manslaughter bill? It is difficult to see beyond the power of the corporate lobby persuading government that 'it would not be a good thing'. Yet in the United States it is possible for corporations to be forced to stop trading because of corporate wrongdoings. Such acts, known as charter revocation acts, are very rarely used, but at least they exist. In the UK no such possibilities exist, other than for the Department of Trade and Industry in special situations and for creditors. In America, however, a private citizen can instigate a winding-up procedure as a result of a corporate wrongdoing. There the death penalty exists for corporate acts of murder as it does for individuals. Notwithstanding that the death penalty for citizens has long been abolished in the UK, the possibility of such a punishment in the corporate field raises very different issues and arguments. The possibilities for a charter revocation law in the UK are discussed in a little more detail in Chapter 13 where we introduce our 'modest proposal' for affecting change in the ethics of business.

## The 'identification principle' and the 'guiding mind'

As it currently stands, the first impediment to criminal prosecution for corporate manslaughter in the UK has been the argument, with which you will by now be familiar, that corporations do not commit acts; only individuals do. Thus, individual employees can be charged with manslaughter, e.g. a train driver involved in a rail crash, but charging the relevant rail company is a more difficult task. To do so, one has to be able to prove that an individual, who sits at the nerve centre of corporate decision making, and who should have acted in ways that could have prevented the accident occurring, was negligent in their duties. This is known in law as the *identification doctrine*, i.e. one has to be able to identify the negligent individual who could be said to represent the failure of the corporation as a whole.

In law, as in many other walks of life, one has to be clear about the precise meaning of words. So, when we use the phrase 'who sits at the nerve centre of corporate decision making', what do we mean? For the corporation to be charged, the identified individual has to be shown to be the person with overall responsibility for this particular aspect of corporate activity, for example health and safety matters, or rail track inspection. The need for this requirement is that because the law has, to date, only viewed corporations as being answerable via their employees, the employee concerned must be recognised as the person who was 'guiding' this aspect of corporate activity. This is the second legal principle to recognise, i.e. to be able to prosecute a corporation for corporate manslaughter, the *guiding mind* of the organisation has to be identified, and be shown to be implicated in the negligent act/s. Some real-life examples of this principle will help to illustrate the issues involved.

| Case study 8.6 | The *Herald of Free Enterprise* |
| --- | --- |

The case has already been mentioned in Chapter 7. It relates to the capsizing of the P&O ferry *Herald of Free Enterprise* outside Zeebrugge harbour in which 192 people lost their lives. It is possible that the captain of the ferry might have been able to be prosecuted for not fully checking that the bow doors were securely closed before the ferry set sail. However, the fact that crew members had, on five previous occasions, expressed concerns to their seniors about the lack of any warning lights on the bridge relating to the position of the bow doors was insufficient to bring a prosecution against the P&O Corporation. It was not possible to prove that these expressions of concern had reached the top echelons of the P&O corporation, the 'guiding mind'. Although comparative evidence was available concerning the (lack of) commitment that P&O was claimed to have towards safety issues, the prosecution lawyers were refused permission by the trial judge to call captains of the Sealink corporation (at the time of the trial Sealink was a rival ferry company), to contrast the safety practices of P&O ferries with those of other ferry operators. Four years after the capsizing of the *Herald of Free Enterprise*, safety issues at P&O were again raised when it was revealed that P&O crew members had to pay for their own basic safety training. One recruit recounted, ' I was sent to a college and given pages of information on things like where lifeboats are kept on a ferry, and how to evacuate in an emergency. But you don't get a chance to practise any of this on a ship. When I worked on a ferry for the first time it was up to me to find out where the evacuation points and passengers' lifejackets were' (Crainer, 1993: 67).

Even actions that might have appeared doubtful did not attract the judge's concerns. For example, while the inquests into the deaths of the 192 passengers and crew were still in progress, the *Herald of Free Enterprise*, which, unaccountably, had been renamed *Flushing Range* and with its bow doors welded together, was being towed to a scrap yard in Taiwan. Members of the Kent police had to fly to South Africa to intercept and inspect the renamed ship. As Crainer (1993) observes, for many concerned in the case, the vessel was 'regarded as an important piece of evidence in a criminal investigation'.

In terms of the 'guiding mind' P&O's marine superintendent admitted that he had misled the original inquiry into the disaster about when he had first heard of a proposal to fit warning lights on ferry bridges. It was also revealed that he discounted warnings from one of the company's senior masters about potential dangers because he thought the captains were exaggerating. Sheen (who chaired the initial enquiry) described Develin's [P&O's marine superintendent] responses to the legitimate concerns of the masters as 'flippant, facetious and fatuous' (Crainer, 1993). Yet Develin was not deemed sufficiently senior to equate with being (or being part of) P&O's 'guiding mind'.

Similar scenarios regarding the chasm that can appear to exist between a corporation's executive and operational management can be seen in other examples. A report in a safety journal during the inquiry into the disaster at *Piper Alpha* oil rig noted,

> The whole management evidence from Occidental [the owners of the oil rig] paints a picture of complete ignorance of the problems which existed. The senior management provided no support to the platform staff. They provided no training. They provided no guidance. The laid down no procedures. They did not participate in discussions with the operators. They did not seek the views of their employees.
>
> (*Safety Management*, December, 1989, reported in Crainer, 1993: 116)

Similarly, King (2001) remarked upon the actions of senior management at British Rail following the 1999 Paddington rail crash.

> It should come as no surprise that soon after the UK suffered its second worse rail disaster of recent times – the 1999 Paddington crash – it was revealed that the rail companies had resisted calls to introduce a confidential reporting procedure, i.e. 'whistleblowing' procedure through which staff could report safety concerns without fear of recrimination.
>
> (King, 2001: 152)

Of course, if a company has an internal grievance/concerns procedure, and issues are raised by employees within this process, senior management cannot later feign ignorance of any problems that subsequently result in injuries or death to consumers or general members of the public.

A little over 12 months after the Paddington rail crash, in October 2000, another serious incident occurred involving rail transport when a train left the track at Hatfield due to faults in the track. This time four people lost their lives and many more were injured. Again management failures regarding reluctance to heed concerns about the quality of the track and its maintenance were suggested to be a significant feature of the case, but on 23 September 2004 a high court judge announced that no charges would be brought against either the company *Railtrack* (which was later renamed *Network Rail*) and three of its directors, including the former chief executive. The reason – lack of evidence.

## The issue of aggregation

Unlike the situation in the United States, UK courts will not accept the principle of *aggregation*. This relates back to the 'guiding mind' principle. In essence the refusal of UK courts to accept aggregation means that the guiding mind of an organisation needs to be held within a tight area of the corporate structure. However, the US Court of Appeal ruled in 1987 that,

> corporations compartmentalise knowledge, subdividing the elements of specific duties and operations into small components. The aggregate of those components constitute the corporation's knowledge of a particular operation.
>
> (Crainer, 1993: 122)

The US Court of Appeal thus recognised the complexity of corporate structures, and allowed that, if responsibility for a particular facet of corporate activity, such as health and safety, was located in many different parts of a corporation, this was not a defence a corporation (as a totality) could employ to deny responsibility for a failure to adhere to acceptable safety practices. As a result of this approach, all the various parts of a corporation that are responsible for safety can be added together (aggregated) to produce the sum of the corporation's health and safety practices (or lack of).

As mentioned above, the past decade has seen calls for a crime of corporate manslaughter grow louder and more frequent in the UK, so much so that in 2000 the UK Government, via the Home Office, published its own proposals, *Reforming the Law on Involuntary Manslaughter*. However, no time in parliamentary sessions could be found. We have already mentioned what happened to the Queen's Speech in the Autumn of 2004. The situation in the UK with regard to corporate manslaughter remains a contentious issue. The influence of industry lobby groups in the stunted progress of a corporate manslaughter bill is a worrying issue for many.

## The UK government's and EU proposals on corporate manslaughter

Notwithstanding the fact that a general election in 2005 frustrated parliamentary time on a bill, the government's proposals do acknowledge the inadequacies of the current law. Four significant disasters were cited in the report *Reforming the Law on Involuntary Manslaughter*. These were: the capsizing of the *Herald of Free Enterprise*; the Kings Cross fire; the Clapham rail crash; and the Southall rail crash, with the implicit view that the law inhibited the successful prosecution of what appeared to be culpability within and of the organisations concerned. The identification doctrine was seen as the principal stumbling block to successful prosecution of companies.

The Government's proposals were based upon the Law Commission Report No. 237, *Legislating the Criminal Code: Involuntary Manslaughters*. The principal proposals were:

- There should be a special offence of corporate killing, broadly corresponding to the proposed offence of killing by gross carelessness.

- The corporate offence should (like the individual offence) be prosecuted only where the corporation's conduct fell far below what could be reasonably expected.

- The corporate offence should not (unlike the individual offence) require that the risk be obvious or that the defendant be capable of appreciating the risk.

- A death should be regarded as having been caused by the conduct of the corporation if it is caused by a 'management failure', so that the way in which its activities are managed or organised fails to ensure the health and safety of persons employed in or affected by its activities.

- Such a failure will be regarded as a cause of a person's death even if the immediate cause is the act or omission of an individual.

- That individuals within a company could still be liable for the offences of reckless killing and killing by gross carelessness, as well as the company being liable for the offence of corporate killing.

## Switching the burden of proof to the corporation

A different approach has been proposed by the Council of Europe (European Union). This proposal would make companies responsible for all offences committed by their employees, but corporations would be allowed a due diligence defence, i.e. corporations would be exempted from liability if they could show that every precaution to avoid or minimise such an act occurring had been implemented. In this proposal the conventional approach to law is turned on its head, i.e. the initial presumption is that of guilt on the part of the accused, and it is then the responsibility of the accused (the corporation) to present evidence of its existing practices that would exempt it from liability. Clarkson (1998) has expressed concern at the implications of this proposal in that (from a legal perspective) it would change the offence committed to one of a lesser order than criminal manslaughter. The new offence would be offset by a possible due diligence defence. The result would be the attribution of lesser sanctions than under a criminal prosecution for manslaughter.

The possibilities for the senior management of corporations to deny personal or corporate responsibility for criminal neglect appear to be entering a new era. In 1993, Crainer observed,

> Sadly the failure of the Zeebrugge corporate manslaughter trial seemed to condone an all-too-prevalent attitude among senior managers: 'Don't tell me what is going on because if I know, I might be held accountable'.
>
> (Crainer, 1993: 142)

Clarkson made a similar point when he observed,

> If the company's structures are impenetrable or if its policies are so 'sloppy' that no person has been made responsible for the relevant area of activity, a company can still shield itself from corporate criminal liability. In the *P&O* case, where there was no safety manager or director, there would be no person whose acts and knowledge could be attributed to the company.
>
> (Clarkson, 1998: 6)

Drawing upon the findings of the Sheen Report into the *Herald of Free Enterprise* disaster, in which the corporation was accused by Sheen of 'being infected with the disease of sloppiness' (Department of Transport, 1987), Clarkson observes, 'the worse the disease of sloppiness, the greater is the immunization against criminal liability'. The inference of Clarkson's comments regarding the 'P&O case' (*Herald of Free Enterprise*) is that the interpretation of the identification principle during the trial was too tight. It is not just the weight of the evidence that determines the outcome of legal prosecutions. The interpretations of law and decisions concerning the admissibility of evidence make the judiciary crucial elements within legal processes.

An example of the power of judges to create legal precedent is exemplified in the ruling relating to *Meridian Global Funds Management Asia Ltd v. Securities Commission* (reported in Clarkson, 1998: 3). The presiding judge ruled that the 'directing mind and will' of a company did not have to be a very senior person, if the person committing the act was authorised to undertake the act on the company's behalf. This ruling still leaves identification necessary, at the present time at least, but the clear implication is that the responsible person does not have to be a very senior person in order for a corporation to be held responsible for an act of negligence (Clarkson, 1998: 3).

Twelve years after the *Herald of Free Enterprise* disaster, and following the high-profile rail crashes involving loss of life at Clapham and Southall, two trains collided just outside Paddington Station in 1999, killing 31 people and injuring over 400. In the report published in June 2001 into the causes of the crash, Lord Cullen, the enquiry Chairman, condemned the entire rail industry for 'institutional paralysis'. He described the failure of the track operator, Railtrack, to act on previous reported incidents of train drivers passing through red signals as 'lamentable'. He was extremely critical of one of the train companies involved, Thames Trains (whose driver passed the red signal), and the company's safety culture which he described as 'slack and less than adequate'. Lord Cullen also spoke of the 'significant failures of communication within the organisation'.

The driver of the train operated by Thames Trains was inexperienced and had not been notified by the company of information that was in its possession that the signal just outside Paddington Station had been passed at danger (i.e. on red) eight times before. The problem appears to have been related to the signal being obscured at certain times of day due to the glare of the sun and/or overhanging foliage.

Lord Cullen was also critical of the quality of training given by Railtrack to its signallers, the 'slack and complacent regime at Slough' (the control centre for the signals in question). He was also extremely critical of the Railway Inspectorate which he deemed 'lacked resources, acted without vigour and placed too much faith in Railtrack'. These words carry echoes of those used by Sheen, the chairman of the Department of Trade inquiry into the *Herald of Free Enterprise* disaster. Sheen spread the blame far more widely than those directly involved on the night of the disaster. Guilt lay with 'all concerned in management. From top to bottom, the body corporate was infected with the disease of sloppiness.' No actions were ever brought against the corporations concerned!

The UK Government's earlier proposals allow for criminal prosecutions of corporations, as well as individuals, if practices that a reasonable and careful corporation would employ are absent. The speed with which the Government's proposals move from discussion paper to actual law will be interesting to observe following the 2005 election. American law would be a good precedent to follow in this case.

Clarkson offered a further variation on the quest to hold corporations to account, by the application of what he describes as 'corporate *mens rea*'. Clarkson offers his proposal because he fears that the doctrines of 'identification' and 'guiding mind' remain problematic within the government's proposals.

**DEFINITION**

*Mens rea* is a legal term that means criminal intention, or knowledge that an act is wrong. Thus, corporate *mens rea* refers to an act or set of practices (or lack of) perpetrated in the name of a corporation that possess the essence of wrongdoing.

Clarkson argued,

> Doctrines – identification, aggregation, etc. – involve fictitious imputations of responsibility. The real question is not whether the question of corporate mens rea involves a fiction, but whether, of all the fictions, it is the one that most closely approximates modern-day corporate reality and perceptions. ... the important point about this approach is that it is not whether any individual within the company would have realised or foreseen the harm occurring but whether in a properly structured and organised, careful company, the risks would have been obvious.
>
> (Clarkson, 1998: 10)

What this argument is saying is, 'Yes, corporate culpability is a fiction, or a problematic concept, but then so are many of the concepts that are involved in this debate'. Clarkson referred to legal concepts such as identification and aggregation as equivalent fictions/problematic concepts, but we could just as easily refer to concepts such as citizenship, democracy, property rights, free trade, a living wage. Property rights are an entirely socially constructed phenomenon, yet this has not prevented millions of lives being lost in its defence over the centuries. It is for societies to decide the laws that are appropriate for their own well-being and development. In many respects the fact that some of the laws relate to human beings, whilst others relate to socially constructed beings, is irrelevant.

**Connexion point**

Earlier in this chapter we discussed one of Milton Friedman's main criticisms of corporations being required to be 'responsible' for their actions beyond economic responsibility. The criticism in question was that as social constructs corporations could not have responsibilities; only people can. The reference, immediately above, to 'It is for societies to decide the laws that are appropriate for their own well-being and development. In many respects the fact that some of the laws relate to human beings, whilst others relate to socially constructed beings, is irrelevant', is extremely apposite in the context of Friedman's objections to calls for CSR.

This still leaves us with the issue of whether corporations can be construed or treated as corporate citizens. From the Heideggerian position (which we discuss in more detail in Chapter 9), corporations cannot be citizens, because the best that can be expected of corporations is that they view nature in exclusively instrumental ways. From a Heideggerian perspective, corporations have to be controlled in ways other than 'wishing' them to act in socially responsible ways. Windsor (2001) supported this view.

> The corporate citizenship notion conflates citizen (which a firm cannot be) and person (which a firm can be, but only as a legal fiction). The portrayal is fictional .... Fictional personhood is not a sound basis for artificial citizenship.
>
> (Windsor, 2001: 41)

The key proposal of the Law Commission report on involuntary manslaughter, which the UK government appears to have accepted, is that management failure to introduce and ensure the application of reasonable safety practices is sufficient to justify the prosecution of corporate manslaughter. This is a fundamental change. Whether it could be cited, retrospectively, against Railtrack and/or Thames Trains is a moot point, but the position of corporations vis à vis the death of their employees and/or members of the public due to actions or inactions of the corporation is undergoing fundamental scrutiny. As mentioned above, whether any alterations to the law will reflect such a fundamental change remains to be seen.

## Summary

In this chapter the following key points have been made:

- The changes in terminology, as reflected in the initial use of corporate social responsibility, which is beginning to mutate into corporate responsibility, while along the way the notion of corporate citizenship has also been employed, reflect an ongoing search for a concept that can encapsulate a business–society set of relationships that satisfies all aspects of the debate, but, particularly, that extends corporate executives' responsibilities beyond those to the providers of equity capital.

- Corporate governance reforms in the UK and America have retained an exclusive focus upon the interests of shareholders, unlike the King Report on corporate governance in South Africa.

- The King Report also raised the issue of values and beliefs as an explicit consideration of corporate governance, which in a South African context emphasised kinship, community and 'an inherent trust and belief in fairness of all human beings'. The issue of values within Anglo-American approaches towards corporate governance is not explicit, but implied. They are underpinned by ethical individualism and (from agency theory) a belief that individuals are self-serving and inherently untrustworthy.

- The 1999 UN Global Compact reflected a frustration with governments to address corporate governance reforms which focused upon basic human rights, such as humane living conditions; freedom of association at work; respectful working conditions, including hours of work; child labour; forced labour; and extreme poverty.

- However, the 2004 *Gearing Up* report reflects a recognition that the initial Global Compact placed too much of the responsibility for making a difference on these issues on to business corporations. The *Gearing Up* report acknowledges that there has to be a genuine bipartisan approach between governments and business if any significant outcome is to be achieved on profound global and national structural problems.

- Integrated Social Contract Theory (ISCT) offers a framework to allow us to begin to identify core organisational values that can stand the test of universalisation, but that retain the flexibility for local variations in customs and values.

- Corporate manslaughter, as a criminal offence, remains profoundly difficult to prosecute under UK law. Proposals to remedy this situation continue to be frustrated and the reasons for this stifling of progress are worrying in terms of democratic principles. The Law Commission and the Council of Europe have both pronounced on the issues and their recommendations await parliamentary time. It is now for government to choose whether or not to act.

- We may be entering, or have already entered, a period when the business–society relationship becomes far more openly debated. As a result we might find that in, say, 10 or 15 years' time the evolution of the limited liability company may have moved on apace from where it was at the turn of the century.

- Within the next 10–15 years, perhaps the notion of shareholder-as-constraint, rather than shareholder-as-maximising-objective, might have become more recognised and part of practice. As a result the notion of stakeholding may have become less of a practical conundrum. Business ethics and values have never been more relevant and centre-stage.

## Quick revision test

1. Have calls for corporations to display greater levels of social responsibility only arisen during the past fifteen years?

2. What was the view of Charles Lindblom regarding the fit of large corporations in democratic states?

3. What is agency theory?

4. What is the paradox concerning non-executive directors that relates to agency theory?

5. What admission was made in the 2004 *Gearing Up* Report concerning the 1999 UN Global Compact?

6. What were Christian Aid's principal criticisms of the UN Global Compact?

## Typical assignments and briefs

1. The ethical principles that underpin official approaches towards corporate governance in South Africa (the King Report) and the UK (2003 Combined Code) both defend issues of rights, but the extent of those rights and to whom they relate varies significantly. Debate, using contrast and comparison, where you believe the weight of ethicality and pragmatics lies.

2. International codes of conduct reflect attempts to move a more socially oriented agenda into the board rooms of corporations. Employing three different international codes,

   (i) compare and contrast the ethical principles upon which each is based; and
   (ii) given the explicit or implicit objectives of the codes you have chosen, provide a reasoned analysis of their respective likely efficacy.

3. You are an advisor to the cabinet minister who has been charged with the responsibility of responding to a parliamentary question as to why the government has chosen not to introduce the crime of corporate manslaughter. You are required to present a paper to the minister that evaluates the ethically based arguments that could be used to defend the government's position during the debate.

4. Critically evaluate Integrated Social Contract Theory as a possible way forward for reconciling a universal code of behaviour in multi-ethnic, multi-national corporations.

5. Critically contrast the 'shareholder as constraint, not objective' proposal, from both the ethical egoist and Rawlsian 'justice as fairness' perspectives.

### Group activity 8

You are asked to work in groups of between three and six members and to assume the role of being the senior decision-making team of a leading institutional investor. Your tasks are as follows, with tasks A and B ideally completed before the commencement of the group session.

A Define the principles that will guide your investment strategy. To do this you will need to consider, among other issues, the following:
   (i) On whose behalf are you making decisions?
   (ii) Are there any types of organisation in which you would not invest?
   (iii) Are there any sectors in which you emphatically wish to invest?
   (iv) What do you expect of the companies in which you invest in terms of communications and information updates?
   (v) Are there any aspects of corporate governance that you would prioritise?
   (vi) What will be your attitudes towards growth and risk?
   (vii) What will be your expectations and attitude towards rates of return?

An example of a leading institutional investor that has published its investment principles is the Hermes organisation. The following website will allow you to access the Hermes Principles, as well as a number of other important corporate governance publications.

http://www.ecgi.org/codes/country_pages/codes_uk.htm

B  Having established your investment principles, you must now select ten quoted companies that will form your investment portfolio. You are not required to worry about how well these organisations have performed in the past year. For now, simply select ten companies that you believe satisfy your investment principles.

C  You should prepare to discuss in open session the basis upon which you established your investment principles and the rationale for selecting the ten companies in your investment portfolio.

## Recommended further reading

You might find the following publications helpful.

Donaldson, T. (1989) *The ethics of international business*, New York: Oxford University Press.

Donaldson, T. and Dunfee, T.W. (1999) *Ties That Bind: A Social Contracts Approach to Business Ethics*, Harvard Business School Press.

Lindblom, C.E. (1977) *Politics and Markets: The World's Political-Economic Systems*, New York: Basic Books Inc.

SustainAbility (2004), *Gearing Up: From corporate responsibility to good governance and scalable solutions*, New York: UN Global Compact.

## Useful websites

| Topic | Website provider | URL |
|---|---|---|
| Corporate governance | European Corporate Governance Institute | http://www.ecgi.org/ |
| International corporate governance | International Corporate Governance Network | http://www.icgn.org/ |
| Corporate governance – The King Report | | http://www.ecseonline.com |
| Gearing Up Report | SustainAbility | http://www.sustainability.com |
| Global Compact | United Nations | http://www.unglobalcompact.org |

## CHAPTER 9

# Sustainability and the responsible corporation

## Learning outcomes

Having read this chapter and completed its associated activities, you should be able to:

- Discuss the importance of sustainability as a concept that applies to social and economic, as well as environmental, aspects of human activity.

- Debate both the principled and consequentialist positions that underpin sustainability arguments.

- Participate in debates concerning various global initiatives on sustainability.

- Evaluate the strength of the ethical egoist arguments for market-based, price-led sustainability solutions.

- Debate the 'enframing of technology' mind-set that represents one of the major obstacles to moving to more sustainable activities, practices and processes.

- Discuss reconceptualising the relationship between shareholder and corporate executives that could allow the stakeholder perspective to become a less problematic issue.

## Introduction

The immediate question we have to address is, 'What do we mean by sustainability?' Sustainability of what, for whom, and over what timescale?

When the term sustainability was first used in the context of social and economic activities it was used exclusively in the context of the use and depletion of environmental resources. There are a number of statements that capture the essence of this notion of sustainability and one of the earliest came from the United Nations Brundtland Commission (1987), which referred to sustainability as

> development that meets the needs of the present without compromising the ability of future generations to meet their own needs.

A variation on this theme is to see members of the human race as always in the role of lessees or guardians of the planet. From this perspective, statements such as the following flow, 'We lease nature from our children, and they from their children. We must all act wisely'.

## Significant political initiatives

There have been a number of political initiatives that have attempted to address pressing (environmental) sustainable development issues, culminating in agreements such as the Rio Declaration (1992); the Kyoto Protocol (1997); and the Johannesburg World Summit (2002). Implementation of the Kyoto Protocol was intended to be a major advance in the global approach to climate change issues, with commitments to reduce by 5.2 per cent the 1990 level of global greenhouse gas (GHG) emissions by 2012 and by 50 per cent by 2050.

As indicated above the protocol was drawn up in 1997, but the base line year for calculations was agreed as 1990. However, the subsequent withdrawal of America and Australia from the protocol undermined its status, and the tenth annual UN Conference on Climate Change, held in Buenos Aires in December 2004, witnessed further erosion of its credibility. The purpose of the conference in Buenos Aires was to gain agreement on Kyoto 2, i.e. post-2012. However, the dominant developing economies of India and China joined forces with the USA and Australia to scupper any talks concerning post-2012 GHG emission levels. India and China considered that such levels of GHG emission controls threatened their economic growth and might just be a ploy by the developed economies to slow the economic growth of India and China.

At the present time it is impossible to see the adjustments required to move to a globally sustainable position on natural resource usage without major adjustments being made to people's perceptions of acceptable ways of living. This statement denies neither the claim that present ways of living for many western societies are unsustainable, nor that the adjusted standard of living required is in any way unacceptable to rational human beings. However, it has to be recognised that, at the present time, with ethical egoism such an apparently powerful descriptive theory of human behaviour, for a political leader to claim that their policies will lead to fundamental adjustments and, some might argue, reduced standards of living would be political suicide.

You might ask what types of 'adjustments' are being referred to here. One of the major areas of potential impact would be in terms of modes of transportation. An interesting example is described in Activity 9.1.

### Activity 9.1

For example, an inter-city train can carry many more passengers than a plane on an internal flight, yet, in early 2005, it costs under £27 (including all taxes) for a scheduled return flight from Nottingham (in England) to [...] (in Scotland), a distance of 260 miles each way. With the round [...]

to 520 miles, this works out at 5p per mile! The cheapest return ticket for a train journey from Nottingham to Edinburgh is an Apex ticket that costs £50, but there are always relatively few of these tickets available. The next cheapest ticket costs £85, while the standard return (not first class) is £135. In addition, the train travel time is three hours longer, even allowing for a one-hour early arrival time at the airport. In this context you might like to make enquiries as to the cost of rail travel versus internal air flights in your own part of the UK or your own country.

With the cost of running an average family motor car estimated to be around 30p per mile and rising, and the accepted mileage rate for car travel approved by the Inland Revenue to be 40p per mile, it is puzzling in the extreme to understand how an airline can charge the equivalent of 5p per mile and still find it economically worthwhile. One of the reasons for the difference in price in the UK is that aviation fuel is not taxed. Even though this concession to the airlines is estimated to cost the UK taxpayer £6bn each year (The *Guardian*, 2005), it is not the only concession. In addition, the cost of an airline ticket is 'subsidised' in the sense that no value added tax (VAT) is levied by the government, despite the fact that air travel is the most polluting form of transportation one can choose. Excluding food products, it is difficult to identify any product or service provided by a private sector organisation that is free of VAT. This situation has to say something about the influence the airline industry has in the corridors of power.

While an element of the price differences may have something to do with the respective efficiency levels of the organisations concerned, any government espousing its commitment to a sustainability agenda has to address the cost of air travel. Interestingly, the owners of airports (often local authorities) sometimes offer incentives to airlines to fly to their destination to facilitate local economic development, which once again illustrates the complex intertwining of governments and business and the vulnerability of sustainability issues to economic, social and political interests.

Likewise, the motor car and its place in modern society cannot be exempt from political attention. The taxation of all the different facets of road travel (e.g. fuel costs, road tolls, recycled materials, fuel types, etc.) is a further issue upon which politicians can be said to be dragging their feet. In many societies the motor car has become a fundamental part of modern living, with public transport sometimes barely a viable option. Changing attitudes to reduce dependency upon the motor car is a monumental task and at the present time, potentially, a political suicide note.

## Activity 9.2

Employing the following scale, think about where your position lies on the scale with regard to each of the questions shown below.

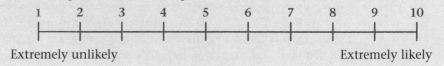

Extremely unlikely                                    Extremely likely

**Questions**

1. Can you envisage *not* owning a car – ever?

2. Would you support an increase in motor fuel tax that would double the price of a litre of fuel?

3. Would you support an increase in motor fuel tax that would quadruple the price of a litre of fuel?

4. Assuming the price adjustment relates to an airline flight that you might take, would you support a levy on aviation fuel that would raise the price of an economy airline ticket from its current price of £300 to £1800?

5. Assuming the price adjustment relates to an airline flight that you might take, would you support a levy on aviation fuel that would raise the price of an internal air flight from, say, £27 to £270?

6. How likely do you think it is that the fuel tax rises suggested in the questions above would address the worldwide issue of GHG emissions?

| Activity 9.3 | A moral choice |
| --- | --- |

In a radio interview of January 2005, Jonathon Porritt, the UK government's advisor on environmental issues, gave an example of the tension between social ethics and environmental ethics. He argued that, whilst it might be a socially moral act to attend one's sister's wedding in New York, the environmentally moral case is not to attend (but with profuse apologies). What is your reaction to this statement?

The changes required to address the environmental problems facing the world in the early stages of the twenty-first century are not all as startling or lifestyle-changing as these examples and questions imply, but it is probable that many required changes do represent changes of a stepped and profound nature.

Returning to the UN Climate Change Conference in Buenos Aires in December 2004, the problems of achieving an outline agreement on a Kyoto 2 accord were further exacerbated when Italy joined the dissenting countries (Australia, China, India and America) and thereby undermined a previously united EU position. This was clearly a significant setback for the coordinated European position, but the UK's position is itself not wholly consistent. For example, the UK government had previously announced that it had set itself the task of achieving the Kyoto target of GHG emissions by 2010 and by a greater amount than the EU as a whole had agreed. The commitment to achieve higher levels of reduction of carbon dioxide emissions, and two years ahead of the time the EU was requiring its member states to achieve the Kyoto targets, was a demanding commitment by the UK government. However, by doing so the UK government was announcing its commitment to environmental issues.

In April 2004 the UK Secretary of State for the Department of Environment, Food and Rural Affairs (DEFRA) announced that for the period 2004–2007 the UK's reduction in carbon dioxide emissions would be 756m tonnes. However, on 27 October 2004, and after significant lobbying by industry groups, the Secretary of State announced that the UK government had made adjustments to the base line number to allow British industry to remain 'competitive' (i.e. to allow it to spend less on GHG-reducing measures). The reduction in carbon dioxide emissions had been recalculated as 736m tonnes. The overall target reduction for 2010 remained unchanged, which meant that the reductions between 2007 and 2010 would have to be even more significant than before, although maybe that was seen as the next government's problem!

## Emissions Trading Scheme

The commitment to the GHG targets may have been initially well intentioned, but the political will appears to have been found lacking when confronted by powerful industrial pressure groups. However, the story does not end there. The EU Commission refused to accept the UK's revised figures and insisted that the original target be reinstated. After much 'discussion' the UK Government acceded to the EU ruling, but announced that it would challenge the ruling in the courts. This decision allowed the UK to enter the Emissions Trading Scheme (ETS) but left unresolved, for the time being, the reduction in GHG emissions that UK companies would need to achieve. As we write this chapter the situation remains unresolved. The ETS officially began operating on 1 January 2005, although the dispute between the UK government and the EU Commission delayed its start.

The ETS is a market-based response to the need to reduce GHG emissions. As part of the Kyoto Protocol, the EU committed its member states to reduce GHG emissions by 8 per cent by 2012, but as mentioned above the UK government committed itself to achieve a 12 per cent reduction by 2010, so relatively speaking this was a far more ambitious, environmentally sensitive and bold stance than the EU had committed its member states to.

Each EU country has had to develop a National Allocation Plan (NAP). Within the respective NAPs organisations generating more than a certain level of carbon dioxide emissions have to apply for a permit, which may or may not represent the organisation's current carbon dioxide emissions level. If during the year an organisation believes it will exceed its permitted allowance then it will need to enter the ETS and buy additional 'credits'. Alternatively, if an organisation believes that it will not require all its allocated credits (maybe as a result of installing equipment and plant that are very energy efficient) then the organisation can consider selling its surplus 'credits' on the ETS.

Environmental pressure groups and other agencies (including governments) may wish to increase the pressure on companies to replace existing plant with more energy-efficient plant by entering the market and buying credits, thereby reducing the available pool of credits and increasing the price of those credits still available. The intention would be that by driving up the price of credits the cost of purchasing energy-efficient plant and equipment becomes more attractive than buying the GHG credits. In addition, by investing in energy-efficient plant and equipment a company may not need all its credits and thus be able to sell them in, ideally, a rising market for credits. It will be interesting to see the extent to which agencies such as pressure groups and governments act as buyers to push up the price of credits. Without such intervention it is difficult to see how the market will stimulate the desired transfer to energy-efficient plant.

Whether this 'solution' to global warming is the ideal solution, or even a suitable one, is a moot point. It is a business solution to a problem that has profound social, political and, ultimately, survival consequences. As discussed above, unless a market price fully reflects all opportunity and externality costs, including those of future societies, it remains incomplete as an expression of societies' preferences. For example, the approach encourages a highly calculative stance with regard to investment in new energy-efficient plant. As an alternative to possessing sufficient credits that equate with one's GHG emissions, a corporation may simply decide to pay whatever fine is levied upon corporations that fail to comply with the ETS and the Kyoto defined emission levels. Thus, to make engagement with the ETS economically logical, non-compliance fines will need to be high, even punitive. Will governments be strong enough to levy fines of this scale? History does not offer encouragement for this prospect.

Thus, ETS credits could remain only a partial solution to the problem, but be presented as if they were the complete answer. Societies and their governments are likely to have important roles still to play on the issue of global warming.

## When is the environment precious?

The perception that nature is simply a resource at our disposal and that the only factor that will shape our usage of, and attitudes towards, it is the exhaustion of these resources is a very specific view. We will explore a counterview to this stance later in the chapter when we consider the ideas and arguments of Martin Heidegger, but for now it is worth reflecting upon a study by Sterman and Sweeney (2002).

The authors conducted a study of American interviewees' understanding of climate change and global warming issues. Their findings were that, while most who took part in the study accepted that the available facts bear out the claims that climate change and global warming are real phenomena, their understanding of the trajectory of the different issues was usually illogical and/or irrational (the researchers' judgement). Coupled with this was a widespread preference on the part of the study's participants for a wait-and-see policy towards implementing environmental protection policies and practices. The arguments of the researchers were that a 'wait-and-see' approach is inadequate and that merely reducing environmental usage, other than a radical step-change, is unacceptable, but that the interviewees would not consider this as an acceptable position. In terms of the questions posed in Activity 9.2 above, the researchers would argue that, with ozone depletion and global warming occurring at such a pace, nothing short of stopping certain actions and practices is required.

### Connexion point

The claims of ethical egoism, as discussed in Chapters 3 and 8, are that neo-liberal economics (including free trade, free markets and no government interventions) offers the best prospect for the protection of individual liberties and freedoms and democratic ideals.

Yet, in terms of Activity 9.2, there are, paradoxically, important aspects of a 'business/market-based' solution to GHG emissions and transportation choices that are profoundly undemocratic. Even the intervention of governments by raising fuel taxes by factors of 2, 3, 10, 20, or whatever, but in doing so employing the price mechanism to shape behaviour and achieve a critical environmental policy, suffers the same undemocratic potential.

At one level, by using the price mechanism as a moderator of behaviour, the notion of individual choice is maintained. This, as we have discussed, is the neoliberal argument regarding the morality of the price mechanism to reflect freedom of choice. However, how democratic is it that only the very wealthy might be able to afford such amenities, and how democratic is it that many, many millions of people may never be able to afford these facilities?

Possibly a more profound question in terms of democratic ideals is, if certain practices and activities are major contributors to ozone depletion and GHG emissions and are thereby harmful to the vast majority of people, possibly even threatening the survival of many species, including *homo sapiens*, why should a few people be allowed to inflict harm upon the vast majority, simply because they are able to use their wealth to exercise their freedom to fly? Is the price mechanism as democratic a tool of resource allocation as it is invariably portrayed?

Redclift (1984, 1987) presented a thoughtful analysis of the tensions and contradictions within the sustainability debates. One of the early statements in his 1987 book asserts, '... the environment, whatever its geographic location, is socially constructed' (1987: 3). What might he have meant by this?

One way to understand this statement is to think of a woodland comprised of ancient trees, glades, brooks, and with special flora and fauna. Today the woodland might be a prized place, maybe designated an SSI (a place of Special Scientific Interest) and consequently protected from exploitation. This is how we see it (socially construct it) today, but that is unlikely to be how it has always been seen by those who have lived by the woodland and in the woodland. At times it might have been seen as a source of social and possibly economic survival. At the social, human existence level, the woodland would have presented wood for building homes and fires, while the animals and bushes would have been the sources of food and sustenance. The notion of a prized place would have been meaningless beyond its relative fruitfulness in terms of hunting, shelter and sustenance. The woodland, and its immediate environs, represented the world as the inhabitants knew it, assuming they had forsaken a nomadic existence. They had neither the time nor the reason to consider the woodland beyond its functionality. If the woodland lacked wildlife it is extremely likely the local people would have held the woodland in low esteem and moved on to more plentiful pastures. A woodland's value would have been determined by its ability to sustain human existence.

At other times the woodland may have been a place of foreboding, a place to be avoided as it could have harboured dangerous and predatory animals and/or people. Highwaymen may have roamed the woodland and trees would have been considered negative elements, providing cover for robbers and brigands. The notion of the woodland as a special place would have been scoffed at and derided. Yet it is the same woodland that we prize today. This is what is meant by the phrase, 'the environment is socially constructed'. In one era the felling of trees (to remove the camouflage that robbers seek) would have been considered desirable and sensible. In another era (today) the felling of many species of trees without special permission is considered a crime and subject to criminal prosecution. With regard to our perceptions of the environment, it is clear that we are once again discussing values, ethics and arguments and not irrefutable and indisputable facts. With regard to issues such as global warming and GHG emissions, while we are discussing (disputed) 'facts', our behaviours and responses to these 'facts' will be reflective of our ethics and our values.

## Broadening the concept of sustainability

For many people the concept of sustainability still refers to the effects of human, particularly corporate, activity on the environment. However, for others the concept needs broadening. With social and political systems so intertwined with economic activity, any hope of addressing the exploitation of people and natural resources has to involve corporate and political forces. In addition, whilst national initiatives on environmental and social issues are important, coordinated international initiatives are equally important, even though the refusal of America and Australia to comply with the Kyoto Protocol (and now India, China and Italy refusing to agree on a Kyoto 2) bears testimony to the problems of achieving meaningful progress on environmental issues. However, the important point is that recognition needs to be given to the engagement of large corporations. It is not enough to highlight that corporate activity (often with governmental support or acquiescence) is the principal cause of many environmental and social problems. The active collaboration of the corporate world has to be an important element in any successful set of initiatives that are implemented to address the world's environmental and social problems.

Part of this argument is that for corporations to remain sustainable (the notion of business sustainability is the interesting twist to current debates) they have to operate within socially acceptable parameters, which include how corporations use and treat the environment and people. This is part of what can be called the 'social contract', as discussed in Chapter 8. The UN Global Compact (1999) and the *Gearing Up* (2004) report are also important documents in attempts to shape thinking, debate and action.

To illustrate some of the tensions that can exist between competitive forces delivering lower prices, but only as the result of what some argue are unsustainable practices, we reflect on the challenges being made against the alleged practices of the supermarkets.

| Case study 9.1 | **Low, low prices – but at whose cost?** |
|---|---|

Tesco has risen from the third most significant food retailer in the UK to the UK's largest retailer (not just food) within a 15-year period. In 2005, for every £8 spent in retail outlets in the UK – on all goods – £1 was spent at Tesco. This is a phenomenal growth record and achievement. Tesco has branched out into ▶

clothes and white goods (e.g. fridges and freezers) and other electrical and electronic goods, with good quality goods being sold at prices that customers judge to be excellent value for money. For example, both Tesco and Asda sell good quality jeans for just £3, and a pint of milk cannot be purchased more cheaply than at these stores. However, the low prices of certain goods (not all goods are so 'competitively' priced) come at costs. There are accusations of unethical practices and in some cases illegal practices.

Farmers' unions and allied pressure groups accuse Tesco (and the other large food retailers) of making the farmer carry the burden of the falling price of milk. Tesco is accused of being able to sell milk at the price that it does only because it pressurises the farmer to sell, in some cases, at less than the costs of production.

Tesco has also accepted that quality garden furniture was sold at 'extremely competitive prices', but was made from illegally logged wood from the Indonesian rain forests. In 2003, Friends of the Earth identified that 70 per cent of Tesco's garden furniture was made from illegally logged timber. The Malaysian timber industry has greatly outstripped the supply of suitable Malaysian timber, and highly profitable, but illegal, trafficking in protected Indonesian timber has flourished through Malaysia. However, this was a known phenomenon and having been a signatory to the 95+ Group, which was set up by the World Wildlife Fund (WWF) to protect endangered rain forests, it might have been expected that great care would have been taken by Tesco to ensure that it did not undermine the WWF campaign. A spokesperson for Tesco stated, 'We didn't knowingly buy timber from illegal sources ... We haven't done such a good job of checking where the material is coming from, and the ability to track it isn't up to our usual standards' (*Independent on Sunday*, 13 July 2003). Just how rigorous 'usual standards' are was not explained.

The issue is, that while the consumer is able to enjoy low prices, it is the food producer, or the inhabitants of the rain forests, or the garment maker in a sweatshop somewhere, or the assembly worker on an electrical goods production line where health and safety standards bear little resemblance to western conditions, who is shouldering the price cuts, not the superstores. 'Low' and declining prices can rarely be explained exclusively by economies of scales, or the learning curve effect. Someone, somewhere, along the supply chain is being squeezed hard and invariably it will be the least powerful links in the chain.

Tesco, and the other supermarkets, refute these claims and a continuing 'debate' moves back and forth between the companies and their critics.

Interestingly, Bennett (2005) questions why consumers show considerable concern for dolphin-friendly tuna, inappropriately reared prawns or battery-farmed chickens, but express few such qualms regarding jeans that retail at £3 per pair and are sold at the rate of 50,000 pairs per week from Tesco stores alone. National newspapers, so quick to focus upon unsatisfactory farming and harvesting practices when it comes to fish or poultry, laud the cheap, but high-quality garments now on sale, not just at Tesco or Asda, but at designer outlets such as Hennes and Top Shop (Bennett, 2005: 5). The big clothing retailers argue that they meet local employment and payment conditions and often exceed them, but a quick study of local laws and conditions should raise important questions regarding the acceptability of these rules. For example, the internationally agreed Sweatshop Code requires the following conditions in terms of hours of work to be respected if companies are to claim compliance with the Code.

> Except in extraordinary business circumstances, employees shall (i) not be required to work more than the lesser of (a) 48 hours per week and 12 hours overtime or (b) the limits on regular and overtime hours allowed by the law of the country of manufacture or, where the laws of such country do not limit the hours of work, the regular work week in such country plus 12 hours overtime and (ii) be entitled to at least one day off in every seven-day period.

Thus, depending upon how vigorously the Code is policed and monitored, company owners can require 60 hours per week as long as they claim that the circumstances are 'extraordinary', or local employment law stipulates a lower ceiling. With regard to the latter, it would be interesting to learn how vigorously the large international corporations lobby for greater employee protection legislation in countries such as Guatemala, Indonesia, China, India, El Salvador and Cambodia, compared with, say, corporate-friendly taxation policies or inward investment incentives.

However, it is not just corporations that should be the focus of attention. As indicated above, while the living conditions of poultry and prawns have grabbed the attention of the media and consumers, the living and working conditions of fellow human beings appear to be less/not important. If we wish markets to reflect different values from those that currently prevail, then it is for individual consumers to exercise their voice. This can be expressed via purchasing decisions or political voting and/or through other media, such as radio and television phone-in programmes etc. These issues are not just issues for businesses to address. Individuals have a part, some would say a responsibility, to express their views. It is too easy to pass all the responsibility for curing the ills of the world on to corporate executives, with consumers accepting no responsibility. If the 'C' in CSR relates only to 'corporate' and not 'consumer' then, should corporations who take their broader social and environmental responsibilities seriously suffer consequential cost increases, but consumers retain price as their primary decision criterion, executives have every right to feel double standards at play in the CSR debate. In such situations the 'market' may need help from governments in the form of differential taxation policies with regard to CSR products or organisations. Contrary to market-fundamentalist belief, maybe this is an example where governments could intervene to reward those companies that operate socially and environmentally sensitive practices and policies, or conversely penalise those organisations that do not. On its own the 'market' cannot equalise the product costs of the different corporate approaches. As the Secretary-General of the United Nations stated at the launch of the UN Global Compact in 1999, 'Markets are not embedded in universal human rights'.

| Activity 9.4 | £3 jeans – a good buy? | | | |
|---|---|---|---|---|
| | | *Yes* | *No* | *Maybe* |
| Having read the above discussion, would you: | | | | |
| 1. Now think twice before purchasing jeans at very low prices? | | ☐ | ☐ | ☐ |
| 2. Wait until you are earning a reasonable wage before being able to be a discriminating consumer? or | | ☐ | ☐ | ☐ |
| 3. Not worry about the possible implications of the low prices on the basis that the 'workers' would be worse off without the work? | | ☐ | ☐ | ☐ |

The issue of consumer responsibility, as distinct from corporate responsibility, is an interesting issue to which we will return. However, for the moment, we will concentrate upon environmental sustainability and its various dimensions.

## Environmental sustainability

It might be assumed that concerns at the rate of environmental depletion and contamination are relatively recent, with the levels of social and economic activity of earlier times too limited to have raised concerns over the environmental impacts of human activity. How long ago do you think the following words were written?

> Human beings have been endowed with reason and a creative power so that they can add to what they have been given. But until now they have not been creative, but destructive. Forests are disappearing, rivers are drying up, wildlife is becoming extinct, the climate's being ruined and with every passing day the earth is becoming poorer and uglier.

These are familiar and contemporary concerns, expressed in modern language, but the words were written not five or ten years ago but in 1897 by the Russian dramatist and short-story writer, Anton Chekhov. Does this mean that current concerns over, for example, global warming, deforestation, changes in sea levels and pollution levels are merely a continuation of long-standing worries, and that these concerns underestimate the ability of the environment to absorb and cope with the worst excesses of man?

Even if the answer to the above questions is agreed to be 'No', that is, the depletion of natural resources and evidence of climate change and global warming do pose a threat to political, social and economic structures, the question remains, 'Are these issues really about ethics and morals?' Can we not simply categorise the arguments about pollution levels, climate change and the depletion of natural resources as commonsense? Will not the logic of adverse developments in any or all of these areas force people to behave sensibly, even if only out of enlightened self-interest?

We will take these questions separately, with our responses shown in italics, before returning to the standard font for the general discussion.

**Question 1** – Are we over-reacting and over-estimating the extent of environmental degradation and despoliation and their effects?

*There are a few voices that argue that most, if not all, of the claims over the effects of environmental degradation and despoliation are misguided and/or exaggerated. An interesting contribution to the debates has been that of the thriller crime writer Michael Crichton, whose book 'State of Fear' (2004) tells a fictional but, it is argued, rigorously researched story of environmental news distortion, exaggeration and manipulation. It reflects most of the arguments, plus new claims, used by the Kyoto dissenting countries. However, the counter-view is supported by a considerable weight of evidence. The latter evidence highlights climate change and global warming and the factors that appear to be triggering these changes, plus the rate of natural resource depletion. All this evidence appears to reflect fundamental and potentially destabilising changes. In view of this, the evidence would argue forcibly for profound changes to our collective and individual behaviours and practices, particularly on behalf of future generations.*

From an ethical perspective, a response to the above statement can be justified using both principled (deontological) and consequentialist (utilitarian) arguments.

## The principled argument

Natural justice would be the basis for opposition to what many would argue to be unsustainable environmental depletion and pollution linked to the double standards of critical decision-makers. An important factor in this debate is the issue of property rights. We (societies) have created the construct of property rights as a way of managing important parts of our lives. This development has been a significant force in economic development, but it has not been a universal approach. Various groups and societies through time, often but not always nomadic, have seen man and nature's relationship as far more respectful and symbiotic than tends to be the case in many contemporary societies. Nature, in its various forms, has often been represented by gods to be revered and worshipped. Taking from the gods was only possible through compensatory offerings and devotion to rituals.

Irrespective of contemporary religious (and secular) perspectives on nature, the social construct of property rights has located control over natural resources (*see* definition below) in the hands of relatively few people, those with great personal wealth, or those in critical decision-making roles in business or political organisations. A natural justice argument would see this 'arrangement', at least as it involves non-politicians, as undemocratic, not just for those members of contemporary societies that are excluded from important decisions by virtue of the existence of property rights legislation (e.g. because they do not own equity shares in companies), but also members of societies that are denied involvement owing possibly to their age, gender or ethnicity, or maybe because they have yet to be born.

The term **resource** is a value-laden concept, carrying with it connotations of something to be used. Even the notion of usage is usually considered in terms of economic usage. This is a particular way of 'seeing' nature – as a resource, as something to be exploited. The notion of nature as a resource will be explored in more depth when we consider the work of Martin Heidegger.

Planning laws have been instituted to address some of these concerns, but the power of 'economic logic' in planning decisions is such that governments, both national and local, are often incapable of resisting proposals to exploit natural resources or to build constructions (including large-scale quarrying) that despoil landscapes or localities. The promise of jobs and the associated economic benefits, or the consequences of losing the proposal to other areas, can be powerful reasons for overriding environmental and other planning considerations. Even Deputy Prime Ministers seem to feel the need to instruct planners to 'take developers' business arguments into account' when considering planning applications (Russell, 2005).

## The double standards argument

This argues that the people who make these decisions rarely live close to, or are affected by, these decisions. Indeed they invariably live in beautiful areas and fight aggressively and generally effectively to defend 'their' environmental habitats. Their access to political networks and their ability to engage influential legal and other resources make their prospects for defending their environments from exploitation by others far greater than is the norm. A defence of this state of affairs might be that it is a system that is open to all, but this would be a very particular form of democratic logic, because many do not possess the networks or financial resources to employ 'the system' so effectively.

The reason that the above is referred to as a principled argument is that it is an argument that is independent of consequentialist issues. No reference has been made to particular decisions being 'wrong' or 'right' because of the specific ramifications of those decisions. To be a principle-based argument, the case has to be that the decisions and/or the processes by which such decisions are made are inadequate and unjust at the general, societal level.

## The consequentialist argument

Opposition to and criticism of current decision-making processes that impact upon sustainability issues that stem from a consequentialist perspective will be as a result of weighing all the ramifications of the decisions in terms of their effects upon various groups. As a result of this calculative approach, the consequentialist perspective is a stance that can be employed to both support and condemn environmental exploitation. Much depends upon how far one draws the boundaries of affected or relevant individuals and groups. Just how far should one allow one's considerations to be stretched before it is agreed that all the relevant parties' interests have been adequately weighed to allow the hypothetical scales of utilitarian justice to show where the balance of the argument lies?

These are often far from easy decisions and decision processes, although utilitarian considerations will often lie at the heart of political and planning decisions. The following case illustrates some of the complexities of such decisions.

| Case study 9.2 | **Removing a mountain on the Isle of Harris** |
| --- | --- |

The Isle of Harris lies to the north-west of the Scottish mainland and is part of the Outer Hebrides. It is an island, along with the attached Isle of Lewis, of significant natural and archaeological interest and beauty. It is also of considerable geological interest because, unlike the other islands that form the Inner and Outer Hebrides, it was not once part of the Scottish mainland. It 'drifted' to its current position over millennia, as a result of the movement of tectonic plates. The only other areas of the world displaying similar rock formation and composition are to be found in New Zealand and South Africa.

Shortly before this case study was written, the Scottish Parliament announced that it had turned down an application to allow mining of a mountain area on the Isle of Harris. The economic, social and political dimensions to the case were considerable and it is unlikely that the recent decision by the Scottish Parliament is the last act in this unfolding drama.

The mountain in question lies in the south-east corner of the island and is composed of rock that is both extremely hard (wearing) and has luminous qualities, ideal qualities of aggregates to be used in the construction of roads and motorways. With the mining completed the mountain would have effectively been removed, leaving an enormous cavity in the ground. The hole would cover a very wide area and the belief/fear was/is that it would then be a convenient site for the dumping of much of Scotland's 'undesirable' waste, which could include toxic waste.

One of the authors visited the island in 2004 for a holiday and was impressed with the level of opposition to the proposal by islanders in the north of the island, particularly those who were relatively recent inhabitants of the island. Their opposition was based upon environmental and, to a lesser extent, economic considerations. The latter reflected concerns over the impact upon tourism of the massive quarrying and then dumping operations. However, when he visited the south of the island the reaction of the locals was far more mixed, with possibly a majority of those he met (in a very unscientific study!) in favour of the proposal. Their reasoning? It reflected the locals' concern over the significant haemorrhaging of young islanders to the mainland in search of work (although there was a strong argument that the jobs issue could be handled by other approaches). The islands were becoming the repositories of elderly (usually English) people, seeking peaceful retirements and those seeking an alternative lifestyle to the pressures and demands of modern life. In the words of those who supported the proposal, the island was dying as its young people continued to migrate to the mainland.

The following are some of the difficult questions that demand attention if adopting a utilitarian approach to the ethically appropriate decision for the Isle of Harris.

1. Where does the balance of the consequentialist argument lie?

2. Is a simple calculative approach adequate?

3. Is it simply a case of counting the number of people likely to be affected, both negatively and positively, by the decision, and opting for the decision that affects the larger number of people positively?

4. Or should the decision be based upon the option that affects the smaller number of people negatively?

5. If a higher value is placed upon avoiding harm, then avoiding negatively affecting people will carry a higher (political) weighting, which might result in a different decision from that suggested by 3 above.

6. How much attention and weight should be given to the financial implications of the decision?

7. How does one take into account those people who live elsewhere in Scotland or other parts of the UK, who might be affected by a landfill site being located near their homes if the planning application for the Isle of Harris site is refused?

8. Within a utilitarian stance should the views of the indigenous islanders be weighed more significantly than those of the 'newcomers'?

This is a real case with which the Scottish Parliament has had to wrestle and which it might have to revisit, should an appeal be lodged against the planning rejection.

To conclude this section we highlight the murkiness and business–political intrigue at play on the critical subject of environmental sustainability with reference to an article written by Lord May, who in 2005 was President of the Royal Society and between 1995 and 2000 was the UK government's chief scientific advisor. The following case summarises the article.

**Case study 9.3**

### An insider's view

During the 1990s, parts of the US oil industry funded – through the so-called Global Climate Coalition (GCC) – a lobby of professional sceptics who opposed action to tackle climate change by cutting greenhouse gas emissions. The GCC was 'deactivated' in 2001, once President Bush made it clear he intended to reject the Kyoto Protocol. But the denial lobby is still active , and today it arrives in London.

The UK has become a target because the government has made climate change a focus of its G8 presidency this year [2005]. A key player in this decision is chief scientific advisor Sir David King, who became public enemy number one for the denial lobby when he described climate change as a bigger threat than terrorism.

> In December [2004], a UK-based group, the Scientific Alliance, teamed up with the George C. Marshall Institute, a body headed by the chairman emeritus of the GCC, William O'Keefe, to publish a document with the innocuous title 'Climate Issues & Questions'. It plays up the uncertainties surrounding climate change science, playing down the likely impact that it will have.
>
> It contrasts starkly with the findings of the Intergovernmental Panel on Climate Change (IPCC) ... the world's most reliable source of information on the effects of greenhouse gas emissions.
>
> (*Source*: Lord May, 2005)

Lord May was pointing out that powerful interest groups in the shape of the major US oil corporations were funding organisations that were seeking to undermine the evidence-based arguments of respected scientific bodies such as the IPCC. You might feel that if the claims being made by organisations such as the George C. Marshall Institute are unfounded and spurious then they will be derided. However, one should not trust reason and logic to prevail when such powerful economic interests are at risk.

Later in his article, Lord May expressed concern that major UK daily newspapers were running articles and leaders in 2005 that undermined the evidence-based arguments of the IPCC. Public opinion becomes influenced by such sources. The American tobacco industry denied for decades the causal link between smoking and different forms of cancer. In the mid-1990s all the CEOs of the seven largest tobacco companies testified before a congressional hearing that in their view there was no causal link, despite the fact the tobacco industries' own (private) research revealed the connections. It was only when one of the tobacco industries' own scientists 'blew the whistle' on the suppressed evidence that the tobacco companies accepted the causal relationship. The oil industry cannot suppress the scientific evidence that is published on climate change, so an alternative strategy is to challenge and undermine the evidence and arguments.

In all discussions on environmental sustainability the American perspective is critical. With America accounting for only 4 per cent of the world's population, but with 22.5 per cent of the world's GHG emissions emanating from the United States, gaining the support of the American political establishment is critical. A different way of looking at this situation is that any American president has an incredibly difficult and high-risk task in making environmental issues a major political issue for the American electorate. Some argue that it would be a political suicide note.

Interestingly, the UK Prime Minister, Tony Blair, when he gave the keynote speech at the opening of the World Economic Forum at Davos, Switzerland, on 26 January 2005, softened his own commitment to making climate change issues his primary challenge, when he asserted that climate change was 'not universally accepted'. Elliot (2005) observed, 'with chief executives of many US firms in the audience, [Blair] said, "the evidence is still disputed"'. Mr Blair went on to state that no significant adjustments to business behaviour towards the environment can be expected if such adjustments threaten economic growth. This may or may not be a realistic assessment of the economic and political power positions (the so-called *realpolitik*), but the assertion is as much puzzling as it is concerning, because it ignores both the morality and the physical consequences of a 'do-nothing' attitude to environmental despoliation and degradation, whether from a principled or consequentialist perspective.

**Question 2** – What are the implications of relying exclusively upon enlightened/rational self-interest to drive sustainable corporate behaviour and practices?

*There has been a variety of evidence available over many years that has highlighted the unsustainability of the rate of environmental depletion and waste across the globe. However, to date, this evidence and official responses have had limited impact upon our practices. For example, in the early 1990s and in response to concerns over carbon dioxide emissions, the Intergovernmental Panel on Climate Change called for carbon dioxide emissions to be 50 per cent lower by 2050 than their 1990 levels. Given the likely increase in global economic activity between 1990 and 2050, such a reduction represents a significant change in consumption and will not be achieved without new technologies and practices, as well as possible revisions to economic growth assumptions. Yet between 1990 and 2004 carbon dioxide emissions actually rose by 8.9 per cent! The implications of these (in)actions and behaviours are likely to affect all members of the human race to some extent, but possibly most significantly, those yet to be born. Thus, a decision based exclusively upon rational self-interest fails to address the wider significance of individual choices and decisions. Whilst our actions and behaviours affect others, they have ethical import.*

The assumptions regarding economic growth rates contained within the calculations regarding carbon dioxide emissions do reflect an economic mind-set that now goes almost unchallenged. Whilst writers such as Dickson (1974), Sawyer (1978) and Schell (1982) presented arguments that challenged the wisdom and sustainability of economic growth assumptions in the 1970s and 1980s, these arguments are far less frequently discussed today, even though the economic growth assumptions have been outstripped – such is the dominance of economic imperatives and their relationships with political objectives. The notion of short-termism in decision making, whether it be related to political or economic decisions (and often they are linked), is a central issue within these debates and can be said to reflect an ethical egoist perspective, as discussed below.

| Activity 9.5 | Putting yourself in the shoes of 'others' |
|---|---|

The refusal to recognise the evidence that exists regarding environmental degradation and depletion represents an act with ethical significance. A decision to do nothing is still a decision. What will be the consequences of maintaining existing rates of resource consumption and thus depletion by 2105? If you were to be living in 2105, what do you think would be your attitude towards those living in 2005 who refused/failed to curb their consumption of finite natural resources and/or did little to address global warming and climate change issues?

Ethical egoism (sometimes referred to as possessive egoism), with its reliance upon market signals to reflect social preferences would, at best, appear to require an ambivalent stance towards environmental issues.

## Ethical egoism and sustainability

From an ethical egoist perspective, market-based forms of coordination of economic and social activity are argued to be at the bedrock of basic freedoms. The more all facets of human interaction can be coordinated by market dynamics, the more the resulting outcomes will reflect the independent, 'free' choices of all participants. As we discussed in Chapter 3, this argument has certain strengths, but it also ignores important structural issues which challenge its integrity (principled-based objection) and efficacy (utilitarian-based objection).

Allowing markets to be the dominant forms for allowing societal preferences and choices to become known assumes that prices contain all relevant information and markets are not unduly skewed owing to power imbalances. Yet, as suggested in the Isle of Harris case, there might be certain situations where the opinions and arguments of particular groups might justify higher weightings than other groups in a decision-making process. If it was left to simple market dynamics to reflect these different weightings, then it is likely that the economically powerful would secure the largest weightings, possibly usurping those with higher, principle-based claims to justice, or deservingness.

As mentioned already in this chapter, the voice of the yet to be born is a complex one to include in such debates, but it is almost impossible to envisage how the price mechanism would incorporate the views of future generations, other than perhaps taxes levied by governments on behalf of future generations, to pay for 'clean-ups' or detoxifying processes, reclamation, compensation payments, etc. However, if the voice of future generations was truly able to be heard, it could be that they would be at one in rejecting the decision in its entirety, thus obviating the need for compensation payments or other such contingency plans. Designating areas of special scientific interest is one way of protecting certain parts of the environment for current and future generations, but these designations are vulnerable to powerful interests and can be overridden. One such example is the opening up of a previously protected region of the Arctic Circle in Alaska for oil drilling, as evidenced in Table 8.1 in the previous chapter.

In the context of environmental protection it would seem that market signals have limited application, an example of what can be called 'market failure', making the intervention of governments essential as the representatives of the people and their adjudicators. However, governments' interventions in economic and social affairs are anathema to market fundamentalists, with any exceptions to this principle seen as the start of a very slippery slope. For those with more acceptance of political intervention in such situations, their concerns are with the corruptibility of political processes. The latter are seen as too susceptible to the influence of powerful individuals and corporations.

**Connexion point**

Refer back to Table 8.1 to refresh your memory on the political donations made to the Republican Party during the US Presidential elections of 2000 and the resulting changes to the law that immediately followed President Bush's inauguration.

## A different perspective on environmental issues

If you refer back to Chapter 1, three of the theories of the firm, *Classical liberal economic, Pluralist (A and B)* and *Corporatist*, each locate the business corporation within a capitalist-driven, market-based economy. Each perspective accepts the need for corporations to legitimately seek out new ways to generate profits on behalf of shareholders, but with other interest groups (employees, customers and suppliers) benefiting in differing ways as a result of these corporate activities. Within these perspectives, nature, in all its various forms, is seen as a resource, at the behest of society in general, and corporations in particular, to be employed in whatever ways are deemed socially and legally permissible to facilitate economic activity.

Before these issues are discussed in more detail, we would like you to take a few minutes to undertake the following task.

| Activity 9.6 | Subjects and objects |
|---|---|

Try to identify a place or an object that has a special significance for you. The place or object might be very commonplace (e.g. a ring, an ornament, a book, a photograph) or it might be a little unusual, a location for example. Whatever it is, for you it is special. If you cannot identify such a place or object, try to identify a place or object that you know to be special to someone else, your mother or father perhaps, or your brother or sister. If you were then asked to place a value on that place or object, how might you express that value as a number, a monetary value?

Prior to Activity 9.6, the perspective that has so far underpinned our discussions in this chapter has been that of a clear distinction between ourselves (subjects) and the world of objects that surround us. We have assumed that we are separate from nature and nature is separate from us. We possess the technologies to control, manipulate and direct nature, and we possess the capabilities, and some would argue the right, to do with nature as we see fit. The law of property rights underpins this belief. Landowners can prohibit access to their lands because laws have been passed that allow such prohibitions. Countries fight over, or at least contest, ownership of areas of land and sea (the Arctic and Antarctic regions for example) because of their mineral deposits and other valued resources. Even the moon is subject to property rights' claims for its mineral deposits. Currently companies are seeking to decode human DNA so that they can patent and thus 'own' the codes. The ability of humanity to benefit from such 'code-breaking' research will then be subject to commercial exploitation of these medical understandings. At one level this is no different from the patent rights and copyright constraints existing in many areas of organisational activity, but deeper philosophical issues can be argued to be at play when one considers knowledge breakthroughs that can possibly alleviate great human suffering, e.g. in the areas of genetically inherited diseases and disabilities.

Practically everything you see around you, can touch, or what you are wearing, represents some form of intervention of human activity on nature. This is not to say that these interventions have been/are bad or wrong. The question is, how do we view nature and, equally importantly, how do we view ourselves with respect to nature?

Martin Heidegger (1959, translation 2000) is the person who is most identified with the perspective we are about to discuss. It is known as Phenomenology.

---

**DEFINITION**

**Phenomenology** is the belief that the world around us can only be understood through our lived experiences. The world does not exist beyond those experiences. We impose understandings and interpretations on that world, or worlds, based upon the values, perspectives and beliefs we hold. The relationship between ourselves and nature is a symbiotic one (i.e. mutually dependent) and not one of independence. This perspective has a strong resonance with the discussion earlier in the chapter concerning the way a woodland might be perceived through time.

---

Whilst Heidegger was not the first to challenge the notion that subjects and objects are distinct and separate entities, his analysis was more radical than those who had come before him, for example, Edmund Husserl (1931, 1965), who was Heidegger's teacher. Heidegger died in 1976, so by the standards of notable philosophers his arguments are quite new.

As the definition above indicates, Heidegger's principal argument was that we cannot understand nature other than how we experience it. Nature does not exist beyond our experiences of it. Those experiences might have come to us via first-hand knowledge, or stories, accounts, films, newspapers, books, the Internet, conversations, whatever. When we look at something or hear something, what we see and hear is filtered through our mental faculties, which in turn process information and understanding through many subtle processes including emotions, memories, existing values, beliefs and understandings – essentially our experiences. For example, when we look at something, say an NHS hospital, what do we see? Some would simply say that they see a place where those who are unwell or injured are taken in order to receive treatment. Others might see the building as representing a symbol of a civilised society that has created facilities to tend to the sick or the injured, irrespective of their ability to pay for their treatment. Others might see the building as representing a bundle of resources, which are outstripped by demand for its services. From the latter perspective, the hospital is a cauldron of ethical dilemmas in terms of the choices over which treatments to prioritise and which to de-prioritise.

The same object can represent different visions to different people. Think back to Acitivity 9.6. Why was the place or object you selected special? The answer will be related to the place or object's history. It is likely to hold memories that are important to you. The place or object keeps you in touch with something or someone you want to hold on to. History and context are central to this debate. Were you able to place a monetary value upon your object or place? For some, the importance of the object or the place will be incalculable because of the memories it reveals, what it represents.

Whilst the argument that different people will have different views about the importance of places and objects is reasonably uncontentious, you might ask, 'Are we moving towards a position that simply admits that all we are likely to agree upon is that we are likely to disagree upon the values we are prepared to place upon various objects?' If so, how is this going to help individuals and corporations make choices over the use of natural resources, whether they be tropical rain forests, a local park, playing field, a set of allotments or the survival of a threatened species of animal? Heidegger does not offer a magic formula, but he does offer a way of thinking, a way of seeing, that could prove helpful.

Heidegger's concern was with what he described as the 'enframing of technology', or what we might call a technology mentality, i.e. the seeing of nature as purely instrumental, as simply a means to an end. If nature represents merely the opportunity to make money, if that is all nature means to us, then, from a Heideggerian perspective, society has become emotionally and spiritually bankrupt.

### DEFINITION

If an object is viewed in purely **instrumental** terms then it possesses no worth beyond its functional use, that is, what might be obtained for it by either selling it as it is or converting it into another form of tradable object. It is purely a means to an end. The end in this case is to make money, although this is not the only 'end' that can be considered.

Heidegger was not anti-technology. He recognised the contributions that technological advancements had made, and continue to make, to people's lives. Improvements in sanitation, health care, education, etc. can be seen as benefiting either directly or indirectly from technology. In Heidegger's view, we have a symbiotic relationship with nature, i.e. the relationship between humans and nature is one of mutual dependency. As we exploit nature, we cannot avoid, to a greater or lesser extent, having an impact upon ourselves. In this context 'ourselves' is used in a very broad sense, reflecting impacts not necessarily upon our own generation, but those that are yet to come.

The treatment of nature in purely instrumental ways is not limited to profit seeking organisations. Neither is the 'enframing of technology' limited to capitalist systems. Examples of the destruction of the environment in the name of 'progress' can be seen in many different political and economic contexts. However, in an economic system in which:

(a) the *raison d'être* (the reason for being) of business enterprises is to maximise profits on behalf of shareholders, and

(b) the nature of competitive capitalism is that a company incurring additional costs by way of laudable, but not legally required, pollution controls that result in its being put at a cost and price disadvantage to its competitors is likely to fail,

the question has to be asked, 'How is it possible for corporations to view nature in anything other than an instrumental fashion'? In addition, if we cannot expect everyone to value the same objects that we regard as important as highly as ourselves, and vice versa:

- How can a corporation place a value upon any object, other than in terms of its instrumental worth to the corporation?

- How can objects have meaning to a corporation beyond their functional or instrumental worth?

- Where is a corporation's memory that might allow it to attach feelings to objects that transcend their instrumental worth?

- What is the market value of the site of the Parthenon of ancient Greece to a property developer or, for a mining company, a spectacular ravine in a site of special scientific interest that contains valuable mineral deposits?

## A moment of reflection

We are approaching a possibly critical point in our consideration of sustainability, corporate social responsibility and corporate citizenship, certainly in terms of Heidegger's view of a 'technology mentality'. Asking where a corporation's memory might lie, or whether a corporation can possess feelings towards objects, is attributing human characteristics to business enterprises that many would regard as simply unrealistic, as silly. The technical term is reification, that is, giving concrete (human) form to an abstract idea (a corporation). When we use the term 'corporation' in the sense being discussed here, we are referring to the senior decision-makers. A corporation's 'memory' will reside with individuals, or possibly in the form of company stories and myths. The use of 'corporation' is in fact a form of shorthand.

If corporations can only ever view objects in instrumental ways, then society cannot expect corporations to value and to treat nature in ways that it (society) might wish or demand. To repeat, this is not to suggest that all members of society will hold the same views on particular aspects of nature, but at least a debate can ensue between interested parties about the various merits of different choices under debate. And the debate will embrace many value systems that go beyond instrumentality.

Following Heidegger, the fundamental objection is that corporations *cannot* fully act in socially responsible ways because they possess a perspective on nature that is extremely limited. A societal perspective on nature that is compatible with a Heideggerian perspective is denied to a corporation, as long as corporations are constituted in their current form. Corporations cannot be citizens because their value systems are highly constrained and unable to handle concepts of value beyond instrumentality. A corporation's perspective is 'enframed by technology'. However, this does not dismiss corporations as irrelevancies to modern life. Clearly, business, in its many forms, is fundamental to the way we live. In many respects it is the dominant force in modern societies. The central issue concerns the relationship between corporations and society, but is citizenship a realistic or appropriate concept in this debate? Welford (1995), when discussing issues of sustainable development, referred to this issue when, in the six areas that are argued to require shifts of thinking, he stated that a key transformation is the move from 'objects to relationships'.

## Thinking about the Self and Others

Central to any debate concerning objects and subjects is the notion of the Self. We have referred to ethical egoism on a number of occasions in this chapter, with an example of its manifestation reflected in the previous chapter in Table 8.2 on page 303. This table contrasted the remuneration of executive directors of FTSE 100 between January 2000 and December 2002 (up 84 per cent), with the movement in the FTSE 100 index (down 40 per cent). It is intriguing how the behaviour of corporate executives, in relation to their own remuneration, or the ownership of many, many gas-guzzling motor cars by certain wealthy individuals, is sometimes accepted on the basis that, 'Well, I would do the same in their shoes'! Why is there this apparent acceptance of such behaviour and the belittling of one's own ethics? It might have something to do with the promulgation of the Self as a self-serving, myopic, selfish individual as exemplified in agency theory and ethical egoism.

**DEFINITION**

**Agency theory**, as used here, refers to the division of ownership and control of corporations, with shareholders the principals and management their agents. With human behaviour assumed to be essentially self-seeking and self-focused and management 'enjoying' a privileged control of information over shareholders, this control is assumed to manifest itself in sub-optimum decision making (from the shareholders' perspective), as reflected in Table 8.2.

This view of human nature was argued for by Thomas Hobbes and David Hume among others. Both were eminent philosophers, but their position on this issue is an argument, not a fact, and it is up to us, individually and collectively, to decide where we stand on this issue. If we are to see as 'natural' a regard for the Self as the primary, maybe sole, driver for determining our collective attitudes towards sustainability, who speaks for those who cannot speak, the dispossessed, the unborn? These tensions are explicitly addressed in the following statement taken from the Sustainability Strategy and Action Plan 2000–2005 of the UK's second largest city, Birmingham. A local authority, like Birmingham City Council, has an immensely difficult task to develop a sustainability strategy or, more accurately, a series of sustainability strategies that cohere and are mutually supportive and sustaining. The statement from which the following extract is taken is headed 'The Challenge'.

> A Sustainability Strategy for the City Council could be huge, involving almost every policy and strategy of every department. Clearly this would be undesirably unwieldy. Suffice it to say that Community Safety and Nature Conservation Strategies, policies on Disability, Employment, Equalities and the City's commitment to lifelong learning are a fraction of the existing policies, strategies and actions which are relevant to our drive towards sustainability (p. 3).

Having hinted at the complexity of the task facing the City Council, the 'challenge' is then articulated.

### The Challenge

Delivering sustainability for a large Metropolitan city in the developed world is not an easy or comfortable matter. It is about making choices about the distribution of benefits between generations, and denying people benefits now, for the yet unborn. Such decisions will never be universally popular. There will always be special reasons for not taking the sustainability route. Indeed tensions will sometimes even exist between alternative sustainability options. Facing up to this dilemma is one of the biggest challenges the Council needs to address.

(Sustainability Strategy and Action Plan 2000–2005, Birmingham City Council, p. 4)

Birmingham City Council cite the Brundtland Commission's definition of sustainability (which was shown at the start of this chapter) to define what they mean by sustainability. An interesting definition of sustainable communities and one that offers an insight into the complexity of the notion of sustainable communities is reflected in the UK Government's Sustainable Communities' initiative.

## Sustainable communities                                      DEFINITION

Places where people want to live and work, now and in the future. They meet the diverse needs of existing and future residents, are sensitive to their environment, and contribute to a high quality of life. They are safe and inclusive, well planned, built and run, and offer equality of opportunity and good services for all.

The above reflects the challenges that a sustainability commitment involves, but the philosophical position of the ethical egoist position is a powerful one in modern western societies and it is important that we study the issues in more depth. The discussion which follows explores the issues through the lens provided by Adam Smith, who is sometimes referred to as the father of market-based capitalism.

Smith lived during the eighteenth century and was an acquaintance of David Hume. Smith was a prominent Scottish academic who applied his intellect to a number of fields, but he is most notably remembered for his seminal work, the title of which is usually shortened to *The Wealth of Nations*. This treatise argues for the primacy of market-based capitalism to be the basis for social and economic coordination. However, while markets were his principal means of releasing the individual from the demands of kings, governments and religious interference, Smith's advocacy was conditional and dependent on two central elements, that of *competitive* market-based capitalism and *constrained self-love*.

Smith is referred to as a 'classical economist', which means that he considered economic issues from a broader, more socially inclusive perspective than is allowed or recognised in neo-classical economics. In 1751 and at the age of 28, Smith was appointed to the Chair of Logic at Glasgow University. One year later he was appointed to the Chair of Moral Philosophy. It was from the perspective of a Professor of Moral Philosophy that Smith wrote his two seminal treatises. *The Wealth of Nations* has already been referred to, but the second major treatise to flow from Smith's pen was *The Theory of Moral Sentiments*. The importance of this is that, within *The Wealth of Nations*, Smith did not elaborate on his notion of self-love. However, the concept is explored by Smith in *The Theory of Moral Sentiments*, which was first published in 1759, sixteen years before *The Wealth of Nations* was first published, while the final edition of *The Theory of Moral Sentiments* was published in 1790, the year of Smith's death. Thus, it can be seen that the notion of self-love would have developed as a result of Smith's work on his two famous treatises over a period of some forty years. *The Theory of Moral Sentiments* allows us to understand that Smith's conception of self-love was not the distorted version that travels today under the banner of selfishness, nor as it appears to have become corrupted by certain writers, e.g. Levitt (1956), who argued,

> What is important is that the pursuit of Self-interest has become institutionalized ... this is of the greatest importance for the future of capitalism.
>
> (Levitt, 1956: 109)

As indicated above, although Smith placed competition at the centre of his economic thought, he did not leave his economic ideal to the mercy of rapacious individuals or groups, or imperfections in market conditions. Smith sympathised with Platonic and Aristotelian notions of self-control as a core human virtue in its own right, but his commitment to the importance of self-control within his economic theorising might be argued to be as much prosaic as principled. Self-control was attributed a key position within his economic schema to buttress situations where economic equilibrium would be less than perfect. Self-control was not argued to be regretted, but rather a necessary constraint on human action. Self-control was recognised in respect of freedoms, but not just those of the Self. In sympathy with Aristotelian arguments, the perception of Others was also important.

Smith's recognition of Others was more than a recognition of the plight of others out of a sense of pity. Smith used the term 'sympathy', with this describing a notion of empathy, a 'fellow-feeling'. The opening sentence of *The Theory of Moral Sentiments* reads as follows:

How selfish soever man may be supposed, there are evidently some principles in his nature, which interest him in the fortunes of others, and render their happiness necessary to him, though he derives nothing from it, except the pleasure of seeing it.

(Smith, 2000: I, 3)

The recognition of Others and their interests, whilst not equating to altruism, leads to Smith's important mechanism for operationalising his conception of self-control. The notion of fellow-feeling has been termed 'imaginative sympathy' (Wilson and Skinner, 1976), allowing an understanding to be developed of the position of other people by trying to view our own conduct through their eyes. As Wilson observed,

To use Smith's own imagery, we learn to observe our own behaviour as it might be seen by an imaginary spectator who is at once impartial and well-informed with regard to our motives.

(Wilson, 1976: 74)

Smith used the idea of a 'stranger' or 'spectator' to convey the imagery of an independent arbiter, unfettered by bias and preconceptions.

The constancy or equality of temper which is more valuable for Smith than virtues like humanity, generosity etc., is obtained through a society where everyone has continuously tried to moderate his emotions … everyone is accustomed to think how Others will judge his action and passion and to act accordingly … and … it must be repeated that Self-control in Smith cannot be established without the judgement of strangers.

(Skinner and Wilson, 1975: 122)

In a footnote Skinner and Wilson add,

The stranger is not a friend from whom we can expect any special favour and sympathy. But at the same time he is not an enemy from whom we cannot expect any sympathy at all. Everyone in society is as independent of every other stranger, and is equal with every other as they can exchange the situations. The famous impartial stranger is no one else but the spectator who is indifferent to, and does not take the part of either side.

(Skinner and Wilson, 1975: 122)

Smith argued that man is keen to obtain the respect of Others, but, because this is insufficient to ensure appropriate behaviour, he also argued that man is subject to two forms of jurisdiction, that of conscience (the man within) and that of the 'spectator' (the man without) (Smith, 1776/1982: 20/1).

The above represents a portrayal of Smith's notions of the Self that runs counter to the *a priori* assumptions of man as self-serving, atomised egoist for whom self-love equates with selfishness, traits that are to be found at the root of ethical egoism and agency theory. However, the atomisation of the individual, so dominant in neo-classical economics, is also observable in other disciplines. In political science the elevation of the Self as consumer, but with little other political relevance, was commented upon by Nisbet over fifty years ago.

> The politics of enslavement of man requires the emancipation of man from all the authorities and memberships ... that serve, one degree or another, to insulate the individual from the external political power ... totalitarian domination of the individual will is not a mysterious process, not a form of sorcery based upon some vast and unknowable irrationalism. It arises and proceeds rationally and relentlessly through the creation of new functions, statuses and allegiances which, by conferring community, makes the manipulation of the human will scarcely more than an exercise in scientific, social psychology ... there may be left the appearance of individual freedom, provided it is only individual freedom. All of this is unimportant, always subject to guidance and control, if the primary social contexts of belief and opinion are properly organized and managed. What is central is the creation of a network of functions and loyalties reaching down into the most intimate recesses of human life where ideas and beliefs will germinate and develop.
>
> (Nisbet, 1953: 202, 208)

Sarason (1986) echoed Nisbet's concerns. The following paraphrases Sarason, setting his argument at the general level of concern about modern conceptions of individualism.

> If *your* ethical dilemma is *your* responsibility according to *my* morality, this is quite consistent with the increasingly dominant ideology of individual rights, responsibility, choice and freedom. If *I* experience the issues as *yours*, it is because there is nothing in my existence to make it *ours*. And by *ours* I mean a social-cultural network and traditions which engender in members an obligation to be part of the problem and possible solution.

One line of thinking has been that the primacy of the Self has been reinforced by the attention given in psychology, and more particularly psychoanalysis, to patients being directed to 'look within' and to see solutions to their personal problems taking the form of much greater attention to the Self – to be far more self-aware and self-actualising. Goodwin (1974: 75), cited in Wallach and Wallach (1983), observed,

> The ideology of individualism is so powerful that we ... look on bonds as restraints; values as opinions and prejudices; customs as impositions.
>
> (Goodwin, 1974: 75)

Within this conception the Self is seen as a fully autonomous unit that should be responsible to no authority in the forming of its relationships beyond the exercise of its own volition – what it voluntarily wills and wishes to do. The social arrangements remaining that permit a sense of community or shared social purpose 'are assaulted as unjust restraints on liberty, impediments to the free assertion of the self' (Goodwin, 1974: 75). The proper mode of living is to be oneself – to find out who one is and to let no one and nothing interfere with one's self-realisation. This is ethical egoism in its raw form.

Challenging psychoanalysis's focus upon the Self, to the exclusion of broader social relationships and behaviours, Wallach and Wallach (1983) asserted,

> If, ..... human beings can be motivated towards ends quite other than them-selves, and it is in fact better for them when this is the case, then perhaps the usual lines of therapeutic advice might well be redirected. The problems and troubles that lead people to seek psychotherapy may derive less than is com-monly supposed from not expressing themselves, fulfilling themselves, or satisfying needs directed toward themselves and more from not having a workable way of living in which they participate in and contribute to matters they care about beyond themselves.
>
> (Wallach and Wallach, 1983: 274)

Maybe we need to think more carefully before accepting the arguments of agency theory and ethical egoism that human beings are by nature self-serving, possessively egoistic, with little other consideration than their own well-being. As in psychoanalysis, we need to think afresh about both the empirical and philosophical justification of this position. The assumptions concerning human behaviour explicit within agency theory and ethical egoism to explain the behaviour of senior corporate executives might simply be philosophical camou-flage to mask the greed of those in privileged and powerful positions.

Smith was not blind to the risks of competitive capitalism, hence his advocacy of self-control, a virtue that appears to be in very short supply in many corporate board rooms (as evidenced by Table 8.2). What might be the issue is that too many corporate executives lack a fundamental quality of Smith's advocacy of competitive market-based capitalism. Do contemporary corporate executives (as well as politicians) possess the requisite qualities and values that issues, develop-ments and challenges such as the GHG emissions, the power of large corporations, global poverty, and the exploitation of weak and corrupt govern-ments, require?

## Is it all doom and gloom?

There is much within modern experiences to make the heart heavy with con-cern, but it would clearly be a fundamental mistake to imply that all corporate executives are greedy individuals with no care for the environment, or that cor-porate activity is exclusively negative, both socially and environmentally. Although one or two examples of impressive individual and/or corporate activity 'do not a summer make', it is important to be aware of the excellent initiatives that are under way at the local and individual (including corporate) level to address sustainability issues, and which in some cases have been established for some time. The following are some examples of organisations that are working with corporations to develop more sustainable processes, practices, attitudes and beliefs. The last two elements are possibly the most important because without them changes to processes and practices are likely to be short-lived and/or poorly implemented and operationalised.

| Case study 9.4 | **Capital *One*** |
|---|---|

In the corporate sector the company Capital *One* is a large credit card organisation. It has a 'corporate responsibility' team of four full-time employees, headed by a 'Corporate Social Responsibility Manager'. The initiative to establish the team came from the main board and replicates its American parent company's belief in corporate responsibility. A 'corporate responsibility' commitment was not the result of the company receiving bad publicity and feeling the need to be 'seen to be doing something'. At one level it might be argued that all the company is displaying is a form of enlightened self-interest, in that by performing good deeds it wishes to attract employment applications from high-quality people who wish to work for such an organisation. The company does not dispute that it hopes to attract 'better' applicants for posts at the company, but the primary stimulus is the belief of the senior management that 'this is the way companies should behave'. The company does not publicise many of the projects in which it becomes involved, the reason being that it does not wish to be accused of merely undertaking the projects to obtain the favourable publicity. It is something of a Catch 22 situation, with the company potentially damned if it does and damned if it doesn't.

An example of one of the projects with which it has been involved relates to the collaboration between the company's programming team and Nottinghamshire Police Force. Following the murder of two young girls in Soham, UK, the Nottinghamshire Police Force wished to create a database of all known paedophiles; however, they lacked the expertise to do this. The programming team of Capital *One*, over a period of some months, developed the database, which has now been adopted by other police forces in the UK. Initially the company kept its involvement in the project low-key. It was only when the system was rolled out to a number of other police forces that it publicly acknowledged its collaboration.

| Case study 9.5 | **The Citizen Group** |
|---|---|

The Citizen Group is an interesting organisation, noted for its watches and other timepieces. The reason for featuring the corporation is not so much for any specific 'good deeds', but rather the company's broader commitment to notions of corporate citizenship. The President of the company heads the 'Citizen CSR Committee', which was instituted in October 2003. The company has developed a 'Citizen Code of Conduct' that speaks to the corporation's values and ethics. The code has eight commitments, with commitments 1–4 concerned with, respectively, products and services; open competition; corporate information; and a respectful environmental policy. These are laudable and hopefully reasonably standard commitments. For our purposes, in terms of corporations that appear to be moving beyond specific but localised CSR initiatives, the Citizen Group displays in commitments 5–8 an articulation of a corporation that does appear to be 'walking the talk' of corporate citizenship (the name of the corporation being highly apposite).

| No. | Commitment |
| --- | --- |
| 5 | Value symbiosis with the regional society as a good corporate citizen, and strive to make a social contribution. |
| 6 | Ensure a safe and good work environment, encourage the development of our employees' abilities and energies while respecting their character and individuality. |
| 7 | Respond to anti-social and corruptive behaviour in a decisive manner. |
| 8 | Value and respect different cultures and customs in foreign countries and contribute to the development of the locale. |

In an extract from the company's 2004 'Environmental and Social Report' (p. 26), the following statements appear.

In my view [Chair of the CSR Committee] CSR initiatives are an integral part of our business activities. It's not something new that we have to begin. Rather, the way I see it, what we need to do is have a fresh look at our business activities in the context of our relationships with the various stakeholders who support Citizen, and ask anew how we can put this new CSR approach into our business activities ... last year when other companies in Japan suffered from various corporate scandals, I felt that Citizen's culture served us well as a precious asset to help us avoid such problems. Now that Citizen has announced CSR as an important pillar of management, I would like to do my best to help preserve our corporate culture, robustness, honesty and openness.

**Case study 9.6**

## The 'DEEP' fish restaurant chain

A fish restaurant chain was established in 2005, trading under the name 'DEEP'. The menu in the restaurants is limited to only those fish that are *not* 'at risk'. So you will not find Atlantic cod, haddock, blue fin tuna, monkfish or halibut on the menu. Instead there are herring, mackerel and pollack, and others whose stocks are not endangered. The restaurant chain is committed to serving only fish that are taken from the sea within a sustainable fishing policy. Interestingly, fish farms, because of health and safety concerns, as well as the practice of feeding fish sprats to the salmon in the form of food pellets, are not regarded as an appropriate source. In addition, the restaurant chain makes an explicit statement that £1 is added to every bill, which will be used as a donation to a named pressure group that is lobbying for sustainable fishing policies throughout the world.

These are encouraging developments from the corporate world. Moving to the non-profit seeking organisation, a number of interesting developments can be cited, of which the following are but illustrative.

| Case study 9.7 | **The Natural Step Organisation** |
| --- | --- |

The Natural Step Organisation was founded in 1989 by Dr Karl-Henrik Robèrt, who at the time was a leading Swedish oncologist (cancer specialist). Dr Robèrt had become concerned about a significant increase in childhood leukaemia cases in particular parts of Sweden, and traced the cause to increasing toxins in the environment. These appeared to have been the result of particular production processes. Dr Robèrt's concern at the production methods used to manufacture so many goods led him to found The Natural Step Organisation to address the systemic causes of environmental problems. Society's apparent preferencing of commercial activity has echoes of Heidegger's 'enframing of technology' or 'technology mindset'.

With the help of fifty Swedish scientists, Dr Robèrt developed a consensus document that described the basic knowledge of the earth's functions and how humans interact with it. The organisation's website tells how the document went through 21 iterations and upon completion was sent to every household and school in Sweden.

In the early 1990s, Dr Robèrt worked with physicist, John Holmberg, to define a set of guiding principles for a sustainable society that are based on the laws of thermodynamics and natural cycles. These principles of sustainability are the foundation of The Natural Step's content and approach. The organisation now has centres in many countries, with its American operations having been established in 1995. The Natural Step Organisation works with corporations and governments in developing sustainable programmes of industrial and commercial activity, but that is not to say that its four guiding principles are easily absorbed within many corporate practices. Changes are required.

| Case study 9.8 | **The Sustainability Institute** |
| --- | --- |

The Sustainability Institute was founded in 1996 and possesses an interesting statement of its philosophy.

> Unsustainability does not arise out of ignorance, irrationality or greed. It is largely the collective consequence of rational, well-intended decisions made by people caught-up in systems – ranging from families and communities to corporations, governments and economies – that make it difficult or impossible to act in ways that are fully responsible to all those affected in the present and future generations.

(http://www.sustainabilityinstitute.org)

Once again the issue of an 'enframing technology' mind-set underpins the perspective. We are dealing with, in many respects, a need to change people's assumptions about what is possible and acceptable in terms of sustainable systems, communities, economies and societies. However, it must be stressed that what sustainable futures will look like is up to people, individually and collectively, to negotiate, debate and work towards. The mission statement of The Sustainability Institute adopts just this line of reasoning. It possesses three elements, namely:

- to shift mind-sets – values, attitudes and beliefs – when they are out of step with the realities of a finite planet and a globally dominant human race;

- to restructure systems when the rewards and incentives of the system are inconsistent with long-term social, environmental and economic goals; and

- to build the capability to manage and learn in complex, environmental, social and economic systems.

| Case study 9.9 | **The Sustainable Business Institute** |

The Sustainable Business Institute (SBI) is another organisation that seeks to work with corporations to address the challenges of sustainable economic, social and environmental systems.

The SBI was founded in 1994 and aims to educate senior executives about 'what is sustainability' and how sustainable practices are working effectively across industries. In sympathy with the Global Compact's approach of disseminating good practice, the SBI places considerable emphasis upon using workshops, forums and the media, particularly television programmes, to spread its ideas and approaches among senior executives.

| Case study 9.10 | **The International Institute for Sustainable Development** |

The International Institute for Sustainable Development (IISD) was established in 1990 and aims to contribute to sustainable development by advancing policy recommendations in a number of areas, *viz.*

- international trade and investment,

- economic policy,

- climate change,

- measurement and indicators, and

- natural resource management.

By using Internet communications the IISD aims to report on international negotiations and broker knowledge gained through collaborative projects with global partners, resulting in more rigorous research, capacity building in developing countries and better dialogue between North and South.

**Case study
9.11**

### The Institute for Market Transformation to Sustainability

The Institute for Market Transformation to Sustainability (MTS) is another organisation with a commitment to exploring, identifying and supporting sustainable economic activity. However, this organisation is much more upbeat and bullish about the power of markets to be the force in activating change, albeit with an initial helping hand. Its website includes the following statement.

MTS brings together a powerful coalition of sustainable products manufacturers, environmental groups, and key state and local government leaders using market mechanisms [to] increase sales and market share of sustainable products. We have identified consensus protocols for sustainable products such as FSC Certified Wood, Certified Organic Products, and the Clean Car Standard. When such a consensus is reached, the next steps are to increase awareness and sales of these products until profit motives and other marketplace incentives kick in and drive the transformation. Awareness and sales are manageable steps. ... Because the 100 largest companies account for more than 90% of the world's products, our mission is attainable. All companies want to increase their profits while contributing to an unpolluted, safer environment, and improved public welfare. ... Sustainable products increase corporate profits while enhancing society as a whole, because they are cheaper to make, have fewer regulatory constraints, less liability, can be introduced to the market quicker, and are preferred by the public.

(http://mts.sustainableproducts.com)

The commitment to the notion of markets being the primary, if not exclusive, driver of sustainable development is contestable, for such an approach requires that:

(a) all the salient facts can be expressed in numerical form;

(b) all the salient information (including that relating to the preferences of future generations) can be articulated in the final 'market' price; and

(c) all decisions are simply the art, or science, of obtaining the 'right balance' of resource usage and that placing the resource in the hands of those who are able to pay the highest price is the most appropriate 'solution'.

The first two points are concerned with the feasibility of developing inclusive and articulate prices. The third and final point is one that raises profound philosophical issues, both political and ethical.

Moving to the academic community, we find that a number of universities have established sustainability research centres such as:

- the **Sustainable Futures Institute** at Michigan Technological University, USA;

- the **Sustainable Development Research Initiative** at the University of British Columbia, Canada;

- the **World Business Council for Sustainable Development**, which has close links with the Royal Melbourne Institute of Technology, Australia;

- the **Institute of Sustainable Development in Business** at Nottingham Trent University, England; and

- the **Sustainable Development Research Centre**, at Forres, Scotland, which has strong links with St Andrews University, Scotland, and the University of the Highlands and Islands, Scotland.

All of these institutes, and the many more that exist, are important developments. Local, grassroots initiatives are necessary developments for sustainable communities and societies. However, for the national and global sustainability agendas to be adequately addressed, there is an unavoidable need for the active and sincere engagement of large corporations and governments. As the MTS website announces, the largest 100 corporations account for 90 per cent of the world's production output. Without these corporations 'on board' and the active support of governments in encouraging and enforcing sustainable economic, social and environmental policies, all the individual initiatives, as important as they are, will not be anywhere near sufficient to address the pressing sustainability problems.

## The triple bottom line

A phrase that was in vogue in the early 2000s was to talk of organisations having a 'triple bottom line', as distinct from the traditional use of the term 'bottom line' meaning simply profit. The triple bottom line encompasses economic, social and environmental concerns, but its articulation and operationalisation has remained problematic. Explanations of what is meant by 'triple bottom line' do not suggest an equal weighting being given to the three elements. Birch (2001), in reviewing a draft charter of corporate citizenship developed by BP Australia, referred to a statement contained within the draft charter. Under the heading 'sustainable development' the following statement appeared.

> BP is committed to a socially, environmentally and economically responsible business. This means maximising profit in order to create wealth and sustainable jobs, always intending to have a positive social and environmental impact.
>
> (Birch, 2001: 62)

The reference to maximising profit is interesting. Within the draft charter no attempt is made to discuss the tension between this commitment and the commitments made to the social and environmental issues mentioned elsewhere in the draft charter. However, Birch does refer to earlier discussions with BP Australia during which these issues appeared to have been raised.

> The tensions between capitalism and democracy as currently defined are irreconcilable without serious change. We agreed that we could not achieve long-term sustainability without change. Business needs, therefore, significant policy directions to enable this change to occur, not just within business practices but also within society overall.
>
> (Birch, 2001: 59)

The phrase 'business needs ... significant policy directions' refers directly to the need for a 'sovereign power', à la Hobbes. There is no suggestion that business can be assumed to resolve these tensions itself. The 'hidden hand' of the market is viewed as too unreliable to be left to its own devices in this context.

The triple bottom line is part of the Global Reporting Initiative (GRI) which in turn is a voluntary initiative that has so far been through two iterations. As we write the second edition of this book, the GRI team is receiving comments and advice from users and preparers as to how the GRI reporting requirements should be developed for the future. The process is open, mirroring the GRI's commitment to a stakeholder approach to corporate reporting. The third version of the GRI is due in 2006.

The current requirements of the GRI require organisations to report on corporate environmental, social and economic performance information, in essence a corporation's sustainability performance. There are five framework documents to the GRI, which are:

- Sustainability reporting guidelines (these are core requirements for all organisations).

- Sector supplements (which indicate additional information for different sectors, if such information is available).

- Technical protocols (these provide details of individual indicators, their definition, formulae and cross-referencing to minimise problems in comparability).

- Issue guidance documents (which are non-sector specific issues affecting a range of organisations, such as 'diversity' and 'productivity'), which all lead to:

- The Sustainability Report.

## A two-way social contract?

What every sustainability and corporate responsibility initiative has to recognise and accept is that with the best will in the world, business corporations, in the form of their chief executives, have to be competitive in their respective marketplaces. Until consumers not only express a wish for corporations to move beyond legal minima, but are prepared, in certain cases, to pay slightly higher prices for products or services produced and delivered in ways that are more socially or environmentally sensitive than rival products, then corporate executives will feel there is too much hypocrisy and double standards in many of the corporate responsibility debates. The social contract, which was discussed in Chapter 8, tends to be presented as a one-way contract, that is, the conditions within the contract are placed exclusively upon corporations for them to maintain their (theoretical) 'licence to operate'. This poses a significant and fundamental question.

## A fundamental question

Do the demands of global environmental and social issues, as articulated in the Global Compact, suggest that we must think more carefully about the notion of a two-way social contract?

What do we mean by this?

The transfer of production capacity to less-developed economies is not only a reflection of capital seeking out the most profitable investment opportunities, but is also evidence of the perpetual downward pressure on prices. The 'real' (inflation adjusted) cost of many products has been and continues downwards. For most customers, assuming the quality differential is not too marked, then price is a/the critical purchase criterion. Corporate executives need to feel reassured that, assuming any price differential between their own products and those of their competitors can be explained by the more environmentally and/or socially sensitive policies of their organisation, then consumers will respect this and not prejudice the more sustainable policies of the company by switching their purchasing allegiance to companies with lower prices but less sustainable policies. In this respect governments have a potentially important part to play in either rewarding companies that operate with leading-edge environmental and social policies or penalising those that do not. Such interventions could be via grants, tax concessions or tax penalties. Such an approach might be anathema to market fundamentalists, but 'the market' (or more particularly 'the consumer') might be too capricious and fickle a coordinating mechanism in these circumstances to be seen as the principal tool for resource allocation. Is there a need for a term such as 'consumer social responsibility'?

These issues reflect the profoundly important debates that need to be increasingly part of political and social agendas.

## Summary

In this chapter the following key points have been made:

- The notion of sustainability should be seen as the symbiotic relationship between social, economic and environmental issues.

- Different ethical stances can be drawn upon to support particular sustainability positions.

- However, weighting the different claims in a utilitarian analysis can be extremely problematic. Not all those involved in or affected by a decision should necessarily attract the same level of importance.

- The leadership required of all political leaders concerning sustainability issues and the global crises of extreme poverty, child labour, inhuman working conditions, global warming, greenhouse gas emissions and political corruption has been found wanting.

- However, the decision by Global Compact to by-pass the political processes in 1999 and to go directly to the largest corporations to gain their active support in addressing the great global challenges of our time has, with hindsight, been recognised as flawed. Notwithstanding their poor track records, governments have to be a critical part of the strategies to address the many sustainability issues.

- Exclusive reliance upon the price mechanism to adjudicate and reflect societal preferences over sustainability issues has a number of profound weaknesses.

- The 'enframing of technology' mindset has to be successfully challenged.

- Current debates and demands concerning sustainable corporate practices tend to exclude the role consumers and governments can/must play in supporting those corporations employing sustainable and responsible practices and processes.

- The choices before us involve many issues, but above all they are choices that speak to the ethics and morals that we wish to underpin our communities and societies.

## Quick revision test

1. Is the price mechanism without blemish as the key mechanism for resolving societies' preferences for addressing global warming issues?

2. What is meant by the phrase 'the enframing of technology'?

3. What is meant by the environment being socially constructed?

4. Who is the philosopher normally associated with the phrase 'the enframing of technology'?

5. What is the difference between Adam Smith's notion of self-love and selfishness?

6. What might be meant by 'consumer social responsibility'?

7. What is the triple bottom line?

## Typical assignments and briefs

1. In the context of global warming, debate the appropriateness of the price mechanism as the primary democratic tool of resource allocation.

2. Critically evaluate Heidegger's notion of the 'enframing of technology' in terms of its contribution to debates concerning global economic growth rate forecasts.

3. Discuss the notion that 'consumer social responsibility is as important as corporate social responsibility'.

4. Evaluate the usefulness of Adam Smith's 'stranger' to debates concerning corporate executive behaviour and sustainable business practices.

## Group activity 9

For Group Activity 8, you established an investment portfolio of ten companies. Having considered the issues covered in Chapter 9, you are now required to carry out the following tasks.

1. Revisit your investment principles to consider whether you wish to amend, add to or subtract from your previously agreed principles.

2. Decide whether you are comfortable with the ten corporations you have in your portfolio. You are allowed to make any changes you wish, but the final number of corporations in your portfolio must remain ten.

3. During the group session you will be provided with two sets of information of the share prices of quoted companies, taken from the financial pages of daily newspapers. One set will be dated within seven days of the group session, while the other will be twelve months old. From these two sets of information you will identify how the share prices of the companies in your portfolio have moved during the past twelve months, both absolutely and in terms of the sector index. You can include the dividend return in your calculations if this information is available, but for the purposes of the exercise it is not crucial.

4. Within your teams, you can briefly discuss your level of satisfaction with your portfolio's performance and whether you would wish to make any further changes to your portfolio.

5. You should prepare to discuss your team's judgement on your portfolio's performance, whether you have intentions to make adjustments and the basis for your decisions.

6. You should consider (with complete honesty and openness) how the issues of sustainability and social practices weighed

   • in your initial portfolio selection; and

   • in your considerations about possible changes your team might make in the light of the first year's financial performance.

7. You should also consider the knowledge that, in your employment as a portfolio manager, 40 per cent of your personal remuneration package is represented by a performance-related payment, based upon the financial performance of your team's portfolio's performance, and this payment is calculated every three months, i.e. it is not based upon the overall performance of your portfolio for the full twelve months, but is calculated for each quarter.

## Recommended further reading

The most useful book on the issues covered in this chapter is Redclift, M. (1987) *Sustainable Development: Exploring the contradictions*, London: Routledge.

## Useful websites

| Topic | Website provider | URL |
| --- | --- | --- |
| Sustainability | The Sustainability Institute | http://www.sustainabilityinstitute.org |
| | The Sustainable Business Institute | http://www.sustainablebusiness.org |
| | The International Institute for Sustainable Development | http://www.iisd.org |
| | The Sustainable Futures Institute | http://www.sustainablefutures.mtu.edu |
| | The Sustainable Development Research Centre | http://www.sustainableresearch.com/about-sustainable-research/news.asp |
| | The Institute for Sustainable Development in Business | http://www2.ntu.ac.uk/susdev/about_us.htm |

# CHAPTER 10

# Ethical conformance: codes, standards, culture, leadership and citizen power

## Learning outcomes

Having read this chapter and completed its associated activities, readers should be able to:

- Discuss the pressures upon organisations to employ codes of practice.

- Differentiate between various types of codes.

- Describe the practical problems faced when drafting codes.

- Understand the arguments for and against the employment of codes of practice within organisations.

- Show an awareness that codes of practice can sometimes conflict with one another, creating organisational tensions.

- Understand the significance and power of organisational culture and unwritten codes of conduct.

- Evaluate the role of ethical leadership.

- Evaluate the role of public pressure on maintaining organisational good behaviour.

## Introduction

This chapter considers the developments that have become evident as the attention paid to ethical issues in business has intensified. Broadly speaking, these developments have reflected reactions to one or more problems affecting either a specific firm or an industrial/commercial sector. Sometimes developments can be seen in the form of organisations and/or groups of companies working in tandem, sometimes with governments and/or pressure groups, to draw up codes of practice and conduct.

The International Labour Organisation (ILO) argued that worldwide interest in corporate codes of conduct was initially awakened in the 1980s by scandals in the US defence industry and the overt greed that was displayed on Wall Street. The ILO sees business ethics as a way for companies to promote self-regulation, thereby deterring government intervention and possible regulatory action.

Corporate interest quickly led to the institutionalisation of business ethics programmes, consisting largely of codes of conduct, ethics officers and ethics training. However, Brytting (1997) cited the Zeiss organisation as having a recognisable code of conduct for its employees in 1896, and Mill, writing in 1861 but cited by Warren (1993: 187), observed that 'it is the business of ethics to tell us what our duties are or by what test we may know them'. It has been argued that the more recent increase in the growth of corporate codes of conduct relates to the potential for such codes to reduce corporate exposure to punitive damages in claims of negligence. As Warren (1993: 109) observed in terms of the situation in the United States,

> The 1984 Sentencing Reform Act and the US Sentencing Commission's 1991 Federal Guidelines for Sentencing Organisations, allow for a fine on a corporation to be reduced by up to 95% if it can show that it has an effective program to prevent and detect violations of law.

Attempts to reduce negligence claims are not the only reason for organisations to be seen to be addressing the ethicality of their practices. Multi-national corporations (MNCs) are not only increasingly powerful, but also open to critical scrutiny of any of their practices in all parts of the world. MNCs thus have a vested interest in harmonising and standardising practices throughout their respective organisations in order to minimise the risk of aberrant behaviour. We consider later in this chapter the initiatives being employed by MNCs to address concerns about their practices and those of their supplier networks.

## An overview of the pressures upon organisations for ethical development

Figure 10.1 reflects the differing pressures on organisations to institute and formalise their ethical practices.

Of all the connections depicted in Figure 10.1, the only unbroken line is that between 'Governments' and 'The organisation'. This reflects the mandatory nature of laws, as opposed to the other relationships that are characterised by frameworks, agreements, codes, understandings or memoranda, none of which is legally binding. The agreements, or framework documents, between governments and MNCs reflect the dilemma faced by many governments, particularly those of developing countries. The presence of MNCs within the host country can bring the prospect of accelerated economic development, but the support, incentives and conditions that must be agreed to by the host government, in the face of alternative offers by other countries to the MNCs, can weaken the host government's bargaining powers. In such circumstances, legislation is unlikely to be deemed 'appropriate' to control the operations of the MNCs, and more adaptive, negotiable instruments such as framework agreements, or codes,

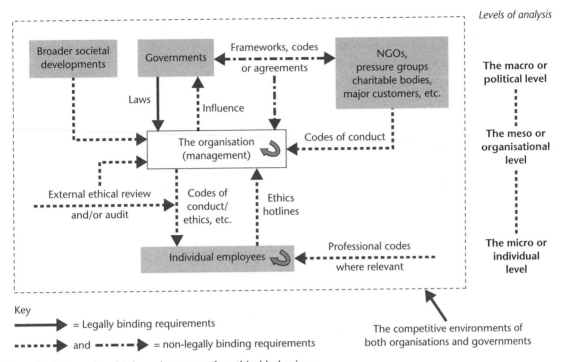

Figure 10.1 Formal and informal pressures for ethical behaviour

become the norm. The non-legally binding agreements or codes of practice may be developed with or without the involvement of pressure groups and interested charitable bodies.

In turn, non-governmental bodies (NGOs), pressure groups and charitable bodies can exert pressure upon organisations independently of governments by developing their preferred codes of practice for business organisations and then contrasting these codes with the behaviour of specific organisations. These comparisons can reveal considerable discrepancies between espoused and actual behaviour and, given the glare of national and international publicity, can involve discussions about change. These relationships are reflected in the additional lines emanating from the 'NGOs, pressure groups'- box and going towards the 'The organisation' box. Organisations such as Greenpeace, Friends of the Earth and the International Baby Food Action Network (IBFAN) are notable in this field.

Business organisations do not have to wait for external pressure before they act to enhance their own practices and behaviour. We illustrate below examples of ethical initiatives that appear to have come from within organisations, although the initiatives may have been in anticipation of government or pressure group involvement if the organisation did not respond in some way to an ethical issue.

There are examples of cooperation and collaboration between governments and pressure groups, between pressure groups and organisations/industries and between governments, pressure groups and business organisations, that appear to be addressing matters of ethical concern in effective ways. We also highlight, however, examples of apparent 'good' practice, which, when carefully scrutinised, are possibly less effective than they might at first appear.

Within Figure 10.1 the introduction of a corporate code of conduct by an employing organisation is shown by the downward-pointing arrow, aimed at 'Individual employees'. This is because such codes are invariably the result of a 'top-down initiative', with relatively little, or no, involvement from non-senior managerial staff. These codes tend to be statements of how employees are required to behave by the company/senior management.

> **Connexion point**
>
> However, companies can also incorporate 'ethics hotlines' to allow those employees with concerns about the ethicality of particular business practices to express their concerns, as we discussed in Chapter 7. These organisational vents can be both important mechanisms for concerned employees to express their worries, and effective early warning systems for organisations about potentially damaging practices and behaviour.

Both the ethics hotlines and the codes of conduct can be supported by external ethical review, e.g. an annual or periodic ethics audit, but because all of these mechanisms are optional they are shown as broken lines.

An important point to emphasise is that the 'Codes of conduct, etc.' link between 'The organisation' and 'Individual employees' is not just about codes of conduct. The 'etc.' encompasses a range of other ways of communicating, inculcating and nurturing corporate values. McDonald and Nijhof (1999) cited:

- training
- story telling
- reward systems
- monitoring systems
- communication channels
- job design
- ethics officers
- information systems
- recruitment and selection policies and processes, and
- organisational strategies

as further examples of ways in which organisations can influence the values and practices that become accepted as 'the ways things are done around here'. Many of these elements come within what is known as organisational culture. This is a very significant area, upon which many books have been written. A consideration of some of the important issues of organisational culture for values and ethics, and vice versa, is undertaken towards the end of this chapter.

The arrows within 'The organisation' and 'Individual employees' boxes that appear to turn on themselves indicate that neither organisations, nor individuals, should expect or passively wait for developments on ethical behaviour to be externally imposed or influenced. If terms such as 'learning organisation' and 'reflective practitioner' are to mean anything, they will need to be evident in the critical reflection of both organisations and individuals on their respective practices. In many respects the integrity with which organisations and individuals reflect upon notions of ethicality are fundamental elements of Figure 10.1. If change is only ever externally stimulated, rather than the result of internal reflection and action, then such change is subject to whims and pressures that will not necessarily be rooted in well-argued principles and values.

The arrow moving from the 'The organisation' to 'Governments' acknowledges that business organisations are not passive or disinterested bystanders in the development of laws affecting corporate practice. This arrow acknowledges the quite significant influence that specific organisations and industrial/commercial sectors can have on governments and the laws that are passed. Equally, it must be emphasised that the whole of Figure 10.1 sits within a commercial and competitive environment that bears upon the practices of individuals, organisations and governments.

## The levels of analysis

Researchers and organisations that study and work with the many issues that comprise business ethics and values tend to do so from one of three perspectives, as reflected in the column on the right-hand side of Figure 10.1. These levels are the macro or political level, the meso or organisational level and the micro or individual level. Those working at the macro-political level are seeking to understand, and possibly influence, the way that political and particularly economic systems impact upon broad national and societal issues. Examples of interesting monitoring organisations that operate at national and international government levels include Transparency International and One World Trust. Their respective websites are provided in the list of business ethics resources on the World Wide Web at the end of the chapter.

At the meso, or organisational, level we find pressure groups, professional associations, trade bodies and labour organisations which are working to monitor, analyse, understand, support, defend and develop the ethicality of business practice within organisations. Researchers working at this level study issues such as ethical awareness and training programmes; the development of corporate codes of conduct and/or ethics; and controversies such as those relating to the production, distribution and selling of bananas; the retailing of breastmilk substitutes in developing countries; and sweatshop and child labour issues. In addition to the material on the websites given at the end of the chapter, there are some interesting ideas and arguments concerning ethical development at the organisational level in Schein (1992); Watson (1994); Fineman and Gabriel (1996); McDonald and Nijhof (1999); Gabriel, Fineman and Sims (2000); and Sternberg (2000).

At the individual level we find debates and research that consider the possibilities for moral agency in organisations. This level is discussed in a number of places in this book, but particularly Chapter 7.

## Codes of conduct and codes of ethics

In market contexts where competitive forces are significant, consistency in all aspects of an organisation's operations is imperative. In order to stimulate, foster and maintain consistency in the behaviour of employees, consistency that also reflects the standards of behaviour that an organisation wishes its employees to adopt, organisations often develop codes of conduct and ethics. A distinction can be made between codes of ethics and codes of conduct that is helpful in examining the roles these types of statements perform. Although this distinction is not universally employed, indeed you may find some organisations employing codes of ethics that by our definition would be classed as codes of conduct, it offers some insight into the purpose of such codes. A study by Farrell and Cobbin (1996) discusses variations between codes of conduct and codes of ethics and the findings of this study add support to the distinction. A much higher level of prescription was found in the codes of conduct studied (average number of rules equalled 30.6), compared with the average number of rules contained in the codes of ethics (16.5).

---

**DEFINITIONS**

*Codes of conduct* tend to be instructions, or sets of rules, concerning behaviour. As a result they are likely to be reasonably prescriptive and proscriptive concerning particular aspects of employee behaviour. They identify specific acts that must be either adhered to (prescription), or avoided (proscription). However, the extent to which all possible situations can be addressed within a code of conduct is problematic.

*Codes of ethics* tend to be reasonably general in their tenor, encouraging employees to display particular characteristics such as loyalty, honesty, objectivity, probity and integrity. They do not normally address specific types of decisions; rather they encourage the application of what might be called 'virtues', although, as noted in Chapter 3, what are regarded as virtues can vary over time. While notions of honesty and integrity remain fairly constant over time, concepts such as justice and loyalty are more contentious.

---

From these definitions it is evident that, where all possible scenarios that an employee might face can be predicted with a high degree of confidence, as well all the circumstances relating to those scenarios, then a specific code of conduct might be possible, because ethical judgement becomes redundant. However, where the likely scenarios that an employee might face cannot be predicted in the requisite detail, then reference to general qualities and principles will be preferred, i.e. codes of ethics become more appropriate.

The risk of confusing these two general positions is that, if a code of conduct fails to address a particular scenario that an employee actually faces, then the silence of the code on the matter in question might be interpreted by the employee as an indication that the employing organisation is at best indifferent to the ethics of the decision in hand.

In this discussion the employee might be said to be (or be treated as) morally immature, requiring a code of conduct or ethics to act as a reference point in times of need, but that is just what codes imply. By issuing such codes, a company is stating that it does not have sufficient confidence in all of its employees to be able to view a code of conduct or ethics as unnecessary. This is an implication that some, perhaps many, employees might find objectionable, but for an organisation that straddles many countries and cultures in its operations the need for an articulation of expected behaviour and practices throughout its operations can be overwhelming.

## The purposes of codes of conduct and ethics

At one level, codes of conduct and ethics can be seen as legitimate and necessary devices for senior management to develop in order to specify expected codes of behaviour of all employees. Each employee of an organisation will be seen as a representative of that organisation by others external to the organisation. Thus, it is important that employees reflect behaviour that is commensurate with the persona and reputation that the organisation wishes to project. In this context some writers see codes of conduct as principally manipulative control devices to achieve managerial ends. Stevens (1994: 65) argued that 'some ethical codes are little more than legal barriers and self-defence mechanisms; others are intended to influence and shape employee behaviour'. These were observations that had been made earlier by, among others, Mathews (1988) and Warren (1993).

Developing and adding to the work of Bowie and Duska (1990), we have listed below eight roles for corporate codes. These are:

- *Damage limitation* – to reduce damages awarded by courts in the event of the company being sued for negligence by one its employees.

- *Guidance* – the 'reference point' role, similar to what Passmore (1984) referred to as 'the reminding role'. An aide-memoire for employees when faced with an ethically complex situation.

- *Regulation* – this is the prescribing and proscribing roles that will stipulate specific qualities that are essential, e.g. independence, objectivity, etc., or acts that are prohibited.

- *Discipline and appeal* – this is the role of a code as a benchmark for an organisation or professional body to decide whether an employee/member has contravened required conduct and what form of punishment might ensue. In addition the code can form the basis of an appeal by the accused.

- *Information* – a code expresses to external audiences standards of behaviour that can be expected of employees/members.

- *Proclamation* – this has echoes of 'information', but it relates more to the role of codes of conduct developed by professional bodies. To achieve 'professional' status trade associations are normally required to assuage public concerns over the granting of monopoly rights to specific areas of commercial/social activity (e.g. auditing, doctoring, etc.). Ethical codes will attempt to reassure that these monopoly powers will not be abused.

- *Negotiation* – this is not dissimilar to *guidance* in that codes can be used as a tool in negotiations and disputes with and between professionals, colleagues, employers, governments, etc.

- *Stifling* – this is the creation of internal procedures for handling the ethical concerns of employees that are more concerned with management keeping a lid on internal dissent than acting as a conduit for internal debate and examination. Hunt's (1995 and 1998) work on whistleblowing in the health and social services reflects a number of examples of this use of codes of conduct and internal whistleblowing processes.

The attention paid to codes of conduct by both organisations and researchers does presume both that codes are a 'good' thing and that they do have a positive impact upon individual and corporate behaviour. With regard to the latter, Mathews (1988) was able to identify only a weak link between the existence of ethical codes and corporate behaviour. This latter point was taken up by Cassell, Johnson and Smith (1997: 1078) who argued that:

> An important, if implicit, assumption of many writings on corporate codes ... is that such codes do have a 'real' effect upon behaviour. This tends to be something that is taken for granted, but it is not empirically validated by subsequent investigation ... recipients of the code: those who are required to make sense of it, and respond to it, often as one more instance of managerially-inspired change, amidst a plethora of pre-existing formal and informal control processes within which the impact of the code must be located. As with any example of formal organisational control, the actual, as opposed to the intended, effect may be subject to processes that entail negotiation and bargaining.

Stevens' (1994) observations were that codes were:

- primarily concerned with employee conduct that might damage the firm, that is, they were thus skewed towards self-protection, and

- preoccupied with the law.

The legalistic orientation of many codes has been noted by a number of writers, including Farrell and Cobbin (1996). The latter identified differences between American, Australian and UK corporate codes of conduct. They concluded that, of the codes they studied, the Australian codes tended to concentrate upon a reiteration of the legal environment within which individuals and organisations operate, emphasising the importance of not doing anything to harm the employing organisation's reputation. American codes included, but went beyond, this orientation, emphasising customers, equal opportunities and insider dealing, while the UK codes made more frequent reference to the community, customer welfare and the environment than the Australian or American codes. However, all of these are relative terms, 'the level of specific guidance on ethical content in each country's codes was very low' (1996: 54). As lawyers were identified as the most frequent developers of such codes (30 per cent), a legalistic orientation to the codes was not surprising.

## Factors that will affect the impact of a code

Cassell *et al.* (1997), combining the work of Hopwood (1974) and Kelman (1961), identified three possible explanations why individuals might display behaviours that conform with desired organisational behaviours. These are:

1. *Internalisation*, in which the behaviours are accepted by the individual as their own, even though they are set externally. This does suggest, however, that the ethical values displayed will be subject to, and influenced by, further external forces, unless the organisational values are held by the individual at a profound and deep level.

2. *Compliance*, in which the displayed behaviour is associated with the desire to achieve some form of reward, or avoid an identifiable punishment. This form of behaviour will last as long as the punishment or reward is regarded as both significant and realisable by the individual/s concerned, but not beyond. This form of behaviour is thus not ethically based, but instrumental, calculating and unreliable.

3. *Identification*, in which behaviour is shaped by, and mirrors, the behaviours of significant others with whom the individual wishes to identify. Again because of the instrumental and externally located locus of a behaviour's rationale, the reliability of the behaviour in question is problematic.

Of these three possible explanations, only the first holds out the prospect of consistency for the organisations, the other two being unreliable due to external corruption. If this is so then the individual must absorb the organisation's values in a conscious and knowing way because either:

- The individual's existing values correspond closely with those espoused by the organisation and, thus, little change is required to the individual's own ethics, or

- The individual recognises in the organisation's values a set of principles that transcend their own and to which they wish to aspire.

Alternatively the internalisation is not conscious, but unconscious, achieved by the constant drip-drip of organisational images and rhetoric. This might seem a very distant possibility in the current day and age, but one of the authors is reminded of an ethics workshop he held for a group of managers on a Master's programme. One of the managers worked for a well-known and respected retail organisation, respected among other things for the apparently strong employee benefits and care provided by the company. However, during the course of the workshop all the participants reviewed different aspects of their organisation's practices, and this particular manager gradually shifted from a view of his employing organisation's paternalistic care as benign, to one which was more oppressive and manipulative. This change in interpretation came not from questioning by the tutors, but from a series of interactive exercises with other members of the course. The manager in question had worked for the retail organisation for over 15 years and during that time had accepted the organisation's house journal, the management conferences he attended and other practices as evidence of his employer's good intent. His now more critical interpretation did not suddenly make his employers 'bad' employers, when for the previous 15 years they had been 'good' employers. What unsettled him was how uncritical he had been in accepting a particular interpretation of some of the organisation's actions and decisions over the years, some of which did not square with his original uncritical, 'rose-tinted' description of his organisation.

Using Goffman's (1959) dramaturgical metaphor, individuals can be said to 'act out' their preferred view of themselves on the stage of life. Information likely to enhance others' opinions of oneself is kept 'centre stage' rather than 'in the wings'. The concept of impression management pervades the literature on business ethics, and is particularly apparent in ethnographic accounts of how managers deal with ethical problems (e.g. Jackall, 1988; Schein, 1992; Toffler, 1991; Watson, 1994). Interestingly, the 'management' and 'organisational behaviour' literature is a much richer and a more academically robust source of material on this point than much of the business ethics literature.

Jackall (1988) argued that the unethical actions of managers do not result from the individual's moral deficiencies, but rather from the bureaucratic structures of modern organisations that encourage managers to behave unethically. This view has been echoed by others within the literature. For example, Liedtka (1991) concluded that many of the managers in her study found themselves forced to choose between preserving their relationships within the firm (operating within the organisational political model) and following their own values (using a value-driven model). We will conclude our consideration of this issue with a quote from Cassell *et al.* (1997: 1088):

> It is our contention that although individual psychological and demographic factors play a role in influencing behaviour in relation to codes, that role is relatively minor given the significance of the organisational context and culture within which behaviour takes place.

Cassell *et al.* (1997) identified three factors they argued would determine the influence a code would have upon the behaviour of organisational members, namely:

1. The nature of the code, its content and the processes by which it has been designed, developed and implemented.

2. The organisational control mechanisms (both formal and informal). For example, will the employees see the introduction of a (new) code as just another mechanism by which the employing organisation wishes to determine individual behaviour, or a genuine attempt to help employees cope with complex ethical issues that they will face during their day-to-day practice?

3. Individual influences which focus upon perceptual and self-control processes.

Thus, if the individual employee acts in keeping with required organisational behaviour out of either compliance or identification motives, and is sceptical about factors (1) and (2) above, the prospects for a newly introduced code of conduct or practice are likely to be unpredictable and variable throughout an organisation, two outcomes the code was presumably intended to obviate.

## Writing a code of ethics

The difficulty of writing a code of ethics is that, when they are completed, they look banal, and people comment, 'Well, that is all just common sense'. Their commonplaceness is intensified when they are reduced to the basics and provided to all employees as laminated cards that can be stored in wallets and purses with the credit cards. Commonplaces of course are mostly true and important statements about trust, integrity, honesty and fairness. The intention is clearly that employees should carry these cards around with them as reminders, thus implying that the staff need constant admonition to be honest and so on. In our research interviews one respondent reported a debate in a focus group set up to discuss what should be included in the new code of ethics. One side of the argument was that 'Employees should act honestly' should be included. The contrary view was that this was such an obvious requirement that it did not need stating, and that if it was it implied that the management thought their employees potentially dishonest. It was decided not to include it.

Most organisations go to great trouble to ensure that their code of ethics is particular to them and their business and circumstances. Yet most codes of ethics look alike. It is unusual for codes to go against convention or the norms and institutions of the surrounding society. Table 10.1 attempts to illustrate this phenomenon by comparing the ethical code for the conduct of pharmaceutical medicine of Johnson and Johnson (n.d.) with that of the Covenant of the Goddess (Center for the Study of Ethics in the Professions, 2003), which is an association of white witches.

As there is much common ground between different organisations' codes of ethics it is possible to identify the topics and themes most commonly mentioned. In the analysis in Table 10.2 the examples are taken from Johnson and Johnson's Credo, the UK Civil Service Code of Conduct (The Cabinet Office, 2004), BP's business policies and the statement of core values of Carbo Ceramics (2002) (which was more or less chosen at random from the many company statements available); note that none of these uses the term code of ethics, but nevertheless that is what they are.

**Table 10.1**  A comparison of the code of ethics for the conduct of pharmaceutical medicine of Johnson and Johnson and the Covenant of the Goddess Code of Ethics

| Common theme | Ethical code for the conduct of pharmaceutical medicine of Johnson and Johnson | Covenant of the Goddess ethical code |
| --- | --- | --- |
| Credo based | 'It is our responsibility to apply Credo-based values and judgment regarding the design, conduct, analysis and interpretation of clinical studies and results.' | 'Members of the covenant should ever keep in mind the underlying unity of our religion as well as the diversity of its manifestations.' 'These ethics shall be understood and interpreted in the light of one another, and especially in the light of the traditional laws of our religion.' |
| The credos are of similar antiquity | The Johnson and Johnson credo was first published in 1943 | Modern witchcraft was probably invented as a religion in the 1920s and 1930s when there was a fashion for magic and druidism. It is only slightly older than the Johnson and Johnson credo. |
| Do no harm | 'It is our fundamental responsibility to place the well-being of the patient first by appropriately balancing risks and benefits and to ensure that the best interests of patients and physicians who use our products receive utmost consideration. ' | 'An ye harm none, do as ye will' |
| Respect the differences and autonomy of others | 'It is our responsibility to understand differences in values across cultures and to appropriately adapt our behaviors without relaxing our ethical principles.' | 'Every person associated with the covenant shall respect the autonomy and sovereignty of each coven, as well as the right of each coven to oversee the spiritual, mental, emotional and physical development of its members and students in its own way, and shall exercise reasonable caution against infringing upon that right in any way.' |
| A position on openness and secrecy | 'It is our responsibility to ensure all Company-based, medically relevant product information is fair and balanced, accurate and comprehensive, to enable well-informed risk-benefit assessments about our products.' | 'All persons associated with this covenant shall respect the traditional secrecy of our religion.' |
| Right to a fair return | Not included in the code but the credo states, 'When we operate according to these principles, the stockholders should realize a fair return.' | 'All persons have the right to charge reasonable fees for the services by which they earn their living, so long as our religion is not thereby exploited.' |
| Professional standards of those who practice the activity | 'It is our responsibility to adhere to the principles of good clinical practice.' | 'Since our religion and the arts and practices peculiar to it are the gift of the Goddess, membership and training in a local coven or tradition are bestowed free, as gifts, and only on those persons who are deemed worthy to receive them.' |

**Table 10.2** Common themes in codes of ethics

| Theme | Example | Source of example |
|-------|---------|-------------------|
| Integrity | The constitutional and practical role of the Civil Service is, with integrity, honesty, impartiality and objectivity, to assist the duly constituted Government [ ] whatever their political complexion, in formulating their policies, carrying out decisions and in administering public services for which they are responsible. | UK Civil Service Code |
| | We conduct our business with the highest ethical standards. We are truthful and honor our commitments and responsibilities. | Carbo Ceramics |
| Loyalty | Civil servants are servants of the Crown. Constitutionally, all the Administrations form part of the Crown and, subject to the provisions of this Code, civil servants owe their loyalty to the Administrations in which they serve. | UK Civil Service Code |
| No harm and risk management | We believe our first responsibility is to the doctors, nurses and patients, to mothers and fathers and all others who use our products and services. In meeting their needs everything we do must be of high quality. | Johnson and Johnson |
| | We will regularly identify the hazards and assess the risks associated with our activities. We will take appropriate action to manage risks and hence prevent or reduce the impact of potential accidents or incidents. | BP |
| Respect for individual employees | We are responsible to our employees, the men and women who work with us throughout the world. Everyone must be considered as an individual. We must respect their dignity and recognize their merit. They must have a sense security in their jobs. Compensation must be fair and adequate, and working conditions clean, orderly and safe. We must be mindful of ways to help our employees fulfil their family responsibilities. Employees must feel free to make suggestions and complaints. There must be equal opportunity for employment, development and advancement for those qualified. We must provide competent management, and their actions must be just and ethical. | Johnson and Johnson |
| Respect for the law | We will respect the law in the countries and communities in which we operate. | BP |
| Trust | Our commitment is to create mutual advantage in all our relationships so that people will trust us and want to do business with BP. | BP |
| Relationship with stakeholders | We will enable customers, governments, communities and our own people to participate in a new constructive dialogue. We aim for a radical openness – a new approach from a new company, transparent, questioning, flexible, restless and inclusive. | BP |
| | Our suppliers and distributors must have an opportunity to make a fair profit. | Johnson and Johnson |
| Developing communities | We are responsible to the communities in which we live and work and to the world community as well. | |
| | We must be good citizens – support good works and charities and bear our fair share of taxes. | |
| | We must encourage civic improvements and better health and education. We must maintain in good order the property we are privileged to use, protecting the environment and natural resources. | Johnson and Johnson |

▶

**Table 10.2** Continued

| Theme | Example | Source of example |
|---|---|---|
| **Goals and achievement** | We set aggressive goals and strive to exceed them. We value and celebrate a high level of individual achievement and team performance. | Carbo Ceramics |
| **Return to shareholders** | Our final responsibility is to our stockholders. Business must make a sound profit. | Johnson and Johnson |
| **Environmental sustainability** | We are committed to [ ] demonstrating respect for the natural environment and work towards our goals of no accidents, no harm to people and no damage to the environment. | BP |
| **Political activity and contributions** | BP will never make political contributions whether in cash or in kind anywhere in the world. | BP |
| **Personal advantage** | Civil servants should not misuse their official position or information acquired in the course of their official duties to further their private interests or those of others. They should not receive benefits of any kind from a third party which might reasonably be seen to compromise their personal integrity or judgement. | Civil Service Code |
| **Commitment to external standards or assurance** | BP supports the principles set forth in the UN Universal Declaration of Human Rights and will respect the 2000 International Labour Organisation, the 'Tripartite Declaration of Principles Concerning Multinational Enterprises and Social Policy' and the 2000 OECD 'Guidelines for Multi-national Enterprises'. | BP |

## Arguments against the employment of codes of conduct and ethics

### Activity 10.1

Although our consideration of codes of conduct and ethics has identified limitations in practice and referred to evidence that casts doubt upon the actual impact of codes 'on the ground', we have not suggested that the development and introduction of a code would be a negative development. There are, however, such arguments, and before discussing these we would like you to think through what these might be.

Identify as many negative aspects as possible associated with the development of a code of conduct or ethics.

While the employment of codes has an intuitive appeal, we can identify five possible objections to their development and employment.

## 1 Justification

This relates to the lack of any universally accepted set of common principles and ethics. If 'everything is relative' is taken to its logical conclusion and codes can only ever be culturally and socially specific, the notion of universal laws is rejected and with it the argument that a corporation can have a single code of conduct. If a multi-national organisation produces a code of conduct that reflects a basic set of values, by definition this implies there are certain basic concepts that it wishes to universalise, at least within its own worldwide operations, but is this possible? The question might become one of distinguishing between negotiable and non-negotiable values – how and when does one balance local customs and traditions with one's own sense of values when the two are in conflict? For example, when is a gift a bribe? We discuss this particular issue in the next chapter.

## 2 The inability of rules to govern actions

If codes cannot guarantee changes in behaviour, and empirical evidence is very limited with respect to examples of codes shaping behaviour in desired ways, will the negative signals being sent out to employees, that the organisation does not trust them, be the abiding impact of the introduction of a code? If so, then the overall impact of a code is likely to be negative.

**Connexion point**

Re-read our discussion of *Integrative Social Contract Theory* in Chapter 8 (pp. 323–6) and consider how it argues the issues relating to universal versus relativist ethics can be handled.

## 3 Support structures

There is a need for, but paucity of, support structures within organisations for employees to feel able to act in accordance with specified codes of behaviour. Where codes of conduct do exist, Warren (1993: 189) argued that:

> All too often ethical codes are handed down to employees from the executive above and the importance of trying to create a community or purpose within the company is ignored.

Warren (1993) referred to the field of industrial relations where evidence indicates that rules governing industrial relations need collective agreement if they are to be honoured in the observance as well as in the breach (e.g. Terry, 1975). This perspective is supported by Bird and Waters (1989: 83). They argued that just talking about ethical issues is unlikely to enhance the significance of the issues unless mechanisms are found for 'connecting this language with the experiences and expectations of people involved in business'. Taking this argument forward, Bird and Waters (1989: 84) argued that

> Business people will continue to shun open discussions of actual moral issues unless means are provided to allow for legitimate dissent by managers who will not be personally blamed, criticised, ostracised, or punished for their views.

They found that talking to managers individually revealed that the managers had many concerns of an ethical nature. However, when asked if these issues were ever raised among managerial colleagues, either formally or informally, the managers replied that they were not. The managers identified a range of explanations for the collective managerial muteness on ethical issues. Such talk was perceived to be a threat to:

- efficiency (i.e. the imposition of rigid rules and regulations);

- the image of power and effectiveness (i.e. previous attempts had resulted in the dissenting manager being shown to be organisationally impotent); and

- organisational harmony (i.e. discussion of moral issues at work was perceived to be dysfunctional).

Thus, the introduction of a code of conduct requires an environment in which expressions of concern over particular practices are not perceived as simplistically 'anti-company' or 'wimpish'. Without such an environment, cynicism is likely to be fuelled, and the overall impact of the code will be negative.

## 4 The marginality of codes

Codes tend to be treated as 'add-ons', as constraints upon action, and thus act at the margins of corporate activity. To be effective, codes need to be at the centre of corporate beliefs or, more particularly, a code becomes redundant if the corporate culture encapsulates those values and beliefs that would be reflected in a corporate code of conduct or ethics. If left at the margins, a code might be interpreted as a necessary accoutrement (garnish) to corporate activities, but one that can be circumvented, or 'negotiated' in certain circumstances. If so, then cynicism about corporate motives would be heightened and the overall effect of the code would be negative.

## 5 The diminution and ultimate invisibility of individual responsibility

Codes that specify behaviour in particular situations seek to take judgement out of ethically charged situations. Whilst this has the advantage of standardising behaviour throughout an organisation and potentially minimising the risk of behaviour that is unacceptable, there is also the risk of the individual using the 'I was only following orders' defence in the event of an enquiry into a dispute over a particular incident. This shifting of responsibility has been termed by Bauman (1994) as 'floating responsibility' and was discussed in Chapter 7. It becomes an organisational defence against individual conscience. The following of rules and adherence to the commands of superiors makes identification of responsibility difficult to isolate. Identification of responsibility for a particular action or inaction falls between the cracks of job descriptions and responsibilities, and codes of conduct. Morality (or the defining of it) thus becomes someone else's responsibility. The actions of individuals become automatic, with little thought or judgement on the part of the individual required. Whilst actual situations will often present complexities and nuances that take the individual into contexts not addressed adequately by a code, the existence and 'failings' of the code present the individual with an escape route from responsibility. To obey instructions is less demanding and far less risky than exercising moral judgement.

Bauman (1994) identified a second tendency, that of organisational actions being deemed amoral, that is neither good nor bad, only correct or incorrect. In this context codes of conduct can be used to make what could be transparent opaque. Codes might be expressed, not so much in moral terms, but in technical terms, implying a moral neutrality to the issues being addressed in the code.

## The difficulties of writing codes of conduct – the ethics of e-communication

With the coming of new forms of electronic communication and diffusion of information, in particular email and the Internet, new forms of ethical problems have appeared in organisations. As this has happened organisations have tried to develop new codes of conduct governing e-communications, to minimise abuse. Their attempts to respond to new problems illustrate many of the problems and difficulties with codes of conduct discussed in the previous section. The matter is not an inconsequential one. In 1998 an IT manager was sacked from her job because she had booked her holiday on the Internet, using the company's computers, during work time (Wakefield, 1999). In 2003 four lawyers lost their jobs at a top London law firm after circulating an email about oral sex among their colleagues; at some point it was emailed to a further 20 million people worldwide. A year later ten clerical workers at the Royal Sun Alliance in Liverpool were dismissed after emailing a risqué cartoon involving Bart Simpson and a donkey (*The Observer*, 2004). People have no control over what they are sent by email, and they may inadvertently, or so they will claim, download a pornographic image for example. Even if they delete it immediately a record will remain, in this networked age, that they received the image. It might be difficult for them subsequently to disprove that they were simply an innocent dupe.

It is estimated that 36 per cent of employees have an email address provided by their employers. As access to email and the Internet grows so the ethical issues become more important. The main problems are listed below.

### 1 Misuse by employers

- Employers have the capacity, but not always the inclination, to monitor every action that employees take while using networked computers at work. Employees' net surfing and email correspondences are all logged. The question is the extent to which such surveillance is ethical and legitimate and when it could be claimed to break an employee's right to privacy. In 2003 the UK government passed the Regulation and Investigatory Powers Act that made it illegal to monitor employees' emails without their consent. Guidelines issued by the Department of Trade and Industry, however, construed the Act as allowing surveillance if contracts of employment included a clause that allowed employers to monitor email and Internet usage. The employers argued that they needed this right as all emails sent from their systems were their legal responsibility, which is why most emails now sent from organisational systems have a disclaimer (often longer than the message) denying any such responsibility.

- Assuming that by emailing all staff they have exhausted their responsibility to communicate effectively with their staff.

## 2 Misuse by employees

- Stealing employers' time by surfing the net when they should be working.

- Using the email and Internet facilities for improper purposes, such as distributing racist messages or obscene materials.

- Conducting a personal business using their employer's systems.

- Harassing or stalking other employees by email, a practice that has been recognised by Industrial Tribunals as illegal behaviour (Taylor, 2001).

- Sending an internal email communication to an external body. For example, an aggrieved employee who had taken Prince Charles to an Industrial Tribunal complaining of sex discrimination used an internal email from the Prince's household as evidence in support of her case.

- Misusing online selection and recruitment testing to misrepresent oneself to a potential employer. In 2003 6 per cent of organisations were using some form of online testing for recruitment and selection purposes (Czerny, 2004).

## 3 Abuses of good communication

- Email communication is anomalous; on the one hand it is seen as quick and informal yet on the other it is a recorded form of communication that can be used in a court of law. This leads people to show a lack of courtesy in their communications with others that they would not think of exhibiting on the telephone or in face-to-face communication (Taylor, 2001).

- People often use emails to avoid giving news, often bad, that ought to be given personally. There was in 2004 a case of a large number of employees being informed by email that they were redundant.

- The informality and distance of emails encourage people to be ruder, especially when they are angry, than they would be if addressing the subjects of their disgust directly. Reliance Industries (RIL) is a very large family firm in India. When the founder died there was a power struggle between his two sons that was conducted almost entirely in emails leaked to the media. The directors of the company thought the dispute would never be resolved by emails and said,

> [we do] not find the mode of e-mail suitable. Instead of e-mail it should be love mail. It is better to sit and talk.
>
> (*Hindustan Times*, 2004: 1)

The extreme email discourtesy is when someone writes an email complaining about some hurt from another and then copies it to the entire company. This may have a beneficial aspect, such as when an email that affects all staff, but which was intended to be confidential to a select group, is forwarded by one of that group to all employees. This can lead to a vigorous and democratic debate about the issue between all staff. Emails can be an effective forum for rapid debate.

- Overusing mailing lists and the 'cc' function to flood people with emails that are of little interest to them.

One of the difficulties of writing a code of conduct to cover these issues is that most employers wish to draw a sensible balance between the employees' rights and those of the companies. Most organisations are happy to allow their employees to use email and Internet access for personal use, but, as one code expresses it,

> this should not interfere with or conflict with business use. Employees should exercise good judgement regarding the reasonableness of personal use.

This particular employer provided a junk mail group so that employees could post messages such as 'looking to rent' or 'something to sell'. Only a few organisations go to the extreme of prohibiting all personal use of the Internet and email. One American University did, and incurred the wrath of its academic staff. (Woodbury, 1998). One of the reasons for employers to exercise some discretion is that the custom and practice, the work culture, of many occupational groups does not see personal use of ICT as an ethical wrong. Stylianou *et al.* (2004) conducted research that shows that R&D staff think it is right to violate both intellectual property (IPR) and privacy rights (when using ICT) to favour open access to data and knowledge. Programmers, more restrictively, think it acceptable to plagiarise (ignore IPR) but not to breach an employee's right to privacy. Some of the standard clauses in a code of conduct on the use of email and the network might be as follows.

- No email or communication should violate the law or company policy.
- Employees should take care to maintain the security of their passwords.
- Accessing and using copyright information in ways that break the law is a disciplinary offence.
- Confidential internal messages should not be posted outside the organisation.
- Chain messages should not be originated or passed on.
- Emails should be brief, courteous and only sent to individuals with an interest in them, and not en bloc to groups.
- Employees should be informed of the level of monitoring of their email and Internet usage that will be carried out.
- The monitoring of an individual's private emails will not be routinely conducted unless it has been specifically authorised by a senior manager in support of a specific allegation of wrongdoing. (This is a particularly contentious clause.)

- Employers should give warnings to staff about misuse and make the penalties clear. Cronin (2004) has carried out some intriguing research on the efficacy of such warnings.

Of course once someone starts to draft such regulations the creation of a rule to prevent one problem, not using email to distribute political messages to staff for example, quickly creates another. Does this mean that Trade Union officials cannot use organisational email to send messages to its members? The other problem is the rate of innovation in e-communication. Each new development probably creates a new opportunity for misuse that had not been anticipated by the writers of codes (*see* the story of the Delhi schoolboy, p. 6).

---

### Activity 10.2

In what ways, if any, might a code of conduct designed to govern email and Internet use at work in a:

- research and consultancy company with a small staff of professional IT employees, and a

- large call centre dealing with service and other enquiries differ? If they do differ, why?

---

## When codes of conduct collide

A fundamental problem within many types of organisation, but particularly those in the public and non-profit seeking sectors, is the issue of the codes of conduct of differing professional groupings and the potential conflicts that the respective codes can create. For example, the role of internal accounting information as a management information support system places the role of accountants within the managerial structures. This does not of itself set accountants and those professionals located within an organisation's managerial structures against those professionals who are outside those structures, but it creates the possibilities of conflict. One of the six principles upon which the International Federation of Accountants' Code of Ethics is based, and which is reflected in the codes of conduct of all the UK professional accountancy bodies, is that of confidentiality. The duty to protect the confidential nature of corporate information is underscored, even after a contract of employment is terminated.

A consideration of the codes of conduct or ethics within which other professionals must operate indicates the potential for conflict. For example, the United Kingdom Central Council for Nursing, Midwifery and Health Visiting (1996) states that 'each registered nurse, midwife and health visitor shall act, at all times, in such a manner as to safeguard and promote the interests of individual patients and clients'. In an environment that has seen health care subjected to considerable financial strictures over the past twenty years, a number of cases have highlighted the extremely difficult situations health care workers face in delivering effective and appropriate medical care 'that is in the interests of individual patients and clients'. The creation of managerial posts for medical staff such as nurses has only served to emphasise these tensions. Hunt (1995 and 1998) recounted cases in health care and social services where individuals have tried to speak out about their concerns, but found their actions thwarted and future career progression blighted.

The very nature of the codes of conduct of nurses and accountants maps out the territory of potential conflict. While the nursing code requires patient advocacy, the accountants' code reflects an orientation of organisational loyalty. Indeed, in the cases of the codes of conduct developed by the American Institute of Internal Auditors and the (American) Government Finance Officers Association (Harris and Reynolds, 1993), explicit reference is made to loyalty to the employer. Even the human resource managers interviewed in the Fisher and Lovell (2000) study displayed a greater organisational orientation than the stereotypical portrayal of human resource managers might suggest.

The respective codes of conduct under which professional accountants and health care workers must operate are both understandable and defensible when viewed separately. However, when placed within a single organisational context, the potential for conflict is evident.

Even within a code of conduct, tensions often exist. Proctor *et al.* (1993: 166) highlight the contradictory situation that confronts social workers:

> The preamble to the Code itself acknowledges that multiple principles could bear on any practice situation ... thus, the potential for conflict is inherent in the profession's values and is reflected in its Code of Ethics.

At least the code of the social workers' professional body recognises these tensions. For accountants, the needs both to respect the confidentiality of corporate information and to respect the public interest are not usually formally recognised as posing any particular dilemma for accountants.

Interestingly, Article IV of the code of conduct of the Project Management Profession (1996: 2) contains the following clause:

> Project management professionals shall protect the safety, health and welfare of the public and **speak out** against abuses in the areas affecting the public interest [emphasis added].

Some would argue that more than a pinch of salt needs to be on hand when considering the pronouncements of aspiring professional associations, but it is quite clear that this aspiring professional body expects its members to take public stands when appropriate. This is an unusually explicit statement from a trade association.

The above discussion has introduced an additional dimension, that of the ethics codes of professional associations. Much has been written on the rise of the professions (*see* Durkheim, 1992; Koehn, 1994; and Larson, 1977, for a discussion of these issues) and the roles of codes of ethics have been influential in this rise. Any trade association that gains the statutory right to control the membership of a particular aspect of human activity (e.g. the British Medical Association and doctoring; the Law Society and particular legal work; and certain professional accountancy bodies and auditing) will possess a code of ethics for its members to follow. The existence of a code of ethics will have been an essential element of the trade association's submission to control the membership of those who wish to practise as specific 'professionals', such as doctors, lawyers and auditors, etc. This is because the trade associations will need to assuage public concern that their state-granted monopolies will not be abused. The 'professional' bodies concerned will commit their members, above all else, to act 'in the public interest' whenever there is a clash of interest.

The 'public interest' is a very slippery concept. It refers to the interests of the public at large, not in a simplistic majority-type way, but rather in terms of what should be in the general interest of civic society if a rational, objective, long-term assessment of a situation is taken. Major scandals involving professional people cast very long shadows over the veracity and intentions of codes of conduct when employed by so-called professional bodies. Examples include the involvement of the international firm of accountants, Arthur Andersen, in the Enron affair. Shortly after Enron's collapse and the complicity of the auditing arm of Andersen's was revealed this part of the company collapsed. Other examples are the failure of the accountancy profession to respond in any meaningful way to the travails of its senior members, or the way that doctors appear to have placed the interests of their profession and fellow colleagues' status above that of the public interest in cases such as the Bristol Heart Surgery Unit, or the body-parts shambles (*see* Case study 2.19). Yet to stay within the membership of a 'profession' the individual member must attempt not to bring the profession into disrepute. As mentioned above, individual professional codes of ethics, while defensible when considered on their own, can present a conflict situation when juxtaposed in particular organisational contexts.

In the Fisher–Lovell (2000) study, few of the accountants and HR professionals had studied their respective professional bodies' code of ethics and little weight seemed to be placed on them. In some senses the issue of the codes of ethics of professional associations has diminished in its relevance as an area of interest and study, as the mantle of professional bodies has slipped, and their claims to be acting in the public interest are seen as little more than façades behind which opaqueness is maintained and vested interests are concealed.

Given the arguments posed in this section against the use of codes, the question might be asked, 'So do codes have a future?' Judging by the increase in the number of organisational codes in evidence, codes certainly have a present. A survey conducted by Arthur Andersen and London Business School (1999) contrasted the prevalence of codes of conduct in 1996 and 1999. Whereas 59 per cent of companies surveyed in 1996 acknowledged the use of a code of conduct, the figure had grown to 78 per cent by 1999, and 81 per cent of companies surveyed in 1999 had values or mission statements. The question is whether this recent upsurge in interest is anything more than a defensive reaction against potential legal claims, or, as in the case of public sector bodies, merely a necessary response to the outcome of the Nolan Committee reports. Does managerial attention to codes of conduct represent anything more than the latest management fad – after quality circles, business process re-engineering, the balanced scorecard, the learning organisation, etc.?

> **Connexion point**
>
> The Nolan principles, which were published in the First Nolan Committee Report on Standards in Public Life, can be read in Chapter 2, p. 71.

So far we have focused upon organisational responses to ethical issues by way of the development and employment of a range of different forms of codes of practice. We now move to a consideration of less overt, more subtle, but possibly more effective ways of shaping behaviour within organisations. This is the notion of corporate cultures, either singular or multiple. The development of a particular culture does not preclude the employment of a code of conduct; indeed the unwritten understandings that invariably comprise a particular culture often act as inviolate rules of conduct. All organisations will have 'ways of working', although those ways may be many and varied, with espoused behaviour sometimes deviating from actual behaviour.

## Ethical culture and ethos

There are ethical issues about the propriety of using culture as a device for encouraging people to behave in one way rather than another. However, if we assume for the moment that it is acceptable for managers to foster a culture that encourages ethical behaviour, what would such a culture look like? Snell (1993 and 2000) used the term moral ethos, rather than ethical culture, when he discussed this issue. He defined moral ethos as comprising a set of 'force-fields',

> all of which impinge on members' understandings, judgements and decisions concerning good and bad, right and wrong.
>
> (Snell, 2000: 267)

Snell argued that the moral ethos emerges from the interactions of such forces. For example, if the demand for loyalty is low this may encourage openness within an organisation that supports criticism and acting with integrity. Contrarily an organisation's demand for loyalty may inhibit the exercise of integrity. From an organisational perspective, loyalty is possibly the most important behaviour to cultivate among employees. Willmott (1998: 83) highlighted the contentious nature of codes of conduct and the implicit role of loyalty within them when he observed:

> the value ascribed to the adoption of codes is made conditional upon their contribution to business objectives. This implies that, in principle, the codes will be refined or discarded according to calculations about their continuing contribution to these objectives.

Integrity is less amenable to codes of conduct. For example, a code or rule to respect the confidentiality of corporate affairs in all circumstances might conflict with a broader social perspective of integrity.

Paralleling Kohlberg's stages of moral reasoning, Snell (1993: Chapter 6) identified six types of moral ethos that could arise within organisations. They are:

1. *Fear-ridden ethos*. Behaviour that is characterised by coercion, blind obedience and a myopic focus on organisational survival at any cost.

2. *Advantage-driven ethos*. Employees are rewarded for getting the best for the organisation even if this might involve deception, gamesmanship and exploitation of others if necessary. The ethos encourages private alliances, secrecy and personal advantage.

3. *Members-only ethos*. This ethos demands loyalty and a shared concern to present a good image to those outside the organisation. Clever upstarts are to be tamed and brought into the fold. Internally the focus on group membership can encourage paternalism, sexism and racism.

4. *Regulated ethos*. Regulation and accountability are typical of this ethos. Codes of conduct are written and employees are often expected to self-certify that they have obeyed the rules.

5. *Quality-seeking ethos*. This ethos seeks to encourage everyone to work to the highest ethical standards. Training and development encourages debate and argument about what those standards should be. The ethos can create a sense of arrogance and over-commitment.

6. *Soul-searching ethos*. The organisational ethos supports a spiritual learning community that emphasises integrity and an ongoing ethical dialogue.

Given that corporate cultures can be employed in manipulative ways, the issues of ethicality that pervade this area ultimately resolve themselves around

> the process of moral thought and self-scrutiny that precedes it. This understanding of ethics puts weight on the process of thought that precedes action, to qualify behaviour as ethical.
>
> (Sinclair, 1993: 69)

Thus, the ethicality of a decision lies not in the behaviour displayed, or the decision taken, but in the forethought that preceded the behaviour or decision. This suggests that we need to think more critically about notions of culture. The 'forces' that Snell referred to can be seen at the visible level (e.g. the behaviour of individuals) or at more subtle, less visible levels (e.g. assumptions and beliefs that inform behaviour). Thus it is argued that culture operates at different levels, with important implications for business ethics.

**Connexion point**

Kohlberg's staged theory of moral development is discussed in detail in Chapter 6, pp. 252–4 ,if you wish to confirm the parallels between the theory and Snell's stages of development of ethical ethos.

## Levels of culture

Schein (1992) offered an analysis that reflects three levels of culture, each with a different level of visibility. The top or first level is the most visible level of culture. Within this category would be included evidence such as signs, symbols, written codes, forms of address (i.e. how seniors, peers and juniors are expected to be addressed), clothing (formal, informal), stories and myths (usually about past leaders), rituals, architecture and décor of the company's premises. These visible signs, practices and images are described as artefacts of culture. Schein argues that while these are the most visible evidence of culture they are not always easy to decipher by the external observer. Forms of initiation and 'apprenticeship' are often required before the full significance of these artefacts is revealed.

The second level of culture is represented by the espoused values of a group. These are the beliefs that are articulated, that are audibly expressed. Sometimes these beliefs can be represented by a 'go-get-'em' philosophy, with staff encouraged to 'take the moment' or to 'go for it'. Whether these values are wholeheartedly believed is a matter of question, but if the stated values or beliefs tend to deliver the outcomes sought, then the credibility of the beliefs will grow and become accepted as 'the way things are done around here'. An interesting example of how language is used to create particular attitudes and cultures is reflected in the refusal of one leading security firm to allow its employees to use the term 'failure'. This reflects a refusal by the senior management to accept any level of underachievement by employees, or for the employees to see any demand as unattainable.

Schein referred to the third level as basic assumptions. These are the unspoken beliefs that exist within an organisation. They are the least visible, yet the most pervasive, form of culture because they represent deeply embedded ways of thinking about such questions as the nature of human nature, humanity's relationship with the environment, the nature of truth and of human activity. Basic assumptions are difficult to bring to the surface and challenge. Consequently they operate below the level of consciousness and can undermine the idea of moral agency, which requires conscious deliberation. If corporations are capable of subliminal influence on their employees' basic assumptions then this would be a potent threat to moral agency. There is much debate (Smircich, 1983), however, about whether top managers do have this power or whether any attempts they make to guide cultures lead only to unanticipated changes. That corporations can shape employees' beliefs is not questioned; whether those influences can be controlled to the organisation's benefit is doubtful, at least in the short term.

How to develop the ethical ethos of organisations leads us to a consideration of ethical leadership.

## Ethical leadership

The direction and example presented by senior management in terms of what is considered to be acceptable practice within an organisation must inform and shape the behaviour of others. Most textbooks argue that it is a leader's role to define the vision and core values of an organisation. The UK government, through an agency called the CSR Academy, has published a set of CSR competencies. These can be seen as a tool for establishing a set of behaviours and core values within organisations that would support the development of a CSR culture within an organisation. In Schein's terms they would be cultural artefacts. The competencies are intended to make CSR an integral part of business practice not only in large companies but also in small ones. The competencies (CSR Academy, 2004)

- focus on the personal qualities, attitudes and mind-sets which managers need to learn and which will in turn drive improvements in business performance.

- should become embedded into the education, training and development of managers and staff,

- are a tool for assessing performance in all business functions.

The competencies are:

1. Understanding society and business's roles and obligations within it

2. Building capacity within an organisation to work effectively in a responsible manner

3. Questioning business as usual

4. Stakeholder relations

5. Strategic view and ensuring that social and environmental concerns are considered in broad decision making

6. Harnessing diversity.

Alongside these competencies are a set of benchmark indicators that can be used to assess whether people in the company

- are aware of CSR

- understand the issues around CSR

- apply the competencies at work

- integrate the competencies into the culture of the company

- provide leadership on CSR across the organisation.

Competencies have normally been defined as an ability to do something. Distinctively, these CSR competencies are about understanding at the lower levels of attainment and only about action at the higher levels. As a cultural artefact the extent to which the competencies will affect the levels of values and basic assumptions in organisations is limited. They are probably best seen as a way of raising the priority given to CSR in businesses, especially smaller ones, and of creating a market for training courses in CSR.

Kanungo and Mendonca (1996) pointed out that employees will not believe leaders who lack ethical integrity and the leaders' values will not be accepted. They suggested that ethical leadership has to be altruistic, putting the well-being of others in the organisation before self-interest. However, they noted that western culture was better known for its emphasis on egoism than on altruism. The human resource management function has been identified (Connock and Johns, 1995: 159) as the natural repository of organisations' consciences, although a survey found that, in those companies that allocated business ethics to a particular department, responsibility was given to a range of departments (Arthur Andersen and London Business School, 1999: 19).

To suggest that where there is a virtuous set of senior managers all employees will automatically follow their examples of desired practice would be naïve. However, negative examples of immoral behaviour by senior executives can act like a cancer on ethical behaviour throughout an organisation, as the example provided in Case study 7.1 illustrated. The organisation in question appeared to harbour unpalatable practices and beliefs at a senior level, which created moral indifference within the headquarters.

A significant problem for any organisation that publicises its commitment to high ethical standards in all its business dealings is that any one single departure from such standards is likely to attract considerable media attention and cast doubt upon the full range of the organisation's activities. If this does happen, the reaction could be both unreasonably harsh (depending of course upon the nature and scale of the alleged infraction), and also a somewhat disingenuous approach to the analysis and reporting of the incident. Even if the infraction in question is finally judged to be an intentional and knowingly unethical act on the part of the individual employee concerned (however senior), the individual transgression might be just that, an individual's error of judgement. It might not be a revelation of institutionally entrenched unethical practices. In such a situation the more telling test of organisational commitment to a broadly accepted notion of corporate ethical behaviour would be how the organisation's senior management respond to the transgression and the steps they take to remedy the problem. In short, no one is perfect, but when errors are made, or misjudgements are revealed, how do we as individuals and corporations react and respond? The openness of individuals and organisations to acknowledge an error or problem, and the learning that ensues from the incident in question, are more likely to reflect the depth of commitment to ethical practice than are pious claims to high ethical standards made in mission statements or corporate reports. It is at times of tension or challenge that ethical credentials are more likely to be revealed. Organisational learning is a much vaunted but also a most demanding and challenging notion. The processual model of managing is commensurate with such an approach, and Buchholz and Rosenthal (1998) adopt it to explain their view of moral development within organisations.

> The adjustment between the self and the other is neither assimilation of perspectives, one to the other, nor the fusion of perspectives into an indistinguishable oneness, but can best be understood as an 'accommodating participation' in which each creatively affects and is affected by the other through accepted means of adjudication ... because of these dynamics, the leader does not 'stand apart' from a following group, nor is the leader an organizer of group ideas, but rather leadership is by its very nature in dynamic interaction with the group, and both are in a process of ongoing transformation because of this interaction.
>
> (Buchholz and Rosenthal, 1998: 418–19)

**Connexion point**

The idea of 'accommodating participation' is closely associated with those of the learning organisation and ethical learning discussed in Chapter 3, pp. 119–21.

Such a processual and 'accommodating participatory' approach would represent a fundamental change of perspective for the type of managers represented in the studies reported by Bird and Waters, 1989; and Lovell, 2002. The processual perspective offers, on the one hand, the prospects for moral chaos, but, on the other, possibly the best hope for moral agency. The former because the type of leadership implied in the processual model requires a degree of maturity and humility, but also a strength of belief and conviction that might be beyond many managers and leaders. However, if some form of accommodation is achievable in ways that eschew indoctrination, the debates that would be evident might do much to address many of the concerns raised throughout this book.

An important caveat with respect to greater openness and transparency in corporate dealings is the issue of litigation. The greater demands made of public corporations in terms of their various impacts are in many respects a sign of a maturing society. However, there has been an attendant increase in the propensity of members of the public to take legal action against corporations when infractions occur. In such a context it should not be surprising that corporations become very wary of revealing their 'failings' in public for fear of how such information might be employed. These complex issues can only be moved forward by debate and a developing sense of balance between:

- on the one hand, reparation for any 'injuries' experienced as a result of substandard performance by an individual or organisation, where culpability is evident; and

- on the other, a recognition that 'things' will and do go less than satisfactorily on occasions and that if the 'failing' was innocent, and all reasonable measures had been taken to avoid its occurrence in the first place, then retribution should be avoided, to encourage and foster learning from the experience.

These words are easy to say and write, but much more difficult to put into practice. Yet this is the challenge facing organisations. No easy compromise or solution is on offer, only the prospect of continued action and attention to the levels of behaviour deemed acceptable within our societies.

## Best practice standards

In the past ten years a number of standards for business ethics have been developed. These differ from codes of conduct and ethics in that they are meant to have a wide application, and are not written for particular organisations or professional groups. More importantly, whereas a code determines rules or principles for behaviour, standards set a minimum benchmark of behaviour against which organisations can be compared and judged. A standard often accredits, or gives a badge to, any organisation that meets the minimum standard. Membership-based organisations, often referred to as compacts, and international agreements concerned with improving the ethical standards of international business are discussed in Chapter 12.

## Accountability 1000 (AA1000)

AA1000 is a quality assurance standard. That is to say it focuses, not on whether an organisation is acting ethically, but on whether it has good systems that will identify whether it is acting unethically and so enable it to put things right. It is like ISO 9000 which is also a process standard, but one concerned with quality assurance systems generally and not just those that focus on ethical matters. It was announced in 1999 by the Institute of Social and Ethical Accountability, which works under the name AccountAbility. It contains both principles and a set of standards against which an organisation can be assessed. The issue of accountability always raises the question of accountability to whom, and in this standard the answer is to stakeholders. The components required in a system that makes an organisation accountable to its stakeholders include:

- planning
- accounting
- auditing and reporting
- embedding and
- stakeholder engagement.

Embedding means ensuring that everyone in the organisation takes the meeting of ethical and social standards seriously and takes it into account in their daily work. This is contrary to the suspicion, about all standards, that organisations only pay attention to them when they are to be accredited or re-accredited and only then to the extent of making sure that the right boxes on the correct forms have been ticked. The standard is also concerned with materiality, that is to say whether the accountability systems include the entire range of topics, such as:

- environmental issues
- work place and employment issues
- health and safety
- behaviour of supply chain partners
- employee involvement
- training and people development
- community involvement
- sustainable development.

In 2004 there were 22 companies using the standard, of which 16 were companies providing assurance services. This was a decrease from the 55 companies who were using the service in 2003 (AccountAbility, 2004). The International Standards Organisation (ISO) reported in 2004 that it was to prepare a set of standards for corporate social responsibility.

## Global Reporting Initiative (GRI)

The GRI was initiated in New York and although originally directed at US businesses it is now based in Amsterdam. The original sponsor was CERES but the initiative was subsequently funded and supported by the UN. Its purpose is to propose guidelines for organisations to report on the economic, environmental and social implications of their business practices. The GRI provides a series of performance indicators that it recommends organisations should publish. Some of these are regarded as core and others as optional. But in either case they are divided between:

- *Economic*: monetary flows to stakeholders, e.g. donations to community, civil society or other groups
- *Environmental*: for example, in the area of bio-diversity the impact of a company's activities on sensitive or protected land
- *Social*: for example, the composition of the senior management team, the number of men and women on it.

The performance indicators are either

- descriptions of policy and procedures or
- numerical measures of impacts and outcomes.

The full list can be seen in the Sustainability Reporting Guidelines. In brief, the Guidelines can be seen as a crib for those who need to write triple-line (*see* p. 371) reporting documents.

## Social Accountability 8000 (SA8000)

SA8000 is an international standard for corporate behaviour that identifies a range of criteria against which the activities and performance of organisations can be mapped and compared. The intention is that the standard (and the beliefs, values and ethics assumed within it) should be applicable throughout the world, with no exceptions. It is thus an attempt to specify a standard of employment conditions and practices with universal application.

The standard was developed by the Council on Economic Priorities Accreditation Agency (CEPAA). In 2000 it changed its name to Social Accountability International (SAI) and it keeps the standard under review, updates it from time to time and invites comments and advice. Indeed, once you have visited the website you may wish to pass on your own thoughts about the standard's comprehensiveness or robustness.

The standard has nine categories. These are:

- Child Labour
- Forced Labour
- Health and Safety
- Freedom of Association and Right to Collective Bargaining
- Discrimination
- Disciplinary Practices
- Working Hours
- Remuneration
- Management Systems.

Each of the categories has sub-headings. For example, 'Forced Labour' has only one, which effectively states, 'Thou shalt not be engaged in, or associated with, forced labour'. 'Management Systems', on the other hand, has 14 sub-headings. The standard is not enforced by any national law, but it is hoped that, as its use grows as a standard against which corporate practices and behaviours are judged, compliance will become the norm.

As the SA8000 standard is a recent development only a small number of companies have been accredited. Although a wide range of companies, governments and NGOs were consulted during the development of the standard some NGOs concerned with international labour standards criticise CEPAA for being too close to the views of industry. Nevertheless the standard is an attempt to formalise universal ethical standards for businesses and organisations.

## The Ethics Compliance Management System Standard (ECS2000)

This standard was developed by the business ethics research project at the Rietaku Centre for Economic Research in Japan. This standard is fully committed to the business case for ethical behaviour in business and assumes that through a continuous improvement process unethical behaviour can be reduced, to the economic and financial benefit of the company. Not surprisingly, since Japan was the home of the Total Quality Management (TQM) movement and the commitment to *Kaizen*, it is not unexpected that they would apply a similar approach to business ethics reporting. The standard proposes four stages in the creation of an ethical compliance system:

- Preparing a legal compliance manual and clarifying the organisation's ethical policy and values.
- Appointing an individual or group to oversee the implementation of the compliance manual.
- An independent audit to check that the manual has been implemented.
- Identifying areas for development and improvement using the audit results.

This standard is a process-centred one. It cannot report on whether a company is acting ethically because each company will produce:

- a set of ethical standards which the organisation will implement according to its own traditions and management beliefs [a code of ethics] and

- a body of rules and regulations [a code of conduct] of specific relevance and importance to the organisation considering its work content, scale and the materials and services in which it deals.

(Reitaku Centre for Economic Studies, 1999: 8)

The standard can only report on whether the company is doing what it says it would do.

## Q-RES

This is an Italian initiative; the documents are available in English. The standard was published in draft form in 2001 and was piloted by seven companies. It aims to provide guidance on how to:

- draw up codes of ethics and conduct;

- improve training and communication on social responsibility matters;

- produce externally verified reports.

The project has identified a number of indicators that can be used to indicate social and ethical performance as far as the following stakeholder groups are concerned (Tencati *et al.*, 2003: 19–21):

- Human resources

- Members/shareholder/financial community

- Clients/customers

- Suppliers

- Financial partners

- Government and local authorities

- Community

- Environment.

The indicators that were identified during the pilot projects were a mixture of qualitative, quantitative, and in particular economic measures.

### Activity 10.3

Compare and contrast the best practice standards just discussed. Identify the relevant strengths and weaknesses of each. Which would you recommend to a multi-national company?

## The challenge of the citizen

In Chapter 8 we considered the possible implications of the notion of corporate citizenship developing along the lines of (theoretical) individual citizenship. We also considered, in Chapter 9, a simultaneous process identified by many commentators as the diminishing and stunted notion of the individual, as reflected solely in the self-seeking consumer. Yet, paradoxically, groups opposed to particular corporate practices have focused their attention upon consumer groups in order to try to change the practices in question. The oil corporations Esso (Exxon in America) and Shell have both been the subject of boycott campaigns. In the case of Esso, the issue was the corporation's oil-drilling activities in the Arctic Circle, whereas for Shell it has been the continuing problems of oil extraction in the Niger delta.

Other specific examples include:

- The picketing of Cartier, one of the premier jewellers on New York's Fifth Avenue, by members of the Campaign to Eliminate Conflict Diamonds, in September 2000.

  As thousands of potential shoppers filed past, the demonstrators brandished signs depicting children whose hands and feet had been amputated by rebels fighting a brutal war in Sierra Leone. 'Did your diamond do this?' the placards screamed. The protest, which was reinforced later by prime-time television advertising, was aimed at forcing the US diamond industry to support legislation to stem the flow of illegal diamonds, thereby robbing rebels in Sierra Leone and Angola of their main funding source. By linking the diamond industry with such extreme violence, the campaign tried to tarnish the image of diamonds as a sign of love and fidelity... NGOs have realised that the quickest way to get the results is to go directly after companies by targeting their customers, their investors, or both.

  (Alden, 2001: 11)

- The picketing of Huntingdon Life Sciences (HLS) is discussed in Chapter 2 (Case study 2.26). In 2002 a number of major clients removed their custom from HLS because of the damage the association was causing the client companies.

- The criticisms levelled at corporations such as Nike for their involvement in Indonesia and other third world countries. In response to adverse publicity and campaigns against their products, some companies, including Nike, have agreed to pay certain non-government organisations (NGOs) to monitor the operations of suppliers to ensure compliance with agreed codes of conduct.

- Conversely the rise of retailing initiatives such as 'Trade Fair' reflects the ability and opportunities that are beginning to occur that allow consumers to display their preferences for ethical practices in business.

- In a similar vein, it can be argued that the significance of US and UK pension funds, unit trusts and investment trusts has increased the importance of the capital and securities markets as potential points of leverage for NGOs. One of the most active, and famous, pension funds in the field of ethical investing is CalPERS (The California Public Employees Pension system). In July 2001 the *Financial Times* announced the launch of four sets of indices that were designed to reflect the ethicality of corporate practices and activities. An ethical share index was launched. One of the indices relates to companies operating in the UK, one relates to Europe, the third to the USA and the fourth to the whole world. The UK-based index was the first to go 'live' in July 2001.

To be included in the index a company must satisfy a range of criteria including employment issues; types of products produced and/or sold; the human rights records of the countries in which the companies operate; health and safety issues; and community involvement. Of the top 100 UK companies, as measured by the traditional *Financial Times* index, 36 were not included in the first publication of the ethical share index. In some way each of these companies had failed against one or more of the index's criteria.

The Confederation of British Industry (CBI) expressed reservations about the index, fearing that those companies omitted from the index would be perceived as 'bad' companies, whereas any exclusion might reflect merely a difference in terminology or definition. However, pressure groups expressed concern at the inclusion of certain companies in the index. The Free Tibet Campaign, for example, objected to BP's inclusion.

A further development comes from the EU. In 2001 the EU part-financed a business organisation called CSR Europe, which was intended to add impetus to the developments in corporate social responsibility. CSR Europe was charged with promoting corporate social responsibility throughout Europe, culminating with 'European Year on corporate social responsibility' in 2005. Whilst free-market critics accused CSR Europe of being anti-capitalist and anti-market, those on the left have been critical of CSR Europe, seeing it as a 'camouflage', 'allowing big business to claim responsibility without doing anything more than paying its subscriptions. Trade unionists worry that voluntarism cannot provide sufficient protection for workers' (Cowe, 2001).

Those companies initially supporting CSR Europe included Nike, Shell and BP, companies with much adverse publicity to overcome. The reasons for joining CSR Europe are varied but Cowe (2001) observed that, 'while social responsibility is much more than philanthropy, it is about money, not morals'. BT's group personnel director made the following observation, 'It is about doing business in a way that persuades our customers to buy from us, our employees to work hard for us and our communities to accept us'.

The phenomenon of the rise of citizen pressure groups, whether they are human or animal rights based, or associated with environmental issues, is a development that contains the seeds of positive and negative potentialities. The positive aspects relate to the challenging (and sometimes overturning) of unethical corporate practices. Campaigns and protests can reflect active citizen participation in the social, political and economic evolution of nation states and super-nation states. However, there is also the downside potential, the risks associated with these developments. These risks are three-fold.

1. The first relates to the ability of the under-represented, the already socially and economically excluded, to be able to articulate their concerns – and be listened to. At least with universal suffrage, each person has only one vote. In pressure group politics, the super-organised, media-wise, politically adept pressure group is likely to have a considerable advantage over less well-organised groups. In the latter scenario, 'might is right' might well prevail, which is hardly an ethically sound approach.

2. The second concern is that, if scarce resources are to be effectively harnessed and utilised (a justifiable ethical concern), decision making in corporations cannot become paralysed by rules, by interminable meetings, or by an inability to achieve consensus on every decision.

3. The third concern is associated with the way opposition to corporate or government practices is expressed. The violence witnessed at the G8 summits at Genoa, Seattle and London shocked many people. Unintentional violence can be seen as one of the possibilities of democratic expression, but a number of the pressure groups present at these summits were also concerned by the violence, not just because it was never their intention that the demonstrations would develop in the ways they did, but also because the violence detracted from their important messages.

The ways societies evolve to handle these aspects of the corporate citizen relationship is of fundamental importance to societal development.

## Reflections

From the Hobbesian view of human behaviour, that people will not behave morally without the fear of retribution, flows the necessity for rules, of which codes of conduct are an obvious example. Bauman saw rules and codes, based upon reason, as leading to a morality associated with law – the laws of business and bureaucracy. This adherence to procedural rationality requires that

> all other emotions must be toned down or chased out of court . . . the most prominent of the exiled emotions are moral sentiments; that resilient and unruly 'voice of conscience'.
>
> (Bauman, 1994: 8)

Interestingly, Bauman argued that when the term ethics appears in the vocabulary of bureaucracy it is invariably in connection with 'professional ethics'. The latter term is considered to be breached when a member shows disloyalty either to the organisation or to (organisational) colleagues. A qualified notion of honesty thus becomes of critical importance, i.e. the keeping of promises and contractual obligations. This leads to predictability and consistency in organisations, an extremely important managerial need. When this is coupled with the notion of 'floating responsibility', an escape route is provided for those seeking a quiet life in the face of an awkward organisational issue.

People's instrumentalism is seen as something to be encouraged by Clutterbuck (1992: 100–1) as he exhorted organisations to reward exemplary behaviour, possibly with cash payments, and to 'punish breaches of the code publicly; use the key motivators of influence, promotion and access to resources'. This simplistic view of human nature and notions of managing assumes that instrumentalism is the only determinant, or at least the dominant explanation, of human behaviour. From a purely instrumental perspective, it is also an expensive option. In the governing of human relationships, trust is a far less expensive option than contractualism or financial incentives. But the problem remains of whether trust can be relied upon. When associated with notions of loyalty, it becomes increasingly problematic. For example, in a situation where it has become known to you that a product of your employing organisation poses health risks to consumers, which is paramount, your loyalty to:

- your work colleagues,

- your employing organisation,

- your family (who depend on your income),

- the consumer, or

- the general public?

The converse of the loyalty question is which of these groups has the right to trust you and your actions in such a situation?

Maybe the least that can be said for codes of ethics is that they give the principled employee a reference point should times become ethically challenged and certain organisational practices give rise to serious cause for concern. At its best a code can reflect an honestly expressed expectation about moral conduct within an organisation, with the code probably written in terms of principles rather than in a prescriptive or proscriptive fashion. Employees would be encouraged to act with moral agency and the codes would be supported by mechanisms that would allow concerned employees to raise concerns in a neutral and anonymous forum, preferably using external counsellors.

The roles of codes and agreements relating to the relationships between MNCs, national governments and supplier networks are important and interesting elements in the debates on codes of conduct. At the same time debates relating to codes of ethics and professions, an area of much academic activity at one time, have become less relevant as the compromised positions of many business professions have come to general attention.

Within the complex arenas that are modern business corporations, codes of conduct, codes of ethics and the prevailing culture/s will be important reference points for many of the players involved with, or affected by, the activities of the corporation. At different times the eight roles of codes discussed in this chapter will be seen in operation. Yet if ethics is at the heart of an organisation's practices and its *raison d'être*, embedded within its culture/s, written codes become less important. They become less defensive in terms of their tenor, being essentially codes of ethics.

## Summary

In this chapter the following key points have been made:

- While not universally or uniformly recognised, distinctions between codes of conduct and codes of ethics help crystallise the intended purpose of a code.

- Codes of practice can be important mechanisms that allow business corporations to negotiate their position in a society.

- Codes of practice have multiple roles within organisations, which will not necessarily be mutually exclusive.

- The development of a code of practice is, at one and the same time, an understandable development by a corporation, but also a reflection of a lack of trust in the integrity and reliability of its employees.

- There are arguments against developing codes of practice that require ethical practice to be at the heart of an organisation's activities and 'ways of working'.

- The various international and public ethical best practice standards that companies can commit to each have separate priorities and emphases.

- Organisational cultures and leadership are critical to understanding an organisation's actual (as distinct from espoused) values.

- The challenges to corporations by organised lobby groups of citizens are also an important means of monitoring the ethical performance of companies and their degrees of adherence to codes.

## Quick revision test

1. Identify the possible roles of codes of ethics.

2. What are the arguments against the employment of codes of practice within organisations?

3. What other means can organisations employ to communicate and inculcate organisational values, in addition to codes of conduct and ethics?

4. How many levels of culture does Edgar Schein identify; which are the most changeable?

## Typical assignments and briefs

1. Why have codes of ethics become so commonplace in corporations and how useful are they?

2. Draft a code of conduct to cover e-communications (email, Web use and so on). Explain and justify your proposed code.

3. What are the drawbacks and problems associated with codes of ethics?

4. Discuss the role of leadership and organisational culture in developing a socially responsible company.

## Group activity 10

Search the World Wide Web to find a code of ethics that you can download. The easiest way might be to think of a company you have heard of and track down its code. Analyse it by answering the following questions.

- Is it a code of ethics, a code of conduct or both?

- Does it look like a standard code, the same as everyone else's, or does it look as if it has been tailored to that organisation?

- Is it a code that recognises that some things within it are likely to be aspirations?

- Is it clear and unambiguous or does it leave lots of 'wriggle room'? If it does is such a 'fudge factor' necessary?

- Does it look like a PR document or one that will be helpful to employees?

- If you were an employee of the organisation what would you think the code implied about the organisation's view of its staff?

## Recommended further reading

A useful text is R.A. Buchholz and S.B. Rosenthal (1998) *Business Ethics: The Pragmatic Path Beyond Principles to Process*, London: Prentice Hall. Deborah Smith's pamphlet, *Demonstrating Corporate Values – which standard for your company?*, published by the Institute of Business Ethics in 2002 is an excellent comparative guide to the various codes and standards of ethical business available to organisations. The following articles will be of interest to those who wish to study the topic further: C. Cassell, P. Johnson and K. Smith (1997), 'Opening the Black Box: Corporate codes of ethics in their organisational context', *Journal of Business Ethics*, 16, 1077–93; G. McDonald and A. Nijhof (1999) 'Beyond codes of ethics: an integrated framework for stimulating morally responsible behaviour in organisations', *Leadership & Organisation Development Journal*, 20(3), 133–46; R.C. Warren (1993) 'Codes of ethics: Bricks without straw', *Business Ethics: A European Review*, 2(4), 185–91. *See also* S. Srivastva and D.L. Cooperrider (1988) *Executive Integrity: The Search for High Human Values in Organisational Life*, San Francisco: Jossey-Bass Inc., 1–28.

## Useful websites

| Topic | Website provider | URL |
| --- | --- | --- |
| The CSR Competency framework | The CSR Academy | http://www.csracademy.org.uk/competency.htm |
| The AA1000 quality standard for corporate social responsibility | AccountAbility | http://www.accountability.org.uk/aa1000/default.asp |
| The One World Trust website | One World Trust | http://www.oneworldtrust.org/ |
| Transparency International website | Transparency International | http://www.transparency.org/ |
| The Global Reporting Initiative Web page | CERES/UN | http://www.globalreporting.org/ |
| Social Accountability SA8000 Web page | Social Accountability International | http://www.cepaa.org/SA8000/SA8000.htm |
| The Ethics Compliance Management System Standard (ECS2000) | Reitaku Centre for Economic Studies | http://www.ie.reitaku-u.ac.jp/~davis/assets/applets/ecs2k-e.pdf |
| Q-RES Report | | http://www.biblio.liuc.it:8080/biblio/liucpap/pdf/95e.pdf |
| This is a good place to find copies of professional, governmental and organisational codes of ethics. Particularly fun is the code of ethics for witches (the Covenant of the Goddess). Most of the codes on this site are utterly serious. | Centre for the Study of Ethics in Professions | http://www.iit.edu/departments/csep/PublicWWW/codes/ |
| An interesting corporate ethics website | Texas Instruments | http://www.ti.com/corp/docs/company/citizen/ethics/benchmark.shtml |
| Issue brief on codes of ethics/values | Business for Social Responsibility | http://www.bsr.org/CSRResources/IssueBriefDetail.cfm?DocumentID=395 |
| Shell Canada: Statement of general business principles | Shell Canada | http://www.shell.ca/code/values/commitments/principles.html |

# PART D

# The international context

## CHAPTER 11

# Global and local values – and international business

Having read the chapter and completed its associated activities, readers should be able to:

- Describe how the ethical and business values of countries and societies differ.

- Argue about the validity of particular values and ethical standards of different countries.

- Evaluate the options for responding to the ethical issues and dilemmas that arise from international business and globalisation.

- Relate these issues to the debates about ethical universalism and ethical relativism.

- Understand the processes of learning that occur when people with partly overlapping but partly distinct values interact.

## Introduction

Societies and countries may differ in their business ethics and values. Any differences or similarities may be internal to societies or countries or between them.

- Different countries may have, in the high ethics established within their religion, philosophical traditions and literature, different ideals about the conduct of business and organisational life. Cultural tradition in one place might see business growth and profitability as an end in itself; in other places economic ends might be seen as subordinate to other goals.

- Within a country or society there may be competing sets of values concerning business and management. Within Muslim countries, for example, there may be differences between modernisers who want to work to the values of global business whereas traditionalists may wish to apply Islamic values to business practices.

- Even if countries and societies share the same values they may vary in the degree to which they practise them. While two countries might, at a formal level, regard bribery as immoral, one country might conduct its business in line with this standard but the second country might not.

- There may be differences within a country and society between the values embodied in its high traditions and those values adopted in everyday life.

---

**Connexion point**

In Chapter 4, pp. 157–63, it was argued that people will have different ideas about whether values are unified in a seamless whole or whether they are fragmented, in the modern world. Those who see values as fragmented do not necessarily believe this to be a problem.

---

Such differences, between and within countries, raise questions that are the subject of this chapter.

1. The first question asks about the similarities and differences between different countries' and societies' ethical principles and practices concerning business.

2. The second question is whether such differences can ever be justified. In ethical terms this question is a particular example of the general debate between ethical relativism and ethical universalism. Ethical universalism, in brief, is the argument that there can only be one set of true ethical principles that must apply everywhere in the world; ethical relativism is the argument that different places can have different values and principles that are valid to that particular locality.

3. The third question is whether diversity of values between societies and communities can be of advantage to international businesses as a source of organisational learning.

---

## Essentialism    DEFINITION

Before we go any further with this chapter we must consider an ethical question that arises from the assumption that has been made that countries and societies have distinctive values and ethical standards that are generally shared by all those within the country or society. This assumption is known as essentialism. According to essentialist theory a society, or even a nation state, has a set of stable, internally consistent values that change only slowly. Essentialists therefore tend to emphasise the differences between the values of different societies and underplay the differences within the society (Holden, 2002: 27). At one level this is just a consequence of the simplification needed to discuss matters of inter-cultural values at a high level of generalisation. Critics argue, however, that such generalisation about different societies' values can have a more pernicious effect. By reducing complex societies to simple labels such as Islamic or African and defining them by a few core ideas, which are often the opposite of those claimed by western business people, the task of managing businesses and organisations in Islamic or African countries is simplified and stereotyped for the western manager. These managers then do not have to deal with the complexity, merely respond to the stereotypes.

The alternative view is to stress the differences of values within societies by focusing on the processes by which individuals make sense of the many influences that bear on their sense of values and of right and wrong. These influences will not only include the influences from the family and community but also from the international media.

This chapter can be accused of essentialism. However, it is not naïve essentialism. Some research, for example, shows that being evasive and not providing all the information you have on a matter is not seen as wrong in Hong Kong (Yeung et al., 1999), but in the USA it is (McCornack et al., 1992). However, it would be silly to say that no one in Hong Kong felt it was wrong to tell less than the whole truth or that no American ever bluffed or spoke the truth only selectively.

A non-naïve view of essentialism depends upon a sensible understanding of the idea of the average. Individual diversity can form a pattern in the aggregate. A statement such as 'people in Hong Kong do not think withholding information is lying' is a statement of that group's average view. Within an average there can be a range of actual views. Many people in Hong Kong will think it a terrible thing to hold back the full truth. Just as likely is that individual people in Hong Kong may take different positions on the matter at different times and in different circumstances. It is also of course important to recognise that when one generalises about large entities, such as India, there will be much regional and local diversity in values and principles. The essentialist statements made in this chapter, indeed in this book, should be taken for what they are, a statement that the view or principle attributed to a group has the highest probability of being taken by individuals within that group at any one time. A belief that individuals construct and adapt their own stories about right and wrong does not preclude generalisations about whole populations. A determined anti-essentialist however would most likely find this argument unacceptable because it does not concede the whole ground to individuality.

The case studies provided in Chapter 2 illustrate many ethical issues that may arise from an international diversity of ethical values. Case study 2.4, for example, deals with the use of child labour, which is seen as acceptable by some people in some countries. The issue is whether universal codes of conduct should be established which carry moral authority, or the sanctions of international law, to prevent companies acting badly in the world market place. Such universal provisions could be seen as ethically necessary but can also be seen as a form of ethical colonialism in which western multinational companies, and even non-governmental organisations (NGOs), use their strength to force societies to accept values that are not their own. Apart from any moral objection to such processes Jaeger and Kanungo (1990: 1) expressed a practical criticism:

> uncritical transfer of management theories and techniques based on Western ideologies and value systems has in many ways contributed to organisational inefficiency and ineffectiveness in the developing country context.

Western organisations' concern for equal opportunities in staff selection processes for example might contradict local obligations to support friends, family and relations. Such situations can lead to employees experiencing psychological conflicts between the values of their society and those imposed on them by their western employers (Tripathi (1990), Viswesvaran and Deshpande (1996)). These issues have not arisen only recently, with the expansion of multinational organisations in the world. The dominance of western values has long been recognised and disputed. Vivekenanda, a nineteenth-century Indian nationalist and religious leader, argued:

> I will tell you something for your guidance in life. Everything that comes from India take as true, until you find cogent reasons for disbelieving it. Everything that comes from Europe take as false, until you find cogent reasons for believing it.
>
> (Quoted in Chakraborty, 1999: 4)

The chapter is divided into three parts that deal with each of the questions raised in the introduction.

- The first part describes the extent to which ethical standards, values and practices of business differ between and within countries. It also discusses attempts to produce universal standards for business ethics.

- The second part offers a normative discussion of whether it matters if different countries have different ethical systems. It raises the philosophical debate between universalists, who believe there can only be one true ethical system, and relativists, who believe that cultural ethical difference is justifiable. It is argued that relativism does not mean that 'anything goes' because there are ways of judging between valid differences in business ethics and invalid ones.

- The third part deals with the question of how people should behave in a world in which a universal business ethic is not established and in which countries may have valid differences in their business ethics.

## Business and managerial values in different countries and societies

This section of the chapter assesses the extent to which values and ethics are universal in the business and organisational arenas and the extent to which they differ between countries and societies.

## Universal values?

There are ethical norms and values that are transnational, shared by many countries. Sometimes these reflect common cultures, as in the Islamic countries. Sometimes they are the result of coincidence or a reflection of the commonalities of human nature and condition (Wines and Napier, 1992). There have been attempts to identify such standards, to codify them and publish them as a universal guide.

One important example is the Declaration of Human Rights, which was published by the United Nations in 1948 and subsequently, in 1966, divided into two separate codes, one covering civil and political rights and one, more relevant to our field, covering economic, cultural and social rights.

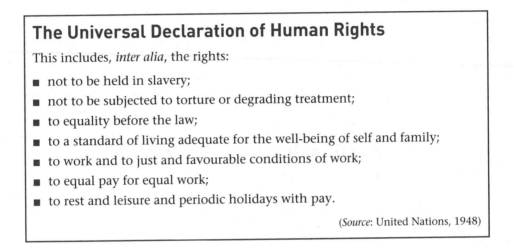

# The Universal Declaration of Human Rights

This includes, *inter alia*, the rights:

- not to be held in slavery;
- not to be subjected to torture or degrading treatment;
- to equality before the law;
- to a standard of living adequate for the well-being of self and family;
- to work and to just and favourable conditions of work;
- to equal pay for equal work;
- to rest and leisure and periodic holidays with pay.

(*Source*: United Nations, 1948)

Other attempts have focused on standards for international business. Sometimes companies and industries publish codes that they believe should govern their business operations worldwide. This sort of standard has been particularly common in relation to the employment practices used by companies' partners in their international supply chains. There are arguments for saying that the World Trade Organisation (WTO), which was set up in 1995 as a successor to the General Agreement on Tariffs and Trade (GATT), should be the body to take on this ethical responsibility as it is the regulatory body for world trade. In particular Tsogas (1999) argued that it should publish and regulate labour standards across the world. The WTO has not taken on this role.

The Caux Round Table is an international body that, with the involvement of the Minnesota Center for Corporate Responsibility, developed a set of ethical principles for international business. It was founded in 1986 by Olivier Giscard D'Estaing of INSEAD, a French business school, and Frederick Philips, chairman of Philips Electronics. They accepted that law and markets provided insufficient guides for conduct. They therefore defined ethical principles based on the Japanese concept of *kyosei* – cooperating to achieve a mutual common prosperity – and human dignity (Caux Round Table, 2001).

**Connexion point**

Universal codes for governing businesses globally are a recurring theme of this book. Such codes are also discussed in Chapter 10 where the practical benefits and uses of codes are discussed and again in Chapter 12 where the relevance of codes in dealing with some of the ethical problems caused by globalisation is considered.

Implicit agreement on transnational standards, or even formal agreement about universal ethical standards, does not, of course, mean that those standards are implemented. The gap between espoused values and values in practice has been conceptualised by Hofstede (1991: 9) as the difference between the desirable and the desired. The desirable is an ethical norm that states what is right and good; the desired is a description of what people actually seek to achieve. Bribery and corruption is a case in point. Most societies in the world see it as undesirable, but that does not prevent large numbers of people in many societies desiring the benefits it can bring them.

It is worth considering bribery and corruption in more detail. Some types of bribery in particular circumstances might not be immoral. A suggested scale of impropriety for the payment of bribes is shown below.

---

## A scale of bribery and corruption

- *Gifts* – expressions of friendship and good faith, openly given, of low value and often reciprocated.

- *Tips* – discretionary rewards for good service.

- *'Grease'* (sometimes known as facilitation payments) – small payments on a customary scale to encourage people to do what their job requires them to do. Not a payment to make them do what they should not do. Grease is often a recompense for the very low wages of those accepting the inducement. The Anti-terrorism, Crime and Security Act 2001 made it a crime in the UK for British firms to make such payments (or any other form of bribe) to officials overseas. The UK government did not anticipate that overseas officials extorting such payments in countries in which it was normal would lead to prosecutions in the UK.

- *Commissions* – often large payments for acting as a go-between and facilitating deals. It could be a fair payment for professional services but if the payment is disproportionate it might be a way of delegating responsibility for paying bribes from the principal to an agent.

- *Bribes* – payments to encourage people to do things that they should not.

---

The following factors should be considered when judging the badness of a bribe.

- Whether it gives the bribe giver an unfair advantage or access to resources or benefits that would not otherwise be available to them.

- Whether the amount of the bribe is greater than is customary.

- Whether the opportunity to offer a bribe is not equally open to all and when different people or groups have to pay different amounts in bribes.

- Whether it is illegal.

- Whether its cultural impact is to undermine trust and probity in a society.

It can be argued that bribery of a government official is worse than bribery of a company or a private individual. This is because a public body or official has a special obligation to the well-being of the population as a whole that cannot be discharged if that body or official responds to private and sectional interests through bribery. The OECD (2001) published a convention that outlawed the bribing of public officials in international business negotiations. A private individual or company in contrast might be thought to have a responsibility only to themselves, their close associates and their shareholders. In this case the damage caused by the giving or taking of bribes may be less.

Nevertheless most countries formally proscribe the giving and taking of bribes for the reasons outlined above. Yet in many countries corruption is endemic. Transparency International is an NGO that researches the level of perceived bribery and corruption, in terms of both offering and receiving bribes, in a wide range of countries. They produce two indices based on surveys of informed persons. The indices do not measure the actual frequency of corruption but people's opinion of its frequency.

Selections from the 2004 Corruption Perceptions Index are shown in Table 11.1. Ninety-nine countries were analysed in the index but they are not all shown for reasons of space. The complete results can be seen on Transparency International's (2004) website. The index uses a 0–10 scale in which 0 means highly corrupt and 10 means very honest.

**Table 11.1** The Transparency International Corruption Perceptions Index (CPI) 2004

| Country | Rank | CPI score | Country | Rank | CPI score |
|---------|------|-----------|---------|------|-----------|
| Finland | 1 | 9.7 | El Salvador | 51 | 4.2 |
| New Zealand | 2 | 9.6 | China | 71 | 3.4 |
| Singapore | 5 | 9.3 | Egypt | 77 | 3.2 |
| United Kingdom | 11 | 8.6 | India | 90 | 2.8 |
| Hong Kong | 16 | 8.0 | Russia | 90 | 2.8 |
| USA | 17 | 7.5 | Indonesia | 133 | 2.0 |
| Italy | 42 | 4.8 | Bangladesh & Haiti | 145 | 1.5 |

*Source*: Transparency International, 2004

The second index produced by Transparency International, the Bribe Payers Index, is based on a survey of 21 countries. The respondents were asked how likely it was that companies from named countries would pay bribes to win or retain business. The results are shown in Table 11.2. Again an index number of 10 represents a perceived low level of bribery and 0 a high level.

Two sectors dominated the bribery table when it came to identifying those sectors in which bribes were most likely to be paid, principally because they would be demanded or expected. These were public works and construction (first), followed by arms and defence. Third and fourth were oil and gas, and banking and finance respectively.

**Table 11.2** The Transparency International Bribe Payers Index (BPI) 2002

| Country | Rank | BPI score | Country | Rank | BPI score |
|---|---|---|---|---|---|
| Australia | 1 | 8.5 | Spain | 11 | 5.8 |
| Sweden | 2 | 8.4 | France | 12 | 5.2 |
| Switzerland | 2 | 8.4 | USA | 13 | 5.3 |
| Austria | 4 | 8.2 | Japan | 13 | 5.3 |
| Canada | 5 | 8.1 | Malaysia | 15 | 4.3 |
| Netherlands | 6 | 7.8 | Italy | 17 | 4.1 |
| Belgium | 6 | 7.8 | Taiwan | 17 | 3.5 |
| United Kingdom | 8 | 6.9 | South Korea | 18 | 3.9 |
| Germany | 9 | 6.3 | China | 20 | 3.5 |
| Singapore | 9 | 6.3 | Russia | 21 | 3.2 |

*Source*: Transparency International, 2002

The final table we will refer to relates to the responses of developing countries and their experiences of donor countries applying pressure other than bribery, for example, diplomatic pressure, financial pressure, tied foreign aid, threat of reduced foreign aid, and tied arms deals. In practically all cases countries receiving the aid reported significant increases in these forms of pressure. All respondents taking part in the survey were asked to identify the three governments they would principally associate with the type of practices mentioned above. In all, there were 567 responses to the survey and 22 countries were identified as employing some or all of these unfair practices. The percentage figures in Table 11.3 indicate the frequency with which the countries were mentioned.

To some extent the countries at the top of the table (or, in some respects, the bottom) are where they might be expected to be because they are the big operators in the construction and armaments' sectors, but the percentage differences are particularly revealing.

More attempts are being made to produce universal ethical codes for international business. But there is still much work to be done. Even if the difficulties of promulgating codes are overcome, the problem of differing degrees of conformance to the codes remains. The gap between intention and implementation connects to a final observation on the search for a universal code. It is that such codes mostly deal with terminal values; that is to say, values about what the end purposes of human life and activity are. The discussion of corruption suggests that in business ethics the emphasis is on instrumental values, which deal with how we should behave with each other. It is in the matter of instrumental values that most cultural differences in business values lie, as we shall see in the next section.

**Table 11.3** The Transparency International table of 'Countries using other unfair means to gain or retain business'

| Country | Rank | % |
|---|---|---|
| USA | 1 | 58 |
| France | 2 | 26 |
| United Kingdom | 3 | 19 |
| Japan | 4 | 18 |
| China | 5 | 16 |
| Russia | 6 | 13 |
| Italy | 10 | 5 |
| Canada | 15 | 3 |
| Australia | 19 | 1 |
| Sweden | 22 | <1 |

*Source*: Transparency International, 2002

**Connexion point**

The terms 'terminal' and 'instrumental' values were coined by Rokeach, whose work on values is discussed in Chapter 4, pp. 152–4.

## Relative values?

This section explores the extent to which different societies and cultures have different values and ethical standards in the fields of business and organisational life. Geert Hofstede (1991 and 2001) carried out the seminal empirical work on national value differences in organisations. He conducted a questionnaire survey of employees in the national subsidiaries of IBM. Responses were obtained from 72 national subsidiaries in 1968 and 1972. The results from the smaller subsidiaries were ignored and so the analysis finally enabled a comparison between the personal values of employees in 53 countries. He identified four dimensions along which the values of employees in different countries varied.

- *Power distance* – the extent to which the less powerful members of organisations expect and accept that power is distributed unequally.

- *Individualism* – high in countries in which the ties between individuals are loose and everyone is expected to look out for themselves. It is low in collectivist countries where people are integrated into strong, cohesive groups and are expected to give loyalty to these groups in return for their protection.

- *Masculinity* – high in those countries in which gender roles are distinct and in which men are expected to be assertive, tough and focused on material success and women are supposed to be more modest, tender and concerned with the quality of life. In societies in which masculinity is low the gender roles overlap and both men and women are supposed to be modest, tender and concerned with the quality of life.

- *Uncertainty avoidance* – the extent to which society members feel threatened by uncertain or unknown situations. Societies in which there is low uncertainty avoidance are comfortable with ambiguity; those in which there is high uncertainty avoidance seek to finesse ambiguity away.

Table 11.4 shows the relative positions of the USA, Great Britain and India, and the highest and lowest scoring countries on each index.

**Table 11.4** Values and rank score for selected countries on four indices of national value differences

| Country | Power distance index | Individualism index | Masculinity index | Uncertainty avoidance index |
|---|---|---|---|---|
| *Highest scoring country* | Malaysia (104) | USA (91) | Japan (95) | Greece (112) |
| USA | 38/53 (40) | – | 15 (62) | 43/53 (46) |
| Great Britain | 42/53 (35) | 3/53 (89) | 9 (66) | 47/53 (35) |
| India | 10/53 (77) | 21/53 (48) | 20 (54) | 40/53 (40) |
| *Lowest scoring country* | Austria (11) | Guatemala (6) | Sweden (5) | Singapore (8) |

Figures in brackets are the countries' scores on the scales.

*Source*: Based on Hofstede, 1991: 26, 53, 84, 113

Differences in values need not cause ethical difficulties. For example, differences in values about uncertainty avoidance or perceptions of time may not raise major ethical problems, but differences in other values do. The identification by Trompenaars and Hampden-Turner (1993: 144–5) of national differences in attitudes towards nature, for example, affects ethical matters such as humanity's use or abuse of the physical world. North American culture, which rose historically from a small society that found itself in a huge continent, developed values that emphasised control over one's environment and destiny as the key to success. In a post-Kyoto world these values appear to be a threat to environmental sustainability. Among the value dimensions identified by Hofstede, power distance, masculinity and individualism all raise ethical questions about the nature of good and moral relationships between people.

The various approaches to leadership in different countries may be related to their values. Hofstede looked at two dimensions in particular to map these differences, and the analysis is shown in Figure 11.1. This shows how four national cultures might be expected to handle conflicts between people in business and

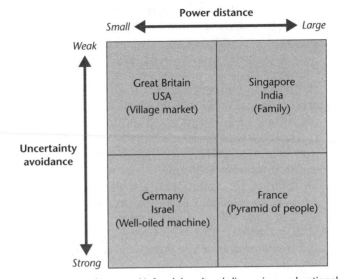

**Figure 11.1** The relationship between Hofstede's cultural dimension and national leadership styles
*Source*: Hofstede, 2001: 377

organisations. In France, where large power distances are accepted and people are ill-disposed towards uncertainty, it would be done through the chain of command. Those higher in the hierarchy would be expected to resolve disputes between their subordinates. German values also favour order and predictability but have a lower acceptance of large power distances. The German approach to conflict would be to improve procedures that would remove the causes of the conflicts. The British, with their tolerance of ambiguity, but not of big power distances, would prefer to tackle the problems through informal negotiations between the opponents. People would negotiate with each other as if they were farmers haggling in the village market place. Other countries, and India is an example, see relationships in a holistic rather than a functional manner. This can be explained by considering attitudes to friendship. Dewey (1993), who studied British civil servants in India, and their relationship with Indians, in the early twentieth century, discovered they had contradictory views of friendship. The British took their idea of friendship from Oxbridge common rooms and gentlemen's clubs and saw it as a relationship that carried little obligation beyond that of good conversation. The Indians, however, saw friendship as a fundamental bond that carried obligations to sacrifice oneself, if necessary, to support a friend in all their endeavours. Unsurprisingly, Dewey found that British officials' attempts to befriend Indians often collapsed in recriminations of faithlessness. The importance Indians place on personal obligations is reflected in Hofstede's suggestion about how managers, in countries like India, might handle conflicts. He argued they would use a metaphor of the family in which problems were resolved by deference to the head of the family or by accepting the demands imposed by a friend.

Hofstede (1991) was concerned that his original IBM survey was conducted using a research questionnaire written from a western cultural perspective. A new survey based on Chinese perspectives was prepared and administered to respondents in 23 countries around the world.

The results from the Chinese Values Survey supported the identification of three of Hofstede's value dimensions. The fourth one, however, uncertainty avoidance, could not be statistically identified in the raw results from the survey. Uncertainty is avoided, Hofstede argued, by establishing the truth. If the Chinese survey did not register this concern then it might be explained by the emphasis in Chinese values on virtue rather than truth. He proposed a fifth value dimension, which he labelled Confucian dynamism. Confucianism, the traditional philosophy of China, is not concerned with establishing religious Truths. Like Hinduism it is more concerned with practice than belief. To follow Confucianism or Hinduism it is not necessary to believe a creed, but it is required to behave in a particular way. This differentiates these religions from Christianity and Islam, which, while providing rules for daily life, require commitment to a creed. Confucianism stresses the importance of subordination in five key relationships (ruler–subject, father–son, older brother–younger brother, husband–wife, senior friend–junior friend), virtuous behaviour towards others and the adoption of key virtues such as thrift, hard work and study. Table 11.5 sets outs the Confucian values.

**Table 11.5** Confucian values

| Long-term Confucian values | Short-term Confucian values |
|---|---|
| • Persistence and perseverance | • Personal steadiness and stability |
| • Ordering relationships by status | • Protecting your 'face' |
| • Thrift | • Respect for tradition, reciprocation of greetings, favour and gifts |
| • Having a sense of shame | |

*Source*: Based on Hofstede, 1991: 165–6

The Confucian dynamism scale effectively measures the extent to which a society values a long-term rather than a short-term orientation. But the acceptance of the whole set of Confucian values marks, according to Hofstede (2001: 363), a major ethical divide between western and eastern ethical approaches. Western ethical approaches are focused on identifying the moral Truth, either by deontological or consequentialist means. The eastern traditions are more concerned with virtuous behaviour, which calls for the development of personal insight and judgement rather than knowledge. As pointed out in Chapter 3, many writers are arguing that a virtue ethics approach would be better suited to western businesses and organisations than that of western moral philosophy.

**Connexion point**

The importance of values in ethical decision making is discussed in Chapter 5.

## Moveable values

The argument so far has been based on the assumption that countries and societies have definable and discrete ethical beliefs and values. It would be wrong, however, to interpret this as meaning that they have fixed and monolithic ethical systems. Within societies and countries there will be competing interpretations of the shared values, and arguments about how they should change and develop. It is always dangerous therefore to talk about American values, British values or Indian values as if they could be authoritatively and definitively defined.

The development of thinking about management values in India can provide an example of how such debates progress. Much business and management education in India is based on American models. It is unsurprising that Indian managers have acquired through their training an American set of business values. Many Indian academics and business people have seen this as demeaning to an ancient civilisation such as India's and have begun to develop an indigenous approach to management that is based in Indian thought and traditions (Gopinath, 1998). This of course is difficult because India has a rich and varied religious and philosophical history from which values might be drawn. Hinduism is the main strand but Islam, Sikhism, Jainism, Zoroastrianism and others share a significant presence in Indian thought. Zoroastrianism is a particularly important element because it is the religion of the Parsi community from which many important Indian entrepreneurs come. We will concentrate on attempts to build modern business values from Hindu philosophy.

In Hindu thought there are four aims for humanity, *dharma* (righteousness), *artha* (wealth creation), *kama* (pleasure or material needs) and *moksha* (salvation from the transient to the eternal and the infinite). This is normally interpreted as making business and wealth creation an ethical imperative as long as it is circumscribed by a sense of duty and ethics. It is therefore opposed to the Friedmanite version of business ethics, which imposes no duty on businesses other than making profits for the shareholders. Chakraborty (1993, 1999) has developed a detailed system of business ethics and values based on the Vedanta and Yoga schools of Hindu philosophy. He has used it as a basis for consultancy and management development in Indian companies. Vedanta is based upon the *Upanishads* which are sacred Hindu scriptures written between the fifth and eighth centuries BC. It is based on the existence of a Supreme Being or absolute called the Brahman. Surprisingly, for those who see Hinduism as a religion with many Gods, Vedanta emphasises a monist belief in a single supreme being. The Brahman is the only reality. The world we perceive through our senses is, more or less depending upon which branch of Vedanta is followed, an illusion. The individual soul, through ignorance of the Brahman, believes in its own independent existence and importance. This sense of ego is the cause of all troubles in life. The end of religious striving is liberation from this false sense of individualism and a practical awareness of oneness with the absolute, with the Brahman. In Yoga this oneness can be expressed by the *purusha–prakriti* pairing. *Purusha* is the worldly and active term and *prakriti* is the still and contemplative term. The aim, according to Aurobindo Ghose, is to create a dual consciousness in which there is 'the one engaged in surface-level activity, caught in obscurity and struggle; the other, behind, remaining calm and strong with effortless insight' (Chakraborty, 1999: 6). It is this sense of oneness that, once achieved, leads to a life of unselfish service, which is the basis of Chakraborty's criticism of western management values and ethics. He argued that management development should not emphasise techniques and calculation but should encourage the spiritual development of managers and employees. Only when people have made a personal psychological journey will they be able to make ethical decisions in their jobs. This is an important theme in much Indian management literature. Mahesh (1995) and Diwedi (in Saini and Khan, 2000) stress the importance of ethical leadership and leaders with 'oriental soul'. Chakraborty argued, to take one specific example, that people who have achieved *moksha* would take a different view of change in business from that advocated by western textbooks. He criticised the fashion for constant change in business, in the name of economic growth, that has only led to disharmony between nations and between individuals. He proposed (Chakraborty, 1999: 24) some Vedantic principles that might be applied to organisational change:

- Natural change, that is the cycle of birth, growth and death, is good but man-made change often goes against natural change and leads to irreparable harm to the environment and to relations between people.

- For people to develop dual consciousness it is necessary for structures and institutions that have been developed from tradition to remain constant. Constant change of organisational structures and processes distracts people from their psychological development.

- Change in organisation and business often implies exchanging a condition closer to the eternal for a position that is more ephemeral and transient. In particular the tendency for organisations to focus on the measurable, at the expense of that which is not, ethically weakens organisations.

Chakraborty's work is a complex attempt to produce business values that are specific to India and which provide a critique of western and American values. It will be subject to debate and challenge within India if for no other reason than that it is based on one of India's religions and on a particular strand of Hinduism.

Other writers have drawn on different sources in Indian classical literature and identified other schemes of business ethics. One common source is the *Arthashastra* of Kautilya (Rangarajan, 1992), sometimes known as Chanyaka. This is a vast treatise on statecraft probably written in the third century BC and designed as a manual for the guidance of kings. Little is known of the author although there are many legends, and it is not even certain that a single person produced the work. This is a practical rather than a scriptural work and it is often compared with Machiavelli's *The Prince* (*see* p. 251). Most commentators on the work recognise that, like Machiavelli, Kautilya accepts that evil things sometimes have to be done in the best interests of the state. Several writers have argued that the lessons from the *Arthashastra* fit well with the values of modern western strategic thinking. Starzl and Dhir (1986) argued that the modern business world resembles the competing feudal states of India in the third century BC and that there is potential for Kautilya's principles to be applied to strategic planning. Kumar and Rao (1996) interpreted the *Arthashastra* as a recipe for modern value-based management. By this they meant the style of management, advocated by Peters and Waterman (1982), that involves defining corporate values and ensuring that staff are committed to them. They did not see Kautilya as being Machiavellian but instead saw his work as a source of 'ethical, moral and value based guidelines ... which will be useful for present day management and organisations'.

Whether Kautilya, as some argue, is seen as providing unethical but practical advice on statecraft or, as others argue, is a source of value-based managerial pre-scriptions, he is still the source of a set of values that are held to be close to those of western management thought. This indigenous approach to management therefore is contrary to Chakraborty's approach, based on Vedanta, which is highly critical of western business values. This contradiction illustrates why it should not be assumed that countries or societies have simple, clear and consen-sual business ethics.

The two Indian perspectives discussed are themselves just particular views from within the Indian managerial and academic community. The bulk of man-agement books published in India take a mainstream approach to management based on, and contributing to, a worldwide general consensus about the matter of management. Indeed Indian managerial technocrats have faced the ethical charge of being instrumentally rational, levelled at management generally, that it is too focused on means and does not concern itself with the proper ends of those means. A study by Sahay and Walsham (1997: 432) of a GIS and satellite imaging system that was designed to benefit Indian farmers identified the scien-tists' lack of interest in anything beyond the working of the new technology. They did not see the exploitation of the technology to ensure the agricultural benefits as their concern. India's pre-eminence in IT and software has brought it much benefit but it also produces a view that the setting up of a software pack-age, such as a customer relations marketing (CRM) system, is the whole solution to the problem of establishing relationships with customers and certainly does not question what the nature of that relationship should be.

Of course, Indian management writers do not simply accept the prescriptions and techniques of western management writers. An example is the Indian response to the American notion of human resource management (HRM) that has almost exclusively replaced the old personnel management in the industri-alised countries. The key theme of HRM is that it is not simply a necessary administrative function, which was how its predecessor personnel management was seen, but it is a strategically central function that makes a direct contribution to organisations' financial and other success. This idea is new in India where the emphasis has been on personnel management, industrial relations and human resource development (Saini and Khan, 2000). Rao (2000) pointed out some ethi-cal problems with the fashion for the adoption of HRM. HRM ignores context, in particular the tradition of strong unions in India and the illegality of retrench-ment, which means that voluntary retirement is the most common method of downsizing in India. To replace this approach with HRM's distrust of unions and with a strategic approach to downsizing (as recommended by the Federation of Indian Chambers of Commerce) on the basis of hunches as to what works in the USA would be unwise. He also points out the ethical hypocrisy of HRM.

Employees may be told that they are the organisations's most valued resource, and soon after they find themselves in a redundancy programme. They may be exposed to various participative management styles, teamwork, cellular working etc., and simultaneously exposed to aggressive anti-union policies.

(Rao, 2000: 116)

Ironically, because in the world of national stereotypes India is a place of spirituality and ashrams, Rao (2000: 133) accuses American concepts of HRM as being 'pseudospiritual' because they are based on American values rather than on scientific research and will, in India, lead to long-term disaster. Other Indian commentators on HRM (Dwivedi, 2000) seek to take aspects of HRM, such as empowerment, and to root them in classical Indian philosophy by seeing the implementation of the concept developing through four stages of *kali*, *dvaper*, *tretya* and *satya* (in Hindi thought these are the four *yuga* or ages that make up a historical aeon and they each have their own spiritual characteristics. We are currently in the *kali-yuga*). The manner of India's adoption of HRM exemplifies the complex relationships between different sets of management values and ethical positions. It is not a simple matter of there being an outright acceptance of American ideas of HRM, or a simple rejection of it and its replacement by an entirely Indian view, rather it is a process of interactive sense-making in which something distinct, but not separate from what preceded it, emerges.

The discussion so far in this section has focused on the formal and normative literature about what Indian business ethics should be. The business values actually adopted in India can be seen in the broad sweep of Indian history in the second half of the twentieth century. From Indian independence in 1947 until 1991 public policy focused on economic isolationism and self-sufficiency. As Nehru, the first prime minister of independent India, said, 'It is better to have a second-rate thing made in one's own country than a first-rate thing one has to import'. The socialism that predominated in these years also led to the development of a Licence Raj in which there were many bureaucratic controls on business. This approach to economic development also reflected Mahatma Gandhi's moral preference for self-sufficiency. At this period policy reflected Hindu values that refused pre-eminence to economic growth.

In 1991 the government of India changed its policy and started a process of liberalisation. The licensing system was abolished, trade barriers were lowered and foreign investment was made easier. The amount of direct foreign investment rose from virtually nothing to US$2 billion a year. Liberalisation encouraged Indian companies to adopt western business values and Indians working for western multi-nationals in India exhibited western business values (Singh, 1990: 92). The change in India's business policies provides the context in which, as we have seen, Indian managers have begun to adopt HRM. The change may also encourage Kautilya's ethics rather than those of Vedanta.

## Section summary

Although there are attempts at producing universal ethical standards they have not yet had a major impact on international business. There is evidence that people in different countries have different values that they apply to business. In broad terms there is a dialogue, a process of sense-making, between the predominant values of western businesses and cultures and the desire of many in developing countries who wish to see business ethics that reflect their indigenous ethical and religious traditions.

## The normative debate about ethical universalism and relativism in the business context

## The normative implications and arguments

The existence of different ethical standards and values in different societies and countries raises difficulties for normative and philosophical thinking about ethics. If different countries have different customary values that each regards as valid then philosophers' attempts to define what is good and right are undermined. All the multi-national company has to do is follow the maxim, 'When in Rome do as the Romans do'. But what if we feel that what is allowed in some countries is wrong? Does a relativist position mean that any practice or value in a society has to be accepted as long as it has a patina of tradition? A number of arguments can be put forward that constrain the apparent arbitrariness of relativist ethics.

### The need for standards is universal

Although societies may have different ethical practices and values they all have a universal requirement to have such norms (Blackburn, 2001: 22). Societies may treat their children differently when they come of age. Some buy them cars and send then as far away as possible to universities, some send them out to find their fortune, some require them to join the family firm and some require them to get married as soon as possible. But all these societies share a need to have some ethical standards about how they treat their new adults. It is a similar situation in organisations. They all need, for example, ethical standards for the treatment of family members working in an organisation. In some cultures they would be seen as an embarrassment and people would feel guilty that they might be seen to be favouring their relatives. In other cultures it would be expected that family members would be favoured. Family members might be less favourably treated in cultures where they are seen as a threat to the status of other family members in the organisation. Yet in all this variety there is an acceptance that there need to be some standards to help people cope with this particular situation. This allows a universal imperative to underlie ethical diversity.

In some cases it really does not matter what the rule is as long as there is one. It is important that all the drivers in a country drive on the right or on the left, but which they choose is of little consequence. Many differences in business and managerial values fall into this category in which value diversity causes no ethical problems. Attitudes to working hours and holidays are an example. Americans generally put more hours into their job than Europeans, and the gap between the two is increasing. Americans also have less entitlement to holidays. The Spanish in contrast to the Americans take two-hour lunch breaks, eat late at night, go to bed late, have lots of public holidays and take extended vacations in July or August (*Director*, 2001: 32). This is often explained by the different cultural values of the Americans and the Europeans. The former value increasing their income over leisure and there is some evidence that the Americans are correct in thinking that extra effort leads to higher income. One study showed that extra effort does result in promotions and pay increases (Koretz, 2001). The Europeans place a premium on leisure. These differences in values may have good and bad economic consequences – the Europeans are poorer than they might be if they had adopted American values – but the differences are ethically neutral. As long as most Europeans are happy with their values, and most Americans happy with theirs, it does not matter ethically which values they choose. It is possible that there is a loss of happiness caused by Americans spending less time with their families but it is by no means certain that the detriment is not counterbalanced by some families being happier when one of their number is at work and by the pleasure they gain from spending the extra money that is earned.

Some value differences between countries do raise ethical problems however. Attitudes towards discrimination at work against certain population groups often differ and they can become points of inter-cultural conflict. For example, the degree to which discrimination against women is accepted varies between countries. The next section begins to describe a way in which such differences might be evaluated.

## A contingency approach

So far it has been argued that the need for some values and standards may be universally present in all societies but that the particular values adopted by different societies may, in practice, vary. This relativism does not mean that anything goes: that because there is no one best scheme of values all contenders may be equally valid. If a system of values is relative it must be relative to something; and if this is so then it must be possible to argue that some sets of ethics are more relevant to the 'thing' than other sets. The difficult question of course is 'what is the thing' to which ethics can be judged relevant. There are several answers. According to situational ethics, which developed from Anglican theology (Fletcher, 1966), that thing is love, the obligation to act lovingly towards others. Another possible answer, which may be of particular use in a business and management context, is the economic and social context people find themselves in. Although it may be possible to argue that a set of ethical standards is more or less suited to particular circumstances, the naturalistic fallacy prevents us from claiming that such standards are true, in the same way that true standards could be derived from the notion of love. This is because it is not possible to derive an 'ought' statement from an 'is' statement. A social and economic account of a society is a descriptive statement and so moral imperatives cannot be derived from it. Love, however, is a normative, moral concept and can be the basis for a definition of universal values. Nevertheless a contingency approach rescues relativist ethics from being undiscriminating; it does allow some ethical schemes to be judged as better than others.

---

**DEFINITION**

The **naturalistic fallacy** was defined by the philosopher G.E. Moore (1873–1958). Naturalism is the belief that the criterion of right action is some feature of the world that can be described, such as the happiness of people. Moore argued that this was wrong and took an intuitionist view that fundamental moral truths are directly understood by a special faculty of moral knowledge or thinking. Moral thinking, just as mathematical thinking, is *a priori* and exists independently of our perceptions of the world. The knowledge that one plus one equals two is not based upon experimentation. The good can be explained but it is too simple to be defined. The good can no more be defined than can the colour yellow. In general terms the naturalistic fallacy is taken to mean that a moral statement about what is good or right (i.e. what ought to be) cannot be inferred from any description of how things in the world are. To say, for example, that a particular ethical code adopted in one country makes its citizens prosperous and happy does not imply that those values and standards are moral.

---

The contingency idea is a common one in management theory. It is the idea that there is no one best way of doing something, no universal answer, but that there will be different best ways for different circumstances. Styles of leadership, organisational structures and cultures and strategic choices may all be contingent upon particular aspects of an organisation's nature and circumstances. This idea might be applied to business ethics.

All societies need a system of ethical values and standards that, with more or less effectiveness, creates circumstances in which people feel safe to do business. These values and standards should encourage the trust necessary for people and organisations to work with others, or at least provide remedies and sanctions if trust is broken. But insurance against untrustworthy business contacts can be achieved by various sets of values and norms. In different places at different times this end might be achieved by:

- reliance on contracts and the rule of law;

- relying on family and friendship and by only doing business with those from whom trust can be taken for granted. In China this is known as *Guanxi*, the network of personal and family connections that cement business relationships;

- developing personal and individual relationships with those with whom business is done;

- deal making so that it is in the mutual self-interest of both parties to show trust.

The ethical end of all of these means is the same, but it could be that each would be effective in particular circumstances. The contingency idea provides a possible yardstick against which the relative merit of a set of ethical standards might be judged. So while it might not be possible to say that a particular set of values is true and definitive and allows room for no other, it could be argued that one set of values is better suited to the contingent circumstances than another. As Umberto Eco (1992: 52) wrote when discussing the wide range of interpretations one can put on a particular text, 'If there are no rules that help ascertain which interpretations are the "best" ones there is at least a rule for ascertaining which ones are "bad"'.

This idea can be explored by looking at Indian and Chinese overseas businesses operating in the Asian arena. A particular feature of businesses in South-east Asia (Hong Kong, Indonesia, Malaysia, Thailand, Indonesia and the Philippines) is the presence of networks of Chinese and Indian family-based firms. The family businesses that make up these networks are often large conglomerates. Haley and Haley (1998) argued that these networks exist in a different strategic environment from that of most large western companies.

- The Chinese and Indians are mostly ethnically separate from the populations of the countries in which their companies do business. They have the uncertainty of being alien, and in the case of the Indian networks the memory of their community's expulsion from Uganda in 1972 provides a reminder of the risks borne by aliens.

- Governments in the region are often whole or part owners of major companies and this increases the importance to strategic success of contacts with, and access to, ministers and public servants.

- There is in South-east Asia an 'informational void'. Relative to the western economies there is a shortage of objective, statistical, research-based market and business information.

- There are doubts about the extent of the rule of law and, in some cases, about the adequacy of the 'background institutions' that support trust in business transactions.

These features make the strategic environment uncertain and difficult for overseas entrepreneurs. In South-east Asia contract and law were thought to provide a poor source of security for the Indian and Chinese networks. Instead they created the trust they needed by working within their family- or community-based networks where trust is ensured by traditional community values and/or by family relationships. Both the Chinese and Indian networks share a belief in filial loyalty to fathers. Chinese Confucianism identifies this as one of the five relationships that are an ethical duty. The intensity of familial loyalty is as strong among the Indian networks. The concept of *dharma* imposes the need to achieve financial success as a duty to the family (Gidoomal and Porter, 1997 and Haley and Haley, 1998: 310). They also pointed out, though, that in their dealings with large western corporations, which generate less uncertainty, the overseas Indian networks do view their contractual obligations as ethically binding. The Chinese networks also place importance on developing personal relationships with individuals outside the family.

The existence of the Chinese and Indian networks allows the businesses within them to operate differently from western corporations. They are secretive and keep low public profiles. They use their family-based networks for support, finance and advice. Rather than base decisions on objective research, network members often use the subjective judgements and experience of trusted members of the network. The Indian overseas businesses often use their own networks to finance their ventures, thus avoiding the conventional banking system. This is a development of a traditional Indian financial instrument known as the *hoondie*. A *hoondie* is a bill of exchange issued within a network and the system is based upon the honour and reputation of those within it. The reliance on internal network resources, including trusted contacts within regional governments, and on qualitative judgements that can be rapidly collated, allows overseas Indian and Chinese businesses to take decisions and actions very rapidly. Haley and Haley (1998: 314) argued that these Indian and Chinese entrepreneurs take an emergent approach to strategy that responds to knowledge of changes in the business environment that are detected and disseminated by the network. Through their webs of contacts these businesses also seek to influence the regional governments so as to acquire and maintain a favourable business environment and government contracts. The choice of the Indian and Chinese networks to give ethical priority to family and personal relationships rather than to legal or corporate relationships is arguably appropriate for their circumstances.

**Table 11.6** Value attributes of overseas business networks in South-east Asia

| Attributes | Chinese | Indian | Japanese |
|---|---|---|---|
| **Firm** | | | |
| *Merchants* | Reviled | Specialised | Exalted |
| *Primogeniture* | None | Very strong | Strong |
| *Firm's lifespan* | Short | Medium | Long |
| **Loyalty** | | | |
| *Family definition* | Blood | Blood | Role |
| *Focus* | Individual | Group | Institution |
| *Intensity* | Low | High | High |
| *Filial piety v. patriotism* | Opposed | No relationship | Equivalent |
| **Commercial trust** | | | |
| *Ethical foundation* | Five relationships and social harmony | Dharma | Mutual self-interest |
| *Ethical focus* | The Way | Family | Service to father figure |
| *Expectations of benefits* | Immediate and up-front | Immediate and up-front | Delayed |

*Source*: Haley and Haley, 1998

As shown in Table 11.6, Japanese business values are different from those of the overseas Indian and Chinese business networks. Japanese society values traders whereas the status of merchants in Chinese and Indian cultures is questionable. The importance of primogeniture in Japan means that Japanese family businesses outlive Chinese ones. In Japan's business culture trust is built upon contractual obligations and personal and corporate self-interest whereas the obligations of personal relations are more important in the Chinese and Indian environments. Japanese business people are more likely to take a long-term view whereas the overseas Indian and Chinese business networks expect more immediate returns. Haley and Haley (1998: 307) argued that Japan's different business values were appropriate to their different strategic environments compared with the Chinese and Indian overseas business networks. Whereas the latter, as has already been argued, worked in an informational void and were operating in regional markets in South-east Asia the Japanese companies aimed their exports at North American and European markets. They have not operated in the informational void experienced by the overseas business networks and their emphasis on contractual obligations and mutual self-interest is arguably well suited to dealings with western economies.

This is not to imply that there may not be cultural clashes between Europe and North America on the one hand and Japan on the other. Trompenaars and Hampden-Turner (1993: 196–7) gave an example of how an American's neglect of role and ritual in his dealings with a Japanese company president caused problems in a negotiation. The American was trying to nail down the specifics of a deal and ignored the largely ceremonial role of presidents of Japanese firms. In his frustration at the evasive answers he was receiving in response to detailed questions he absent-mindedly rolled up the president's business card that had been formally presented to him, and scraped his fingernails clean with it. The Japanese president was apparently displeased. Nevertheless the common emphasis of Americans and Japanese on contractual obligations and corporate mutual self-interest as an ethical basis for trust would generally be of benefit to the business relations between the two countries.

## Activity 11.1

The discussion above has identified a number of different bases upon which trust in others, in business dealings and negotiations, can be developed.

- Contracts and mutual self-interest
- Family and clan relationships
- Personal relationships (as in *guanxi*).

What problems or benefits might emerge if business people from different social and cultural backgrounds were to find themselves in a business negotiation in which they based their trust in others on different factors?

1. Contracts & mutual self-interest ................ Family & clan relationships

2. Contracts & mutual self-interest ................ Personal relationships

3. Family & clan relationships ......................Personal relationships

4. Family & clan relationships ..................... Family & clan relationships

   (but both are from different family networks)

A contingent approach to ethics does not mean that circumstances cause the acceptance of particular values or ethical norms. The business conditions found in South-east Asia did not cause the overseas Indian and Chinese business networks to adopt their particular values. These came, as much as from anywhere, from the traditional values of their communities. The fit between their values and the strategic environment did however create an 'evolutionary' pressure that maintained them.

The relationship between situational factors and a society's ethical norms is mediated by people's thinking, debating and power games. People will only begin to change their values if they think there is a misfit between their values and their circumstances. Such awareness does not come easy for an individual and may only have an impact through generational changes. The direction of the influence between situation and ethical norms may also alternate. The situation might influence changes in norms, or norms may encourage changes in the situation. These processes tend to operate over long periods of time. They can be illustrated by the history of Christian and Islamic attitudes towards the payment of interest on loans.

Interest is the money paid for the use of money. It is an essential feature of modern financial systems. The Bible however clearly states that taking interest on a loan is wrong. Usury is the formal term for charging any interest on a loan although it is now only used for extortionate rates of interest. The Old Testament forbade the Israelites to charge each other usury but they were allowed to levy usury on 'foreigners' (Deuteronomy 23: 20). The logic appears to be that in ancient societies most loans were for consumption, to help people survive hard times, rather than to finance entrepreneurial activities. In this circumstance it was wrong to charge interest. The New Testament also finds usury wrong. It is implied that even charging usury to 'foreigners' is wrong. As part of loving one's enemy interest-free loans should be made to any who needed them. In medieval times these Biblical injunctions were taken very seriously. Interest was seen as unjust because it meant charging a continuing rent for the use of money that could only be spent once (Buckley, 1998).

Such an ethical position was not helpful to the growing number of merchants and entrepreneurs who emerged in Europe during the Reformation. Slowly the official position on usury began to change to one that was more conducive to business enterprise. It was recognised that there was a legitimate difference between loans for consumption and loans for investment. The idea developed, for example, that a creditor could receive compensatory payments for the loss of use of their money from the start of the loan and not simply, as was traditional, for failure to pay off the loan at the agreed date. But it was not accepted that the creditor who loaned for entrepreneurial purposes should have a risk-free entitlement to interest whilst the merchant bore all the commercial risk of the enterprise. It was felt that the financier should share the risk in a partnership agreement.

Jean Calvin, who lived in the highly commercial city of Geneva in the sixteenth century, triggered a change in the Christian view of interest although his writings were not a great change on the traditional position. He argued that the poor should still be given loans without interest but that otherwise it was acceptable to charge interest on a loan as long as the rate was reasonable and the security taken was not excessive. He dismissed the Biblical strictures against interest because they were designed for a society very different from the mercantile one in which he lived (Tawney, 1966: 115–16). Although Calvin's ethical adjustment was small it led to a widespread acceptance of the justness of interest as long as the rate was fair. The issue moved from the ethics of interest to the ethics of the rate of interest. This example illustrates how ethical norms might change under the influence of new circumstances.

Such changes, however, are not inevitable. Islam, for example, has the same view of interest as that expressed in the Bible. But in Islam, unlike in Christianity, the injunction has survived into modern times so that practising Muslims have developed financial techniques that work without the concept of interest. Interest (*riba*), defined as any risk-free or guaranteed rate of return on a loan or investment, is prohibited. Loans must be made without interest according to Islamic law (*Sharia*) (Failaka International, 2001). Islam defines money as a means of exchange that has no intrinsic value. Value is only generated by the human effort behind exchanges and transactions. It follows that money should not be made from money, because that is the same as receiving something for nothing. Islam is not against entrepreneurial activity but it should properly be conducted through partnership financing (*Mudaraba*) in which the entrepreneur and the financier share profits or losses according to a pre-agreed ratio.

The prohibition against *riba* makes contact with western banks and financial instruments, based as they are on the idea of interest, improper for practising Muslims. Credit cards are a particular problem. Some scholars argue that Muslims can open credit card accounts as long as they always pay off the debt each month and so avoid incurring interest charges. Others (Al Andalusia, 2001) argue that when a credit card account is opened a contract is signed which commits the cardholder to paying interest in certain circumstances. Muslims should not sign such a contract in which they agree, in principle, to sin. However, financial techniques can be developed that avoid *riba*. For example the *Bai Muajjal* form of contract is permissible. The bank or provider of capital buys goods or assets on behalf of a business owner. They then sell the goods to the client at an agreed price that involves a percentage for profit. This is proper because, as in Christian thought, it is acceptable to charge a higher price if the payment is to be deferred. At least one bank provides an Islamic credit card based on this form of contract (Failaka International, 2001). Many banks now offer personal and business financing that avoids *riba* (Arif, 1988; Lariba.com, 2001). According to some reports (Anon., 1995) the deposit assets held by Islamic banks increased from $US5 billion in 1985 to over $US60 billion in 1994. The development of Islamic financial instruments is an example of how situations and circumstances can be adapted contingently to a set of ethical principles.

# A stakeholder approach

In addition to the contingency principle there is another criterion that can be used to judge the relative merits of a system of business ethics and values. It is the question of who benefits from a particular scheme of ethics. This criterion depends upon drawing a stakeholder map of all the groups and constituencies who may be affected by, or have a concern with, an ethical proposition. Identifying who benefits and who suffers from its application can test the validity of the proposition. This can be explained by reference to a Rawlsian perspective, as discussed in Chapter 2. One of the principles Rawls proposed was that social and economic inequalities are to be arranged so that they are both (a) reasonably expected to be to everyone's advantage, and (b) attached to positions and offices open to all. Rawls calls the first part of this statement the difference principle. Different systems of business ethics could be tested against the difference principle and if they do not benefit all the stakeholders involved then they could be judged invalid.

An example can be taken from current Indian recruitment practice. Traditional Indian society was divided into *jati* or castes. These were extended kinship groups that could be classified under four main *varna* – the priestly castes, the warrior castes, the merchants and the farmers. A person's caste no longer determines their occupation but it still carries social and status significance in India. This is particularly so for the groups who are excluded from the caste categories. These are the *dalits*, in traditional terms the untouchables, and people from the tribal areas of India. These groups are normally the most economically and socially excluded groups in India (Dhesi, 1998). Caste discrimination is illegal in India. The government operates a system of positive discrimination in which quotas of jobs in public organisations and nationalised industries and places in colleges and universities are reserved for *dalits* and tribals. How would this policy stand against the difference principle? It clearly benefits a group of people, the *dalits* and the tribals, who would be disadvantaged if the policy were not in place. It could be argued that it is to the advantage of all to overcome discrimination against the worst-off in society if for no other reason than to prevent the civil unrest that such discrimination might lead to. However, the policy might contravene Rawls' second principle, that positions should be open to all. Blackburn (2001: 27) suggests that when judging whether a local ethical standard is acceptable it is not enough simply to consider the views of the 'Brahmins, mullahs, priests and elders who hold themselves to be spokesmen for *their* culture'. A wider group of stakeholders needs to be considered, especially those who are oppressed or disadvantaged by that ethical standard. A stakeholder analysis based on Rawls' difference principle provides a mechanism for judging the validity of a particular ethical position in business.

The diversity of business values and ethics in different societies and countries does not mean that any ethical position can be justified. An acceptance of an ethical relativist position does not imply that any value or practice has to be accepted as long as it can be shown to be indigenous or traditional. In this section a number of tests have been suggested which could be used by managers to decide whether a particular local ethical stance should be regarded as valid or not. It has to be accepted of course that this might not be enough for a convinced ethical universalist who would want to argue that there can only be one true ethical system, and that everyone ought to adopt it.

## When different sets of organisational and managerial values meet

### Introduction

The normal view of the different values and standards in different countries is that at a time of increasing world trade it is a problem. The experience of coming from one country and suddenly working in a different culture is described as culture shock. For multi-national companies and organisations therefore the existence of different national values is a management problem to be overcome.

Holden (2002: 284–285) points out that this traditional view is unhelpful and unnecessarily negative. He argues that the old view was based on an over-simple idea that national cultures and sets of values were entirely distinct from each other and were separate objects that bumped and scraped against each other. He illustrates in his book that different cultures are best understood as overlapping networks of ideas and values both within and between countries. Indeed many individuals will have an accumulation of sets of values that may not necessarily fit together neatly in their own minds. A manager in a western-owned company operating in India may have been born in India but brought up and educated in the USA, have worked for a time in the UK and Azerbaijan and holiday frequently in Spain. Such a person's values will form a complex network. They will have some values based on their upbringing in a Hindu family of a particular caste. Their education and admiration for the USA will probably reinforce some aspects of their values at the expense of others. Their work experience in Azerbaijan may have highlighted their dislike of some traditional aspects of Soviet and Hindu values such as automatic respect for those grown old. Experiences while a junior would have similarly buttressed these views but their more recent jobs as a senior manager may have modified the value they attach to experience. For such a person this interlocking set of values can only be an asset when they found themselves confronting the task of managing their new team in the company in India. Their cultural awareness would help make them skilled at negotiating a range of issues from the role of bribery to the appropriate leadership style. The point that Holden (2002: 284) makes is that a cultural mix should be seen as an organisational resource. For him cross-cultural management in MNCs should be seen as an aspect of knowledge management that enables people to learn from the surrounding diversity of cultures.

In the next section an attempt is made to analyse the process of learning that takes place when people have sets of values that partly overlap but are in part distinct.

### A dialectical analysis

Since the disintegration of the Soviet Union into many smaller independent states the attempts by western trainers to inculcate western business values into managers in the new countries have provided many case studies of what happens when competing sets of values clash. In this section it is argued that the process, seen in a case study from Azerbaijan, can best be understood as an aspect of Hegel's dialectic.

## Dialectics of self-consciousness, Lord and bondsman and of the unhappy consciousness

**DEFINITION**

The basic structure of the dialectic is explained on p. 223. In this definition box we will describe a particular sequence of dialectics, part of a wider set of dialectics described in the *Phenomenology of Spirit* (Hegel 2003: 104–30). The three dialectic processes are;

1. The dialectic of self-consciousness
2. The dialectic of master and slave and
3. The dialectic of unhappy consciousness.

The first dialectic, of self-consciousness, begins when the idea of consciousness 'as pure abstraction of self-consciousness' is challenged 'by the particularity everywhere characteristic of existence as such' (Hegel, 2003: 107). This duality brings self-consciousnesses into a life and death conflict (as Hegel expresses it, hyperbolically, for our purposes). The presence of various others contradicts each self-consciousness' sense of its own absolute existence and so it must cancel out the other. This dialectic will be used to explore the initial relationships between western experts and the trainees they appointed to the new college, and between the intermediaries and the local managers they sought to influence.

This first duality is overcome by one self-consciousness cancelling the other by gaining power and control over it. This then begins the dialectic of the master and the slave, or Lord and bondsman in some translations.

> They stand as two opposed forms or modes of consciousness. The one is independent, and its essential nature is to be for itself: the other is dependent, and its essence is life or existence for another. The former is the master, or Lord, the latter the bondsman.
>
> (Hegel, 2003: 108)

In such a hierarchical relationship the dominant party confirms its superiority by comparing their high status with the subordinate partner's low status. Contradictorily this makes the dominant party dependent on the subordinate. This mirror imaging, in which the greater is reflected in the lesser and vice versa, contradicts the master's formal superiority by revealing their dependence on the slave for practicalities and for confirmation of their status. As the slave becomes aware of their importance to the master through their practical labour the dualism is resolved thus:

> In labour where there seemed to be merely some outsider's [the master's] mind and ideas involved, the bondsman becomes aware, through this rediscovery of himself by himself, of having and being a 'mind of his own'.
>
> (Hegel, 2003: 111)

▶

> This dialectic will be used to analyse the stage in the relationship when the western experts discover themselves dependent on the Azerbaijani trainees, in their role as intermediaries; and the trainees find themselves dependent on the Azerbaijani managers they are training and developing.
>
> In the dialectic of the unhappy consciousness the newly self-aware consciousness experiences, within themselves (and not between themselves and others as was the case in the preceding dialectic), a conflict between stoicism and scepticism that resolves itself as an acceptance of a thing for lack of something better. The conflict between stoicism and scepticism is again one between empty form and chaotic particularity.
>
> Scepticism is the realisation of that of which stoicism is merely the notion, and is the actual experience of what freedom of thought is...
>
> This consciousness [ ] is here neither more nor less than an absolutely fortuitous embroglio, the giddy whirl of a perpetually self-creating disorder.
>
> (Hegel, 2003: 118, 119–120)

The mutual learning that happened when imported western experts met the Azerbaijanis who were to be trained as the new academic faculty of the School of Public Administration will be explored using a case study of a project to set up a new School for Public Administration in Azerbaijan. The project was one of many, begun after the collapse of the Soviet Union, that were designed to modernise the new post-Soviet republics by replacing their institutions with western, democratic and free-market ones. The School for Public Administration was to deliver a range of programmes to government officials, including a Master's degree, that were intended to create western style public service organisations. The school was to be a new faculty within the rump of a former Soviet institute that had retained its Rector, who had been appointed in Soviet times, its administrative and technical staff, but not its academic staff. A number of local trainees were recruited whom the western experts would train to become the academic faculty of the new school.

The project was based on a cascade model that was analogous to, but not knowingly based upon, a process that had its classical formulation in Macaulay's minute on education in India. The intention in India was to use an English education to form

> a class of persons, Indian in colour and blood, but English in tastes, opinions, in morals and in intellect ... who may be interpreters between us and the millions we govern.
>
> (Keay, 2000: 431)

This model necessarily implies three main stakeholders, the western experts (as the European Union officials insisted they be called), the Azerbaijanis who were recruited to the college and who were to be trained to become its academic faculty (and who would be the intermediaries) and the managers in Azerbaijani organisations who would be trained by the new staff of the new school. As these managers were mostly appointed in the Soviet period they fell under the two categories of the *nomenklatura* (privileged elite who held their posts through Communist party patronage) and the *apparatchiks* (party functionaries who implemented policy). However, in this section only the relationship between the western experts and the Azerbaijani trainees will be considered.

The manner in which this relationship develops is outlined in Table 11.7.

---

**Table 11.7** The dialectic of western experts and local change agents

*The dialectic of self-consciousness*

**Thesis ⟶ Antithesis ⟶ Synthesis**

| Thesis | Antithesis | Synthesis |
|---|---|---|
| The western experts express an undiscriminating and universalised philanthropy that assumes that the local and western parties can have an equal and mutually beneficial partnership. | In practice both the local and western parties are self-conscious and wary of the other. They accuse each other of individualism, each party seeking to fulfil their own selfish ambitions. This leads to a lack of trust. | The lack of trust is overcome by the development of a hierarchical relationship between the two parties. The western experts are seen as dominant. |

*The dialectic of master and slave*

**Thesis ⟶ Antithesis ⟶ Synthesis**

| Thesis | Antithesis | Synthesis |
|---|---|---|
| The western experts are seen as high status individuals whose role is to introduce locals to new western values and techniques. | Although formally superior the western experts are practically dependent upon the local trainees' cooperation. Socially the locals' demands upon the westerners were greater than the westerners' demands of friendship. | The western experts and local change agents recognise their mutual dependence and develop a more equal working relationship based upon the assumption of shared western values. |

*The dialectic of unhappy consciousness*

**Thesis ⟶ Antithesis ⟶ Synthesis**

| Thesis | Antithesis | Synthesis |
|---|---|---|
| Both western experts and local change agents stoically accept that it is necessary to bring Azerbaijani organisations into line with a western free market model. | But sceptically both now doubt whether a simple transfer of western values and practices into Azerbaijan is feasible or workable. They struggle over how the two institutional templates should be meshed. | A reasoned concatenation of the two templates based upon some concept of unity-in-diversity; however this process was still ongoing, and might last for some time. |

---

## The dialectic of self-consciousness

In the Azerbaijan project the relationship between the western experts and local trainees (the change agents to be) was intended to be equal and open. In the early days this ideal relationship was contradicted by both parties' perception of the other as separate and distinct from themselves. There was a mutual suspicion and lack of empathy as in the dialectic of self-consciousness (Mabbott, 1967: 38). The dialectic begins with the abstract, undiscriminating philanthropy of the western experts. In formal terms they saw their role as bringing the benefits of democracy, public service and markets to the former Soviet state. They expressed a formal and universal benevolence but their ignorance of the local context made their efforts unfocused. The impossibility of direct transplantation of western ideals into post-Soviet soil, combined with their ignorance of local conditions, meant that the western experts found it easier to proselytise than to generate practical proposals. As Mabbott, (1967: 38–39) noted of the consequences of this contradiction, if such people do good (as opposed to talking about it), it is only by chance.

The western experts, made self-conscious by the combination of universal benevolence and practical impotence, externalised their frustration and thought their good intentions were undermined by the self-interestedness of the local agents. They believed that the trainees were only involving themselves with the project so that they could gain access to resources (dollars, cars and computers) or a job with a western organisation in Azerbaijan or, even better, employment in Europe or the USA. It was the local staff's enthusiasm for trips to the UK and Europe and for developing marketable skills in IT and English language that encouraged the western experts' suspicions of the trainees' private motives. Others involved in similar projects however have pointed to the importance of visits to western countries. Bedward *et al.*, (2003) saw them as a means of allowing people from the former command economies to learn from the west without having the lessons imposed upon them. The private interests of the local trainees can be seen in the career paths they followed during and after the project. Of the 23 local trainees recruited to the new school, six left Azerbaijan to work or study in the west and nine obtained jobs with western organisations based in Baku within the time span of the project.

The western experts' suspicions of the trainees were mirrored by the trainees' doubts about the experts. The local agents noted the contradiction between the western experts' professed intentions and their suspicious attitude towards them. They concluded that the western experts were not in their country out of altruism. They believed the western experts were there for the benefits of expatriate employment and to improve their personal circumstances. This was not an isolated phenomenon of this particular project. As Lenke and Davies (1995: 23) reported about a western-led management development programme in Hungary, the locals commented on the western experts' superior, colonialist and expatriate attitudes, their ignorance of the Hungarian context and their social segregation.

This suspicion can be illustrated by another incident. Two of the western experts had boasted, while working in Azerbaijan, that they were having an affair and that they had only agreed to work on the project because it gave them a holiday overseas and a chance to be together away from their respective spouses. Two other team members complained about the couple. As a matter of principle, they objected to the way the couple's freeloading was disrespectful of other team members' efforts. They also expressed a more important concern that our Azerbaijani partners, who had learnt of the affair, were asking questions about the pair's lack of commitment, and this was threatening the credibility of the project.

The cumulative effect of such mutual suspicions, developed out of a self-conscious suspicion each of the other, led to mistrust between the two groups. Abramson (1999) identified a similar dialectic, of acceptance and subversion, in his analysis of western-funded attempts to build institutions of civil society in Uzbekistan. He argued that western agencies, by creating NGOs (that would provide an alternative to the state as the focus of social action), formed new elites. These new elites retained the tendency, developed during Soviet rule, to subvert systems to their personal advantage. Consequently the formal 'concept of civil society loses any universally understood meaning and value' (Abramson, 1999: 241) as the new elites, in their concrete implementation of the ideal of civil society, merely saw western programmes as a means to benefit themselves, as indeed do the 'young Americans with fat pay-checks and [western corporations] with fat contracts'. The many individual acts of self-interest negated the formal intentions of the development projects.

The synthesis of the contradictions was an acceptance of a hierarchical relationship between western experts and local change agents in which the experts were dominant (they after all controlled the flow of resources from the funding body) and the local agents were dependent. Lack of trust is one such absence. The removal of self-consciousness, which constrained the formation of any relationship between western experts and local agents, allowed the emergence of a hierarchical relationship between them. The absence of trust was replaced by a mutual and conscious commitment between the two parties, albeit an unequal one. This synthesis becomes the starting point, the thesis, of the next dialectic.

## The dialectic of master and slave

In this second dialectic, in the development of the relationship between western experts and trainees, the formal term, the thesis, was that the experts were dominant over the locals because they were the source of the new ideas and values that were required to modernise Azerbaijani public services. The antithesis was that, in practice, the experts were dependent upon the trainees because they could not work without their cooperation, or indeed without their presence. This latter point became a major cause of conflict. The local trainees were paid only a small salary by the Azerbaijan government and they needed time to earn extra money to support themselves and their families. The westerners, however, needed them to attend the classes and seminars and to turn up on time. The project team were constantly trying to find ways to improve the local trainees' attendance record, always with limited success. The formal dominance of the western experts was negated by their practical dependence upon the local agents, who displayed a disregard for punctuality.

Tensions could be seen in the relationship between the western experts and the local trainees. The Middle Eastern courtesies and respect given by the locals to the western experts gave the latter a sense of status that they would not have received from others in their own culture. This led to an asymmetry in the social relations between the western experts and local agents. As discussed earlier, Dewey (1993) identified different notions of friendship in western and eastern societies. The western, and middle class, notion saw friendship as a limited relationship, which required little more than mutual entertainment and polite, constrained civilities. This was the view of most of the western experts. The eastern view, one that was shared by the Azerbaijanis, was that the expectations of friendship were almost without limit. They saw friendship as creating personal obligations such that the western friend would be obliged to help them find jobs in western companies or places to study in overseas universities. The local staff saw the experts as potential patrons and so offered them deference. However, in return for deference the Azerbaijanis anticipated a large and bankable return. The westerners were formally dominant but were under heavier demands of friendship. This inversion in the social relationships is another version of the master/slave dialectic because the Azerbaijanis' expectations of the western experts outweighed the social obligations that the westerners put on their Azerbaijani friends.

The contradiction between western expert as 'master' and the local trainer as 'slave' diminished as the latter came to realise that the experts depended on them. As the experts' superiority diminished the two were brought nearer to equality. Master and slave recognised that they would each benefit from mutual cooperation. As Jankowicz and Dobosz-Bourne (2003) reported, in their study of modernising projects in the countries of the former Warsaw Pact, effective cross-cultural transfer of knowledge can only occur when there is a negotiation of mutual meanings between the western experts and the local learners. Several local participants in the project moved from being trainees to becoming academic colleagues over the three and a half years of the project, replacing the hierarchical relationship of patron and client. The western experts' developing respect for some of the local trainees led to an attempt by the western project team to shift power from the institution's Rector, who had held this post since Soviet times, to one of the younger local staff. It was necessary to appoint a Director of the School of Public Administration. The person appointed was a young woman selected from among the local staff. It was recognised that she would have difficulties dealing with the older, and male, culture of top government officialdom. It was also a recognition by the western project team that some of the local trainees were capable of taking on such a job. The new director was seen as someone with whom the experts could work as a partner.

## The dialectic of unhappy consciousness

The last observed stage of the relationship between the western experts and the local trainers may be viewed as a dialectic of unhappy consciousness. The newly independent trainees, who should now be called trainers, stoically accepted that there could be no mean between vice and virtue, and accepted the western institutional template, but their scepticism about the application of this template to Azerbaijan led them to a state of unhappy consciousness, a form of melancholic acceptance. The contradiction was not then between experts and local colleagues but within the minds of both. They were struggling with the ethical question of relativism and universalism: Is the western business and managerial template applicable everywhere or should each society develop its own business values and institutions? Holden (2002) would see this situation as a helpful one because it has moved away from insisting on a single universal set of values that must be true everywhere and has moved to a situation that requires mutual learning. As the dialectical analysis suggests, however, this process of learning is not straight-forward; rather it proceeds by working through a series of contradictions and misunderstanding. This requires both good manners and the ability to partici-pate with others' values and ethical principles.

## Activity 11.2

If you were a human resource manager responsible for improving cooperation and communication between employees (who come from different cultural backgrounds but who work together in teams in your transnational company), what practical recommendations would you make for training or development activities that would help them move smoothly through the difficulties of developing a mutual understanding and appreciation of each other's values?

## Good manners and participative competence

How should managers cope with the kinds of tensions described in the previous section? How should the manager, and corporately the organisation they work for, respond to this complexity? One possible response is that managers working with, or in, other countries should show good manners by accepting others' cul-tures. This does not mean that managers should become promiscuous in the manner in which they take up and put down values. Indeed, Hofstede argued (1991: 237), a person cannot show tolerance of others' values unless they are secure in their own values. Tolerance is necessary, the more so when differences in priorities and practice do not raise serious ethical difficulties. Good manners imply trying to see situations from other people's perspective, empathising with their anxieties and taking what actions you can to put them at ease. A more formal term for good manners might be participative competence (Holden, 2002: 273–4). He defines this as:

> the ability to interact on equal terms in multicultural environments in such a way that knowledge is shared and that the learning experience is profession-ally enhancing.

The ability to participate competently in different countries calls for different skills and sensitivities. In India a happy receipt of compliments given, without taking them too seriously, and in France a glad acceptance that the lunch break is more important than the meeting that was abruptly stopped for it, add to par-ticipative competence. There are common understandings that are vital to such competence however. They are that, despite apparent problems of mutual under-standings, the others with whom you are dealing share with you the basic structures of communication and the ability to infer not just from the spoken language but from the interaction of voice, expression, stance and actions. Both people in a multicultural encounter are seeking to make sense of the encounter and are using a wide range of cues to make a common understanding

The following suggestions for helping to develop participative competence, largely based on those developed by De George (1999), are all variations on a famous ethical precept – first of all do no harm.

> **DEFINITION**
>
> **First, do no harm** is an ancient moral precept. It is often claimed to be taken from the Hippocratic oath that doctors in classical times were required to take. This is not so. The nearest the oath gets to it is in the following statement, 'I will follow that system of regimen which, according to my ability and judgement, I consider for the benefit of my patients, and abstain from all that is deleterious and mischievous'. Today few doctors are required to take the oath.

## Empathy and humour

There are various disciplines that can be learned for acquiring good manners. One is to recognise that we all possess a wide range of values that we can use to understand others' positions. For example, fear of losing 'face' is often cited as a matter of great importance to the Chinese. But there cannot be a western manager who has not also felt shame when they made a fool of themselves in front of colleagues or bosses. Recognising the humour in a conflict of values can also aid their reconciliation.

**Case study 11.1**

### The college principal's new car

This case was part of the experience of the project to set up a new college of public administration in Azerbaijan (*see* pp. 446–51). It concerns the Rector, who had built his career in the old Soviet regime but was now to be Rector of the new college. He was in his late sixties and was, every inch of his substantial frame, a Soviet *apparatchik*. As part of the package the project delivered two brand-new western-built vehicles to the college. One was a minibus, the other was a good quality car. Both vehicles were, according to the project specification, for the use of the western project team. In practice the minibus was the more useful vehicle because it coped well with the difficult road conditions and could be used to move all the team around, complete with their equipment. The principal began to use the car more and more as if it were his personal vehicle. It was easy for him to do this because both of the drivers were on his staff and took their orders from him. This became an issue because the principal clearly saw the car as his 'commission' for facilitating the project. If the western funding body were to discover this they would think it a misuse of project funds. The issue became a matter of dispute between the principal and the project team. Then one day the team saw that some cowboy builders had been brought in and were rapidly constructing a ramshackle garage in the college grounds. The strongest part of the garage was the padlocked steel doors to which only the principal held the key. The project team saw the funny side and could remember occasions when they had tried to guard hard-won privileges and perks that they had won from their organisations. Humour discharged the project team's anger and a compromise deal was made about the use of the car.

## Responding to the particularness of host countries' ethical standards and values

This guideline goes a little beyond good manners. It suggests that, unless there are good ethical reasons for not doing so, organisations should learn and respect the values and ethical practices of the host country. This is not an easy thing to achieve. Expatriate staff are often criticised because they try to recreate their pattern of life from their own country rather than learn about and come to terms with the culture of their host country. This has been recognised as a problem for international NGOs. Lewis (2001: 105) has raised the question of defining the management challenges that arise from employing expatriate NGO staff from the northern world to work in partnership with southern-world NGO partners. He asks, but does not answer, the question of whether such staff should be driven by their own values or by the values of their partner organisations.

### Connexion point

The argument about the importance of the particulars of individual cases when deciding how to respond to an ethical issue is related to the discussion of casuistry in Chapter 13.

---

**Case study 11.2**

### Testing Maori employees for drugs in a New Zealand company

A company that employed Maoris and non-Maoris decided that they wanted to start a programme of testing employees for drug abuse. Their reasons were to improve the safety record at their plant and to fulfil their obligations under New Zealand's health and safety laws. Carrying out drugs testing on employees, however, raised ethical questions about employees' rights to privacy, and the question of the legality of such testing under New Zealand law was uncertain. The Maori employees appeared to be more critical of the proposal than the other staff. A particular point of conflict however was that the company tried to negotiate with employees separately to gain their consent to the testing. Maori culture is collectivist and the staff demanded that the issue between them and the company should be negotiated collectively.

(*Source*: Blackburn, 2000)

## Activity 11.3

When should the demands, expectations or values of the state outweigh the values and social expectations of religious, national or ethnic groups? Consider the following examples.

- When the state's health and safety laws imply that the wearing of a certain national dress in a production plant would be a health and safety hazard.

- When the state's belief in secularism is challenged by Muslim women's insistence on wearing the *hijab* (head scarf). This issue was highlighted in 2004 when France passed a law that prohibited Muslim schoolgirls wearing the *hijab* at school.

## Reflections

The international work of companies and organisations involves an engagement with different values and ethical standards. This chapter has concerned the ethical validity of such diversity and the question of how people in organisations should respond to it. There are two processes in operation. One is an attempt to universalise, to create core principles that can be accepted worldwide. The other is localisation in which values, which some think are universal, are adapted and modified to meet particular circumstances. Both processes however involve judgement and choice. They do not represent an uncritical acceptance that all values and principles that exist must be of equal worth and must be protected. What managers are involved in is a process termed 'sense-making' by Weick (1995 and 2001). According to Weick, sense-making is a retrospective activity triggered by actions and influenced by cues and heuristics. If these processes are to be seen, as Holden suggests, as an organisational resource then it is necessary for organisations to bring the process of learning to the surface that is open to multicultural interaction. It is worth considering some aspects of developing participative competence in terms of Weickian sense-making.

### Connexion point

Weick's theory of the process of sense-making is also discussed in Chapter 4, pp. 155–6.

- **Action and social context.** People only make sense of situations when their circumstances force them to. Putting people in multicultural forums requires them to interact and reform their views.

- **Identity formation.** Historically, people from particular communities have defined their identities in contrast to an assumed and poorly understood 'other' (*see* the definition of orientalism on p. 485). Denying people access to stereotypes by confronting them with real people will ease the learning resulting from the coming together of different value sets.

- **Cues**. The way that people make sense of value differences is by observing the cues created by the ways in which others deal with them, and by noting the results. If those who take a traditional 'expat' view of other countries gain promotion then the cues will be readily read.

- **Plausibility**. The sense that people may make of their experiences must be plausible to them. The sense they make of others' cultures and values may be wrong but seem plausible unless they have had to work with those from other communities and societies.

Managers who make sense of the world's diversity of values only from the cues and circumstances provided by their own organisational, group or national cultures may simply develop stereotypes rather than acquire participative competence.

## Summary

In this chapter the following key points have been made:

- Universal standards for international business have been written but they are not universally accepted; nor do they cover all the issues relevant to business.

- Different countries and societies have some ethical standards and values concerning business in common, but they differ on others.

- In countries outside the western industrialised zone there is a process of dialogue in which, predominantly, American business values are integrated and challenged in a process of sense-making.

- An acceptance of ethical plurality does not mean that any value has to be accepted as long as it can be shown to be authentically indigenous to a place.

- Although extreme universalists and relativists might reject the idea, it is arguable that a contingency approach or, alternatively a stakeholder and Rawlsian approach, can be used to distinguish appropriate from inappropriate local ethical standards.

- If this is so, then transnational and multinational companies have to make moral judgements about whether they should adopt or challenge the business standards of the countries they are working in. In this process it is helpful if managers in such companies see the value diversity they face as an asset and an opportunity for organisational learning rather than as a culture shock problem that has to be overcome.

- This process of mutual learning from different values in different places and among different groups can be understood as a dialectical process.

- In dealing with these matters transnational and multinational organisations need to show:
  - good manners,
  - a willingness to respond to the particularness of the host countries' ethical standards and values.

## Quick revision test

1. What is the naturalistic fallacy?
   (a) All natural things are morally good
   (b) Natural laws are the basis of human rights
   (c) The belief that statements about what is ethical can be derived from a statement about people's behaviours

2. Which is the least corrupt country in the world according to Transparency International's Corruption Perception Index?
   (a) Finland
   (b) USA
   (c) Germany

3. When was the United Nation's Universal Declaration of Human Rights published?
   (a) 2000
   (b) 1995
   (c) 1948

4. What is the Islamic position on the payment of interest?
   (a) It is morally wrong
   (b) It is morally acceptable
   (c) It is morally acceptable as long as the rate is not excessive

## Typical assignments and briefs

1. In what circumstances should a company accept local values and practices that differ from its own core values and when should it not? Illustrate your answer with particular examples.

2. How useful and valid is it to argue that countries can be classified by the different managerial and organisational values they exhibit?

3. What is likely to happen when managers from different societies with different values come into contact? How should this process be managed?

4. Are there some areas of business and management where universal standards and principles apply to all? What are they?

## Group activity 11

If you have a group of students who have different ethnic backgrounds, or have lived in different countries, choose two of those countries to concentrate on. Discuss and compare the views of:

- teenagers and young adults in each country
- and their parents' generation in each country

on

- McDonald's and other fast food outlets
- Multi-national companies as employers
- Credit cards
- Reserving quotas of jobs for people of a particular social or ethnic category in universities, government agencies and state-owned enterprises.
- The importance of personal relationships in the conduct of business.

## Recommended further reading

F. Trompenaars and C. Hampden-Turner (1993) *Riding the Waves of Culture*, 2nd edn, London: Nicholes Brealey, is good on the problems of managing intercultural misunderstandings. Nigel Holden (2002) *Cross Cultural Management. A Knowledge Management Perspective*, Harlow: Pearson Education, provides an interesting perspective based on the principles of knowledge management. He challenges the common assumption that cultural differences are simply a cause of problems.

## Useful websites

| Topic | Website provider | URL |
| --- | --- | --- |
| Transparency International home page | Transparency International | http://www.transparency.org/ |
| The Universal Declaration of Human rights | United Nations | http://www.unq.org/Overview/rights.htm |
| The Ethical Values Project in India | Institute of Management Development and Research (IMDR), Pune, India | http://www.imdr.edu/research/values_project.htm |

| Topic | Website provider | URL |
|---|---|---|
| Islamic Finance | Sala@m | http://www.salaam.co.uk/themeof themonth/november02_index.php |
| A Web page concerned with the work of Geert Hofstede | The International Business Centre | http://geert-hofstede.international-business-center.com/index.shtml |
| The 'Inspirations' section of the website, run by a private consultancy, has interesting self-tests and materials | Trompenaars Hampden-Turner, Consultants | http://www.7d-culture.nl/index1.html |
| The website of the Caux Round Table | Caux Round Table | http://www.cauxroundtable.org/about.html |

# CHAPTER 12

# Globalisation and international business

## Learning outcomes

Having read the chapter and completed its associated activities, readers should be able to:

- Define globalisation and the ethical issues that it raises.

- Evaluate the evidence and arguments concerning the fairness of the economic impact of world trade liberalisation.

- Evaluate the roles of multinational enterprises in relation to developing the institutions of ethical business practice.

- Identify the potential for close relationships between multinational enterprises and governments to damage ethically responsible business practices.

- Identify the risks to peace and stability that multinational enterprises may cause by their operations in politically and militarily unstable regions.

- Judge the arguments for multinational enterprises remaining within ethically dubious countries, and trying to change things from the inside, or for withdrawing.

- Rehearse the argument about the social and cultural impact of globalisation.

- Identify the strengths and weaknesses of various approaches to developing codes and compacts for the conduct of international business.

## Introduction

The ethics of globalisation, for most, rests on a fine point of utilitarianism. Does globalisation result in more harm than good? If it creates both harm and good in large measures, but the harm and the good are felt by different groups of people, how should the benefits experienced by some be weighed against the disadvantages heaped on others? It would probably not be sufficient to quieten the disadvantaged to simply point out that in aggregate the good outweighs the bad.

**Connexion point**

Utilitarianism is one of the major ethical theories. It is discussed in detail in Chapter 3, pp. 127–36. Those who take a human rights perspective, which is also discussed in Chapter 3, do not approach the ethical issues of globalisation from a utilitarian perspective but simply argue that companies operating in the global marketplace should take care to respect human rights.

A consideration of the ethics of globalisation, and of the role of multi-national enterprises (MNEs) within it, must therefore include an analysis of its impact. The likely areas of impact can be deduced from the definition of globalisation.

**DEFINITIONS**

**Globalisation** is a process which is bringing societies that were previously economically, politically and culturally diverse into convergence. This is being achieved by a combination of the success of capitalism, the growth of a common mass culture (McLuhan and Powers' (1989) 'global village') and the wish of people in all societies, through their rational choices, to choose the same goals. It is a process that affects three domains, the political, the economic and the cultural and social.

The World Commission on the Social Dimension of Globalization (WCSDG, 2004: §132–5) identified the following characteristics of globalisation.

- Liberalisation of international trade.
- Growth of foreign direct investment (FDI) and massive cross-border financial flows.
- Growth of the new technology of IT and communications that makes communication between countries easier.
- The greater ease of transporting goods and people around the world that now makes it possible for markets to be global in scope.

This last characteristic gives rise to a different definition of globalisation that sees it not as a description of a process but as a strategy that a company can choose to adopt. Companies may decide to produce and market their goods and services for a global market (Holden, 2002: 44).

In this chapter the impacts and ethical considerations of globalisation will be reviewed under the following headings.

- Trickle down or just trickery? Does the opening of national markets to world trade and an increase in international trade benefit all countries?

- Developing institutions or taking advantage? Do multi-national companies seek to improve the institutional arrangements (by advocating and practising good employment practices and operating to high standards of business) in host companies or do they seek to benefit from the weak institutional and legal frameworks governing business in many developing countries?

- Creating political tensions between and within states. Does the involvement of multi-national companies, many of which have a higher turnover than developing countries have gross domestic product (GDP), exacerbate regional political instabilities and create political disturbances and unrest?

- Staying put or withdrawing? Multi-national enterprises may find themselves operating in countries where they become complicit with intolerable unfairness and abuses of human rights, and they have to decide whether to remain or withdraw.

- Cultural diversity or cultural homogenisation? Does the global reach of multi-national companies threaten indigenous cultures and values and lead all societies to a standardised culture that diminishes the variety of human cultures?

The remainder of the chapter will consider the various attempts to create a worldwide framework of global governance to guide and police the propriety and fairness of international trade and its globalising consequences.

However, the ethical issues of globalisation are not new. They could be found in the actions of colonial companies, such as the Dutch and English East India Companies, which were as powerful and globally dominating in the eighteenth and nineteenth centuries as multi-nationals are today. The modern themes listed above for this chapter had their equivalents in the eighteenth- and early nineteenth-century history of the British East India Company in particular.

- **The charge that the East India Company impoverished India.** In the eighteenth century it was a common charge that the Company was draining India of its wealth and transferring it to Britain. It was accused of enriching new elites, both Indian and British (called nabobs), while the mass of the Indian population suffered intermittent famines. The charges were crystallised when Warren Hastings, the Governor-general, was impeached by Parliament in 1786 over issues that would today be termed corporate governance. He was found not guilty in 1795.

- **Exploiting weak institutions in host countries.** When the East India Company was establishing itself in India in the eighteenth century the nominal sovereign power was the Moghul Empire, which by that time was in decline. The company was able to exploit the empire's institutional weaknesses to its own commercial advantage by acquiring formal government roles, such as the tax collecting function of the *diwani* of Bengal.

- **Increasing political tensions in a region.** The decline of the Moghul Empire created military and political tensions as different groups sought to fill the political vacuum. The East India Company was one of these and it developed its own armies and spent much of the eighteenth century fighting wars in India.

- **Staying in or withdrawing decision.** The company's business stretched as far as China, from where it imported tea to Britain. The tea had to be paid for and conveniently the Company had a monopoly of opium production in India. It was convenient to ship the opium to China, where there was a good market, and use the proceeds to buy the tea. Unfortunately the Chinese government banned the sale of opium in 1729 because of its damaging effects on the users.

The Company formally withdrew from the illegal trade, but it would sell the opium to private traders in Calcutta and then turn a blind eye when they exported it at their own risk to China. However, by the 1830s the revenues from the opium trade which in the eighteenth century had been only about 5 per cent of the Company's turnover had become much more important and Britain engaged in gunboat diplomacy in China, not just to protect the opium trade but to protect its much more important general monopoly of trade with China.

- **Cultural diversity or cultural globalisation?** William Dalrymple's (2002) book on the interaction between the Company's officials and the Mughal elite in India in the eighteenth century tells an intriguing history of how originally many of the British in India were fascinated by the culture of the Mughal courts, adopted its customs, married Mughal women and became 'white Mughals'. But in the late eighteenth century, and certainly during the Victorian era, the British came to despise Indian culture and kept aloof from it so that those Indians who wished to benefit from the opportunities that the Company offered had to adapt to British ideas, values and customs.

The World Commission (WCSDG, 2004: §134) has pointed out that one difference between eighteenth- and nineteenth-century globalisation and that of today is that the earlier period involved large migrations of people – Africans to the Americas, Indians to East and South Africa, the Welsh to Patagonia and so on. Many of these movements themselves raised moral questions because the migrations were enforced by the slave trade. In the current phase of globalisation money and goods are free to cross borders but in general people are not. However, this is not to say that globalisation does not still create some problems associated with migration. The ethical charge is still that people are moved to the advantage of the first world and the disadvantage of the third world. One particular instance concerns the National Health Service (NHS) in the United Kingdom. The NHS is short of doctors and it will be several years before the expansion of medical education delivers the needed fully qualified doctors. To fill the immediate gap the NHS has recruited doctors from other countries, from Africa in particular. In 2004 two-thirds of newly registered doctors in the UK came from abroad. Many African countries desperately need the doctors they train to remain, not least to help deal with the AIDS epidemic they face. Yet in Zambia, to take one example, only 50 of the 600 doctors trained there since independence are still practising in the country. This migration also has the advantage for the UK that it does not have to bear the cost of training many of the doctors it employs. This movement of doctors is seen by both the British government and the British Medical Association as an ethical problem. In this case, however, the migration is not an enforced one. Doctors trained in Africa are inevitably attracted by the better salaries and working conditions that they would experience in the UK (BBC, 2005).

Although the claims that globalisation has brought new ethical problems need to be seen in historical context, globalisation has increased the velocity and awareness of the ethical problems of worldwide economic integration. As Petrick (2000: 1) expressed it, the 'high velocity global market place is complex and challenging'. The international marketplace can now operate in real time – as do the world's stock exchanges as trading moves through time zones from one exchange to another – and not have to deal with the time lags in communication that characterised earlier times. This is the other main difference between the current and the historical periods of globalisation.

The networks of global, multi-national and transnational companies and organisations and NGOs form the arenas in which such problems may arise and the business cultures of different societies and countries may come into contact with each other. It will be useful to define the differences between them.

---

**DEFINITIONS**

**Multi-national enterprises** (MNEs) have been divided into three types (Harzing, 2000):

- **Multi-domestic companies** are federations of autonomous subsidiaries that operate in different countries.

- **Global companies**, by comparison, view themselves as operating in a world market and their products and services make relatively little concession to the particularities of different national markets.

- **Transnational companies** are networks and tend to have little specific national identification or base, although they do have a legal base in a particular country. Worldwide consultancy and accountancy firms are a good example of this type of organisation. They are run by international managements and are willing to move their capital and operations to any favourable location (Hirst and Thompson, 1996: 11).

---

Now that the key terms have been defined we can consider the ethical issues of globalisation in turn.

## Trickle down or just trickery?

Does the evidence we have of the effects of globalisation and trade deregulation on world markets display an improvement of people's well-being? The available evidence is at best mixed. At worst we are experiencing even greater concentrations of power within corporations over resources that lie outside the political arena, with fundamental questions regarding authority, responsibility and accountability remaining unanswered. The observations of Anita Roddick, founder of the Body Shop organisation, are interesting in this context. She was responding to an article by Philippe Legrain that had appeared in the *Guardian* (on the day before the publication of her letter). The latter had made the case that the deregulation of world markets, in line with the actions of the WTO, should be welcomed by all, as ultimately all would benefit. Case study 12.1 presents the words of Ms Roddick.

Case study
12.1

## Anita Roddick's views on globalisation

I went to Seattle in November 1999 to speak at a teach-in on globalisation and to peacefully protest against the WTO. Probably the only international retailer on the 'wrong' side of the police lines. I was baton-charged and tear-gassed by riot police. It was a frightening experience of what corporate controlled reality might look like. Perhaps it prejudiced me against the WTO, it certainly re-radicalised me. Mr Legrain trots out the free traders' familiar falsehood that globalisation is all about making the poor richer. No, Mr Legrain, it's about making the rich even richer ... I can only presume his travels haven't taken him out of the international conference centres into the slums and shanty towns where the poorest and most exploited people live. How else could he glibly state that seamstresses in Bangladesh are not exploited because 'they earn more than they would as farmers'? I recently visited Nicaragua, a country restructured to comply with the WTO and IMF vision of economic progress. There I met workers from the free trade zone, who are paid less than $5 a day to make jeans and shirts exported to the US and sold at obscene mark-ups. Does their pay afford them [the means] to live decently? Depends if a 10 ft square, dirt floored, shack with no plumbed in water or sanitation is decent.

I also visited a cooperative of peasant farmers who grow sesame seed in a remote part of Nicaragua. The price of sesame crashed in 1993. Working with Christian Aid, Body Shop now community trades with the cooperative, sustaining the farmers' livelihoods and culture. They may not be rich, but they do lead dignified lives off the rollercoaster of the commodity market. When the WTO promotes such fair trade, I may 'dump my prejudices'.

(*Source*: Anita Roddick, Letter to the *Guardian*, 13 July 2001)

## Discussion activity 12.1

What were the positions taken on international free trade and its impact on developing countries at the Gleneagles G8 meeting in 2005? Had postions changed since Seattle in 1999?

The two sides of this debate are:

1. The trickle down case – that freeing international trade from restrictions increases the total wealth of the world and that, while this will inevitably reward the elites, the benefits will also trickle down to everyone. This argument is based on standard economic theory which proposes that free international trade encourages countries to specialise in exporting those services and products in which they have a competitive advantage and not to produce those that other countries can produce more efficiently. This leads to a situation in which all countries are producing the most added value they can and are not wasting resources on producing things inefficiently that could better be imported from elsewhere. This maximises the world's wealth, and all benefit.

2. The contrary case argues that, whilst the trickle down case may be logical, the international trade market has a number of imperfections that can prevent the anticipated benefits for all emerging. The first is that large companies from the industrialised countries have greater bargaining power than the small-scale companies and traders in the developing world from whom they buy goods. The former therefore gain the most advantage from international trade. The second imperfection is that the industrialised countries demand that the developing countries place no barriers on international trade but do not return the favour. The most obvious example is that the European Union's Common Agricultural Policy subsidises food production in Europe and so makes it difficult for food producers in the developing world to export their produce to Europe. The third imperfection is that the global institutions set up to regulate international trade, notably the World Trade Organisation (WTO), do not fairly represent the interests of the many parties to them. The institutions respond more to the needs of the industrialised countries, which have their own global institutions such as the G8, and less to the voices of the countries of the developing world. The consequence of these imperfections is that international trade does not necessarily deliver what it promises, and that its promises are sleight of hand and trickery to disguise the fact that the poor in the poorest countries do not benefit from the liberalisation of foreign trade. Even if international trade does make some poor countries better off there is no guarantee that those benefits will be fairly enjoyed by the whole population. Most of the oil exported from Nigeria comes from the Niger delta region. The major oil companies are inevitably active in the region and the Government of Nigeria receives most of its revenues from the oil industry, but the population of the delta has not benefited economically. Indeed the environmental damage to agricultural land caused by the oil operations has worsened even that poor standard of living it used to have.

It is necessary to consider the evidence relating to this debate. Some researchers have focused on identifying whether there is a statistical correlation between growth in world trade and changes in the level of income inequality between countries. As is often the case, research studies do not agree. Lundberg and Squire (2003) found that increasing the openness of international trade makes for greater income inequality between countries. Dollar and Kraay (2002 and 2004), however, found that increasing international trade had little or no impact on income inequality. The figures for countries' poverty levels (percentage of people living on less than $1.08 a day at 1993 purchasing levels) and countries' growth in international trade (measured by exports as a percentage of GDP) was studied by Ravallion (2004). He found a negative correlation between the two, namely as a country's trade increases the amount of poverty decreases, but the correlation was too weak to carry conviction.

China has often been cited as a case where the expansion of its international trade following the start of its 'Open Door 'policy in the early 1980s was a major factor in its success against poverty (World Bank, 2002). An analysis of the statistics by Ravallion and Chen (2004) gives a negative correlation of –0.75 between trade increases and decreases in poverty. As always with correlations, however, it may be dangerous to assume that statistical association implies a cause and effect relationship. The greatest decrease in poverty in China occurred in the early

1980s when trade was liberalised. The poverty rate fell from 76 per cent in 1980 to 23 per cent in 1985 (Ravallion, 2004: 9). However, this was also a period of great increases in agricultural production following the de-collectivisation of agriculture. Conversely the greatest changes in China's openness to international trade occurred after 1985 when poverty had already fallen. It is at least arguable that the reduction in poverty was more to do with agrarian reform than with trade liberalisation. Ravallion also studied the differential impact of China's accession to the WTO in 2001 which involved massive reductions in China's tariff barriers to trade. His analysis suggests that between 2001 and 2007

- 75 per cent of rural households are predicted to lose income but only 10 per cent of urban households would suffer similarly.

- Some areas of China will lose income while other areas will gain.

- In rural areas larger households will benefit more from trade liberalisation than small ones.

- In urban areas smaller households will benefit more than larger ones.

Similar patterns can be found in other countries. In India some states have benefited massively from trade liberalisation and the growth of the IT industry. Other states, notably Bihar on the Gangetic plain, continue with a subsistence economy with increasing levels of poverty. Equally it is the urban areas that benefit from increasing international trade and the rural populations that mostly suffer. The World Bank completed a study of the likely impact of a decrease in the tariffs protecting cereal production in Morocco. The impact of a 30 per cent reduction in tariffs would have been to increase rural poverty while improving the lot of urban households.

The general conclusion concerning the relationship between the opening up of countries to international trade and the level of poverty is that trade openness may not be the key issue in decreasing poverty but that its impact within a particular country is likely to be variable between regions and groups within the country.

It seems unlikely therefore that world trade liberalisation can be morally justified by its impact on reducing poverty. Rather, the consequence of world trade liberalisation for developing countries may be to create a two-track economic and social system, sometimes known as dualism and sometimes as the informal economy.

## Dualism or the informal economy

Dualism was first observed in the British and Dutch empires in South Asia, the British in India and the Dutch in what is now Indonesia. The term means that two economic systems exist in one place in parallel with one another but with little connection or interaction between them. In the nineteenth-century Asian empires there would typically be a capitalist plantation economy that was integrated into international trade by exporting raw material to the west and which used hired labour. Alongside it would be a subsistence agricultural sector that ate what it produced and participated very little in markets. An argument was often made that the plantation managers acted in an economically rational way while the peasant producers exhibited a backward sloping supply curve for labour; in other words the more they earned the less inclined they were to work. However, subsequently it was recognised that this phenomenon was explained by structural barriers that made it too difficult for subsistence producers to put effort into the production of risky cash crops that they would not be able to eat if the market failed to offer them a worthwhile price, quite a likely consequence as they were forced to sell to monopsonistic middlemen. The modern equivalent of this situation is known as the informal economy, which exists in many countries. It consists of small-scale manufacturing, service provision and agricultural work. It is characterised by:

- A lack of recognition and formality: these enterprises do not submit accounts or have legal recognition, they do not recognise laws and regulations and, in many countries, will obtain their electricity by tapping into the grid illegally. The informal market will often specialise in pirated goods such as tapes and CDs. They are a tolerated, but therefore fragile, form of enterprise.

- No access to the formal sources of credit.

- They do not have access to wider regional, national and international markets.

- A lack of rights and legal protections for the people within it.

- Women forming a large proportion of the informal workforce.

- Wages and income being at or close to poverty levels.

- An entrepreneurial creativity and energy that helps respond very quickly to market demand.

The World Commission on the Social Dimension of Globalisation (WCSDG, 2004) reported that globalisation had a great potential for good but that this potential was not yet being fulfilled. Their vision was a moral one.

> We have come to an agreement on a common goal: a fair globalisation which creates opportunities for all. We wish to make globalisation a means to expand human well-being and freedom, and to bring democracy and development to local communities where people live. [ ] Our primary concerns are that globalisation should benefit all countries and should raise the welfare of all people throughout the world.
>
> (WCSDG, 2004: §3 and 171)

It is clear that the liberalisation of international trade will not automatically meet that vision through a trickle down process.

- Between 1985 and 2000 16 developing countries had a per capita income growth of more than 3 per cent, 32 developing countries grew at less than 2 per cent, 23 countries showed negative growth. China and India were transitional countries with high growth rates.

- The gap between GDP per capita in the poorest and richest countries has increased. In the early 1960s per capita income was 50 times higher in the 20 richest countries than in the 20 poorest. By the new millennium this figure had increased to 110.

- In the developed countries, particularly in the UK and the USA, the ratio between the top 10 per cent highest earners and the lowest 10 per cent earners has increased between the mid-1980s and the mid-1990s by 35.1 per cent in the UK and 36.8 per cent in the USA.

- In the developing countries the volatility of flows of foreign direct investment has brought new jobs to countries, most obviously in the movement of call centres from the West to South Asia, but has also decreased the security of jobs in these mobile industries. (WCSDG, 2004: §210)

If there is no global action to help spread the undoubted benefits of increasing trade then unfairness will result.

## Developing institutions or taking advantage?

Many of the ethical criticisms of multinationals and transnationals arise from their tendency to exploit local conditions for commercial advantage. In practice, developing countries may have lower expectations, and weaker laws, concerning acceptable conditions of employment, minimum wage rates, pollution control, health and safety, and many other factors concerning management and business. The problem is to determine to what extent it is right and proper to exploit these circumstances to gain a commercial advantage. There will be extreme cases when it would be uncontroversial to say that such exploitation is bad. A company dumping in third world markets a product that has been declared unfit for use or consumption in the country of origin is such as case. It is perhaps a little more difficult when we consider companies that move their manufacturing operations to new countries where the cost of labour is much lower. It would be clear that they are taking advantage of the lower wages; the question is whether this is simply the market working effectively or an unethical taking of advantage. The typical corporate response to this charge is that inward investment gives jobs to those who would not otherwise have them. The company is thus doing good by giving people jobs and ought not to be expected to pay them wages above the going rates. Local employers would also object and claim they were being harmed if a multi-national started to pay its staff above the labour market rate. Often, however, a form of dual economy emerges in which the multinational companies in a developing country exist in parallel with the local companies but occupy a separate economic 'world', paying higher wages and granting better employment conditions than companies in the local economy. Such a development seems to have happened with the development of the IT industry in India. As the *Economist* (2001) reported, most of India's new economy holds aloof from the old Indian economy. Software engineers in Bangalore, the capital of India's IT industry, work in good conditions in state-of-the-art corporate campuses whereas the rest of the economy operates in poor to bad conditions. Such dual economies produce their own ethical problems and critics demand to know why the benefits of inward investment are not being spread more widely in society.

Chakraborty (1999: 20) laments the impact of western companies employing Indian MBAs at a salary three times that which an Indian company would pay, but still lower than an equivalent person would be paid in the USA, because of the disaffection produced among those not lucky enough to be employed by a multi-national.

| Case study 12.2 | **The Bhopal disaster** |

This episode is a tragic and classic case study in business ethics. Union Carbide, an American-owned company, owned 50.9 per cent of a pesticide plant in Bhopal, central India. The government of India had apparently been so keen to receive this inward investment that it had found a way around its own legislation, which at that time allowed overseas companies to own no more than 40 per cent of any Indian company in which they invested. On the night of the 2–3 December 1984, 40 tonnes of poisonous gases were thrown into the air over Bhopal from the plant. The gases burned the eyes and lungs of people on whom it settled and, when it crossed into their blood stream, it damaged many physiological systems. Over 3,000 people died and 20,000 were injured. At least that was one estimate; the death and morbidity rates of the accident are still the subject of controversy. Campaigners claim that the accident has caused 20,000 deaths in the twenty years since the accident and that half a million have become chronically ill (Ramesh, 2004).

There appear to have been a number of contributory factors that led to the leakage. They mostly related to a cost-cutting culture in a factory that at that time was making a loss and only working at a third of its capacity. On the night of the disaster six safety measures designed to prevent a leak were inadequate, malfunctioning or switched off. Safety audits had been done that had revealed major safety concerns but no action had been taken. These all raise the question of the extent to which Union Carbide had taken advantage of low levels of safety monitoring and expectations to save costs.

It can be argued that a concern to save costs characterised the company's behaviour during the aftermath of the disaster. On one account the company's legal team arrived in Bhopal days before their medical team (Bhopal.net, 2001). One of the issues after the accident was whether the case should be settled in an American court, as the government of India wanted, or in an Indian court, as the company wished, and as was in fact the case. The company fought liability for the accident and agreed an out-of-court settlement five years later with the government of India for $470m. The families of those who died received an interim payment of $550 per fatality. Had the deaths occurred in the USA the families might have received a hundred times that amount (De George, 1999: 511). Associations of the injured are still fighting for further compensation (Corpwatch, 2001). The Bhopal.com website (2001), owned by the Union Carbide Corporation, argues that the 1989 settlement has provided sufficient money from its investment to provide the compensation, and that the compensation was much higher than any settlement that would have been payable under Indian law. The company saw this settlement as complete and final.

▶

It was the twentieth anniversary of the incident in 2004 and this became a time for taking stock. The site of the plant in 2004 belonged to the government of India. The site had not been cleared and there were reports that it still contained potentially damaging chemicals. Dow Chemicals, which had taken over Union Carbide, claimed that it had no further responsibilities in India while the government of India was still pursuing its demand, that Dow Chemicals should clean up the site, through the Indian Courts.

There is an outstanding criminal case against Warren Anderson, the former Chief Executive of Union Carbide. The Indian CBI (Criminal Branch Investigations) had sought Anderson's extradition from his retirement in the United States to stand trial in India. However, the American Government had not responded, pointing to technical difficulties in the claim. The CBI was still pursuing the case, however (*Times of India*, 2004).

The poor of Bhopal, who had borne the brunt of the toxic effects of the discharge, were often still living close to the plant. Only part of Union Carbide's payment had been distributed to the victims. By 2004 there was a balance of £174m (the compensation fund had been swelled by interest over fifteen years). The problems of identifying the victims and deciding what proportion of the compensation sum each should receive had brought the payments to a standstill. In 2004, however, the Supreme Court of India demanded that the government should pay the money out on a per-capita basis (Brown, 2004); which would mean that each victim would receive about $300. There was some scepticism among the activists in Bhopal as to whether the money would appear in the victims' hands.

A group of activists, the 'Yes Men Group', arranged an elaborate hoax so that when BBC producers arranged an interview with a representative of Dow Chemicals (the successor company to Union Carbide) they were actually talking to one of the hoaxers who stated, when interviewed on radio, that Dow Chemicals was accepting full responsibility for the Bhopal disaster. He later said that he was 'speaking on behalf of Dow in a certain way. I was expressing what they should express' (Wells and Ramesh, 2004). Residents of Bhopal had broken down in tears when they heard that Dow had finally accepted their responsibilities, a collapse that was no doubt repeated when they learnt it was not true.

## Discussion activity 12.2

The harm caused by an event such as the Bhopal gas leak can have consequences for many years; yet the corporations, who may be liable for the harm through their negligence, cannot, as commercial organisations, tolerate having long-term, open-ended liabilities on their balance sheets. Discuss whether the belief that responsibility can be ended by a one-off payment in final settlement can be sustained when the harm may be so extensive and widespread?

The Bhopal case illustrates the ability of MNEs to exercise some choice over which legal jurisdiction they choose to submit to, as a way of taking advantage of the different institutional contexts of different countries. Sometimes organisations attempt to do this but fail to achieve the hoped for advantage. An example is the giant Russian oil company Yukos. Yukos was accused by the Russian government of having evaded the payment of taxes. The Government enforced the sale of Yukos's largest asset, a company called Yuganskneftegaz that produced two-thirds of Yukos's oil production. It was likely that Gazprom, the Russian state-owned oil company, would become the purchaser and it had arranged financial backing for the deal from Deutsche Bank. It so happens that the United States courts claim worldwide bankruptcy jurisdiction for companies that operate in the United States. Consequently Yukos opened an office in Dallas and put $2m into its American bank account. It then applied to the courts in Dallas for temporary bankruptcy protection. This was granted and a restraining order was issued to stop the sale of Yugansk. The sale went ahead but the displeasure of the US legal system was enough to frighten away Gazprom's western financial backers, and Deutsche Bank withdrew its financial support. The restraining order made it illegal for any company to work with Gazprom, and Deutsche Bank has a large American operation. The bank has applied to the American courts to have the restraining order removed (Mortished, 2004).

There have been cases where MNEs have avoided the institutional arrangements of industrialised countries. One such case is McDonald's operations in Europe. Most European countries have legislation on worker participation that is designed to give employees some influence on company decision making. This is known as co-determination and in Germany the legislation allows for both supervisory boards and works councils. Supervisory boards are strategic bodies within a company, and companies with more than 2,000 employees should have employee representatives on the supervisory board. If McDonald's operations in Germany were registered in Germany it would have to have a supervisory board; however, it is a fully owned subsidiary of the American parent company and so has avoided the necessity (Royle, 2000: 124). McDonald's are however obliged to allow, and meet with, a plant level Works Council if the employees request it. The company had 350 fully owned restaurants in Germany and 650 franchises and each one was entitled to have a Works Council as well as a company level and a group level Works Council. In practice, in 1999, there was no group or company Council and there were only between 40 and 50 plant level Councils in the 1,000 restaurants. McDonald's management had used a number of tactics to discourage its employees setting up Works Councils. The simplest was sending flying squads of managers to restaurants to dissuade staff from setting up a Works Councils and to use McDonald's own systems of communication and feedback. On occasion the company would transfer the ownership of a company between holding companies, an action that had the effect of delaying the election of a Works Committee. Most commonly they would 'buy out' Works Council representatives with cash and then nominate their own candidates to capture the Council and keep it compliant with management's wishes (Royle, 2000: 126–127). It was reported in 1995 that McDonald's spent £250,000 buying out 46 works councillors and their supporters. US companies, used to unregulated labour markets, would inevitably find continental European labour markets uncongenial, sufficiently so for them on occasion to seek to avoid the legal and institutional requirements.

However, most examples of MNEs taking advantage of easier institutional conditions refer to developing countries that have a strong desire for foreign direct investment (FDI). It is arguable that the exploitation of institutional weaknesses is an unsatisfactory form of advantage. The problems of investing and operating in a country that has weak institutions and poor governance outweigh, in the long term, the advantages. As the Report of the Commission for Africa (2005: 24–5) points out, both MNEs and developing countries would benefit if those countries could develop an effective form of governance that encourages investment. By effective governance is meant

- security and peace
- sound economic policies under the law
- collecting taxes and providing adequate public services
- adequate physical infrastructure such as transport and telecommunications
- effective legal systems and respect for contracts and property rights
- maintenance of human rights
- appropriate constitutional checks on the actions of government.

Multi-national and transnational countries should act as good corporate citizens in the host countries in which they operate. They should play a part in developing the ethical codes, norms and practices of business. This may be particularly important in developing countries which, through lack of resources or of opportunity, have poorly developed legal and voluntary frameworks intended to encourage ethical business behaviour.

## Collusion between governments and corporations

Since Eisenhower invented the term 'military–industrial complex' in 1961 there have been concerns that the American government and large American companies, especially those involved in strategic industries, have become mutually dependent in a way that damages government's ability to ensure that the market-place operates fairly and ethically. Governments anywhere may use their discretion to take decisions that unfairly advantage companies based in their countries. Very often the criticisms concern the actions of government to support domestic companies' export sales.

An example occurred in the UK in 2005 when the Government was found to have been publicly supporting moves to prevent UK companies paying facilitation payments overseas while, at the same time, supporting the business lobby's opposition to the controls (Eaglesham and Tait, 2005). In May 2004 the government's Export Credits Guarantee Department (which underwrites British companies' export deals) introduced tough anti-corruption rules. Among other provisions these would have forced companies to guarantee that their joint venture partners would not act corruptly and to disclose commissions paid to agents. A number of British companies, including Airbus, Rolls Royce and BAE Systems, lobbied against the rules. They argued that if these rules stood major contracts would be lost. The Secretary of State for Trade and Industry relented and agreed a new set of rules in which these requirements were dropped, even though her civil servants had advised that any changes should have been put out for public consultation. However, Corner House, an anti-corruption group, threatened to go to Court to have the old rules reinstated because the anti-corruption groups had not been consulted. On this occasion the Secretary of State relented to the demands of the anti-corruption lobby and a process of public consultation was agreed. If it had not been for some leaked documents however the regulations would have been quietly changed in order to protect the interests of some major companies, and consequently, as some would argue, the interests of the UK. The price would have been tacit collusion with bribery in the world marketplace.

**Connexion point**

The nature of bribery and of grease payments in particular is discussed in Chapter 11, pp. 424–7. This particular case is also raised in Chapter 13, p. 00.

**Case study 12.3**

## Indonesia

The situation regarding the fate of Indonesia since 1965/6, as documented by Pilger (2001), is one of the most troublesome examples of corporate capital and western governments working in tandem, first to engineer a change in political leadership, and then to dictate both economic policy and the way ownership and control of a nation state's natural resources would be allowed to develop. It involves the overthrow of the then leader President Sukarno in 1965/6 by General Suharto, with significant western support. The prize in ousting Sukarno was great. Of Indonesia, Richard Nixon, a former President of the United States, said, 'With its 100 million people, and its 300-mile arc of islands containing the region's richest hoard of natural resources, Indonesia is the greatest prize in southeast Asia.'

The UK also had a vested interest in seeing a regime in power that was friendlier to the West than Sukarno and his ruling Communist party. In 1964 the UK Foreign Office produced an analysis of the region and 'called for the "defence" of western interests in south-east Asia, a major producer of essential commodities. The region produces nearly 85% of the world's natural rubber, over 45% of the tin, 65% of the copra and 23% of the chromium ore' (Pilger, 2001: 26).

The complicity of America and the UK in the bloody aftermath of the Suharto take-over (it is claimed that as many as one million have been murdered) appears to have been considerable and is documented by Pilger (2001). The American Central Intelligence Agency (CIA) reported that, 'in terms of the numbers killed the massacres rank as one of the worst mass murders of the 20th century' (Pilger, 2001: 24).

With Suharto in power, a conference took place between corporations, predominantly American, but also including some UK and other European corporations, and the Indonesian government. In Pilger's words, 'the Indonesian economy was carved up, sector by sector. In one room, forests; in    ▶

another minerals. The Freeport Company got a mountain of copper in West Papua. A US/European consortium got West Papua's nickel. The giant Alcoa company got the biggest slice of Indonesia's bauxite. A group of US, Japanese and French got the tropical forests of Sumatra, West Papua and Kalimantan. In addition a foreign investment law was hurried on to the statute books by Suharto, allowing all profits made by foreign companies to be tax-free for at least the first five years of operations.'

Over the next thirty years the World Bank provided loan finance amounting to £30bn to Indonesia. Of this, it is estimated by the World Bank itself that up to £10bn went into Suharto's own pockets, or those of his family and associates.

'In 1997 an internal World Bank report confirmed that at least 20–30% of the bank's loans [to Indonesia] are diverted through informal payments to GOI [Government of Indonesia] staff and politicians' (Pilger, 2001: 22).

In recent years attention has been drawn to the working conditions (e.g. up to 36-hour shifts) and pay (equivalent to 72p per hour) of factory workers in Indonesia making products for major companies such as Nike, Adidas, Reebok and GAP, and the squalor of the living conditions they endure in the camps located next to the 'economic processing zones' (i.e. the factories). In 1998, following mounting demonstrations in the Indonesian capital of Jakarta by large crowds protesting at their poverty and their desperate living conditions, Suharto left office, taking with him many billions of pounds sterling provided for his country over the years by the World Bank. These are monies that the country is obliged to keep paying the interest on, before it can even start repaying the capital.

The fall of Suharto might have marked the end of Indonesia's plight, but it may not have done. In 2000 the IMF offered the post-Suharto government a 'rescue package' of multi-million-dollar loans. However, there were conditions. These included the elimination of tariffs on staple foods. 'Trade in all qualities of rice has been opened to general importers and exporters' (Pilger, 2001: 24), decreed the IMF's letter of intent. Fertilisers and pesticides lost their 70 per cent subsidy, thereby ending for many farmers the prospect of staying on their land. They too will be forced to try to find work in the cities, which are already overburdened with unemployed 'citizens' looking for work. However, 'it gives the green light to the giant food grains corporations to move into Indonesia' (Pilger, 2001: 24).

## Discussion activity 12.3

Use a World Wide Web search engine to find material on the relationships between the American oil company Halliburton and the American administration of President Bush concerning the re-building of Iraq after the defeat of Saddam Hussein. Discuss the issues the case raises about close connections between governments and global businesses.

## Creating political tensions between and within states

As MNEs are often bigger than many states they frequently begin to act as sovereign bodies and players in international power politics or realpolitik.

> **DEFINITION**
>
> The term **Realpolitik** originated in Germany in 1853 to describe an approach to relations with other countries. It does not mean a naked self-interest or use of power but it does imply that ethical considerations have to be balanced against what is possible, where the balance of power lies, and self-interest. The idea of course is an ancient one. It can be found in the Arthrashastra of Kautilya.
>
> > A King whose territory has a common boundary with that of an antagonist is an ally.
> >
> > (Rangarajan, 1992: 555)
>
> In other words, my enemy's enemy is my friend. This is the principle that MNEs may have to follow. It would explain why the oil companies in the following case study found themselves in alliance with the federal Nigerian government, which was then a military dictatorship.

The natural aim of trading companies is to achieve political stability so that their trading plans are not inconvenienced. However, since the days of the European colonial trading companies – the Dutch East India Company, The English East India Company, the Hudson Bay Company and many others – international trading companies have been drawn into regional power struggles between and within states. Their ambition may be profit but the pursuit of that goal often requires them to act as political entities and, in some cases, to take on aspects of sovereignty. Inasmuch as they become additional factors in regional conflicts they have the opportunity to act to diminish or inflame these disputes. When companies intervene in local and regional politics and conflict in support of their commercial objectives they cannot be certain that the outcomes will be the ones they wished for. Companies may have good intentions but their actions may make matters worse. Consequently, serious ethical implications attach to companies' decisions to act politically; they may seriously disturb the peace and prosperity of communities and societies.

---

**Case study 12.4**

### The oil industry and the Niger Delta

The Nigerian oil fields are in the Niger Delta in the south-eastern part of the country, and this has been a politically troubled area for many years. Since 2001 there has been ethnic violence in the area between Muslims and Christians with 5,000 people killed in four years. There is conflict between tribes indigenous to the area and the Nigerian government and consequently a large military presence in the region. Much of the political instability however ▶

is a consequence of the presence of the international oil industry in the region. The peoples of the delta feel that they have not benefited from, and in fact have been damaged by, the presence of the oil industry. A sense of deprivation is often expressed as resentment against other groups who, it is felt, have fared better. Link this relative sense of deprivation to the tribal diversity of the delta and the probability of civil unrest is much increased. This of course is the opposite of what the oil companies wanted and they allied themselves with the Nigerian government, then a military dictatorship, by supporting a military crack-down against what they saw as greed by the communities in the delta who were prepared to foment unrest to extract the maximum benefits from and damage an oil industry that was necessary to the economic well-being of the whole of Nigeria.

Two of the major ethnic groups in the delta are the Ogoni and the Ijaw. The Ogoni started a campaign against the environmental damage, social exclusion and poverty caused by the oil industry. These troubles came to the world's notice in 1995 when activists linked Shell to the military government's trial and execution of the Ogoni activist Ken Saro-Wiwa (Planet Ark, 2004). It was also argued that the government encouraged violent conflicts between the Ogoni and neighbouring communities – the Andoni, the Okrika and the Ndoki. This violence then gave the government an excuse to use the security forces against the Ogoni whose uprising ended when the Ogoni leadership split amidst mutual accusations that competing leaders were only interested in furthering their own financial and political ambitions. By the late 1990s the struggle against the petro-business had been taken up by a youth movement among the Ijaw. This developed into what became known as the first and second Egbusu wars.

The presence of the international oil industry was the focus of violent conflicts between sections of the Nigerian population and its government and between Nigerian communities. It is not claimed that there would have been only peace if there had been no oil industry. But it can be claimed that by allying themselves to the government, rather than responding to the concerns of the communities, the presence of the oil industry made the problems worse. A class action being prepared against Shell will accuse the company directors of supporting military operations by Nigeria's former government against Ogoniland separatists in the Niger Delta in the 1990s.

In 2003 Shell commissioned a conflict resolution consultancy based in Lagos to prepare a report on its troubles in the Niger River Delta. The 93-page report was published in 2004. In that year's annual sustainability report the Community Development manager, Emmanuel Etomi, wrote that he accepted that the oil industry was 'inadvertently contributing' to conflict in the country; and

> How we sometimes feed conflict by the way we award contracts, gain access to land and deal with community representatives; how ill-equipped our security is to reduce conflict; and how drastically conflict reduces the effect of our community development programmes.

The consultants' report argued that ethnic violence would cause Shell to withdraw from the area by 2009 (Hope, 2004).

(*Sources*: Ibeanu (2000); Ojefia (n.d.))

## Discussion activity 12.4

Corporations working in politically troubled areas will often need the support of the local government. This might lead such corporations to assume that their ally's enemy is also their enemy, and cause them to come into conflict with local communities, who are antagonistic towards the government, but whose support they also need to conduct their business. Discuss how corporations might avoid this dilemma.

The oil industry is the natural one to consider in this section because it deals with the most strategically important product in the world. Oil has become the driving force of much international politics as the USA seeks to protect its sources of oil from the inconvenient fact that much of the oil comes from countries with which it is out of sympathy, Russia seeks to maintain its control over central Asian oil fields, and China desperately seeks the oil it needs to finance its rapid industrialisation. Whereas the previous case study dealt with the impact of the oil industry on the internal politics of a country, Case study 12.5 deals with its impact on the relationships between states.

**Case study 12.5**

### The Baku – Tblisi – Ceyhan (BTC) oil pipeline

The Caucasus region, like the Balkans, has long been an area of nationalist, ethnic and religious rivalries. When the region was part of the Soviet Union these tensions were held in check. Now that each of the groups within the region has its own sovereign territory, and the few who do not, the South Ossetians and the Chechens for example, are seeking it, the conflicts between them have again become palpable. If to this mixture is added the internationally strategic significance of the new oil fields discovered under the Caspian Sea then the industrialised countries, who need the oil and the multinational oil companies, who need the business, also become involved in what has become called the New Great Game, in homage to the strategic conflict between Britain and Russia in the nineteenth century over who was to control the region (Kleveman, 2003).

Azerbaijan is a central player in this game. The modern oil industry had its origin in the Azerbaijani capital Baku in the 1880s and the city experienced an oil boom that lasted until 1905. The industry revived after the Second World War when Azerbaijan was an important component of the Soviet Union's oil industry. When Azerbaijan gained independence in 1991 it wished to assert its actual as well as legal independence from Russia. Its only asset for achieving this was the state-owned oil company SOCAR. The new state went into partnership with BP and Amoco by forming the Azerbaijan International Operating Company (AIOC). BP later took over Amoco and so became the major western oil company operating in Azerbaijan.

If Azerbaijan were more conveniently located, so that oil could be easily taken to the west, there would be few problems. However, the country is landlocked and a long pipeline is needed. There were several possible routes. ▶

- To a port on Turkey's Black Sea coast; but Turkey rejected this option because it would have involved oil tankers going through the narrow Bosporus that links the Black Sea to the Mediterranean and the danger of pollution was unacceptable.

- Through Armenia to either the Black Sea or Mediterranean coast; but Azerbaijan and Armenia had fought a war over, and Armenia still occupies, the Azerbaijani province of Nagorno-Karabakh. Although hostilities have ceased peace talks between the two countries make little progress.

- Through Russia; but Azerbaijan is trying to assert its independence from its former masters.

- Through Iran; but the United States would not wish to entrust the security of a pipeline from which it drew oil to a fundamentalist Shiite state with which it is already in diplomatic dispute.

- Through Georgia; but Georgia is politically unstable with intrusions from Chechen rebels in the north and its own internal separatist movements among the Abkhazians and the South Ossetians.

The route finally chosen was from Baku, through Georgia and then through Turkey to the Mediterranean coast. BP and the other oil companies grumbled about the cost of the pipeline which was inevitably taking a circuitous route. The additional costs also made the oil companies feel more anxious about the potential political problems of building and operating the pipeline.

This insecurity was perhaps what led the oil companies to insist on international treaties, rather than commercial contracts, to govern the pipeline. Consequently an inter-governmental agreement and three host government agreements (HGAs) were drafted, largely by BP's lawyers, and signed by the governments. Pressure groups such as Corner House (*et al.*, 2003) have argued that these agreements give the oil companies virtual sovereign powers over the territory that the pipeline will traverse in its long journey through Turkey, Georgia and Azerbaijan. They effectively exempt BP and its partners from any laws in the three countries, present or future, that would conflict with the pipeline project. The governments have to compensate BP if any law or tax damages the financial viability of the pipeline. The consortium is also given the right to prevent building development in the pipeline zone and to restrict the movement of livestock. Amnesty International (2003) argued that the HGA signed by Turkey creates a disincentive for Turkey to improve its human rights record. Turkey has to pay the consortium compensation if there is any economic disruption to the project. Such disruption might take the form of local protests against the pipeline, especially as 30,000 people will have to give up their property rights to make way for the pipeline. The government of Turkey might be prepared to sacrifice the human rights of any protestors to avoid paying compensation. The agreements were a revival of the OECD proposals for a Multilateral Agreement on Investment that was dropped in 1998 because of the public outcry it caused (Friends of the Earth, 1997).

Despite these treaty provisions some of the Caucasian states are flexing their muscles against the oil companies. In 2003 Edward Shevardnadze was forced out of government by popular pressure. In 2004 the new government ordered BP to stop work on the pipeline in Borjormi, an area of Georgia that is classified as an area of natural beauty and in which are located mineral water springs that provide a good proportion of Georgia's exports. The government argued that BP had not provided a full environmental assessment (Malhiason, 2004).

There is a danger that the presence of the pipeline will exacerbate the political and military tensions in the areas it traverses. The pipeline passes near to Nagorno-Karabakh, near to South Ossetia and near to the Kurdish area of Turkey where there is a conflict between the PKP and the Turkish military. All the countries in the region are also the seats of conflict between Russia and western nations as to who can include the region in its sphere of influence. The pipeline could become a focal point for military or terrorist attack, and to protect from this possibility it is likely that western troops will be posted to protect it and create a militarised strip running through the region. The oil companies could only be grateful for the support even if they knew that the military presence might increase the probability of an attack on the pipeline.

There is a dilemma for companies pursuing projects in politically unstable areas. Their presence makes them an object of contention between competing political factions and interests. This causes them to seek means of protecting their investment. But the means they use, presence of foreign troops, HGAs, creates local objections and protests making them even more the focus of political and, possibly military, conflict.

(*Additional sources*: baku-ceyhan campaign, 2003a, 2003b and n.d.)

## Discussion activity 12.5

In the past western governments have sometimes assumed sovereign powers in other countries to secure vital trade links. Two examples are the US government and the Panama Canal and the British and French governments who had control over the Suez Canal. Use a World Wide Web search engine to discover what the historical outcomes were in these two cases. Then discuss what lessons, if any, can be drawn from these examples for projects such as the BTC pipeline.

## Staying put or getting out?

The issue facing multi-national companies, however, may not just be that the norms of business behaviour in the countries they operate in are undeveloped. Companies may find themselves in countries where the regimes are commonly regarded as oppressive and human rights are being denied. This situation raises the question of what obligations private companies might have to challenge unethical behaviour by states. Murphy (2001) proposed a theory of benevolence in which people (he was not discussing companies) are not morally obliged to do more to solve the world's problems than would be their portion if everyone else were doing their share. In other words people (and companies?) should only do their portion even if others are not doing theirs and so there remains much that the individual or company could do.

Unethical states may, however, seek to influence how international companies conduct their business. If such regimes demand that companies use unacceptable employment practices, for example, or direct their investments in ways that reward their political supporters, then companies may be forced to consider whether it is ethical to remain in that country

Lord Browne (Browne of Madingley, 2004), Group Chief executive of BP, put forward an unambiguous principle.

> Companies must obey the law in every jurisdiction in which we operate and if we find the law unacceptable and at odds with our own values we shouldn't be operating in that jurisdiction.

Withdrawing from a failed or oppressive state may meet ethical requirements because the organisation would cease to be complicit in wrongdoing, but such a move may make the situation of the population in the state worse. Talisman is a Canadian oil company that was active in Sudan, a country that has been suffering a civil war between its Muslim north and its Christian and Animist south for two decades. Talisman was charged by human rights groups that its presence exacerbated the civil war, that the money it paid for the oil was used to buy arms and that its oil development had displaced thousands of people. In 2003 Talisman withdrew from the Nile Petroleum Operation Company (NPOC), which it owned in partnership with the China National Petroleum Corporation, Petronas the Malaysian oil company and the Sudanese state-owned oil company. Talisman sold its share of NPOC to an arm of India's Oil and Natural Gas Corporation. The organisations that now own NPOC are all state owned. They do not raise their capital on the international markets nor are they accountable to shareholders. Seymour (2003) argued that these organisations benefited from the political turmoil in Sudan, which acted to keep their western competitors out. (Since a peace deal brought the civil war to an end in 2005 western oil companies have shown a renewed interest in Sudan.) He also argued that because they are companies owned by governments, which were often intolerant of critical voices within their own countries, these corporations are immune from the demands of human rights groups such as had encouraged Talisman to quit Sudan.

> [ ] with the sale of Talisman's share, a company that its critics had ensured had an interest in attempting to moderate the government of Sudan's policies has left. What remains are companies that actively support the government of Sudan and its war against southerners, with all its attendant human rights abuses. The moral calculus is thus vastly more complex, and our celebration of Talisman's departure utterly displaced.
>
> (Seymour, 2003: 5)

| Case study 12.6 | **Businesses and South Africa in the apartheid era** |

In the 1950s the apartheid regime in South Africa was created by a series of laws that enforced racial segregation by restricting the areas in which blacks and coloureds could live and by limiting the jobs they could apply for. There were many foreign-owned companies that had long been present in South Africa. These companies had to obey the apartheid laws. As, by common consensus in the world beyond South Africa, apartheid was evil, and the foreign-owned companies were not in a position to change it, the question arose as to whether in conscience they should disinvest from South Africa. In 1977 Leon Sullivan, a director of General Motors, a company that had a subsidiary in South Africa, proposed a set of principles to govern its business in South Africa (Minnesota Center for Corporate Responsibility, 2001). They amounted to a refusal to obey the apartheid laws. Segregation was not to be practised in its plants and staff were to be paid and promoted according to merit not race. They also imposed an obligation to improve the quality of life in those communities in which companies did business. Many American companies trading in South Africa signed up to the principles. It was hoped that such large numbers would discourage the South African government from prosecuting the companies for breaking the apartheid laws and that their efforts might lead to the collapse of apartheid.

However, in 1987 Sullivan declared that the experiment was showing no sign of undermining apartheid. He claimed that American companies should withdraw from their South African operations. In that year General Motors sold its holdings in South Africa. In 1991 the South African government began to repeal the apartheid regime. Nelson Mandela was elected President of South Africa in 1994.

The issue of the moral, and perhaps legal, responsibility of MNEs for the apartheid era has remained. The issue came into prominence in 2004, as in the Yukos case (*see* p. 471), because the United States judiciary was claiming a worldwide jurisdiction in certain circumstance. The American Alien Tort Claims Act of 1789 allows American companies to be sued in the American courts for certain classes of wrong that were committed in other countries. The validity of this law was confirmed by a Supreme Court ruling in 2004. An American law firm proposed to start a case on behalf of the Khulumani Support Group of South Africa against IBM. The allegation is that IBM supplied the then South African government with the computers that enabled them to put the pass laws, which allocated individuals to a racial category that determined where they might go and what they might do, into effect. The pass laws were at the heart of the apartheid system. In case it be argued that in supplying the hardware IBM cannot be liable because they could not determine the use to which the computers might be put, the allegation also argues that IBM supplied the software (Robins, 2004).

The South African government is opposed to the case although many human rights groups are supporting it. They point out that the MNEs are fully cooperating in rehabilitating the lives of those damaged by apartheid. It is also no doubt seen to be in the country's national interest to keep the MNEs engaged with South Africa's economic growth.

**Discussion activity 12.6**

Draw up and discuss guidelines that could be used to help a company decide whether a country it was working in had such a corrupt government and institutions that they should withdraw from it.

## Cultural diversity or cultural homogenisation?

The World Commission on the Social Dimension of Globalisation (WCSDG, 2004) identified a number of broadly cultural aspects of globalisation. The major impact concerns what they term interconnectivity (WCSDG, 2004: §218). The rapid spread of telecommunications and the Internet, and in particular of television and the global entertainment industry, has made people everywhere more conscious of each other's ambitions, expectations and circumstances. For the relatively poor this process creates a sense of missing out that they would not have if their horizons were more local and circumscribed. For the relatively rich it increases their sense of privilege, which may create a feeling of obligation to those less fortunate. This may well explain the growth of NGOs and international charities and indeed the increase in anti-globalisation activisms. Travel is an aspect of this increasing interconnectivity and the fact that many Europeans had travelled to Thailand, in particular, explains both the high loss of life of European tourists in the 2004 Asian tsunami and the huge and sympathetic response from the western world.

A common cliché is that travel broadens the mind. However, ironically, as we travel more, taking advantage of the spread of budget airlines, our ethical horizons can become narrower. If we visit the places much frequented we may only see a Disney-fied version of the local culture – folkloric evenings in Greece, having lunch with the inhabitants of the floating islands on Lake Titicaca – and mistakenly think it true. Julian Barnes' (1998) comic novel *England, England* explores the idea of a replica England built on the Isle of Wight to attract the tourists. Merely flying to broaden our minds may show a lack of awareness of sustainability issues. Aviation fuel is untaxed, which makes flying cheaper than if it were taxed as are other forms of transport. Therefore as the demand for air travel, especially for holidays, increases aeroplanes become a major source of the greenhouse gases that may contribute to global warming. Therefore our desire to travel may be harming us all.

A particular criticism of globalisation is the tendency of powerful countries and companies to impose their values on weaker societies. This is sometimes called McDonaldisation, a process by which western brands and organisational methods and structures replace local products and thereby reduce choice and variety.

The charges of McDonaldisation and Logo-isation define the ethical questions surrounding the cultural and social aspects of globalisation. Do these processes destroy local cultures and replace them with North American values, and if they do is this a bad thing?

DEFINITION

Ritzer (1993) in his book *The McDonaldization of Society* took the global success of McDonald's as an example of the growth of a common, worldwide, mass culture. Ritzer argued that the process of **McDonaldisation** represents the expansion of instrumental rationality – a drive for efficiency, predictability, calculability and control – with no questioning of the ends being sought. The criticism of mass culture, of which McDonaldisation is a modern example, is that it causes people to be satisfied with a 'vulgar simplicity' (Harrington, 1965: 188). Advertising and sound-bite communications, it is alleged, diminish the masses' ability to exercise moral agency. They lose the ability to distinguish the good from the bad, gourmet cooking from burgers, the noble life from consumerism.

This criticism was taken up and popularised by Naomi Klein (2000) in her book *No Logo*. She argues that globalisation, and in particular the branding of consumer goods, has limited people's choices throughout the world. This has been done by:

- Replacing culture and education by marketing. Brands divert people from the product or service they are buying and focus them on purchasing the perceived status and values that are associated with the brand. People buy coffee from Starbucks, she argues (Klein, 2000: 21), for the sense of being a member of a warm, bookish, jazz listening, armchair lounging community; and not for the coffee. The purchase of coffee therefore ceases to be a rational expression of personal values but an entrapment by emotional lures. It may of course have always been so. If one replaces jazz and armchairs with tobacco fug, cosy booths and clubbable warmth one has a description of the original coffee shops in eighteenth-century London.

- Creating less secure, less fulfilling and poorly paid jobs for people, not just in the developing world but in the industrialised worlds as well. This has been achieved by the casualisation of labour through outsourcing, flexible work and part-time employment. Interestingly, again, a return to the nature of the work force in eighteenth-century England.

Klein however is not simply an observer; her intention is to report on and encourage the forces of anti-globalisation and the activities of anti-brand warriors.

**Connexion point**

The discussion of McDonaldisation and Logo-isation is a particular aspect of a more general issue that is discussed in Chapter 11, namely the extent to which different countries or cultural groups wish to develop or maintain their own values and priorities in relation to business and management.

## Does globalisation damage indigenous and local cultures?

The first of these questions is slightly easier to address because it is a practical matter. MNEs may take a range of actions concerning the introduction of their international brands into new countries.

- Introduce the brand and product in its traditional form. Such is the case with Coca Cola that is marketed as a global product.

- Introduce the brand but adapt the product to local tastes and preferences. In Greece, for example, McDonald's burgers are mostly lamb, in recognition of local tastes; in India they sell no beef or pork patties at all in response to religious prohibitions.

- Decide not to enter the market but wait to see if local demand develops. No major western coffee chain has yet opened in India to sell espressos and lattes. However, in Delhi and other metropolitan areas local chains such as Barista are expanding.

- In some cases an MNE may prevent the importation of a western product or service into a country. China has opened its market but its government is concerned that this should not present any threat to its ideology and policies. MNEs therefore will take care not to offend the Chinese government lest they experience some problems with their licences to operate in China. The country is a vast potential market for satellite television and other services and News Corporation International is a major provider through its Star TV service. News Corporation International dropped the BBC World Service from the range of channels it provided to China because the government objected to a documentary that the BBC had broadcast on Mao Tse-tung (Klein, 2000: 171).

- The case of what the WCSDG calls indigenous and tribal peoples (WCSDG, 2004: §311) is a particularly difficult one. There are a few communities in the world that are totally separated from life in the rest of the world. The question is whether these societies should be protected not only from intrusion by companies but also from all other forms of contact including tourism.

| Case study 12.7 | **McDonald's fries** |
|---|---|

The original McDonald's fries were cooked in beef fat. This of course made them objectionable to vegetarians and to Hindus for whom the cow is sacred. In 1990 McDonald's announced that in future all its fries would be cooked in vegetable oil. It emerged in 2001, however, that this was only part of the story. In North America the fries were first cooked in centralised plants using beef fat. They were then frozen and transported to the restaurants for further frying in vegetable oil. McDonald's announced that it was 'not too big to apologise' and that it had given incomplete information to its customers. American Hindus have started seeking damages. Other customers have no problem with the use of beef fat and may even think that it improves the taste of the fries. McDonald's has nearly thirty restaurants in India, where its burgers are made from lamb rather than beef. It assured its Indian customers that its cooking methods were strictly vegetarian.

(*Source*: Evans, 2001)

The situation is not a simple one therefore of the imposition of western brands and products, and by implication western consumer values, on local cultures. Such an argument in any case implies a naïve and orientalist distinction between the spiritual east and the materialist west, and presumes a story in which the simple and non-materialist lives of the east are destroyed by crass western commercial values. Social and economic histories point out that people and communities in the east are as concerned with material things and profits as those in the west. For a detailed and very local account of the importance of the market – the bazaar – in the lives of local people in the Gangetic plain of India in the nineteenth and twentieth centuries, read Yang (1998).

## Orientalism  `DEFINITION`

This term was coined by Edward Said (1978) to explain the stereotyped view that the western imperial powers had of the eastern societies they were colonising.

> This is the apogee of Orientalist confidence. No merely asserted generality is denied the dignity of truth; no theoretical list of oriental attributes is without application to the behaviour of orientals in the real world. On the one hand there are Westerners, and on the other there are Arab-orientals; the former are (in no particular order) rational, peaceful, liberal, logical, capable of holding real values, without natural suspicion; the latter are none of these things.
>
> (Said, 1978: 49)

Said argued that such stereotyping was an ideological device to support colonialist exploitation of the east.

### Connexion point

The concept of orientalism is closely associated with that of essentialism, which is discussed in Chapter 11, p. 420.

## Globalisation and consumer choice

Let us assume, and it is a big assumption, that western brands and products are changing the local and family values of developing countries. Is this a bad thing? We will not answer the question but we will try to lay out the form that an argument about the matter might take. The process would be bad

- if it were accepted unwittingly by those affected, who were unaware of the changes and their significance.

- or if it broke some generally accepted ethical principle.

The main commentators on these questions take different positions.

- Klein argues that branding and marketing are devices to circumvent people's tendency to make rational choice by appealing to them through symbolism and emotion. She would also argue that this effect is just as strong, and perhaps stronger, in the industrialised west than it might be in developing countries. Branding is therefore to be regarded as a bad thing because people are unconscious of the changes they were experiencing. This argument is a version of the Marxist concept of false consciousness (Sklair, 1995). This states that in capitalist societies the masses are exploited but are lured into believing that they are living in the best of all possible worlds. They are not able to recognise their own oppression.

- The Ritzer argument in McDonaldisation (*see* p. 483) is not that people do not make rational choices in a consumer society, simply that they use the wrong sort of rationality. Instrumental rationality, which is what it is argued consumers use, is conscious and calculated but it is focused on achieving the wrong ends. Instead of seeking the good life, as Aristotle demanded in the west and as is required by many other philosophies and religions, modern consumers satisfy themselves with designer labels and the newest gadgets. This is essentially a Weberian analysis in which the day-to-day operations of modern organisations constrain people's actions to implementing means, and mistakenly assuming them to be ends. On this basis consumerism can be seen as breaking an important ethical principle and thus is to be seen as a bad thing.

- The third position believes that in the new global village people in different societies choose freely to enjoy the benefits and comforts provided by iPods, computer games, Internet access and coffee lattes. This view was taken by Kerr *et al.* (1960). On this argument globalisation, and the standardisation of tastes it brings, are to be thought a good thing.

**DEFINITION**

**Weberian** is the adjectival form of the name of the sociologist Max Weber. He defined bureaucracy (the following definition is heavily dependent on Watson (2002: 240–2)) as a distinctive form of organisation and decision making that had replaced traditional methods. In bureaucracies decisions are made using instrumental or formal rationality that involves a calculation as to which option would best meet the desired objectives. This approach has many benefits; it enables, for example, doctors to develop ever more complex means of assisting human conception. However, Weber also noted that a fixation on techniques would lead to a neglect of discussion of the value of the ends being sought. This was his idea of the *stalhartes Gehäuse* (meaning steel-hard house but often translated as iron cage). In the example given instrumental rationality could mean that if the technology to clone human beings is developed it would be used without considering whether it was right to do so.

The net effect of globalisation would seem to be one in which the populations of the developing and the transitional countries are increasingly sharing common expectations and demands for services and products. The expansion of international trade and foreign direct investment (FDI) that fuels globalisation has increased the wealth of the world. However, the distribution of these beneficial impacts has been skewed. Some areas, notably Asia and Latin America and the Caribbean, have received much larger inflows of FDI than other areas such as Africa and Eastern Europe (International Labour Organisation, ILO 2004: 28). Within the developing countries the elite have benefited more than the bulk of the populations, who in some cases have become worse off. At an ethical level these outcomes offend against Rawls' fairness principle (*see* p. 115); in practice it creates a destabilising situation in which many people's expectations are increasing while their conditions are worsening. There is recognition among international institutions, such as the United Nations, The Group of Eight (G8) and many others, that this situation is unfair and potentially a source of conflict within the world. There is consequently much discussion about the governance of international businesses, and it is to this topic that we now turn.

## Global governance

At the close of the second world war a series of international conferences set up the basic institutions of global governance, namely the United Nations, the World Bank, the International Monetary Fund and the General Agreement on Tariffs and Trade (GATT). There have been changes since; GATT was replaced in 1995 by the World Trade Organisation (WTO) for example. Although the number of sovereign states has increased, from about 50 after 1945 to 190 now, the system of global governance has remained much the same. A number of deficiencies in this system of governance have been recognised by the WCSDG (ILO: §340–52).

- The western industrialised companies have an excessive influence in the formal bodies of global governance. The emergent industrialised countries such as China, India and Brazil can exert influence in such bodies when they act in concert, but the western countries still have the greatest influence and the developing countries have little. This is so even in organisations like the WTO where the developing countries have a formal equality with the industrialised ones.

- The developing countries often cannot afford to attend the many international conferences that influence global governance and do not have the technical expertise necessary to make their cases as strong as they might be.

- An international civil society has emerged since the end of the second world war formed of non-governmental organisations (NGOs) such as international charities and lobby organisations such as Greenpeace. These organisations have no formal role in the institutions of governance.

- The MNEs have become much more significant in the world. They have become bigger and more globally extensive. They have great influence on global governance through private lobbying and public relations activities. They are not however formally involved in the institutions and do not carry the accountability that formal membership would imply.

- Many decisions that affect global governance are made by exclusive bodies, such as the G8 and the Organisation for Economic Cooperation and Development (OECD).

- The system of global governance is disjointed and unconnected. There are many bodies operating separately – and often doing much good, such as the development of international accountancy standards. However, these initiatives are often unconnected and carry differing levels of authority. Some aspects of global governance have the status of international law and treaty obligations: there are voluntary agreements backed by public bodies such as the United Nations and voluntary agreements between any permutation of private companies, NGOs and governments.

Global governance is the set of rules set up by the international community of governments, companies and NGOs and formal bodies to govern political, economic and social affairs. Some of these are discussed in the next section of the chapter.

**Connexion point**

There is a general discussion of ethical codes in Chapter 10. In this chapter we concentrate on those standards and codes that are concerned with the consequences of international trade.

## Voluntary codes

Mention was made earlier in the chapter of the dilemma that national governments, particularly those of developing countries, sometimes face when wishing to encourage inward investment by MNEs, but also wishing to maintain some form of influence, if not control, over the activities of the MNEs in the host country. Some form of middle ground is often required between the polar extremes of legislation governing particular aspects of economic or corporate activity on the one hand, and a totally laissez-faire approach on the other. Codes of conduct, agreements and framework documents are examples of such 'middle ground'.

If a code of conduct for MNEs has the support of sovereign states, this does not mean the issues encompassed by the code have become international law. Until they do the codes are not legally binding on MNEs. Thus, the obligations cited by a code will be moral, but not legal.

An example of such a code of practice that has received much publicity concerns the selling of breastmilk substitutes in developing countries.

**Case study 12.8**

## The International Code of Marketing of Breastmilk Substitutes

The International Code of Marketing of Breastmilk Substitutes, the first international code of its kind, was adopted by the World Health Organisation (WHO) in 1981 and by the World Health Assembly (WHA) in 1984. The code was intended to control the practices of those producing and selling breastmilk substitutes and related products (e.g. feeding bottles), particularly in developing countries. These countries tend to have relatively high birth rates but weak economies. It can be argued that expenditure on breastmilk substitutes is a misuse of a nation's resources, when the natural alternative is cost free and more nutritious for the child. However, to the large corporations producing these products the markets of the developing world represent significant profit opportunities. The problem had become so acute in certain African countries that breastfeeding had become almost eradicated. The international code bans free supplies of breastmilk substitutes in hospitals, because once mothers leave hospital the breastmilk substitutes are no longer free. Yet in 1996 Nestlé, a significant producer of breastmilk substitutes, was reported to be providing free and low-cost supplies of infant formula to hospitals in Kunming Province in China. Save the Children reported:

> Nestlé has made Lactogen widely available in six hospitals in Kunming, where it has targeted health professionals with both free and discounted supplies of the formula. This helps to create an incentive for the health workers, not only to use the formula within the hospitals, but also actively to encourage its use among mothers of newborn children. Lactogen has been displayed in some of the hospitals for sale. The report prepared by our China staff and local health workers alleged that there had been an increase in the consumption of Lactogen and that breastfeeding rates had fallen.

Despite getting companies to sign up to the International Association of Infant Food Manufacturers (IFM) and in 1991 pledging to eradicate the supply of free and discounted supplies, a monitoring report entitled 'Breaking the Rules, Stretching the Rules' found that in 19 of 31 countries surveyed contraventions of the pledge were evident. In addition, a study in Pakistan in 1998 found widespread use and distribution of free supplies, with doctors being 'purchased by the companies'.

*(Source: IBFAN, n.d.)*

Even when codes of practice are established, compliance by MNEs is not necessarily automatic, and enforcement can be difficult, as evidenced by the selling of breastmilk substitutes in Malawi.

**Case study 12.9**

## Breastmilk substitutes in Malawi

In 1994 the Health Ministry of Malawi had discussed with Nestlé the need to have the instructions on their products written in Chichewa, the national language of Malawi, a requirement that was in compliance with Article 9.2 of ▶

the International Code of Marketing of Breastmilk Substitutes. Despite these discussions, Nestlé did not respond positively and the instructions remained in English. The level of literacy is not high in Malawi and, of those women who could read at the time, it was estimated that only a little over one-half could read English.

Under Article 9.1 of the Code, labels on breastmilk substitutes should not discourage breastfeeding. However, on its Bona infant formula, Nestlé continued to assert in a section headed 'Important Notice', 'Infant formula can be used from birth onwards when breastfeeding is not possible, or as a supplement to breastfeeding'. This statement was retained on the packaging despite there being general recognition that supplementing breastfeeding with breastmilk substitutes brings forward the time when a mother's natural milk dries up, thereby bringing forward the time when breastmilk substitutes will be required as the sole source of infant nutrition.

## Discussion activity 12.9

Should the response to the difficulties in implementing voluntry codes illustrated in Case studies 12.8 and 12.9 be:

- Work harder at convincing companies to adhere to the codes

or

- pass legislation in the companies' base countries that make it illegal not to adhere to the codes?

Humanitarian aid provides another opportunity for breastmilk substitute products to be introduced into vulnerable, but lucrative, markets. The International Baby Food Action Network (IBFAN) claims that:

> The baby food industry has used emergencies generally to promote its products and used 'humanitarian aid' as a way of entering into the emerging markets of Europe and the former Soviet Union.

(IBFAN, n.d.)

These cases illustrate some of the problems inherent within a 'pledge', 'code' or 'framework agreement' that is not supported by legal or meaningful sanctions.

Another area of contention relates to the use of child labour. Corporate policy statements of MNEs on the use of child labour within its supplier networks tend to reflect one of four options:

1. Stipulate a minimum age for employment by their suppliers.

2. Refer to national laws of the host country regarding minimum age of working.

3. Refer to international standards, or

4. A combination of some or all of the above.

However, some company policy statements that prohibit the use of child labour in the production of their products do not define what they mean by child labour, thus leaving discretion and judgement to local suppliers. This takes us to the issue of the rigour with which codes of practice are implemented and monitored, particularly those relating to overseas suppliers.

## Putting MNE codes of practice into effect

Codes of conduct for MNEs can take various forms and the ILO cites three factors that tend to determine the credibility with which codes for MNEs are regarded.

1. The specific governments that have adopted and support the codes, and the particular MNEs that have 'signed up' to the codes.

2. Whether a code actually addresses the critical issues of the business activity being considered.

3. The effectiveness of the monitoring mechanisms employed and the sanctions available.

The International Chamber of Commerce (ICC) is active in pursuing a self-regulatory framework for business operations on the world stage. It sets standards that recognise the tensions inherent within any competitive market setting. The following statement is drawn from one of its publications.

> The globalisation of the world's economies, and the intense competition which ensues therefrom, require the international business community to adopt standard rules. The adoption of these self-disciplinary rules is the best way that business leaders have of demonstrating that they are motivated by a sense of social responsibility, particularly in light of the increased liberalization of markets.
>
> (International Chamber of Commerce, 1997)

A number of initiatives and codes have been developed to address specific global business issues. Examples include the following:

- The 1990s saw the scope of some agreements expand to take in broader social issues. An example is the Japan Federation of Economic Organisations. Established in 1996, it covered a number of issues including philanthropic activities, resistance against organisations that undermine social cohesion, policies to enrich the lives of employees, safe and comfortable work environments, a respect for individual dignity and 'specialness' and corporate transparency.

- In 1996 the British Toy and Hobby Association developed a code of practice that forbids the use of forced, indentured or under-age labour in the production of toys. The agreement also speaks to the working and living conditions of employees. An amended form of this code was adopted by the International Council of Toy Industries later in 1996.

- In February 1997, the ILO, the Sialkot Chamber of Commerce (SCCI) in Pakistan and UNICEF formed an agreement to eliminate child labour in the production of footballs by 1999. This specific initiative was the result of worldwide publicity of the use of child labour in the production of footballs, although no other products or industries were specifically targeted. It appears that this initiative has been largely, if not completely, successful. It does appear that high-profile media coverage is conducive to, and possibly necessary for, change to be levered and achieved.

- In the USA similar codes have been developed in relation to other industries, e.g. the Apparel Partnership on Sweatshops and Child Labour which was adopted in 1997.

- The Organisation for Economic Cooperation and Development (OECD) has also produced guidelines for MNEs covering labour relations.

- A variety of organisations have sponsored the Sweatshop and Clean Clothes Codes, which cover labour relations, health and safety issues, freedom of association, wages and benefits and hours of work.

- The Declaration of Principles concerning Multinational Enterprises, developed in 1997 and involving the ILO, is a code that addresses issues such as freedom of association, terms and conditions of work.

At first sight the existence of such codes presents a preferable state of affairs to that of no codes at all. However, a closer inspection of such codes poses some uncomfortable challenges to this assumption. For example, within the Sweatshop Code, the wording relating to 'wages and benefits' specifies:

> Employers shall pay employees, as a floor, at least the minimum wage required by local law or the prevailing industry wage, whichever is the higher, and shall provide legally mandated benefits.

This leaves much responsibility with governments to institute laws that enhance working and employment conditions. The lobbying of governments by business organisations, including MNEs, will clearly be listened to in government circles. Those employed in sweatshop conditions are not often well represented at the political negotiating table. In the meantime global organisations and western customers of the manufacturing output of developing countries remain free to exploit the cost differentials of sourcing their production capacity overseas. Indeed, the very reason why many western apparel companies have closed their western production capability and transferred production to locations in the Philippines, India, Honduras, etc. has been to exploit the cost advantages of the developing world, cost advantages that have often involved sweatshop conditions and child labour.

With regard to 'hours of work' the Sweatshop Code states:

> Except in extraordinary business circumstances, employees shall (i) not be required to work more than the lesser of (a) 48 hours per week and 12 hours overtime or (b) the limits on regular and overtime hours allowed by the law of the country of manufacture or, where the laws of such country do not limit

the hours of work, the regular work week in such country plus 12 hours over-time and (ii) be entitled to at least one day off in every seven day period.

Thus, unless local laws state otherwise, an employer can require their workers to work 60 hours per week, and stay within the obligations of the code. Employees might be entitled to one day off per week, but whether they will get this is another matter. In addition, when demand is high, the working week can extend beyond the 60 hours. This should be constrained to 'extraordinary business circumstances', but the latter is not defined and less than scrupulous employers will use this as a loophole to work employees for all seven days of the week and exceed the 60 hours per employee. The code could be far more stringent in its demands on behalf of the employees (the majority of whom tend to be women), but of course, the closer wage rates and working conditions are pushed towards western levels, the less the original decision to source production to the developing country makes economic sense.

There are examples of organisations appearing to make serious efforts to put their codes into practice. The ILO reported that Levi-Strauss, for example, conducts annual global training programmes to ensure its audit managers are familiar with their internal code, and has conducted five-day training programmes in the Dominican Republic for 'terms of engagement' auditors. Liz Claiborne (an American retail organisation of women's fashion clothes) has also reported that it had intensified its efforts to identify and remove labour abuses.

An example is provided by McDonald and Nijhof (1999: 140) of an organisation that employed 6,000 people, and whose CEO sought to roll out an ethics awareness-raising programme across the whole organisation. This involved writing the associated code of conduct in both English and Chinese and then training a series of trainers to deliver the associated workshops. The latter included a video message from the CEO, in which he stated that he would rather the organisation lose a contract than undermine the code. The programme was delivered throughout the company. For the CEO, 'the code needs to come off the pages and into people's lives'. As McDonald and Nijhof report, elements that were not included in the initiative were an annual ethics audit and an ethics hotline. Whether these have since been instituted is unknown.

The rigour with which MNEs police their own codes of conduct (particularly those they apply to their suppliers) does appear to vary. Of the organisation Liz Claiborne, the plant manager of Primo Industries, an apparel contractor based in El Salvador, stated, 'they are the toughest on child labour'. The plant manager told US Department of Labor officials that inspectors from Liz Claiborne visited the plant 'approximately twice a month to check on quality control and see whether rules and regulations are being implemented'. Such vigilance by the Claiborne organisation must involve costs that some other organisations (maybe its competitors) do not appear to incur, at least not to the same extent. A manager with the Indian company, Zoro Garments, 75 per cent of whose output goes to US markets, is quoted as saying that:

> Representatives of US customers have visited Zoro's factory occasionally for quality control inspections, [but] most of the visits were walk-throughs with some general questions raised about the use of child labour, but no check-list of requirements was administered.
>
> (ILO, n.d.)

A complicating issue occurs where the MNE sources products from a variety of overseas suppliers, with some of these suppliers being in monopsony relationships with the MNE, while for other suppliers the MNE in question might be only one among a range of customers. Thus, can an MNE be held responsible for the work conditions and labour practices of a supplier from which it sources relatively few orders? Whatever one's position on this question, it has to be taken for granted that, for production costs of suppliers in developing countries to be so much lower than those of their western competitors, wage rates and employment conditions cannot be equal. Thus, for MNEs, or any other form of organisation, to feign ignorance of the working conditions of some of its suppliers ignores the logic of the situations. Rather than assuming that all is satisfactory, they must know that the cost differentials between suppliers in developing and developed countries would suggest a default position that all is not satisfactory, and that evidence is required to disprove this assumption.

Establishing a corporate code of conduct is one thing; making it a part of everyday practice is another. Of the 42 apparel companies surveyed by the US Department of Labor in 1996, to establish how many of them had endeavoured to ensure that workers in their overseas suppliers were aware of their code of conduct, 'very few respondents indicated that they had tried'. Only three companies insisted on their codes being posted on their suppliers' notice boards. In a further study reported by the ILO, of 70 supplier companies, 23 (33 per cent) indicated that they were not aware of corporate codes of conduct issued by their US customers.

The US Department of Labor also undertakes company visits and the ILO website gives information on ILO visits to a variety of countries including El Salvador, the Dominican Republic, Honduras, India and the Philippines. In a study of 70 companies, managers at only 47 of these stated an awareness of such codes, and of these only 34 could produce a copy of a code. Thus, less than half of the sites visited could produce a principal customer's code, yet the US retailers refer to their supplier codes as evidence of their (the apparel retailers') commitment to ethical practices at their overseas suppliers.

Awareness of such codes was highest in El Salvador, where managers at six out of the nine companies visited were aware of such codes, whereas in India managers at only two of the seven producer sites visited were aware. Even where awareness was acknowledged, awareness was not the same as accepting the codes and adhering to them. As the ILO observed,

> Although a significant number of suppliers knew about the US corporate codes of conduct, meetings with workers and their representatives in the countries visited suggested that relatively few workers were aware of the existence of codes of conduct, and even fewer understood their implications.

## The UN Global Compact

This international standard is worth separate consideration because it was initiated by the UN Secretary-General at the Davos World Economic Forum in 1999. This is an informal conference at which politicians, MNE chief executives, NGO representatives and high-profile lobbyists meet. The Compact is supported by the International Labour Office (ILO), The Office of the UN Commissioner for

Human Rights (OHCHR), the United Nations Environment Programme (UNEP), the UN Industrial Development Organisation (UNIDO) and others. It therefore carries the support of many of the world's institutions of global governance. It is however also a voluntary code.

---

**Connexion point**

The principles that companies have to sign up to when they join the Global Compact are discussed in Chapter 8, pp. 308–10. The chapter also provides an evaluation of the Compact's impact.

---

A major criticism of the Global Compact from a globalisation perspective is that it covers only a narrow range of issues. For example, several of the matters raised in this chapter, such as the justice and fairness of the governance of international trade, and the effect the operations of MNEs might have on exacerbating political and military tensions in regions in which they operate are not covered.

The Global Compact, however, is developing in a different form from that of other ethical and CSR standards which take an assurance based ('ticking the box') approach. The Compact is more like a learning network in which understanding and learning about the problems of behaving in a socially and environmentally responsible way are discussed and explored. Those who have signed up to the Compact are encouraged to take part in seminars, act as mentors, join networks and enter into partnerships to carry out projects. Many of the world's well-known companies have signed up including BT, BMW, Standard Chartered Bank, Nike, Novartis, Shell, Warburg and Unilever.

In 2001 the theme of the Global Compact policy dialogue was 'the role of the public sector in zones of conflict'. So, despite the criticism often made of it, it does address the issues of globalisation and conflict. The participants were from businesses, NGOs, trade unions and the UN. Tools and techniques for ameliorating conflict, such as risk assessment and multi-stakeholder processes of community development (*see* the Shell case study on p. 475). It was also agreed that partnership projects would be set up to try to make practical changes in selected regions (McIntosh *et al.*, 2003: 182). The Global Compact also undertakes outreach activities and tries to involve small and medium-sized companies as well as city governments.

---

## Reflections

Individual MNEs have, in many cases, become so large that as individual corporations they can have a major impact on the prosperity and the peacefulness of the communities, countries and regions they work within. This gives them a power equivalent to that of governments. If they have the influence of governments then they ought also to have the accountability that goes with it.

Historically large corporations have become governments. The British East India Company, for example, formed in the seventeenth century as a company of merchants, became by degrees the government of India in the nineteenth century. The task for the development of global governance is to find the institutions and mechanisms by which large corporations can be brought to account for their global impacts.

Corporations may have an ethical responsibility to behave well in their international dealings but it is the individual managers in multinationals, transnationals and international NGOs who exercise that responsibility. In Case study 12.6 it was an individual, Leon Sullivan, who drove forward the response to apartheid.

## Summary

In this chapter the following key points have been made:

- Globalisation concerns the economic, political and cultural impact of the expansion of international trade and international interconnectivity.

- The ethical issues surrounding globalisation include whether MNEs do or do not offend against human rights and/or benefit themselves and certain others but only at the cost of making others worse off in their pursuit of global business.

- The standard argument in favour of the liberalisation of world trade is that it increases the total sum of wealth in the world, which through a 'trickle down' effect benefits all. The evidence suggests that the benefits of increasing world trade are patchily distributed. Some countries, notably China, Brazil and India, have benefited but others have experienced a worsening of their relative economic performance. Within developing and transitional countries some sections of the population have paid a price for trade liberalisation while other groups have benefited.

- MNEs are tempted to choose the location of their operations to gain the benefits of institutions and legal jurisdictions that will give them better financial returns.

- The foreign and domestic policies of the governments of countries can be distorted by the needs and demands of MNEs that are based in those countries in ways that diminish the public good.

- The operations of MNEs in developing countries can make internal political and ethnic tensions worse. When their operations stretch over several mutually antagonistic countries in a region the presence of the MNEs can either make the tensions worse or, at the least, act as a focus of discontent for the disaffected.

- MNEs may find themselves operating in countries whose governments are thought to be tyrannical and dismissive of human rights. This raises the ethical question of when the situation is so bad that the company should withdraw from that country.

- Globalisation is in part a diminution of cultural diversity across the world and the growth of a worldwide consumerist and brand led culture. The ethical issue is whether this change is one that people have entered into freely and in full knowledge or whether they have been manipulated into acceptance because it suits the purposes of the MNEs.

- Cultural change is an unpredictable process, however, and it is likely that different cultures will absorb western consumerist values and adapt and change them in unexpected ways.

- There has been much development of voluntary codes that are intended to provide a framework for the global governance of MNEs and world trade. Although this is a good development the implementation of such standards and codes is a difficult one when the demands conflict with commercial imperatives.

- The Global Compact is a development that promises a new type of approach to global governance, one based on networks of learning rather than the assurance of adherence to bureaucratic standards.

## Quick revision test

1. What is a trans-national company?
   (a) A company that trades globally
   (b) A company that trades internationally but makes little concession to the particularities of national markets.
   (c) A network-based international organisation that has little or no identification with a particular country.

2. What are the Sullivan principles?
   (a) Companies should not continue to operate in countries whose systems of government and governance are below minimum, acceptable ethical standards.
   (b) Companies should work to meet the human rights of their employees even when they are operating in countries where those rights are ignored or undermined.
   (c) Companies should strive to change the system of government and governance in countries where those systems are below minimum, acceptable ethical standards.

3. What does dualism mean when applied to developing countries?
   (a) Where an advanced and international economic system coexists, but does not connect, with an informal local economy.
   (b) An economic system that meets the objective of both national economies and international companies.
   (c) A business strategy that adapts international brands to local market conditions.

4. The host government agreement (HGA) that governs the Baku-Tblisi-Ceyhan oil pipeline…
   (a) requires the governments to compensate the oil companies if there is any disruption to the pipeline project
   (b) requires the oil companies to invest in the social and cultural development of the host countries
   (c) gives local communities a veto over the specific location of the pipeline.

## Typical assignments and briefs

1. In what circumstances should an MNE withdraw from a country for ethical reasons? Illustrate your argument with examples.

2. To what extent does the UN Global Compact represent an innovative and effective approach to the governance of MNEs?

3. What responsibilities, if any, do MNEs have in helping countries develop fair and effective systems of governance?

4. Does the expansion of international trade benefit everybody? Does it matter if it does not?

## Group activity 12

For the purposes of this activity, you should assume that most desktop computers are made in a variety of Asian countries. Three parties are in discussions over the development of a code of practice that might cover the activities of the local suppliers to the multinational corporate purchasers of the computers.

The code of practice would cover the operations of the MNEs in **one** of the countries concerned. The three parties are a spokesperson for the Society of Computer Manufacturers and Assemblers, a representative from the host country's Ministry for trade and industry and a representative from the pressure group Workers in the Manufacture and Assembly of Computers (WMAC), who is also a local trade union representative.

Divide the seminar group into three sub-groups (one for each of the parties involved). Each sub-group should decide its position, in terms of what is:

(a) morally justifiable, and

(b) likely to be achieved,

on the following issues:

- standard hours of work;

- acceptable overtime working;

- pension rights;

- accident and injury protection and benefits for dependants;

- number of continuous working days in normal and abnormal circumstances;

- health and safety standards (equivalent to western standards?);

- employment rights (e.g. period of notice required by both employer and employee);

- minimum employment age;

- social infrastructure support (e.g. support for local schools, sports clubs, youth clubs, medical facilities);

- grievance procedures.

Then, as a complete group, debate the contrasts between the three perspectives.

## Recommended further reading

Jan Aart Scholte's book *Globalisation: a critical introduction* (2000) provides a good introduction to the topic, as does Held and McGrew (2000) *The Global Transformations Reader*. Another very popular book is *Globalisation and its Discontents* by Joseph Stiglitz (2004). *Living Corporate Citizenship* by McIntosh, Thomas, Leipziger and Coleman (2003) is a good read and describes most of the main standards for international business but it also has a particularly extensive discussion of the Global Compact and lots of case studies of projects undertaken by companies. Unusually, two semi-official publications make good introductions to the topic of globalisation. The first is the World Commission on the Social Dimension of Globalisation (2004) *A Fair Globalisation: Creating Opportunities for All* and the second is the Report of the Commission for Africa (2005) that was instigated by the British government.

## Useful websites

| Topic | Website provider | URL |
|---|---|---|
| A very useful site providing links to materials on businesses and human rights. The materials are classified by topicality, regions, sectors, individual companies, laws and principles | Business & Human Rights Resource Centre | http://www.business-humanrights.org/Home |
| International poverty measures | Povcal website | http://iresearch.worldbank.org/povcalnet |
| The Corner House anti-corruption organisation | The Corner House | http://www.thecornerhouse.org.uk/ |
| Global Compact | The Global Compact Secretariat | www.unglobalcompact.org |
| Businesses and human rights | Amnesty International Business group | www.amnesty.org.uk/business |
| Private sector initiatives on labour and social conditions | The Business and Social Initatives Database (BASI) | www.oracle02.ilo.org/dyn/basi/vpisearch.first |
| The Sullivan principles website | The Sullivan principles organisation | www.globalsullivanprinciples.org |
| World Trade Organisation | World Trade Organisation | www.wto.org/ |
| International Forum on Globalisation web page | International Forum on Globalisation | http://www.ifg.org/ |
| A vast list of resources on globalisation | The Róbinson Rojas Archive | http://www.rrojasdatabank.org/dev3000.htm |

## CHAPTER 13

# Moral agency at work and a modest proposal for affecting ethics in business

## Introduction

The title of this final chapter – moral agency at work – has a deliberate ambiguity. It can refer to the role and importance of moral agency in organisations and work. Alternatively, it might mean how moral agency works, the processes that moral agency involves. We are concerned with both aspects in this chapter. The two levels of analysis, the individual and the corporate, that have been shuttled between throughout this book are brought together in this final chapter. Both perspectives must be addressed if organisations in business and management are to operate socially, ethically and environmentally responsibly. We want to make a case, and a series of proposals, for taking moral agency seriously at a corporate level, and also to suggest some ways in which individuals might approach choosing and taking the ethical action on difficult moral issues at work. Our modest proposal addresses both.

## Challenges to moral agency in modern organisations

Throughout the book we have endeavoured to present the full range of perspectives on each of the critical issues. This has not meant that we have given each perspective equal weight, because each perspective may not have warranted such attention, either because of the weight of evidence or arguments relating to competing perspectives or because of the complexities involved.

What must be clear from the issues and arguments we have examined is that there are a number of challenges that have to be handled in an adequate form if already significant problems are not to become overpowering and out of control, assuming they are not already. We would identify the following as matters of significant import, although not in any order of rank.

- The relationship between corporations and democratic ideals and the relationships between business, society and the state.

- The sustainability of business practices and business organisations.
  - global warming and its implications.
  - the raising to a public level, once again, of debates concerning the defensibility and wisdom of preferencing economic growth above all other considerations.

- Challenging narrow conceptions of the self, in particular:
  - the enframing of the technological mindset;
  - the myopic fixation upon the Self, a form of 'Cult of the Self', with little if any regard for Others; and
  - the defining of individuality within notions of consumerism, but little else.

- Underpinning all the above, the ability of individuals to exercise moral agency without fear of retribution or recrimination.

It has been a theme of this book that in business organisations there can be great tensions between how an ethical theory says people should behave and how their social values and a specific organisational culture can incline them to behave. All the issues we raise in this final chapter, whether set at an individualistic, organisational, national or international level, will ultimately be addressed, or not, by the actions of individuals, acting independently, or collectively in groups of varying sizes. This does not deny the significance of structures such as ideology, discourses, group values and, most critically, issues of power. We tend towards Giddens' (1984) notion of structuration, that is, while recognising the dominance of structures, we would argue that agency can effect change, particularly at moments of crisis, but also at other times. By recognising the significance of agency in change processes we thereby recognise and bring into sharp focus the issue of moral agency.

**The structure/agency debate**    **DEFINITION**

## The structure/agency debate    DEFINITION

This question is of concern to social sciences, philosophy and history as well as to business ethics which draws from all these disciplines. When people act, which has the greater influence on their actions:

- things (broadly called structures) that are external to them such as social and cultural norms, economic structure and circumstances, and historical forces and trends, or
- their own will and powers of detached analysis (broadly termed agency)?

In terms of historical study the question refines to whether only certain people – who used to be referred to as great men, a category that extends now to include great women – act as agents and others simply follow the flow of long-term historical movements. As in most such debates, and as Giddens intimates, the answer is that there is a complex interaction between agency and structures. Structuration is the idea that there is a duality to human action. It can be seen as guided by rules, resources and social relationships, but from the second perspective it can be seen that human actions can both define and change those structures.

We have also argued that, whilst there are competing positions on practically any point of issue within business ethics, the arguments supporting each position are unlikely to be equally robust, defensible or contain the same quality of ethical argument. Our stance has been to explore the different ethical positions to allow you to make informed judgements. We do not seek or offer a Holy Grail of business ethics, but we have outlined some modest proposals for business ethics that we would like you to consider. However, before doing so, we will consider the broad issues raised above.

## The corporation and democratic ideals

You will recall that a key criticism, made by Milton Friedman, against calls for corporate social responsibility beyond profit making was that to encourage and support such developments would undermine democratic ideals. As indicated in our analysis of Friedman's criticisms, we would agree that in this respect Friedman has a 'justice' argument on his side with respect to this particular criticism. Indeed, one of the central arguments of neo-liberal economics is its integrity in sustaining democratic ideals, most notably individual freedoms. Yet, paradoxically, and leaving the CSR argument to one side, the role and place of the corporation in modern society raises profound and disturbing questions regarding democratic ideals. The democratic pretensions of neo-liberal economics are, for others, its great deceit.

In Chapter 8 we referred to the observation of Charles Lindblom that

It has been a curious feature of democratic thought that it has not faced up to the private corporation in an ostensible democracy. Enormously large, rich in resources ... they can insist that government meet their demands, even if these demands run counter to ... citizens ... Moreover they do not disqualify themselves from playing the role of citizen ... they exercise unusual veto powers .... The large private corporation fits oddly into democratic theory and vision. Indeed it does not fit.

(Lindblom, 1977: 356)

Bakan (2004), in an acclaimed book that was the basis of the film *The Corporation* (Achbar, Abbott and Bakan, 2003), went further, likening the corporation to a monster that has become uncontrollable.

Governments create corporations, much like Dr. Frankenstein created his monster, yet once they exist, corporations, like the monster, threaten to overpower their creator.

(Bakan, 2004: 149)

Bakan argued that if the corporation was to take human form it would be a psychopath – cheating, lying, even killing to serve the interests of its shareholders. A recent example of the unattractiveness of some corporations is the British MG Rover volume car producer (*Financial Times*, 2005). The company had been owned by BMW who had decided that Rover's Longbridge plant did not have the capacity to produce cars at the volume necessary to achieve the economies of scale enjoyed by other volume car makers. BMW sold the company to Phoenix for £10. In addition to gaining the company, Phoenix also received a large amount of cash and assets from the former owner. The four partners of Phoenix did not use this money to introduce new models and so keep the marque competitive, nor did they fill the hole in the employees' pension fund. Instead, the partners ensured they were personally well remunerated, awarded themselves a £10m loan note, set up a £12m pension fund for themselves, gained personal control of a lucrative financing business, and asset stripped the company by selling off its land and intellectual property rights. As the *Financial Times* pointed out,

> **FT** This is capitalism at its ugliest. There is no suggestion that the Phoenix team broke any laws. They did what any ruthless entrepreneur would have done in their situation: incentivise, strip assets, take cash out early.
> But they betrayed the trust placed in them by their workers, the government and the public. Yes they kept the business afloat for five years. But they did so by burning through someone else's money and without delivering the new generation of models that might have given Rover a slim chance.

(*Financial Times*, 2005: 10 Copyright © Financial Times Limited. Reproduced with permission.)

This level of hyperbole can attract reactions of disdain and dismissal, although Bakan cites evidence of each to support his description. Using less emotive language Basu, Mintzberg and Simons (2002) wrote an open letter to CEOs arguing that capitalism is facing a crisis and that simply repeating the mantra 'shareholder interests and only shareholder interests' (which for too many might more accurately be 'executives' interests and only executives' interests') is not acceptable. For Basu *et al.* (2002), change has to take place and it has to be fundamental.

For J.K. Galbraith (2004), one of the leading economists of the twentieth century, neo-liberal economics has been fraudulent in the naïveté of its assumptions and the camouflage it has provided for individual greed. For Galbraith, the initial deceit was evident as early as the late nineteenth century/early twentieth century, when the search took place for an alternative phrase for capitalism, following the problems of corporate collapses and fraud during this period.

> Because of the problems with 'capitalism' the search was underway for a new term. 'Free Enterprise' had a trial in the United States. It did not take. In Europe there was 'Social Democracy' – capitalism and socialism in a companionate mix. In the United States, however, socialism was (as it remains) unacceptable. In the next years reference was to the New Deal; this however, was too clearly identified with Franklin D. Roosevelt and his cohorts. So in reasonably learned expression there came 'the market system'. There was no adverse history here, in fact no history at all. It would have been hard, indeed, to find a more meaningless designation – this a reason for the choice.
>
> (Galbraith, 2004: 18)

Galbraith continued,

> Reference to the market system as a benign alternative to capitalism is a bland, meaningless disguise of the deeper corporate reality – of producer power extending to influence over, even control of, consumer demand. This, however, cannot be said. It is without emphasis in contemporary economic discussion and instruction ... But no one can doubt that the renaming of the system, the escape from the unacceptable term 'capitalism', has been somewhat successful ... Reference to a market system is, to repeat, without meaning, erroneous, bland, design. ... No individual firm, no individual capitalist, is now thought to have power; that the market is subject to skilled and comprehensive management is unmentioned even in most economic teaching. Here is fraud. Sensitive friends and beneficiaries of the system do not wish to assign definitive authority to the corporation. Better the benign reference to the market.
>
> (Galbraith, 2004: 19–20)

A further subtle change in language is commented upon by Galbraith, indicative of the way public discourses are shifted/manipulated.

> The phrase 'monopoly capitalism' once in common use, has been dropped from the academic and political lexicon. The consumer is no longer subordinate to monopoly power; he or she is now sovereign or is so described. ... As the ballot gives authority to the citizen, so in economic life the demand curve accords authority to the consumer. In both instances there is a significant measure of fraud. With both ballot and buyer, there is a formidable, well-financed management of the public response. And so especially in the age of the advertising and modern sales promotion. Here an accepted fraud, not least in academic instruction.
>
> (Galbraith, 2004: 24)

We stress that the demise of the corporation is neither predicted, nor required, but if democratic ideals and aspirations are important and to be taken seriously, then, like Bakan, Basu *et al.* and Galbraith, we would argue that changes have to be debated, and then acted upon, although the prospects for such open, balanced and informed debates are not propitious. For example, in 2003, when a female grocers' cooperative in the State of Oregon, USA, sought to gain sufficient names on a petition at a federal election that would have allowed a vote to have been taken on food products in the state having to have upgraded labelling to bring them in line with the labelling requirements that exist in the EU (revealing, for example, the proportion of genetically modified elements in the products), the multi-national GM food corporations mounted a $5M advertising campaign against the proposal, claiming the labelling would cost jobs. The proposal never received the required number of signatures and the 'debate' was still-born.

Globalisation is invariably portrayed as an inevitable consequence of technological developments, an unavoidable reality. What are more contestable are the ramifications of the developments. The problem of externalities has long been an issue concerning business–society relationships. Deregulation can be seen as a way of transferring ever more corporate costs to society. Externalities are those costs caused as a result of corporate activity, but which are not borne by the corporation. They are paid for by individuals and broader societal groups. Examples of externalised costs are the effect of air and noise pollution caused by corporations involved in transport services. Unhealthy and unsafe corporate practices are usually paid for by employee or consumer injuries, unless adequate compensation can be obtained, although whether the loss of a loved one can be adequately compensated is a moot point. Despoliation of water courses, forests and environmental habitats is controlled to a certain extent in developing economies, although not always adequately, as is illustrated below with regard to waste disposal. The situation in many developing economies is far less regulated, so the costs of the despoliation are carried by the indigenous people and their descendents. As a consequence of all the above examples and the many, many more that exist, corporate profits are overstated and shareholders receive inflated returns because 'Others' are bearing some of the corporate costs.

Companies are very rarely forced to close by governments, even when they have been found criminally negligent in their practices. Enron, for example, has not been formally required to cease trading. However, an interesting case is cited by Bakan (2004), involving charter revocation laws in America, long forgotten statutes, the re-discovery of which has raised some intriguing issues and cases. The important point is that corporations are increasingly using legal protection designed to protect individual citizens, such as the American Constitution, but in many other respects the corporation is seen as above the law, or in some form 'different'. For example, unlike in the United States, it is extremely difficult to bring a case of corporate manslaughter in the UK. The UK government has threatened to 'bring in' corporate manslaughter legislation since 1997, but has so far procrastinated and obfuscated its way past its critics for its lack of action. Corporate influence remains strong in political corridors and politicians remain highly receptive to corporate needs.

| | |
|---|---|
| **Case study 13.1** | **A law professor, as citizen, takes action** |

Robert Benson, a Professor of Law at Loyola University, petitioned the Californian state attorney to dissolve the Union Oil Company of California (Unocal) by revoking its charter. Bakan writes,

> Benson listed Unocal's transgressions in his 127 page application to the attorney general: the company had collaborated on a pipeline project with the outlaw Burmese military regime, which had allegedly used slave labor on the pipeline and forced whole villages to relocate: it had allegedly collaborated on projects with Afghanistan's former Taliban regime, which was notorious for its violations of human rights long before the United States waged war against it; it had, the application claimed, persistently violated California's environmental and employee safety regulations.
>
> (Bakan, 2004: 157)

Unsurprisingly, not least to Benson, the application was rejected by the attorney general, after only three working days, but Benson's objective was to gain public recognition that corporations are not above the law and are even subject to the corporate 'death penalty'.

> We're letting the people of California in on a well-kept secret, ... the people mistakenly assume that we have to try to control these giant corporate repeat offenders one toxic spill at a time, one layoff at a time, one human rights violation at a time. But the law has always allowed the attorney general to go to court to simply dissolve a corporation for wrongdoing and sell its assets to others who will operate in the public interest.
>
> (Mokhiber, 1998)

Benson's action is an example of an individual taking action. In response to any thoughts that he might be naïve Benson explained

> We are not politically naïve. We don't think that this is going to get so far along the road that Unocal will actually be broken up anytime soon, although it should be. The petition was filed to change the legal and political culture. Our fundamental goal here is to change the public discourse and the media perception of the power of corporations versus people, to float the idea that people are sovereign over corporations.
>
> (Mokhiber, 1998)

| | |
|---|---|
| **Case study 13.2** | **A judge, as citizen, takes action** |

An Alabama Circuit Judge, William Wynn, took out an action to revoke the charters of America's five major cigarette companies. Wynn filed a complaint in a state court in Birmingham, Alabama, demanding that the corporate charters of Philip Morris, Brown & Williamson, R.J. Reynolds, The Liggett Group and Lorillard Corporation be revoked. Wynn was angry that Alabama had refused to join 22 states in suing the tobacco companies, and had spent the ▶

better part of a year researching the law, to find a way to force the state to act. He stumbled across a nineteenth-century statute giving any citizen the right to petition the state for a 'writ of quo warranto' – a Latin phrase meaning 'by what authority?' The writ of quo warranto allows a citizen to file a lawsuit against any corporation, posing the question: By what authority are you holding a corporate franchise to do business, when you are in fact breaking the law?

Judge Wynn uncovered a number of laws he believed the cigarette companies had violated, including contributing to the dependency of a minor, unlawful distribution of material harmful to a minor, endangering the welfare of a child, assault in the third degree, recklessly endangering another, deceptive business practice, and causing the delinquency of a child. Though the companies have not been charged with these crimes in Alabama, Judge Wynn says that he is 'calling for the criminal enforcement of these misdemeanors.' And upon a finding that the companies have broken the law, he is then calling for charter revocation.

Perhaps the most surprising response to the lawsuit was that of the state's most influential paper, the *Birmingham News*. The paper not only ran a news story about the lawsuit, but published a very long opinion piece by Richard Grossman (a long-time advocate of using charter revocation laws), titled 'Slaying Big Tobacco.' Mainstream readers were thus exposed to the characteristically radical Grossman style, arguing that Judge Wynn is on 'solid legal ground when he demands the state of Alabama provide its sovereign people with a proper remedy to end the corporate usurpation of the people's authority'.

(Mokhiber, 1998)

The above evidence and examples are used to illustrate that, far from being a mainstay of democratic ideals, the large corporation at least represents a profound and formidable obstacle to democratic aspirations.

## Sustainability

We will now move to a consideration of the issues loosely coupled under the broad banner of sustainability, although they are also separable issues.

The notion of sustainability has a number of sub-headings. First there is the issue of *environmental sustainability*. We referred in Chapter 9 to the ideas and arguments of Martin Heidegger in exploring the notion of 'Being', which is essentially the value, the importance, the meaning which something or someone has in the eyes of others. Being is very much a social construct, a sense of intrinsic value, and the latter is itself socially constructed. For example, in the early twentieth century a coin, known as a florin (with a face value of 10p in current exchange), contained an element of silver. At particular times, when the price of silver was high on the metals' commodity market, the intrinsic value of a florin could exceed its face value. The intrinsic value existed because we as a society valued silver as a valuable metal. If we had not, then the intrinsic value of the coin would have been zero. Thus, both the intrinsic and face values of the coin were what they were because we, as a society, decided to act as if they had those values.

In a similar fashion the face value/economic value of an area of, say, scrubland could be very low and a property developer may purchase it for a smallish sum of money in order to build houses, office blocks or some other amenity. However, the scrubland may also be the habitat of a rare and possibly endangered species of plant, insect or mammal. What is the value of the endangered species? We cannot say specifically, because each case would have to be considered on its merits and in some cases the arguments may show that the ecological or environmental considerations should not hold sway. Our intention is not to prejudge events but to raise a number of standards that are consistent across each of the sustainability areas.

The first standard is the issue of *property rights*. This social construct has been a significant engine in economic development over the past two hundred years, allied to the creation of the limited liability company in the United Kingdom in 1856. Are we arguing that the notion of property rights should be abolished and that all possessions should be 'held in common'? The answer is no, but neither are we arguing that the present situation is acceptable.

The laws that societies construct and, particularly for our purposes, the demands, constraints and remit of business corporations can vary and have varied through time. Equally the autonomy of the individual has varied through time, as have the dominant values. However, as we said in Chapter 4, while different organisations, different groups, different cultures and different countries may have different values, ethical theories are disdainful of societies. It does not matter to the validity of a theory if it is not accepted by the generality of people. The truth of an ethical theory cannot be judged by an opinion poll.

The issue of waste generation and disposal may not sound like an obvious candidate for inclusion in a book on business ethics, but as one studies the subject it reveals itself as a series of major ethical issues. The vast majority of the waste generated is the result of individual consumption that is associated with lifestyle choices. For example, a high proportion of purchases are made, not because existing possessions are exhausted or inoperable, but because of the desire to own the latest model or gadget (for example, motor cars or mobile phones). Lives are so busy and/or allocation of time is so skewed that we find it more convenient to purchase ready-cooked meals with all the associated processing costs than to prepare meals ourselves. Vegetables and fruits, capable of being grown locally, are sourced from across the world, with the associated impact upon global warming of long-haul transportation. Yet to buy locally may in turn deny farmers in developing economies the markets they so desperately need. The ethical choices are not always harmonious and the ethical implications of our actions not always palatable.

In 2004 German citizens recycled 40 per cent of their waste. The equivalent percentage in the UK in 2004 was 17 per cent, explaining why the UK is still described as 'the dirty man of Europe'. However, by elevating the analysis to the 'UK' somehow absolves individuals from their culpability. That is why we referred to German citizens recycling 40 per cent of their waste, rather than Germany recycling 40 per cent of its waste. A nation state does not act as such, but its individual citizens do.

The disposal of plastic wrappings and containers remains a major problem. Landfill sites are becoming exhausted and new ones difficult to obtain because of planning permission problems. If incineration is used to dispose of waste, harmful dioxins are released into the air, particularly as a result of incinerating chemically based products like plastic bottles and other plastic packaging. Dioxins are hazardous, carcinogenic agents – they cause cancers.

To try to control the disposal of hazardous waste, the UK government has employed a twin strategy, the first element being a concentration of the disposal of toxic waste into a few highly controlled sites, the second element being the price mechanism. The cost of disposing of all waste, but particularly toxic waste, has risen sharply since 2000, presumably to try to temper the use of chemical-based products, but the result has been an example of an unintended consequence, although not a particularly difficult one to predict. With legal disposal becoming specialised and localised (there is no official toxic waste disposal site for London) and increasingly expensive, illegal disposal has proliferated and on a grand scale. The companies operating the illegal disposal of waste, both toxic and non-toxic, are referred to as the eco-mafia. They operate fleets of lorries and look to all intents and purposes like bona fide operators. They obtain contracts by bidding at below market rates, but having collected the waste they then dump it on open land, in rivers, or anywhere that is accessible, pocketing the disposal fee they would otherwise have had to pay to the official disposal site. They are ruthless and shameless.

Toxic waste is disposed of into river courses and streams and thus enters the water table and ultimately our drinking water. Solid waste (including the ash from incinerators which contains dioxins) is dumped brazenly on open land, but with no record of the waste's contents or from where the waste was acquired. Waste management and disposal is the most unregulated of industries. On a television programme – *If... the toxic timebomb goes off* (BBC, 2005), the value of illegal waste disposal, in the UK alone, between 1994 and 2004 was estimated at £90 billion! The stakes are high, the profits huge, the ramifications horrific. In Italy it was estimated that 30 per cent of all waste disposal is done illegally.

In Ireland supermarkets are required to charge customers 10p per plastic bag used. As a result the usage of plastic bags has dropped remarkably and the acquisitions of 'bags-for-life' have increased dramatically. In this case the price mechanism has affected behaviour in the desired way because there was no alternative, the costs and profits are small, and the effects upon lifestyles minuscule. However, in the case of the disposal of industrial waste the eco-mafia has entrenched itself in a profound way.

Part of the 'solution' has to involve a re-think of disposal methods, locations and price, but more significantly attention has to be concentrated upon the generation of waste and this includes and involves the individual citizen. They, we, have to accept our part in shaping solutions to these profound problems. Just as we can express our 'voice' via our purchasing choices, as we discussed with regard to a two-way social contract between corporations and consumers in Chapter 9, these 'conversations' need to include the packaging choices that companies make. Thus, the second standard that we raise is the role of the individual, as employer, as employee, as consumer, as citizen.

## Business sustainability

Any discussion of business sustainability would include the issues raised above, but it would also bring into focus two other sets of relationships. The first is the set of relationships between the corporation and its external contexts. These would include the notion of stakeholding interests, but, as discussed above, the way a corporation conducts its affairs with regard to political processes and politicians, and its treatment of environmental resources may have an increasing bearing upon the way it is perceived and respected by important groups. The second is the set of relationships between the corporation and its internal contexts. These would include the employees of the corporation and, where they were applicable, supervisory boards.

As discussed in Chapters 8–12, (global) corporations are increasingly subject to scrutiny via international codes of conduct, such as the UN Global Compact, the OECD's Guidelines for Multinational Enterprises, the Ethical Trading Initiative as well as various industry-specific or issue-specific codes, such as the Sweatshop Code and the Breastmilk Substitutes Code. However, while the number of codes increases, concerns regarding the efficacy of such codes also grows.

Christian Aid (2004) provided three case studies of alleged double standards, hypocrisy and/or duplicity by, respectively, Shell and the continuing problems of the people of the Niger delta from Shell's oil exploration there; BAT and the medical ailments of the tobacco pickers of Kenya and Brazil; and Coca Cola and its alleged (mis)use of a village water source in Plachimada, India.

### Connexion point

The case of Shell and its oil operations in the Niger delta is described in more detail in Chapter 12, pp. 475–6.

Each of these companies claims high ethical standards. They each produce a social accountability report and BAT and Shell have been recognised as in the van of social reporting. However, the form of voluntary reporting and accountability argued for in the Global Compact has been criticised by Christian Aid as, at best, of little significance, but, at worst, providing a façade of social responsibility for its members, while behind the façade little appears to change. The comments of David Millar, of the Stirling Media Research Institute, provide evidence for the lack of faith in CSR articulated by Christian Aid.

> One of the key functions of CSR is to enable further deregulation by pointing to the involvement of business in ethical and sustainable activities and to indicate that 'multi-stakeholder dialogue' with civil society obviates the need for binding regulation.
>
> (Christian Aid, 2004: 15)

In a similar fashion, but this time in response to the CSR initiatives emanating from the European Union, the personnel director of BT (the UK's largest telecoms corporation) observed,

> It [CSR] is about doing business in a way that persuades our customers to buy from us, our employees to work hard for us and our communities to accept us.
>
> (Cowe, 2001)

Thus, at its most cynical, CSR and voluntary social reporting requirements provide the façade that allows statutory regulation to be held at bay, politicians to claim that positive developments are taking place, while the operational activities of the corporations are left to get on with their *raison d'être*, the business of business.

There are notable exceptions to this pessimistic view of developments and some of these are referred to in Chapters 8 and 9, but the concern is that the evidence revealed by studies such as those reported by Christian Aid (2004) are possibly more reflective of general practices and attitudes. What fuels these concerns is that companies such as Shell, BAT and Coca Cola are high-profile, multi-national corporations, with the resources to undertake the type of social and environmental engagements that the so-called socially responsible corporation is being 'encouraged' to undertake. They are also corporations with much to lose should they alienate their public by revelations of the kind of evidence revealed by Christian Aid. In this context, what price the activities of corporations that are less high-profile and with less public scrutiny than these three MNCs?

Business sustainability has to relate to a state of affairs that has at its centre a notion of symbiosis. This refers to a mutual dependency between the social (including the company's relationships with its employees); the environmental; the political (and here the 'mutual dependency' needs to be more circumspect and distant than it sometimes is), and the undoubted competitive nature of business. Because there are in-built tensions within these sets of relationships, tensions that sometimes may become very troublesome, there is required a binding agent, or series of binding agents, that can hold the relationships together when the tensions are at their most profound and destabilising. These 'glues' will have to be multi-faceted, being comprised of processes, rules, laws, voluntary initiatives and far greater accountability, with that accountability possessing adequate penalties for individuals and corporations who fail or choose not to comply.

Possibly the most significant element of the binding agents, we would argue, has to be the ethics and morals that inform individual, social and corporate behaviour. The ethics and morals will invariably be articulated via, and filtered through, an individual's values and beliefs, as we discussed in Chapters 4–7. We have also recognised that the organisational contexts in which an individual is located will undoubtedly shape the extent to which a person's values are ultimately able to be reflected in their decisions and actions. The Public Interest Disclosure Act (1998) has gone some way to providing protection for those employees who speak out about organisational malpractices, but the Act may need strengthening, as it has done since it entered the statute books with the removal of the ceiling on awards that can be made. More significantly, however, the Act will need protection from those who may endeavour to weaken its scope and protection.

## Challenging central assumptions of economics, politics and human behaviour

The matters under this heading refer to profound issues, which if not addressed adequately will make irrelevant many of the other issues/concerns. Neo-liberal economics informs the actions of significant world institutions, notably the IMF, WTO and World Bank. Under the guise of 'free trade/markets' to benefit everyone via the trickle down effect, the ideology overrides social and political objections. By encouraging everyone to focus upon themselves, neo-liberalism argues, the broad economy will benefit and flourish. Selfishness is not the devil it is made out to be. It leads to an overall benefit, or that is the mantra.

### Connexion point

The trickle down arguments are discussed in detail in Chapter 12, pp. 463–7.

Some anomalies might be explained as the result of unintended consequences. For example, EU farm subsidies (and those paid by other governments to their landowners) can be explained as 'transition payments', moving farming practices into a more efficient, modern era, while minimising social disruption in the farming communities. However, the distinction between 'transition payments' and trade barriers or anti free-trade subsidies is not always clear. The waters of this particular issue are further muddied when one considers the strictures the western-funded institutions, the World Bank, the IMF and the World Trade Organisation, place upon less developed economies and their exported food produce. With regard to the latter, a fundamental element of many, if not most, loans is that the loans are subject to local subsidies being removed and the local markets opened up to worldwide competition. Deregulation of local markets is imposed, as is privatisation.

**Case study 13.3** | **Malawi and the consequences of deregulating and privatising the grain market**

In 2002 Malawi experienced its worst famine since 1949. The primary reason for the famine was laid at the feet of the IMF (and to a lesser extent the World Bank) in a report published by the World Development Movement (2002). The Malawi Agricultural Development and Marketing Corporation had been state owned and maintained a central stock of grain and regulated the prices of the grain. The report's authors (Owusu and Ng'ambi) accepted that the corporation was ripe for reform, but argued that the IMF ignored the need to protect the social aims of the corporation. Since 1996 the IMF, World Bank and other donors had pursued a programme of austerity, deregulation and privatisation in Malawi, but without the attendant infrastructure of accountability and good governance. In 2002 Malawi spent $70M servicing its debt, which represented 20 per cent of the national budget, more than the combined spend of the government on education, health and agriculture. The harvests failed (not for the

▶

first time), but the grain stocks were totally inadequate to cope with the needs of the people. The donors washed their hands of responsibility, claiming that 'the causes of the food shortages are complex, including lapses in the government's early warning systems, distortions in domestic markets, and mismanagement of food reserves'. What was not acknowledged was that the enforced privatisation and deregulation were not accompanied by a grain market that bore any resemblance to the conditions normally required for a market to operate effectively. There was asymmetry of information, exploitation of a lack of multiple buyers and sellers, a lack of product substitution, a lack of an effective mechanism to establish a market clearing price, and no contingency planning to cope with market failure for such an essential human right, i.e. food to eat.

Without any form of market regulation, other forms of regulation should have been insisted upon by the donor institutions, but they were not. A regulator was required to stand in the place of inadequate market dynamics, as is the case with the regulators of gas, water and electricity supply in the UK. Transparent accountability and effective governance regimes neither existed, nor were demanded. These forms of regulation should have been insisted upon by the donor institutions, but such action went against neo-liberal ideology.

Reference was made in Chapter 9 to the response given by the Commerce and Industry Minister of Malawi, Mr Mpasu, who, when asked by the UK government to speak to a meeting of G7 ministers in Cancun of the benefits of liberalising the Malawi economy, stood up and said, 'We have opened our economy. That's why we are flat on our backs.' However, Elliot (2003: 25) went further when he asked,

> How is it that the G7 can export neo-liberal policies to Africa yet the United States would not dream of accepting 'structural adjustments' for its own malfunctioning economy? Isn't it strange that if a country like Zambia deviates from its IMF-imposed programme it gets punished, but if France thumbs its nose at the stability and growth pact (like Germany), nothing happens? ... The language of globalization is all about democracy, free trade and the sharing of technological advances. The reality is about rule by elites, mercantilism and selfishness.

In addition to the lack of justice inherent in the above example, with the commitment to place neo-liberal ideology above democratic principles, there is a second important democratic consideration.

In the developed economies, particularly the UK and USA, it is common for financial institutions (e.g. banks and pension funds) to own substantial tracts of land, with the result that the majority of farm subsidies paid out by the European Union and other western governments go not to individual farmers, but to the financial institutions. Although it is the lone farmer that is invariably depicted as in receipt of the subsidies, protecting the rural idyll as they till the soil, the reality is different. Eighty per cent of farm subsidies paid out in America are paid to corporations. In the UK and America the ubiquitous taxpayer pays money to various national and supernational governments, which in turn distribute a

significant proportion of these taxes in the form of farm subsidies t(
porate landowners. Thus, the claimed protection of local fai
transition payments and against imported food produce, in fact pri
large corporate interests. The commitment of the corporations to
however, purely instrumental. Their commitment is not to the l_
pound, the euro or the dollar. Where is the democratic integrity or vision in so
much of the assets of modern societies being beyond the control of the various
polities or their elected representatives? One must ask whether the power of large
corporations, their sweep of influence, or the extent of corporate, not public or
private individual, ownership of societies' assets and levers of power is acceptable.

## A modest proposal for affecting ethics in business

The following draws upon the work of Bakan (2004), but also reflects our suggestions for addressing the anti-democratic nature of current business–society
relationships. The proposals are presented in four parts.

## 1 The need to strengthen the regulatory systems

In line with Bakan (2004) and Galbraith (2004) we cannot see any significant
improvements to the issues raised above without more robust regulatory frameworks. As Galbraith (2004: 67) observed, 'No one should suppose that supervisory
participation by directors and shareholders is sufficient. Remedy and safeguard
must have the force of law.' To this end we argue for:

- strengthened government regulations on corporate governance, reflecting a
  more inclusive approach to defining corporate obligations in line with the
  King Report (*see* p. 307);
- an elevation of the primary rights of citizens over corporations;
- regulatory agencies to be resourced appropriately, for example, but not confined to, the health and safety inspectorates;
- regulatory agencies being held to more effective public account, possibly via
  parliamentary scrutiny;
- fines for corporate non-compliance with penalties being set at punitive levels;
- repeat offending corporations being subject to the equivalent of charter revocation legislation, with directors barred from obtaining future directorships;
- the crime of corporate manslaughter to be introduced and wanton violations
  of specific legislation subject to the equivalent of charter revocation legislation, with directors barred from obtaining future directorships;
- environmental and health and safety laws being based upon the precautionary principle, making legislation anticipatory, rather than reactive;

- where appropriate, regulatory systems being more decentralised to minimise regulatory capture and over-bureaucracy;

- the monitoring roles of workers' associations/trade unions, consumer groups being enhanced.

## 2 The need to strengthen political infrastructures

- All political elections must be publicly funded. The financial support given to political parties by corporations and the involvement of corporations in political processes (and vice versa) is more of an issue in America than Europe but it is becoming an issue in Europe, particularly Italy.

- A comprehensive review of the lobbying system, with much heightened levels of transparency, must take place.

- 'New voices' should be encouraged to participate into parliamentary and/or public scrutiny of corporate affairs.

## 3 The need to create a robust public sphere

- A public debate is required regarding the sphere of human activity and development that should not be subject to corporate exploitation. Although this does not exclude private provision of public services, it does envisage a greater public involvement in determining the quality and levels of those services and assessing their actual delivery. Areas such as health, education, power and water, genes and other biological materials fall into this category.

  The caveat of a public debate is central to our argument. We do not claim to have a monopoly on knowing the 'right' system or where the boundaries should be unequivocally drawn. The growing national debate in 2005 over the very poor quality of school meals in the UK, as a result of school dinner services being privatised and deregulated during the early 1980s and 1990s, is an example of the type of debate we would hope to see.

## 4 The need to challenge international neo-liberalism

- Nations should work together to shift the ideologies and practices of international institutions such as the WTO, IMF and World Bank away from market fundamentalism and its facilitation of deregulation and privatisation, in the interests of western corporations, but against the interests of less developed economies. Such developments are unlikely to happen without the significant involvement of pressure groups, including consumer rights perspectives, but also NGOs such as Christian Aid, The Red Cross, World Wildlife Fund, Greenpeace, Friends of the Earth, Oxfam and World Vision.

- Of course those NGOs that seek to challenge the neo-liberal consensus should also be accountable. There is a danger that as people become less trusting of governments and international institutions the NGOs will compete with each other to have their alternative view become the consensus. In competing with each other the NGOs may seek to discredit other's views and present their own with a greater rhetorical certainty than is justified. As Beck (1999: 137) puts it,

> the more threatening the shadows that fall on the present day from a terrible future looming in the distance, the more compelling the shock that can be provoked by dramatizing risk today.
>
> (Beck, 1999: 137)

In view of this danger NGOs need to be accountable for their claims and the unintended consequences these may have.

- The last proposal is to some extent an observation of what might actually be happening, although to suggest that it become accepted theory would be considered a heresy by many. It is that the shareholder be seen as a first-order preference shareholder, as a constraint rather than the dominant or sole corporate objective. As discussed above, a constraint is in many respects more demanding than an objective. In mathematical speak, a constraint is an independent variable, say a 12 per cent return on capital employed, whereas an objective is a dependent variable, the latter only being able to be achieved within constraints laid down, such as return on capital employed. So at one level the shareholders remain important business considerations and the market for capital is recognised as an important business issue/constraint. However, the proposal moves us from the sterile debate that companies cannot do X or Y because they (the senior executives) have to act solely in the interests of shareholders. What at one level might seem a small change in perspective offered by this proposal in fact moves us to begin discussing business possibilities and options that are currently not allowed on to (official) boardroom agendas.

## The processes of moral agency

Throughout the book we have often returned to the question of whether the business system – the free market, capitalist system – is in itself moral. Some argue that free markets, which are based on the exercise of individual choice, are intrinsically good. Some argue the opposite while others yet believe markets are not inevitably immoral but that they need to be regulated. Some argue that no answer to the question of the morality of business is possible. They claim that business ethics is an impossibility (Parker, 1998b: 294) because every attempt to define what ethical business means draws us into an agony of philosophical debate or creative accounting.

If we were to assume pessimistically that the market system were immoral, or that it is impossible to define how it should behave to be moral, does that mean it is impossible to behave ethically within it? Can good deeds be done in a bad world or does accepting one's existence within a bad world taint everything?

Such pessimism denies the potential of agency, that is the ability of individuals (and collectives of individuals) to effect change by way of direct action or indirect action, such as the lobbying of governments to effect greater legal controls over business activity.

Although the focus of this chapter has so far been upon the large corporation, and so much of business ethics literature is focused upon corporate social responsibility, no discernible changes will take place as long as the individual can be counted upon to be a passive, detached, disconnected bystander to the contests that take place on a regular basis that shape our social, environmental, economic and political lives. This is why we have devoted a large part of our attention in this book to the issues of business ethics as they affect and are affected by individuals. Developments will take place, for the better or for the worse, and they will be shaped by, instigated by and ultimately implemented by many individuals. Some will act in groups, some individually and alone. Some will argue for one outcome, others for other outcomes. The issues will often be complex, multifaceted, conflicting and not easily resolved. A unique solution will not always be an option, but rather a compromise may need to be sought. This prospect may be unattractive to some, requiring as it does a more active engagement with different decision-making processes and issues than might be appealing. However, the more that individuals opt out of decision-making processes, including those within business organisations, the more the democratic ideal is sacrificed and ultimately lost.

Active engagement with ethical issues at work has two component parts:

1. Thinking through the issues and deciding whether something is sufficiently bad that something should be done, and deciding what exactly one should do.

2. Summoning up the will to take the action that should be done.

We want to make some proposals on both of these matters.

## Thinking through the issues and deciding on the best action

Most people, in their working lives, do not consciously apply ethical theories and philosophical arguments. Values provide the means for thinking about ethical issues. Values are the common sense reflections of ethical theories that we accept without argument and use heuristically in our thinking. Plato used the metaphor of the cave to explain how our perceptions are inadequate representations of the true world. Imagine people who live in a cave that they never leave. They are constrained to look only at the back wall of the cave on to which the sun projects the silhouettes of the world beyond the cave. They believe what they see to be the world. The metaphor identifies values as dim reflections of the ethical theories debated in Chapter 3. This may not be a bad thing. It implies that people muddle through ethical issues at work. The alternative would be an approach to choosing what to do, when faced with difficult moral issues, on the basis of a mechanical application of pre-determined rules or principles. There are, no doubt, some ethical issues in business and organisational life that are clear-cut and what it is right to do is unambiguous. Our discussions of cases in this book, and our interviews with managers and employees, indicate that in many matters there are, at the least, contrary views on what is right and wrong and often, in the perceptions of those involved, the issues are seen as dilemmas. The particulars of a case often defy our values and ethical principles. Our contention is that a better understanding of theories of ethics and moral behaviour, and an encouragement to think more critically about the values that inform our behaviour, will provide each of us with a greater opportunity for reducing the intractability of complex ethical situations. As Oscar Wilde (1996) quipped, 'generalities in morals mean absolutely nothing'.

Intriguingly it seems that computer software based on Artificial Intelligence (AI), which uses neural nets to make decisions, is also muddled, inefficient yet effective. Neural nets have a capacity for induction. That is to say, they can learn. They evolve as they process many particular cases and their consequences. Two neural nets developed from the same case material will not necessarily be the same but they will share the characteristics of being 'wastefully redundant and strangely ordered' (6, 2001: 410). They will also do the job. Neural nets work by enriching systems of classification; they begin by trying to fit situations into pre-existing categories but then, as they note distinguishing peculiarities, they create new categories. Something similar to this process will form the basis of our proposal.

We propose that a good approach to thinking about ethical issues can be constructed from the following three elements.

1. Moral imagination – which challenges the tendency to fit new problems into old categories of problems we have dealt with in the past (known as paradigm cases) and that provide us with tried and tested solutions.

2. Casuistry – which requires that each ethical issue be treated as a separate case and the particularities and peculiarities of each be understood.

3. Dialogue and debate – with all the various interest groups who may have different perspectives on the issues.

Moral imagination is a term developed by Werhane (1999) to describe a way of thinking about messy moral matters that uses creativity to avoid moral morasses. Her argument starts from the position that we all view the world through socially constructed mind-sets or schemas. When we come across a problem we unconsciously associate it with similar problems that we have experienced in the past. If we can conveniently categorise the problem as the same as those of the past it is easy to draw the conclusion that what worked in the past will work for the current problem. Werhane points out that every situation will differ from others in some particulars and that those differences may be more important in determining what should be done than the similarities with past cases. Moral imagination is the process of looking for new ways of thinking about the current problems that enable new solutions and options for action to emerge. William Hazlitt (2004: 84–5) expressed this point with insightful imagery in an essay he wrote in 1826. People without imagination stick to the table of contents and never open the volume of the mind. They are for having maps, not pictures of the world we live in: as much as to say that a bird's-eye view of things contains the truth, the whole truth, and nothing but the truth.

Moral imagination requires pictures, and passion, not maps alone.

> **Connexion point**
>
> The importance of mind-sets and schemas in thinking about ethical issues has been treated extensively in Chapter 5 which deals with heuristics. Heuristics are a form of schema, derived from past experiences, that provides an efficient way of deciding what should be done. It is argued in that chapter that heuristics can be both efficient and effective as decision-making devices, but in difficult moral dilemmas it may be that they are more prone to be counter-productive. In Chapter 6 the same concerns are explored through the notions of categorisation and particularisation.

Bowie with Werhane (2005: 120–1) includes the following in their definition of moral imagination:

- Perceiving the ethical nuances of the case.
- Disengaging from the immediate issue and understanding the mental models (to use Senge's term) that limit one's understanding of the issues.
- Fantasising about new possibilities.
- Evaluating the new possibilities from a moral perspective.

Casuistry, in its everyday sense, is something to be avoided. It means twisting and distorting arguments to support a conclusion that has been previously agreed for other, and often ignoble, reasons. Casuistry does have a more formal and less pejorative meaning. According to Jonsen and Toulmin (1988: 341), casuistry is a method of moral reasoning that is based on consideration of particular cases and not on the application of general ethical theories or principles. As they express it,

> A morality built from general rules and universal principles alone too easily becomes a tyrannical disproportioned thing, and ... only those people who have learned to 'make equitable allowances' for the subtle individual differences among otherwise similar circumstances have developed a true feeling for the deepest demand of ethics.

> **Connexion point**
>
> There are many similarities between the notion of casuistical thinking and the highest level of moral development described in Kohlberg's theory of moral development discussed on p. 253.

There are significant points of connection between the ideas of moral imagination and casuistry. The key points are:

- moral issues should be considered on a case by case basis;

- an emphasis on the subtle difference between apparently similar cases;

- particularities can be identified by making case by case comparisons;

- the differences between cases can be used as the basis for moral double-loop learning. This is a concept developed by Argyris (1993) to define the kind of learning that challenges our customary mental models. Double-loop learning occurs when we challenge the assumptions, goals and rules that contributed to the emergence of a problem and do not simply find an operational way of overcoming the problem, which is called single-loop learning

All of the themes raised so far suggest that questions of business ethics cannot be resolved by a rigid application of rules and codes. This makes dialogue and debate about business ethics necessary, but here we have a paradox. While the importance of dialogue and debate has been stressed throughout the book, we have also referred to research studies that indicate that moral behaviour is not, in practice, something managers discuss much. The continuing moral muteness of managers is a cause for concern and a significant impediment to enhancing the prospects for moral agency within business organisations.

With whom should this dialogue take place? The answer is: with the stakeholders. The dialogue should not be restricted to only those stakeholders who have property rights in the matter. Nor should the dialogue simply be bilateral, between the central organisation involved and the various interested parties. The central organisation in the stakeholder map should also enable discussions to take place between the various stakeholder groups. Bowie and Werhane (2005: 117, 131–3) give an interesting example related to ExxonMobil's project, in conjunction with other oil companies, to drill for oil in the African country of Chad and transport it through a pipeline that passes through neighbouring Cameroon. Within these countries there are tensions between the Bantu and the Bakula Pygmy tribes over whose territory is affected by the drilling and the pipeline, and who should be compensated by the oil companies and to what degree. These tribes have fought each other in the past. In such a situation it would be important to encourage dialogue between the two tribes and, because there are weak legal and institutional infrastructures in the two countries, there may be a need for ExxonMobil to support dialogue between the two African governments and between the governments and international NGOs, which may be able to help the countries develop institutional arrangements that could monitor and sustain any agreements reached between the governments and between the tribes.

**Connexion point**

Stakeholder theory has been a recurrent theme in this book. It is discussed on the following pages: 16–18, 131, 315–18, 443.

Dialogue and debate are, on their own, insufficient to enhance moral agency. They require support structures such as formal mechanisms to raise ethical concerns at work, as well as organisational cultures that are conducive to well-intentioned expressions of concern and the fostering of ethical behaviour. Without these support structures, debate and dialogue become merely additional justifications for cynicism, suspicion and pessimism.

Figure 13.1 is an attempt to integrate the three themes of:

- moral imagination,

- casuistry,

- dialogue and debate among stakeholders

into a series of questions that could be used to guide the consideration of tricky moral issues at work according to the processes of principled judgement.

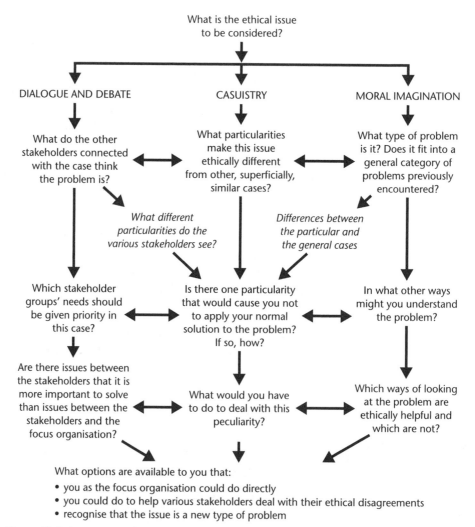

**Figure 13.1** A sequence of questions for guiding principled judgement

## Activity 13.1

What follows is a case loosely based on the MG Rover story described earlier in this chapter (p. 504). The details given are largely invented.

> You are the board of China Xian Automotive Company (CXAC), a very large, state-owned, Chinese car manufacturer. You have been involved for nearly a year in negotiations with the owners of Anglian Lanchester, the last remaining British-owned volume car manufacturer. Five years ago Anglian Lanchester had belonged to Deutsche Vehicles who had decided the company was not viable as a volume car producer. Deutsche Vehicles wanted to turn it into a niche producer of sports cars. This would have lost many jobs in the Middle England region and, with the encouragement of the government, Anglian Lanchester was sold instead to the Raven Consortium for a nominal sum. The new owners did not manage in the subsequent five years to develop the new range of models that were the only chance for the company to regain viability. The talks between Raven and CXAC explored the possibility that in return for investment to develop new models the Chinese would acquire the brands and technology of Anglian Lanchester's range which they would produce in China.
>
> CXAC, however, were not really interested in acquiring a marginal car plant in England. They wanted the brand, models and production technology to produce cars in China to meet a rapidly expanding domestic market. During the negotiations they did purchase from Raven the intellectual property rights associated with Anglian Lanchester's range of cars. CXAC were not unaware of the fact that if they withdrew from the deal Anglian Lanchester would most likely go into liquidation and they would then be able to buy what they needed at knock-down prices from the administrator. However, if the deal goes through the British government would provide some substantial soft loans to ease the survival of Anglian Lanchester.

The question is whether you should:

- complete the deal, and so keep Anglian Lanchester afloat and protect the jobs of the many who work for it;

- or withdraw from the deal.

Now consider the following sets of particular circumstances. How would any of the following particulars affect your decision? Decide whether it would make any difference to your view of what it would be right to do in the case, if one or the other of the following pairs of particulars were true.

▶

| | |
|---|---|
| There is a large population of people of Chinese origin living in Middle England, who migrated to the UK when the Chinese population of an Indian Ocean country that was once part of the British Empire were thrown out by the majority indigenous population. Many of these people work for Anglian Lanchester. | ←→ | There are no great ethnic or cultural connections between Middle England and China. |
| Britain is a richer country than China and so might be expected to take responsibility for the well-being of its own citizens. | ←→ | Imagine that, instead, China was the rich industrialised country and Britain was a developing country for whom the loss of the Anglian Lanchester jobs would be a major blow. |
| The intellectual property rights had been bought by CXAC as a confidence building measure, as a mark of good faith that it intended to complete the deal. | ←→ | CXAC had bought the intellectual property rights because the owners of Anglian Lanchester had lobbied hard for the sale in order to keep the company solvent. |
| The owners of Anglian Lanchester, the four partners in the Raven Consortium, had made substantial fortunes from Anglian Lanchester even while the company had been failing. | ←→ | The owners of the Raven Consortium had heavily invested their personal money in Anglian Lanchester in order to keep it going. |
| There are adequate funds in the employees' pension fund that will provide the employees with better pensions than your Chinese employees might expect. | ←→ | The pension fund will be insolvent if the company ceases trading. The staff of Anglian Lanchester will lose their pensions if you withdraw from the deal. |

We have placed considerable emphasis upon the notion of moral agency because without this the individual is diminished. Organisations represent the places that the majority of people inhabit for most of their waking lives. If they are unable to exercise moral agency, to follow their consciences, and are required to do things they believe are wrong for fear of reprisals if they do not, then we have created, at best, amoral communities, and at worst immoral communities.

Employing Aristotle's use of the mean to identify a balance of behaviour that avoids the extremes of indulgence or neglect with respect to moral agency we argue for a form of moral agency that recognises and avoids the excesses of priggishness or self-righteousness. We call this mean 'principled judgement'. To see the correction of a 'wrong' as justifiable because it assuages the moralist's conscience, irrespective of the harm that might be caused by righting the wrong, would be an example of moral agency transgressing into the indulgence of self-righteousness. Principled judgement is the mean, or balance, between moral impotence and self-righteousness.

Self-righteousness demands a reflexive wrestling with one's conscience that implies a greater concern for the state of one's soul than for the state of the world. It seems imbalanced to others because

> ... we feel so extremely uncomfortable in the presence of people who are noted for their special virtuousness, for they radiate an atmosphere of the torture to which they subject themselves.
>
> (Jung, 1953)

Moral impotence, on the other hand, implies a failing that is not necessarily the fault of the individual. While feelings of impotency can be the result of individual failing, it can also be the consequence of factors beyond the control of the individual. In the latter case, an authoritarian regime, coupled with an unsupportive organisational culture, may render the individual employee seemingly helpless in the face of practices with which they are uncomfortable. However, much will depend upon the circumstances of individual cases before one can make judgements about the sources of the moral impotency.

## Summoning up the will to take the action that should be done

Knowing what should be done is one thing. Doing it is something else again. The problem to be faced in business ethics is that people often do not do what they know they ought to do. The Kew Gardens case, which was mentioned in Chapter 6, p. 250, provides a classic formulation of the problem. In 1984 in Kew Gardens in New York Kitty Genovese was murdered in full view of 38 onlookers in the nearby apartment block. None of the observers took any action. They did not go to Genovese's aid nor did they phone the police. Was this because people were callous and unconcerned or was it perhaps because they were afraid for their own safety if they became involved? One interesting interpretation of the onlookers' lack of action involves the idea of social proof (Silk, 1999). In a situation where something bad is apparently happening people assume that it cannot be so and look for a more benign interpretation. Perhaps it is not a murder being witnessed but a scene being shot for a film and there is surely a camera crew just out of sight. Before they accept the worst-case interpretation people look for social evidence or proof that it is in fact a murder. As Silk points out, if the fire alarm sounds at work we all look around us to see if others are taking it seriously before we decide there really might be some danger and evacuate the building. In the

Kew Gardens case perhaps all the observers were waiting for someone else to start the hue and cry before they could feel sure that they were in fact witnessing a murder. A related aspect of social proof is that, if there are a number of witnesses who are aware of each other, but not in direct communication with each other, as was the case with the Kew Gardens observers who were each looking out of their separate apartment windows, people tend to assume that others will take action and so they do not.

---

**Connexion point**

The notion of social proof or social evidence is very close to Bauman's concept of *'floating responsibility'* that is discussed in Chapter 7, p. 283.

---

A Cambridge academic published in 1908 a tongue-in-cheek guide to university politics. He also attributed people's inclination to act against their natural preference to be honest and good to their anticipation of the actions or inactions of others.

> The number of rogues is about equal to the number of men who always act honestly; and it is very small. The majority would sooner behave honestly than not. The reason why they do not give way to this natural preference of humanity is that they are afraid that others will not; and the others do not because they are afraid that they will not. Thus it comes about that, while behaviour that looks dishonest is fairly common, sincere dishonesty is about as rare as the courage to evoke good faith in your neighbours by shewing that you trust them.
>
> Cornford in Johnson (1994: 103)

If it is true that people's tendency not to see the bad behaviour under their noses is a consequence of their perception of the social situation then they may be encouraged to take ethical responsibility by creating organisational and institutional contexts that reinforce individual responsibility. From this perspective, as an aside, the current focus on teams as the basic units of organisations may contribute to the failure of employees to recognise and respond to the ethical problems because the responsibility to do so is diffused throughout the team.

An example of how institutional changes might encourage individual responsibility can be illustrated by the story of Bernie Ebbers. He was the CEO of Worldcom. He had built it up from a small telecoms company to the second largest long-distance phone company in the USA. Following the dotcom crash the business came under pressure and it coped in part by fraud. It exaggerated its revenue and misreported its expenses in an effort to maintain its share price. When it collapsed it was the largest bankruptcy in American history. In 2005 Bernie Ebbers was found guilty of conspiracy and fraud, in particular of filing false documents (BBC News, 2005). He had used the 'Aw Shucks' defence, unsuccessfully, during his trial (Evans, 2005). Ebbers had portrayed himself as a chief executive who did not know the details of his company's accounts. He was just a simple salesman who knew how to cut costs but he was not clever enough to understand the complexities of corporate finance and accounts. That sort of thing he left to his finance director who must be the person who was guilty of fraud, whereas – Aw shucks – Ebbers was not sophisticated enough to have committed the fraud. The prosecution in his trial thought it beyond belief that Ebbers could have built up the company from nothing and yet have been ignorant of finance. The defence can be interpreted as an example of the social proof theory. Ebbers would have looked at his senior finance managers and, if they were acting as if nothing was wrong, then there was nothing wrong. Although Ebbers will appeal against his conviction the success of the prosecution sent out an institutional message to other CEOs that the 'Aw shucks' defence will not work. This may incline them to recognise and react to ethical issues because they know that they cannot use the lack of actions from others to excuse their own inactivity. At both an institutional level and an organisational level, we should be setting up structures and establishing norms that make it less easy for managers to evade their moral obligations.

## Summary

In this chapter the following key points have been made:

- There are strong arguments that corporations represent a brake on the achievement of democratic aspirations and that they should be made more accountable within democratic processes.

- A response to the problems of sustainability needs the privileges accruing to property rights to be reviewed and market mechanisms to be designed so that they discourage corporations from unsustainable practices.

- There is a need to raise public debate worldwide about the ideological assumptions and preferences that are built into the international organisations that oversee the world's trade and economic development.

- In ethical matters 'the devil is in the detail' and issues should be tackled on a case by case basis and their particularities and peculiarities attended to.

- Decision-makers in organisations should be encouraged to adopt a 'moral imagination' approach when they review issues that have ethical dimensions, as most managerial decisions do.

- At both societal and organisational levels institutions and structures should be developed that overcome the natural human tendency to underrate or fail to respond to ethical problems.

## Quick revision test

1. When was limited liability for public companies introduced in the United Kingdom?
   (a) 1920
   (b) 1856
   (c) 1578

2. What percentage of waste disposal in Italy is estimated to be done illegally?
   (a) 95%
   (b) 68%
   (c) 30%

3. The Kew Gardens effect is...?
   (a) the belief that talking to people, as to plants, encourages healthy growth and development
   (b) the tendency of people to ignore wrongdoing that they witness
   (c) evidence that people take action against wrongdoing they witness directly

4. Oscar Wilde quipped...
   (a) 'a gentleman prefers manners to morals'
   (b) 'a little morality is a dangerous thing; a lot of it is fatal'
   (c) 'generalities in morals mean absolutely nothing'.

## Typical assignments and briefs

1. Are NGOs who work to improve the social and environmental responsibility of corporations more ethical, and less in need of being brought to account, than the corporations they criticise?

2. Should the law make it easier for corporations to be wound up if they are found to have acted unethically and caused great harm?

3. What is moral imagination and how might it be applied in corporate decision making?

4. In what ways, at both the institutional and the organisational levels, might changes be made that would encourage managers to recognise and respond to ethical issue in organisations?

### Group activity 13

Watch a video or DVD of the feature film documentary *The Corporation* based on Bakan's book of the same name. Discuss, as suggested on the film's website, whether the approach to corporations should be:

- to rewrite – change the legal form and privileges of corporations;

- to regulate – create more methods and bodies to monitor and regulate corporations;

- to reform – encourage organisations to manage themselves better and more ethically; perhaps (returning to the introductory theme of this book) corporations could be so encouraged by disseminating good and heroic stories of organisations and CEOs who chose to act ethically.

## Recommended further reading

The two key books for this chapter are Bakan, J. (2004) *The Corporation: The Pathological Pursuit of Profit and Power*, London: Constable, and Patricia Werhane (1999) *Moral Imagination and Management Decision-making*, New York: Oxford University Press. If you do not read Bakan, watch the film *The Corporation*.

## Useful websites

| Topic | Website provider | URL |
|---|---|---|
| Lots of information about the film including synopses and educational resources | The website for the film *The Corporation* | http://www.thecorporation.com/index.php |
| The murder of Kitty Genovese in Kew Gardens in 1964 triggered much ethical debate. The Wikipedia site gives the context; the other site is a more partisan one in which a Randian objectivist worries about the consequences of the case for her ethical philosophy. | Wikipedia | http://en.wikipedia.org/wiki/Kitty_Genovese |
| | Christine Silk, The Objectivist Centre | http://www.objectivistcenter.org/navigator/articles/nav+csilk_why-kitty-genovese-die.asp |

# References

6, P. (2001) 'Ethics, regulation and the new artificial intelligence, part II', *Information, Communication & Society*, 4(3), 406–34.

ABC News Online (2005a) *Shareholders' group opposes tsunami donations*, World Wide Web, http://www.abc.nrt.au/news/newsitems/200501/s1278005.html. Site visited 17 January 2005.

ABC News Online (2005b) *Shareholders' group clarifies tsunami donation stance*, World Wide Web, http://www.abc.nrt.au/news/newsitems/200501/s1278362.html. Site visited 17 January 2005.

Abramson, D.M. (1999) 'A critical look at NGOs and civil society as a means to an end in Uzbekistan', *Human Organisation*, 58(3), Fall, 240–50.

Account Ability (2004) *AA1000 series*, World Wide Web, http://www.accountability.org.uk/aa1000/default.asp. Site visited 19 September 2004.

Achbar, M., Abbott, J. and Bakan, M. (Directors) (2003) *The Corporation*, a film, New York: Zeitgeist Films.

Adair, J. (1980) *Management and Morality. The Problems and Opportunities of Social Capitalism*, Farnborough: Gower.

Al Andalusia, S.C. (2001) *Credit Cards*, World Wide Web, http://www.islamzine.com/carlo/shari33.html. Site visited 20 August 2001.

Alden, E. (2001) 'Brands feel the impact as activists target customers', *Financial Times*, 18 July: 11.

Alvesson, M. and Willmott, H. (1996) *Making Sense of Management. A Critical Introduction*, London: Sage.

Amnesty International (1997) *The 'Enron project' in Maharashtra – protest suppressed in the name of development*, World Wide Web, http://web.amnesty.org/802568F7005C4453/0/73E2D8C20C9F126F8025690000693183?Open&Highlight=2,enron. Site visited 22 January 2002.

Amnesty International UK (2003) *Baku-Tbilisi-Ceyhan Pipeline Project Puts Human Rights on the Line*, World Wide Web, http://www.amnesty.org.uk/business/btc/press.shtml. Site visited 12 March 2005.

Anon. (1995) *Principles of Islamic Banking*, World Wide Web, http://cwis.usc.edu/deptMSA/economics/nbank1.html. Site visited 20 August 2001.

Anon. (1997) 'Branson to tell EU of "illegal" BA practices', *Financial Times*, 11 November.

Anon. (1999a) 'Brussels gets tough with British Airways', *Financial Times*, 15 July.

Anon. (1999b) 'US judge throws out last Virgin complaint against BA', *Financial Times*, 26 October.

Anon. (2001) 'Cancer research hampered after Alder Hey', *Guardian Unlimited*, 22 May, World Wide Web, http://www.societyguardian.co.uk/alderhey/story/0,7999,494612,00hl. Site visited 12 March 2003.

Argyris, C. (1993) *Knowledge for Action. A Guide to Overcoming Barriers to Organizational Change*, San Francisco: Jossey-Bass.

Arif, M. (1988) 'Islamic Banking', *Asian-Pacific Economic Literature*, 2(2), September: 46–62.

Aristotle (1976) *The Ethics of Aristotle*, trans. J.A.K. Thompson, Harmondsworth: Penguin.

Armstrong, M. (1998) *Performance Management*, London: Kogan Page.

Arthur Andersen and London Business School (1999) *Ethical Concerns and Reputation Risk Management. A Study of Leading UK Companies*, London: Arthur Andersen.

Badaracco, J.L. Jr (1997) *Defining Moments: When Managers Must Choose Between Right and Right*, Boston: Harvard Business School Press.

Bakan, J. (2004) *The Corporation: The Pathological Pursuit of Profit and Power*, London: Constable.

baku-ceyhan campaign (2003a) *Conflict, militarization, human rights and the Baku-Ceyhan Pipeline*, World Wide Web, http://www.bakuceyhan.org.uk/more_info/humanrights.htm. Site visited 24 January 2005.

baku-ceyhan campaign (2003b) *Environmental Risks in the BTC*, World Wide Web, http://www.bakuceyhan.org.uk/more_info/impacts.htm. Site visited 24 January 2005.

baku-ceyhan campaign (n.d.) *Colonialism and the Baku-Ceyhan Pipeline*, World Wide Web, http://www.bakuceyhan.org.uk/more_info/colonialism.htm. Site visited 24 January 2005.

Baldwin, S., Godfrey, C. and Propper, C. (eds) (1990) *Quality of Life: Perspectives and Policies*, London: Routledge.

Barber, T. and Parker, A. (2004) 'Parmalat suspects deny fraud role', *Financial Times*, 5 January 2004, 1.

Barlow, T. (2001) 'Body and mind: Treatments that cost an arm and a leg', *Financial Times*, 7 April.

Barnes, J. (1999) *England, England*, London: Picador.

Barr, N. (1985) 'Economic Welfare and Social Justice', *Journal of Society and Politics*, 14(2), 175–87.

Barry, B. (1989) *Theories of Justice: A Treatise on Social Justice*, Hemel-Hempstead: Harvester-Wheatsheaf.

Bartlett, R. (2000) *England under the Norman and Angevin Kings, 1075–1225*, Oxford: The Clarendon Press.

Basu, N., Mintzberg, H. and Simons, R. (2002) 'Memo to: CEOs'. Reprinted in *Fast Company*, 59, April: 117.

Bauman, Z. (1993) *Postmodern Ethics*, Oxford: Blackwell.

Bauman, Z. (1994) *Alone Again: Ethics After Certainty*, London: Demos.

Bauman, Z. (1995) *Life in Fragments: Essays in Postmodern Moralities*, Oxford: Blackwell.

BBC News Online (2004a) *Dizaei to face a police tribunal*, 30 March, World Wide Web, http://www.bbc.co.uk/1/hi/England/London/3583107. Site visited 10 February 2005.

BBC News Online (2004b) *Cleared officer returns to work*, 30 October, World Wide Web, http://www.bbc.co.uk/1/hi/England/London/3226687. Site visited 8 February 2005.

BBC News Online (2005) 'NHS 'taking away Africa's medics'', 15 March, World Wide Web, http://www.bbc.co.uk/go/pr/fr/-/1/hi/health/4349545. Site visited 16 February 2005.

BBC News Online (2005) 'Ebbers guilty of Worldcom fraud', 15 March, World Wide Web, http://news.bbc.co.uk/1/hi/business/4351975.stm. Site visited 17 March 2005.

Beardshaw, V. (1981) *Conscientious Objectors at Work*, London: Social Audit.

Beck, L.W. (1959) *Immanuel Kant: Foundations of the Metaphysics of Morals*, Indianapolis: Bobbs-Merrill Educational Publishing.

Beck, U. (1999) *World Risk Society*, Cambridge: Polity Press.

Bedward, D., Jankowicz, A.D. and Rexworthy, C. (2003) 'East meets West: a case example of knowledge transfer', *Human Resource Development International*, 6(4), 527–46.

Belbin, R.M. (1981) *Management Teams: Why they Succeed or Fail*, London: Heinemann.

Bennett, C. (2005) 'Where's the fair trade in £3 jeans?', G2, *Guardian*, 31 March: 5.

Bennett, R. and Voyle, S. (2001) 'Supermarkets facing more scrutiny after election: The relationship between food suppliers and retailers is likely to be probed', *Financial Times*, 11 April.

Bentham, J. (1982) *An Introduction to the Principles of Morals and Legislation*, eds J.H. Burns and H.L.A. Hart, London: Methuen. Original edition 1781.

Bentham, J. (1994) 'The Commonplace Book', in *The Works of Jeremy Bentham*, Vol. X, ed. J. Bowring, Bristol: Thoemnes Press. Original edition (1843), Edinburgh: Tait.

Berle, A. and Means, G. (1932) *The Modern Corporation and Private Property*, New York: Macmillan.

Beyond Strategy (1998–2001) *Feng Shui and the Beyond Strategy Logo*, World Wide Web, http://beyondstrategy.com/aboutus/ourlogo.htm. Site visited 24 April 2001.

Bhopal.com (2001) *Bhopal incident review and the settlement*, World Wide Web, http://www.bhopal.com. Site visited 15 October 2001.

Bhopal.net (2001) *The Union Carbide Disaster. Quick Fact Tour*, World Wide Web, http://www.bhopal.net/intro2.html. Site visited 25 October 2001.

Billig, M. (1996) *Arguing and Thinking: A Rhetorical Approach to Social Psychology*, 2nd edition, Cambridge: Cambridge University Press.

Birch, D. (2001) 'Corporate Citizenship: Rethinking Business beyond Corporate Social Responsibility', in Andriof, J. and McIntosh, M. (eds), *Perspectives on Corporate Citizenship*, 53–65, Sheffield: Greenleaf Publishing.

Bird, F.B. and Waters, J.A. (1989) 'The Moral Muteness of Managers', *California Management Review*, Fall: 73–88.

Blackburn, M. (2000) 'Managing the cross-cultural aspect of workplace privacy', paper presented at *Cross-cultural Business Ethics*, 2nd *International Conference*, 17–19 April, University of Westminster, London.

Blackburn, S. (2001) *Being Good. A Short Introduction to Ethics*, Oxford: Oxford University Press.

Blanchard, K. and Peale, N. (1988) *The Power of Ethical Management*, New York: Fawcett Crest.

Borrie, G. (1996) 'Business Ethics and Accountability', in Brindle, M. and Dehn, G., *Four Windows on Whistleblowing*, 1–23, London: Public Concern at Work.

Borrie, G. and Dehn, G. (2002) *Whistleblowing: The New Perspective*, London: Public Concern at Work, World Wide Web, http://www.pcaw.co.uk/policy_pub/newperspective.html.

Bosanquet, B. (1906) *A Companion to Plato's Republic*, London: Rivingtons.

Boseley, S. (2001a) 'Arrogance of Doctors led to organ scandal', *Guardian*, 11 January: 3. *Guardian* and *Observer* on CD-ROM.

Boseley, S. (2001b) '50,0000 Organs Secretly Stored in Hospitals', *Guardian*, 11 January: 1. *Guardian* and *Observer* on CD-ROM.

Bowe, C. (2001) 'Firestone cuts ties with Ford over tyre recall', *Financial Times*, 22 May: 36.

Bowie, N.E. and Duska, R. (1990) *Business Ethics*, Englewood Cliffs, NJ: Prentice Hall.

Bowie, N.E. (1999) *Business Ethics: A Kantian Perspective*, Oxford: Blackwell Publishers.

Bowie, N.E. with Werhane, P.H. (2005) *Management Ethics*, Oxford: Blackwell.

BP (2001) *BP's 2001 Environmental and Social Report*, World Wide Web, http://www.bp.com/environ_social/review_2001/index.asp. Site visited 28 March 2002.

Bradley, S. (2000) 'Villagers not sweet on 7-day sugar plan', *Bury Free Press*, 30 June.

Bridges, J. (Director) (1979) *The China Syndrome* (DVD), UCA.

Brigley, S. and Vass, P. (1997) *Privatised Ethics. The Case of the Regulated Industries*, in Davies, P.W.F. (ed.), *Current Issues in Business Ethics*, London: Routledge.

Brindle, M. and Dehn, G. (1996) *Four Windows on Whistleblowing*, London: Public Concern at Work.

British Airways (2000) *British Airways Social and Environmental Report 2000*, London: British Airways.

Brown, P. (2004) 'India ordered to pay out Bhopal fund', *Guardian*, 20 July: 11.

Brown, J.M. (1972) *Gandhi's Rise to Power: Indian Politics 1915–1922*, Cambridge: Cambridge University Press.

Brown, M. (2001) 'Capitalism: Reconstruction theory', *Financial Management*, November, 20.

Browne of Madingley (2004) *The Ethics of Business – The Botwinick Lecture*, Columbia Business School, 19 November 2004, World Wide Web, http://www.bp.com/genericarticle.do?categoryId=98*contended-7002497. Site visited 2 December 2004.

Brunsson, N. (1986) 'Organising for Inconsistencies: On Organisational Conflict, Depression and Hypocrisy as Substitutes for Action', *Scandinavian Journal of Management Studies*, May: 165–85.

Brunsson, N. (1989) *The Organisation of Hypocrisy: Talk, Decisions and Actions in Organisations*, Chichester: John Wiley & Sons.

Brytting, T. (1997) 'Moral support structures in private industry – The Swedish case', *Journal of Business Ethics*, 16, 663–97.

Buchholz, R.A. and Rosenthal, S.B. (1998) *Business Ethics: The Pragmatic Path Beyond Principles to Process*, London: Prentice Hall.

Buckley, S.L. (1998) *Usury Friendly? The Ethics of Moneylending – a Biblical Interpretation*, Cambridge: Grove Books.

Burgo, E. and Stewart, H. (2002) 'IMF policies led to Malawi famine', *Guardian*, 29 October.

Burns, J. and Shrimsley, R. (2000) 'Racism "remains rife" in the Met: Complaints of discrimination at all levels add to ethnic recruitment crisis says report', *Financial Times*, 14 December.

Burrell, G. (1997) *Pandemonium: towards a Retro-organizational Theory*, London: Sage.

Burt, T. (2004) 'Breeden report opens the floodgates: Hollinger Chronicles', *Financial Times*, 4 September: 11.

Cabinet Office (2004) *The Civil Service Code*, World Wide Web, http://www.cabinet-office.gov.uk/central/1999/cscode.htm. Site visited 13 March 2002.

Cadbury Schweppes (2004) *Cocoa procurement: Free Trade*, World Wide Web, http://www.cadburyschweppes.com/EN/EnvironmentSociety/EthicalTrading/CocoaProcurement/fair_trade.htm. Site visited 22 December 2004.

Cantor, N., Mischel, W. and Schwartz, J. (1982) 'Social Knowledge: Structure, Content, Use and Abuse', in Hastorf, A.H. and Isen, A.M. (eds), *Cognitive Social Psychology*, New York: Elsevier.

Carbo Ceramics (2002) *Mission Statement*, World Wide Web, http://www.carboceramics.com/1024/company/mission.html. Site visited 10 December 2004.

Carey, J.L. (1984) 'The Origins of Financial Reporting' in Lee, T.A. and Parker, R.H. (eds), *The Evolution of Corporate Financial Reporting*, 241–64, New York & London: Garland Publishing Inc.

Carr, A.Z. (1968) 'Is Business Bluffing Ethical?', *Business and Society Review*, 100(1), 1–7.

Carroll, A.B. (1990) 'Principles of Business Ethics: their Role in Decision Making and an Initial Consensus', *Management Decision*, 28(8), 20–4.

Carter, C. (2004) 'Parmalat subsidy superior to CAP', *Financial Times*, 25 February, Letters to the Editor: 18.

Cassell, C., Johnson, P. and Smith, K. (1997) 'Opening the Black Box: Corporate Codes of Ethics in Their Organisational Context', *Journal of Business Ethics*, 16, 1077–93.

Casson, M. (1991) *The Economics of Business Culture: Games Theory, Transaction Costs and Economic Performance*, Oxford: Oxford University Press, Clarendon Paperbacks.

Caulkin, S. (2004) 'Money for less than nothing', *The Observer, Business*, 12 December: 10.

Caux Round Table (2001) *Caux Round Table Principles for Business*, World Wide Web, http://www.cauxroundtable.org/ENGLISH.HTM. Site visited 26 October 2001.

Center for Public Enquiry (2000) *The Public I: Major tobacco multinational implicated in cigarette smuggling, tax evasion, documents show*, World Wide Web, http://www.public-i.org/story_01_013100.htm. Site visited 3 June 2000.

Center for the Study of Ethics in the Professions (2003) *Covenant of the Goddess Code of Ethics*, World Wide Web, http://www.iit.edu/departments/csep/codes/coe/COG-CoE.html. Site visited 2 December 2004.

CEPAA (1997) *Guidance Document for Social Accountability 8000*, London: CEPAA.

Chakraborty, S.K. (1993) *Managerial Transformations by Values*, New Delhi: Sage.

Chakraborty, S.K. (1999) *Values and Ethics for Organisations. Theory and Practice*, New Delhi: Oxford University Press.

Chandler, D. (2001) *Semiotics: the Basics*, London: Routledge.

Chang, H.-J. (2002) *Kicking away the Ladder*, London: Anthem Press.

Chaudhuri, N.C. (1987) *Thy Hand, Great Anarch! India 1921–1952*, London: Chatto and Windus.

Christian Aid (2004) *Behind the mask: The real face of corporate social responsibility*, London: Christian Aid.

Clark, A. and Borger, J. (2001) 'Cheaper drugs for Africa: Manufacturer to relax its patent on two Aids remedies', *Guardian*, 15 March: 3. *Guardian* and *Observer* on CD-ROM.

Clark, D. (2004) *The Rough Guide to Ethical Shopping*, London: Rough Guides.

Clarke, K. (2000) 'Dilemma of a cigarette exporter', *Guardian Unlimited*, 3 February, World Wide Web, http://www.newsunlimited.co.uk/bat/0,2763,131913,00.html. Site visited 12 August 2001.

Clarkson, C.M.V. (1998) 'Corporate Culpability', *Web Journal of Legal Issues*, Blackstone Press Ltd, World Wide Web, http://webjcli.ncl.uk/1998/issue2/clarkson2.html.

Clean Clothes Campaign (n.d.), World Wide Web, http://www.cleanclothes.org/companies/levi5-5-98.htm

Clutterbuck, D. (1992) *The Role of the Chief Executive in Maintaining an Ethical Climate*, London: Clutterbuck Associates.

CNN International (2003) *Parmalat to decide on bankruptcy*, World Wide Web, http://editioncnn.com/2003/BUSINESS/italy.parmalat/index.html. Site visited 8 February 2005.

Commission for Africa (2005) *Our Common Interest. Report of the Commission for Africa*, World Wide Web, http://news.bbc.co.uk/1/shared/bsp/hi/pdfs/11_03_05africa.pdf. Site visited 2 April 2005.

Connock, S. and Johns, T. (1995) *Ethical Leadership*, London: Institute of Personnel Development.

Corpwatch (2001) *Personal Appeal from Bhopal to Shareholders of Union Carbide: You Can Still End the Disaster in Bhopal*, World Wide Web, http://www.corpwatc.org/trac/bhopal/shareholder.html. Site visited 25 October 2001.

Covey, S.R. (1991) *Principle-centred Leadership*, New York: Summit Books.

Covey, S.R. (1992) *The Seven Habits of Highly Effective People: Powerful Lessons in Personal Change*, London: Simon and Schuster.

Cowe, R. (2001) 'Europe Rises to Social Challenge: Corporate Citizenship', *Financial Times*, 19 July.

Crainer, S. (1993) *Zeebrugge: Learning from Disaster*, London: Herald Charitable Trust.

Crichton, M. (2004) '*State of Fear*', New York; HarperCollins.

Cronin, J. (2004) *DBA dissertation*, Nottingham Business School, Nottingham Trent University.

Crouch, C. and Marquand, D. (eds) (1993) *Ethics and Markets: Co-operation and competition within capitalist economies*, Oxford: Blackwell Publishers.

CSR Academy (2004) *The CSR Competency Framework*, London: CSR Academy, World Wide Web, http://www.csracademy.org.uk/competency.htm. Site visited 28 February 2005.

Cyert, R.M. and March, J.G. (1992) *A Behavioral Theory of the Firm*, 2nd edition, New Jersey: Blackwell.

Czarniawska, B. (2004) *Narratives in Social Science Research*, London: Sage.

Czerny, A. (2004) 'Support for "ethical" testing', *People Management*, 11 March: 10.

D'Entreves, A.P. (1965) *Aquinas. Selected Political Writings*, trans. J.G. Dawson, Oxford: Basil Blackwell.

Dallas, M. (1996) 'Accountability for Performance – Does Audit have a Role?' in *Adding Value? Audit and Accountability in the Public Services*, Public Finance Foundation and Chartered Institute of Public Finance and Accountancy (CIPFA): London.

Dalrymple, W. (1999) *The Age of Kali. Travels and Encounters In India*, London: Flamingo Press.

Dalrymple, W. (2002) *The White Mughals*, London: Flamingo.

Davies, P.W.F. (ed.) (1997) *Current Issues in Business Ethics*, London: Routledge.

De George, R.T. (1999) *Business Ethics*, 5th edition, New Jersey: Prentice Hall.

De Pelsmacker, P., Driesen, L. and Rayp, G. (2003) *Are Fair Trade Labels Good Business? Ethics and Coffee Buying Intentions*, University of Ghent, Faculty of Economics and Business Administration, Working Paper, World Wide Web, http://www.feb.ugent.be/fac/research/WP/Papers/wp_03_165.pdf. Site visited 22 December 2004.

Degli Innocenti, N. and Reed, J. (2004) 'Anger at delay to AIDS drugs in South Africa', *Financial Times*, 21 January: 9.

Department of Transport (1987) *MV Herald of Free Enterprise, Formal Investigation by Hon. Mr Justice Sheen, Wreck Commissioner, Court Report 8074* (The Sheen Report), London: HMSO.

Derrida, J. with Bennington, G. (1985) 'On Colleges and Philosophy', in Appignanesi, L. (ed.), *Postmodernism. ICA Documents*, London: Free Associates Books.

Dewey, C. (1993) *Anglo-Indian Attitudes: the Mind of the Indian Civil Service*, London: The Hambledon Press.

Dhesi, A.S. (1998) 'Caste, Class Synergies and Discrimination in India', *International Journal of Social Economics*, 25(6, 7, 8), 1030–48.

Dickson, D. (1974) *Alternative Technology and the Politics of Technical Change*, Fontana/Collins.

*Director* (2001) 'Spanish Shuffle', *Director*, February: 29.

Dollar, D. and Kraay, A. (2002) 'Growth **is** Good for the Poor', *Journal of Economic Growth*, 7(3), 195–225.

Dollar, D. and Kraay, A. (2004) 'Trade, Growth and Poverty', *Economic Journal*, 114(493), F22–49.

Donaldson, T. (1982) *Corporations and Morality*, Englewood Cliffs, NJ: Prentice Hall.

Donaldson, T. (1989) *The Ethics of International Business*, New York: Oxford University Press.

Donaldson, T. (1990) 'Morally privileged relationships', *Journal of Value Enquiry*, 24, 1–15.

Donaldson, T. (1996) 'Values in tension: Ethics away from home', *Harvard Business Review*, 74(5), 48–56.

Donaldson, T. and Dunfee, T.W. (1994) 'Toward a unified conception of business ethics: Integrative social contracts theory', *Academy of Management Review*, 19(2), 252–84.

Donaldson, T. and Dunfee, T.W. (1995) 'Integrative social contracts theory: A communitarian conception of economic ethics', *Economics and Philosophy*, 11(1), 85–112.

Donaldson, T. and Dunfee, T.W. (1999) *Ties That Bind: A Social Contracts Approach to Business Ethics*, Boston, MA: Harvard Business School Press.

Donaldson, T. and Preston, L.E. (1995) 'The Stakeholder Theory of the Corporation; Concepts, Evidence and Implications', *Academy of Management Review*, 22(1), 65–91.

Donaldson, T. and Werhane, P.H. (1979) *Ethical Issues in Business: A Philosophical Approach*, New Jersey: Prentice Hall.

Done, K. (2003) 'Branson's Concorde bid grounded by Airbus Chief', *Financial Times*, 30 April: 3.

Done, K. (2004) 'Airlines battle for profitable Indian routes', *Financial Times*, 11 November: 6.

Donner, W. (1991) *The Liberal Self: John Stuart Mill's Moral and Political Philosophy*, New York: Cornell University Press.

Doran, J. (2004) 'The bank in American backwaters that has the answers to your prayers', *The Times, Business section*, 11 December: 70.

Doran, J. and Mansell, I. (2004) 'Shell settlements "bolster" billion-dollar class actions', *The Times*, 26 August: 50.

Dorff, E.N. (1997) 'The implications of Judaism for business and privacy', *Business Ethics Quarterly*, 7(2), 31–44.

Dugatkin, L. (2000) *Cheating Monkeys and Citizen Bees*, Cambridge, MA: Harvard University Press.

Dunfee, T.W. (1991) 'Business Ethics and extant social contracts', *Business Ethics Quarterly*, 1(1), 23–51.

Dunfee, T.W. (1996) *Ethical challenges of managing across cultures*, Invited plenary paper presented at the Ninth Annual European Business Ethics Networks Conference, Seeheim, Germany.

Dunfee, T.W. and Donaldson, T. (1995) 'Contractarian business ethics: Current status and next steps', *Business Ethics Quarterly*, 5(2), 173–86.

Durkheim, E. (1992) *Professional Ethics and Civic Morals*, trans. C. Brookfield, London: Routledge.

Dwivedi, R.S. (2000) 'The paradox of employee empowerment: Illusion or reality?' in Saini, D.S. and Khan, S.A. (eds) *Human Resource Management. Perspectives for a new era*, New Delhi: Response Books, Sage.

Dworkin, R. (1977) *Taking Rights Seriously*, London: Duckworth.

Dyer, G. (2003a) 'Taking action to head off its critics', *Financial Times*, 28 November, FT Report, Business and AIDS section: 18.

Dyer, G. (2003b) 'South Africa revives patent drugs issue', *Financial Times*, 17 October, International economy section: 12.

Eaglesham, J. and Tait, N. (2005) 'DTI backs down on bribery rules', *Financial Times*, 14 January: 1.

Eagleton, T. (1996) *The Illusions of Postmodernism*, Oxford: Blackwell.

Eastwood, A. and Maynard, A. (1990) 'Treating Aids. Is it Ethical to be Efficient', in Baldwin, S., Godfrey, C. and Propper, C. (eds), *Quality of Life: Perspectives and Policies*, London: Routledge.

Eco, U. (1985) *Reflections on the Name of the Rose*, London: Secker and Warburg.

Eco, U. with Richard Rorty, Johnathan Culler and Christine Brooke-Rose, ed. Stefan Collini (1992) *Interpretation and Overinterpretation*, Cambridge: Cambridge University Press.

*Economist* (2001) *The Plot Thickens: A Survey of India's Economy*, 2 June.

Eden, C., Jones, S. and Sims, D. (1979) *Thinking in Organisations*, London: Macmillan Press.

Edey, H.C. (1984) 'Company Accounting in the Nineteenth and Twentieth Centuries' in Lee, T.A. and Parker, R.H. (eds), *The Evolution of Corporate Financial Reporting*, New York and London: Garland Publishing Inc. pp. 225–30.

Elkington, J. (1999) 'Triple Bottom Line Reporting: Looking for Balance', *Australian CPA*, March, World Wide Web, http://www.cpaonline.com.au/03_publications/02_aust_cpa_magazine/1999/03_mar/3_2_3_31_reporting.asp. Site visited 12 June 2001.

Elliot, L. (2003) 'Policy made on the road to perdition', *Guardian*, 13 October: 25.

Elliot, L. (2005) 'Oil firms fund campaign to deny climate change', *Guardian*, 27 January: 1.

Elshtain, J.B., Aird, E., Etzioni, A., Galston, W., Glendon, M.A., Minow, M. and Rossi, A. (n.d.) *The Communitarian Network. A Communitarian Position Paper on the Family*, World Wide Web, http://www.gwu.edu/~ccps/pop_fam.html. Site visited 15 November 2001.

Erturk, J., Froud, J., Sukhdev, J. and Williams, C. (2004) *Pay for corporate performance or pay as social division: re-thinking the problem of top management pay in giant corporations*, University of Manchester and Royal Holloway College, London University.

Etzioni, A. (1988) *The Moral Dimension: Towards a New Economics*, New York: The Free Press.

Etzioni, A. (1993) *The Spirit of Community*, New York: Crown.

Evans, R. (2004) 'Hewitt weakened rules against corporate graft', *Guardian*, 23 December: 8.

Evans, S. (2001) 'McDonald's grilled over "veggie" fries', *BBC News Online*, World Wide Web, http://news.bbc.co.uk. Site visited 24 May 2001.

Evans, S. (2005) 'Blow dealt to the "Aw Shucks!" defence', *BBC News Online*, 16 March, World Wide Web, http://news.bbc.co.uk/1/hi/business/4337543.stm. Site visited 17 March 2005.

ExecutiveCaliber (2004) *Parmalat*, World Wide Web, http://executivecaliber.ws/sys-tmp/parmalat/. Site visited 8 February 2005.

Failaka International Inc. (2001) *Glossary of Islamic Financial Terms*, World Wide Web, http://www.failaka.com/Glossary.html. Site visited 20 August 2001.

Farrell, B.J. and Cobbin, D.M. (1996) 'A Content Analysis of Codes of Ethics in Australian Enterprises', *Journal of Managerial Psychology*, 11(1), 37–55.

Festinger, L. (1957) *A Theory of Cognitive Dissonance*, New York: Row Peterson.

*Financial Times* (2000) 'Leading article: Spy trap', *Financial Times*, 22 August.

*Financial Times* (2001) 'Leading article: Changing Track', *Financial Times*, 9 May.

*Financial Times* (2005) 'Leading article: A tale of greed and gullibility', *Financial Times*, 9 April: 10.

Fineman, S. and Gabriel, Y. (1996) *Experiencing Organisations*, London: Sage.

Firestone Tire Resource Center (n.d.), World Wide Web, http://www.citizen.org/fireuf/index7.htm. Site visited 22 May 2001.

Fischer, F. (1983) 'Ethical Discourse in Public Administration', *Administration and Society*, 15(1), 5–42.

Fischoff, B., Slovic, P. and Lichtenstein, S. (1977) 'Knowing with certainty: the appropriateness of extreme confidence', *Journal of Experimental Psychology*, 3(4), 552–64.

Fisher, C. and Lovell, A.T.A. (2000) *Accountant's Responses to Ethical Issues at Work*, London: CIMA Publishing.

Fisher, C.M. (1998) *Resource Allocation in the Public Sector: Values, Priorities, and Markets in the Management of Public Services*, London: Routledge.

Fisher, C.M. (1999) 'Ethical Stances: The Perceptions of Accountants and HR Specialists of Ethical Conundrums at Work', *Business Ethics: A European Review*, 18(4), 236–48.

Fisher, C.M. (2000) 'The ethics of inactivity: human resource managers and Quietism', *Business and Professional Ethics Journal*, 19, 55–72.

Fisher, C.M. (2001) 'Managers' Perceptions of Ethical Codes: Dialectics and Dynamics', *Business Ethics: A European Review*, 10(2), 145–57.

Fisher, C.M. and Rice, C. (1999) 'Managing Messy Moral Matters', in Leopold, J., Harris, L. and Watson, T.J. (1999) *Strategic Human Resources. Principles, Perspectives and Practices*, London: Pearson Education.

Fletcher, J. (1966) *Situation Ethics*, London: SCM Press.

Floodgate, J.F. and Nixon, A.E. (1994) 'Personal development plans: The challenge of implementation – a case study', *Journal of European Industrial Training*, 18(11) 43–7.

Forster, E.M. (1975) *Two Cheers for Democracy*, New York: Holmes & Meier.

Foster, N. (2001) *The Foster Catalogue 2001*, London: Prestel.

Francis, D. and Young, D. (1979) *Improving Work Groups: A Practical Manual for Team Building*, La Jolla, CA: University Associates.

Friedman, J. (1994) *Cultural Identity and Global Process*, London: Sage.

Friedman, M. (1970) 'The Social Responsibility of Business is to Increase its Profits', *The New York Times Magazine*, 13 September, 33, 122–6.

Friends of the Earth – US (1997) *OECD Multilateral Agreement on Investment: Fact Sheet*, World Wide Web, http://www.globalpolicy.org/socecon/bwi-wto/oecd-mai.htm. Site visited 25 January 2005.

Fukuyama, F. (1993) *The End of History and the Last Man*, Harmondsworth: Penguin.

Gabriel, Y., Fineman, S. and Sims, D. (2000) *Organizing & Organizations*, 2nd edition, London: Sage.

Galbraith, J.K. (2004) *The Economics of Innocent Fraud: Truth for Our Time*, Allen Lane: Penguin Books.

Galton, M. and Delafield, A. (1981) 'Expectancy Effects in Primary Classrooms', in Simons, B. and Willcocks, J. (eds) (1981) *Research and Practice in the Primary Classroom*, London: Routledge, Kegan and Paul.

Gamble, P.R. and Kelliher, C.E. (1999) 'Imparting Information and Influencing Behaviour: An Examination of Staff Briefing Sessions', *Journal of Business Communications*, 36(3), 261–80.

Giddens, A. (1984) *The Constitution of Society*, Cambridge: Polity Press.

Giddens, A. (1985) 'Reason Without Revolution? Habermas's Theorie des Kommunikativen Handelns', in Bernstein, R.J. (ed.), *Habermas and Modernity*, Cambridge: Polity Press in association with Oxford: Blackwells.

Gidoomal, R. and Porter, D. (1997) *The UK Maharajahs: Inside the South Asian Success Story*, London: Nicholas Brealey.

Gigerenzer, G., Todd, P. and the ABC Research Group (1999) *Simple Heuristics that Make us Smart*, Oxford: Oxford University Press.

Gilligan, C. (1982) *In a Different Voice: Psychological Theory and Women's Development*, Cambridge, MA: Harvard University Press.

Goffman, E. (1959) *The Presentation of the Self in Everyday Life*, New York: Doubleday Anchor Books.

Gompers, P., Ishii, J. and Metrick, A. (2004) *Incentives vs. Control: An Analysis of U.S. Dual-Class Companies*, NBER Working papers no. 10240, Cambridge, MA: National Bureau of Economic Research.

Gonella, C., Pilling, A. and Zadek, S. (1998) *Making Values Count*, Research Report No. 57 of the Association of Chartered Certified Accountants, London: Certified Accountants Educational Trust.

Goodwin, R.N. (1974). *The American Condition*, New York: Doubleday.

Gopinath, C. (1998) 'Alternative Approaches to Indigenous Management in India', *Management International Review*, 38(3), 257–75.

Gosling, P. (2004) *Accountability in the Public Services*, London: ACCA.

Greenawalt, K. (1987) *Conflicts of Law and Morality*, Oxford: Oxford University Press.

Gregory, M. and Rufford, N. (1994) *Dirty Tricks: Inside Story of British Airways' Secret War Against Richard Branson's Virgin Atlantic*, London: Little Brown.

Greimas, A. (1987) *On Meaning: Selected Writings in Semiotic Theory* (trans. Paul J. Perron & Frank H. Collins), London: Frances Pinter.

Griseri, P. (1998) *Managing Values*, London: Palgrave.

Gross, J. (1987) *Oxford Dictionary of Aphorisms*, Oxford: Oxford University Press.

*Guardian* (1999) 'Leading article: 'Mr Aitken pays the price', *Guardian*, 9 June: 21. *Guardian* and *Observer* on CD-ROM.

*Guardian* (2004a) 'Damned in detail – but let off lightly', *Guardian Unlimited*, 25 August, World Wide Web, http://www.guardian.co.uk/online/news/0,12597,1377968,00.html. Site visited 21 December 2004.

*Guardian* (2004b) 'Solitary part-timer conducted group audit', *Guardian*, 25 August: 22.

Gudex, C. (1986) *QALYs and their Use by the Health Service*, Discussion paper No. 20, Centre for Health Economics, York: Centre for Health Economics, University of York.

Guerrera, F. (2001a) 'Hit squad to tackle animal rights activists', *FT.com*, 27 April.

Guerrera, F. (2001b) 'Huntingdon seeks nominee structure to protect holders', *Financial Times*, 12 May.

Gustafson, A. (2000) 'Making sense of postmodern business ethics', *Business Ethics Quarterly*, 10(3), 645–58.

Haidt, J. (2003) 'The Moral Emotions', in Davidson, R.J., Scherer, K.R. and Goldsmith, H.H. (eds) *Handbook of Affective Sciences*, 852–70, Oxford: Oxford University Press.

Haley, G.T. and Haley, U.C.V. (1998) 'Boxing with Shadows: Competing Effectively with the Overseas Chinese and the Overseas Indian Business Networks in the Asian Arena', *Journal of Organisational Change Management*, 11(4), 301–20.

Harding, L. (1999) 'The fall of Aitken: from Eton and Oxford to the Ritz and the Old Bailey', *Guardian*, 9 June: 4. *Guardian* and *Observer* on CD-ROM.

Harding, L. 'Delhi Schoolboy sparks global porn row', *Guardian Online*, 21 December 2004.

Harrington, M. (1965) *The Accidental Century*, Harmondsworth: Penguin.

Harrington, S. (2003) 'Stringing us along?' in *AccountancyAge.com*, World Wide Web http://www.accountancyage.com/Features/1137242. Site visited 13 September 2004.

Harris, C. and Michaels, A. (2004) 'Shell Board blames crisis on human failings', *FT.com*, 19 April, World Wide Web, http://www.FT.com. Site visited 12 June 2004.

Harris, J.E. and Reynolds, M.A. (1993) 'Formal Codes: The Delineation of Ethical Dilemmas', *Advances in Public Interest Accounting*, 5, 107–20.

Harris, L.C. and Ogbonna, E. (1999) 'Developing a Market Oriented Culture: A Critical Evaluation', *Journal of Management Studies*, 36(2), 177–96.

Hartley, R.E. (1993) *Business Ethics: Violations of the Public Trust*, Chichester: John Wiley & Sons.

Harvey, D. (1989) *The Condition of Postmodernity*, Oxford: Blackwell.

Harzing, A.-W. (2000) 'An empirical test and extension of the Bartlett and Ghoshal typology of multinational companies', *Journal of International Business Studies*, 31(1), 101–20.

Hazlitt, W. (2004) *William Hazlitt on 'The Pleasure of Hating'*, London: Penguin Books.

Heelas, P. and Morris, P. (1992) (eds), *The Values of the Enterprise Culture: The Moral Debate*, London: Routledge.

Hegel, G.W.F. (2003) *The Phenomenology of Mind*, trans. J.B. Baillie, a reprint of the 1910 2nd, revised edition, New York: Dover.

Heidegger, M. (2000) *Introduction to Metaphysics*, trans. G. Fried and R. Polt, Yale: Nota Bene.

Held, D. (1987) *Models of Democracy*, Oxford: Polity Press.

Held, D. and McGrew, A.G. (2000) *The Global transformations reader: An Introduction to the Globalization debate*, Cambridge: Polity Press.

Helson, R. and Wink, P. (1992) 'Personality Change in Women from the Early 40s to the Early 50s', *Psychology and Ageing*, 7(1), March.

Herman, S.M. (1994) *The Tao at Work: On Leading and Following*, San Francisco: Jossey-Bass.

*Hindustan Times* (2004) 'Ambanis told to talk', *The Hindustan Times*, 2 December: 1.

Hirst, P. and Thompson, G. (1996) *Globalisation in Question*, Oxford: Polity Press.

Hobbes, T. (1968) *Leviathan*, Harmondsworth: Penguin.

Hobbes, T. (n.d.) ed. M. Oakeshott, *Leviathan or the Matter, Forme and Power of a Commonwealth Ecclesiastical and Civil*, Oxford: Blackwell.

Hoffman, W.M. and Moore, J.M. (1990) *Business Ethics: Readings and Cases in Corporate Morality*, London: McGraw-Hill.

Hofstede, G.H. (1991) *Cultures and Organisations. Software of the Mind*, London: McGraw-Hill.

Hofstede, G.H. (2001) *Culture's Consequences*, 2nd edition, London: Sage.

Hogarth, R. (1980) *Judgement and Choice*, New York: John Wiley & Sons.

Holden, N.J. (2002) *Cross Cultural Management. A Knowledge Management Perspective*, Harlow: Pearson Education.

Holland, L. and Gibbon, J. (2001) 'Processes in Social and Ethical Accountability: External reporting mechanisms', in Andriof, J. and McIntosh, M. (eds), *Perspectives on Corporate Citizenship*, 278–95, Sheffield: Greenleaf Publishing.

Hollinger International Inc. (n.d.) Hollinger International Inc. home page, World Wide Web, http://www.hollingerinternational.com/. Site visited 15 September 2004.

Hollinshead, G. and Michailova, S. (2001) 'Blockbusters or bridge-builders? The role of western trainers in developing new entrepreneurialism in Eastern Europe', *Management Learning*, 32(4), 419–36.

Home Office (2000) *Reforming the Law on Involuntary Manslaughter*, London: The Home Office.

Hope, C. (2004) 'Shell advised to retreat from Nigeria', *Business Telegraph*, 11 June.

Hopwood, A. (1974) *Accounting and Human Behaviour*, London: Prentice-Hall.

Hosking, P. (2004) 'Ousted Shell chief takes FSA to court', *The Times*, 17 September, Business section: 25.

House of Commons (2004) *The Future of the Railways*, Select Committee on Transport, seventh report, HC 145, London: The Stationery Office, World Wide Web, http://www.guardian.co.uk/business/story/0,3604,821285,00.html. Site visited 3 November 2004.

Hunt, G. (1995) *Whistleblowing in the Health Service: Accountability, Law & Professional Practice*, London: Edward Arnold.

Hunt, G. (1998) *Whistleblowing in the Social Services: Public Accountability and Professional Practice*, London: Edward Arnold.

Husserl, E. (1931) *Ideas: General Introduction to Pure Phenomenology*, trans. W.R. Boyce-Gibson, London: George Allen & Unwin.

Husserl, E. (1965) *Phenomenology and the Crisis of Philosophy: Philosophy as Religious Science and Philosophy and the Crisis of European Man*, trans. Q. Lauer, New York: Harper Torchbooks, Harper & Row.

Ibeanu, O. (2000) 'Oiling the friction: Environmental Conflict Management in the Niger Delta, Nigeria', *Environmental Change and Security Project Report*, Issue 6, Summer.

IBFAN (International Baby Food Action Network) (n.d.) *How Breast Feeding is Undermined*, World Wide Web, http://www.ibfan.org/english/issue/bfundermined01.html. Site visited 17 February 2002.

Independent Police Complaints Commission (IPCC) (2004) *IPCC decision on Superintendent Dizaei*, World Wide Web, http://wwwipcc.gov.uk/news/pr160604_dizaei. Site visited 8 February 2005.

International Chamber of Commerce (ICC) (1997) *International Code of Advertising Practice*, World Wide Web, http://www.iccwbo.org/home/statements_rules/rules/1997/advercod.asp. Site visited 13 March 2002.

International Labour Organisation (ILO) (2004) *Codes of Conduct for Multinationals*, World Wide Web, http://www.itcilo.it/english/actrav/telearn/global/ilo/guide/main.htm. Site visited 17 February 2002.

Investor Responsibility Research Centre (IRRC) (2004) *Investigation of governance at Hollinger reveals 'corporate kleptocracy'*, IRRC news item 10 September 2004, World Wide Web, http://www.irrc.org/index.html. Site visited 15 September 2004.

IRC (International Relations Centre) (1998) *The Fair Trade Movement: Making Commerce Work for the Poor Majority*, Bulletin No. 50, World Wide Web, http://www.irc-online.org/content/bulletin/bull50.php. Site visited 22 December 2004.

Jackall, R. (1988) *Moral Mazes: The World of Corporate Managers*, New York: Oxford University Press.

Jaeger, A.M. and Kanungo, R.N. (eds) (1990) *Management in Developing Countries*, London: Routledge.

Jankowicz, A.D. and Dobosz-Bourne, D. (2003) 'How are meanings negotiated? Commonality, sociality, and the travel of ideas', in Scheer, J. (ed.), *Crossing Borders, Going Places*, Giessen: Fischer-Verlag.

John Paul II (1991) *Centesimus Annus: Encyclical Letter of the Supreme Pontiff John Paul II on the One Hundredth Anniversary of Rerum Novarum*, World Wide Web, http://listserv.american.edu/catholic/church/papal/jp.ii/jp2hundr.txt. Site visited 11 June 2001.

Johnson, G. (1994) *University Politics*, Cambridge: Cambridge University Press.

Johnson and Johnson (n.d.) *Our Company, Our Credo*, World Wide Web, http://www.jnj.com/our_company/index.htm. Site visited 2 December 2004.

Jones, J.E. and Pfeiffer, J.W. (eds) (1974) *The 1974 Handbook for Group Facilitators*, Iowa City: University Associates.

Jonsen, A. and Toulmin, S. (1988) *The Abuse of Casuistry*, Berkeley: University of California Press.

Jos, P.H. (1988) 'Moral autonomy and the modern organisation', *Polity: The Journal of the North-Eastern Political Science Association*, XXI(2), Winter.

Joyce, J. (1996) *Portrait of the Artist as a Young Man*, London: Penguin.

Jung, C.G. (1953) *Psychological Reflections, An Anthology of the Writings of C.G. Jung*, J. Jacobi (ed.), London: Kegan Paul.

Kahneman, D., Slovic, P. and Tversky, A. (eds) (1982) *Judgement under Uncertainty: Heuristics and Biases*, Cambridge: Cambridge University Press.

Kaler, J. (1999) 'What's the good of ethical theory?' *Business Ethics – A European Review*, 8(4), 206–13.

Kanungo, R.N. and Mendonca, M. (1996) *Ethical Dimensions of Leadership*, London: Sage.

Kapner, F. and Minder, R. (2004) 'Police arrest three more of the Tanzi family', *Financial Times*, 18 February, Companies International section: 28.

Kapner, F. (2004a) 'A hole dug over 30 years', *Financial Times*, 20 February, Companies section: 26.

Kapner, F. (2004b) 'Fast-track Parmalat trial rejected', *Financial Times*, 25 March, Companies section: 30.

Kärreman, D. and Alvesson, M. (1999) 'Ethical Closure in Organisational Settings – the Case of Media Organisations', paper presented at the 15th EGOS Colloquium, *Organisations in a Challenging World: Theories, Practices and Societies*, The University of Warwick, 4–6 July.

Keats, R. (1993) 'The Moral Boundaries of the Market', in Crouch, C. and Marquand, D. (eds), *Ethics and Markets: Co-operation and Competition within Capitalist Economies*, 6–20, Oxford: Blackwell Publishers.

Keay, J. (2000) *India: A History*, London: HarperCollins.

Kell, G. (2004) *Gearing Up: From corporate responsibility to good governance and scalable solutions* in SustainAbility, New York: UN Global Compact.

Kelman, H. (1961) 'The Process of Opinion Change', *Public Opinion*, 25, 57–78.

Kemm, J.R. (1985) 'Ethics of Food Policy', *Community Medicine*, 7, 289–94.

Kerr, C., Dunlop, T.J., Harbison, F. and Myers, C.A. (1960) *Industrialism and Industrial Man*, Cambridge, MA: Harvard University Press.

King Committee on Corporate Governance (2002), Institute of Directors, South Africa.

King, C. (2001) 'Providing Advice on Whistleblowing', in Lewis, D.B. (ed.), *Whistleblowing at Work*, London: The Athlone Press.

Kirchenbaum, H. (1977) *Advanced Value Clarification*, La Jolla, CA: University Associates.

Kirk, G.S. (1974) *The Nature of the Greek Myths*, Harmondsworth: Penguin.

Kirkpatrick, J. (1994) *In Defense of Advertising: Arguments from Reason, Ethical Egoism and Laissez-Faire Capitalism*, Westport: Greenwood.

Kjonstad, B. and Willmott, H. (1995) 'Business Ethics: Restrictive or Empowering', *Journal of Business Ethics*, 14, 445–64.

Klein, N. (2000) *No Logo*, London: Flamingo.

Kleveman, L. (2003) *The New Great Game. Blood and Oil in Central Asia*, London: Atlantic Books.

Knights, D. and Willmott, H. (1999) *Management Lives: Power and Identity in Work Organizations*, London: Sage.

Koehn, D. (1994) *The Ground of Professional Ethics*, London: Routledge.

Kohlberg, L. (1969) *Stages in the Development of Moral Thought and Action*, New York: Holt Rinehart and Winston.

Kohlberg, L. (1984) *Essays in Moral Development, Volume 2, The Psychology of Moral Development*, New York: Harper and Row.

Koretz, G. (2001) 'Why Americans work so hard. How pay inequality galvanizes effort', *Business Week*, issue 3736, 6 November.

Kumar, N.S. and Rao, U.S. (1996) 'Guidelines for Value Based Management in Kautilya's Arthashastra', *Journal of Business Ethics*, 15(4), 415.

Lambur, M., Rajgopal, R., Lewis, E., Cox, R. and Ellerbrock, M. (2003) *Applying Cost benefit Analysis to Nutrition Education Programs: Focus on the Virginia Expanded Food and Nutrition Education Program*, Virginia Cooperative Extension, publication no. 490–403, World Wide Web, http://www.ext.vt.edu/pubs/nutrition/490-403/490-403.html. Site visited 2 March 2005.

Lane, J.-E. (1995) *The Public Sector. Concepts, Models and Approaches*, 2nd edition, London: Sage.

Lariba.com (2001) *Lariba Concept*, World Wide Web, http://www.lariba.com/concepts.shtn. Site visited 20 August 2001.

Larson, M.S. (1977) *The Rise of Professionalism: A Sociological Analysis*, Berkeley, CA: University of California Press.

Lee, T.A. (1984) 'Company Financial Statements: An Essay in Business History 1890–1950' in Lee, T.A. and Parker, R.H., (eds), *The Evolution of Corporate Finanacial Reporting*, New York and London: Garland Publishing Inc., pp. 15–29.

Legge, K. (1995) *Human Resource Management: Rhetoric and Realities*, London: Macmillan.

Legge, K. (1998) 'Is HRM Ethical? Can HRM be Ethical?' in Parker, M. (ed.), *Ethics & Organisations*, 150–72, London: Sage.

Lenke, S. and Davies, G. (1995) 'Cultural, social and organizational transitions: the consequences for the Hungarian manager', *Journal of Management Development*, 14(10), 14–31.

Lessnoff, M. (1986) *Social Contract*, London: Macmillan.

Levitt, T. (1956) 'The Lonely Crowd and the Economic Man', *Quarterly Journal of Economics*, February: 109.

Lewis, D. (2001) *The Management of Non-Governmental Development Organisations*, London: Routledge.

Lewis, D. B. (2000) *Whistleblowing at Work*, London: The Athlone Press.

Liedtka, J. (1991) 'Organisational Value Contention and Managerial Mindsets', *Journal of Business Ethics*, 10, 543–57.

Lindblom, C.E. (1977), *Politics and Markets: The World's Political-Economic Systems*, New York: Basic Books Inc.

Locke, J. (1952) *The Second Treatise of Government*, The Library of Liberal Arts.

Lookatch, R.P. (1991) 'HRD's failure to sell itself', *Training and Development*, 45(7), July, 47–50.

Lovell, A.T.A. (2002) 'The vulnerability of autonomy that denies the exercise of moral agency', *Business Ethics: A European Review*, 11(1), 62–76.

Lovell, A.T.A. and Robertson, C. (1994), 'Charles Robertson: In the Eye of the Storm', in Vinten, G. (ed.), *Whistleblowers*, 146–73, London: Chapman and Hall.

Lundberg, M. and Squire, L. (2003) 'The Simultaneous Evolution of Growth and Inequality', *Economic Journal*, 113, 326–44.

Lyons, D. (1984) *Ethics and the Rule of Law,* Cambridge: Cambridge University Press.

Lyotard, J.-F. (1988) *Le Postmodernisme Expliqué aux Enfants, Correspondance 1982–85*, Paris: Editions Galilée.

Mabbott, J.D. (1967) *The State and the Citizen*, 2nd edition, London: Hutchinson and Co.

Machiavelli, N. (1950) *The Prince and the Discourses*, introd. by M. Lerner, New York: Modern Library.

MacIntyre, A. (1967) *A Short History of Ethics: A History of Moral Philosophy from the Homeric Age to the Twentieth Century*, London: Routledge.

MacIntyre, A. (1987) *After Virtue: A Study in Moral Theory*, London: Duckworth.

Mackie, J.L. (1990) *Ethics: Inventing Right and Wrong*, Harmondsworth: Penguin.

Maclagan, P. (1996) 'The organisational context for moral development: questions of power and access', *Journal of Business Ethics*, 15(6), 645–54.

Maclagan, P. (1998) *Management & Morality*, London: Sage.

Maclagan, P. and Snell, R. (1992) 'Some Implications for Management Development of Research into Managers' Moral Dilemmas', *British Journal of Management*, 3, 157–68.

Maguire, K. (2000) 'Clarke admits BAT link to smuggling', *Guardian Unlimited*, 3 February, World Wide Web, http://www.newsunlimited.co.uk/bat/article/0,2763,131957,00.html. Site visited 24 August 2001.

Mahesh, V.S. (1995) *Thresholds of Motivation*, New Delhi: Tata McGraw Hill.

Mahoney, J. (1990) *Teaching Business Ethics in the UK, Europe and the USA: A Comparative Study*, London: The Athlone Press.

Malhiason, N. (2004) 'BP's pipeline to nowhere: Georgia halts oil giant's $2.4b project', *The Observer*, 25 July.

Marchington, M., Parker, P. and Prestwich, A. (1989) 'Problems with Team Briefing in Practice', *Employee Relations*, 11(4), 21–30.

Marcuse, A.H. (1991) *One-Dimensional Man*, 2nd edition, London: Routledge.

Marx, K. (1963) *The Eighteenth Brumaire of Louis Bonaparte*, first published 1852, International Publishers.

Marx, K. and Engels, F. (1962) 'Critique of the Gotha Programme' in *Selected Works*, vol. II, Moscow: Progress Publishers.

Maslow, A.H. (1987) *Motivation and Personality*, 3rd edition, New York: Harper Collins.

Mathews, M.C. (1988) *Strategic Intervention in Organizations*, Sage Library of Social Research, No. 169, London: Sage.

Matthews, J.B., Goodpaster, K.E. and Nash, L.I. (1991) *Policies and Person: A Casebook in Business Ethics*, 2nd edition, London: McGraw-Hill.

May, B. (2005) 'Under-informed, over here', 'Life', *Guardian*, 10.

McCornack, S.A., Levine, T.R., Solowczuk, H.I., Torres, H.I. and Campbell, D.M. (1992) 'When the alteration of Information is viewed as deception: an empirical test of information manipulation theory', *Communication Monographs*, 59, 17–29.

McDonald, G. and Nijhof, A. (1999) 'Beyond codes of ethics: an integrated framework for stimulating morally responsible behaviour in organisations', *Leadership & Organisation Development Journal*, 20(3), 133–46.

McGreal, C. (2001) 'Crucial drug case opens in Pretoria', *Guardian*, 6 March: 17.

McIntosh, M., Thomas, R., Leipziger, D. and Coleman, G. (2003) *Living Corporate Citizenship. Strategic Routes to socially responsible business*, Harlow: FT Prentice Hall.

McKinley, A. and Starkey, K. (1998) *Foucault, Management and Organization Theory: From Panopticon to Technologies of Self*, London: Sage.

McLuhan, M. and Powers, B.R. (1989) *The Global Village. Transformations in World Life and Media in the Twentieth Century*, Oxford: Oxford University Press.

McMylor, P. (1994) *Alisdair MacIntyre: Critic of Modernity*, London: Routledge.

Meade, J.E. (1973) *Theory of Economic Externalities: The Control of Environmental Pollution and Similar Social Costs*, Leiden: Sijhoff.

Meikle, J. (2001) 'Professor quits over tobacco firm's £3.8m gift to university', *Guardian*, 18 May: 6.

Meirovich, G. and Reichel, A. (2000) 'Illegal but ethical: an inquiry into the roots of illegal corporate behaviour in Russia', *Business Ethics: A European Review*, 9(3), 126–35.

Miceli, M.P. and Near, J.P. (1992) *Blowing the Whistle: The Organisational & Legal Implications for Companies and Employees*, New York: Lexington Books.

Michaels, A. (2001) 'Inside Track: Big pharma and the golden goose: interview Hank Mckinnell, Pfizer: Cheaper drugs would mean less money to spend on research and innovation, Pfizer's chief tells Adrian Michaels', *Financial Times*, 26 April.

Mihil, C. (1990) 'Thatcher shuns out of court deal for haemophiliacs with HIV', *Guardian*, 9 November: 2.

Mill, J.S., (1971) *Utilitarianism*, Harmondsworth: Penguin (reprint of 1861 edition).

Mill, J.S. (1998) *On Liberty and other Essays*, ed. John Gray, Oxford: Oxford University Press.

Milmo, C. (2001) 'Watchdog warns Virgin over misleading adverts', *Independent*, 30 May.

Minnesota Center for Corporate Responsibility (2001) *The Global Sullivan Principles*, World Wide Web, http://tigger.stthomas.edu.mcer/SullivanPrinciples.htm. Site visited 26 October 2001.

Mokhiber, R. (1998) 'The Death Penalty for Corporations Comes of Age', *Business Ethics*, 12, November–December.

Monks, R.A.G. (2003) 'Equity Culture at Risk: the threat to Anglo-American prosperity', *Corporate Governance: An International Review*, 11(3), July, 164–70.

Moon, C.J. (2003) 'ENRON: economics and ethics', Proceedings of the 7th EBEN-UK Annual Conference *The Challenge of Business Ethics*, Selwyn College, Cambridge, 7–8 April.

Moore, G. (2001) 'Corporate social and financial performance: an investigation in the UK supermarket industry', *Journal of Business Ethics*, 34(3, 4), 299–315.

Moore, G. (2003) 'Hives and horseshoes, Mintzberg or MacIntyre: what future for corporate and social responsibility?', *Business Ethics: A European Review*, 12(1), 41–53.

Moore, G. and Robson, A. (2002) 'The UK supermarket industry: an analysis of corporate social and financial performance', *Business Ethics: A European Review*, 11(1), 25–39.

Moore, O. (2000) 'Day of peace plea to sugar factory', *Great Yarmouth Mercury*, 7 July.

Moray Sustainability Forum (2005) *Moray Sustainability Forum: The Rough Guide to Moray's Future*, Keith, Banffshire: Moray Sustainability Forum.

Morgan, O. (2004) 'Dutch helm disease gets blame at Shell', *Observer*, 25 April.

Mortished, C. (2004) 'Deutsche Bank attacks Yukos court protection', *The Times, Business section*, 30 December: 43.

Mounce, H.O. (1997) *The Two Pragmatisms: from Peirce to Rorty*, London: Routledge.

Murphy, L.B. (2001) *Moral Demands in Non-ideal Theory*, Oxford: Oxford University Press.

Myers, A. and Dehn, G. (2000) *Whistleblowing: The first cases and practical issues*, World Wide Web, http://www.pcaw.co.uk/news/press/_14.html. Site visited 17 February 2002.

NICE (National Institute for Clinical Excellence) (2001) *Interferon Beta/glatiramer Speculation*, World Wide Web, http://www.nice.org.uk/nice-web/rticle.asp?a=1370. Site visited 23 May 2001.

NICE (National Institute for Clinical Excellence) (2002) *NICE issues guidance on drugs for multiple sclerosis*, World Wide Web, http://www.nice.org.uk/article.asp?a=27619. Site visited 7 March 2002.

Niebuhr, R. (1932) *Moral Man and Immoral Society*, New York: C. Scribner.

Nisbet, R.A. (1953) *The Quest for Community*, Oxford: Oxford University Press.

Nolan Committee (1995) *Standards in Public Life, Volume 1. First Report of the Committee on Standards in Public Life*, London: HMSO.

Nozick, R. (1974) *Anarchy, State, and Utopia*, New York: Basic Books.

Oberman, W.D. (2000) Book review of Mitchell: 'The Conspicuous Corporation', (1997) *Business and Society*, 329(2), 239–44.

*Observer* (2000) Leader article 'The mob should never rule', *Observer*, 17 September.

*Observer* (2001) 'Beware – you've got mail', *Observer*, 7 January, World Wide Web, at *Guardian Unlimited*, http://www.guardian.co.uk/freespeech/article/0,2763,418935,00.html. Site visited 18 March 2004.

*Observer* (2004) 'Noble gesture', *Observer*, 2 September.

OECD (Organisation for Economic Co-operation and Development) (2000) *The OECD Guidelines for Multi-national Enterprises*, World Wide Web, http://www1.oecd.org/daf/ investment/guidelines/mnetext.htm#6. Site visited 12 December 2001.

Ojefia, I.A. (n.d.) 'The Nigerian State and the Niger Question' *22nd Annual Conference of the Association of Third World Studies*, Americus, Georgia. Paper available on the World Wide Web, http://www.deltastate.gov.ng/oyefia.htm. Site visited 17 December 2004.

Pagels, E. (1982) *The Gnostic Gospels*, Harmondsworth: Penguin.

Paris, G.A., Savage, G.W. and Seitz, G.H. (2004) *Report of the Investigation by the Special Committee of the Board of Directors of Hollinger International Inc. (The Breeden report)*, Washington DC: US Securities and Exchange Commission. Available on the World Wide Web, http://www.sec.gov/Archives/edgar/data/868512/000095012304010413/y01437exv99w2.htm. Site visited 16 September 2004.

Parker, A. (2004) 'Audit team had "lack of warnings": Hollinger Inquiry', *Financial Times*, 2 September: 28.

Parker, M. (1998a) 'Business Ethics and Social Theory: Postmodernizing the Ethical', *British Journal of Management*, 9, September: 27–36.

Parker, M. (1998b) 'Against Ethics', in Parker, M. (ed.), *Ethics & Organisations*, London: Sage.

Parsons, T. (1999) 'The traditional square of opposition', *The Stanford Encyclopedia of Philosophy (Spring 1999 Edition)*, Zalta, Edward N. (ed.), World Wide Web, http://plato.stanford.edu/archives/spr1999/entries/square/. Site visited 25 October 2003.

Passmore, J. (1984) 'Academic Ethics', *Journal of Applied Philosophy*, 1(1).

Pateman, C. (1985) *The Problem of Political Obligation: A Critique of Liberal Theory*, New York: John Wiley & Sons.

Pava, M.L. (1999) *The Search for Meaning in Organisations: Seven Practical Questions for Ethical Managers*, Westport: Quorum Books.

Pereira, J. (1989) *What does Equity in Health Mean?* Centre for Health Economics, Discussion paper No. 61, York: Centre for Health Economics.

Peters, T.J. and Waterman Jnr, R. (1982) *In Search of Excellence*, New York: Harper Row.

Petrick, J.A. (2000) 'Global human resource management competence and judgement integrity: towards a human centred organisation, paper presented at Third Conference on Ethics and Human Resource Management, Towards a Human Centred Organisation, Imperial College, London, 7 June.

Petrick, J.A. and Quinn, J.F. (1997) *Management Ethics. Integrity at Work*, London: Sage.

Pilger, J. (2001) 'Spoils of a massacre', *Guardian Weekend*, 14 July: 18–29.

Pilling, D. and Timmins, N. (2000) 'Medicines arbiter delays decision on beta-interferon clinical excellence. Multiple Sclerosis Society angry that drug ruling is only likely after election', *Financial Times*, 23 December.

Planet Ark (2004) 'Shell says it unwittingly fed conflict in Nigeria', World Wide Web, http://www.planetark.com/avantgo/dailynewsstory.cfm?newsid=25486. Site visited 1 November 2004.

Plant, R. (1992) 'Enterprise in its place: the moral limits of markets', in Heelas, P. and Morris, P. (eds) *The Values of the Enterprise Culture: The Moral Debate*, Routledge, 85–99.

Plender, J. (2004) 'The insidious charms of Shell's dual votes: But just one factor in the foul up', *Financial Times*, 21 June: 22.

Pojman, L.P. (1998) *Classics of Philosophy*, Oxford: Oxford University Press.

Pollitt, M. and Ashworth, H. (2000) 'Beet lorry victory for villages', *Eastern Daily Press*, 21 July: 63–77.

Porter, M. and Kramer, M.R. (2002) 'The Competitive Advantage of Corporate Philanthropy', *Harvard Business Review*, December, 56–68.

Preston, L. and O'Bannon, D. (1997) 'The corporate social-financial performance relationship. A typology and analysis', *Business and Society*, 36(4), 419–29.

Preuss, L. (1999) 'Ethical theory in German business ethics research', *Journal of Business Ethics*, 18, 407–19.

Proctor, E.K., Morrow-Howell, N. and Lott, C.L. (1993) 'Classification and Correlates of Ethical Dilemmas in Hospital Social Work', *Social Work*, 38(2), 166–77.

Project Management Profession (1996) *Code of Ethics for the Project Management Profession*, World Wide Web, http://www.pmi.orh/pmi/mem_info/pmpcode.htm.

Pusey, M. (1987) *Jürgen Habermas*, London: Routledge.

Ramesh, R. (2004) 'Bhopal is still suffering, 20 years on', *Guardian*, 29 November, available at *Guardian Unlimited*, World Wide Web, http://www.guardian.co.uk/international/story/0,,1361551,00.html. Site visited 25 Jannuary 2005.

Rangarajan, L.N. (ed.) (1992) *Kautilya: The Arthrashastra*, New Delhi: Penguin Books India.

Rao, E.M. (2000) 'Human Resource Management: The Road to neo-Taylorism in Management Thought', in Saini, D.S. and Khan, S.A. (eds), *Human Resource Management. Perspectives for a new era*, New Delhi: Response Books, Sage.

Raphael, D.D. (1970) *Problems of Political Philosophy*, London: Methuen.

Ravallion, M. (2004) *Looking beyond Averages in the Trade and Poverty debate*, World Bank Policy Research working paper 3461, Washington DC: World Bank Development Research Group.

Ravallion, M. and Chen, S. (2004) *China's (Uneven) Progress against Poverty*, Policy Research Working paper 3408, Washington DC: World Bank, World Wide Web, http://econ.worldbank.org/files/38741_wps3408.pdf. Site visited 10 January 2005.

Rawls, J. (1971) *A Theory of Justice*, Cambridge, MA: Harvard University Press.

Rawls, J. (1999) *A Theory of Justice* (revised edition), Cambridge, MA: Harvard University Press.

Redclift, M.R. (1984) *Development and the Environmental Crisis: Red or Green Alternatives?*, London: Methuen.

Redclift, M.R. (1987) *Sustainable Development: Exploring the Contradicitons*, London: Routledge.

Redfern Report (2001) *The Royal Liverpool Children's Hospital Report*, House of Commons Parliamentary Papers, World Wide Web, http://www.rlcinquiry.org.uk/.

Rees-Mogg, W. (2004) 'Not quite as Black as he's been painted', *Mail on Sunday*, 5 September: 59.

Reitaku Centre for Economic Studies (1999) *Ethics Compliance Management Systems. ECS 2000. Ethics Compliance Standard*, Reitaku Centre for Economic Studies, World Wide Web, http://www.ie.reitakuu.ac.jp/~davis/assets/applets/ecs2k-e.pdf. Site visited 12 December 2004.

Ritzer, G. (1993) *The McDonaldization of Society*, California: Sage.

Robins, J. (2004) 'Should business bat for apartheid?', *The Times, Law section*, 28 September: 5.

Rokeach, M. (1973) *The Nature of Human Values*, New York: The Free Press.

Rorty, R. (1985) 'Habermas & Lyotard on postmodernity', in Bernstein, R. (ed.), *Habermas and Modernity*, Cambridge: Cambridge University Press.

Rorty, R. (1989) *Contingency, Irony and Solidarity*, Cambridge: Cambridge University Press.

Rorty, R. (1990) *Philosophy and the Mirror of Nature*, Oxford: Blackwell.

Rorty, R. (1992) 'The Pragmatist's Progress', in Eco, U. with Richard Rorty, Johnathan Culler and Christine Brooke-Rose, ed. Stefan Collini (1992) *Interpretation and Overinterpretation*, Cambridge: Cambridge University Press.

Ross, W.D. (1930) *The Right and the Good*, Oxford: Oxford University Press.

Rotter, J.B. (1966) 'General Expectancies for Internal versus External Control of Reinforcement', *Psychological Monographs; General and Applied*, 80, 1–28.

Rousseau, J.-J. (1913) *The Social Contract*, London: J.M. Dent & Sons Ltd.

Royle, T. (2000) *Working for McDonald's in Europe: The Unequal Struggle?*, London: Routledge.

Rubin, S. (2004) 'Hollinger trial to test dual-class structures', *National Post*, 18 February.

Russell, J.B. (1985) *The Devil in the Middle Ages*, Cornell: Cornell University Press.

Russell, J. (2005) 'The glue is coming unstuck', *Guardian*, 23 April: 20.

Sahay, S. and Walsham, G. (1997) 'Social structure and managerial agency in India', *Organisation Studies*, 18(3), 414–44.

Said, E.W. (1978) *Orientalism*, London: Routledge, Kegan Paul.

Saini, D.S. and Khan, S.A. (eds) (2000) *Human Resource Management: Perspectives for the New Era*, New Delhi: Sage.

Sarason, S.B. (1986) 'And what is the public interest?' *American Psychologist*, August.

Sartre, J.-P. (1957) *Existentialism and Human Emotions*, trans. B. Frechtman, New York: Philosophical Library.

Sawyer, G.C. (1978) *Business and Society: Managing Corporate Social Impact*, Boston, MA: Houghton Mifflin.

Schein, E.H. (1985) *Career Anchors: Discovering Your Real Values*, San Diego, CA: University Associates.

Schein, E. (1992), *Organizational Culture and Leadership*, San Francisco: Jossey-Bass.

Schein, E. (1993) *Career Anchors: Discovering your Real Values*, revised edition, San Diego: Pfeiffer.

Schell, J. (1982) *The Fate of the Earth*, Picador, in association with Jonathan Cape.

Scholte, J.A. (2000) *Globalisation: A critical introduction*, London: Palgrave.

Schreier, M. and Groeben, N. (1996) 'Ethical Guidelines for the Conduct in Argumentative Discussions: An Exploratory Study', *Human Relations*, 49(1), 123–32.

Schwartz, M. (1998) 'Peter Drucker and the denial of business ethics', *Journal of Business Ethics*, 17(15), 1685–92.

Scruton, R. (2000) *Animal Rights and Wrongs*, 3rd edition, London: Metro.

Seedhouse, D. (1988) *Ethics: The Heart of Healthcare*, London: John Wiley & Sons.

Senge, P.M. (1990) *The Fifth Discipline. The Art and Practice of the Learning Organisation*, London: Century.

Seymour, L. (2003) 'Talisman is out... What now?' *Review: The North-South Institute Biannual Newsletter*, Winter 2002–2003: 5, World Wide Web, http://www.nsi-ins.ca/english/pdf/review_winter_2002.pdf. Site visited 6 April 2005.

Shaw, W.H. and Barry, V. (1998) *Moral Issues in Business*, 7th edition, Belmont, CA: Wadsworth Publishing Company.

Shell Group (2004) *Notes to corporate governance arrangements, Shell Annual Report 2003*, World Wide Web, http://www.shell.com/html/investor-en/reports2003/st/g/g8.html. Site visited 13 September 2004.

Showalter, E. (1997) *Hystories: Hysterical Epidemics and Modern Culture*, New York: Columbia University Press.

Silk, C. (1999) 'Why did Kitty Genovese die?', *The Navigator. An Objectivist review of Politics and Culture*, World Wide Web, http://www.objectivistcenter.org/navigator/articles/nav+silk_why-kitty-genovese-die. Site visited 8 March 2005.

Simon, H.A. (1952) 'Comments on the Theory of Organizations', *American Political Science Review*, 46, 1130–39.

Simon, H.A. (1953) 'Notes on the Observation and Measurement of Political Power', *Journal of Politics*, 15, 500–16.

Simon, H.A. (1955) 'A Behavioural Model of Rational Choice', *Quarterly Journal of Economics*, 69, 99–118.

Simon, H.A. (1983) *Reason in Human Affairs*, Oxford: Basil Blackwell.

Simpson, D. (2005) 'Caring big business or a wolf in sheep's clothing?', *Online Opinion* (email journal), World Wide Web, http://www.onlineopinion.com.au/print.asp?article=2913. Site visited 17 January 2005.

Sinclair, A. (1993) 'Approaches to Organisational Culture and Ethics', *Journal of Business Ethics*, 12, 63–73.

Singer, P. (1983) *Hegel*, Oxford: Oxford University Press.

Singh, J.P. (1990) 'Managerial Culture and Work-related Values in India', *Organisation Studies*, 11(1), 75–101.

Skapinker, M. (1998) 'BA says sorry to Branson', *Financial Times*, 17 May.

Skapinker, M. (2001) 'Michael Skapinker examines the issues raised by Luc Vandevelde's recent decision to turn down a generous pay bonus', *FT.com*, 4 May, World Wide Web, FT.com. Site visited 23 June 2004.

Skinner, A.S. and Wilson, T. (1975). *Essays on Adam Smith*, Oxford: Clarendon Press.

Sklair, L. (1995) *Sociology of the Global System: Social Change in Global Perspective*, Hemel Hempstead: Harvester Wheatsheaf.

Slapper, G. and Tombs, S. (1999) *Corporate Crime*, London: Longman.

Sloan, K. and Burnett, A. (2004) *Enlightenment: Discovering the World in the Eighteenth Century*, London: British Museum Press.

Smircich, L. (1983) 'Concepts of Culture and Organisational Analysis', *Administrative Science Quarterly*, 28, 339–58.

Smith, A., 1776/1982, *An Inquiry into the Nature and Causes of the Wealth of Nations*, with an introduction by Skinner, A., London: Penguin Books.

Smith, A. (2000) *The Theory of Moral Sentiments* (originally published 1799), New York: Prometheus Books.

Smith, M. (1977) *A Practical Guide to Value Clarification*, La Jolla, CA: University Associates.

Snell, R.S. (1993) *Developing Skills for Ethical Management*, London: Chapman and Hall.

Snell, R.S. (2000) 'Studying Moral Ethos Using an Adapted Kohlbergian Model', *Organisation Studies*, 21(1), 267–95.

Soeken, K. and Soeken, D. (1987) *A Survey of Whistleblowers: Their Stresses and Coping Strategies*, Laurel, MD: Association of Mental Health Specialties.

Sokal, A. and Bricmont, J. (2003) *Intellectual Impostures*, London: Profile Books.

Solomon, R.C. (1993) *Ethics and Excellence: Cooperation and Integrity in Business*, Oxford: Oxford University Press.

Spaemann, R. (1989) *Basic Moral Concepts*, trans. T.J. Armstrong, London: Routledge.

SpeakersUK (2005) *home page*, World Wide Web, http://speakers-uk.com/. Site visited 15 February 2005.

Spurlock, M. (2004) *Super Size Me*, film, Samuel Goldwyn Films.

Srivastva, S. and Cooperrider, D.L. (1988) 'The Urgency for Executive Integrity' in Srivastva, S. (ed.), *Executive Integrity: The Search for High Human Values in Organisational Life*, 1–28, San Francisco: Jossey-Bass.

Starzl, T.W. and Dhir, K.S. (1986) 'Strategic planning 2,300 years ago', *Management International Review*, 26(4), 70–8.

Sterman, J.D. and Sweeney, L.B. (2002) 'Cloudy Skies: Assessing Public Understanding of Global Warming', *Systems Dynamic Review*, 18(2).

Sternberg, E. (1996) 'A Vindication of Whistleblowing in Business', in Brindle, M. and Dehn, G., *Four Windows on Whistleblowing*, 24–39, London: Public Concern at Work.

Sternberg, E. (2000) *Just Business: Business Ethics in Action*, 2nd edition, Oxford: Oxford University Press.

Stevens, B. (1994) 'An Analysis of Corporate Ethical Code Studies: "Where Do We Go From Here?"', *Journal of Business Ethics*, 13, 63–9.

Stewart, D.W. (1984) 'Managing Competing Claims: An Ethical Framework for Human Resource Decision Making', *Public Administration Review*, 44(1), January/February, 14–22.

Stiglitz, J. (2004) *Globalisation and its Discontents*, London: Penguin.

Stokes, E. (1959) *The English Utilitarians and India*, Oxford: The Clarendon Press.

Stylianou, A.C., Winter, S. and Giacalone, R.A. (2004) 'Accepting unethical information practices: the interactive effects of individual and situational factors', paper presented at the *Academy of Management Conference: OCIS division*, New Orleans, August.

SustainAbility (2004) *Gearing Up: From corporate responsibility to good governance and scalable solutions*, New York: UN Global Compact.

Tait, N. (2003) 'Cleared police chief accuses Met of witch-hunt', *Financial Times*, 16 September: 5.

Taki (2004) 'A publisher and a gentleman', *The American Conservative*, 15 March.

Tawney, R.H. (1966) *Religion and the Rise of Capitalism*, Harmondsworth: Penguin.

Taylor, C. (2001) 'How to be diverse. The need for a "looser" us to accommodate "them"', *Times Literary Supplement*, No. 5116, 20 April: 4.

Taylor, D. (2001) 'E-mail: good, bad and ugly', *Computer Weekly*, 8 March.

Tencatti, A., Perrini, F. and Pougtz, S. (2003) 'New Tools to foster corporate socially responsible behaviour', *European Business Ethics network – 16th Annual Conference*, Budapest, 29–31 August, World Wide Web, http://ethics.bkae.hu/html/documents/Tencattietalpapernew.doc. Site visited 9 December 2004.

Terry, M. (1975) 'The Inevitable Growth of Informality', *British Journal of Industrial Relations*, 1(3), 76–90.

Tester, K. (1991) *Animals and Society: The Humanity of Animal Rights*, London: Routledge.

Texas Instruments (1999) *Ethics in the Global Market*, World Wide Web, http://www.ti.com/corp/docs/company/citizen/ethics/market.shtn. Site visited 12 November 1999.

Texas Instruments (2001) *The TI Ethics Quick Test*, World Wide Web, http://www.ti.com/corp/docs/company/citizen/ethics/quicktest.shtml. Site visited 19 November 2001.

The Cabinet Office (2004) *The Civil Service Code*, World Wide Web, http://www.cabinetoffice.gov.uk/propriety_and_ethics/civil_service/civil_service_code.asp. Site visited 2 December 2004.

The Corner House and 14 other NGOs (2003) *Review of the Environmental Impact Assessment for the Baku-Tbilisi-Ceyhan oil pipeline*, World Wide Web, http://ifiwatchnet.org/doc/btceiareview.pdf. Site visited 28 November 2004.

*The Times of India* (2004) 'CBI struggling to extradite Anderson', 20 July, World Wide Web, http://timesofindia.inditimes.com/articleshow/784941.cms. Site visited 25 January 2005.

Thomson, A. (1999) *Critical Reasoning in Ethics. A Practical Introduction*, London: Routledge.

Tilney, L.H. (2000) 'Peter Pan and the big bad wolf', *Financial Times*, 5 August, Book section: 4.

Tinker, T. (1985) *Paper Prophets*, Eastbourne: Holt, Reinhart and Winston.

Titmuss, R.M. (1970) *The Gift Relationship: From Human Blood to Social Policy*, London: Allen & Unwin.

Todd, E. (2003) *After the Empire*, New York: Columbia University Press.

Toffler, B.L. (1991) *Managers Talk Ethics: Making Tough Choices in a Competitive World*, New York: John Wiley & Sons.

Transparency International (2002) *Bribe Payers Index 2002*, World Wide Web, http://www.transparency.org/cpi/2002/bpi2002.en.html#bpi. Site visited 13 February 2005.

Transparency International (2004) *Corruption perceptions Index 2004*, World Wide Web, http://www.transparency.org/cpi/2004/cpi2004.en.html#cpi2004. Site visited 13 February 2005.

Trevino, L.K. (1986) 'Ethical Decision making in Organisations: A Person-Situation Interactionist Model', *Academy of Management Review*, 11(3), 601–17.

Trevino, L.K. and Youngblood, S.A. (1990) 'Bad Apple in Bad Barrels: A Causal Analysis of Ethical Decision-Making Behaviour', *Journal of Applied Psychology*, 75(4), 378–85.

Tripathi, R.C. (1990) 'Interplay of Values in the Functioning of Indian Organisations', *International Journal of Psychology*, 25, 715–34.

Trompenaars, F. and Hampden-Turner, C. (1993) *Riding the Waves of Culture. Understanding Cultural Diversity in Business*, 2nd edition, London: Nicholas Brealey.

Tsogas, G. (1999) 'Labour Standards in International Trade Agreements: A Critical Assessment of the Arguments', *International Journal of Human Resource Management*, April, 10(2), 351–75.

Turner, C.T. (2001) *The Real Root Cause of the Ford–Firestone Tragedy: Why the Public is Still at Risk*, Public Citizen and safetyforum.com, World Wide Web, http://www.citizen.org/fireweb/index7.htm. Site visited 3 June 2001.

United Kingdom Central Council for Nursing, Midwifery and Health Visiting (UKCC) (1996) *Code of Professional Conduct*, World Wide Web, http://www.ukcc.org.uk/codecon.html. Site visited 8 May 2002.

United Nations (1948) *Universal Declaration of Human Rights*, World Wide Web, http://www.un.org/Overview/rights.html. Site visited 8 February 2002.

United Nations (1989) *Convention on the Rights of the Child*, World Wide Web, http://www.unicef.org/crc/crc.htm. Site visited 30 March 2002.

United States District Court: Southern District of New York (2003) *Opinion in the case of Pelman and Bradley against McDonald's Corporation*, World Wide Web, http://tajnedokumenty.com/MDpelmandismissal.html. Site visited 29 September 2004.

Van Buitenen, P. (2000) *Blowing the Whistle. One Man's Fight Against Fraud in the European Commission*, London: Politico's Publishing.

Vardy, P. and Grosch, P. (1999) *The Puzzle of Ethics*, revised edition, London: Fount.

Verbeke, W., Ouwerkerk, C. and Peelen, E. (1996) 'Exploring the Contextual and Individual Factors on Ethical Decision Making of Salespeople', *Journal of Business Ethics*, 15, 1175–87.

Viswesvaran, C. and Deshpande, S.P. (1996) 'Ethics, Success and Job Satisfaction: a Test of Dissonance Theory in India', *Journal of Business Ethics*, 15(10), 1065–9.

Vroom, V.H. (1964) *Work and Motivation*, New York: Wiley.

Wakefield, J. (1999) 'Surfing results in sacking', *ZDNet UK News*, 16 June, World Wide Web, http://news.zdnet.co.uk/intrnet/0,390220369,2072304,00.htm. Site visited 18 March 2004.

Wallach, M.A. and Wallach, L. (1983) *Psychology's Sanction for Selfishness: The Error of Egoism in Theory and Therapy*, San Francisco: W.H. Freeman and Company.

Walzer, M. (1983) *Spheres of Justice: A Defence of Pluralism and Equality*, Oxford: Martin Robertson.

Warren, R.C. (1993) 'Codes of Ethics: Bricks without Straw', *Business Ethics: A European Review*, 2(4), 185–91.

Watchman, R. (2004) 'FSA probes scandal of "missing" Shell reserves', *Observer*, 14 March.

Watson, T.J. (1994) *In Search of Management. Culture, Chaos and Control in Managerial Work*, London: Routledge.

Watson, T.J. (1998) 'Ethical Codes and Moral Communities: the Gunlaw Temptation, the Simon Solution and the David Dilemma', in Parker, M. (ed.), *Ethics & Organisations*, 253–69, London: Sage.

Watson, T.J. (2002) *Organising and Managing Work. Organisational, Managerial and Strategic Behaviour in Theory and Practice*, Harlow: Pearson Education.

Weaver, M. (2000) 'Chummy protest hides drivers' grim resolution', *Daily Telegraph*, 14 September.

Webley, S. and More, E. (2003) *Does Business Ethics Pay?*, London: Institute of Business Ethics (IBE).

Weick, K.E. (1995) *Sensemaking in Organizations*, London: Sage.

Weick, K.E. (2001) *Making Sense of the Organization*, Oxford: Blackwell.

Welford, R. (1995) *Environmental Strategy and Sustainable Development: The Corporate Challenge for the Twenty-first Century*, London: Routledge.

Wells, M. and Ramesh, R. (2004) 'BBC reputation hit by Bhopal interview hoax', *Guardian*, 4 December: 1.

Werhane, P.H. (1999) *Moral Imagination and Management Decision-making*, New York: Oxford University Press.

Wheen, F. (2003) *How Mumbo-Jumbo Conquered the World*, London: HarperPerennial.

Whysall, P. (2000) 'Addressing the Issues in Retailing: a Stakeholder Perspective', *International Review of Retail, Distribution and Consumer Research*, 10(3), 305–18.

Wilde, O. (1996) *A Woman of No Importance*, Harmondsworth: Penguin.

Willmott, H. (1998) 'Towards a New Ethics? The Contributions of Poststructuralism and Posthumanism', in Parker, M. (ed.), *Ethics and Organisations*, London: Sage.

Wilson, B. (2004) 'Proximate cause and fries to go', *Times Literary Supplement*, 24 September: 17.

Wilson, J. (1999) 'Aitken "will not be a priest" ', *Guardian*, 10 June: 10.

Wilson, T. and Skinner, A.S. (1976), *The Market and the State: Essays in Honour of Adam Smith*, Oxford: Clarendon Press.

Windsor, D. (2001) 'Corporate Citizenship, Evolution and Interpretation', in Andriof, J. and McIntosh, M. (eds), *Perspectives on Corporate Citizenship*, 39–52, Sheffield: Greenleaf Publishing.

Wines, A.W. and Napier, N.K. (1992) 'Towards an Understanding of Cross-cultural Ethics: A Tentative Model', *Journal of Business Ethics*, 11, 831–41.

Winfield, M. (1990) *Minding Your Own Business: Self-regulation and Whistleblowing in British Companies*, London: Social Audit.

Winstanley, D. and Woodall, J. (eds) (2000) *Ethical Issues in Contemporary Human Resource Management*, London: Macmillan.

Winstanley, D., Clark, J. and Leeson, H. (2001) 'Approaches to Child Labour in the Supply Chain', paper presented at *4th Conference on Ethics and Human Resource Management: Professional Development and Practice*, Middlesex University Business School, 20 April.

Winter, R. (1989) *Learning from Experience. Principles and Practice in Action Research*, Lewes: Falmer.

Wolf, M. (2000) 'Sleepwalking with the Enemy: Corporate Social Responsibility Distorts the Market by Deflecting Business from its Primary Role of Profit Generation', *Financial Times*, 16 May: 21.

Wood, D.J. and Logsdon, J.M. (2001) 'Theorising Business Citizenship', in Andriof, J. and McIntosh, M. (eds), *Perspectives on Corporate Citizenship*, 83–103, Sheffield: Greenleaf Publishing.

Woodall, J. and Douglas, D. (1999) 'Ethical Issues in Contemporary Human Resource Development', *Business Ethics: A European Review*, 8(4), October, 249–61.

Woodbury, M. (1998) 'Email, Voicemail, and privacy: What policy is ethical?', paper presented to *The Fourth International Conference on Ethical Issues of Information Technology*, Erasmus University, The Netherlands, 25–27 March, World Wide Web, http://www.cpsr.org/~marsha-w/emailpol.html. Site visited 18 March 2004.

Woodcock, M. (1979) *The Team Development Manual*, Aldershot: Gower Press.

Woodcock, M. (1989) *50 Activities for Team Building*, Aldershot: Gower.

World Bank (2002) *Globalization, Growth and Poverty*, Washington DC: World Bank.

World Commission on the Social Dimension of Globalization (2004) *A fair Globalization: Creating Opportunities for All*, Geneva: International Labour Organization.

Wyschogrod, E. (1990) *Saints and Postmodernism*, Chicago: University of Chicago Press.

Wyver, J. (1989) 'Television and postmodernism', in Appignanesi, L. (ed.), *Postmodernism: ICA Documents 4*, London: Free Association Books.

Yang, A.A. (1998) *Bazaar India: Markets, Society, and the Colonial state in Gangetic Bihar*, University of California Press.

Yeung, L.N.T., Levine, T.R. and Nishiyama, K. (1999) 'Information manipulation theory and perceptions of deception in Hong Kong', *Communication Reports*, 12(1), 1–13.

Young, K. (1977) 'Values in the Policy Process', *Policy and Politics*, 5, 1–22.

# Answers to quick revision tests

## Chapter 1

1. Moral agency is the ability of individuals to exercise moral judgement and behaviour in an autonomous fashion, unfettered by fear for their employment and/or promotional prospects.

2. (i) **Reason** – Reality is only knowable through a process of objective reason that begins with sensory perception and follows the laws of logic;

   (ii) **Rational self-interest** – Objectivism rejects altruism (i.e. the greatest good is service to others) as an unhelpful and illogical human attribute. Individuals are required to pursue their own happiness, so long as it does not negatively affect anyone else's. This is compatible with negative freedom, one of Isaiah Berlin's two forms of freedom. It relates to a 'freedom from' approach that grants people a right to be free from interference by others, including, and in particular, government;

   (iii) **Laissez-faire capitalism** – This is the objective social system (note, not just economic system).

3. The assumptions regarding human preferences and human behaviour that are at the bedrock of neo-liberal economics do not reflect the complexity and variability of actual human behaviour.

4. Normative theories are theories of how things should be (such as the classical-libertarian-economics perspective), whereas descriptive theories are theories of how things actually appear to be.

## Chapter 2

Objective test answers:  Q1 – b; Q2 – b; Q3 – a and b; Q4–a

## Chapter 3

Objective test answers: Q1 – a; Q2 – c; Q3 – a; Q4 – a

## Chapter 4

Objective test answers: Q1 – b; Q2 – b; Q3 – a; Q4 – c

## Chapter 5

Objective test answers: Q1 – a and b; Q2 – a; Q3 – b; Q4 – all three options, a, b and c

## Chapter 6

Objective test answers: Q1 – c; Q2 – b; Q3 – all three options, a, b and c depending on which of Kohlberg's works or commentators you read. The theory was developed over time; Q4 – a

## Chapter 7

1. No, an act of whistleblowing can be treated as having happened by the mere act of revealing to a work colleague one's concerns about a particular (mal)practice or individual, rather than registering one's concerns with the organisation's internal grievance/whistleblowing procedures.

2. In our opinion, no. Referees are officially appointed individuals who are charged with upholding the laws of a game or a community (if we extend the notion of a referee to a judge). Whistleblowers are not officially appointed. Indeed, their unofficial, invariably reluctantly assumed role of upholding written or written codes or laws is one of their key problems. However, neither should whistleblowers be tarred with the brush of 'self-appointed' judges. Such a term carries with it connotations of a righteous, superior attitude, which, in our experience, is a misplaced assumption. Whistleblowers are invariably embroiled by context, circumstance and (mis)timing.

3. The *Public Interest Disclosure Act*, often referred to as the *PIDA*, which was given parliamentary approval in 1998 and passed on to the statute book in 1999.

4. No. A person who profits, say, by selling their story to a newspaper loses the protection of the PIDA. That person can still bring a case of wrongful dismissal through the courts, but it would be a lawsuit without the protection of the PIDA.

## Chapter 8

1. No. Oberman (2000) identifies concerns being expressed in the 1920s.

2. They do not fit. Thus if large corporations are to exist within democratic states there have to be certain developments that democratise the corporations and other developments that make them less of a threat to political and social democracy.

3. Agency theory reflects the division of the ownership of corporations (which many argue rests with the shareholders) from the control of corporations (which few would disagree rests with senior management). However, agency theory goes further than this in that it assumes that all individuals are self-serving and that the asymmetry of power that exists between management and shareholders allows management to follow practices and policies that, while serving their own interests, do not always correlate with those of the shareholders (e.g. executive pay).

4. Non-executive directors (NEDs) play a fundamental role in Anglo-American developments in corporate governance. NEDs are seen as the force that will keep executive directors on the straight and narrow when they otherwise might act in exclusively self-serving ways (agency theory). However, the majority of NEDs are also executive directors in other companies, so what is the transformation process that turns an untrustworthy executive director into a trustworthy NED?

5. That corporations/business cannot be expected to address the great world problems, such as extreme poverty, child and slave labour, bribery and corruption, etc., on their own. Despite previous frustrations with member governments, the UN must work towards a resolution of these seemingly intractable problems thorough a partnership between business and governments.

6. The Global Compact is a toothless tiger because it lacks the resources and/or brief to effectively monitor and verify claims made by its members. Christian Aid has also been critical of the Compact because of its lack of transparency regarding membership and what the member organisations have achieved to both warrant membership and to maintain their involvement.

# Chapter 9

1. Neo-liberalist economics argues that the price mechanism is the most democratic form of market (and social) coordination. However, in the context of global warming only the wealthy may be able to afford air travel in the future, which may in itself be considered to be an ethically uncomfortable situation, but more significant from an ethical perspective is the ethics of use. Air travel is the most polluting form of travel, yet the price mechanism would not prevent the few inflicting harm (adding to global warming) upon the majority. How can this be democratic?

2. The environment can be seen in different ways in different times. The example was given in the chapter of a wood and how its status and value might change through time. The physical aspects of the wood (or any other element we might consider) may remain reasonably constant, but the way it is treated might differ significantly. This argument might seem to suggest an instrumental view of nature, but the point is that once again our future lies in our hands. It is up to us, both individually and collectively, to shape the world we inhabit and the legacy we will leave for others.

3. The 'seeing' of nature in purely instrumental terms, as simply a means to an end, with that end usually, but not always, making money.

4. Martin Heidegger.

5. Smith's notion of self-love represented a belief in the interests of the Self, but not at the unfair expense of Others. Smith's self-love was bounded by self-control, whereas selfishness tends to represent an unbounded and myopic focus upon the Self. For Smith the self was a part of society, whereas selfishness sees the self as apart from society.

6. Corporations can rightly point to a too often glossed over aspect of corporate social responsibility, that is, the role of consumers in supporting corporations that take their corporate impacts seriously and which go beyond their competitors in trying to create a set of working practices and relationships that reflect a more sensitive, civil and respectful approach to business deals and relationships. However, if consumers are so concerned about notions of equity, respect and justice operating in the supply chains of large corporations, they should also be prepared to pay the extra cost that such practices might require. Thus, do consumers have a social responsibility to support corporations that practise and champion corporate social responsibility?

7. The triple bottom line is an attempt to move away from an exclusive focus upon profit, the latter being the so-called 'bottom line'. The triple bottom line requires attention and consideration to be given in a corporation's published accounts to profit performance, but also to the social and environmental impacts of the corporation's activities.

## Chapter 10

1. Possible roles for codes of ethics are:

- Damage limitation
- Guidance
- Regulation
- Discipline and appeal
- Information
- Proclamation
- Negotiation
- Stifling.

2. Arguments against the employment of codes of practice within organisations will include:

- **Justification** – can we collectively agree upon values, ethics, ways of behaving that can be universally accepted?
- **The inability of rules to govern actions** – the concern (and weak evidence) that codes do actually influence behaviour.
- **Support structures** – or lack of to support codes.

- **The marginality of codes** – codes are rarely part of executive management's modus operandi.
- **The diminution and ultimate invisibility of individual responsibility** – externally imposed codes might detract from individual responsibility.
- **Contradiction** – codes can contradict one another.

3. In addition to codes of conduct and ethics, organisations can employ the following mechanisms to inculcate their desired ethics, values and beliefs.

- Training programmes
- Story telling
- Reward systems
- Monitoring systems
- Communication channels
- Job design
- Ethics officers
- Information systems
- Recruitment and selection policies and processes, and
- Organisational strategies.

## Chapter 11

Objective test answers: Q1 – c; Q2 – a; Q3 – c; Q4 – a

## Chapter 12

Objective test answers: Q1 – c; Q2 – b; Q3 – a; Q4 – a

## Chapter 13

Objective test answers: Q1 – b; Q2 – c; Q3 – b; Q4 – c

# Country and region index

# Index